PORTFOLIO MANAGEMENT, ETHICAL AND PROFESSIONAL STANDARDS

CFA® Program Curriculum
2023 • LEVEL 1 • VOLUME 6

©2022 by CFA Institute. All rights reserved. This copyright covers material written expressly for this volume by the editor/s as well as the compilation itself. It does not cover the individual selections herein that first appeared elsewhere. Permission to reprint these has been obtained by CFA Institute for this edition only. Further reproductions by any means, electronic or mechanical, including photocopying and recording, or by any information storage or retrieval systems, must be arranged with the individual copyright holders noted.

CFA®, Chartered Financial Analyst®, AIMR-PPS®, and GIPS® are just a few of the trademarks owned by CFA Institute. To view a list of CFA Institute trademarks and the Guide for Use of CFA Institute Marks, please visit our website at www.cfainstitute.org.

This publication is designed to provide accurate and authoritative information in regard to the subject matter covered. It is sold with the understanding that the publisher is not engaged in rendering legal, accounting, or other professional service. If legal advice or other expert assistance is required, the services of a competent professional should be sought.

All trademarks, service marks, registered trademarks, and registered service marks are the property of their respective owners and are used herein for identification purposes only.

ISBN 978-1-953337-03-0 (paper)
ISBN 978-1-953337-28-3 (ebook)

SKYCE79E490-50BD-4C02-A375-01F10E459B45_032522

Please visit our website at
www.WileyGlobalFinance.com.

Logo Applies to Text Stock Only

CONTENTS

How to Use the CFA Program Curriculum		xv
	Errata	xv
	Designing Your Personal Study Program	xv
	CFA Institute Learning Ecosystem (LES)	xvi
	Feedback	xvi

Portfolio Management

Learning Module 1		**Basics of Portfolio Planning and Construction**	**3**
		Introduction	3
		The Investment Policy Statement	4
		The Investment Policy Statement	4
		Major Components of an IPS	5
		IPS Risk and Return Objectives	6
		Return Objectives	12
		IPS Constraints	14
		Liquidity Requirements	14
		Time Horizon	15
		Tax Concerns	15
		Legal and Regulatory Factors	16
		Unique Circumstances and ESG Considerations	16
		Gathering Client Information	18
		Portfolio Construction and Capital Market Expectations	21
		Capital Market Expectations	22
		Strategic Asset Allocation	22
		Portfolio Construction Principles	30
		New Developments in Portfolio Management	34
		ESG Considerations in Portfolio Planning and Construction	34
		Summary	*38*
		Practice Problems	*40*
		Solutions	*44*
Learning Module 2		**The Behavioral Biases of Individuals**	**47**
		Introduction	47
		Behavioral Bias Categories	48
		Cognitive Errors	48
		Belief Perseverance Biases	49
		Processing Errors	54
		Emotional Biases	61
		Loss-Aversion Bias	61
		Overconfidence Bias	63
		Self-Control Bias	64
		Status Quo Bias	65
		Endowment Bias	65
		Regret-Aversion Bias	67

◘ indicates an optional segment

	Behavioral Finance and Market Behavior	70
	Defining Market Anomalies	70
	Momentum	71
	Bubbles and Crashes	72
	Value	73
	Summary	*74*
	References	*76*
	Practice Problems	*77*
	Solutions	*80*
Learning Module 3	**Introduction to Risk Management**	**83**
	Introduction	83
	Risk Management Process	85
	Risk Management Framework	87
	Risk Governance - An Enterprise View	93
	An Enterprise View of Risk Governance	93
	Risk Tolerance	96
	Risk Budgeting	98
	Identification of Risk - Financial Vs. Non-Financial Risk	101
	Financial Risks	101
	Non-Financial Risks	103
	Interactions Between Risks	107
	Measuring and Modifying Risk: Drivers and Metrics	110
	Drivers	111
	Metrics	112
	Risk Modification: Prevention, Avoidance, and Acceptance	116
	Risk Prevention and Avoidance	116
	Risk Acceptance: Self-Insurance and Diversification	117
	Risk Modification: Transferring, Shifting, and How To Choose	118
	Risk Shifting	120
	How to Choose Which Method for Modifying Risk	124
	Summary	*126*
	Practice Problems	*129*
	Solutions	*132*
Learning Module 4	**Technical Analysis**	**135**
	Introduction	135
	Principles, Assumptions, and links to Investment Analysis	136
	Principles and Assumptions	138
	Technical Analysis and Behavioral Finance	138
	Technical Analysis and Fundamental Analysis	140
	The Differences in Conducting/Interpreting Technical Analysis in Various Types of Markets	142
	Chart Types	144
	Types of Technical Analysis Charts	145
	Trend, Support, and Resistance	156
	Common Chart Patterns	159
	Reversal Patterns	159
	Continuation Patterns	169

◙ indicates an optional segment

Contents

Technical Indicators: Moving Averages and Bollinger Bands	179
Technical Indicators	181
Technical Indicators: Oscillators, Relative Strength, and Sentiment	186
Rate of Change Oscillator	187
Relative Strength Index	189
Stochastic Oscillator	191
Moving-Average Convergence/Divergence Oscillator (MACD)	193
Sentiment Indicators	194
Intermarket Analysis	200
Principles of Intermarket Analysis	201
Technical Analysis Applications to Portfolio Management	204
The Role of the Technical Analyst in Fundamental Portfolio Management	215
Summary	*217*
Practice Problems	*220*
Solutions	*227*

Learning Module 5   **Fintech in Investment Management**   **233**

Introduction	233
What Is Fintech?	234
Big Data	237
Sources of Big Data	239
Big Data Challenges	240
Advanced Analytical Tools: AI and Machine Learning	240
Types of ML	242
Data Science: Extracting Information from Big Data	243
Data Processing Methods	243
Data Visualization	244
Applying Fintech to Investment Management	246
Text Analytics and Natural Language Processing	246
Robo-Advisory Services	247
Risk Analysis	249
Algorithmic Trading	250
DLT and Permissioned and Permissionless Networks	251
Permissioned and Permissionless Networks	253
Applications of DLT to Investment Management	253
Cryptocurrencies	253
Tokenization	254
Post-Trade Clearing and Settlement	254
Compliance	254
Summary	*255*
Practice Problems	*257*
Solutions	*259*

Ethical and Professional Standards

Learning Module 1   **Ethics and Trust in the Investment Profession**   **263**

Introduction	263
Ethics	265

◙ indicates an optional segment

	Ethics and Professionalism	267
	How Professions Establish Trust	268
	Professions Are Evolving	270
	Professionalism in Investment Management	270
	Trust in Investment Management	271
	CFA Institute as an Investment Management Professional Body	271
	Challenges to Ethical Conduct	273
	Ethical vs. Legal Standards	276
	Ethical Decision-Making Frameworks	278
	The Framework for Ethical Decision-Making	279
	Applying the Framework	281
	Conclusion	287
	Summary	*287*
	Practice Problems	*289*
	Solutions	*291*
Learning Module 2	**Code of Ethics and Standards of Professional Conduct**	**293**
	Preface	293
	Evolution of the CFA Institute Code of Ethics and Standards of Professional Conduct	294
	Standards of Practice Handbook	294
	Summary of Changes in the Eleventh Edition	295
	CFA Institute Professional Conduct Program	297
	Adoption of the Code and Standards	298
	Acknowledgments	298
	Ethics and the Investment Industry	299
	Why Ethics Matters	299
	CFA Institute Code of Ethics and Standards of Professional Conduct	303
	Preamble	303
	The Code of Ethics	304
	Standards of Professional Conduct	304
	Practice Problems	*308*
	Solutions	*311*
Learning Module 3	**Guidance for Standards I–VII**	**315**
	Standard I(A): Professionalism - Knowledge of the Law	315
	Standard I(A) Knowledge of the Law	315
	Guidance	316
	Standard I(A): Recommended Procedures	320
	Members and Candidates	320
	Distribution Area Laws	320
	Legal Counsel	320
	Dissociation	320
	Firms	321
	Standard I(A): Application of the Standard	321
	Example 1 (Notification of Known Violations):	321
	Example 2 (Dissociating from a Violation):	322
	Example 3 (Dissociating from a Violation):	322
	Example 4 (Following the Highest Requirements):	322

◉ indicates an optional segment

Example 5 (Following the Highest Requirements):	323
Example 6 (Laws and Regulations Based on Religious Tenets):	323
Example 7 (Reporting Potential Unethical Actions):	323
Example 8 (Failure to Maintain Knowledge of the Law):	324
Standard I(B): Professionalism - Independence and Objectivity	324
Guidance	324
Standard I(B): Recommended Procedures	330
Standard I(B): Application of the Standard	331
Example 1 (Travel Expenses):	331
Example 2 (Research Independence):	332
Example 3 (Research Independence and Intrafirm Pressure):	332
Example 4 (Research Independence and Issuer Relationship Pressure):	332
Example 5 (Research Independence and Sales Pressure):	333
Example 6 (Research Independence and Prior Coverage):	333
Example 7 (Gifts and Entertainment from Related Party):	333
Example 8 (Gifts and Entertainment from Client):	334
Example 9 (Travel Expenses from External Manager):	334
Example 10 (Research Independence and Compensation Arrangements):	335
Example 11 (Recommendation Objectivity and Service Fees):	335
Example 12 (Recommendation Objectivity):	336
Example 13 (Influencing Manager Selection Decisions):	336
Example 14 (Influencing Manager Selection Decisions):	337
Example 15 (Fund Manager Relationships):	337
Example 16 (Intrafirm Pressure):	337
Standard I(C): Professionalism – Misrepresentation	338
Guidance	338
Standard I(C): Recommended Procedures	342
Factual Presentations	342
Qualification Summary	342
Verify Outside Information	342
Maintain Webpages	343
Plagiarism Policy	343
Standard I(C): Application of the Standard	343
Example 1 (Disclosure of Issuer-Paid Research):	343
Example 2 (Correction of Unintentional Errors):	344
Example 3 (Noncorrection of Known Errors):	344
Example 4 (Plagiarism):	344
Example 5 (Misrepresentation of Information):	345
Example 6 (Potential Information Misrepresentation):	345
Example 7 (Plagiarism):	345
Example 8 (Plagiarism):	346
Example 9 (Plagiarism):	346
Example 10 (Plagiarism):	346
Example 11 (Misrepresentation of Information):	347
Example 12 (Misrepresentation of Information):	347
Example 13 (Avoiding a Misrepresentation):	348
Example 14 (Misrepresenting Composite Construction):	348
Example 15 (Presenting Out-of-Date Information):	348

◙ indicates an optional segment

Example 16 (Overemphasis of Firm Results):	349
Standard I(D): Professionalism – Misconduct	349
Guidance	349
Standard I(D): Recommended Procedures	350
Standard I(D): Application of the Standard	351
Example 1 (Professionalism and Competence):	351
Example 2 (Fraud and Deceit):	351
Example 3 (Fraud and Deceit):	351
Example 4 (Personal Actions and Integrity):	352
Example 5 (Professional Misconduct):	352
Standard II(A): Integrity of Capital Markets - Material Nonpublic Information	352
Standard II(A) Material Nonpublic Information	353
Guidance	353
Standard II(A): Recommended Procedures	357
Achieve Public Dissemination	357
Adopt Compliance Procedures	357
Adopt Disclosure Procedures	357
Issue Press Releases	358
Firewall Elements	358
Appropriate Interdepartmental Communications	358
Physical Separation of Departments	358
Prevention of Personnel Overlap	359
A Reporting System	359
Personal Trading Limitations	359
Record Maintenance	360
Proprietary Trading Procedures	360
Communication to All Employees	360
Standard II(A): Application of the Standard	361
Example 1 (Acting on Nonpublic Information):	361
Example 2 (Controlling Nonpublic Information):	361
Example 3 (Selective Disclosure of Material Information):	361
Example 4 (Determining Materiality):	362
Example 5 (Applying the Mosaic Theory):	362
Example 6 (Applying the Mosaic Theory):	363
Example 7 (Analyst Recommendations as Material Nonpublic Information):	363
Example 8 (Acting on Nonpublic Information):	363
Example 9 (Mosaic Theory):	364
Example 10 (Materiality Determination):	364
Example 11 (Using an Expert Network):	365
Example 12 (Using an Expert Network):	365
Standard II(B): Integrity of Capital Markets - Market Manipulation	365
Guidance	366
Standard II(B): Application of the Standard	367
Example 1 (Independent Analysis and Company Promotion):	367
Example 2 (Personal Trading Practices and Price):	367
Example 3 (Creating Artificial Price Volatility):	368
Example 4 (Personal Trading and Volume):	368
Example 5 ("Pump-Priming" Strategy):	368

◘ indicates an optional segment

Contents

Example 6 (Creating Artificial Price Volatility):	369
Example 7 (Pump and Dump Strategy):	370
Example 8 (Manipulating Model Inputs):	370
Example 9 (Information Manipulation):	370
Standard III(A): Duties to Clients - Loyalty, Prudence, and Care	**371**
Standard III(A) Loyalty, Prudence, and Care	371
Guidance	371
Standard III(A): Recommended Procedures	**375**
Regular Account Information	375
Client Approval	375
Firm Policies	375
Standard III(A): Application of the Standard	**376**
Example 1 (Identifying the Client—Plan Participants):	376
Example 2 (Client Commission Practices):	377
Example 3 (Brokerage Arrangements):	377
Example 4 (Brokerage Arrangements):	378
Example 5 (Client Commission Practices):	378
Example 6 (Excessive Trading):	378
Example 7 (Managing Family Accounts):	379
Example 8 (Identifying the Client):	379
Example 9 (Identifying the Client):	379
Example 10 (Client Loyalty):	380
Example 11 (Execution-Only Responsibilities):	380
Standard III(B): Duties to Clients - Fair Dealing	**380**
Guidance	381
Standard III(B): Recommended Procedures	**383**
Develop Firm Policies	383
Disclose Trade Allocation Procedures	385
Establish Systematic Account Review	385
Disclose Levels of Service	385
Standard III(B): Application of the Standard	**385**
Example 1 (Selective Disclosure):	385
Example 2 (Fair Dealing between Funds):	386
Example 3 (Fair Dealing and IPO Distribution):	386
Example 4 (Fair Dealing and Transaction Allocation):	387
Example 5 (Selective Disclosure):	387
Example 6 (Additional Services for Select Clients):	387
Example 7 (Minimum Lot Allocations):	388
Example 8 (Excessive Trading):	388
Example 9 (Limited Social Media Disclosures):	388
Example 10 (Fair Dealing between Clients):	389
Standard III(C): Duties to Clients – Suitability	**389**
Guidance	390
Standard III(C): Recommended Procedures	**393**
Investment Policy Statement	393
Regular Updates	393
Suitability Test Policies	393
Standard III(C): Application of the Standard	**394**
Example 1 (Investment Suitability—Risk Profile):	394

◉ indicates an optional segment

Example 2 (Investment Suitability—Entire Portfolio):	394
Example 3 (IPS Updating):	395
Example 4 (Following an Investment Mandate):	395
Example 5 (IPS Requirements and Limitations):	395
Example 6 (Submanager and IPS Reviews):	396
Example 7 (Investment Suitability—Risk Profile):	396
Example 8 (Investment Suitability):	397
Standard III(D): Duties to Clients - Performance Presentation	397
Guidance	397
Standard III(D): Recommended Procedures	398
Apply the GIPS Standards	398
Compliance without Applying GIPS Standards	398
Standard III(D): Application of the Standard	399
Example 1 (Performance Calculation and Length of Time):	399
Example 2 (Performance Calculation and Asset Weighting):	399
Example 3 (Performance Presentation and Prior Fund/Employer):	400
Example 4 (Performance Presentation and Simulated Results):	400
Example 5 (Performance Calculation and Selected Accounts Only):	400
Example 6 (Performance Attribution Changes):	401
Example 7 (Performance Calculation Methodology Disclosure):	401
Example 8 (Performance Calculation Methodology Disclosure):	402
Standard III(E): Duties to Clients - Preservation of Confidentiality	402
Guidance	402
Standard III(E): Recommended Procedures	404
Communicating with Clients	404
Standard III(E): Application of the Standard	404
Example 1 (Possessing Confidential Information):	405
Example 2 (Disclosing Confidential Information):	405
Example 3 (Disclosing Possible Illegal Activity):	405
Example 4 (Disclosing Possible Illegal Activity):	405
Example 5 (Accidental Disclosure of Confidential Information):	406
Standard IV(A): Duties to Employers – Loyalty	407
Standard IV(A) Loyalty	407
Guidance	407
Standard IV(A): Recommended Procedures	410
Competition Policy	410
Termination Policy	411
Incident-Reporting Procedures	411
Employee Classification	411
Standard IV(A): Application of the Standard	411
Example 1 (Soliciting Former Clients):	411
Example 2 (Former Employer's Documents and Files):	412
Example 3 (Addressing Rumors):	412
Example 4 (Ownership of Completed Prior Work):	412
Example 5 (Ownership of Completed Prior Work):	413
Example 6 (Soliciting Former Clients):	413
Example 7 (Starting a New Firm):	414
Example 8 (Competing with Current Employer):	414
Example 9 (Externally Compensated Assignments):	414

◘ indicates an optional segment

Contents

Example 10 (Soliciting Former Clients):	415
Example 11 (Whistleblowing Actions):	415
Example 12 (Soliciting Former Clients):	415
Example 13 (Notification of Code and Standards):	416
Example 14 (Leaving an Employer):	417
Example 15 (Confidential Firm Information):	417
Standard IV(B): Duties to Employers - Additional Compensation Arrangements	418
Guidance	418
Standard IV(B): Recommended Procedures	418
Standard IV(B): Application of the Standard	419
Example 1 (Notification of Client Bonus Compensation):	419
Example 2 (Notification of Outside Compensation):	419
Example 3 (Prior Approval for Outside Compensation):	420
Standard IV(C): Duties to Employers - Responsibilities of Supervisors	420
Guidance	420
Standard IV(C): Recommended Procedures	422
Codes of Ethics or Compliance Procedures	423
Adequate Compliance Procedures	423
Implementation of Compliance Education and Training	424
Establish an Appropriate Incentive Structure	424
Standard IV(C): Application of the Standard	425
Example 1 (Supervising Research Activities):	425
Example 2 (Supervising Research Activities):	425
Example 3 (Supervising Trading Activities):	426
Example 4 (Supervising Trading Activities and Record Keeping):	426
Example 5 (Accepting Responsibility):	427
Example 6 (Inadequate Procedures):	427
Example 7 (Inadequate Supervision):	428
Example 8 (Supervising Research Activities):	428
Example 9 (Supervising Research Activities):	429
Standard V(A): Investment Analysis, Recommendations, and Actions - Diligence and Reasonable Basis	429
Standard V(A) Diligence and Reasonable Basis	429
Guidance	430
Standard V(A): Recommended Procedures	433
Standard V(A): Application of the Standard	434
Example 1 (Sufficient Due Diligence):	434
Example 2 (Sufficient Scenario Testing):	434
Example 3 (Developing a Reasonable Basis):	435
Example 4 (Timely Client Updates):	435
Example 5 (Group Research Opinions):	436
Example 6 (Reliance on Third-Party Research):	436
Example 7 (Due Diligence in Submanager Selection):	436
Example 8 (Sufficient Due Diligence):	437
Example 9 (Sufficient Due Diligence):	437
Example 10 (Sufficient Due Diligence):	438
Example 11 (Use of Quantitatively Oriented Models):	438
Example 12 (Successful Due Diligence/Failed Investment):	439

◘ indicates an optional segment

Example 13 (Quantitative Model Diligence):	439
Example 14 (Selecting a Service Provider):	440
Example 15 (Subadviser Selection):	440
Example 16 (Manager Selection):	440
Example 17 (Technical Model Requirements):	441
Standard V(B): Investment Analysis, Recommendations, and Actions - Communication with Clients and Prospective Clients	442
Guidance	442
Standard V(B): Recommended Procedures	445
Standard V(B): Application of the Standard	445
Example 1 (Sufficient Disclosure of Investment System):	445
Example 2 (Providing Opinions as Facts):	446
Example 3 (Proper Description of a Security):	446
Example 4 (Notification of Fund Mandate Change):	447
Example 5 (Notification of Fund Mandate Change):	447
Example 6 (Notification of Changes to the Investment Process):	447
Example 7 (Notification of Changes to the Investment Process):	448
Example 8 (Notification of Changes to the Investment Process):	448
Example 9 (Sufficient Disclosure of Investment System):	448
Example 10 (Notification of Changes to the Investment Process):	448
Example 11 (Notification of Errors):	449
Example 12 (Notification of Risks and Limitations):	450
Example 13 (Notification of Risks and Limitations):	450
Example 14 (Notification of Risks and Limitations):	451
Standard V(C): Investment Analysis, Recommendations, and Actions - Record Retention	451
Guidance	451
Standard V(C): Recommended Procedures	453
Standard V(C): Application of the Standard	453
Example 1 (Record Retention and IPS Objectives and Recommendations):	453
Example 2 (Record Retention and Research Process):	453
Example 3 (Records as Firm, Not Employee, Property):	454
Standard VI(A): Conflicts of Interest - Disclosure of Conflicts	454
Standard VI(A) Disclosure of Conflicts	454
Guidance	454
Standard VI(A): Recommended Procedures	457
Standard VI(A): Application of the Standard	458
Example 1 (Conflict of Interest and Business Relationships):	458
Example 2 (Conflict of Interest and Business Stock Ownership):	458
Example 3 (Conflict of Interest and Personal Stock Ownership):	458
Example 4 (Conflict of Interest and Personal Stock Ownership):	459
Example 5 (Conflict of Interest and Compensation Arrangements):	459
Example 6 (Conflict of Interest, Options, and Compensation Arrangements):	459
Example 7 (Conflict of Interest and Compensation Arrangements):	460
Example 8 (Conflict of Interest and Directorship):	460
Example 9 (Conflict of Interest and Personal Trading):	461
Example 10 (Conflict of Interest and Requested Favors):	461

◙ indicates an optional segment

Contents

Example 11 (Conflict of Interest and Business Relationships):	462
Example 12 (Disclosure of Conflicts to Employers):	462
Standard VI(B): Conflicts of Interest - Priority of Transactions	463
Guidance	463
Standard VI(B): Recommended Procedures	464
Standard VI(B): Application of the Standard	466
Example 1 (Personal Trading):	467
Example 2 (Trading for Family Member Account):	467
Example 3 (Family Accounts as Equals):	467
Example 4 (Personal Trading and Disclosure):	467
Example 5 (Trading Prior to Report Dissemination):	468
Standard VI(C): Conflicts of Interest - Referral Fees	468
Guidance	469
Standard VI(C): Recommended Procedures	469
Standard VI(C): Application of the Standard	469
Example 1 (Disclosure of Referral Arrangements and Outside Parties):	469
Example 2 (Disclosure of Interdepartmental Referral Arrangements):	470
Example 3 (Disclosure of Referral Arrangements and Informing Firm):	470
Example 4 (Disclosure of Referral Arrangements and Outside Organizations):	471
Example 5 (Disclosure of Referral Arrangements and Outside Parties):	471
Standard VII(A): Responsibilities as a CFA Institute Member or CFA Candidate - Conduct as Participants in CFA Institute Programs	472
Standard VII(A) Conduct as Participants in CFA Institute Programs	472
Guidance	472
Standard VII(A): Application of the Standard	474
Example 1 (Sharing Exam Questions):	475
Example 2 (Bringing Written Material into Exam Room):	475
Example 3 (Writing after Exam Period End):	475
Example 4 (Sharing Exam Content):	475
Example 5 (Sharing Exam Content):	476
Example 6 (Sharing Exam Content):	476
Example 7 (Discussion of Exam Grading Guidelines and Results):	476
Example 8 (Compromising CFA Institute Integrity as a Volunteer):	477
Example 9 (Compromising CFA Institute Integrity as a Volunteer):	477
Standard VII(B): Responsibilities as a CFA Institute Member or CFA Candidate - Reference to CFA Institute, the CFA Designation, and the CFA Program	478
Guidance	478
Standard VII(B): Recommended Procedures	480
Standard VII(B): Application of the Standard	481
Example 1 (Passing Exams in Consecutive Years):	481
Example 2 (Right to Use CFA Designation):	481
Example 3 ("Retired" CFA Institute Membership Status):	482
Example 4 (Stating Facts about CFA Designation and Program):	482
Example 5 (Order of Professional and Academic Designations):	482
Example 6 (Use of Fictitious Name):	482
Practice Problems	*484*
Solutions	*495*

◙ indicates an optional segment

Learning Module 4	**Introduction to the Global Investment Performance Standards (GIPS)**	**503**
	Introduction	503
	Why Were the GIPS Standards Created, Who Can Claim Compliance, & Who Benefits from Compliance?	504
	Who Can Claim Compliance?	505
	Who Benefits from Compliance?	505
	Composites	506
	Fundamentals of Compliance	507
	Verification	507
	Practice Problems	*509*
	Solutions	*511*
Learning Module 5	**Ethics Application**	**513**
	Introduction	513
	Professionalism	513
	Knowledge of the Law	514
	Independence and Objectivity	516
	Misrepresentation	518
	Misconduct	520
	Integrity of Capital Markets	522
	Material Nonpublic Information	522
	Market Manipulation	524
	Duties to Clients	525
	Loyalty, Prudence, and Care	525
	Fair Dealing	528
	Suitability	529
	Performance Presentation	531
	Preservation of Confidentiality	532
	Duties to Employers	533
	Loyalty	533
	Additional Compensation Arrangements	536
	Responsibilities of Supervisors	537
	Investment Analysis, Recommendations, and Actions	539
	Diligence and Reasonable Basis	539
	Communication with Clients and Prospective Clients	540
	Record Retention	542
	Conflicts of Interest	543
	Disclosure of Conflicts	543
	Priority of Transactions	544
	Referral Fees	546
	Responsibilities as a CFA Institute Member or CFA Candidate	547
	Conduct as Participants in CFA Institute Programs	547
	Reference to CFA Institute, the CFA Designation, and the CFA Program	548
	Glossary	**G-1**

◉ indicates an optional segment

How to Use the CFA Program Curriculum

The CFA® Program exams measure your mastery of the core knowledge, skills, and abilities required to succeed as an investment professional. These core competencies are the basis for the Candidate Body of Knowledge (CBOK™). The CBOK consists of four components:

- A broad outline that lists the major CFA Program topic areas (www.cfainstitute.org/programs/cfa/curriculum/cbok)
- Topic area weights that indicate the relative exam weightings of the top-level topic areas (www.cfainstitute.org/programs/cfa/curriculum)
- Learning outcome statements (LOS) that advise candidates about the specific knowledge, skills, and abilities they should acquire from curriculum content covering a topic area: LOS are provided in candidate study sessions and at the beginning of each block of related content and the specific lesson that covers them. We encourage you to review the information about the LOS on our website (www.cfainstitute.org/programs/cfa/curriculum/study-sessions), including the descriptions of LOS "command words" on the candidate resources page at www.cfainstitute.org.
- The CFA Program curriculum that candidates receive upon exam registration

Therefore, the key to your success on the CFA exams is studying and understanding the CBOK. You can learn more about the CBOK on our website: www.cfainstitute.org/programs/cfa/curriculum/cbok.

The entire curriculum, including the practice questions, is the basis for all exam questions and is selected or developed specifically to teach the knowledge, skills, and abilities reflected in the CBOK.

ERRATA

The curriculum development process is rigorous and includes multiple rounds of reviews by content experts. Despite our efforts to produce a curriculum that is free of errors, there are instances where we must make corrections. Curriculum errata are periodically updated and posted by exam level and test date online on the Curriculum Errata webpage (www.cfainstitute.org/en/programs/submit-errata). If you believe you have found an error in the curriculum, you can submit your concerns through our curriculum errata reporting process found at the bottom of the Curriculum Errata webpage.

DESIGNING YOUR PERSONAL STUDY PROGRAM

An orderly, systematic approach to exam preparation is critical. You should dedicate a consistent block of time every week to reading and studying. Review the LOS both before and after you study curriculum content to ensure that you have mastered the applicable content and can demonstrate the knowledge, skills, and abilities described by the LOS and the assigned reading. Use the LOS self-check to track your progress and highlight areas of weakness for later review.

Successful candidates report an average of more than 300 hours preparing for each exam. Your preparation time will vary based on your prior education and experience, and you will likely spend more time on some study sessions than on others.

CFA INSTITUTE LEARNING ECOSYSTEM (LES)

Your exam registration fee includes access to the CFA Program Learning Ecosystem (LES). This digital learning platform provides access, even offline, to all of the curriculum content and practice questions and is organized as a series of short online lessons with associated practice questions. This tool is your one-stop location for all study materials, including practice questions and mock exams, and the primary method by which CFA Institute delivers your curriculum experience. The LES offers candidates additional practice questions to test their knowledge, and some questions in the LES provide a unique interactive experience.

FEEDBACK

Please send any comments or feedback to info@cfainstitute.org, and we will review your suggestions carefully.

Portfolio Management

LEARNING MODULE 1

Basics of Portfolio Planning and Construction

by Alistair Byrne, PhD, CFA, and Frank E. Smudde, MSc, CFA.

Alistair Byrne, PhD, CFA, is at State Street Global Advisors (United Kingdom). Frank E. Smudde, MSc, CFA, is at APG Asset Management (Netherlands).

LEARNING OUTCOME	
Mastery	The candidate should be able to:
☐	describe the reasons for a written investment policy statement (IPS)
☐	describe the major components of an IPS
☐	describe risk and return objectives and how they may be developed for a client
☐	explain the difference between the willingness and the ability (capacity) to take risk in analyzing an investor's financial risk tolerance
☐	describe the investment constraints of liquidity, time horizon, tax concerns, legal and regulatory factors, and unique circumstances and their implications for the choice of portfolio assets
☐	explain the specification of asset classes in relation to asset allocation
☐	describe the principles of portfolio construction and the role of asset allocation in relation to the IPS
☐	describe how environmental, social, and governance (ESG) considerations may be integrated into portfolio planning and construction

INTRODUCTION 1

To build a suitable portfolio for a client, investment advisers should first seek to understand the client's investment goals, resources, circumstances, and constraints. Investors can be categorized into broad groups based on shared characteristics with respect to these factors (e.g., various types of individual investors and institutional investors). Even investors within a given type, however, will invariably have a number of distinctive requirements. In this reading, we consider in detail the planning for investment success based on an individualized understanding of the client.

This reading is organized as follows: Section 2 discusses the investment policy statement, a written document that captures the client's investment objectives and the constraints. Section 3 discusses the portfolio construction process, including the first step of specifying a strategic asset allocation for the client. Section 4 concludes and summarizes the reading.

2. THE INVESTMENT POLICY STATEMENT

- [ ] describe the reasons for a written investment policy statement (IPS)
- [ ] describe the major components of an IPS

Portfolio planning can be defined as a program developed in advance of constructing a portfolio that is expected to define the client's investment objectives. The written document governing this process is the investment policy statement (IPS). The IPS is sometimes complemented by a document outlining policy on responsible investing—the broadest (umbrella) term used to describe principles that typically address one or more environmental, social, and governance themes that an investor requires to be considered when evaluating whether to invest in a particular company, as well as during the period of ownership. Sustainable investing, a term used in a similar context to responsible investing, focuses on factoring in sustainability issues during the investment process. Policies on responsible investing may also be integrated within the IPS itself. In the remainder of this reading, the integration of responsible investing within the IPS will be our working assumption.

The Investment Policy Statement

The IPS is the starting point of the portfolio management process. Without a full understanding of the client's situation and requirements, it is unlikely that successful results will be achieved. "Success" can be defined as a client achieving his important investment goals using means that he is comfortable with (in terms of risks taken and other concerns). The IPS essentially communicates a plan for achieving investment success.

The IPS is typically developed following a fact-finding discussion with the client. This discussion can include the use of a questionnaire designed to articulate the client's risk tolerance as well as address expectations in connection with specific circumstances. In the case of institutional clients, the fact finding may involve asset–liability management reviews, identification of liquidity needs, and a wide range of tax, legal, and other considerations.

The IPS can take a variety of forms.[1] A typical format will include the client's investment objectives and the constraints that apply to the client's portfolio.

The client's objectives are specified in terms of risk tolerance and return requirements. These elements must be consistent with each other: a client is unlikely to be able to find a portfolio that offers a relatively high expected return without taking

---

[1] In this reading, an IPS is assumed to be a document governing investment management activities covering all or most of a client's financial wealth. In many practical contexts, investment professionals work with investment mandates that cover only parts of a client's wealth or financial risk. Governance documents such as "Limited Partnership Agreements" and "Investment Management Agreements" will govern such mandates. Their contents are to a large degree comparable to the contents of the IPS as described in this reading.

on a relatively high level of expected risk. As part of their financial planning, clients may specify specific spending goals, which need to be considered when setting risk tolerance and return requirements.

The constraints section covers factors that need to be taken into account when constructing a portfolio for the client that meets the objectives. The typical categories are liquidity requirements, time horizon, regulatory requirements, tax status, and unique needs. The constraints may be either internal (i.e., set by the client) or external (i.e., set by law or regulation), as we discuss in detail later.

Having a well-constructed IPS for all clients should be standard procedure for an investment manager. The investment manager should build the portfolio with reference to the IPS and be able to refer to it to assess a particular investment's suitability for the client. In some cases, the need for the IPS goes beyond simply being a matter of standard procedure. In certain countries, the IPS (or an equivalent document) is a legal or regulatory requirement. For example, UK pension schemes must have a statement of investment principles under the Pensions Act 1995 (Section 35), and this statement is in essence an IPS. The UK Financial Services Authority also has requirements for investment firms to "know their customers." The European Union's Markets in Financial Instruments Directive ("MiFID") requires firms to assign clients to categories (eligible counterparties, institutional clients, or retail clients), with the category type determining the types of protections and limitations relevant for the client by law.

In the case of an institution, such as a pension plan or university endowment, the IPS may set out the governance arrangements that apply to the investment portfolio. For example, this information could cover the investment committee's approach to appointing and reviewing investment managers for the portfolio, and the discretion that those managers have.

The IPS should be reviewed on a regular basis to ensure that it remains consistent with the client's circumstances and requirements. For example, the UK Pensions Regulator suggests that a pension scheme's statements of investment principles—a form of IPS—should be reviewed at least every three years. The IPS should also be reviewed if the manager becomes aware of a material change in the client's circumstances, as well as on the initiative of the client when her objectives, time horizon, or liquidity needs change.

Major Components of an IPS

There is no single standard format for an IPS. Many IPS and investment governance documents with a similar purpose (as noted previously), however, include the following sections:

- *Introduction.* This section describes the client.
- *Statement of Purpose.* This section states the purpose of the IPS.
- *Statement of Duties and Responsibilities.* This section details the duties and responsibilities of the client, the custodian of the client's assets, and the investment managers.
- *Procedures.* This section explains the steps to take to keep the IPS current and the procedures to follow to respond to various contingencies.
- *Investment Objectives.* This section explains the client's objectives in investing.
- *Investment Constraints.* This section presents the factors that constrain the client in seeking to achieve the investment objectives.

- *Investment Guidelines.* This section provides information about how policy should be executed (e.g., on the permissible use of leverage and derivatives) and on specific types of assets excluded from investment, if any.
- *Evaluation and Review.* This section provides guidance on obtaining feedback on investment results.
- *Appendices*: (A) Strategic Asset Allocation and (B) Rebalancing Policy. Many investors specify a strategic asset allocation (SAA), also known as the policy portfolio, which is the baseline allocation of portfolio assets to asset classes in view of the investor's investment objectives and the investor's policy with respect to rebalancing asset class weights. This SAA may include a statement of policy concerning hedging risks such as currency risk and interest rate risk.

The sections that are most closely linked to the client's distinctive needs, and probably the most important from a planning perspective, are those dealing with investment objectives and constraints. An IPS focusing on these two elements has been called an IPS in an "objectives and constraints" format.

In the following sections, we discuss the investment objectives and constraints format of an IPS beginning with risk and return objectives. The process of developing the IPS is the basic mechanism for evaluating and trying to improve an investor's overall expected return–risk stance. In a portfolio context, return objectives and expectations must be tailored to be consistent with risk objectives. The risk and return objectives must also be consistent with the constraints that apply to the portfolio. A growing proportion of investors explicitly include non-financial considerations when formulating their investment policies. This approach is often referred to as responsible investing (discussed earlier alongside related terms), which reflects environmental, social, and governance (ESG) considerations. Responsible investing recognizes that ESG considerations may eventually affect the portfolio's financial risk–return profile and may express the investor's societal convictions. In this reading, we discuss responsible investing aspects of investment policy, where relevant.

3. IPS RISK AND RETURN OBJECTIVES

☐ describe the major components of an IPS
☐ describe risk and return objectives and how they may be developed for a client
☐ explain the difference between the willingness and the ability (capacity) to take risk in analyzing an investor's financial risk tolerance

When constructing a portfolio for a client, it is important to ensure that the risk of the portfolio is suitable for the client. The IPS should state clearly the risk tolerance of the client. Risk objectives are specifications for portfolio risk that reflect the client's risk tolerance. Quantitative risk objectives can be absolute, relative, or a combination of the two.

Examples of an absolute risk objective would be a desire not to suffer any loss of capital or not to lose more than a given percentage of capital in any 12-month period. Note that these objectives are unrelated to investment market performance, good or bad, and are absolute in the sense of being self-standing. The fulfillment of such

IPS Risk and Return Objectives

objectives could be achieved by not taking any risk—for example, by investing in an insured bank certificate of deposit at a creditworthy bank. If investments in risky assets are undertaken, however, such statements could be restated as a probability statement to be more operational (i.e., practically useful). For example, the desire not to lose more than 4% of capital in any 12-month period might be restated as an objective that with 95% probability the portfolio not lose more than 4% in any 12-month period. Measures of absolute risk include the variance or standard deviation of returns and **value at risk**.[2]

Some clients may choose to express relative risk objectives, which relate risk relative to one or more benchmarks perceived to represent appropriate risk standards. For example, investments in large-cap UK equities could be benchmarked to an equity market index, such as the FTSE 100 Index. The S&P 500 Index could be used as a benchmark for large-cap US equities; for investments with cash-like characteristics, the benchmark could be an interest rate such as Treasury bill rate. For risk relative to a benchmark, the measure could be **tracking risk**, or **tracking error**.[3] In practice, such risk objectives are used in situations where the total wealth management activities on behalf of a client are divided into partial mandates.

Other clients take both the investor's assets and liabilities into consideration when establishing an IPS risk objective. In some cases where the size, timing and/or relative certainty of future investor financial obligations are known, an IPS may be tailored to meet these objectives in what is called a **liability-driven investment (LDI)** approach. Examples of LDI include life insurance companies, defined benefit pension plans or an individual's budget after retirement. For example, a pension plan must meet the pension payments as they come due, and the risk objective will be to minimize the probability that it will fail to do so. A related return objective might be to outperform the discount rate used in finding the present value of liabilities over a multi-year time horizon.

When a policy portfolio (that is, a specified set of long-term asset class weightings and hedge ratios) is used, the risk objective may be expressed as a desire for the portfolio return to be within a band of plus or minus X% of the benchmark return calculated by assigning an index or benchmark to represent each asset class present in the policy portfolio. Again, this objective may be more usefully interpreted as a statement of probability—for example, a 95% probability that the portfolio return will be within X% of the benchmark return over a stated period. Example 1 reviews this material.

EXAMPLE 1

Types of Risk Objectives

A Japanese institutional investor has a portfolio valued at ¥10 billion. The investor expresses her first risk objective as a desire not to lose more than ¥1 billion in the coming 12-month period. She specifies a second risk objective of achieving returns within 4% of the return to the TOPIX stock market index, which is her benchmark. Based on this information, address the following:

1.
   A. Characterize the first risk objective as absolute or relative.

---

[2] **Value at risk** is a money measure of the minimum value of losses expected during a specified period at a given level of probability.
[3] **Tracking risk** (sometimes called **tracking error**) is the standard deviation of the differences between a portfolio's returns and its benchmark's returns.

> **B.** Give an example of how the risk objective could be restated in a practical manner.
>
> **Solution**
>
> **A.** This is an absolute risk objective.
>
> **B.** This risk objective could be restated in a practical manner by specifying that the 12-month 95% value at risk of the portfolio must be no more than ¥1 billion.

> 2.
>
> **A.** Characterize the second risk objective as absolute or relative.
>
> **B.** Identify a measure for quantifying the risk objective.
>
> **Solution**
>
> **A.** This is a relative risk objective.
>
> **B.** This risk objective could be quantified using the tracking risk as a measure. For example, assuming returns follow a normal distribution, an expected tracking risk of 2% would imply a return within 4% of the index return approximately 95% of the time. Remember that tracking risk is stated as a one standard deviation measure.

A client's overall risk tolerance is a function of the client's ability to bear (accept) risk and her "risk attitude," which might be considered as the client's willingness to take risk. For ease of expression, from this point on we will refer to ability to bear risk and willingness to take risk as the two components of risk tolerance. Above-average ability to bear risk and above-average willingness to take risk imply above-average risk tolerance. Below-average ability to bear risk and below-average willingness to take risk imply below-average risk tolerance. These interactions are shown in Exhibit 1.

Exhibit 1: Risk Tolerance

	Ability to Bear Risk	
Willingness to Take Risk	**Below Average**	**Above Average**
Below Average	Below-average risk tolerance	Resolution needed
Above Average	Resolution needed	Above-average risk tolerance

The *ability* to bear risk is measured mainly in terms of objective factors, such as time horizon, expected income, and level of wealth relative to liabilities. For example, an investor with a 20-year time horizon can be considered to have a greater ability to bear risk, other things being equal, than an investor with a 2-year horizon. This difference is because over 20 years, there is more scope for losses to be recovered or other adjustments made to circumstances than there is over 2 years.

Similarly, an investor whose assets are comfortably in excess of their liabilities has more ability to bear risk than an investor whose wealth and expected future expenditure are more closely balanced. For example, a wealthy individual who can sustain a comfortable lifestyle after a very substantial investment loss has a relatively high ability to bear risk. A pension plan that has a large surplus of assets over liabilities has a relatively high ability to bear risk.

The *willingness* to take risk, or risk attitude, is a more subjective factor based on the client's psychology and perhaps also his current circumstances. Although the list of factors related to an individual's risk attitude remains open to debate, it is believed that some psychological factors, such as personality type, self-esteem, and inclination to independent thinking, are correlated with risk attitude. Some individuals are comfortable taking financial and investment risk, whereas others find it distressing. Although there is no single agreed-upon method for measuring risk tolerance, a willingness to take risk may be gauged by discussing risk with the client or by asking the client to complete a psychometric questionnaire. For example, financial planning academic John Grable and collaborators have developed 13-item and 5-item risk attitude questionnaires that have undergone some level of technical validation. The five-item questionnaire is shown in Exhibit 2.

Exhibit 2: A Five-Item Risk Assessment Instrument

1. Investing is too difficult to understand.
   a. Strongly agree
   b. Tend to agree
   c. Tend to disagree
   d. Strongly disagree
2. I am more comfortable putting my money in a bank account than in the stock market.
   a. Strongly agree
   b. Tend to agree
   c. Tend to disagree
   d. Strongly disagree
3. When I think of the word "risk," the term "loss" comes to mind immediately.
   a. Strongly agree
   b. Tend to agree
   c. Tend to disagree
   d. Strongly disagree
4. Making money in stocks and bonds is based on luck.
   a. Strongly agree
   b. Tend to agree
   c. Tend to disagree
   d. Strongly disagree
5. In terms of investing, safety is more important than returns.
   a. Strongly agree
   b. Tend to agree
   c. Tend to disagree
   d. Strongly disagree

Source: Grable and Joo (2004).

The responses, a), b), c), and d), are coded 1, 2, 3, and 4, respectively, and summed. The lowest score is 5 and the highest score is 20, with higher scores indicating greater risk tolerance. For two random samples drawn from the faculty and staff of large US universities (n = 406), the mean score was 12.86 with a standard deviation of 3.01 and a median score (i.e., the middle score) of 13.

Note that a question, such as the first one in Exhibit 2, indicates that risk attitude may be associated with non-psychological factors (such as level of financial knowledge and understanding and decision-making style) as well as psychological factors.

The adviser needs to examine whether a client's ability to accept risk is consistent with the client's willingness to take risk. For example, a wealthy investor with a 20-year time horizon, who is thus able to take risk, may also be comfortable taking risk; in this case the factors are consistent. If the wealthy investor has a low willingness to take risk, there would be a conflict.

The conflict between ability and willingness to take risk can also arise in the institutional context. In addition, different stakeholders within the institution may take different views. For example, the trustees of a well-funded pension plan may desire a low-risk approach to safeguard the funding of the scheme and beneficiaries of the scheme may take a similar view. The sponsor, however, may wish a higher-risk/higher-return approach in an attempt to reduce future funding costs. When a trustee bears a fiduciary responsibility to pension beneficiaries and the interests of the pension sponsor and the pension beneficiaries conflict, the trustee should act in the best interests of the beneficiaries.

When both the ability and willingness to take risk are consistent, the investment adviser's task is the simplest. When ability to take risk is below average and willingness to take risk is above average, the investor's risk tolerance should be assessed as below average overall. When ability to take risk is above average but willingness is below average, the portfolio manager or adviser may seek to counsel the client and explain the conflict and its implications. For example, the adviser could outline the reasons why the client is considered to have a high ability to take risk and explain the likely consequences, in terms of reduced expected return, of not taking risk. The investment adviser, however, should not aim to change a client's willingness to take risk that is not a result of a miscalculation or misperception. Modification of elements of personality is not within the purview of the investment adviser's role. The prudent approach is to reach a conclusion about risk tolerance consistent with the lower of the two factors (ability and willingness) and to document the decisions made.

Example 2 is the first of a set that follows the analysis of an investment client through the preparation of the major elements of an IPS.

EXAMPLE 2

The Case of Henri Gascon: Risk Tolerance

1. Henri Gascon is an energy trader who works for a major French oil company based in Paris. He is 30 years old and married with one son, aged 5. Gascon has decided that it is time to review his financial situation and consults a financial adviser, who notes the following aspects of Gascon's situation:

    - Gascon's annual salary of €250,000 is more than sufficient to cover the family's outgoings.
    - Gascon owns his apartment outright and has €1,000,000 of savings.
    - Gascon perceives that his job is reasonably secure.
    - Gascon has a good knowledge of financial matters and is confident that equity markets will deliver positive returns over the long term.
    - In the risk tolerance questionnaire, Gascon strongly disagrees with the statements that "making money in stocks and bonds is based on luck" and "in terms of investing, safety is more important than returns."

IPS Risk and Return Objectives

- Gascon expects that most of his savings will be used to fund his retirement, which he hopes to start at age 50.

Based only on the information given, which of the following statements is *most* accurate?

A. Gascon has a low ability to take risk but a high willingness to take risk.

B. Gascon has a high ability to take risk but a low willingness to take risk.

C. Gascon has a high ability to take risk and a high willingness to take risk.

Solution:

C is correct. Gascon has a high income relative to outgoings, a high level of assets, a secure job, and a time horizon of 20 years. This information suggests a high *ability* to take risk. At the same time, Gascon is knowledgeable and confident about financial markets and responds to the questionnaire with answers that suggest risk tolerance. This result suggests he also has a high *willingness* to take risk.

EXAMPLE 3

The Case of Jacques Gascon: Risk Tolerance

1. Marie Gascon is so pleased with the services provided by her financial adviser that she suggests to her brother Jacques that he should also consult the adviser. Jacques thinks it is a good idea. Jacques, a self-employed computer consultant also based in Paris, is 40 years old and divorced with four children, aged between 12 and 16. The financial adviser notes the following aspects of Jacques' situation:

   - Jacques' consultancy earnings average €40,000 per annum but are quite volatile.
   - Jacques is required to pay €10,000 per year to his ex-wife and children.
   - Jacques has a mortgage on his apartment of €100,000 and €10,000 of savings.
   - Jacques has a good knowledge of financial matters and expects that equity markets will deliver very high returns over the long term.
   - In the risk tolerance questionnaire, Jacques strongly disagrees with the statements "I am more comfortable putting my money in a bank account than in the stock market" and "When I think of the word 'risk', the term 'loss' comes to mind immediately."
   - Jacques expects that most of his savings will be required to support his children at university.

   Based only on the information given, which statement is correct?

   A. Jacques has a low ability to take risk but a high willingness to take risk.

   B. Jacques has a high ability to take risk but a low willingness to take risk.

   C. Jacques has a high ability to take risk and a high willingness to take risk.

> **Solution:**
>
> A is correct. Jacques does not have a particularly high income, his income is unstable, and he has reasonably high outgoings for his mortgage and maintenance payments. His investment time horizon is approximately two to six years given the ages of his children and his desire to support them at university. This finely balanced financial situation and short time horizon suggests a low ability to take risk. In contrast, his expectations for financial market returns and risk tolerance questionnaire answers suggest a high willingness to take risk. The financial adviser may wish to explain to Jacques how finely balanced his financial situation is and suggest that, despite his desire to take more risk, a relatively cautious portfolio might be the most appropriate approach to take.

Return Objectives

A client's return objectives can be stated in a number of ways. Similar to risk objectives, return objectives may be stated on an absolute or a relative basis.

As an example of an absolute objective, the client may want to achieve a particular percentage rate of return. This objective could be a nominal rate of return or could be expressed in real (inflation-adjusted) terms.

Alternatively, the return objective can be stated on a relative basis—for example, relative to a benchmark return. The benchmark could be an equity market index, such as the S&P 500 or the FTSE 100, or a cash rate of interest such as the market reference rate (MRR). A relative return objective might be stated as, for example, a desire to outperform the benchmark index by one percentage point per year.

Some institutions also set their return objectives relative to a peer group or universe of managers—for example, an endowment aiming for a return that is in the top 50% of returns of similar institutions, or a private equity mandate aiming for returns in the top quartile among the private equity universe. This objective can be problematic when limited information is known about the investment strategies or the return calculation methodology being used by peers, and we must bear in mind the impossibility of *all* institutions being "above average." Furthermore, a good benchmark should be investable—that is, able to be replicated by the investor—and a peer benchmark typically does not meet that criterion.

In each case, the return requirement can be stated before or after fees. Care should be taken that the fee basis used is clear and understood by both the manager and client. The return can also be stated on either a pre- or post-tax basis when the investor is required to pay tax. For a taxable investor, the baseline is to state and analyze returns on an after-tax basis.

The return objective could be a required return—that is, the amount the investor needs to earn to meet a particular future goal—such as a certain level of retirement income.

The manager or adviser must ensure that the return objective is realistic. Care should be taken that client and manager are in agreement on whether the return objective is nominal (which is more convenient for measurement purposes) or real (i.e., inflation-adjusted, which usually relates better to the objective). It must be consistent with the client's risk objective (high expected returns are unlikely to be possible without high levels of risk) and also with the current economic and market environment. For example, 15% nominal returns might be possible when inflation is 10% but will be unlikely when inflation is 3%.

IPS Risk and Return Objectives

When a client has unrealistic return expectations, the manager or adviser will need to counsel her about what is achievable in the current market environment and within the client's tolerance for risk.

> **EXAMPLE 4**
>
> ### The Case of Marie Gascon: Return Objectives
>
> Having assessed her risk tolerance, Marie Gascon now begins to discuss her retirement income needs with the financial adviser. She wishes to retire at age 50, which is 20 years from now. Her salary meets current and expected future expenditure requirements, but she does not expect to be able to make any additional pension contributions to her fund. Gascon sets aside €100,000 of her savings as an emergency fund to be held in cash. The remaining €900,000 is invested for her retirement.
>
> Gascon estimates that a before-tax amount of €2,000,000 in today's money will be sufficient to fund her retirement income needs. The financial adviser expects inflation to average 2% per year over the next 20 years. Pension fund contributions and pension fund returns in France are exempt from tax, but pension fund distributions are taxable upon retirement.
>
> 1. Which of the following is closest to the amount of money Gascon will have to accumulate in nominal terms by her retirement date to meet her retirement income objective (i.e., expressed in money of the day in 20 years)?
>
>   **A.** €900,000
>
>   **B.** €2,000,000
>
>   **C.** €3,000,000
>
> ### Solution to 1:
>
> C is correct. At 2% annual inflation, €2,000,000 in today's money equates to €2,971,895 in 20 years measured in money of the day [€2,000,000 × (1 + 2%)^{20}].
>
> 2. Which of the following is closest to the annual rate of return that Gascon must earn on her pension portfolio to meet her retirement income objective?
>
>   **A.** 2.0%
>
>   **B.** 6.2%
>
>   **C.** 8.1%
>
> ### Solution to 2:
>
> B is correct. €900,000 growing at 6.2% per year for 20 years will accumulate to €2,997,318, which is just above the required amount. (The solution of 6.2% comes from €2,997,318/€900,000 = (1 + X)^{20}, where X is the required rate of return.)

4 IPS CONSTRAINTS

☐ describe the major components of an IPS

☐ describe the investment constraints of liquidity, time horizon, tax concerns, legal and regulatory factors, and unique circumstances and their implications for the choice of portfolio assets

In the following sections, we analyze five major types of constraints on portfolio selection: liquidity, time horizon, tax concerns, legal and regulatory factors, and unique circumstances.

Liquidity Requirements

The IPS should state what the likely requirements are to withdraw funds from the portfolio. Examples for an individual investor would be outlays for covering healthcare payments or tuition fees. For institutions, it could be spending rules and requirements for endowment funds, the existence of claims coming due in the case of property and casualty insurance, or benefit payments for pension funds and life insurance companies.

When the client does have such a requirement, the manager should allocate part of the portfolio to cover the liability. This part of the portfolio will be invested in assets that are liquid—that is, easily converted to cash—and have low risk when the liquidity need is actually present (e.g., a bond maturing at the time when private education expenses will be incurred), so that their value is known with reasonable certainty. For example, the asset allocation in the insurance portfolios of US insurer Progressive Corporation (see Exhibit 3) shows a large allocation to fixed-income investments (called "Fixed maturities" by the company), some of which are either highly liquid or have a short maturity. These investments enable the company, in the case of automobile insurance, to pay claims for which the timing is unpredictable.

Exhibit 3: Asset Allocation of Progressive Corporation

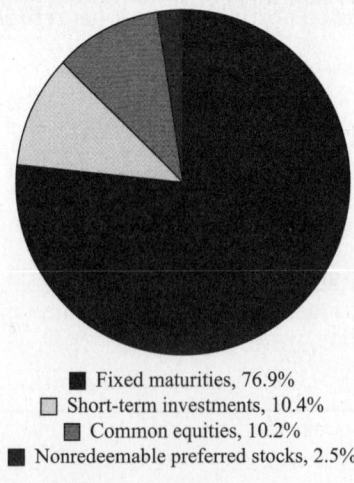

■ Fixed maturities, 76.9%
☐ Short-term investments, 10.4%
■ Common equities, 10.2%
■ Nonredeemable preferred stocks, 2.5%

Source: Progressive Corporation, 2018 Second Quarter Report.

Time Horizon

The IPS should state the time horizon over which the investor is investing. It may be the period over which the portfolio is accumulating before any assets need to be withdrawn; it could also be the period until the client's circumstances are likely to change. For example, a 55-year-old pension plan investor hoping to retire at age 65 has a 10-year horizon. The portfolio may not be liquidated at age 65, but its structure may need to change, for example, as the investor begins to draw an income from the fund.

The time horizon of the investor will affect the nature of investments used in the portfolio. Illiquid or risky investments may be unsuitable for an investor with a short time horizon because the investor may not have enough time to recover from investment losses, for example. Such investments, however, may be suitable for an investor with a longer horizon, especially if the risky investments are expected to have higher returns.

EXAMPLE 5

Investment Time Horizon

1. Frank Johnson is investing for retirement and has a 20-year horizon. He has an average risk tolerance. Which investment is likely to be the *least* suitable for a major allocation in Johnson's portfolio?

   A. Listed equities
   B. Private equity
   C. US Treasury bills

Solution to 1:

C is correct. With a 20-year horizon and average risk tolerance, Johnson can accept the additional risk of listed equities and private equity compared with US Treasury bills.

2. Al Smith has to pay a large tax bill in six months and wants to invest the money in the meantime. Which investment is likely to be the *least* suitable for a major allocation in Smith's portfolio?

   A. Listed equities
   B. Private equity
   C. US Treasury bills

Solution to 2:

B is correct. Private equity is risky, has no public market, and is the least liquid among the assets mentioned.

Tax Concerns

Tax status varies among investors. Some investors will be subject to taxation on investment returns and some will not. For example, in many countries, returns to pension funds are exempt from tax. Some investors will face a different tax rate on income (dividends and interest payments) than they do on capital gains (associated with increases in asset prices). Typically, when there is a differential, income is taxed more highly than gains. Gains may be subject to a lower tax rate, or part or all of the gain may be exempt from taxation. Furthermore, income may be taxed as it is earned, whereas gains may be taxed when they are realized. Hence, in such cases there is a time value of money benefit in the deferment of taxation of gains relative to income.

In many cases, the portfolio should reflect the tax status of the client. For example, a taxable investor may wish to hold a portfolio that emphasizes capital gains and receives little income. A taxable investor based in the United States is also likely to consider including US municipal bonds ("munis") in his portfolio because interest income from munis, unlike from Treasuries and corporate bonds, is exempt from taxes. A tax-exempt investor, such as a pension fund, will be relatively indifferent to the form of returns.

Legal and Regulatory Factors

The IPS should state any legal and regulatory restrictions that constrain how the portfolio is invested.

In some countries, such institutional investors as pension funds are subject to restrictions on portfolio composition. For example, there may be a limit on the proportion of equities or other risky assets in the portfolio or on the proportion of the portfolio that may be invested overseas. The United States has no limits on pension fund asset allocation, but some countries do, examples of which are shown in Exhibit 4. Pension funds also often face restrictions on the percentage of assets that can be invested in securities issued by the plan sponsor, so called **self-investment limits**.

Exhibit 4: Examples of Pension Fund Investment Restrictions

Country	Listed Equity	Real Estate	Government Bonds	Corporate Bonds	Foreign Currency Exposure
Switzerland	50%	30%	100%	100%	Unhedged 30%
Japan	100%	Not permitted	100%	100%	No limits
South Africa	75%	25%	100%	75%	25%

Source: OECD "Survey of Investment Regulations of Pension Funds," July 2018.

When an individual has access to material nonpublic information about a particular security, this situation may also form a constraint. For example, the directors of a public company may need to refrain from trading the company's stock at certain points of the year before financial results are published. The IPS should note this constraint so that the portfolio manager does not inadvertently trade the stock on the client's behalf.

Unique Circumstances and ESG Considerations

This section of the IPS should cover any other aspect of the client's circumstances, including beliefs and values, that is likely to have a material impact on portfolio composition. A client may have considerations derived from her faith or moral values that could constrain investment choices. For instance, an investor seeking compliance with Shari'a (the Islamic law) will avoid investing in businesses and financial instruments inconsistent with Shari'a, such as casinos and bonds, because Shari'a prohibits gambling and lending money on interest. Similarly, an investor may wish to avoid investments that he believes are inconsistent with his faith. Charitable and pension fund investors may have constituencies that want to express their values in an investment portfolio.

Whether rooted in religious beliefs or not, a client may have personal objections to certain products (e.g., weapons, tobacco, gambling) or practices (e.g., environmental impact of business activities, human impact of government policies, labor standards), which could lead to the exclusion of certain companies, countries, or types of securities (e.g., interest-bearing debt) from the investable universe as well as the client's benchmark. Investing in accordance with such considerations is referred to as socially responsible investing (SRI).

Specific ESG investment approaches can be classified in a variety of ways, and the investment community lacks clear consensus on terminology. We define six generic ESG investment approaches:

- *Negative screening*: Excluding companies or sectors based on business activities or environmental or social concerns;
- *Positive screening*: Including sectors or companies based on specific ESG criteria, typically ESG performance relative to industry peers;
- *ESG integration*: Systematic consideration of material ESG factors in asset allocation, security selection, and portfolio construction decisions;
- *Thematic investing*: Investing in themes or assets related to ESG factors;
- *Engagement/active ownership*: Using shareholder power to influence corporate behavior to achieve targeted ESG objectives along with financial returns; and
- *Impact investing*: Investments made with the intention to generate positive, measurable social and environmental impact alongside a financial return.

These ESG investment approaches may impact a portfolio manager's investment universe and may also require the investment management firm to put in place a process to systematically incorporate ESG factors into the investment process.

EXAMPLE 6

Ethical Preferences

The BMO Responsible UK Equity Fund is designed for investors who wish to have ethical and ESG principles applied to the selection of their investments. The fund's managers apply both positive (features to be emphasized in the portfolio) and negative (features to be avoided in the portfolio) screening criteria:

Product-Based Screening Criteria

- Alcohol
- Arctic and oil sands
- Coal mining
- Gambling
- Nuclear power generation
- Pornography
- Tobacco
- Weapons

> **Conduct-Based Screening Criteria**
>
> *Environmental*
>
> - Environmental management
>
> *Social*
>
> - Animal welfare
> - Health and safety
> - Human rights and oppressive regimes
> - Labor standards
>
> *Governance*
>
> - Business ethics
>
> [Excerpted from BMO Responsible UK Equity Fund documents; https://www.bmogam.com/gb-en/intermediary/bmo-responsible-uk-equity-2-inc/.]

When the portfolio represents only part of the client's total wealth, there may be aspects or portions of wealth not under the control of the manager that have implications for the portfolio. For example, an employee of a public company whose labor income and retirement income provision are reliant on that company, and who may have substantial investment exposure to the company through employee share options and stock holdings, may decide that his portfolio should not invest additional amounts in that stock. An entrepreneur may be reluctant to see her portfolio invested in the shares of competing businesses or in any business that has risk exposures aligned with her entrepreneurial venture.

A client's income may rely on a particular industry or asset class. Appropriate diversification requires that industry or asset class to be de-emphasized in the client's investments. For example, a stockbroker should consider having a relatively low weighting in equities, as his skills and thus his income-generating ability are worth less when equities do not perform well. Employees should similarly be wary of having concentrated share positions in the equity of the company where they work. If the employer encounters difficulties, not only may its employees lose their jobs but their investment portfolios could also suffer a significant loss of value.

5. GATHERING CLIENT INFORMATION

- [ ] describe risk and return objectives and how they may be developed for a client
- [ ] describe the investment constraints of liquidity, time horizon, tax concerns, legal and regulatory factors, and unique circumstances and their implications for the choice of portfolio assets

As noted earlier, it is important for portfolio managers and investment advisers to know their clients. For example, in the EU, MiFID II requires financial intermediaries to undertake substantial fact finding. This is required not only in the case of full-service wealth management or in the context of an IPS but also in "lighter" forms of financial intermediation, such as advisory relationships (in which clients make investment decisions after consultation with their investment adviser or broker) or execution-only relationships (in which the client makes investment decisions independently).

Gathering Client Information

An exercise in fact finding about the customer should take place at the beginning of the client relationship. This process will involve gathering information about the client's circumstances as well as discussing the client's objectives and requirements.

Important data to gather from a client should cover family and employment situation as well as financial information. If the client is an individual, it may also be necessary to know about the situation and requirements of the client's spouse or other family members. The health of the client and her dependents is also relevant information. In an institutional relationship, it will be important to know about key stakeholders in the organization and what their perspective and requirements are. Information gathering may be done in an informal way or may involve structured interviews, questionnaires, or analysis of data. Many advisers will capture data electronically and use special systems that record data and produce customized reports.

Good recordkeeping is very important and may be crucial in a case in which any aspect of the client relationship comes into dispute at a later stage.

EXAMPLE 7

Marie Gascon: Description of Constraints

Marie Gascon continues to discuss her investment requirements with her financial adviser. The adviser begins to draft the constraints section of the IPS.

Gascon expects that she will continue to work for the oil company and that her relatively high income will continue for the foreseeable future. Gascon and her husband plan to have no additional children but expect that their son will go to a university at age 18. They expect that their son's education costs can be met out of their salary income.

Gascon's emergency reserve of €100,000 is considered to be sufficient as a reserve for unforeseen expenditures and emergencies. Her retirement savings of €900,000 has been contributed to her defined-contribution pension plan account to fund her retirement. Under French regulation, pension fund contributions are paid from gross income (i.e., income prior to deduction of tax), and pension fund returns are exempt from tax, but pension payments from a fund to retirees are taxed as income to the retiree.

With respect to Gascon's retirement savings portfolio, refer back to Example 2 as needed and address the following:

1. As concerns liquidity,
   A. a maximum of 50% of the portfolio should be invested in liquid assets.
   B. the portfolio should be invested entirely in liquid assets because of high spending needs.
   C. the portfolio has no need for liquidity because there are no short-term spending requirements.

Solution to 1:

C is correct. The assets are for retirement use, which is 20 years away. Any short-term spending needs will be met from other assets or income.

2. The investment time horizon is closest to
   A. 5 years.
   B. 20 years.
   C. 40 years.

Solution to 2:

B is correct. The relevant time horizon is to the retirement date, which is 20 years away. The assets may not be liquidated at that point, but a restructuring of the portfolio is to be expected as Gascon starts to draw an income from it.

3. As concerns taxation, the portfolio
   A. should emphasize capital gains because income is taxable.
   B. should emphasize income because capital gains are taxable.
   C. is tax exempt and thus indifferent between income and capital gains.

Solution to 3:

C is correct. Because no tax is paid in the pension fund, it does not matter whether returns come in the form of income or capital gains.

4. The principle legal and regulatory factors applying to the portfolio are
   A. US securities laws.
   B. European banking laws.
   C. French pension fund regulations.

Solution to 4:

C is correct. Management of the portfolio will have to comply with any rules relating to French pension funds.

5. As concerns unique needs, the portfolio should
   A. have a high weighting in oil and other commodity stocks.
   B. be invested only in responsible and sustainable investments.
   C. not have significant exposure to oil and other commodity stocks.

Solution to 5:

C is correct. Gascon's human capital (i.e., future labor income) is affected by the prospects of the oil industry. If her portfolio has significant exposure to oil stocks, she would be increasing a risk exposure she already has.

Example 8, the final one based on Marie Gascon, shows how the information obtained from the fact-finding exercises might be incorporated into the objectives and constraints section of an IPS.

EXAMPLE 8

Marie Gascon: Outline of an IPS

Following is a simplified excerpt from the IPS the adviser prepares for Marie Gascon, covering objectives and constraints.

Risk Objectives:

- The portfolio may take on relatively high amounts of risk in seeking to meet the return requirements. With a 20-year time horizon and significant assets and income, the client has an above-average ability to

> take risk. The client is a knowledgeable investor, with an above-average willingness to take risk. Hence, the client's risk tolerance is above average, explaining the aforementioned portfolio risk objective.
> - The portfolio should be well diversified with respect to asset classes and concentration of positions within an asset class. Although the client has above-average risk tolerance, his investment assets should be diversified to control the risk of catastrophic loss.
>
> *Return Objectives:*
>
> - The portfolio's long-term return requirement is 6.2% per year, in nominal terms and net of fees, to meet the client's retirement income goal.
>
> *Constraints:*
>
> - *Liquidity*: The portfolio consists of pension fund assets, and there is no need for liquidity in the short to medium term.
> - *Time Horizon*: The portfolio will be invested with a 20-year time horizon. The client intends to retire in 20 years, at which time an income will be drawn from the portfolio.
> - *Tax Status*: Under French law, contributions to the fund are made gross of tax and returns in the fund are tax-free. Hence, the client is indifferent between income and capital gains in the fund.
> - *Legal and Regulatory Factors*: Management of the portfolio must comply with French pension fund regulations.
> - *Unique Needs*: The client is an executive in the oil industry. The portfolio should strive to minimize additional exposures to oil and related stocks.

PORTFOLIO CONSTRUCTION AND CAPITAL MARKET EXPECTATIONS

6

- [ ] explain the specification of asset classes in relation to asset allocation
- [ ] describe the principles of portfolio construction and the role of asset allocation in relation to the IPS

Once the IPS has been compiled, the investment manager can construct a suitable portfolio. Strategic asset allocation is a traditional focus of the first steps in portfolio construction. The strategic asset allocation is stated in terms of percentage allocations to asset classes. An **asset class** is a category of assets that have similar characteristics, attributes, and risk–return relationships. The **strategic asset allocation** (SAA) is the set of exposures to IPS-permissible asset classes that is expected to achieve the client's long-term objectives given the client's risk profile and investment constraints. An SAA could include a policy of hedging portfolio risks not explicitly covered by asset class weights. The obvious examples are hedge ratios for foreign currency exposure, or the management of interest rate risk resulting from asset-liability mismatch, and the hedging of inflation risk. So-called "overlay" portfolios of derivatives are often used for this purpose.

The focus on the SAA is the result of a number of important investment principles. One principle is that a portfolio's systematic risk accounts for most of its change in value over the long term. **Systematic risk** is risk related to the economic system (e.g., risk related to business cycle) that cannot be eliminated by holding a diversified portfolio. This risk is different from **nonsystematic risk**, defined as the unique risks of particular assets, which may be avoided by holding other assets with offsetting risks. A second principle is that the returns to groups of similar assets (e.g., long-term debt claims) predictably reflect exposures to certain sets of systematic factors (e.g., for the debt claims, unexpected changes in the interest rate). Thus, the SAA is a means of providing the investor with exposure to the systematic risks of asset classes in proportions that meet the risk and return objectives.

The process of formulating a strategic asset allocation is based on the IPS, already discussed, and capital market expectations.

Capital Market Expectations

Capital market expectations are the investor's expectations concerning the risk and return prospects of asset classes, however broadly or narrowly the investor defines those asset classes. When associated with the client's investment objectives, the result is the strategic asset allocation that is expected to allow the client to achieve his investment objectives (at least under normal capital market conditions).

Traditionally, capital market expectations are quantified in terms of asset class expected returns, standard deviation of returns, and correlations among pairs of asset classes. Formally, the expected return of an asset class consists of the risk-free rate and one or more risk premium(s) associated with the asset class. Expected returns are in practice developed in a variety of ways, including the use of historical estimates, economic analysis, and various kinds of valuation models. Standard deviations and correlation estimates are frequently based on historical data and risk models.

7 STRATEGIC ASSET ALLOCATION

- [ ] explain the specification of asset classes in relation to asset allocation
- [ ] describe the principles of portfolio construction and the role of asset allocation in relation to the IPS

Traditionally, investors have distinguished cash, equities, bonds (government and corporate), and real estate as the major asset classes. In recent years, this list has been expanded with private equity, hedge funds, high-yield and emerging market bonds, and commodities. In addition, such assets as art and intellectual property rights may be considered asset classes for those investors prepared to take a more innovative approach and to accept some illiquidity. Combining such new asset classes as well as hedge funds and private equity under the header "alternative investments" has become accepted practice.

As the strategic asset allocation is built up by asset classes, the decision about how to define those asset classes is an important one. Defining the asset classes also determines the extent to which the investor controls the risk and return characteristics of the eventual investment portfolio. For example, separating bonds into government bonds and corporate bonds, and then further separating corporate bonds into investment grade and non-investment grade (high yield) and government bonds

Strategic Asset Allocation

into domestic and foreign government bonds, creates four bond categories. For these categories, risk–return expectations can be expressed and correlations with other asset classes (and, in an asset–liability management context, with the liabilities) can be estimated. An investment manager who wants to explicitly consider the risk–return characteristics of those bond categories in the strategic asset allocation may choose to treat them as distinct asset classes. Similarly, in equities, some investors distinguish between emerging market and developed market equities, between domestic and international equities, or between large-cap and small-cap equities. In some regulatory environments for institutional investors, asset class definitions are mandatory, thereby forcing investment managers to articulate risk–return expectations (and apply risk management) on the asset classes specified. Conversely, a broader categorization of asset classes leaves the allocation between different categories of bonds and equities, for example, to managers responsible for these asset classes.

When defining asset classes, a number of criteria apply. Intuitively, an asset class should contain relatively homogeneous assets while providing diversification relative to other asset classes. In statistical terms, risk and return expectations should be similar, and paired correlations of assets should be relatively high within an asset class but should be lower versus assets in other asset classes. Also, the asset classes, while being mutually exclusive, should add up to a sufficient approximation of the relevant investable universe. Applying these criteria ensures that the strategic asset allocation process has considered all available investment alternatives.

EXAMPLE 9

Specifying Asset Classes

The strategic asset allocations of many institutional investors make a distinction between domestic equities and international equities or between developed market equities and emerging market equities. Often, equities are separated into different market capitalization brackets, resulting, for example, in an asset class such as domestic small-cap equity.

The correlation matrix in Exhibit 5 shows the paired correlations of monthly returns between different equity asset classes and other asset classes. Specifically, these correlations are measured over the period from December 2000 through August 2018. In addition, the exhibit shows the annualized volatility of monthly returns.

Exhibit 5: Asset Class Correlation Matrix

Correlations	US Equities	Emerging Markets	European Equities	Japanese Equities	US Small-Cap Equities	Commodities	European Gov't. Bonds	US Treasuries	US Credits	US High-Yield Credit
US Equities	1.00	0.78	0.88	0.59	0.89	0.32	0.08	−0.37	0.19	0.66
Emerging Markets Equities	0.78	1.00	0.84	0.64	0.75	0.46	0.21	−0.24	0.34	0.70
European Equities	0.88	0.84	1.00	0.64	0.79	0.43	0.16	−0.28	0.29	0.68
Japanese Equities	0.59	0.64	0.64	1.00	0.57	0.32	0.24	−0.18	0.29	0.52
US Small-Cap Equities	0.89	0.75	0.79	0.57	1.00	0.32	0.09	−0.36	0.19	0.69

Correlations	US Equities	Emerging Markets	European Equities	Japanese Equities	US Small-Cap Equities	Commodities	European Gov't. Bonds	US Treasuries	US Credits	US High-Yield Credit
Commodities	0.32	0.46	0.43	0.32	0.32	1.00	0.13	−0.18	0.12	0.36
European Gov't. Bonds	0.08	0.21	0.16	0.24	0.09	0.13	1.00	0.45	0.60	0.30
US Treasuries	−0.37	−0.24	−0.28	−0.18	−0.36	−0.18	0.45	1.00	0.58	−0.19
US Credits	0.19	0.34	0.29	0.29	0.19	0.12	0.60	0.58	1.00	0.54
US High-Yield Credit	0.66	0.70	0.68	0.52	0.69	0.36	0.30	−0.19	0.54	1.00
Volatility	14.3%	21.6%	18.4%	15.6%	18.4%	22.3%	4.9%	4.4%	5.5%	9.3%

Correlations and volatilities have been calculated using monthly returns from December 2000 through August 2018, unhedged, in USD.

Source: MSCI Bloomberg, S&P

Based only on the information given, address the following:

1. Contrast the correlations between equity asset classes with the correlations between equity asset classes and US Treasuries.

Solution to 1:

The matrix reveals very strong correlation between the equity asset classes. For example, the correlation between European equities and US equities is 0.88. The correlation of equities with bonds, however, is much lower. For example, US equities, emerging markets equities, European equities, and Japanese equities all have negative correlation with US government bonds (−0.37, −0.24 and −0.28, and −0.18, respectively). It is worth noting, however, that correlations can vary through time and the values shown may be specific to the sample period used.

2. The monthly returns of which equity asset class differ the most from US equities?

Solution to 2:

Among equity asset classes as listed in the table, the correlation between US and Japanese equities is the lowest, at 0.59. By contrast, correlations between US equities and emerging markets, European, and US small cap equities are 0.78 or higher.

Using correlation as a metric, Example 9 tends to indicate that only emerging markets were well differentiated from European equities. So, why do investors still often subdivide equities? Apart from any regulatory reasons, one explanation might be that this decomposition into smaller asset classes corresponds to the way the asset allocation is structured in portfolios. Many investment managers have expertise exclusively in specific areas of the market, such as emerging market equities, US small-cap equity, or international investment-grade credit. Bringing the asset class definitions of the asset allocation in line with investment products actually available in the market may simplify matters from an organizational perspective.

The risk–return profile of the strategic asset allocation depends on the expected returns and risks of the individual asset classes, as well as the correlation between those asset classes. In general, adding assets classes with low correlation improves the risk–return trade-off (more return for similar risk). Typically, the strategic asset allocation for risk-averse investors will have a large weight in government bonds and cash, whereas those with more willingness and ability to take risk will have more of their assets in risky asset classes, such as equities and many types of alternative investments.

It is customary to represent asset classes using benchmarks and universes calculated by providers such as FTSE, MSCI, or Bloomberg. An negative screening or a **best-in-class** policy (discussed previously) limits the number of securities to choose from, potentially impacting the risk and expected return estimates for these asset classes. Some examples of exclusions may be controversial weaponry or tobacco companies, or investments in certain countries. When such exclusions apply, risk and return estimates based on non-traditional ("off-the-shelf") asset class benchmarks may not be applicable. Separate benchmark indices reflecting the exclusions may be available from the providers to mitigate this issue.

> ABP is the pension fund for the Dutch government sector employees. The fund offers teachers, police officers, members of the military, and other civil servants a defined benefit pension plan, aiming for a pension of 70% of the average career real income for employees. As of the first quarter of 2018, ABP had €405 billion under management. The strategic asset allocation as of this period is shown in Exhibit 6.

Exhibit 6: Strategic Asset Allocation for ABP

Equity	
Equities, developed countries	27%
Equities, emerging markets	9%
Total equity	*36%*
Alternatives	
Real estate	10%
Private equity	5%
Hedge funds	4%
Commodities	5%
Infrastructure	3%
Total alternatives	*27%*
Fixed-income securities	
Government bonds	13%
Corporate bonds	13%
Inflation-linked bonds	8%
Emerging market bonds	3%
Total fixed income	*37%*
Total	100%

Source: ABP Quarterly Report Q1 2018

A strategic asset allocation results from combining the constraints and objectives articulated in the IPS and long-term capital market expectations regarding the asset classes. The strategic asset allocation or policy portfolio will subsequently be implemented into real portfolios. Exhibit 7 illustrates conceptually how investment objectives and constraints and long-term capital market expectations combine into a policy portfolio.

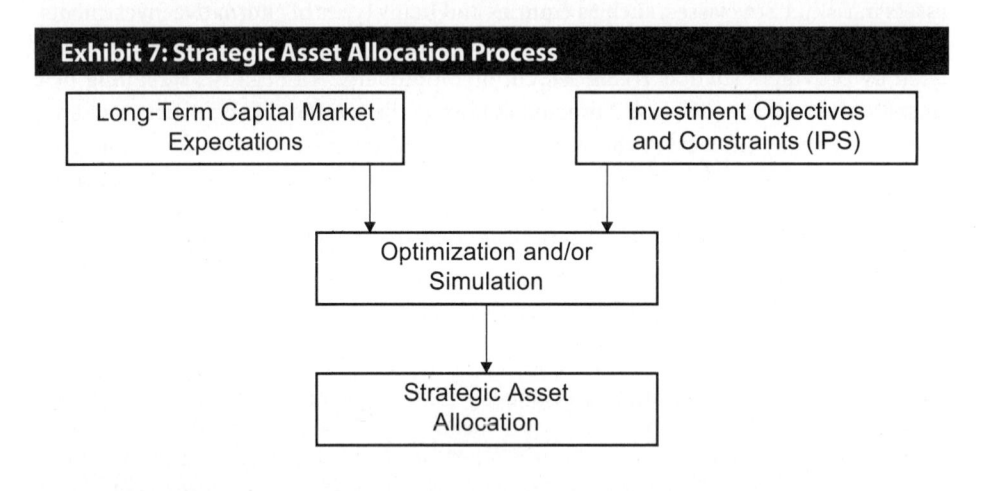

Exhibit 7: Strategic Asset Allocation Process

Long-Term Capital Market Expectations → Optimization and/or Simulation ← Investment Objectives and Constraints (IPS)

Optimization and/or Simulation → Strategic Asset Allocation

In some frameworks used in practice, the asset allocation is an integral part of the investment policy statement. This presentation, however, keeps the asset allocation separate from the investment policy statement because clients' investment objectives and constraints qualitatively differ in nature from capital market expectations, thus requiring different types of analysis, different sources of information, and different review cycles.

The combination of investment objectives/constraints and capital market expectations theoretically occurs using optimization techniques. In this section, we apply mean–variance optimization to a sample set of investment objectives and constraints, using an investment universe with associated market expectations. We assume that investors choosing from a range of asset allocations with similar returns would prefer those with lower risk. Choosing from allocations with similar levels of risk, investors would prefer those with the highest return. Formally, investors' risk and return objectives can be described as a utility function, in which utility increases with higher expected returns and lower risk. This assumption could yield an expected utility equation such as that shown in Equation 1.[4]

$$U_p = E(R_p) - \lambda \sigma_p^2 \tag{1}$$

where

U_p = the investor's expected utility from the portfolio

$E(R_p)$ = the expected return of the portfolio

σ_p = the standard deviation of returns of the portfolio

λ = a measure of the investor's risk aversion

This utility function expresses a positive relationship between utility and expected portfolio return (i.e., higher expected return increases utility, all else equal) and a negative relationship between utility and volatility of portfolio return as measured by

---
[4] Sharpe, Chen, Pinto, and McLeavey (2007).

the variance of portfolio returns. The stronger the negative relationship, the greater the investor's risk aversion. The portfolio is understood to represent a particular asset allocation. The asset allocation providing the highest expected utility is the one that is optimal for the investor given his or her risk aversion.

For different values of U_p, a line can be plotted that links those combinations of risk and expected return that produces that level of utility: an indifference curve. An investor would attain equal utility from all risk–return combinations on that curve.

Capital market expectations, specified in asset classes' expected returns, standard deviations of return, and correlations, translate into an efficient frontier of portfolios. A multi-asset class portfolio's expected return is given by

$$E(R_p) = \sum_{i=1}^{n} w_i E(R_i) \tag{2}$$

where w_i equals the weight of asset class i in the portfolio, and its risk is given by

$$\sigma_p = \sqrt{\sum_{i=1}^{n}\sum_{j=1}^{n} w_{p,i} w_{p,j} \text{Cov}(R_i, R_j)} \tag{3}$$

The covariance between the returns on asset classes i and j is given by the product of the correlation between the two asset classes and their standard deviations of return:

$$\text{Cov}(R_i, R_j) = \rho_{i,j}\sigma_i\sigma_j \tag{4}$$

where

$\text{Cov}(R_i, R_j)$ = the covariance between the return of asset classes i and j

$\rho_{i,j}$ = the correlation between the returns of asset classes i and j

The resulting portfolios can be represented as a scatter of dots in a chart depicting their risk and expected return. Because a portfolio's risk is a positive function of the risk of its assets and the correlations among them, a portfolio consisting of risky assets with low correlation has lower risk than one with similarly risky assets with high correlation. It is therefore possible to construct different portfolios with equal expected returns but with different levels of risk. The line that connects those portfolios with the minimal risk for each level of expected return (above that of the **minimum-variance portfolio**—the portfolio with the minimum variance for each given level of expected return) is the efficient frontier. Clearly, the efficient frontier will move "upward" as more low-correlation assets with sufficient expected return are added to the mix because it lowers the risk in the portfolios for equal expected returns. Similarly, when return expectations increase for asset classes while volatility and correlation assumptions remain unchanged, the efficient frontier will move upward because each portfolio is able to generate higher returns for the same level of risk.

Both the efficient frontier and a range of indifference curves can be plotted in the risk–return space. In Exhibit 8, the dark-colored curves that are concave from below represent efficient frontiers associated with different assumed expected returns. The lighter-colored curves are indifference curves. The point where the efficient frontier intersects with the indifference curve with the highest utility attainable (i.e., the point of tangency) represents the optimal asset allocation for the client/investor. In Exhibit 8, efficient frontier 1 has a point of tangency with indifference curve 1. Higher levels of utility, such as those associated with indifference curve 0, can apparently not be reached with the assets underlying the efficient frontier. It is clear that when capital market expectations change, this change moves the efficient frontier away from its original location. In the chart, this movement is illustrated by efficient frontier 2, which incorporates different capital market expectations. This new efficient frontier has a point of tangency with indifference curve 2, which is associated with a lower level of expected utility. Because the point of tangency represents the strategic asset allocation, it implies the asset allocation should be adjusted. Similarly, should investment objectives or constraints change, the indifference curves will change their shape and location. This change will again move the point of tangency, and hence change the asset allocation.

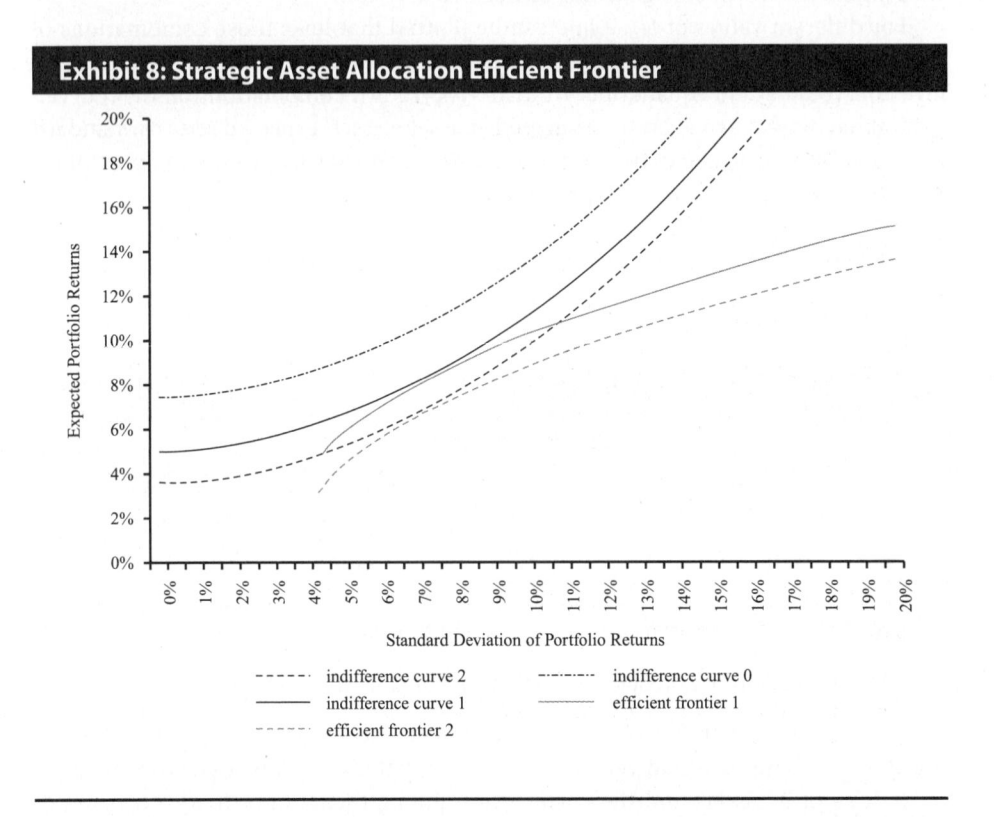

Exhibit 8: Strategic Asset Allocation Efficient Frontier

[Chart showing Expected Portfolio Returns (0%–20%) on y-axis vs Standard Deviation of Portfolio Returns (0%–20%) on x-axis, with curves labeled: indifference curve 2, indifference curve 1, efficient frontier 2, indifference curve 0, efficient frontier 1]

This framework describes how investor objectives and capital market expectations should theoretically be reconciled. It will, however, not be the exact procedure that in practice will be followed. First, an IPS does not necessarily translate the client's investment objectives and constraint into a utility function. Rather, an IPS gives threshold levels for risk and expected return, combined with a number of additional constraints that cannot be captured in this model. Second, the model illustrated is a single-period model, whereas in practice, the constraints from the IPS will make it more appropriate to use multi-period models. Multi-period problems can be more effectively addressed using simulation.

EXAMPLE 10

Approaching a SAA for a Private Investor

1. Rainer Gottschalk recently sold his local home construction company in the south of Germany to a large homebuilder with a nationwide reach. Upon selling his company, he accepted a job as regional manager for that nationwide homebuilder. Gottschalk is now considering his and his family's financial future. He looks forward to his new job—he likes his new role, and the position provides him with income to fulfill his family's short-term and medium-term liquidity needs. Gottschalk feels strongly that he should not invest the proceeds of the sale of his company in real estate because his income already depends on the state of the real estate market. Also, reflecting family values, he feels strongly that his savings should not support the

tobacco industry. He therefore wants his equity allocation to exclude any stocks of tobacco product manufacturers or retailers. Gottschalk consults a financial adviser from his bank about how to invest his money to retire in good wealth in 20 years.

The IPS developed by his adviser suggests a return objective of 5%, with a standard deviation of 10%. The bank's asset management division provides Gottschalk and his adviser with the following data (Exhibit 9, Panel 1) on market expectations. The adviser estimates that excluding the tobacco industry from the investment universe affects expected equity returns of European equities by –0.2% and annual standard deviation by +0.1%. The impact on emerging market equities, and on the correlation structure, was considered negligible. Gottschalk accepts the results of these calculations as shown in Exhibit 9, Panel 2.

Exhibit 9: Risk, Return, and Correlation Estimates

	Expected Return	Standard Deviation	European Equities	Emerging Mkt Equities	European Govt Bonds
Panel 1					
European equities	6.0%	15.0%	1.00	0.78	–0.08
Emerging market equities	8.0%	20.1%	0.78	1.00	–0.07
European government bonds	2.0%	7.8%	–0.08	–0.07	1.00
Panel 2					
European equities	5.8%	15.1%	1.00	0.78	–0.08
Emerging market equities	8.0%	20.1%	0.78	1.00	–0.07
European government bonds	2.00%	7.8%	–0.08	–0.07	1.00

Standard deviation and correlation calculated over the period March 1999–August 2018. All data in unhedged euros.

Sources: MSCI, Bloomberg

To illustrate the possibilities, the adviser presents Gottschalk with the following plot (Exhibit 10), in which the points forming the shaded curve outline the risk–return characteristics of the portfolios that can be constructed out of the three asset classes. An imaginary line linking the points with the lowest standard deviation for each attainable level of return would be the efficient frontier. The two straight lines show the risk and return objectives. Gottschalk should aim for portfolios that offer an expected return of at least 6% (the straight horizontal line or above) and a standard deviation of return of 12% or lower (the straight vertical line to the left).

Exhibit 10: Efficient Frontier

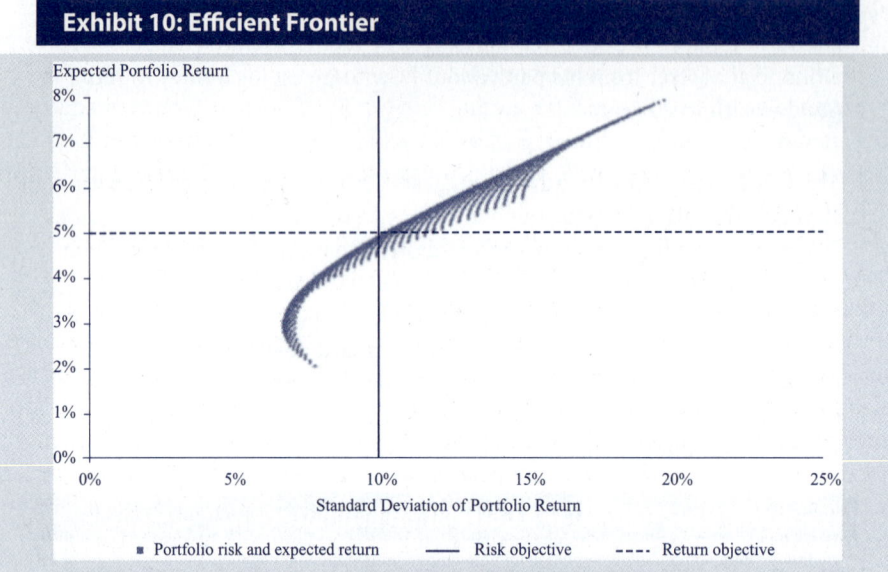

Exhibit 10 shows that no portfolio satisfies the two objectives (return of 5% and standard deviation of 10%) exactly, because the highest expected return that can be attained at a maximum volatility of 10% is 4.9%. This difference, Gottschalk and the adviser agree, is acceptable. The portfolio that would correspond with this expected return consists of 16% European stocks, 38% emerging market equities, and 46% government bonds.

8. PORTFOLIO CONSTRUCTION PRINCIPLES

☐ describe the principles of portfolio construction and the role of asset allocation in relation to the IPS

The strategic asset allocation in itself does not yet represent an actual investment portfolio. It is the first step in implementing an investment strategy. For quantitatively oriented portfolio managers, the next step is often risk budgeting.

As used in this reading, **risk budgeting** is the process of deciding on the amount of risk to assume in a portfolio (the overall risk budget) and subdividing that risk over the sources of investment return (e.g., strategic asset allocation, tactical asset allocation, and security selection). Because the decision about the total amount of risk to be taken is made in constructing the IPS, at this stage we are concerned about the subdivision of that risk.

Apart from the exposures to systematic risk factors specified in the strategic asset allocation, the returns of an investment strategy depend on two other sources: tactical asset allocation and security selection. **Tactical asset allocation** is the decision to deliberately deviate from the policy exposures to systematic risk factors (i.e., the policy weights of asset classes) with the intent to add value based on forecasts of the near-term returns of those asset classes. For instance, an investor may decide to temporarily invest more of the portfolio in equities than the SAA prescribes if the investor anticipates that equities will deliver a higher return over the short term than other asset classes. **Security selection** is an attempt to generate higher returns than the asset class benchmark by selecting securities with a higher expected return. For example, an investment manager may decide to add more IBM stock in her portfolio than the weight in her equity benchmark if she expects this stock to do better than the benchmark. To fund this purchase, she may sell another stock expected to do worse than either the benchmark or IBM. Obviously, deciding to deviate from policy weights or to select securities aiming to beat the benchmark creates additional uncertainty about returns. This risk is over and above the risk inherent in the policy portfolio. Hence, an investment policy should set risk limits and desired payoffs for each of these three activities.

Risk budgeting implies that the portfolio manager has to choose, for every asset class, whether to deploy security selection as a return generator. This choice is generally referred to as the choice between active or passive management. Contrary to strategic asset allocation, where exposures to sources of systematic risk are selected and sized, security selection is not rewarded with a long-run payoff to risk. Security selection is a zero-sum game: All investors in an asset class are competing with each other to identify a typically limited number of assets that are misvalued. In total, the gross returns of all market participants average out to the market return (the reward for taking systematic risk). This implies that the average active investor will match the market return and that one investor's gain versus the market return is the other investor's loss versus the market return. Because active managers tend to trade more and have to pay people (including themselves) to generate investment ideas or information leading to such ideas, however, the average active manager will underperform the market, net of costs. This fact does not imply that there are no skillful investment managers who, with some consistency, beat their benchmarks. Neither does it imply that all passive managers will be able to match the benchmark. The higher the turnover of an index, the more trading costs a passive manager will incur, making the task of matching the return of an index more difficult.

The likelihood of adding a significant amount of value from security selection depends on the skills of the manager and the informational efficiency of the market for the asset class his skill relates to. The more efficient an asset class or a subset of that asset class (such as a regional stock, bond, or real estate market or a size category within the stock market), the more skillful an asset manager has to be to add value. Broadly speaking, an efficient market is a market in which prices, on average, very quickly reflect newly available information. That requires a sizeable participation of investors trading risk against expected return, acting on rational expectations, using the same or similar pricing models, and having equal opportunities to access relevant information. Clearly, the market for US large-capitalization equities would be quite efficient. By contrast, some regional bond and equity markets do not have the technical and regulatory systems for information dissemination that are sufficient to serve all investors on a timely basis. Skilled managers should be able to exploit the resulting inefficiencies.

Sometimes the choice between active and passive management is actually made implicitly when the asset class is included in the asset allocation. The markets for some assets—such as those for non-listed real estate and infrastructure assets—are so illiquid that it is very difficult to buy a diversified exposure. As a result, participating in that market is not possible without engaging in security selection.

As the portfolio is constructed and its value changes with the returns of the asset classes and securities in which it is invested, the weights of the asset classes will gradually deviate from the policy weights in the strategic asset allocation. This process is referred to as drift. Periodically, or when a certain threshold deviation from the policy weight (the bandwidth) has been breached, the portfolio should be rebalanced back to the policy weights. The set of rules that guide the process of restoring the portfolio's original exposures to systematic risk factors is known as the **rebalancing policy**. Even absent a formal risk budget, formulating a rebalancing policy is an important element of risk management, as the following example illustrates.

> **EXAMPLE 11**
>
> ## Strategic and Tactical Asset Allocation for a European Charity
>
> A European charity has an asset allocation at the beginning of the year consisting of the asset classes and weights shown in Exhibit 11.
>
> **Exhibit 11: Asset Allocation of a European Charity (beginning of year)**
>
> | Asset Class | Policy Weight | Corridor (+/–) | Upper Limit | Lower Limit |
> |---|---|---|---|---|
> | European equities | 30.0% | 2.0% | 32.0% | 28.0% |
> | International equities | 15.0% | 2.0% | 17.0% | 13.0% |
> | European government bonds | 20.0% | 2.0% | 22.0% | 18.0% |
> | Corporate bonds | 20.0% | 2.0% | 22.0% | 18.0% |
> | Cash and money market instruments | 15.0% | 2.0% | 17.0% | 13.0% |
> | Total | 100.0% | | | |
>
> As Exhibit 11 reveals, the charity has a policy that the asset class weights cannot deviate from the policy weights by more than 2% (the corridor). The resulting upper and lower limits for the asset class weights are shown in the rightmost columns of the table. There are two reasons for asset class actual weights to deviate from policy weights: by deliberate choice (tactical asset allocation or market timing) and as a result of divergence of the returns of the different asset classes (drift). In this example, the asset class weights start the year exactly in line with policy weights.
>
> After half a year, the investment portfolio is as shown in Exhibit 12.
>
> **Exhibit 12: Asset Allocation for a European Charity (six months later)**
>
> | Asset Class | Policy Weight | Corridor (+/–) | Upper Limit | Lower Limit | Period Return | Ending Weight |
> |---|---|---|---|---|---|---|
> | European equities | 30.0% | 2.0% | 32.0% | 28.0% | 15.0% | 32.4% |
> | International equities | 15.0% | 2.0% | 17.0% | 13.0% | 10.0% | 15.5% |
> | European government bonds | 20.0% | 2.0% | 22.0% | 18.0% | 0.5% | 18.9% |
> | Corporate bonds | 20.0% | 2.0% | 22.0% | 18.0% | 1.5% | 19.1% |
> | Cash and money market instruments | 15.0% | 2.0% | 17.0% | 13.0% | 1.0% | 14.2% |
> | Total | 100.0% | | | | 6.6% | 100.0% |
>
> 1. Discuss the returns of the portfolio and comment on the main asset weight changes.
>
> ## Solution to 1:
>
> The investment portfolio generated a return calculated on beginning (policy) weights of 6.55%, rounded to 6.6% (= 0.30 × 15% + 0.15 × 10% + 0.20 × 0.5% + 0.20 × 1.5% + 0.15 × 1.0%), mainly driven by a strong equity market.

Portfolio Construction Principles

Bond returns were more subdued, leading to considerable drift in asset class weights. In particular, the European equity weight breached the upper limit of its allowed actual weight.

The investment committee decides against reducing European equities back to policy weight and adding to the fixed income and cash investments toward policy weights. Although this rebalancing would be prudent, the committee decides to engage in tactical asset allocation based on the view that this market will continue to be strong over the course of the year. It decides to just bring European equities back to within its bandwidth (a 32% portfolio weight) and add the proceeds to cash. Exhibit 13 shows the outcome after another half year.

Exhibit 13: Asset Allocation for a European Charity (an additional six months later)

Asset Class	Policy Weight	Starting Weight	Corridor (+/−)	Upper Limit	Lower Limit	Period Return	Ending Weight
European equities	30.0%	32.0%	2.0%	32.0%	28.0%	−9.0%	29.7%
International equities	15.0%	15.5%	2.0%	17.0%	13.0%	−6.0%	14.9%
European government bonds	20.0%	18.9%	2.0%	22.0%	18.0%	4.0%	20.0%
Corporate bonds	20.0%	19.1%	2.0%	22.0%	18.0%	4.0%	20.2%
Cash and money market instruments	15.0%	14.6%	2.0%	17.0%	13.0%	2.0%	15.2%
Total		100.0%				−2.0%	100.0%

The prior decision not to rebalance to policy weights did not have a positive result. Contrary to the investment committee's expectations, both European and international equities performed poorly while bonds recovered. The return of the portfolio was −2.0%.

2. How much of this return can be attributed to tactical asset allocation?

Solution to 2:

Because tactical asset allocation is the deliberate decision to deviate from policy weights, the return contribution from tactical asset allocation equals the difference between the actual return and the return that would have been made if the asset class weights were equal to the policy weights. Exhibit 14 shows this difference to be −0.30%.

Exhibit 14: Returns to Tactical Asset Allocation

Asset Class	Policy Weight I	Starting Weight II	Weights Difference III (= II − I)	Period Return IV	TAA Contribution V(= III × IV)
European equities	30.0%	32.0%	2.0%	−9.0%	−0.18%
International equities	15.0%	15.5%	0.5%	−6.0%	−0.03%
European government bonds	20.0%	18.9%	−1.1%	4.0%	−0.05%
Corporate bonds	20.0%	19.1%	−0.9%	4.0%	−0.04%
Cash and money market instruments	15.0%	14.6%	−0.4%	2.0%	−0.01%
Total	100.0%			−2.0%	−0.30%

The process of executing an investment strategy continues with selecting the appropriate manager(s) for each asset class and allocating funds to them. The investment portfolio management process is then well into the execution stage.

The investment managers' performance will be monitored, as well as the results of the tactical and strategic asset allocation. When asset class weights move outside their corridors, money is transferred from the asset classes that have become too large compared with the SAA to those that fall short. Managers as well as the strategic asset allocation will be reviewed on the basis of the outcome of the monitoring process. In addition, capital market expectations may change, as may the circumstances and objectives of the client. These changes could result in an adjustment of the strategic asset allocation.

New Developments in Portfolio Management

The portfolio planning and construction framework presented so far relies on a somewhat rigid process. Nonetheless, there are two newer, less structured developments that deserve specific mention.

The first development is the growth in the offering of exchange traded funds, or ETFs, in combination with algorithm-based financial advice (or robo-advice). ETFs are funds that track the performance of an asset class index or sub-index, are easily tradable, and are relatively cheap compared with actively managed funds or managed accounts. The broad array of ETF offerings, covering the main equity and fixed-income indices as well as commodities, enable retail investors to obtain fast, inexpensive, and liquid exposure to asset classes. Robo-advice has further reduced the costs for retail investors to create a well-diversified portfolio.

The second development relates to criticism of asset class return forecasts over relevant time horizons, as well as the perceived instability of asset class correlations and volatilities. Some market participants argue that poor investment portfolio results reflect the sensitivity of modern portfolio theory-based portfolio construction methodologies to small errors in return forecasts or estimated correlations. In response, practitioners developed an investment approach where asset classes were weighted according to risk contribution. This approach is known as *risk parity investing*. Proponents of risk parity investing argue that traditionally constructed portfolios have considerable risk from equities. That is, the typically high (60% or more) weight of equities in institutional portfolios understates the risk impact: equities tend to be much more volatile than fixed income. Opponents of risk parity argue that following the global financial crisis of 2007–2009, favorable results of risk parity portfolios were caused by the long period of decline in interest rates that benefited bond market performance.

9 ESG CONSIDERATIONS IN PORTFOLIO PLANNING AND CONSTRUCTION

☐ describe how environmental, social, and governance (ESG) considerations may be integrated into portfolio planning and construction

The implementation of a policy on responsible investing affects both strategic asset allocation and implementation of the portfolio construction process. The ESG investment approaches described previously require a set of instructions for investment managers with regard to the selection of securities, the exercise of shareholder rights, and the selection of investment strategies. Examples of issues driving the integration of environmental and social factors in the investment process include scarcity of natural resources, physical impacts of climate change, global economic and demographic trends, diversity and inclusion, and the rise of social media. ESG investment approaches can be implemented with structured, numeric data for many of these issues (e.g., executive salaries and bonuses, carbon footprint, employee turnover, lost time injuries and fatalities, and employee absenteeism). Although companies often are not required to disclose such data, that is changing as many stock exchanges and other regulatory bodies across developed and emerging markets have set up guidelines related to corporate sustainability disclosures for listed companies. In addition, many organizations and regulatory bodies have derived frameworks setting out standards on a number of these issues—examples include the Principles of Responsible Investment, the UN Global Compact, and the OECD Guidelines for Multinational Enterprises. These standards help form the basis of responsible investing policies for asset owners. In turn, asset owners may exclude or engage with companies in accordance with these issues, or demand from their selected investment managers consider these issues in their investment process.

We previously discussed that the limitation in the investment universe from using negative screening policies affects the expected returns and risk. When selecting or instructing active or passive managers, these managers will clearly prefer to see their performance measured against a benchmark that reflects the limited universe. There are benchmarks and investment vehicles (both active and passive) available, particularly in equities, that reflect many commonly excluded companies or sectors. It is also worth noting that with the proliferation of the ESG integration approach, more and more asset owners expect their asset managers to beat the regular benchmarks, because integration of ESG factors into traditional financial analysis and portfolio construction is viewed more as a process enhancement rather than an entirely new way to invest.

EXAMPLE 12

ESG Factors Directly Impacting Portfolio Construction

1. Based in South Africa, Mountain Materials (Mountain) is a fictitious cement manufacturing company that ranks as one of the largest cement and concrete manufacturers in the world. Mountain operates mostly in South Africa, where environmental regulations have been gradually strengthening since 2015. Because of the large scale of its operations, Mountain is a significant emitter of greenhouse gases (GHGs). During 2019, by setting a carbon price on the country's largest GHG emitters, South Africa launched a new, crucial endeavor in its efforts to tackle air pollution and climate change. Despite having some ad hoc initiatives to manage its carbon emissions, the company lacks firmwide programs to limit energy use or carbon emissions, thereby remaining exposed to increased costs to offset excess emissions. The average price on carbon across seven pilot markets in South Africa was between $5 and $15 per ton of carbon dioxide. In addition, the company's performance in managing toxic air emissions as well as employee health and

safety falls short of industry best practices, leaving Mountain exposed to related risks.

Ved Disha, CFA, is analyzing the effects of the environmental and social factors on Mountain's financial statements. Exhibit 15 illustrates Disha's expected internal rate of return (IRR) in the base, bear, and bull case scenarios for Mountain based on his fundamental analysis, and Exhibit 16 illustrates the same scenarios following the integration of these material environmental and social risks.

Exhibit 15: Pre-ESG Integration: Bear/Base/Bull Case Scenario

	Bear Case	Base Case	Bull Case
Revenue growth	0.0%	10.0%	15.0%
Margin improvement	−5.0%	3.0%	5.0%
Cash dividend	1.0%	2.0%	2.0%
Multiple expansion	−10.0%	0.0%	5.0%
IRR	−14.0%	15.0%	27.0%

Exhibit 16: Post-ESG Integration: Bear/Base/Bull Case Scenario

	Bear Case	Base Case	Bull Case
Revenue growth	−5.0%	10.0%	20.0%
Margin improvement	−10.0%	−3.0%	0.0%
Cash dividend	0.0%	0.0%	2.0%
Multiple expansion	−5.0%	−2.0%	0.0%
IRR	−20.0%	5.0%	22.0%

Disha assumed that compliance with national and provincial carbon regulations would require the company to increase spending on equipment, resulting in a 1% erosion in operating margin. Moreover, to limit toxic emissions, the company would have to switch to relatively cleaner sources of energy such as gas-based powered plants. This change is expected to further dampen operating margin by 2% because of increased fuel costs. As a result of higher spending, it was assumed that the previously stable cash dividend policy would turn conservative in the short term, and hence Disha reduced the expected dividend from 2% to 0% for the base case. Lastly, there is a downside to multiples as a result of the concerns related to management of health and safety risks, because the company's performance is below that of its peers and capital markets tend to discount the share price in the event of safety incidents. Based on all of these changes, the base case IRR for the cement company case became less attractive. This outlook led Disha to undertake a relatively smaller position of 0.5% (versus 1.5% in the absence of ESG risks) in his portfolio because of the various unmanaged ESG risks at Mountain. Disha also decided to engage with company management to influence better disclosures and management of these environmental and social risks. In this manner, key ESG risks and growth opportunities were

> integrated with traditional financial analysis to help arrive at a more robust investment decision.
>
> In this example, a high level of unmanaged ESG risks led to a significant change in expected IRR following the ESG integration and hence impacted the position size significantly. It is prudent to note, however, that ESG is one of the many factors that influence investment decision making. Therefore, in many cases, ESG risk and opportunities may have limited effect on a company's financial attractiveness and thereby may not cause a large change in the portfolio. These risks and opportunities have to be analyzed and interpreted on a case-by-case basis.

Shareholder engagement requires good cooperation between investor (client) and investment manager. Engagement efforts are time-consuming, and the interest in such efforts is often that of the clients rather than that of the investment managers. Clients and investment managers must be clear with each other about the exercise of voting rights, filing of shareholder proposals, or entering into conversations with company management. It may be that the engagement and voting is delegated by the client to the investment manager and implemented according to the manager's stewardship policy. Alternatively, the client may instruct some proxy agent to vote on its behalf and according to its own stewardship policies, or the client may instruct voting and maintain dialogue with its investee companies through either individual engagements or collaborative engagements. Collaborative engagement initiatives have gained popularity because it is easier to gain the attention of and encourage positive action from corporations on material ESG issues through collective action. Climate Action 100+ is one such initiative that aims to ensure the world's largest corporate GHG emitters take necessary action on climate change. The initiative aims to engage with more than 100 systemically important carbon emitters, accounting for two-thirds of annual global industrial emissions, alongside more than 60 other companies with significant opportunity to drive the clean energy transition.

Selecting thematic investments, particularly in liquid asset classes, requires finding specialist managers who can identify the right opportunities and manage thematic investment portfolios. In particular, an allocation to thematic investments will bias the total asset class portfolio toward a particular theme, so it is important for the investment manager to demonstrate the impact of the thematic investment on the total risk–return profile of the portfolio. Impact investing specifically selects investment opportunities based on their intention to create a positive environmental and social impact.

The effort and costs associated with limiting the investment universe as part of responsible investing may suggest a negative impact on investment returns. Responsible investing proponents argue, however, that potential improvements in governance, as well as the avoidance of material risks by companies that screen, favorably improve returns. Significant empirical research has been conducted on the performance of ESG factors in equities, including the return differences of ESG equity portfolios relative to mainstream equity portfolios. Academic research remains mixed on the impact of ESG factors on portfolio returns. Nevertheless, ESG investing continues to see strong adoption, with nearly US$31 trillion of AUM dedicated toward responsible investment mandates at the start of 2018. The ESG integration approach that integrates material qualitative and quantitative environmental, social, and governance factors into traditional security and industry analysis as well as portfolio construction is now widely adopted across mainstream funds and not just limited to client-specific separate accounts.

SUMMARY

In this reading, we have discussed construction of a client's investment policy statement, including discussion of risk and return objectives and the various constraints that will apply to the portfolio. We have also discussed the portfolio construction process, with emphasis on the strategic asset allocation decisions that must be made.

- The IPS is the starting point of the portfolio management process. Without a full understanding of the client's situation and requirements, it is unlikely that successful results will be achieved.
- The IPS can take a variety of forms. A typical format will include the client's investment objectives and also list the constraints that apply to the client's portfolio.
- The client's objectives are specified in terms of risk tolerance and return requirements.
- The constraints section covers factors that need to be considered when constructing a portfolio for the client that meets the objectives. The typical constraint categories are liquidity requirements, time horizon, regulatory requirements, tax status, and unique needs.
- Clients may have personal objections to certain products or practices, which could lead to the exclusion of certain companies, countries, or types of securities from the investable universe as well as the client's benchmark. Such considerations are often referred to as ESG (environmental, social, governance).
- ESG considerations can be integrated into an investment policy by negative screening, positive screening, ESG integration, thematic investing, engagement/active ownership, and impact investing.
- Risk objectives are specifications for portfolio risk that reflect the risk tolerance of the client. Quantitative risk objectives can be absolute, relative, or a combination of the two.
- The client's overall risk tolerance is a function of both the client's ability to accept risk and the client's "risk attitude," which can be considered the client's willingness to take risk.
- The client's return objectives can be stated on an absolute or a relative basis. As an example of an absolute objective, the client may want to achieve a particular percentage rate of return. Alternatively, the return objective can be stated on a relative basis—for example, relative to a benchmark return.
- The liquidity section of the IPS should state what the client's requirements are to draw cash from the portfolio.
- The time horizon section of the IPS should state the time horizon over which the investor is investing. This horizon may be the period during which the portfolio is accumulating before any assets need to be withdrawn.
- Tax status varies among investors, and a client's tax status should be stated in the IPS.
- The IPS should state any legal or regulatory restrictions that constrain the investment of the portfolio.
- The unique circumstances section of the IPS should cover any other aspect of a client's circumstances that is likely to have a material impact on portfolio composition. Certain ESG implementation approaches may be discussed in this section.

- Asset classes are the building blocks of an asset allocation. An asset class is a category of assets that have similar characteristics, attributes, and risk–return relationships. Traditionally, investors have distinguished cash, equities, bonds, and real estate as the major asset classes.
- A strategic asset allocation results from combining the constraints and objectives articulated in the IPS and capital market expectations regarding the asset classes.
- As time goes on, a client's asset allocation will drift from the target allocation, and the amount of allowable drift as well as a rebalancing policy should be formalized.
- In addition to taking systematic risk, an investment committee may choose to take tactical asset allocation risk or security selection risk. The amount of return attributable to these decisions can be measured.
- ESG considerations may be integrated into the portfolio planning and construction process. ESG implementation approaches require a set of instructions for investment managers with regard to the selection of securities, the exercise of shareholder rights, and the selection of investment strategies.

PRACTICE PROBLEMS

1. Which of the following is *least* important as a reason for a written investment policy statement (IPS)?
   A. The IPS may be required by regulation.
   B. Having a written IPS is part of best practice for a portfolio manager.
   C. Having a written IPS ensures the client's risk and return objectives can be achieved.

2. Which of the following *best* describes the underlying rationale for a written investment policy statement (IPS)?
   A. A written IPS communicates a plan for trying to achieve investment success.
   B. A written IPS provides investment managers with a ready defense against client lawsuits.
   C. A written IPS allows investment managers to instruct clients about the proper use and purpose of investments.

3. A written investment policy statement (IPS) is *most* likely to succeed if:
   A. it is created by a software program to assure consistent quality.
   B. it is a collaborative effort of the client and the portfolio manager.
   C. it reflects the investment philosophy of the portfolio manager.

4. The section of the investment policy statement (IPS) that provides information about how policy may be executed, including restrictions and exclusions, is *best* described as the:
   A. *Investment Objectives.*
   B. *Investment Guidelines.*
   C. *Statement of Duties and Responsibilities.*

5. Which of the following is *least* likely to be placed in the appendices to an investment policy statement (IPS)?
   A. *Rebalancing Policy.*
   B. *Strategic Asset Allocation.*
   C. *Statement of Duties and Responsibilities.*

6. Which of the following typical topics in an investment policy statement (IPS) is *most* closely linked to the client's "distinctive needs"?
   A. *Procedures.*
   B. *Investment Guidelines.*
   C. *Statement of Duties and Responsibilities.*

Practice Problems

7. An investment policy statement that includes a return objective of outperforming the FTSE 100 by 120 basis points is *best* characterized as having a(n):

    A. relative return objective.

    B. absolute return objective.

    C. arbitrage-based return objective.

8. Risk assessment questionnaires for investment management clients are *most* useful in measuring:

    A. value at risk.

    B. ability to take risk.

    C. willingness to take risk.

9. Which of the following is *best* characterized as a relative risk objective?

    A. Value at risk for the fund will not exceed US$3 million.

    B. The fund will not underperform the DAX by more than 250 basis points.

    C. The fund will not lose more than €2.5 million in the coming 12-month period.

10. In preparing an investment policy statement, which of the following is *most* difficult to quantify?

    A. Time horizon.

    B. Ability to accept risk.

    C. Willingness to accept risk.

11. A client who is a 34-year old widow with two healthy young children (aged 5 and 7) has asked you to help her form an investment policy statement. She has been employed as an administrative assistant in a bureau of her national government for the previous 12 years. She has two primary financial goals—her retirement and providing for the college education of her children. This client's time horizon is *best* described as being:

    A. long term.

    B. short term.

    C. medium term.

12. The timing of payouts for property and casualty insurers is unpredictable ("lumpy") in comparison with the timing of payouts for life insurance companies. Therefore, in general, property and casualty insurers have:

    A. lower liquidity needs than life insurance companies.

    B. greater liquidity needs than life insurance companies.

    C. a higher return objective than life insurance companies.

13. A client who is a director of a publicly listed corporation is required by law to refrain from trading that company's stock at certain points of the year when dis-

closure of financial results are pending. In preparing a written investment policy statement (IPS) for this client, this restriction on trading:

A. is irrelevant to the IPS.

B. should be included in the IPS.

C. makes it illegal for the portfolio manager to work with this client.

14. After interviewing a client in order to prepare a written investment policy statement (IPS), you have established the following:

- The client has earnings that vary dramatically between £30,000 and £70,000 (pre-tax) depending on weather patterns in Britain.
- In three of the previous five years, the after-tax income of the client has been less than £20,000.
- The client's mother is dependent on her son (the client) for approximately £9,000 per year support.
- The client's own subsistence needs are approximately £12,000 per year.
- The client has more than 10 years' experience trading investments including commodity futures, stock options, and selling stock short.
- The client's responses to a standard risk assessment questionnaire suggest he has above average risk tolerance.

The client is *best* described as having a:

A. low ability to take risk, but a high willingness to take risk.

B. high ability to take risk, but a low willingness to take risk.

C. high ability to take risk and a high willingness to take risk.

15. After interviewing a client in order to prepare a written investment policy statement (IPS), you have established the following:

- The client has earnings that have exceeded €120,000 (pre-tax) each year for the past five years.
- She has no dependents.
- The client's subsistence needs are approximately €45,000 per year.
- The client states that she feels uncomfortable with her lack of understanding of securities markets.
- All of the client's current savings are invested in short-term securities guaranteed by an agency of her national government.
- The client's responses to a standard risk assessment questionnaire suggest she has low risk tolerance.

The client is *best* described as having a:

A. low ability to take risk, but a high willingness to take risk.

B. high ability to take risk, but a low willingness to take risk.

C. high ability to take risk and a high willingness to take risk.

16. Returns on asset classes are *best* described as being a function of:

A. the failure of arbitrage.

Practice Problems

B. exposure to the idiosyncratic risks of those asset classes.

C. exposure to sets of systematic factors relevant to those asset classes.

17. Consider the pairwise correlations of monthly returns of the following asset classes:

	Brazilian Equities	East Asian Equities	European Equities	US Equities
Brazilian equities	1.00	0.70	0.85	0.76
East Asian equities	0.70	1.00	0.91	0.88
European equities	0.85	0.91	1.00	0.90
US equities	0.76	0.88	0.90	1.00

Based solely on the information in the above table, which equity asset class is *most* sharply distinguished from US equities?

A. Brazilian equities.

B. European equities.

C. East Asian equities.

18. In defining asset classes as part of the strategic asset allocation decision, pairwise correlations within asset classes should generally be:

A. equal to correlations among asset classes.

B. lower than correlations among asset classes.

C. higher than correlations among asset classes.

19. Tactical asset allocation is *best* described as:

A. attempts to exploit arbitrage possibilities among asset classes.

B. the decision to deliberately deviate from the policy portfolio.

C. selecting asset classes with the desired exposures to sources of systematic risk in an investment portfolio.

SOLUTIONS

1. C is correct. Depending on circumstances, a written IPS or its equivalent may be required by law or regulation and a written IPS is certainly consistent with best practices. The mere fact that a written IPS is prepared for a client, however, does not *ensure* that risk and return objectives will in fact be achieved.

2. A is correct. A written IPS is best seen as a communication instrument allowing clients and portfolio managers to mutually establish investment objectives and constraints.

3. B is correct. A written IPS, to be successful, must incorporate a full understanding of the client's situation and requirements. As stated in the reading, "The IPS will be developed following a fact finding discussion with the client."

4. B is correct. The major components of an IPS are listed in Section 2 of the reading. *Investment Guidelines* are described as the section that provides information about how policy may be executed, including restrictions on the permissible use of leverage and derivatives and on specific types of assets excluded from investment, if any. *Statement of Duties and Responsibilities* "detail[s] the duties and responsibilities of the client, the custodian of the client's assets, the investment managers, and so forth." *Investment Objectives* is "a section explaining the client's objectives in investing."

5. C is correct. The major components of an IPS are listed in Section 2 of the reading. Strategic Asset Allocation (also known as the policy portfolio) and Rebalancing Policy are often included as appendices to the IPS. The *Statement of Duties and Responsibilities*, however, is an integral part of the IPS and is unlikely to be placed in an appendix.

6. B is correct. According to the reading, "The sections of an IPS that are most closely linked to the client's distinctive needs are those dealing with investment objectives and constraints." *Investment Guidelines* "[provide] information about how policy may be executed, including investment constraints." *Procedures* "[detail] the steps to be taken to keep the IPS current and the procedures to follow to respond to various contingencies." *Statement of Duties and Responsibilities* "detail[s] the duties and responsibilities of the client, the custodian of the client's assets, the investment managers, and so forth."

7. A is correct. Because the return objective specifies a target return *relative to* the FTSE 100 Index, the objective is best described as a relative return objective.

8. C is correct. Risk attitude is a subjective factor and measuring risk attitude is difficult. Oftentimes, investment managers use psychometric questionnaires, such as those developed by Grable and Joo (2004), to assess a client's willingness to take risk.

9. B is correct. The reference to the DAX marks this response as a relative risk objective. Value at risk establishes a minimum value of loss expected during a specified time period at a given level of probability. A statement of maximum allowed absolute loss (€2.5 million) is an absolute risk objective.

10. C is correct. Measuring willingness to take risk (risk tolerance, risk aversion) is an exercise in applied psychology. Instruments attempting to measure risk attitudes exist, but they are clearly less objective than measurements of ability to take risk. Ability to take risk is based on relatively objective traits such as expected income,

Solutions

time horizon, and existing wealth relative to liabilities.

11. A is correct. The client's financial objectives are long term. Her stable employment indicates that her immediate liquidity needs are modest. The children will not go to college until 10 or more years later. Her time horizon is best described as being long term.

12. B is correct. The unpredictable nature of property and casualty (P&C) claims forces P&C insurers to allocate a substantial proportion of their investments into liquid, short maturity assets. This need for liquidity also forces P&C companies to accept investments with relatively low expected returns. Liquidity is of less concern to life insurance companies given the greater predictability of life insurance payouts.

13. B is correct. When a client has a restriction in trading, such as this obligation to refrain from trading, the IPS "should note this constraint so that the portfolio manager does not inadvertently trade the stock on the client's behalf."

14. A is correct. The volatility of the client's income and the significant support needs for his mother and himself suggest that the client has a low ability to take risk. The client's trading experience and his responses to the risk assessment questionnaire indicate that the client has an above average willingness to take risk.

15. B is correct. On the one hand, the client has a stable, high income and no dependents. On the other hand, she exhibits above average risk aversion. Her ability to take risk is high, but her willingness to take risk is low.

16. C is correct. Strategic asset allocation depends on several principles. As stated in the reading, "One principle is that a portfolio's systematic risk accounts for most of its change in value over the long run." A second principle is that, "the returns to groups of like assets… predictably reflect exposures to certain sets of systematic factors." This latter principle establishes that returns on asset classes primarily reflect the systematic risks of the classes.

17. A is correct. The correlation between US equities and Brazilian equities is 0.76. The correlations between US equities and East Asian equities and the correlation between US equities and European equities both exceed 0.76. Lower correlations indicate a greater degree of separation between asset classes. Therefore, using solely the data given in the table, returns on Brazilian equities are most sharply distinguished from returns on US equities.

18. C is correct. As the reading states, "an asset class should contain homogeneous assets… paired correlations of securities would be high within an asset class, but should be lower versus securities in other asset classes."

19. B is correct. Tactical asset allocation allows actual asset allocation to deviate from that of the strategic asset allocation (policy portfolio) of the IPS. Tactical asset allocation attempts to take advantage of temporary dislocations from the market conditions and assumptions that drove the policy portfolio decision.

LEARNING MODULE 2

The Behavioral Biases of Individuals

by Michael M. Pompian, CFA.

Michael M. Pompian, CFA, is at Sunpointe Investments (USA).

LEARNING OUTCOME

Mastery	The candidate should be able to:
☐	compare and contrast cognitive errors and emotional biases
☐	discuss commonly recognized behavioral biases and their implications for financial decision making
☐	describe how behavioral biases of investors can lead to market characteristics that may not be explained by traditional finance

INTRODUCTION

Research has demonstrated that when people face complex decisions, they often rely on basic judgments and preferences to simplify the situation rather than acting completely rationally. Although such approaches are quick and intuitively appealing, they may lead to suboptimal outcomes. In contrast to this body of research, traditional economic and financial theory generally assumes that individuals act rationally by considering all available information in the decision-making process, leading them to optimal outcomes and supporting the efficiency of markets. Behavioral finance challenges these assumptions by incorporating research on how individuals and markets actually behave. In this reading, we explore a foundational concept of behavioral finance: behavioral biases. Investment professionals may be able to improve economic outcomes by understanding these biases, recognizing them in themselves and others, and learning strategies to mitigate them.

The reading proceeds as follows. Section 2 describes and broadly characterizes behavioral biases. Sections 3 and 4 discuss specific behavioral biases within two broad categories: cognitive errors and emotional biases. The discussion includes a description of each bias, potential consequences, and guidance on detecting and mitigating the effects of the bias. Section 5 discusses market anomalies, which are essentially aggregate expressions of individual biases among financial market participants. A summary and practice problems conclude the reading.

2. BEHAVIORAL BIAS CATEGORIES

☐ compare and contrast cognitive errors and emotional biases

In general, behavioral biases come in two forms: faulty cognitive reasoning, known as **cognitive errors**, and those based on feelings or emotions, known as **emotional biases**. Both forms of bias, regardless of their source, may cause decisions to deviate from what is assumed by traditional finance theory.

Cognitive errors can often be corrected or eliminated through better information, education, and advice. Emotional biases, on the other hand, are harder to correct because they stem from impulses and intuitions. They arise spontaneously rather than through conscious effort and may even be undesired to the individual feeling them. Thus, it is often possible only to recognize an emotional bias and adapt to it. The cognitive–emotional distinction will help us determine when and how to adjust for behavioral biases in financial decision making.

Researchers have identified numerous behavioral biases. This reading does not attempt to catalog all of them. Rather, it discusses some of the more publicized and recognized biases within the cognitive–emotional framework. Additionally, we limit our focus to gauging the presence or absence—not the magnitude—of each bias discussed. That is, we will not try to measure how strongly the bias is exhibited, but rather we will describe the behavioral bias, its potential consequences, and the detection of and correction for the behavioral bias. In detecting a bias, we will identify statements or thought processes that may indicate the bias. Diagnostic tests of varying degrees of complexity are available to detect biases but are beyond the scope of this reading.

Finally, the individuals of interest in this reading are "financial market participants" (FMPs) engaged in financial decision making. These include both individual investors and financial services professionals.

3. COGNITIVE ERRORS

☐ discuss commonly recognized behavioral biases and their implications for financial decision making

We classify cognitive errors into two categories: "belief perseverance biases" and "processing errors."

Belief perseverance is the tendency to cling to one's previously held beliefs by committing statistical, information-processing, or memory errors. The belief perseverance biases discussed are conservatism, confirmation, representativeness, illusion of control, and hindsight.

Processing errors describe how information may be processed and used illogically or irrationally in financial decision making. The processing errors discussed are anchoring and adjustment, mental accounting, framing, and availability.

Belief Perseverance Biases

Belief perseverance biases result from the mental discomfort that occurs when new information conflicts with previously held beliefs or cognitions, known as **cognitive dissonance**. To resolve this discomfort, people may ignore or modify conflicting information and consider only information that confirms their existing beliefs or thoughts.

Conservatism Bias

Conservatism bias is a belief perseverance bias in which people maintain their prior views or forecasts by inadequately incorporating new, conflicting information. In Bayesian terms, they tend to overweight their prior probability of the event and underweight the new information, resulting in revised beliefs about probabilities and outcomes that underreact to the new information.

Consequences of Conservatism Bias

As a result of conservatism bias, FMPs may do the following:

- Maintain or be slow to update a view or a forecast, even when presented with new information; and
- Maintain a prior belief rather than deal with the mental stress of updating beliefs given complex data. This behavior relates to an underlying difficulty in processing new information.

Detection of and Guidance for Overcoming Conservatism Bias

The effect of conservatism bias may be corrected for or reduced by properly analyzing and weighting new information. The first step is to be aware that a bias exists, especially about information that is technical, abstract, and/or statistical, because the **cognitive cost** involved in processing those forms of information is higher than for other types.

When new information is presented, the FMP should ask such questions as, "How does this information change my forecast?" or "What effect does this information have on my forecast?" FMPs should conduct careful analysis incorporating the new information and then respond appropriately. This updating of prior beliefs in light of new information is consistent with the tenets of Bayes' Rule, in which updated probabilities are derived by systematically combining previous estimates and new information.

If information is difficult to interpret or understand, FMPs should seek guidance from someone who can either explain how to interpret the information or can explain its implications.

Confirmation Bias

Confirmation bias refers to the tendency to look for and notice what confirms prior beliefs and to ignore or undervalue whatever contradicts them. A response to cognitive dissonance, confirmation bias reflects a predisposition to justify to ourselves what we want to believe.

Most experienced private wealth advisers have dealt with a client who conducts some research and insists on adding a particular investment to the portfolio. The client may insist on continuing to hold the investment, even when the adviser recommends otherwise, because the client's follow-up research seeks only information that confirms his belief that the investment is still a good value. The confirmation bias is not limited to individual investors; all FMPs should be wary of the potential confirmation biases within themselves.

> **EXAMPLE 1**
>
> ### Confirmation Bias
>
> A portfolio manager at Sarter Investment Advisors recommended shares of Real Media Inc., a hypothetical television production and distribution company, largely on the basis of compelling analytical and valuation work from a top equity research analyst. Sarter's clients have owned the shares for several years.
>
> Recently, the shares have underperformed significantly as a result of the company missing analysts' earnings estimates and also in response to executive management turnover. The portfolio manager's colleagues believe this underperformance is a result of Real Media losing market share to a competitor with superior technology and distribution. The competitor is publicly traded, but Sarter's portfolio managers and analysts have not done research on it.
>
> After another poor earnings release from Real Media, the portfolio manager speaks with the equity research analyst whose work was the primary source of the investment. The equity research analyst, who maintains a buy rating on the stock, believes that Real Media is now a more compelling investment than ever because its share price has fallen while its earnings estimates remain unchanged. As a result of the conversation, the portfolio manager feels reassured and holds the position.
>
> The portfolio manager is subject to confirmation bias. Rather than speaking with a research analyst who has a sell rating on the stock or conducting research on the competitor to consider a different perspective, the portfolio manager speaks with someone who has an opinion she already shares.

Consequences of Confirmation Bias

As a result of confirmation bias, FMPs may do the following:

- Consider only the positive information about an existing investment while ignoring any negative information about the investment.
- Develop screening criteria while ignoring information that either refutes the validity of the criteria or supports other criteria. As a result, some good investments that do not meet the screening criteria may be ignored, and conversely, some bad investments that do meet the screening criteria may be made.
- Under-diversify portfolios. FMPs may become convinced of the value of a single company's stock. They ignore negative news, and they gather and process only information confirming that the company is a good investment. They build a larger position than appropriate and hold an under-diversified portfolio.
- Hold a disproportionate amount of their investment assets in their employing company's stock, because they believe in their company and are convinced of its favorable prospects. Favorable information is cited, and unfavorable information is ignored. If the employee were to acknowledge unfavorable information, the associated mental discomfort might make work very difficult for the employee.

Detection of and Guidance for Overcoming Confirmation Bias

The effect of confirmation bias may be corrected for or reduced by actively seeking out information that challenges existing beliefs.

Cognitive Errors

Another useful step is to corroborate an investment decision. For example, if investment selections are based on criteria confirming an existing belief, such as stocks breaking through 52-week highs, it is usually advisable to corroborate that decision with research from another perspective or source (e.g., fundamental research on the company, industry, or sector).

Representativeness Bias

Representativeness bias refers to the tendency to classify new information based on past experiences and classifications. New information may resemble or seem *representative* of familiar elements already classified, but in reality, it can be very different. In these instances, the classification reflex can deceive, producing an incorrect understanding that biases all future thinking about the information. *Base-rate neglect* and *sample-size neglect* are two types of representativeness bias that apply to FMPs.

In **base-rate neglect**, a phenomenon's rate of incidence in a larger population—its base rate—is neglected in favor of specific information. The specific, individual information may be misleading relative to the more appropriate base rate or general information. FMPs often follow this erroneous path because diligent research is often conducted on an individual security or strategy, leading FMPs to overlook or ignore general information about the "class" to which an investment belongs, such as an industry, sector, or geography.

A second type of representativeness bias is **sample-size neglect**, in which FMPs incorrectly assume that small sample sizes are *representative* of populations. Individuals prone to sample-size neglect are quick to treat properties reflected in small samples as properties that accurately describe large pools of data, overweighting the information in the small sample.

EXAMPLE 2

Representativeness Bias

Jacques Verte is evaluating the future prospects of APM Company, a large auto parts manufacturer having some difficulties. During the last 50 years, very few auto part manufacturers have failed, even during periods of difficulty. A number of recent headlines have highlighted APM's business and financial difficulties, however, with some commentators suggesting that APM may go out of business.

1. Which of the following scenarios is more likely? Explain why.

    A. APM will solve its difficulties.

    B. APM will go out of business.

Solution to 1:

Scenario A is more likely. The base rate, based on 50 years of data, is that more auto parts companies survive difficult times than fail. Thus, it is more likely that APM will solve its difficulties than go out of business.

2. If Verte is subject to representativeness bias, is he more likely to classify APM into A or B? Explain why.

Solution to 2:

If Verte is subject to representativeness bias, he is likely to choose Scenario B, predicting that the company will go out of business because of the headlines he has read. In classifying APM as likely to go out of business, Verte would be guilty of base-rate neglect by ignoring the low base rate of auto parts manufacturers failing even during times of difficulty.

Consequences of Representativeness Bias

As a result of representativeness bias, FMPs may do the following:

- Adopt a view or a forecast based almost exclusively on individual, specific information or a small sample; and
- Update beliefs using simple classifications rather than deal with the mental stress of updating beliefs given the high cognitive costs of complex data.

Detection of and Guidance on Overcoming Representativeness Bias

When FMPs sense that base-rate or sample-size neglect may be a problem, they should ask the following question: "What is the probability that X (the investment under consideration) belongs to Group A (the group it resembles or is considered representative of) versus Group B (the group it is statistically more likely to belong to)?" This question, or a similar question, will help FMPs think through whether they are failing to consider base-rate probabilities or neglecting the law of small numbers and thus inaccurately assessing a particular situation. It may be necessary to do more research to obtain base-rate information and/or widen the sample size of observations.

Illusion of Control Bias

In **illusion of control bias**, people tend to believe that they can control or influence outcomes when, in fact, they cannot. Many researchers have uncovered situations where people perceived themselves as possessing more control than they did, inferred causal connections where none existed, or displayed surprisingly great certainty in their predictions for the outcomes of chance events. A classic example is that people prefer choosing their own lottery numbers over random numbers selected for them.

> **EXAMPLE 3**
>
> ### Illusion of Control Bias
>
> Adelia Scott is a wealth adviser at Sarter Investment Advisors (Sarter), an investment advisory firm for high-net-worth individuals. Scott meets with a client who has 30% of his account in shares of his employer's stock. The client is not subject to any employee holding requirement.
>
> Prior meeting notes indicate that the client initially agreed to diversify the concentrated position over a five-year period. Scott recommends a faster schedule, however, based on recent research indicating that the company's future growth prospects have considerably worsened as a result of industry trends and macroeconomic conditions.
>
> When presented with this information, the client is reluctant to change his diversification plan, citing the company's history of double-digit growth and his belief that this rate of growth will continue for the foreseeable future. The client remarks, "Trust me, my team and I are not going to let those forecasts you're citing come true."
>
> The client is subject to illusion of control bias. He is unwilling to believe Scott's opinion because he believes that he and his team can control the company's performance and stock price.

Cognitive Errors

Consequences of Illusion of Control

As a result of illusion of control bias, FMPs may do the following:

- Inadequately diversify portfolios. Research has found that some investors prefer to invest in companies that they feel they have control over, such as the companies they work for, leading them to hold concentrated positions. In fact, most investors have little or no control over the companies they work for. If the company performs poorly, these investors may experience both the loss of employment and investment losses.
- Trade more than is prudent. Researchers have found that portfolio turnover is negatively correlated with investment returns.
- Construct financial models and forecasts that are overly detailed. FMPs may require detailed models before making an investment decision, believing that forecasts from these models control uncertainty. Although a greater understanding of an investment, issuer, or industry is often useful, increased model complexity does not control the inherent risk and uncertainty of investment outcomes.

Detection of and Guidelines for Overcoming Illusion of Control Bias

The first and most basic idea that investors need to recognize is that investing is a probabilistic activity. Even the largest investment management firms have little control over the outcomes of the investments they make. Companies are subject to macroeconomic and industry forces, as well as the actions of competitors, customers, and suppliers.

Second, it is advisable to seek contrary viewpoints. As you contemplate a new investment, take a moment to think about considerations that might weigh against making the investment. Ask yourself: What are the downside risks? What might go wrong? When will I sell? It is often useful to speak with someone who has an opposing view, such as an equity research analyst with a sell rating on the subject stock.

Hindsight Bias

Hindsight bias refers to believing past events as having been predictable and reasonable to expect. This behavior results from the obvious fact that outcomes that did occur are more readily evident than outcomes that did not. Similarly, people tend to remember their own predictions of the future as more accurate than they actually were because they are biased by the knowledge of what actually occurred. Poorly reasoned decisions with positive results may be remembered as brilliant tactical moves, and poor results of well-reasoned decisions may be described as avoidable mistakes.

EXAMPLE 4

Hindsight Bias

Beverly Bolo, an analyst at an investment advisory firm, is giving a presentation to clients that, among other topics, explains the firm's investment results during past macroeconomic downturns. In the presentation, Bolo points out that the "occurrence of the last recession was obvious upon inspection of the yield curve and other leading indicators eight months before the downturn started."

Bolo's comment exhibits hindsight bias. Recessions, like any other event, appear obvious in hindsight but are hardly ever accurately predicted. Bolo could augment her remarks by exploring how often these leading indicators suggested that a recession is imminent against how often a recession subsequently occurred.

Consequences of Hindsight Bias
As a result of hindsight bias, FMPs may do the following:

- Overestimate the degree to which they correctly predicted an investment outcome, or the predictability of an outcome generally. This bias is closely related to overconfidence bias, which is discussed later in the reading.
- Unfairly assess money manager or security performance. Based on the ability to look back at what has taken place in securities markets, performance is compared against what has happened as opposed to expectations at the time the investment was made.

Detection of and Guidelines for Overcoming Hindsight Bias
Once understood, hindsight bias should be recognizable. FMPs should ask such questions as, "Am I re-writing history or being honest with myself about the mistakes I made?"

To guard against hindsight bias, FMPs should carefully record their investment decisions and key reasons for making those decisions in writing at or around the time the decision is made. Consulting these written records rather than memory will often produce a far more accurate examination of past decisions.

Processing Errors

Processing errors refer to information being processed and used illogically or irrationally. As opposed to belief perseverance biases, processing errors are less related to errors of memory or in assigning and updating probabilities; rather, they relate more closely to flaws in how information itself is processed.

Anchoring and Adjustment Bias

Anchoring and adjustment bias refers to relying on an initial piece of information to make subsequent estimates, judgments, and decisions. When required to estimate a value with unknown magnitude, people generally begin with some initial default number—an "anchor"—which they then adjust up or down. Regardless of how the initial anchor was chosen, people tend to adjust their anchors insufficiently and produce end approximations that are, consequently, biased. Anchoring and adjustment bias is closely related to conservatism bias. Bayes Rule again provides guidance for how new information should be incorporated into changing prior beliefs.

> **EXAMPLE 5**
>
> ### Anchoring and Adjustment Bias
>
> Aiden Smythe is an equity research analyst at a brokerage firm. Smythe covers Industrial Lift Plc, a company that manufactures construction machinery. The company's business is sensitive to macroeconomic conditions, particularly non-residential construction activity. Last year, Industrial Lift reported £1.00 in EPS amid mostly strong non-residential construction activity levels. Smythe is updating his EPS estimate for this year. Non-residential construction activity has severely declined in the last two months, and some economists fear that a recession is likely. As a result, Smythe forecasts that EPS will fall 10% from the prior-year level, publishing a £0.90 estimate for the year.
>
> Smythe's estimate exhibits anchoring and adjustment. Smythe's anchor is the prior year's EPS of £1.00, despite the possibility of a material change in underlying conditions.

Consequences of Anchoring and Adjustment Bias

As a result of anchoring and adjustment bias, FMPs may stick too closely to their original estimates when learning new information. This mindset is not limited to downside adjustments; the same phenomenon occurs with upside adjustments as well.

Detection of and Guidelines for Overcoming Anchoring and Adjustment Bias

The primary action FMPs can take is consciously asking questions that may reveal an anchoring and adjustment bias. Examples of such questions include, "Am I holding onto this stock based on rational analysis, or am I trying to attain a price that I am anchored to, such as the purchase price or a high water mark?" and "Am I making this forecast based on previously observed quantities or based on future expected conditions?"

It is important to remember that a company's revenues and earnings for a given period reflect conditions in that period. If the conditions in the future differ from the past, revenues and earnings will likely differ as well, sometimes radically. Similarly, security prices reflect investors' perception of the future at a given point in time; a given investor's cost basis, past market levels, and other conditions based in the past are often irrelevant. FMPs should look at the basis for any investment recommendation to see whether it is anchored to previous estimates or some "default" number.

Mental Accounting Bias

Mental accounting bias refers to mentally dividing money into "accounts" that influence decisions, even though money is **fungible** (Thaler 1980). Despite traditional finance theory assuming that FMPs consider their entire portfolio holistically in a risk–return context, Statman (1999, 2008) contends that the difficulty individuals have in addressing the interaction of different investments leads to mental accounting: Investors construct portfolios in a layered pyramid format, with each layer addressing a specific financial goal.

> **EXAMPLE 6**
>
> ### Mental Accounting Bias
>
> Kendra Liu, an individual investor, owns shares in New Horizons Ltd., a pharmaceutical company. A drug in that company's research and development pipeline unexpectedly succeeds in a clinical trial, resulting in the shares doubling overnight. Liu sells half of her position in New Horizons and uses the proceeds to purchase shares of Cutting Edge Ltd., a small-cap biotechnology company. Liu believes that an investment in Cutting Edge is a "high-risk, high-reward bet" that could result in a total loss, but she is comfortable making the investment because she is using the proceeds from the sale of New Horizons Ltd., money that she did not expect to have anyway.
>
> Liu's investment in Cutting Edge exhibits mental accounting bias. She has sorted the gains from New Horizons into a mental account based on its source, even though the money is fungible. Liu should invest the proceeds in a manner consistent with a holistic portfolio strategy.

Consequences of Mental Accounting Bias

As a result of mental accounting bias, FMPs may do the following:

- Neglect opportunities to reduce risk by combining assets with low correlations. Offsetting positions across various portfolio layers or mental accounts can lead to suboptimal aggregate performance.

- Irrationally distinguish between returns derived from income and those derived from capital appreciation. Although many investors feel the need to preserve principal, they focus on the idea of spending income that the principal generates. As a result, many FMPs chase income streams, unwittingly risking principal in the process.
- Irrationally bifurcate wealth or a portfolio into investment principal and investment returns. Some FMPs may believe that greater risk can be taken with returns (from either income or capital appreciation) than the principal initially contributed. A common euphemism for this scenario, from the casino world, is "playing with house money."

Detection of and Guidelines for Overcoming Mental Accounting Bias

An effective way to detect and overcome mental accounting behavior is to recognize its drawbacks. The primary drawback is that correlations between investments are not considered, leading to unintentional risk taking. FMPs should go through the exercise of combining all of their assets onto one spreadsheet (without headings or account labels) to see the holistic asset allocation. This exercise often produces information that is surprising when seen as a whole, such as higher cash balances than expected. The logical next step would be to create a portfolio strategy taking all assets into consideration.

Framing Bias

Framing bias is an information-processing bias in which a person answers a question differently based on the way in which it is asked or framed. It is often possible to frame a given decision problem in more than one way.

For example, a situation may be presented within a *gain* context (one in four start-up companies succeed) or within a *loss* context (three out of four start-ups fail). Given the first frame, an FMP may adopt a positive outlook and make venture capital investments. Given the second frame, the FMP might not.

Narrow framing occurs when people evaluate information based on a *narrow frame* of reference—that is, losing sight of the big picture in favor of one or two specific points. For example, an investor might focus solely on a company's executive management team, overlooking or even dismissing other important properties such as industry characteristics, fundamental performance, and valuation.

> **EXAMPLE 7**
>
> ### Effects of Framing Bias
>
> Decision-making frames are quite prevalent in the context of investor behavior. Risk tolerance questionnaires can demonstrate how framing bias may occur in practice and how FMPs should be aware of its effects.
>
> Suppose an investor is to take a risk tolerance questionnaire for the purpose of determining which "risk category" she is in. The risk category will determine asset allocations and the appropriate types of investments. The following information is provided to each questionnaire taker:
>
> Over a 10-year period, Portfolio ABC has averaged an annual return of 10% with an annual standard deviation of 16%. Assuming a normal return distribution, in a given year there is a 67% probability that the return will fall within one standard deviation of the mean, a 95% probability that the return will fall within two standard deviations of the mean, and a 99.7% probability that the return will fall within three standard deviations of the mean. Thus, there is a

67% chance that the return earned by Portfolio ABC will be between −6% and 26%, a 95% chance that the return will be between −22% and 42%, and a 99.7% chance that the return will be between −38% and 58%.

The following two questions focus on hypothetical Portfolio ABC, DEF, and XYZ. The risk and return for each portfolio are the same in each of the two questions, but the presentation of information differs.

1. Based on the following chart, which investment portfolio fits your risk tolerance and desire for long-term return?

Portfolio	95% Probability Return Range	10-Year Average Return
XYZ	0.5% to 6.5%	3.5%
DEF	−18.0% to 30.0%	6.0%
ABC	−22.0% to 42.0%	10.0%

2. Based on the following chart, which investment portfolio fits your risk tolerance and desire for long-term return?

Portfolio	10-Year Average Return	Standard Deviation of Returns
XYZ	3.5%	1.5%
DEF	6.0%	12.0%
ABC	10.0%	16.0%

An investor may choose different portfolios when asked Question 1 compared with Question 2. Portfolio XYZ may appear more attractive in the first question, which uses two standard deviations to define the range of returns and show the risk, than in the second, which shows only the standard deviations. Also, in the second question, the returns are presented first and the measure of risk second. Thus, how questions are framed and the order in which they are presented can significantly affect how they are answered. FMPs should be acutely aware of how framing can affect investment choices.

Consequences of Framing Bias

As a result of framing bias, FMPs may do the following:

- Misidentify risk tolerances because of how questions about risk tolerance were framed, becoming more risk-averse when presented with a gain frame of reference and more risk-seeking when presented with a loss frame of reference. This misidentification may result in suboptimal portfolios.
- Focus on short-term price fluctuations, which may result in long-run considerations being ignored in the decision-making process.

Detection of and Guidelines for Overcoming Framing Bias

Framing bias is detected by asking such questions as, "Is the decision the result of focusing on a net gain or net loss position?" As discussed earlier, an investor who has framed the decision as a potential net loss is more likely to select a riskier investment; if the decision is framed as a potential net gain, however, the investor is more likely to go with a less risky investment. When making decisions, FMPs should try to eliminate any reference to gains and losses already incurred. Instead, they should focus on the future prospects of an investment and try to be as neutral and open-minded as possible when interpreting investment-related situations.

Availability Bias

Availability bias is an information-processing bias in which people estimate the probability of an outcome or the importance of a phenomenon based on how easily information is recalled. Various sources of availability bias exist; the four most applicable to FMPs are retrievability, categorization, narrow range of experience, and resonance.

Retrievability: If an answer or idea comes to mind more quickly than another answer or idea, the first answer or idea will likely be chosen as correct even if it is not the reality.

Categorization: When solving problems, people gather information from what they perceive as relevant search sets. Different problems require different search sets, which are often based on familiar categorizations. If it is difficult to come up with a search set, because the object of the search is difficult to characterize, the estimated probability of an event may be biased.

Narrow Range of Experience: When making an estimate, a person may use only a narrow range of experience instead of considering multiple perspectives. For example, assuming a product or service that has launched successfully in one country will be globally successful.

Resonance: People are often biased by how closely a situation parallels their own personal situation.

> **EXAMPLE 8**
>
> ## Availability Bias
>
> A portfolio manager asks an analyst to research and present a list of companies that have "strong growth potential." The manager suggests looking for companies that sell a product or service different from its competitors—but with a compelling value proposition for customers—and that have a small share of a large market.
>
> The analyst is familiar with technology companies, software in particular, based on prior work experience. The analyst has also seen a lot of news articles covering various software companies that, he believes, fit the criteria. The analyst begins screening among technology companies that have high revenue growth rates for the last two quarters. Although the analyst is aware that other companies in other sectors probably fit the criteria as well, the criteria are qualitative and vague such that they cannot be easily translated as screening input.
>
> The analyst's behavior exhibits availability bias from by considering only technology companies in the search because he is familiar with them. The analyst should consult colleagues and/or external resources to widen his search to include all sectors and for help with creatively specifying screening criteria.

Consequences of Availability Bias

As a result of availability bias, FMPs may do the following:

- Limit their investment opportunity set. This limitation may result because they use familiar classification schemes. They may restrict investments to stocks or bonds, securities of one country or one sector, and so on.

- Choose an investment, investment adviser, or mutual fund based on advertising or the quantity of news coverage. For instance, when asked to name potential mutual fund companies to invest with, many people will name only the funds that do extensive advertising. The choice of mutual fund should be based on a variety of factors that make it a good fit given the investor's objectives and risk–return profile.

- Fail to diversify. This failure may occur because they make their choices based on a narrow range of experience. For example, an investor who works for a company in a particular industry may overweight investments in that industry.

Detection of and Guidelines for Overcoming Availability Bias

To overcome availability bias, investors need to develop an appropriate investment policy strategy, carefully research and analyze investment decisions before making them, and focus on long-term historical data. Questions such as, "How did you decide which investments to consider? Did you choose investments based on your familiarity with the industry or country? Did you see them in an article or research report?" and "Did you choose your investments because you like the companies' products?" can help identify issues of categorization, narrow range of experience, and resonance as sources of availability bias. Availability bias may cause FMPs to think that events that receive heavy media attention are more important than they actually are.

EXAMPLE 9

The following information relates to Questions 1–5

Luca Gerber recently became the chief investment officer for the Ludwigs Family Charity, a mid-size private foundation in Switzerland. Prior to assuming this role, Gerber was a well-known health care industry analyst. The Ludwigs's family fortune is primarily the result of entrepreneurship. Gerhard Ludwigs founded ABC Innovations (ABC), a biotech company dedicated to small cell lung cancer research. The foundation's portfolio is 15% invested in ABC.

Gerber initially feels that the 15% investment in ABC is high. Upon review, however, he decides it is appropriate based on the Ludwigs's involvement and their past success with similar ventures. Gerber makes a mental note to closely monitor the investment in ABC because he is unfamiliar with small-cap start-up companies. The remaining 85% of the foundation's portfolio is invested in equity of high-quality large-cap pharmaceutical companies. Gerber deems this allocation appropriate and is excited that he can continue to use his superior knowledge of the health care industry.

For the past two years, ABC has been dedicated to Project M, an effort directed at developing a drug to treat relapses in small cell lung cancer. Project M has delayed its Phase Two trials twice. Published results from Phase One trials have raised some concerns regarding the drug. In its last two quarterly investors' conference calls, ABC's CEO was very cautious in discussing expectations for Project M. ABC's stock price decreased by more than 20% during the past six months. Gerber believes that the research setbacks are temporary because of ABC's past success with projects. He expects that ABC will begin Phase Two within a year, and he also believes that once Project M goes into Phase Two, ABC's stock price should reach a new 52-week high of CHF80.

Soon after deciding to hold the stock, Gerber reads an article by ABC's chief scientist that details certain scientific results from Project M. As a conclusion, the article states: "Although we still have some major obstacles to overcome, the Project M team has seen positive signs that a treatment for small cell lung cancer is achievable." Although Gerber has difficulty interpreting the scientific results, he feels reassured after reading the concluding statement.

Today, ABC announces the news that it will no longer pursue Project M, citing early signs of the project's failure. In response to the announcement, the stock price drops by 50%. Gerber is stunned. He reviews the company's history and notes that ABC had made numerous comments on its struggles to solve Project M issues, which make the failure seem predictable at the time.

1. Gerber's assessment of the foundation's 100% allocation to biotechnology and pharmaceutical companies is most likely an example of which bias?

    A. Framing
    B. Availability
    C. Hindsight

    B is correct. A consequence of availability bias is a limited investment opportunity set, based on the narrow range of experience of the FMP. Gerber's prior experience has likely resulted in perceiving a portfolio concentrated in a single sector as appropriate because that sector reflects what he knows.

2. Gerber's belief that the research setbacks were merely temporary given ABC's success with past projects is most likely an example of which bias?

    A. Availability
    B. Mental accounting
    C. Conservatism

    C is correct. Conservatism bias can result in FMPs maintaining or only slowly updating their views when presented with new information, especially when the information is complex. Faced with complex information in the form of clinical trial delays that should have reduced his assessment of Project M's probability of success, Gerber elected to maintain his original views.

3. Researching the biotechnology industry average probability of success of Phase 2 trials, particularly those that have experienced delays, is a strategy that Gerber could have used to most likely mitigate which behavioral bias?

    A. Hindsight
    B. Representativeness
    C. Framing

    B is correct. A form of representativeness bias is base-rate neglect, in which general information, such as the rate of incidence of a phenomenon for its "reference class" of phenomena, is ignored in favor of individual, specific information. Gerber did not consider the "base rate" of the success of Phase 2 trials.

4. Gerber's approach to reading the article by ABC's chief scientist could best be described by exhibiting which behavioral bias?

    A. Representativeness
    B. Confirmation
    C. Mental accounting

    B is correct. Confirmation bias refers to the tendency to seek confirming information and ignore contradictory information. Gerber did not adequately interpret the scientific results or the broader message of the article, choosing instead to focus on the reassuring concluding message that confirmed his existing beliefs.

> 5. Gerber's conclusion, upon re-examining ABC's history, is most likely an example of which behavioral bias?
>
>   **A.** Confirmation
>
>   **B.** Hindsight
>
>   **C.** Conservatism
>
> B is correct. Hindsight bias is the result of selectively interpreting the past using knowledge of the present. Although Gerber should have implemented various mitigation strategies over the life of the investment, it is also true that investing, especially investing in a small-cap biotechnology company, is a probabilistic activity. Had Project M succeeded, Gerber may have been tempted to see the investment as evidence of his investment acumen, which would also be biased. The most useful examination of the past for Gerber would be investigating whether any mitigating actions or strategies would have been useful and putting them in place for subsequent investments.

EMOTIONAL BIASES

☐ discuss commonly recognized behavioral biases and their implications for financial decision making

We will now review six emotional biases, their implications for investment decision making, and suggestions for managing the effects of these biases. Emotional biases are harder to correct than cognitive errors because they originate from impulse or intuition rather than conscious calculations. It is often possible only to recognize the bias and adapt to it. The six emotional biases discussed are loss aversion, overconfidence, self-control, status quo, endowment, and regret aversion.

Loss-Aversion Bias

Loss-aversion bias refers to the tendency to strongly prefer avoiding losses to achieving gains. Rational FMPs should accept more risk to increase gains, not to mitigate losses. Paradoxically, in real life, FMPs instead tend to accept more risk to avoid losses than to achieve gains. Loss aversion leads FMPs to hold their losers to avoid recognizing losses and sell their winners to lock in profits.

Kahneman and Tversky (1979) describe loss-averse investor behavior as the evaluation of gains and losses based on a reference point. A utility function that passes through this reference point appears in Exhibit 1. It is S-shaped and asymmetric, implying a greater impact of losses than of gains on utility for the same variation in absolute value. This utility function implies risk-seeking behavior in the domain of losses (below the horizontal axis) and risk avoidance in the domain of gains (above the horizontal axis). An important concept embedded in this utility representation is what has been termed the **disposition effect**: the holding of investments that have experienced losses too long, and the selling of investments that have experienced gains too quickly (i.e., holding on to losers and selling winners). The resulting portfolio may be riskier than the optimal portfolio based on the investor's risk–return objectives.

Exhibit 1: Value Function of Loss Aversion

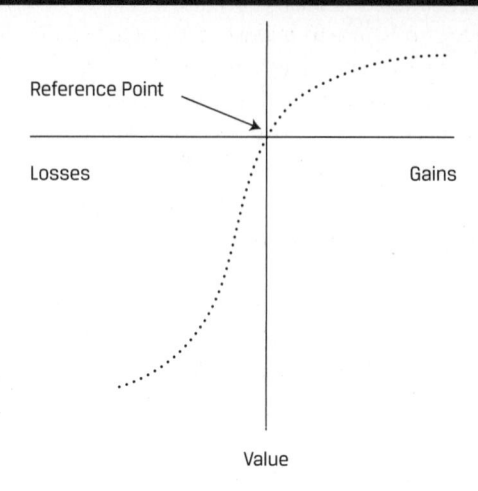

[Graph showing an S-shaped value function curve with Reference Point at origin. Horizontal axis labeled "Losses" on left and "Gains" on right. Vertical axis labeled "Value".]

EXAMPLE 10

Effects of Loss-Aversion Bias

Loss-aversion bias, executed in practice as the disposition effect, is observed often by wealth management practitioners. The classic case of this bias is when an investor opens her monthly account statement and scans the individual investments for winners and losers. Seeing that some investments have lost money and others have gained, the investor is likely to respond by continuing to hold the losing investments. The idea of actually losing money is so painful that the first reaction is to hold the investment until it breaks even.

The investor is acting based on emotions, not cognitive reasoning. In this case, if she did some research, the investor might learn that the company in question is experiencing difficulty and that holding the investment actually adds to the risk in the portfolio (hence the term risk-seeking in the domain of losses).

Conversely, the winners are making money. Loss-averse FMPs tend to sell these investments and realize their gains to avoid seeing gains evaporate. In this case, if the investor did some research, she might learn that the company in question actually improves the portfolio's risk–return profile. By selling the investment, not only is the potential for future losses eliminated but the potential for future gains is also eliminated. Combining the added risk of holding the losers with the elimination of potential gains from selling the winners may make investors' portfolios less efficient than portfolios based on fundamental analysis.

Consequences of Loss Aversion

As a result of loss-aversion bias, FMPs may do the following:

- Hold investments in a loss position longer than justified by fundamental analysis, in the hope that they will return to breakeven.
- Sell investments in a gain position earlier than justified by fundamental analysis, out of fear that the gains will erode.

Emotional Biases

Detection of and Guidelines for Overcoming Loss Aversion

A disciplined approach to investment is a good way to alleviate the impact of the loss-aversion bias. It is impossible to make experiencing losses any less painful emotionally, but analyzing investments and realistically considering the probabilities of future losses and gains may help guide the FMP to a rational decision.

Overconfidence Bias

Overconfidence bias is a bias in which people demonstrate unwarranted faith in their own abilities. Overconfidence may be intensified when combined with **self-attribution bias**, in which people take too much credit for successes (*self-enhancing*) and assign responsibility to others for failures (*self-protecting*). Overconfidence has aspects of both cognitive and emotional errors but is classified as emotional because the bias primarily results from emotion.

Overconfidence bias has two forms: *prediction overconfidence* and *certainty overconfidence*. Both types demonstrate faulty reasoning combined with "gut feel" and hope. Prediction overconfidence occurs when the confidence intervals that FMPs assign to their investment predictions are too narrow. For example, when estimating the future value of a stock, overconfident FMPs will incorporate far too little variation—using a narrower range of expected payoffs and a lower standard deviation of returns—than justified by historical results and fundamental analysis.

Certainty overconfidence occurs when the probabilities that FMPs assign to outcomes are too high. This certainty is often an emotional response rather than a cognitive evaluation.

EXAMPLE 11

Overconfidence Bias

An analyst estimates that the price of oil will increase by 40% over the next 12 months because prevailing prices are lower than many oil producers' cost of production. Unprofitable producers reducing production will eventually put upward pressure on prices so long as oil demand remains stable or increases. Based on this forecast, the analyst recommends several high-yield bonds of oil producers to a portfolio manager.

The portfolio manager asks the analyst for an estimate of downside risk: "How much could we lose if, say, the oil price falls another 10%?" The analyst replies, "That is unrealistic. The current oil price is as low as it can go, and yields on these bonds are as attractive as they will ever be. We must make the investment now. There is no credible downside case."

The analyst is exhibiting overconfidence bias by placing excessive certainty in his prediction and not considering the likelihood or impact of variance from that prediction.

Consequences of Overconfidence Bias

As a result of overconfidence bias, FMPs may do the following:

- Underestimate risks and overestimate expected returns.
- Hold poorly diversified portfolios, which may result in significant downside risk.

Detection of and Guidelines for Overcoming Overconfidence Bias

FMPs should review their trading records, identify *both* the winners and losers, and calculate portfolio performance over at least two years. Investors with an unfounded belief in their own ability to identify good investments may recall winners and their results but underestimate the number and results of their losers. This review will also identify the amount of trading. Overconfidence is also a cognitive error, and so more-complete information can often help FMPs understand the error of their ways.

It is critical that investors be objective when making and evaluating investment decisions. As an old Wall Street adage states, "Don't confuse brains with a bull market." It is advisable to view the reasoning behind and the results of investments, both winners and losers, as objectively as possible. When did you make money? When did you lose money? Mentally separate your good money-making decisions from your bad ones. Then, review the beneficial decisions and try to discern what, exactly, you did correctly. Did you purchase an investment at a particularly advantageous time based on fundamentals, or did you luck out by timing a market upswing? Similarly, review the decisions that you categorized as poor. Did you invest aptly based on fundamentals and then make an error when it came time to sell, or was the market going through a correction?

When reviewing unprofitable decisions, look for patterns or common mistakes that perhaps you were unaware you were making. Note any such tendencies that you discover, and try to remain mindful of them by brainstorming a rule or reminder such as: "I will do X in the future" or "I will not do Y in the future."

Self-Control Bias

Self-control bias is a bias in which people fail to act in pursuit of their long-term, overarching goals in favor of short-term satisfaction. For example, individuals pursuing the CFA charter may fail to study sufficiently because of short-term competing demands on their time. Rational behavior suggests that people would do whatever is necessary to achieve their long-term goals, but it often does not happen.

When it comes to money, many people are willing and able to save for the future, but they often have difficulty sacrificing present consumption because of a lack of self-control. This apparent lack of self-control may also be a function of hyperbolic discounting, the human tendency to prefer small payoffs now compared with larger payoffs in the future. Sacrifices in the present require much greater payoffs in the future; otherwise, people will be unwilling to make current sacrifices.

Consequences of Self-Control Bias

As a result of self-control bias, FMPs may do the following:

- Save insufficiently for the future, which may, in turn, result in accepting too much risk in portfolios in an attempt to generate higher returns.
- Borrow excessively to finance present consumption.

Detection of and Guidelines for Overcoming Self-Control Bias

FMPs should ensure that a proper investment plan is in place and should have a personal budget. Plans need to be in writing, so that they can be reviewed regularly. Similarly, FMPs should look to maintain a strategic asset allocation based on a thorough evaluation.

Status Quo Bias

Status quo bias is an emotional bias in which people choose to do nothing (i.e., maintain the "status quo") instead of making a change, even when change is warranted. Status quo bias is often discussed in tandem with endowment and regret-aversion biases because an outcome of the biases, maintaining existing positions, is similar. The reasons for maintaining the existing positions differ, however. In the status quo bias, positions are maintained largely because of inertia rather than conscious choice. In endowment and regret-aversion biases, positions are maintained because of conscious, but possibly incorrect, choices.

> **EXAMPLE 12**
>
> ### The Path of Least Resistance
>
> Using data from three firms, Choi et al. (2001) studied the impact of automatically enrolling employees in a defined contribution pension plan and how default contribution rates and investment options affect participants' behavior.
>
> Automatic enrollment increased employee participation in the defined contribution plan from 26%–43% after six months' tenure and 57%–69% after three years' tenure to >85% for both tenures at all three firms.
>
> Although automatic enrollment increased participation, more than 65% of employees tended to contribute the employer-specified default amount—2% or 3%—and remained in the default investment option. Although this percentage declined slowly over time, even after two years of tenure, more than 40% of participants continued to use the default.

Consequences of Status Quo Bias

As a result of status quo bias, FMPs may do the following:

- Unknowingly maintain portfolios with risk characteristics that are inappropriate for their circumstances.
- Fail to explore other opportunities.

Detection of and Guidelines for Overcoming Status Quo Bias

Status quo bias may be exceptionally strong and difficult to overcome. Education is essential. FMPs should quantify the risk-reducing and return-enhancing advantages of diversification and proper asset allocation. For example, with a concentrated stock position, showing what can happen to overall wealth levels if the stock collapses may persuade an FMP to diversify.

Endowment Bias

Endowment bias is an emotional bias in which people value an asset more when they own it than when they do not. Endowment bias is inconsistent with standard economic theory, which asserts that the price a person is *willing to pay* for a good should equal the price at which that person would be *willing to sell* the same good. Psychologists have found, however, that people tend to state minimum selling prices for a good that exceed maximum purchase prices that they are willing to pay for the same good. Effectively, ownership "endows" the asset with added value.

Endowment bias may be the result of several other behavioral biases, such as loss aversion, anchoring and adjustment, and overconfidence. Despite the name, purchased as well as inherited securities can be subject to endowment bias.

> **EXAMPLE 13**
>
> ### Endowment Bias
>
> Several of an investment analyst's recommended stocks have done well for the past five years, prompting the portfolio manager to ask for a brief update on each, including valuations. For each stock, the analyst estimates that fair value is at least another 40% above the current price. The portfolio manager challenges the analyst by pointing out that the fair value estimates imply valuation multiples that are at least two standard deviations above the five-year average and are well above even the most bullish sell-side analyst's target price. The analyst responds by saying that the market is overlooking these companies' fundamentals. The portfolio manager then asks, "Would you buy these shares today?" The analyst answers, "Probably not."
>
> The analyst is likely exhibiting endowment bias by overestimating the value of shares already owned in the portfolio. This bias is likely the result of having successfully invested in the shares.

Consequences of Endowment Bias

Endowment bias may lead FMPs to do the following:

- Fail to sell certain assets and replace them with other assets.
- Continue to hold classes of assets with which they are familiar. FMPs may believe they understand the characteristics of the investments they already own and may be reluctant to purchase assets with which they have less experience. Familiarity adds to owners' perceived value of a security.
- As a result, the FMP may maintain an inappropriate asset allocation. The portfolio may be inappropriate for investors' levels of risk tolerance and financial goals.

Detection of and Guidelines for Overcoming Endowment Bias

Many wealth management practitioners have encountered clients who are reluctant to sell securities bequeathed by previous generations. Often in these situations, investors cite feelings of disloyalty associated with the prospect of selling inherited securities, general uncertainty in determining the right choice, and concerns about tax issues. An FMP should ask, "If an equivalent sum to the value of the investments inherited had been received in cash, how would you invest the cash?" Often, the answer is into a very different investment portfolio than the one inherited. It may also be useful to explore the deceased's intent in owning the investment and bequeathing it. "Was the primary intent to leave the specific investment portfolio because it was perceived to be a suitable investment based on fundamental analysis, or was it to leave financial resources to benefit the heirs?" Heirs who affirm the latter conclusion are receptive to considering alternative asset allocations.

An effective way to address endowment bias for purchased securities, when an estimated "sell price" is far higher than any reasonable FMP's estimate of a "buy price" is to ask, "Would you buy this security today at the current price?" A similar question is, "Why are you not buying more of this security today?" Answering these questions can turn the focus away from the past to the present, toward considering the upside from the current price.

Regret-Aversion Bias

Regret-aversion bias is an emotional bias in which people tend to avoid making decisions out of fear that the decision will turn out poorly. Regret-aversion bias has two dimensions: actions that people take and actions that people *could have* taken. Regret is more intense when the unfavorable outcomes are the result of an action taken versus the result of an action not taken. Thus, no action becomes the default decision.

Consequences of Regret-Aversion Bias
As a result of regret-aversion bias, FMPs may do the following:

- Be too conservative in their investment choices as a result of poor outcomes on risky investments in the past. FMPs may wish to avoid the regret of making another bad investment and decide that low-risk instruments are better. This behavior can lead to long-term underperformance and failure to reach investment goals.

- Engage in herding behavior. FMPs may feel safer in popular investments in order to limit potential future regret. It seems safe to be with the crowd, and a reduction in potential emotional pain is perceived. Regret aversion may lead to preference for stocks of well-known companies even in the face of equal risk and return expectations. Choosing the stocks of less-familiar companies is perceived as riskier and involves more personal responsibility and greater potential for regret. As John Maynard Keynes (1936) wrote, "Worldly wisdom teaches that it is better for reputation to fail conventionally than to succeed unconventionally."

Detection of and Guidelines for Overcoming Regret-Aversion Bias
FMPs should quantify the risk-reducing and return-enhancing advantages of diversification and proper asset allocation. Regret aversion can cause some FMPs to invest too conservatively or too riskily depending on the current trends. With proper diversification, FMPs will accept the appropriate level of risk in their portfolios depending, of course, on return objectives. To prevent investments from being too conservative, FMPs must recognize that losses happen to everyone and keep in mind the long-term benefits of including risky assets in portfolios. Recognizing that bubbles happen and keeping in mind long-term objectives will prevent a client from making investments that are too risky.

> **EXAMPLE 14**
>
> Tiffany Jordan is a hedge fund manager with a history of outstanding performance. For the past 10 years, Jordan's fund has used an equity market–neutral strategy (a long–short strategy that strives to eliminate market risk—i.e., beta should be zero), which has proved effective as a result of Jordan's hard work. An equity market–neutral strategy normally generates large daily trading volume and shifts in individual security positions. Jordan's reputation has grown over the years as her fund has consistently beaten its benchmark. Employee turnover

on her team has been high; Jordan tends to be quick to blame and rarely gives credit to team members for success. During the past 12 months, her fund has been significantly underperforming its benchmark.

One of Jordan's junior analysts, Jeremy Tang, is concerned about the underperformance and notes the following:

Observation 1: Certain positions are significantly underwater, have very high risk profiles, and have been held for much longer than normal.

Observation 2: The fund's trading volume has decreased by more than 40% during the past year.

Observation 3: The portfolio is more concentrated in a few sectors than in the past.

Worried that the portfolio may be in violation of the fund's investment policy statement (IPS), Tang brings this concern to Jordan's attention during a regular weekly team meeting. Jordan dismisses Tang's analysis and tells the team not to worry because she knows what she is doing. Jordan indicates that because she believes the pricing misalignment will correct itself, the portfolio would be unable to take advantage of the reversion to the mean if she were to sell certain losing positions. She reassures the team that this strategy has performed well in the past and that the markets will revert, bringing the fund's returns back to normal levels.

Tang tactfully suggests that the team review the fund's IPS together, and Jordan interrupts him and reminds the team that she has memorized the IPS by heart. Tang contemplates his next step. He is concerned that Jordan is displaying behavioral biases that are affecting the fund's performance.

1. By taking credit for successes but assigning blame for failures, Jordan is *most likely* demonstrating:

    A. loss-aversion bias.

    B. self-attribution bias.

    C. illusion of control bias.

    B is correct. In self-attribution bias, people take credit for successes and assign responsibilities for failure. Jordan claims successful decisions for herself while attributing poor decisions to the team. Her self-esteem affects how she looks at success and failure. Self-attribution and illusion of knowledge biases contribute to overconfidence bias, which Jordan clearly demonstrates later when she tells the team that she knows what she is doing.

2. Which of Tang's observations is *least likely* to be the consequence of Jordan demonstrating loss-aversion bias?

    A. Observation 1

    B. Observation 2

    C. Observation 3

    C is correct. Loss aversion by itself may cause a sector concentration; however, a market-neutral strategy tends to focus on individual stocks without regard to sector. The sector exposure would be mitigated with the balancing of the individual long and short positions.

3. Which of Jordan's actions *least* supports that she may be affected by the illusion of control bias?

    A. Her dismissal of Tang's analysis

Emotional Biases

    B. Her routine of holding weekly team meetings

    C. Her comment on market turnaround and current holdings

B is correct. Holding weekly team meetings, which indicates a willingness to listen to feedback from others, is not representative of the illusion of control bias. In the illusion of control bias, people believe they can control outcomes to a greater extent than is possible. Individuals exhibiting this bias display great certainty in their predictions of outcomes of chance events and ignore others' viewpoints. Jordan is sure that the market will turn around even though it is out of her control. She chooses not to listen to Tang, who is questioning her viewpoint.

4. How does Jordan *most likely* demonstrate loss-aversion bias?

    A. Telling the team not to worry

    B. Reducing the portfolio turnover this year

    C. Deciding to hold the losing positions until they turn around

C is correct. Jordan's behavior is a classic example of loss aversion: When a loss occurs, she holds on to these positions longer than warranted. By doing so, Jordan has accepted more risk in the portfolio. In loss-aversion bias, people exhibit a strong preference to avoid losses versus achieving gains. One of the consequences of loss aversion bias is that the financial management professional (in this case, Jordan) may hold losing investments in the hope that they will return to breakeven or better.

5. Which of the following emotional biases has Jordan *mostlikely* exhibited?

    A. Endowment

    B. Regret aversion

    C. Overconfidence

C is correct. Jordan exhibits overconfidence in several ways. She ignores the analysis done by Tang. This may be because Jordan believes she is smarter and more informed than her team members, which is typical of an individual with an illusion of knowledge bias. The certainty she demonstrates that the market will revert is evidence of overconfidence. Her overconfidence is intensified by her self-attribution bias, which is demonstrated through her dealings with her team when she blames them for losses while taking credit for gains. Finally, her portfolio's underperformance against the benchmark is a consequence of overconfidence bias.

6. Which of the following biases did Jordan *not* demonstrate?

    A. Self-attribution

    B. Representativeness

    C. Illusion of knowledge

B is correct. Nowhere in the scenario did it mention that Jordan classified certain information into a personalized category. Representativeness bias is a cognitive bias in which people tend to classify new information based on past experiences and classifications. Jordan is not relating her certainty about the future or her decision to hold losing positions back to anything she has done or experienced in the past.

7. Which of Tang's findings is *not* a typical consequence of self-control bias?

    A. Failure to explore other portfolio opportunities

> **B.** Asset allocation imbalance problems in the portfolio
> **C.** A higher risk profile in the portfolio resulting from pursuit of higher returns
>
> A is correct. Failing to explore other opportunities is a demonstration of status quo bias, not self-control. Self-control bias occurs when individuals deviate from their long-term goals—in this case, the IPS—because of a lack of self-discipline. Jordan is not adhering to the strategy that has succeeded in the past. The consequences of self-control bias include accepting too much risk in the portfolio (C) and asset allocation imbalance problems (B) as Jordan attempts to generate higher returns.

5. BEHAVIORAL FINANCE AND MARKET BEHAVIOR

> describe how behavioral biases of investors can lead to market characteristics that may not be explained by traditional finance

Some persistent market patterns run counter to market efficiency. This section focuses on the contributions of behavioral finance to understanding these exceptions to market efficiency, such as momentum, value, bubbles, and crashes, by explaining them as functions of behavioral biases.

Defining Market Anomalies

Anomalies are apparent deviations from the efficient market hypothesis, identified by persistent abnormal returns that differ from zero and are predictable in direction. Not every deviation is anomalous. Misclassifications tend to stem from three sources: choice of asset pricing model, statistical issues, and temporary disequilibria.

Classifying returns as "abnormal" presupposes a definition of "normal returns," which generally depends on the asset pricing model used. If a reasonable change in the method of estimating normal returns causes an anomaly to disappear, then it is reasonable to suggest that the anomaly is an illusion. Fama (1998) includes in this category apparently low returns following initial public offerings (called the "IPO puzzle") and the positive abnormal returns apparent in the 12 months after a stock split. Similarly, when high returns persist on a particular class of securities, or relative to a specific factor in valuation, it might simply be compensation for excess risk rather than an anomaly.

Other apparent anomalies may be explained by the small samples involved, a statistical bias in selection or survivorship, or data mining that overanalyzes data for patterns and treats spurious correlations as relevant. The magnitude of any over- or underperformance also depends critically on the choice of benchmark, which can make it hard to interpret results.

Finally, from time to time, markets can present *temporary disequilibrium behavior*, unusual features that may survive for a period of years but ultimately disappear. Publication of the anomaly, which draws attention to the pattern, usually starts the arbitrage that removes the behavior. For example, the small company January effect, part of the turn-of-the-year effect, does not appear persistent once appropriate adjustment for risk is made. The weekend effect, involving lower stock market returns on Mondays, appears to have diminished in the United States and United Kingdom.

The anomalies discussed in this section reflect behavior that has been identified and analyzed in a number of markets around the world and during different periods. The patterns have been documented in many academic studies, with broadly similar conclusions. Behavioral finance can help provide good explanations by identifying underlying behavioral biases.

Momentum

Studies have documented, in a range of markets globally, *momentum* or *trending effects* in which future price behavior correlates with that of the recent past (Jegadeesh and Titman 1993; Dimson, Marsh, and Staunton 2008). The positive correlation typically lasts for up to two years before showing a reversal or reversion to the mean, evident in two- to five-year return periods.

EXAMPLE 15

The Momentum Effect: London Business School Study

The study involves buying the top 20% of a performance-ranked list of stocks and selling short the bottom 20%. In the 52 years to 2007 in the UK market, the stocks that had outperformed the market most in the previous 12 months went on to generate an annualized return of 18.3%, whereas the market's worst underperformers rose by 6.8% on average. During that period, the market as a whole rose by 13.5% a year. In a subsequent study using data from 2000 to 2007, the momentum effect was also evident in each of the 16 other international markets researched.

The authors noted, "The momentum effect, both in the United Kingdom and globally, has been pervasive and persistent. Though costly to implement on a standalone basis, all investors need to be acutely aware of momentum. Even if they do not set out to exploit it, momentum is likely to be an important determinant of their investment performance."

Source: Dimson, Marsh, and Staunton (2008).

Momentum can be partly explained by availability, hindsight, and loss aversion biases.

Studies have identified faulty learning models within traders, in which reasoning is based on their recent experience. Behaviorally, this is *availability bias*. In this context, availability bias is also called the *recency effect*, which is the tendency to recall recent events more vividly and give them undue weight. In such models, if the price of an asset rises for a period of time, investors may simply extrapolate this rise to the future. Research points to a tendency for individual private investors to extrapolate trends and to suffer more from recency bias, whereas many investment professionals expect reversion to the mean.

Regret is the feeling that an opportunity has been missed and is typically an expression of *hindsight bias*, which reflects the human tendency to see past events as having been predictable. Regret can be particularly acute when the market is volatile and investors feel they could have predicted the significant market moves, thereby increasing profit or reducing loss. Faced with regret from not owning a mutual fund or stock when it performed well in the previous year, investors may be driven emotionally to remedy this regret. These behavioral factors can explain short-term year-on-year trending and contribute to overtrading.

Bubbles and Crashes

Although bubbles and crashes have been documented for a long time (Mackay's *Extraordinary Popular Delusions and the Madness of Crowds* was published in 1841), their existence presents a challenge to the concept of market efficiency. Historical examples include the technology bubble of 1999–2000 and the residential property boom of 2005–2007, evident in a range of economies globally including the United States, the United Kingdom, and Australia. Exhibit 2 illustrates the residential property boom in the United Kingdom.32

Exhibit 2: UK House Price Average Multiple of Average Family Income

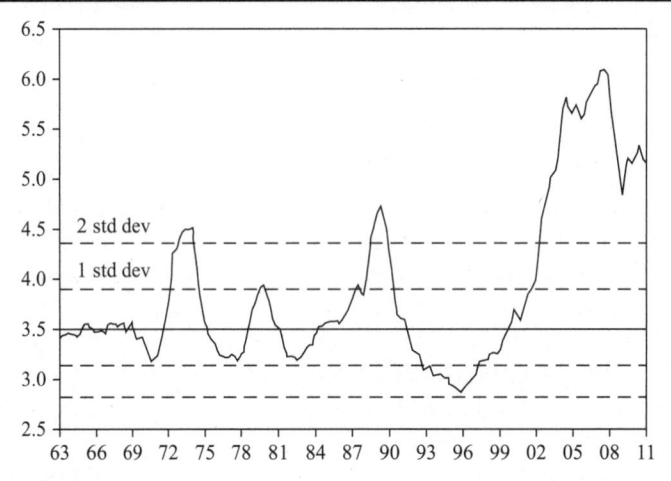

Source: Datastream.

First, note that some bubbles may have rational explanations. Rational investors may expect a future crash but not know its exact timing. For periods of time, there may not be effective arbitrage because of the cost of selling short, unwillingness of investors to bear extended losses, or simply unavailability of suitable instruments. These factors were considerations in past technology and real estate bubbles. Investment managers incentivized on, or accountable for, short-term performance may even rationalize their participation in the bubble in terms of commercial or career risk.

Investors' behaviors and incentives during bubbles are illustrated in Exhibit 16. The manager of Fund A believed he could exit a bubble profitably by selling near the top. The manager of Fund B correctly avoided the bubble, but clients held the manager accountable for short-run performance, which resulted in the fund's closure.

EXAMPLE 16

Investor Behavior in Bubbles

Consider the differing behavior of two managers of major hedge funds during the technology stock bubble of 1998–2000:

The manager of Hedge Fund A was asked why he did not get out of internet stocks earlier even though he knew by December 1999 that technology stocks were overvalued. He replied, "We thought it was the eighth inning, and it was the ninth. I did not think the NASDAQ composite would go down 33% in 15 days." Faced with losses, and despite his previous strong 12-year record, he resigned as Hedge Fund A's manager in April 2000.

> The manager of Hedge Fund B refused to invest in technology stocks in 1998 and 1999 because he thought they were overvalued. After strong performance over 17 years, Hedge Fund B was dissolved in 2000 because its returns could not keep up with the returns generated by technology stocks.

Behavioral finance does not yet provide a full explanation for bubbles and crashes, but a number of specific cognitive biases and emotional biases prevalent during such periods can be identified.

In bubbles, investors often exhibit symptoms of *overconfidence*; overtrading, underestimation of risks, failure to diversify, and rejection of contradictory information. With overconfidence, investors are more active and trading volume increases, thus lowering their expected profits. For overconfident investors (active traders), studies have shown that returns are less than returns to either less active traders or the market while risk is higher. At the market level, volatility also often increases in a market with overconfident traders.

The overconfidence and excessive trading that contribute to a bubble are linked to *confirmation bias* and *self-attribution bias*. In a rising market, sales of stocks from a portfolio will typically be profitable, even if winners are being sold too soon. Investors can have faulty learning models that bias their understanding of this profit to take personal credit for success, a form of *hindsight bias*. Selling for a gain appears to validate a good decision in an original purchase and may confer a sense of pride in locking in the profit. This dynamic fuels overconfidence that can lead to poor decisions. Regret aversion can also encourage investors to participate in a bubble, believing they are "missing out" on profit opportunities as stocks appreciate.

As a bubble unwinds, markets may underreact because of anchoring when investors do not sufficiently update their beliefs. The early stages of unwinding a bubble can involve investors in cognitive dissonance, who ignore losses and attempt to rationalize flawed decisions. Eventually, investors capitulate, which accelerates price declines.

Value

Value stocks are typically characterized by low price-to-earnings ratios, high book-to-market equity, and low price-to-dividend ratios. Growth stock characteristics are generally the opposite of value stock characteristics. For example, growth stocks are characterized by low book-to-market equity, high price-to-earnings ratios, and high price-to-dividend ratios. A number of studies have identified outperformance of value stocks relative to growth stocks over long periods. Fama and French (1998) found that value stocks (high book-to-market equity) outperformed growth stocks (low book-to-market equity) in 12 of 13 major markets during the 1975–1995 period.

Fama and French have also found, however, that the value stock anomaly disappears in a three-factor asset pricing model. This result suggests that size and book-to-market factors are not mispricing but instead represent compensation for risk exposures, such as the greater potential of companies with these characteristics to suffer distress during economic downturns.

A number of other studies have offered behavioral explanations for value anomalies, presenting the anomalies as mispricing rather than compensation for increased risk. These studies recognize the emotional factors involved in appraising stocks. The **halo effect**, for example, extends a favorable evaluation of some characteristics to other characteristics. A company with a good growth record and good previous share price performance might be seen as a good investment, with higher expected returns than its risk characteristics merit. This view is a form of representativeness that can lead investors to extrapolate recent past performance into expected returns. Overconfidence can also be involved in predicting growth rates, potentially leading growth stocks to be overvalued.

Studies have also identified that emotions play a role in estimating risk and expected return of stocks. The impact of emotional biases may be greater with less sophisticated or retail investors, but it has also been identified as a bias in analysts and professional investors. The emotional attraction of a stock can be enhanced by personal experience of products, the value of the brand, marketing expenditures, and the proximity of the headquarters to the analyst or investor. This last issue reflects the **home bias** anomaly, by which portfolios exhibit a strong bias in favor of domestic securities in the context of global portfolios. The effect has also been noted within geographical boundaries, favoring companies headquartered nearer the investor. Home bias may reflect a perceived relative informational advantage, a greater feeling of comfort with the access to company executives that proximity brings (either personal or local brokerage), or a psychological desire to invest in a local community.

To the extent to which less sophisticated investors are influenced by emotions, they may value growth companies more highly. Stock returns of funds that are rated as popular in a *Fortune* magazine survey are found to be subsequently low. A more positive emotional rating in a company leads investors to perceive the company's stock as less risky. Although the capital asset pricing model assumes risk and expected return are positively correlated, many investors behave as if the correlation is negative, expecting higher returns with lower risk.

SUMMARY

Behavioral biases potentially affect the behaviors and decisions of financial market participants. By understanding these biases, financial market participants may be able to moderate or adapt to them and, as a result, improve upon economic outcomes. Behavioral biases may be categorized as either cognitive errors or emotional biases. The type of bias influences whether its impact may be moderated or adapted to.

Among the points made in this reading are the following:

- Individuals do not necessarily act rationally and consider all available information in the decision-making process because they may be influenced by behavioral biases.
- Biases may lead to suboptimal decisions.
- Behavioral biases may be categorized as either cognitive errors or emotional biases. A single bias may have aspects of both, however, with one type of bias dominating.
- Cognitive errors stem from basic statistical, information-processing, or memory errors; cognitive errors typically result from faulty reasoning.
- Emotional biases stem from impulse or intuition and tend to result from reasoning influenced by feelings.
- Cognitive errors are more easily corrected for because they stem from faulty reasoning rather than an emotional predisposition.
- Emotional biases are harder to correct for because they are based on feelings, which can be difficult to change.
- To adapt to a bias is to recognize and accept the bias and to adjust for the bias rather than to attempt to moderate the bias.
- To moderate a bias is to recognize the bias and to attempt to reduce or even eliminate the bias within the individual.
- Cognitive errors can be further classified into two categories: belief perseverance biases and information-processing biases.

- Belief perseverance errors reflect an inclination to maintain beliefs. The belief is maintained by committing statistical, information-processing, or memory errors. Belief perseverance biases are closely related to the psychological concept of cognitive dissonance.
- Belief perseverance biases include conservatism, confirmation, representativeness, illusion of control, and hindsight.
- Information-processing biases result in information being processed and used illogically or irrationally.
- Information-processing biases include anchoring and adjustment, mental accounting, framing, and availability.
- Emotional biases include loss aversion, overconfidence, self-control, status quo, endowment, and regret aversion.
- Understanding and detecting biases is the first step in overcoming the effect of biases on financial decisions. By understanding behavioral biases, financial market participants may be able to moderate or adapt to the biases and, as a result, improve upon economic outcomes.
- Behavioral finance has the potential to explain some apparent deviations from market efficiency (market anomalies).

REFERENCES

Fama, Eugene. 1998. "Market Efficiency, Long-Term Returns, and Behavioral Finance." Journal of Financial Economics 49 (3): 283–306. doi:10.1016/S0304-405X(98)00026-9

Keynes, John Maynard. 1936. The General Theory of Employment, Interest, and Money. New York: Harcourt, Brace.

Statman, Meir. 1999. "Behavioral Finance: Past Battles and Future Engagements." Financial Analysts Journal 55 (6): 18–27. doi:10.2469/faj.v55.n6.2311

Statman, Meir. 2008. "What Is Behavioral Finance?" In Handbook of Finance, ed. Fabozzi, Frank. Hoboken, NJ: John Wiley & Sons.

Thaler, Richard H. 1980. "Toward a Positive Theory of Economic Choice." Journal of Economic Behavior & Organization 1 (1): 39–60. doi:10.1016/0167-2681(80)90051-7

PRACTICE PROBLEMS

1. Under-diversified portfolios are <u>not</u> a potential implication of which of the following behavioral biases?

    A. Representativeness

    B. Illusion of control

    C. Confirmation

2. The advice "Don't confuse brains with a bull market" is aimed at mitigating which of the following behavioral biases?

    A. Self-control

    B. Conservatism

    C. Overconfidence

3. Status quo bias is <u>least</u> similar to which of the following behavioral biases?

    A. Endowment

    B. Regret aversion

    C. Confirmation

4. Which strategy would best mitigate or prevent endowment bias?

    A. Actively seeking out information that challenges existing beliefs

    B. When new information is presented, asking "How does this information change my forecast?"

    C. Asking "Would you buy this security today at the current price?"

5. Jun Park, CFA, works at a hedge fund. Most of Park's colleagues are also CFA charterholders. At an event with recent university graduates, Park comments, "Most CFA charterholders work at hedge funds." Park's remark exhibits which behavioral bias?

    A. Availability

    B. Conservatism

    C. Framing

6. In the 1980s, Japan was viewed by many FMPs as the model economy. Although its growth began to decelerate sharply by 1990, it was not until the mid to late 1990s that FMPs' GDP forecasts were consistently achieved. By taking several years to adapt their forecasts to the lower growth environment, FMPs exhibited which behavioral bias?

    A. Mental accounting

    B. Overconfidence

    C. Conservatism

The following information relates to questions 7-10

Caitríona Daosri is a portfolio manager for an international bank, where she advises high-net-worth clients. Daosri is meeting with a new client, Estêvão Kai, a 40-year-old surgeon with €4 million across various accounts and a salary of €500,000 per annum. Kai explains to Daosri that he has four accounts at four different banks, each with specific sources and uses of funds, as shown in the following table:

Bank Account	Source of Deposits	Use of Funds
1	Salary	Living expenses
2	Bonus	Charitable gifts
3	Portfolio interest	Savings for retirement
4	Portfolio dividends	Mother's living expenses

7. Based on the description of how Kai manages his finances as outlined in Exhibit 1, Kai most likely exhibits the behavioral bias of:

    A. endowment.

    B. mental accounting.

    C. framing.

8. Which of the following is a likely consequence of Kai's approach to managing his finances?

    A. Concentrated portfolio positions

    B. Forgone opportunities to reduce risk by combining assets with low correlations

    C. Excessive trading

9. Which strategy should Daosri use or recommend to Kai?

    A. Keep written records of investment decisions.

    B. Ask questions such as, "Is the decision the result of focusing on a net gain or net loss position?"

    C. Aggregate all accounts and portfolios into a single spreadsheet.

10. Which of the following individual behavioral biases is most strongly associated with market bubbles?

    A. Overconfidence

    B. Representativeness

    C. Framing

11. The halo effect, which may be evident in FMP's assessments of a company with a history of high revenue growth, is a form of which behavioral bias?

    A. Endowment

B. Representativeness

C. Regret aversion

12. All of the following are reasons that an apparent deviation from the efficient market hypothesis might not be anomalous except:

    A. The abnormal returns represent compensation for exposure to risk.

    B. Changing the asset pricing model makes the deviation to disappear.

    C. The deviation is well known or documented.

13. Investment managers incentivized or accountable for short-term performance by current and prospective clients is a potentially rational explanation for which of the following?

    A. Home bias

    B. Bubbles

    C. Value stocks outperforming growth stocks

14. Momentum, can be partly explained by the following behavioral biases except:

    A. availability.

    B. home bias.

    C. regret.

15. All of the following are reasons that the historical outperformance of value stocks versus growth stocks may not be anomalous except:

    A. Abnormal returns represent compensation for risk exposures, such as the heightened risk of value stocks to suffer distress during downturns.

    B. Companies with strong historical growth rates are viewed as good investments, with higher expected returns than risk characteristics merit.

    C. The deviation disappears by incorporating a three-factor asset pricing model.

SOLUTIONS

1. A is correct. Under-diversified portfolios are a consequence of both illusion of control and confirmation biases. Researchers have found that some investors prefer to invest in companies that they feel they have control over, such as the companies they work for, leading them to hold concentrated positions. Confirmation bias may lead to FMPs ignoring negative news, paying attention only to information confirming that a company is a good investment, which may result in large positions. Representativeness bias is not typically associated with under-diversified portfolios.

2. C is correct. This advice is specifically aimed at reducing self-attribution bias, a form of overconfidence bias. This bias may result in FMPs taking credit for investment success, as well as assigning responsibility to others for investment failures, when in reality the investment results reflect exogenous market forces.

3. C is correct. Both endowment bias and regret-aversion bias often result in indecision or inertia—a typical outcome of status quo bias, in which people prefer to not make changes even when changes are warranted.

4. C is correct. Endowment bias refers to people attributing additional, unwarranted value to things they possess versus things they do not. This bias is evident in FMPs that systematically and materially overvalue securities in their portfolio versus securities not in their portfolio. The question "Would you buy this security today at the current price?" turns the investor's attention to assessing the reasonableness of the current price as a buy price rather than solely as a selling price.

5. A is correct. Park is extrapolating his observation based on a narrow range of experience (working at a hedge fund that employs many CFA charterholders) to the entire population of CFA charterholders. Using a narrow range of experience is a form of availability bias.

6. C is correct. Conservatism bias results in maintain or only slowly updating views and forecasts despite the presence of new information. FMPs in the 1990s were reluctant to update forecasts, despite materially different new information for several years.

7. B is correct. Kai has segregated money into four different accounts based on the sources and uses of his funds. Although intuitively appealing, this approach is irrational because money is fungible across the four accounts. Nothing is stopping Kai from collapsing them into a single "account" with a holistic portfolio strategy.

8. B is correct. The most common consequence of mental accounting is neglecting opportunities to reduce risk by combining assets with low correlations, because each account's asset allocation is examined discretely. Offsetting positions across accounts, or an overall inefficient allocation with respect to risk, can lead to suboptimal aggregate performance.

9. C is correct. Aggregating mental accounts is a logical strategy to combat mental accounting. It is the opposite of disaggregating money into separate accounts.

10. A is correct. The overconfidence and excessive trading that contribute to a bubble are linked to self-attribution bias, a form of overconfidence. In a rising market, sales of stocks from a portfolio will typically be profitable, even if winners are being sold too soon, and FMPs will attribute profits and strong performance to

Solutions

their investment acumen and subsequently underestimate risks.

11. B is correct. Representativeness refers to the tendency to adopt a view or forecast based on individual information or a small sample, as well to use simple classifications. The halo effect is an example of representativeness, because FMPs extend an overall favorable evaluation to an investment (e.g., a "good company") based on one or few characteristics (e.g., a "visionary CEO").

12. C is correct. Bubbles and crashes are well-known and well-documented phenomena yet represent market anomalies.

13. B is correct. Investment managers' incentives—or perhaps more accurately, their perception of their incentives—for short-term performance were named as considerations in the technology and real estate bubbles. Not participating in the bubble presented certain FMPs with commercial or career risk.

14. B is correct. Home bias refers to FMPs preferentially investing in domestic securities, likely reflecting perceived relative informational advantages, a greater feeling of comfort with the access to company executives that proximity brings (either personal or through a local brokerage), or a psychological desire to invest in a local community. Momentum, on the other hand, has been documented in a range of markets around the world, in a time-dependent manner, and reflects some FMPs' availability bias, manifested as a belief that stocks will continue to rise because recently they have only risen, as well as regret aversion by those who invest in past winners because they regret not investing in them in the past.

15. B is correct. This choice describes the halo effect, which does offer a behavioral explanation for the poor performance of growth stocks versus value stocks. Growth stocks are mispriced relative to their risk characteristics, because FMPs focusing on just a few properties, such as a high historical revenue growth rate, while neglecting other characteristics.

LEARNING MODULE
3

Introduction to Risk Management

by Don M. Chance, PhD, CFA, and Michael E. Edleson, PhD, CFA.

Don M. Chance, PhD, CFA, is at Louisiana State University (USA). Michael E. Edleson, PhD, CFA, is at the University of Chicago (USA).

LEARNING OUTCOME	
Mastery	The candidate should be able to:
☐	define risk management
☐	describe features of a risk management framework
☐	define risk governance and describe elements of effective risk governance
☐	explain how risk tolerance affects risk management
☐	describe risk budgeting and its role in risk governance
☐	identify financial and non-financial sources of risk and describe how they may interact
☐	describe methods for measuring and modifying risk exposures and factors to consider in choosing among the methods

INTRODUCTION

Risk—and risk management—is an inescapable part of economic activity. People generally manage their affairs to be as happy and secure as their environment and resources will allow. But regardless of how carefully these affairs are managed, there is risk because the outcome, whether good or bad, is seldom predictable with complete certainty. There is risk inherent in nearly everything we do, but this reading will focus on economic and financial risk, particularly as it relates to investment management.

All businesses and investors manage risk, whether consciously or not, in the choices they make. At its core, business and investing are about allocating resources and capital to chosen risks. In their decision process, within an environment of uncertainty, these organizations may take steps to avoid some risks, pursue the risks that provide the highest rewards, and measure and mitigate their exposure to these risks as necessary. Risk management processes and tools make difficult business and financial problems easier to address in an uncertain world. Risk is not just a matter of fate; it is something that organizations can actively manage with their decisions, within a risk management framework. Risk is an integral part of the business or investment process. Even in the earliest models of modern portfolio theory, such as mean–variance portfolio optimization and the capital asset pricing model, investment return is linked directly to risk but requires that risk be managed optimally. Proper identification and measurement of risk, and keeping risks aligned with the goals of the enterprise, are key factors in managing businesses and investments. Good risk management results in a higher chance of a preferred outcome—more value for the company or portfolio or more utility for the individual.

Portfolio managers need to be familiar with risk management not only to improve the portfolio's risk–return outcome, but also because of two other ways in which they use risk management at an enterprise level. First, they help to manage their own companies that have their own enterprise risk issues. Second, many portfolio assets are claims on companies that have risks. Portfolio managers need to evaluate the companies' risks and how those companies are addressing them.

This reading takes a broad approach that addresses both the risk management of enterprises in general and portfolio risk management. The principles underlying portfolio risk management are generally applicable to the risk management of financial and non-financial institutions as well.

The concept of risk management is also relevant to individuals. Although many large organizations formally practice risk management, most individuals practice it more informally and some practice it haphazardly, oftentimes responding to risk events after they occur. Although many individuals do take reasonable precautions against unwanted risks, these precautions are often against obvious risks. The more subtle risks are often ignored. Unfortunately, many individuals do not view risk management as a formal, systematic process that would help them achieve not only their financial goals but also the ultimate goal, or maximum utility as economists like to call it, but they should.

Although the primary focus of this reading is on institutions, we will also cover risk management as it applies to individuals. We will show that many common themes underlie risk management—themes that are applicable to both organizations and individuals.

Although often viewed as defensive, risk management is a valuable offensive weapon in the manager's arsenal. In the quest for preferred outcomes, such as higher profit, returns, or share price, management does not usually get to choose the outcomes but does choose the risks it takes in pursuit of those outcomes. The choice of which risks to undertake through the allocation of its scarce resources is the key tool available to management. An organization with a comprehensive risk management culture in place, in which risk is integral to every key strategy and decision, should perform better in the long-term, in good times and bad, as a result of better decision making.

The fact that all businesses and investors engage in risky activities (i.e., activities with uncertain outcomes) raises a number of important questions. The questions that this reading will address include the following:

- What is risk management, and why is it important?
- What risks does an organization (or individual) face in pursuing its objectives?
- How are an organization's goals affected by risk, and how does it make risk management decisions to produce better results?
- How does risk governance guide the risk management process and risk budgeting to integrate an organization's goals with its activities?
- How does an organization measure and evaluate the risks it faces, and what tools does it have to address these risks?

The answers to these questions collectively help to define the process of risk management. This reading is organized along the lines of these questions. Sections 2 and 3 describe the risk management process, and Sections 4–6 discuss risk governance and risk tolerance. Sections 7 and 8 cover the identification of various risks, and Sections 9–11 addresses the measurement and management of risks.

RISK MANAGEMENT PROCESS

☐ define risk management

Risk, broadly speaking, is exposure to uncertainty. Risk is also the concept used to describe all of the uncertain environmental variables that lead to variation in and unpredictability of outcomes. More colloquially, risk is about the chance of a loss or adverse outcome as a result of an action, inaction, or external event.

This last view may make it sound as if risk is something to be avoided. But that is not at all the case. Risk is a key ingredient in the recipe for business or investment success; return without risk is generally a false hope and usually a prescription for falling short of one's goals. Risks taken must be carefully chosen, understood, and well-managed to have a chance at adding value through decisions. Risk and return are the interconnected forces of the financial universe. Many decision makers focus on return, which is not something that is easily controlled, as opposed to risk, or exposure to risk, which may actually be managed or controlled.

Risk exposure is the extent to which the underlying environmental or market risks result in actual risk borne by a business or investor who has assets or liabilities that are sensitive to those risks. It is the state of being exposed or vulnerable to a risk. Risk exposure results from the decisions of an organization or investor to take on risk-sensitive assets and liabilities.

Suppose there is an important announcement in Japan that will result in the yen either appreciating or depreciating by 1%. The range of possible outcomes in real situations is clearly not as simple as the up-or-down 1% case used here, but we will use a simplified example to make an important point. The risk is the uncertain outcome of this event, and the currency risk to a non-Japanese business is the uncertain return or variation in return in domestic currency terms that results from the event. The risk can be described as the range of resulting outcomes and is often thought of in terms of a probability distribution of future returns. Suppose that the underlying amount is ¥1,000,000. The risk exposure of a business may be zero or it could be sizable, depending on whether the business has assets or liabilities tied to this risk—in this case, exposure to that currency. One million yen would, in this example, result in ¥10,000 of risk exposure (1% of ¥1,000,000). Risk management would include, among other things, quantifying and understanding this risk exposure, deciding how and why to have the exposure and how much risk the participant can bear, and possibly mitigating this risk by tailoring the exposure in several ways. The risk management process would inform the decision of whether to operate or invest in this risky currency.

> The word "risk" can be confusing because it is used by different people at different times to mean so many different things. Even when used properly, the term has three related but different meanings, which this example illustrates well. Risk can mean, in turn, the underlying uncertainty, the extent of the risky action taken, or the resulting range of risky outcomes to the organization. In this example, the first meaning is the uncertain

> +1% or −1% movement of the currency. The second meaning is the ¥1,000,000 worth of risky currency, the position taken by the business. The third meaning is the +¥10,000 or −¥10,000 risky outcome that might accrue to the business for having engaged in this risky activity. A common way of more precisely distinguishing among these three "risks" in usage is: *risk driver* for the underlying risk, *risk position* to describe or quantify the risky action taken, and *risk exposure* for the potential valuation change that may result. In the oversimplified example above, the risk exposure is simply the risk position multiplied by the risk driver. In practice the term "risk" is used interchangeably for all three meanings.

> ***Risk management*** *is the process by which an organization or individual defines the level of risk to be taken, measures the level of risk being taken, and adjusts the latter toward the former, with the goal of maximizing the company's or portfolio's value or the individual's overall satisfaction, or utility.*

Said differently, risk management comprises all the decisions and actions needed to *best* achieve organizational or personal objectives while bearing a tolerable level of risk. Risk management is *not* about minimizing risk; it is about actively understanding and embracing those risks that best balance the achievement of goals with an acceptable chance of failure, quantifying the exposure, and continually monitoring and modifying it. A company that shied away from all risk would find that it could not operate. In trying to create wealth, all organizations will find themselves "in the risk business." Risk management is not about avoiding risks any more than a practical diet is about avoiding calories. Risk management is not even about predicting risks. "The Doctrine of No Surprises" is a key mantra among many risk managers, but it does not mean they are expected to predict what will happen. Instead, it means that if an unpredictable event, either positive or negative, happens in an uncertain world, the *impact* of that event on the organization or portfolio would not be a surprise and would have been quantified and considered in advance.

For example, a risk manager of a bank would not have been expected to know that a real estate crisis was going to occur and cause significant defaults on the bank's real estate securities. But a good risk manager would help the bank's management decide how much exposure it should have in these securities by quantifying the potential financial impact of such a crisis destroying, say, 60% of the bank's capital. A good risk management process would include a deep discussion at the governance level about the balance between the likely returns and the unlikely—but sizable—losses and whether such losses are tolerable. Management would ensure that the risk analysis and discussion actively affects their investment decisions, that the potential loss is continuously quantified and communicated, and that it will take actions to mitigate or transfer any portion of the risk exposure that cannot be tolerated. The only surprise here should be the market shock itself; the risk manager should have prepared the organization through stress-testing and scenario analysis, continuously reporting in advance on the potential impact of this sizable risk exposure.

A poor risk management process would have ignored the possibility, though small, of such a significant market event and not quantified the potential loss from exposure to a real estate crisis. As such, the bank's management would have had no idea that more than half of the bank's capital could be at risk, not addressed this risk in any governance/risk appetite discussion, ignored these risks in its investment decisions, and not taken any action to mitigate this risk. In a good risk management process, most of the work is done before an adverse event happens; in a poor risk management process, perhaps just as much work gets done, but it all comes after the event, which is after the damage has been done.

Good risk management does not prevent losses, but provides a full top-to-bottom framework that rigorously informs the decision-making process—before, during, and after a risk event. Because risks and exposures are dynamic, risk management is a continuous process that is always being reevaluated and revised. If this process is done well, it provides management and staff with the knowledge to navigate as efficiently as possible toward the goals set by the governing body. In turn, this effort increases *ex ante* the value of the business or investment decisions undertaken. Good risk management may allow managers to more quickly or effectively act in the face of a crisis. But *ex post*, even the best risk management may not stop a portfolio from losing money in a market crash nor prevent a business from reduced profits in an economic downturn.

RISK MANAGEMENT FRAMEWORK

☐ describe features of a risk management framework

☐ define risk governance and describe elements of effective risk governance

A **risk management framework** flows logically from the definition of risk management that was previously given: It is the infrastructure, process, and analytics needed to support effective risk management in an organization. This process should fully integrate the "risk" and "return" aspects of the enterprise into decisions in support of best achieving its goals within its tolerance for risk. Risk management is not a "one size fits all" solution; it is integral to the enterprise's goals and needs. Thus, it is best achieved through a custom solution. Despite customization, every risk management system or framework should address the following key factors:

- Risk governance
- Risk identification and measurement
- Risk infrastructure
- Defined policies and processes
- Risk monitoring, mitigation, and management
- Communications
- Strategic analysis or integration

Not surprisingly, these factors often overlap in practice. They are defined and discussed here.

Governance is the top-level system of structures, rights, and obligations by which organizations are directed and controlled. Normally performed at the board level, governance is how goals are defined, authority is granted, and top-level decisions are made. The foundation for risk management in the organization is set at the board level as well. **Risk governance** is the top-down process and guidance that directs risk management activities to align with and support the overall enterprise and is addressed in more detail in Sections 4–6. Good governance should include defining an organization's risk tolerance and providing risk oversight. Governance is often driven by regulatory concerns, as well as by the fiduciary role of the governing body. A risk management committee is another facet of governance; it provides top decision makers with a forum for regularly considering risk management issues. To achieve the best results for an organization, risk governance should take an enterprise-wide view. **Enterprise risk management** is an overarching governance approach applied throughout the organization and consistent with its strategy, guiding the risk management framework to focus risk activities on the objectives, health, and value of the *entire* organization.

Risk identification and measurement is the main quantitative core of risk management; but more than that, it must include the qualitative assessment and evaluation of all potential sources of risk and the organization's risk exposures. This ongoing work involves analyzing the environment for relevant risk drivers, which is the common term used for any fundamental underlying factor that results in a risk that is relevant or important to an organization, analyzing the business or portfolio to ascertain risk exposures, tracking changes in those risk exposures, and calculating risk metrics to size these risks under various scenarios and stresses.

Risks are not limited to what is going on in the financial markets. There are many types of risk that can potentially impact a business, portfolio, or individual.

The power of technology has allowed for risk management to be more quantitative and timely. Management can measure and monitor risk, run scenarios, conduct statistical analysis, work with more complex models, and examine more dimensions and risk drivers as well as do it faster. This use of technology needs to be balanced with and supplement—not supplant—experienced business judgment. Technology has made risk infrastructure even more important and beneficial in managing risks.

Risk infrastructure refers to the people and systems required to track risk exposures and perform most of the quantitative risk analysis to allow an assessment of the organization's risk profile. Infrastructure would include risk capture (the important operational process by which a risk exposure gets populated into a risk system), a database and data model, analytic models and systems, a stress or scenario engine, and an ability to generate reports, as well as some amount of skilled and empowered personnel resources dedicated to building and executing the risk framework. With increased reliance on technology, more time and effort must be allotted to test data, models, and results in order to avoid the ironic outcome of the risk of errors coming from within risk systems.

Obviously, the scope of risk infrastructure will be related to the resources, or potential losses, of the organization. Individuals and smaller businesses may rely heavily on an external partner or provider for much of their risk infrastructure and analysis.

Policies and processes are the extension of risk governance into both the day-to-day operation and decision-making processes of the organization. There may be limits, requirements, constraints, and guidelines—some quantitative, some procedural—to ensure risky activities are in line with the organization's predetermined risk tolerance and regulatory requirements. Much of this is just common-sense business practice: updating and protecting data, controlling cash flows, conducting due diligence on investments, handling exceptions and escalations, and making checklists to support important decisions. In a good risk framework, processes would naturally evolve to consider risk at all key decision points, such as investment decisions and asset allocation. Risk management should become an integrated part of the business and not just a policing or regulatory function.

The process of *risk monitoring, mitigation, and management* is the most obvious facet of a risk framework, but also one of the most difficult. Actively monitoring and managing risk requires pulling together risk governance, identification and measurement, infrastructure, and policies and processes and continually reviewing and reevaluating in the face of changing risk exposures and risk drivers. It requires recognizing when risk exposure is not aligned with risk tolerance and then taking action to bring them back into alignment.[1]

Communication of critical risk issues must happen continually and across all levels of the organization. Governance parameters, such as risk tolerances and associated constraints, must be clearly communicated to, and understood by, managers. Risk metrics must be reported in a clear and timely manner. Risk issues must be reviewed and discussed as a standard part of decision making. Changes in exposure must be

---

[1] Risk mitigation and management is discussed in more detail in Sections 9–11.

Risk Management Framework

discussed so that action can be taken as appropriate. There should also be a feedback loop with the governance body so that top-level risk guidance can be validated or updated and communicated back to the rest of the organization.

Strategic analysis and integration help turn risk management into an offensive weapon to improve performance. Good risk management is a key to increasing the value of the overall business or portfolio. A risk management framework should provide the tools to better understand the how and why of performance and help sort out which activities are adding value, and which are not. In investing, rigorous analysis can support better investment decisions and improve strategy and risk-adjusted returns.

Exhibit 1: The Risk Management Framework in an Enterprise Context

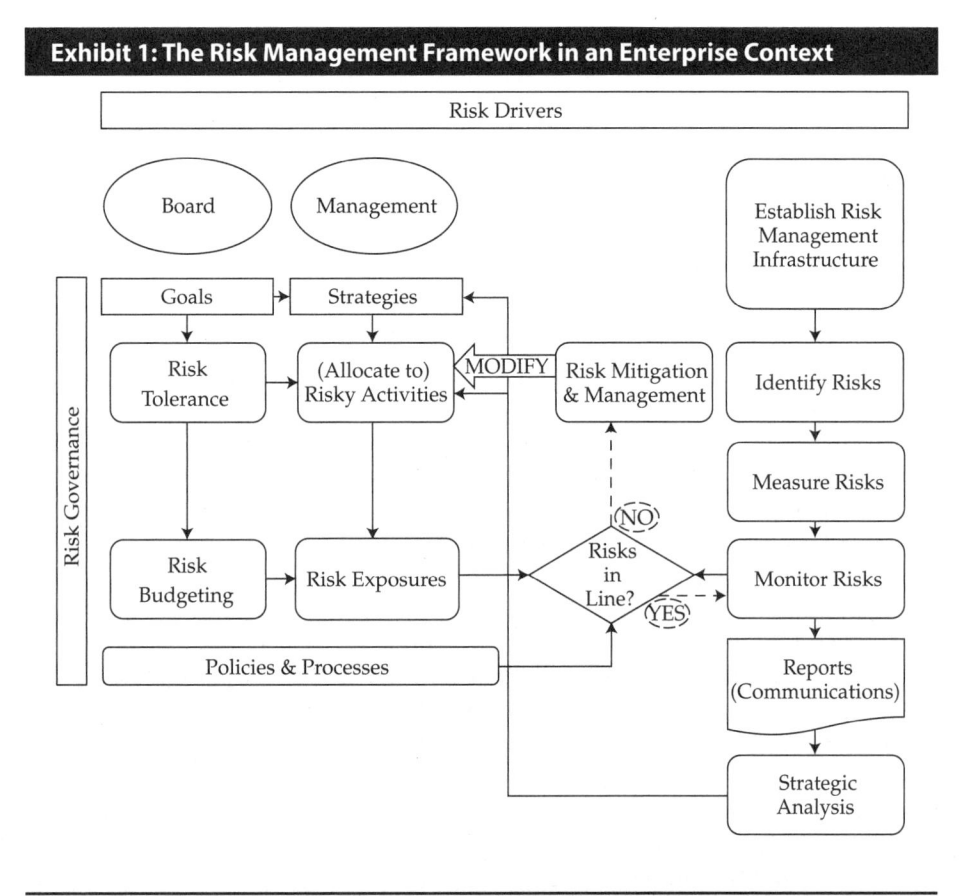

Exhibit 1 illustrates the process of risk management for an enterprise, pulling all the described elements of the risk framework together. Although there are a very high number of risks faced by every organization, most organizations are primarily affected by a small number of key risk drivers, or primary underlying factors that create risk. Along the left side is risk governance, which represents board-level decisions and encompasses and affects the boxes immediately to its right. The governance body, often called a board, defines the goals of the organization and, in turn, decides on its risk tolerance. It may additionally provide guidance on how or where that risk is taken (risk budgeting). The board is also involved in setting high-level policies that will affect most risk management processes. These risk governance activities are a crucial keystone of the risk framework and will be discussed in detail in the next section. When the rest of the risk framework hinges off of these top-down governance elements and is focused on the goals of the entire enterprise (as shown here), the end result is effective enterprise risk management.

The role of management, shown in the middle column, is to plan and execute value-maximizing strategies consistent with their governance guidance. Each management activity in the framework flows not only from management (shown with the arrows) but also from the governance activities on the left. Thus, not only are management's strategies designed to achieve the board's goals, but management also allocates capital to risky activities (its business or investing choices) to execute its strategies consistent with the defined risk tolerance. The risk exposures that result from management's choice of activities should also be aligned with the governing body's risk budget. In addition, management participates actively in setting or implementing policies and establishing procedures that relate to when, how, how much, and by whom each of the other elements of the risk framework are performed.[2]

The rest of the risk management framework comprises a number of important risk activities to help the business achieve all of its strategic and governance goals and mandates. These other elements to implement risk management are shown in the far right column of the illustration. Driven by its need to establish a risk management program to support the enterprise's goals, management would provide the requisite resources for risk management activities by establishing a risk management infrastructure. With risk processes defined and risk infrastructure in place, risks are then identified and measured, which is a regular and continual process of translating risk exposures (produced by the risky activities) into meaningful and generally quantitative risk metrics.

The next major steps—risk monitoring, mitigation, and management—are where much of a firm's day-to-day risk management activity is focused. These activities are split across three boxes in the illustration. Risk levels are continuously monitored, having just been measured.[3] There is a major decision at the monitoring stage: Management must check that all the risks are in line and not outside the limits of the defined risk tolerance or budget.[4] This process involves evaluating the actual risk exposures compared with the organization's risk policies and procedures to ensure that everything is in compliance. If the answer is "no," then risk mitigation and management actions need to be taken to modify risk levels and to bring them back into compliance. There are a variety of methods to accomplish this task, which are addressed in Sections 9–11. Whatever the method, management's allocation of the risk budget to risky activities will be altered by this modification, which includes changing the organization's risk exposures, starting the circle again through the steps on the right, and re-checking to see if risk levels are now consistent with risk policies.

When risks *are* in line with limits, policies, tolerances, mandates, and so on, then the process moves back to continuous monitoring followed by communicating risk levels.[5] This communication, at a minimum, includes reporting key risk metrics on a regular and timely basis across the organization to assist management in its decision-making process and the board in fulfilling its governance duties. Finally, strategic analysis is supported by the risk measurement, reporting, and other steps of the enterprise risk management process. By analyzing all of the enterprise's strategies and risky activities via the risk measurement lens, management can improve its decision-making process and ascertain where to invest its limited capital and risk budget most fruitfully. This

---

2 In essence, there could be an arrow from policies and processes to every other box to the right, but these rather obvious relationships are intentionally omitted in the diagram to avoid clutter. Likewise, risk exposures inform nearly all the boxes to the right. Risk management is innately quite interrelated.

3 Continuous usually does not mean real-time; the frequency of monitoring is based on the resources available, the level of systems support, and the need for risk information in the decision process. At large financial firms, this monitoring will generally be daily; for small businesses and individuals it might be quarterly.

4 This task is generally delegated to a risk manager; but whatever the title, someone must be accountable for this important check.

5 While not obvious in the illustration, communication and reporting should happen whether or not risk levels are in compliance; such communications are even more important when risk levels are out of alignment with tolerances.

step is generally underappreciated and is an inexpensive and beneficial by-product of having built a risk framework. The last two boxes or steps (reports and strategic analysis) represent important feedback loops to inform and improve both governance and the portfolio of risky activities that make up the business.

There are many feedback loops in properly executed risk management. In practice, most of these steps overlap most of the time and are being performed simultaneously. Good risk management ties together all these steps from the highest governance decisions to lower-level specifics, such as models, reports, and operational checklists.

The risk environment is dynamic, and many of our notions of probabilities and likely risk outcomes change in ways we probably could not predict. The risk management framework should be robust enough to anticipate this dynamism—to expect the unexpected. It should be evolutionary—flexible enough to grow with a company or individual and its new challenges.

The complexity of the risk management framework depends on the complexity of an organization's risk exposures and their resources. But that does not mean that smaller organizations or individuals should skip the risk management process; they may simply be able to do less, or have to work with external partners to assist with large portions of the framework, or be less formal about the process. Ultimately, the key principles just covered are still important even to the smallest organization, even if the specific components do not get assembled as described.

> **THE RISK MANAGEMENT PROCESS FOR AN INDIVIDUAL**
>
> Although an individual has neither the resources nor the organizational overhead of a large business, the importance of risk management is not diminished and the risk management framework still applies, albeit most likely in a scaled-down form. Though nearly all of the essential elements of the process illustrated in Exhibit 1 are still useful, the individual can reduce the recipe to six essential ingredients, consistent with the reduced scope of the individual's risk exposures.
>
> The first step for an individual is much like that shown in Exhibit 1 for the most complex organization: the determination of goals or objectives. This step would include most of the elements associated with risk governance, just without all the organizational complexity. The next functional step involves choosing investments (or other assets) and identifying their risks. Lacking any risk infrastructure, the individual may at this stage already require the services of an investment professional or financial adviser. This step and subsequent steps will probably be executed by the adviser, although the individual principal still needs to stay knowledgeable and involved. In the context of the illustration in Exhibit 1, the individual is effectively their own governance body and the adviser serves the role of management.
>
> The next steps for the individual are equivalent to the heart of the risk management process: risk monitoring and risk mitigation and management. The individual would first evaluate their risk exposure (like the diamond or decision step in the illustration), then consider various alternative approaches to modify the risk if necessary, followed by implementing the risk management solution (insuring, hedging, trading, etc.).
>
> The final functional step for an individual's risk management process would be evaluation and review. This step is parallel to the back-end of the risk management illustration, the boxes at the bottom right. This process may occur with much less frequency for an individual—but it is no less important.
>
> Each individual should simplify the risk management process as required so that they do not end up considering it "too esoteric and complicated to worry about" and thus ignoring risk management altogether. The potential costs of avoiding risk management are essentially the same for an individual as for a large corporation or a hedge fund, although perhaps with less money involved.

At its core, business and investing are about allocating resources and capital to chosen risks. Understanding which risks drive better outcomes should be one of the goals of risk management, and it makes good *risk* management inextricably linked with good management generally. When effective risk management is truly integrated at all levels of the decision-making process and the overall management process, the organization has developed an effective *risk culture*. This culture generally produces better results than just considering risk issues as a separate afterthought, and, in turn, it produces *much* better results than ignoring risk issues altogether in the decision-making process. For individuals, the adoption of a risk culture should result in a personal awareness of the many types of risks, their rewards, the costs, the relationships between them, and the methods of aligning the risks borne with the risks and outcomes desired. This awareness should lead to better investment return and/or smaller losses for the risk taken, resulting in higher satisfaction.

There are a number of other benefits from establishing good risk management: (1) Most obvious is less frequent surprises and a better notion of what the damage would be in the event of a surprise; (2) more decision discipline leading to better consideration of trade-offs and better risk–return relationships; (3) better response and risk mitigation stemming from more awareness and active monitoring, which should trim some of the worst losses; (4) better efficiency and fewer operational errors from policies and procedures, transparency, and risk awareness; (5) better relations, with more trust, between the governing body and management, which generally results in more effective delegation; (6) a better image or reputation because analysts and investors perceive a company as prudent and value-focused. Together, all these benefits should lead to higher value for the enterprise.

> **EXAMPLE 1**
>
> ### Risk Management and Risk Management Framework
>
> 1. Which of the following is *not* a goal of risk management?
>
>   **A.** A. Measuring risk exposures
>
>   **B.** B. Minimizing exposure to risk
>
>   **C.** C. Defining the level of risk appetite
>
>   **Solution**
>
>   B is correct. The definition of risk management includes both defining the level of risk desired and measuring the level of risk taken. Risk management means taking risks actively and in the best, most value-added way possible and is not about minimizing risks.
>
> 2. Which element of a risk management framework sets the overall context for risk management in an organization?
>
>   **A.** A. Governance
>
>   **B.** B. Risk infrastructure
>
>   **C.** C. Policies and processes
>
>   **Solution**
>
>   A is correct. Governance is the element of the risk management framework that is the top-level foundation for risk management. Although policies, procedures, and infrastructure are necessary to implement a risk management framework, it is governance that provides the overall context for an organization's risk management.

> 3. Which element of risk management makes up the analytical component of the process?
>   - **A.** A. Communication
>   - **B.** B. Risk governance
>   - **C.** C. Risk identification and measurement
>
> **Solution**
>
> C is correct. Risk identification and measurement is the quantitative part of the process. It involves identifying the risks and summarizing their potential quantitative impact. Communication and risk governance are largely qualitative.
>
> 4. Which element of risk management involves action when risk exposures are found to be out of line with risk tolerance?
>   - **A.** A. Risk governance
>   - **B.** B. Risk identification and measurement
>   - **C.** C. Risk monitoring, mitigation, and management
>
> **Solution**
>
> C is correct. Risk monitoring, mitigation, and management require recognizing and taking action when these (risk exposure and risk tolerance) are not in line, as shown in the middle of Exhibit 1. Risk governance involves setting the risk tolerance. Risk identification and measurement involves identifying and measuring the risk exposures.

RISK GOVERNANCE - AN ENTERPRISE VIEW

☐ define risk governance and describe elements of effective risk governance

Risk governance is the foundation for risk management. As defined earlier, it is the top-down process and guidance that directs risk management activities to align with and support the goals of the overall enterprise. It typically emanates from a board of directors with fiduciary obligations and risk oversight and who prescribe goals and authorities. Referring back to the definition of risk management, note that risk management is keenly focused on the risk and value of the overall enterprise.

An Enterprise View of Risk Governance

In addition to the responsibility for risk oversight, there are two other important areas in which the governing body drives the risk framework. First, it determines the organization's goals, direction, and priorities, which combined serve as a key foundation for enterprise risk management. Recall that enterprise risk management is an overarching governance approach applied across the organization that focuses risk activities on the objectives, health, and value of the whole organization. Second, it spells out the risk appetite or tolerance, meaning which risks are acceptable, which risks are to be mitigated and to what extent, and which risks are unacceptable. Risk governance should also provide a sense of the worst losses that could be tolerated in various scenarios, and management should manage risk accordingly. These considerations should flow naturally into decisions about risk budgeting to guide implementation of an optimal program that is consistent with that risk tolerance.

Risk governance is the impact of the governing body of an organization on the risk management framework. It provides context for and clarity on an organization's value drivers and risk appetite, specifies clear authority to management to execute risk management, and ensures risk oversight to continually determine whether risk management is functioning well and consistent with the organization's value maximization. It is the governing body's job to tie the organizational goals and risk framework together; thus, risk governance happens within an enterprise context. Risk governance and risk oversight also entail compliance with regulatory requirements. Risk governance is a difficult and demanding discipline, and if it is going to flourish in an organization, it needs visible commitment from the top.

Providing clear guidance with sufficient leeway to execute strategy is often a difficult balance. Even more challenging is providing for advance discussion and a clear decision and statement of organizational risk appetite. There is usually substantial discussion about this risk appetite *after* a crisis, but too often there is very little discussion during periods of normalcy, when it would be much more beneficial. Because risk is one of the main strategic tools that management can regulate, it is especially important for governing bodies to openly discuss risk, consider scenarios, understand the impact of negative outcomes on the organization, and make it clear where they are not willing to venture. Much like an automobile that comes with a red zone on some dials to establish boundaries for safe operation, risk governance bodies should likewise establish hypothetical red zones to ensure the safe operation of their enterprise.

Enterprise risk management (focusing risk activities on the objectives, health, and value of the *whole* organization) requires that the entire economic balance sheet of the business be considered, not just the assets or one part of the business in isolation. A narrower view of risk management is unlikely to meet the goal of maximizing the value of the entire enterprise.

Pension fund management provides a classic example of the importance of considering enterprise risk management: "Funds" are the assets and "pension" is the liability. But a true enterprise view requires an even broader outlook. A corporate pension fund's manager might try to maximize only the fund's assets, but this would generally do a disservice to the corporation. The assets and liabilities of a pension fund are both sensitive to market variables, so ignoring the liabilities would be ignoring half the risk. With liabilities that are quite bond-like, a pension fund manager using all equities for maximum growth would potentially make the overall fund insolvent in a market collapse with declining interest rates because, in such a situation, the liabilities would increase substantially in value while the assets fell. Risk tolerance for the assets in isolation would be far different from the risk tolerance of the entire enterprise. One should look beyond just the pension liabilities, which are likely to be a small part of the overall enterprise. Broader still, a true enterprise risk view in this case would *also* consider the parent corporation's business risk profile and not just the pension assets and liabilities. In a market collapse, the overall business might be in a recessionary phase, rendering increasing contributions from the corporation to its pension fund quite painful. Factoring the corporate risk profile into the pension fund investment strategy may cause the risk tolerance to be lower in this case.

Risk governance that focuses on the entire enterprise will result in risk management that is much less likely to be at odds with the goals of the organization and more likely to enhance long-run value. Likewise, consideration of a full spectrum of risks, and not just the most obvious quantitative risks, will result in better risk governance.

The enterprise view of risk management is equally applicable and important to an individual, even if the term "enterprise" is not often used in an individual context.[6] The appropriate set of risks for an individual must be viewed not in isolation, but in consideration of the goals and characteristics of the individual in a holistic view. For example, an adviser may be designing an investment portfolio to maximize a client's wealth and optimize the risk–return trade-off at some perceived comfortable level of risk.[7] But the client, whose wealth consists not only of financial assets but also of valuable **human capital**, might prefer that risk allocation decisions be made in view of both forms of capital, optimizing her total wealth. For example, a client with a career in real estate would most likely benefit if her financial portfolio is invested in a way that considers her earnings exposure to real estate related risks. Holdings of real estate securities above a certain level, even if optimal from an isolated portfolio perspective, might make this individual less than optimally diversified from a total wealth perspective. In another example, Investor X, who has substantial inflation-adjusted pension benefits, is different from Investor Y, who has a fixed pension benefit, and different still from Investor Z, who has no pension benefit and retires with solely his own investment portfolio. These three investors will require remarkably different investment solutions, not only to deal with inflation but also to deal with the uncertainty surrounding lifespans. Individuals with different goals and characteristics will need differing investment and risk solutions that are best suited to their individual situations. In fact, because of the extremely variable life cycle of an individual and the discrete nature of many individuals' goals, the enterprise view is even more important to risk management for individuals than it is for institutions.

Risk governance extends into management to include ways to ensure that the risk framework of an organization stays consistent with top-level guidance. One useful approach is to provide a regular forum to discuss the risk framework and key risk issues at the management level. In other words, a risk management committee would be a key element of good risk governance. Its activities could parallel the governance body's risk deliberations, but at an operational level as opposed to high-level oversight. In this forum, governance overlaps with many of the other aspects of the organization's risk framework as discussed in Sections 2–3. In fact, if done well, it integrates all of them.

In the same vein, another element of good risk governance is the formal appointment of a responsible executive as chief risk officer (CRO). This officer should be responsible for building and implementing the risk framework for the enterprise and managing the many activities therein. In the same manner that risks are inextricably linked with the core business activities, the CRO is likewise a key participant in the strategic decisions of the enterprise—this position is not solely a policing role. Although the chief executive is responsible for risk as well as all other aspects of an enterprise, it makes no more sense for the CEO to perform the role of the CRO than it would be for the CEO to perform the role of the CFO. Many financial firms now have a CRO in executive management,[8] which had become best practice even in the years prior to the 2008 crisis.

---

6 Enterprise risk management is an easier concept for an individual; compared with an organization in which deciding, coordinating, and communicating goals can be a big challenge, the scope of risk management efforts for an individual is smaller and more manageable.
7 Here, the individual is the governing body, setting individual goals and risk appetite; the financial professional or wealth manager is the "management team" executing much of the rest of the risk framework.
8 Although this is common for financial firms or other large organizations, many less-complex companies will forgo a formal risk structure. The board still maintains its risk governance responsibilities; and it is up to them to work out with management as to how, and to what extent, to meet these responsibilities.

5. RISK TOLERANCE

☐ explain how risk tolerance affects risk management

Perhaps the most important element of good risk governance is the **risk tolerance** discussion and decision within the governing body. Business and investment strategy centers on selecting a portfolio of acceptable risk activities that will maximize value and produce the highest returns possible for the given risk level. At the governance level, the duty is generally not to select these activities—a job that usually falls to management—but to establish the organization's risk appetite. Certain risks or levels of risks may be deemed acceptable, other risks deemed unacceptable, and in the middle are risks that may be pursued in a risk-limited fashion. Said differently, risk tolerance identifies the extent to which the organization is willing to experience losses or opportunity costs and to fail in meeting its objectives.

> The risk tolerance decision *for an individual* is similar, but not identical, to that of a business enterprise. In traditional finance theory, the individual focuses on maximizing unobservable utility, whereas the business maximizes a generally observable value—the market value or equity price of the company. Although individuals are facing life and certain death on an uncertain timetable, most businesses tend to be relatively short-lived organizations, but with an expectation of immortality. The decisions about risk tolerance from those two very different viewpoints can be expected to differ—for example, risk tolerance in organizations often treats its continued existence as a major consideration. In many ways, the individual's risk tolerance decision is the harder one.

The enterprise risk management perspective is the right lens through which to view the risk appetite question. The risk tolerance decision begins with two different analyses that must be integrated—an "inside" view and an "outside" view. First, what shortfalls within an organization would cause it to fail, or at least fail to achieve some critical goals? Second, what uncertain forces is the organization exposed to? That is, what are its risk drivers? With the answers to these two difficult questions in hand, a board could begin defining dimensions and levels of risk that it finds too uncomfortable to take on. This risk tolerance should be formally chosen and communicated *before* a crisis, and will serve as the high-level guidance for management in its strategic selection of risks. Many organizations will do this *after* a crisis, which is better than not doing it at all but is much like buying insurance after the loss occurs. It is best to take care of it when there seems to be no particularly pressing reason to do so. Similarly, some individuals may not give much thought to their own risk tolerance until after a crisis occurs, when they belatedly decide that the risk was not worth taking.

For example, suppose a Spanish construction equipment manufacturing company's board is determining its risk tolerance. From the inside perspective, it has two main concerns: revenue and liquidity. It determines that it can tolerate a 5%–10% drop in revenue, but that a 20% drop would trigger its debt covenants and put the launch of its new flagship product at risk. Related to this strategy, it needs €40 million of cash flow annually for the next three years for critical capital expenditures and can leave almost none of this cash flow at risk. From the outside perspective, it realizes that there are three main uncertainties or risk drivers over which it has no control: changes in the value of the US dollar, interest rate changes, and market returns on industrial sector equities. Both its business results and its own stock price are strongly correlated with these three risks and could be adversely affected by any of them.

Rather than taking a passive approach as a risk observer, the board in this example uses a top-level analysis to formulate its risk tolerance. In this case, it may decide to limit maximum cash flow variation to €10 million annually and revenue exposure to −10% in a global recession. In addition, it may specify other stated limits, such as the maximum exposure to currency or other risks. This guidance may affect the riskiness of other product strategies that management may pursue. The company may require more expensive financing options to reduce cash flow uncertainty. The governance restrictions may drive risk mitigation programs, such as a hedging strategy, especially for the primary risk drivers that are stated areas of concern.

Governance guidance is important in helping an enterprise target where it should actively pursue risk and where it should mitigate or modify risk. Strategic goals centered on core competencies should be pursued, which leads the company into taking risks that best position the enterprise for success and value creation. Companies sometimes take risks in areas where they have no expertise, which puts their core value creation and their entire organization at peril. A well-functioning risk program would limit or hedge those non-core risks in areas where they have no comparative advantage. Modifying risk is covered in detail in Sections 9–11.

How does a company determine its risk tolerance? There is certainly no formula. Most importantly, a company's goals, its expertise in certain areas, and its strategies will help a board determine which risks the company may pursue and with how much intensity. The ability of a company to respond dynamically to adverse events may allow for a higher risk tolerance. The amount of loss a company can sustain without impairing its status as a going concern should factor into its risk tolerance; some companies are more fragile than others. The competitive landscape matters because both the board's and investors' expectations are usually developed in the context of how a company is positioned in its industry. The government and regulatory landscape is important too, both in their *ex ante* demands on how companies approach risk and in the likely *ex post* reaction in the event of disasters. Quantitative analyses such as scenario analysis, economic models, and sensitivities to macro risk drivers might be used to assess where a board's zone of comfort is bounded. There are other factors that should *not* determine risk tolerance, but in many cases they do. Personal motivations, beliefs, and agendas of board members (the agency problem); company size; whether the market environment seems stable; short-term pressures; and management compensation often affect risk tolerance in ways that might not be in line with the owners' best interests.

Once risk tolerance is determined, the overall risk framework should be geared toward measuring, managing, and communicating compliance with this risk tolerance—getting the risk exposure in line with the enterprise's risk appetite.

This sort of governance exercise not only helps ensure that the organization survives through the worst of times, but also helps ensure a strategic trade-off between risk and return in the decision process, which, in turn, improves potential returns for the given level of risk and value. It is quite easy to find business strategies and investment approaches that produce apparently outsized returns, but they might be at the cost of putting the organization at extreme risk. A somewhat extreme example would be a company selling put options on its own equity, which could produce higher short-term profits but would dramatically increase the chance of the company failing in a steep market decline. Excessive leverage is another risky strategy for boosting short-term profits that may decrease value or lead to failure in the long run. A formal risk governance process with a stated risk tolerance would naturally result in avoidance of many easier, less well-reasoned strategies that entail excessive risk compared with the firm's risk tolerance. Instead, it would lead the strategic discussion into alternative strategies that are more likely to add value while taking reasonable risk within the enterprise's risk tolerance and not simply trade ruin for return. Sincere, good risk governance and risk culture can avoid excessively risky strategies that might put the long-term enterprise value at risk. This approach should produce enhanced value for the enterprise.

6. RISK BUDGETING

> describe risk budgeting and its role in risk governance

Risk budgeting picks up where risk tolerance leaves off. Whereas risk tolerance focuses on the appetite for risk and what is and is not acceptable, risk budgeting has a more specific focus on how that risk is taken. Risk budgeting quantifies and allocates the tolerable risk by specific metrics; it extends and guides implementation of the risk tolerance decision.

Risk budgeting applies to both business management and portfolio management. Its foundation is the perspective that business or portfolio management involves assembling a number of risk activities or securities, which can be collated into an assemblage of various risk characteristics. For example, a traditional view of a portfolio might be that it is allocated 20% to hedge funds, 30% to private equity, and the remaining 50% is split between stocks and bonds. An alternative risk view of the same portfolio might be 70% driven by global equity returns, 20% by domestic equity returns, with the remaining 10% driven by interest rates. The equity component might be allocated 65% to value and 35% to growth. The portfolio might also have 45% illiquid securities and the remainder liquid. Other allocations can be stated in terms of exposures to inflation, long-term interest rates, currencies, and so on. These multiple dimensions for viewing the allocation of a portfolio are not mutually exclusive: they co-exist. If one is evaluating the risk exposure of a portfolio and trying to keep it in line with a stated risk tolerance, one would be far more concerned with the risk characteristics of the investment assets and portfolio rather than their common classifications of stocks, hedge funds, real estate, private equity, and so on. These terms tell us a little about risk but not enough. Equity is traditionally riskier than hedge funds, but some equities are of quite low risk and some hedge funds are of quite high risk. The risk view may be more meaningful and useful in understanding the portfolio risk than the traditional asset allocation view.

Risk budgeting is any means of allocating a portfolio based on some risk characteristics of the investments. In the purest sense, the term "budget" implies that there is a total risk limit for the organization. Although this approach is not formally required,[9] it would certainly be good practice to have a risk budget that is consistent with the organization's risk tolerance. A risk budget provides a means of implementing the risk tolerance at a strategic level, or in other words, a means of bridging from the high-level governance risk decision to the many management decisions, large and small, that result in the actual risk exposures.

A risk budget can be complex and multi-dimensional, or it can be a simple, one-dimensional risk measure. Even the simplest measure can provide significant benefits in developing an effective risk culture. Four well-known single-dimension measures that are often used are standard deviation, beta, value at risk (VaR), and scenario loss, but there are many others. It is common for some hedge funds to budget

---

9 One could do risk budgeting even if there were no other risk governance guidance.

risk using standard deviation, managing to a fixed-risk fund target, and evaluating individual investments based on their returns and risks as they affect the *ex ante* standard deviation.

More complex forms of risk budgeting use multiple dimensions of risk. One popular approach evaluates risks by their underlying risk classes, such as equity, fixed income, commodity risk, and so on, and then allocates investments by their risk class. Also common are risk factor approaches to risk budgeting, in which exposure to various factors is used to attempt to capture associated risk premiums. An example would be to budget an allocation to give greater emphasis to value stocks based on the belief that they may provide a higher risk-adjusted return than growth stocks. This tactic might be layered over a strategic budget with a certain "beta" as the overall equity risk, supplemented with value and additional factor tilts specified up to some level.

Risk budgeting, although a desirable element of risk governance, cuts across the entire risk management framework, providing a focal point for each of the facets of risk management described in Sections 2 and 3. And although it is true that in practice many organizations operate without a risk budget, it is generally because there has been no specific declaration of their risk tolerance. If a board has a clear understanding of its risk appetite, both the board and management will want some means of implementing a strategic allocation that is consistent with it. Thus, the risk budget becomes a critical overarching construct for the organization's risk framework.

Some individuals may, often through the assistance of a financial planner, engage in some form of risk budgeting, but many do not execute it well or carry it far enough. A classic example of this failure is the tendency of many individuals to invest their financial portfolios in their employers. The risk budget for their total wealth—financial and human capital—is extremely concentrated in one firm and/or one industry. Not surprisingly, such risk budgets typically occur not through formal planning because most formal plans would recognize the problem, but through inaction or inattention.

One major benefit of even the most basic risk budgeting is that it forces risk trade-offs and supports a culture in which risk is considered as a part of all key decisions. Suppose that all the activities a business wants to pursue are in excess of the risk budget. The budgeting of risk should result in an approach, whether explicit or not, of choosing to invest where the return per unit of risk is the highest. Better still, it should also result in a market-benchmarked choice of risk intensity, between possibly doing less of each risky investment or doing more, but with a risk-mitigating hedge. This benefit is extremely important. By choosing between a market hedge or less of a risky investment, one ends up evaluating the investment directly against the market risk–return benchmark. Thus, one is not only comparing risk–return relationships among one's investment choices, but also comparing active versus passive strategies; that is, evaluating investment choices as a whole against the "market return" on a risk-equivalent basis. In other words, one ends up attempting to add active value in each of one's decisions while still staying within the confines of the organization's risk tolerance. The result is even more powerful than merely ensuring that the business is compensated well for the risks they decide to accept. Just having a risk budget in place, forces decision makers to try to add value to the enterprise in every risky decision they make. The risk-budgeting framework makes this consideration innate to the decision process.

EXAMPLE 2

Risk Governance

1. Which of the following approaches is *most* consistent with an enterprise view of risk governance?

    A. A. Separate strategic planning processes for each part of the enterprise

    B. B. Considering an organization's risk tolerance when developing its asset allocation

    C. C. Trying to achieve the highest possible risk-adjusted return on a company's pension fund's assets

    Solution

    B is correct. The enterprise view is characterized by a focus on the organization as a whole—its goals, value, and risk tolerance. It is not about strategies or risks at the individual business line level.

2. Which of the following statements about risk tolerance is *most* accurate?

    A. A. Risk tolerance is best discussed after a crisis, when awareness of risk is heightened.

    B. B. The risk tolerance discussion is about the actions management will take to minimize losses.

    C. C. The organization's risk tolerance describes the extent to which the organization is willing to experience losses.

    Solution

    C is correct. Risk tolerance identifies the extent to which the organization is willing to experience losses or opportunity costs and fail in meeting its objectives. It is best discussed before a crisis and is primarily a risk governance or oversight issue at the board level, not a management or tactical one.

3. Which of the following is *not* consistent with a risk-budgeting approach to portfolio management?

    A. A. Limiting the beta of the portfolio to 0.75

    B. B. Allocating investments by their amount of underlying risk sources or factors

    C. C. Limiting the amount of money available to be spent on hedging strategies by each portfolio manager

    Solution

    C is correct. Risk budgeting is any means of allocating a portfolio by some risk characteristics of the investments. This approach could be a strict limit on beta or some other risk measure or an approach that uses risk classes or factors to allocate investments. Risk budgeting does not require nor prohibit hedging, although hedging is available as an implementation tool to support risk budgeting and overall risk governance.

4. Who would be the *least* appropriate for controlling the risk management function in a large organization?

    A. A. Chief risk officer

    B. B. Chief financial officer

> **C.** C. Risk management committee
> **Solution**
> B is correct. A chief risk officer or a risk management committee is an individual or group that specializes in risk management. A chief financial officer may have considerable knowledge of risk management, may supervise a CRO, and would likely have some involvement in a risk management committee, but a CFO has broader responsibilities and cannot provide the specialization and attention to risk management that is necessary in a large organization.

IDENTIFICATION OF RISK - FINANCIAL VS. NON-FINANCIAL RISK

☐ identify financial and non-financial sources of risk and describe how they may interact

Having laid the framework for understanding the concept of risk management and risk governance, we now move into the implementation of the process. One of the first important parts of the process is the identification of risks. In this reading, we identify two general categorizations of risks. The first is the set of risks that originate from the financial markets. Accordingly, we refer to this type of risk as **financial risks**. The second group of risks includes those that emanate from outside the financial markets. As such, we refer to these as **non-financial risks**. Although most risks ultimately have monetary consequences, we reserve the term "financial risks" to refer to the risks that arise from events occurring in the financial markets, such as changes in prices or interest rates.[10] In this reading, we will consider the types of financial and non-financial risks faced by organizations and individuals.

Financial Risks

The risk management industry has come to classify three types of risks as primarily financial in nature. The three primary types of financial risks are market risk, credit risk, and liquidity risk. **Market risk** is the risk that arises from movements in interest rates, stock prices, exchange rates, and commodity prices. This categorization is not to say that these four main factors are the underlying drivers of market risks. Market risks typically arise from certain fundamental economic conditions or events in the economy or industry or developments in specific companies. These are the underlying risk drivers, which we will cover later.

Market risks are among the most obvious and visible risks faced by most organizations and many individuals. The financial markets receive considerable attention in the media, and information on financial market activity is abundant. Institutional investors and many corporations devote considerable resources to processing this information with the objective of optimizing performance. Many individuals also

---
[10] We use the term "financial markets" in a very broad sense. A company may also be exposed to commodity price risk, which we would include as a financial risk.

devote considerable attention to market risk, and financial publications and television and radio shows are widely followed in the general population. The state of knowledge in risk management is probably greatest in the area of market risk.

The second primary financial risk is credit risk. **Credit risk** is the risk of loss if one party fails to pay an amount owed on an obligation, such as a bond, loan, or derivative, to another party. In a loan, only one party owes money to the other. In some types of derivatives, only one party owes money to the other, and in other types of derivatives, either party can owe the other. This type of risk is also sometimes called default risk and sometimes counterparty risk. As with market risk, the root source of the risk can arise from fundamental conditions in the economy, industry, or weakness in the market for a company's products. Ultimately, default is an asset-specific risk. Bond and derivatives investors must consider credit risk as one of their primary decision tools.[11] Similar to market risk, credit risk is also a highly visible risk with considerable attention paid to defaults, bankruptcies, and the stresses arising from inadequate cash flow in relation to leverage. Credit risk is a particularly significant risk in that although market prices can go down and bounce back up, defaults and bankruptcies have extremely long-term implications for borrowers.

Although market and credit risk are extremely common risks to institutions, they are also assumed by individuals in their personal investments. One other financial risk, however, is much more common to institutions, although it can be faced by individuals, often unknowingly. This third risk is **liquidity risk**, which is the risk of a significant downward valuation adjustment when selling a financial asset. In order to sell an asset, a party may need to reduce the price to a level that is less than the marked value or the seller's assessment of the asset's true value based on the fundamentals of the asset. In certain market conditions, the seller must make a significant price concession. Having to make price concessions is not necessarily unusual and does not imply a poorly functioning market. Indeed, given no shift in demand, a rightward shift of a supply curve in order to sell a larger quantity is entirely consistent with the notion that a seller must lower the price to sell a greater quantity.

All assets have transaction costs in the market, such as the bid–ask spread. The existence of a sell price that is less than a buy price, however, is not a risk but simply a cost. It is the *uncertainty* of that valuation spread that creates this type of risk. Thus, liquidity risk could also be called "transaction cost risk." The liquidity risk of a $10 stock purchased for $10 is not the risk that one would receive the "bid" price of only $9.99 right after one bought it. That $0.01 spread is a known cost when the stock is purchased, so it is not a risk. The risk is that this spread cost might increase dramatically as a result of either changing market conditions or attempting to maintain a position significantly larger than the normal trading volume for the stock. This problem becomes a serious issue for risk management when the liquidation price falls to less than the seller's estimate of the fundamental value of the asset. Although this risk is often associated with illiquid assets,[12] it really stems from a couple of sources. First, market liquidity varies over time and the market for specific assets may become less liquid; second, as the size of a position increases, the cost and uncertainty associated with liquidating it will increase. In some extreme cases, there may be no price above zero at which the seller can sell the asset.

---

11 With certain derivatives (swaps and forwards), either party could be forced to pay off to the other, so each party is concerned about whether its counterparty will pay off, meaning that for some products, credit risk is bilateral.

12 The illiquid nature of an asset is not itself the risk because that is a direct cost borne immediately upon purchase. Still, uncertainty around the valuation of illiquid assets is a pervasive issue, so it is natural to associate liquidity risk with liquidity characteristics. More importantly, though, the term *liquidity risk* also commonly refers to a much broader set of risks for the organization, which are addressed in the next section.

Of course, one might argue that the cost of illiquidity, and liquidity risk, should thus be part of the investor's assessment of fundamental value, and indeed it is for many analysts. If not, liquidity risk can sometimes be confused with a form of valuation denial in which investors believe that they paid an appropriate price and that the market has not converged to its true value. But less liquidity means a thin market and a lack of investor interest, which may be fertile ground for investment opportunities. Although lack of liquidity can offer benefits, such as the opportunity to buy an asset well before everyone else sees that it is an attractive investment, liquidity risk is generally considered to be a negative factor with which risk managers and indeed all investors must contend.

Non-Financial Risks

Recall that we refer to financial risks as those arising primarily from events occurring in the financial markets. Although most risks have monetary consequences, there are a number of risks that are typically classified as non-financial in nature. These risks arise from a variety of sources, such as from actions within the organization or from external origins, such as the environment as well as from the relationship between the organization and counterparties, regulators, governments, suppliers, and customers.

One important risk of this type is closely related to default risk but deals more with the settling of payments that occur just before a default. This risk is called settlement risk. As an example, suppose Party A enters into a forward contract to purchase ¥200 million of Japanese government bonds from Party B. At expiration if all goes well, Party A would wire the money and Party B would transfer the bonds. Each party fulfills its obligation expecting that the other will do so as well. However, suppose Party A wires the money but Party B does not send the bonds because it has declared bankruptcy. At this point, Party A cannot get the money back, except possibly much later through the potentially slow and cumbersome bankruptcy process.[13] Although the financial consequences are very high, the root source of this risk is the timing of the payment process itself.

Organizations face two types of risks related to the law, and as such, this risk is referred to as legal risk. One risk is simply the risk of being sued over a transaction or for that matter, anything an organization does or fails to do. In financial risk management, however, the major legal concern is that the terms of a contract will not be upheld by the legal system. For example, suppose Bank E enters into a derivatives contract with Party F. Assume that as the underlying changes in price, Party F incurs a loss, whereas there is a corresponding gain to Bank E. But suppose that Party F then identifies a legal issue that it interprets as giving it the right to refuse to pay. If the court upholds Party F's position, Bank E could incur a loss. Litigation always involves uncertainty because even a seemingly weak case can prevail in court.

The following three non-financial risks are related: regulatory risk, accounting risk, and tax risk. They could even be collectively referred to as compliance risk because they all deal with the matter of conforming to policies, laws, rules, and regulations as set forth by governments and authoritative bodies, such as accounting governing boards. Obviously the regulatory, accounting, and tax environment is always subject to change, but the rapid expansion of financial products and strategies in relation to the relatively slow manner in which government and private regulators are able to respond means that laws and regulations are nearly always catching up with the financial world. When these laws and regulations are updated, it can result in significant unexpected costs, back taxes, financial restatements, and penalties.

---

13 This type of risk often arises because of significant time zone differences. Settlement risk is also called Herstatt risk; Herstatt was the name of a German bank that failed in 1974 after receiving "overnight" payments and then defaulting.

Another type of non-financial risk is model risk, which is the risk of a valuation error from improperly using a model. This risk arises when an organization uses the wrong model or uses the right model incorrectly. A simple example applicable to both a portfolio manager and a corporate analyst is the assumption of constant dividend growth in the dividend discount model when, in fact, growth is not constant.

Closely related to model risk is tail risk—more events in the tail of the distribution than would be expected by probability models. This risk is a facet of market risk, but it also infects valuations and models when it is ignored or mishandled. Tail risk is known to be especially severe for the normal distribution, which tends to be overused in modeling. As an example, consider the monthly returns on the S&P 500 Index from January 1950 to October 2018. The monthly average return was 0.70%, and the monthly standard deviation was 4.10%. If we rank the monthly returns, we would find that the largest negative return was −21.76%, which occurred in the well-known market crash of October 1987. With a normal distribution, we would find that a return that low would occur only once every 2,199,935 years.[14] The second and third worst monthly returns of −16.94% (October 2008) and −14.58% (August 1998) would occur only once every 6,916 and 654 years respectively. If the normal distribution is a realistic descriptor of returns, results of these magnitudes should *never* have occurred in recorded market history, and yet we have seen three such instances. Interestingly, according to the normal distribution, the largest positive return of 16.30% in October 1974 would occur only once every 888 years. Technically, one could argue that if we go another 2,199,935 years and do not observe a monthly return as low as −21.76%, then the assumption of a normal distribution might seem reasonable, but it seems safe to reject the normal distribution for at least another two million years. Similar comments can apply to the second and third worst returns albeit over shorter periods.

Many quantitative models (e.g., option models) and decision models (e.g., portfolio construction and asset allocation, relying on variances and covariances in analysis and decisions) ignore the existence of fat tails in returns; as a result, market risk is often considered and dealt with in an oversimplified fashion. Tail risk, as the term is used in practice, is important and is discussed separately because financial professionals realize the implicit failure of modeling market risk. More plainly, ignoring tail risk is a form of model risk. And although tail risk might seem more of a financial risk than a non-financial risk, the mistake occurs internally, arising from poor choices made in modeling.

Most of the internal risks faced by an organization are often grouped together and referred to as operational risk. **Operational risk** is the risk that arises from inadequate or failed people, systems, and internal policies, procedures, and processes, as well as from external events that are beyond the control of the organization but that affect its operations. Although the factors that give rise to such risks can arise externally, the risks themselves are largely internal to an organization because it would be expected to have its people, systems and internal policies, procedures, and processes functioning effectively regardless of pressures placed on it by external forces.

Employees themselves are major sources of potential internal risks. Banks are keenly aware of the vulnerability to employee theft, given the ease with which so many employees have access to accounts and systems for making entries. But even perfectly honest employees make mistakes, and some can be quite costly. The employee who credits someone's account $100,000 for a $100 deposit may have made an honest mistake, but it is a mistake that could quickly lead to the rapid disappearance of money. In the past, employees up to senior management have been guilty of perpetrating accounting fraud, not necessarily for their own direct benefit but to make the company look better.

---

14 This calculation and those that follow are based on determining the probability of the given return or less.

In banks and other companies that trade in the financial markets, there is the risk that a trader or portfolio manager will fail to follow laws, rules, or guidelines and put the company at great financial risk. This individual is commonly described as a "rogue trader." Personified by Nick Leeson of Barings Bank, who in 1995 destroyed the 200-year old company by engaging in a series of highly speculative trades to cover up losses, the rogue trader has become a standard concern of risk managers. Although it was never clear if Leeson's trades were truly unauthorized, his legacy left the fear that institutions bear the risk that one trader can imperil the entire organization by making large and highly speculative trades that put the bank's entire capital base at risk. In essence, a rogue trader is a trader who engages in risky transactions without regard for the organization's limits or conforming to its controls.

Organizations are also threatened by business interruptions, such as those caused by extreme weather and natural disasters. Events such as floods, earthquakes, or hurricanes can cause significant damage and temporarily shut down an organization. Although extreme weather and natural disasters are external forces that are completely out of the control of an organization, it does not excuse the organization from having the appropriate internal procedures for managing problems caused by their external environment. Simple and fairly low-cost actions, such as having generators, backup facilities, or providing employees the option to work remotely, can go a long way toward keeping employees working during extreme weather events and when natural disasters strike. Yet, some organization have not heeded inclement weather forecasts. Failing to react to warnings can result in considerable loss.

In a world that is increasingly digital, cyber risk is a major operational risk that spares no organization and that can have significant consequences. Organizations are expected to understand and manage the risk associated with the disruption of or failure related to their information technology (IT) systems. For example, a hacker breaking into a company's IT system and stealing customer or client data is an external threat. Hacking, however, is not simply a random act of mischief. Companies are aware of the threat of hackers, and hackers can break in to a system only if that system is vulnerable. An organization is responsible for ensuring cyber security and establishing sufficiently robust IT safeguards, such as data encryption, to deter hackers from breaking in and either stealing or causing disruption. Cyber-attacks and data breaches can have serious reputational and compliance consequences. For example, all organizations targeting European citizens must comply with the General Data Protection Regulation (GDPR) and notify regulators and data subjects of any data breaches regarding sensitive personal information within 72 hours. Failure to do so can lead to fines of several million euros, including for organizations based outside the European Union. In addition to the threats posed by hackers and viruses, even secure IT systems themselves are a particular source of risk. Programming errors and bugs can create the possibility of costly mistakes.

Terrorism is another form of operational risks that poses a threat to organizations and individuals. The 1993 attacks on the World Trade Center led many companies to recognize that the New York City financial district was a major terrorist target and that, as such, their operations could be shut down by these acts of violence. When the more destructive attacks of 11 September 2001 occurred, many organizations had already established backup facilities sufficiently far away from that area. Of course, such risk is not confined to major financial centers, and indeed, organizations worldwide have begun to take security measures that address this operational risk.

Some of these operational risks are insurable, at least to a modest extent. We will briefly discuss insurance later, but most companies would much prefer to take proactive steps toward prevention than to incur the inconvenience of losses and then have an outside organization compensate them for their losses.

Solvency risk is the risk that the organization does not survive or succeed because it runs out of cash, even though it might otherwise be solvent.[15] This was probably the most underappreciated component of risk prior to the financial crisis of 2008.[16] The collapse of Lehman Brothers was often associated with an excess of leverage, which was certainly a key factor in its failure. But it was solvency risk that forced the company into bankruptcy. Almost overnight, Lehman's liquidity disappeared because most funding sources would no longer willingly bear Lehman's counterparty risk. Even if it had experienced large market gains on the day it went under, it had already been destroyed by solvency risk. Across the entire financial industry, from hedge funds to pension funds, painful but valuable lessons were learned about the critical importance of funds availability and solvency risk, even if all other risks were well-aligned. Solvency risk is now viewed as one of the key factors in running a successful hedge fund because investors are extremely sensitive to not recovering their investment in the event of a "run on the fund."

Solvency, in the personal or institutional sense, is the availability of funding to continue to operate without liquidating—or at a less extreme level, to be able to make good on liabilities and meet one's cash flow requirements. Solvency risk is the ultimate example of the importance of taking an enterprise view of risk management. For example, a university's investment officer might have a perfectly well-balanced set of risks in the endowment portfolio when viewed in isolation. But as a part of a university, the portfolio may be affected by a deep recession because the university's professional degree revenue, grant money, and donations will fall at the same time as the portfolio's investment value and cash distributions are in decline. Although the endowment and university may survive, it might be necessary for the endowment to take many emergency actions that impair its value, simply attributable to the overall solvency risk and the ultimate need of the enterprise to not run out of cash.

Solvency risk is easily mitigated, though never eliminated, by a large number of possible safeguards, none of which is free. Many businesses produce short-term higher returns by essentially ignoring solvency risk, but in doing so, they are not managing risk very well. Since the 2008 crisis, most businesses are keenly aware of the consequences of bad solvency management, and have taken such steps as using less leverage, securing more stable sources of financing, investing in models to provide more transparency on solvency risk, incorporating solvency risk at an enterprise level in risk governance, and holding more cash equivalents and assets with less liquidity risk.

Individuals can also face a number of risks of an operational nature. These include hackers breaking into one's computer and the threat of burglary and robbery. One of the most commonly cited risks for individuals is identity theft. For individuals, however, we consider their primary non-financial risks to be related to their life and health as well as other life-changing events.

Obviously, the health of an individual is an extremely important risk. Poor health can result from poor choices in life, but it can also arise from factors that are outside the control of the individual. These risks can result in direct health care expenses, reduced income because of disability, and reduced lifespan or quality of life. People vary widely in the risk management strategies they undertake to control their health, such as in their choices in diet, exercise, preventive health care, and avoidance of undue health risks. Some individuals address only their financial exposure to health risks, and still others do not take proactive steps to address this risk at all.

---

15 Solvency risk is often referred to as liquidity risk by industry professionals, even though the expression *liquidity risk* was used earlier to refer to the risk of valuation shock when selling a security. Although the term "liquidity risk" is used in practice in both contexts, in this reading we will refer to the risk relating to the cash position of an organization as "solvency risk."

16 Bank runs are perhaps the simplest example of solvency risk. An otherwise solvent bank can easily be ruined by a bank run that wipes out its ability to make good on short-term liabilities.

Closely related to health risk is mortality risk—the risk of dying relatively young—and longevity risk—the risk of outliving one's financial resources. Not only are these risks a primary determinant of the quality of life, they are also critical factors in investment planning. Although it is probably desirable not to know when one will die, financial planning for one's years in retirement is heavily dependent on one's mortality assumption. Insurance companies, defined benefit pension plans, and vendors of retirement annuities need only know the group average mortality. Mortality tables are reasonably accurate, so these institutions have relatively precise estimates of death rates for groups as a whole. Individuals themselves, however, clearly do not know how long they will live. People who use defined contribution plans must therefore build portfolios and control retirement distributions so that their assets outlive them, which is difficult to do when they do not know when they will die. No one wants to outlive their money, but with an increasingly aging population and good health care, this problem is becoming a greater concern.

There are a number of other major non-financial risks that individuals face, which are generally involved with some sort of life-changing disaster. The largest ones—fire, natural disaster, or massive liability stemming from harming others, such as in a car accident—are generally considered "property and casualty" risks and are insured as such.

INTERACTIONS BETWEEN RISKS   8

☐ identify financial and non-financial sources of risk and describe how they may interact

In some cases, a risk classified into one category could easily have been classified into another. Indeed, the interactions between risks are numerous. It has been said that market risk begets credit risk, which begets operational risk. That is, given unexpected market moves, one party then owes the other party money. Given the debtor–creditor nature of the relationship, the two parties must have internal operations that process the transactions and pay or collect the money. Thus, whenever there is credit risk, there is settlement risk. If there were no market risk, the other risks in the chain would likely be relatively minor. Legal risk often arises from market or credit risk. Large market moves create losses for one party. There is a long history of parties searching for loopholes in contracts and suing to avoid incurring the loss.

One simple example of an adverse risk interaction is counterparty risk. When trading a derivative contract, it is important to consider the cost of counterparty risk. Suppose Party A buys an out-of-the-money put option with a strike price of ¥1000—a contract theoretically worth ¥100 entitling him to as much as ¥1000 from Counterparty C if an underlying equity index is down. But there is a 2% chance that C could default; and assume that the possibility of default is considered independent of the performance of the equity market. This transaction, with payoffs adjusted for the possibility of default, might price at, say, ¥98 to A. But in reality, the credit risk of C's default is likely dependent on the equity market return. If the probability distribution of default risk overlaps substantially with that of the market being down, which is a likely scenario, then the risks interact, and the cost of risk is higher. In this example, perhaps the probability of C defaulting is 10% or more when the put option is in the money. So, A's expected payoff is lower as a result of facing a credit risk that is compounded by market risk. In fact, it is quite likely that in the extreme event—a deep decline in the equity market when A would presumably receive ¥1000—Party

A will in all likelihood get nothing. Thus, the investor bears much more risk than initially thought as a result of the failure to consider the interaction of the two risks. And in doing so, Party A overpaid for the contract. This sort of risk interaction is so common in markets that practitioners have given it a very fitting term—"wrong-way risk." In fact, it was extremely common in the financial crisis of 2008, when holders of many securities based on mortgage credit believed that the risks were well-diversified when in truth, the risks were quite systematic.

Another example of interacting risks was experienced by many banks, funds, and private investment partnerships in 2008, as well as the hedge fund Long-Term Capital Management in 1998. Leverage, which manifested itself in higher market risk, interacted in an extremely toxic manner with liquidity risk and solvency risk and impaired or shuttered many investment firms.[17]

In most adverse financial risk interactions, the whole is much worse than the sum of its parts; the combined risk compounds the individual risks in a non-linear manner. For this example, a 2× levered organization might produce a 2% loss when its unlevered twin or baseline risk bears a 1% loss. If liquidity is a serious issue for the organization, then at a 10% baseline loss, the organization might face some moderate distress from liquidity or funding problems that it ends up losing 25% instead of 20%. It would not be surprising if this organization failed at a 30% baseline loss because of the toxic interplay between levered risk and liquidity problems. This resulting non-linear reaction to risk drivers exists across many risk interactions in many markets, making up-front scenario planning even more valuable to the risk process, a point we will return to later.

Earlier, we briefly described a common example of interacting risks for individuals. Suppose an individual works for a publicly traded company and, through an incentive program, receives shares of the company in her company retirement portfolio or for her personal holdings. Company policies may require that employees hold on to these shares for a number of years. When that time has elapsed, however, many individuals fail to recognize the incredibly concentrated risk they are assuming, so they hold on to their shares. An employee's reasoning for not selling the shares is often that the company she works for has been a solid performing company for many years, so she feels no reason to worry. Moreover, the team spirit often imbued in employees generates pride that can make employees believe that there is no better place in which to work and to invest their money. But if something goes wrong in the company or the industry, the employee may lose her job *and* her savings—an incredibly adverse interaction between market risk and human capital risk. The 2003 collapse of Enron remains a powerful historical example, with many loyal and honest employees losing virtually all of their retirement savings by failing to recognize this risk.

In sum, it is important to recognize that risks do not usually arise independently, but generally interact with one another, a problem that is even more critical in stressed market conditions. The resulting combined risk is practically always non-linear in that the total risk faced is worse than the sum of the risks of the separate components. Most risk models and systems do not directly account for risk interactions, which makes the consequences of the risk interaction even worse. Governance bodies, company management, and financial analysts should be keenly aware of the potential risk and damage of risks in combination, and be aware of the dangers of treating risks as separate and unrelated.

---

17 This example illustrates yet another risk, systemic risk, that is a significant concern to regulators and governments. Stresses and failures in one sector transmit to stresses and failures in other sectors, which can ultimately impact an entire economy. Systemic risk is the ultimate example of interactions among risks.

EXAMPLE 3

Financial and Non-Financial Sources of Risk

1. Which of the following is *not* a financial risk?
   - **A.** A. Credit risk
   - **B.** B. Market risk
   - **C.** C. Operational risk

   Solution

   C is correct. Operational risk is the only risk listed that is considered non-financial, even though it may have financial consequences. Credit and market risks derive from the possibility of default and market movements, respectively, and along with liquidity risk, are considered financial risks.

2. Which of the following *best* describes an example of interactions among risks?
   - **A.** A. A stock in Russia declines at the same time as a stock in Japan declines.
   - **B.** B. Political events cause a decline in economic conditions and an increase in credit spreads.
   - **C.** C. A market decline makes a derivative counterparty less creditworthy while causing it to owe more money on that derivative contract.

   Solution

   C is correct. Although most risks are likely to be interconnected in some way, in some cases the risks an organization is exposed to will *interact* in such a way that a loss (or gain) in one exposure will lead directly to a loss in a different exposure as well, such as with many counterparty contracts. Conditions in A and B are much more directly linked in that market participants fully expect what follows—for example, in B, an outbreak of war in one region of the world could well cause widespread uncertainty; a flight to quality, such as to government-backed securities; and a widening in spreads for credit-risky securities. In C, in contrast, the reduction in creditworthiness following the market decline may be expected, but owing more money on an already existing contract as a result comes from the interaction of risks.

3. Which of the following *best* describes a financial risk?
   - **A.** A. The risk of an increase in interest rates.
   - **B.** B. The risk that regulations will make a transaction illegal.
   - **C.** C. The risk of an individual trading without limits or controls.

   Solution

   A is correct because this risk arises from the financial markets.

4. Which of the following is *not* an example of model risk?
   - **A.** A. Assuming the tails of a returns distribution are thin when they are, in fact, fat.
   - **B.** B. Using standard deviation to measure risk when the returns distribution is asymmetric.

C. Using the one-year risk-free rate to discount the face value of a one-year government bond.

Solution

C is correct. The risk-free rate is generally the appropriate rate to use in discounting government bonds. Although government bonds are generally default free, their returns are certainly risky. Assuming a returns distribution has thin tails when it does not and assuming symmetry in an asymmetric distribution are both forms of model risk.

5. Which of the following is the risk that arises when it becomes difficult to sell a security in a highly stressed market?

   A. Liquidity risk
   B. Systemic risk
   C. Wrong-way risk

Solution

A is correct. Securities vary highly in how liquid they are. Those with low liquidity are those for which either the number of agents willing to invest or the amount of capital these agents are willing to invest is limited. When markets are stressed, these limited number of investors or small amount of capital dry up, leading to the inability to sell the security at any price the seller feels is reasonable. Systemic risk is the risk of failure of the entire financial system and a much broader risk than liquidity risk. Wrong-way risk is the extent to which one's exposure to a counterparty is positively related to the counterparty's credit risk.

6. The risks that individuals face based on mortality create which of the following problems?

   A. The risk of loss of income to their families.
   B. Covariance risk associated with their human capital and their investment portfolios.
   C. The interacting effects of solvency risk and the risk of being taken advantage of by an unscrupulous financial adviser.

Solution

A is correct. The uncertainty about death creates two risks: mortality risk and longevity risk. The mortality risk (risk of dying relatively young) is manifested by a termination of the income stream generated by the person. In contrast, longevity risk is the risk of outliving one's financial resources.

9 MEASURING AND MODIFYING RISK: DRIVERS AND METRICS

☐ describe methods for measuring and modifying risk exposures and factors to consider in choosing among the methods

The core element of risk management is the measurement and modification of risk. One cannot modify risk without measuring it. The primary purpose of measuring risk is to determine whether the risk being taken, or being considered, is consistent with the pre-defined risk tolerance. To understand how risk is measured, it is important to understand the basic elements that drive risk.

Drivers

This section illustrates the origins of risk. Risk is a part of life itself. None of us knows from one day to the next everything that will happen to us in the next 24 hours, let alone over a longer period. We may get a phone call that a relative is extremely sick, or we may be contacted by a head-hunter about an attractive job possibility. We may learn that we are going to be given an award from a prestigious organization, or we may find that our identity has been stolen. All of us can almost surely name something that happened the previous day that was not anticipated. Most of these happenings are minor and often quickly forgotten. Others are serious. Some are good. Some are bad. Some are unpredictable outcomes of known events, such as whether we get an offer following a job interview or whether a medical test reveals that we are healthy or ill. Some events are completely unanticipated, such as getting a phone call from an old friend we have not talked to in many years or having a flat tire on the drive home. Fortunately, the vast majority of risks in life are minor. The ones that are not minor, however, have the potential to be highly unpredictable and financially, and sometimes physically and emotionally, quite costly.

In a conceptual sense, financial risks are no different from the other risks we face in life. All risks arise from the fact that the future is unknown. Financial risks largely emanate from economic risks, and economic risks emanate from the uncertainties of life.

Financial markets generate prices that fluctuate as investors absorb information about the global and domestic state of the economy, the company's industry, and the idiosyncratic characteristics of the company itself. Global and domestic macroeconomies are driven by the companies that operate within them, but much of the tone as well as the ground rules are set by governments and quasi-governmental agencies, such as central banks. Taxes, regulations, laws, and monetary and fiscal policy establish a legal and economic environment and a set of ground rules that greatly affect the degree and quality of economic activity that takes place. Attempts by governments and central banks of different countries to coordinate economic policies can lead to some degrees of success if harmonized, but if not, they can create an environment in which companies engage in practices designed to seek favorable treatment in some countries and avoid unfavorable treatment in others.[18]

All economies, in turn, are composed of industries. Government policies also affect industries, in some cases encouraging economic activity in some industries while discouraging it in others. Some industries are stable, weathering macroeconomic storms quite well, whereas others are highly cyclical.

The uncertainties of global and domestic macroeconomic and central bank policies create risks for economies and industries that we often treat as systematic. Seemingly minor events, such as filling the position of central bank chairperson, are often viewed by investors as major events, signaling possibly a change in policy that can greatly affect the macroeconomy and possibly certain industries.

---

18 This practice is sometimes called regulatory arbitrage. The policies of certain countries can be more conducive to establishing operations. Examples are the flow of money into countries whose banking laws are less restrictive and more conducive to secrecy and incorporation in or moving a company to a country with lighter regulations or more favorable tax treatment.

Moving down to a more fundamental level, investors face the unsystematic or idiosyncratic risks of individual companies. Modern investment analysis prescribes that diversified portfolios bear no unsystematic risk. We are then led to believe that unsystematic risk does not matter in a well-diversified portfolio. But unsystematic risk does matter to the management of a company. It also matters to poorly diversified investors. And it certainly matters to the financial analysts who cover specific companies. And what would appear to be unsystematic risk can oftentimes actually be systematic. For example, poor credit risk management by a major bank can turn into a global financial crisis if that bank is "too big to fail."

In sum, the basic drivers of risk arise from global and domestic macroeconomies, industries, and individual companies. Risk management can control some of this risk, but it cannot control all of it. For example, the risk manager of a company may be able to reduce the likelihood that his company will default, but he cannot control movements in interest rates. For the latter risk, he must accept that interest rate volatility is a given and that he can only position the company to be able to ensure that its risk exposure is aligned with its objective and risk tolerance. In order to do so, he must first be able to measure the risk.

Metrics

The notion of metrics in the context of risk refers to the quantitative measures of risk exposure. The most basic metric associated with risk is probability. Probability is a measure of the relative frequency with which one would expect an outcome, series of outcomes, or range of outcomes to occur. One can speak about the probability of rolling a six in one roll of a die as 1/6, the chance of rain in the next 24 hours as 20%, or the odds of a central bank taking actions to increase interest rates of 50%. These are all probabilities, differing in concept by the fact that the die roll is associated with an objective probability measure, whereas the other two examples are subjective probabilities. It is important to note that probability, in and of itself, is not a sufficient metric of risk. A chance of financial loss of 25% does not tell us everything we need to know. There are other measures of risk that incorporate probability but give us more information.

The standard deviation is a measure of the dispersion in a probability distribution. Although there is a formal mathematical definition of standard deviation, at this point we need only understand the conceptual definition. Standard deviation measures a range over which a certain percentage of the outcomes would be expected to occur. For example, in a normal distribution, about 68% of the time the outcomes will lie within plus or minus one standard deviation of the expected value. Two standard deviations in both directions would cover about 95% of the outcomes, whereas three would encompass 99% of the outcomes. Although standard deviation, or volatility, is widely used in the financial world, it does have significant limitations. In particular, standard deviation may not be an appropriate measure of risk for non-normal distributions. Standard deviation may not exist for return distributions with fat tails.

Moreover, according to modern portfolio theory, the risk captured by an asset's standard deviation overstates the risk of that asset's returns in the context of a diversified portfolio. Investors can easily diversify their holdings, thereby eliminating a portion of the risk in their portfolios by diversifying away the security-specific risk. As a result, most financial valuation theories assert that the ability of investors to eliminate security-specific risk, or non-systematic risk, means that investors should not expect to earn a premium to compensate them for the assumption of this risk. As a consequence, the risk of a security may be better measured by its **beta**, a measure

Measuring and Modifying Risk: Drivers and Metrics

of the sensitivity of a security's returns to the returns on the market portfolio. Beta measures relative risk, meaning how much market risk an asset contributes to a well-diversified portfolio.[19]

Beta describes risk well for a portfolio of equities, but other sources of risk may require other descriptive risk metrics. The risk associated with derivatives is one example of this. Although derivatives are widely used to manage risk, they do so by assuming other risks. Even if the derivative is being used to establish a hedge of an existing exposure to risk, it would still result in the assumption of additional risk because the assumed risk is being used to offset an existing risk. For example, if one purchases a call option denominated in euros to buy Russian rubles, one would be assuming the risk of the ruble/euro exchange rate. Because most derivatives exposures are highly leveraged, it is critical that the risk of derivatives be properly measured. There are several specialized measures of derivatives risk.

The sensitivity of the derivative price to a small change in the value of the underlying asset is called the **delta**. It is perhaps the most important measure of derivatives risk. Yet delta is limited to capturing only small changes in the value of the underlying. Large changes are captured by the concept of **gamma**. Whereas delta is a first-order risk, gamma is considered a second-order risk because it reflects the risk of changes in delta.[20] Some derivatives, such as options, are also sensitive to changes in the volatility of the underlying. This risk is captured by a concept called **vega**, which is a first-order measure of the change in the derivative price for a change in the volatility of the underlying. Derivatives are also sensitive to changes in interest rates, which are reflected in a measure called **rho**. Most options have relatively low sensitivity to interest rates.[21] These, and other mathematically derived derivatives metrics, are collectively referred to as "the Greeks."

Other asset classes may have their own special metrics to describe risk. One well-known example, **duration**, is a measure of the interest rate sensitivity of a fixed-income instrument. Analogous to delta, it is a first-order risk. The wide variety of financial instrument types and asset classes leads to a proliferation of terminology and risk measures, with most of them having no meaning outside their asset class. As financial organizations and asset risk modeling became more sophisticated and computer power increased, an approach was needed to measure and describe financial risk across the broad spectrum of asset classes. Spurred by the onset of global bank capital regulation, this led to the development of value at risk.

Value at risk or **VaR** is a measure of the size of the tail of the distribution of profits on a portfolio or for an organization. A VaR measure contains three elements: an amount stated in units of currency, a time period, and a probability. For example, assume a London bank determines that its VaR is £3 million at 5% for one day. This statement means that the bank expects to lose a minimum of £3 million in one day 5% of the time. A critical, and often overlooked word, is *minimum*. In this example, the bank expects that its losses will be at least £3 million in one day with 5% probability. In a VaR measure, there is no ultimate maximum that one can state. VaR is thus a minimum extreme loss metric. With a probability of 5% and a measurement period of one day, we can interpret the bank's VaR as expecting a minimum loss of £3

---

[19] Earlier, we discussed the fact that unsystematic risk matters to some parties. Here we seem to be saying that it should not matter to anyone. Capital market models almost always assume that investors can diversify quite easily and, as a result, they should not expect to earn a premium for bearing diversifiable risk. This assumption does not mean that everyone's wealth is well-diversified. Investors who do not diversify probably cannot expect to earn a return for bearing diversifiable risk, but it does not mean that these investors should not care about measuring the risk they choose to assume by not diversifying.

[20] The notion of a first-order risk versus a second-order risk can be seen by considering the following. Suppose A affects B and B, in turn, affects C. A does not affect C directly but does so only indirectly. A is a first-order risk for B and a second-order risk for C.

[21] Options on interest rates, however, have a high sensitivity to interest rates, but only because interest rates are the underlying, and thus, the source of market risk.

million once every 20 business days. VaR can also be used to measure credit losses, although the construction of the measure is considerably more difficult given the extreme asymmetry of the risk.

VaR is a simple but controversial measure. There are several ways to estimate VaR, each of which has its own advantages and disadvantages. The different measures can lead to highly diverse estimates. Moreover, VaR is subject to the same model risk as derivative pricing models. VaR is based on a particular assumption about the probability distribution of returns or profits. If that assumption is incorrect, the VaR estimate will be incorrect. VaR also requires certain inputs. If those inputs are incorrect, the VaR estimate will be incorrect. Many critics of VaR have argued that naive users of VaR can be lulled into a false sense of security. A presumably tolerable VaR can give the illusion that the risk is under control, when in fact, it is not. Yet, VaR is accepted as a risk measure by most banking regulators and is approved for disclosure purposes in typical accounting standards. As with any risk measure, one should supplement it with other measures.

As emphasized earlier, VaR does not tell the maximum loss. The maximum loss is the entire equity of an organization or the entire value of a portfolio, but the statistics used to estimate VaR can be used to gauge average extreme losses. Conditional VaR or **CVaR** is a common tail loss measure, defined as the weighted average of all loss outcomes in the statistical distribution that exceed the VaR loss. Another tail risk metric in the credit risk space that is analogous to CVaR is expected loss given default, which answers the question for a debt security, "If the underlying company or asset defaults, how much do we lose on average?"

VaR focuses on the left tail of the distribution and purports to tell us the expected frequency of extreme negative returns, but it can understate the actual risk. For example, the normal distribution gives us a well-defined measure of extreme negative returns, which are balanced by extreme positive returns. Yet, actual historical return distributions have shown that there are more extreme negative returns than would be expected under the normal distribution. We previously described this concern in the form of tail risk. In response to this concern, statisticians have developed a branch of study that focuses primarily on extreme outcomes, which is called **extreme value theory**, and leads to measures of the statistical characteristics of outcomes that occur in the tails of the distribution. There are mathematical rules that define the statistical properties of such large outcomes, and these rules have been widely used for years in the insurance business. In the past 20 years or so, risk managers have taken to using them to help gauge the likelihood of outcomes that exceed those that would normally be expected.

Two measures in particular that are often used to complement VaR are **scenario analysis** and **stress testing**. These are common sense approaches that ask "If this happens, then how are we affected?" Scenario analysis can be thought of as a package of stress tests, usually with some common underlying theme. A scenario defines a set of conditions or market movements that could occur and would put some pressure on a portfolio. An example might be a sharp increase in interest rates coupled with a significant decline in the value of a currency. The portfolio is then evaluated to determine its expected loss under these scenarios. A different means of posing a scenario analysis is stress testing, which is done by proposing specific asset price moves generally involving extremely large and high pressure scenarios that would occur only rarely but would have the potential for destabilizing the entire organization. The US Federal Reserve and other central banks have begun requiring major banks to stress test their portfolios. Although scenario analysis and stress testing can provide some information, they are, as noted previously for other measures, subject to model risk.

Of course, the measures just mentioned focus primarily on market risk. Credit risk, which is covered in more detail in readings on fixed-income analysis, has long relied heavily on the credit ratings provided by private companies, such as Moody's

Analytics, Standard & Poor's, and Fitch Ratings. In effect, a large part of credit analysis for many lenders has been outsourced since the early part of the 20th century. Most lenders, however, do not rely exclusively on these rating companies. They do their own analysis, which focuses on the creditor's liquidity, profitability, and leverage. Liquidity measures, such as the current ratio, may indicate how well a borrower can cover short-term obligations. Solvency ratios, such as cash flow coverage or interest coverage, may reveal whether a borrower generates enough cash or earnings to make its promised interest payments. Profitability measures, such as return on assets, estimate whether a company is sufficiently profitable so that it can easily accommodate debt. Leverage measures, such as the ratio of debt to total assets, reflect whether a company has sufficient equity capital in relation to its debt to absorb losses and negative cash flows without defaulting. Credit analysis also examines the strength and cyclicality of the macroeconomy and the company's industry. Other widely used measures of credit risk include credit VaR, probability of default, expected loss given default, and the probability of a credit rating change.

One of the problems of credit risk measurement is that credit events, such as a ratings downgrade or a default, are relatively rare for a particular organization. Certainly, in the aggregate there are many credit losses, but very few companies that default have a history of defaulting. Without a history to go by, estimating the likelihood of an event that has never actually occurred is extremely difficult. Imagine the challenge of assigning a default probability to Lehman Brothers in 2007. It had been in operation since 1850 and had never defaulted. Yet in 2008, Lehman Brothers, one of the most successful financial companies of all time, filed for bankruptcy. Because of the infrequency of default, risk managers normally attempt to assess default probability by aggregating companies with similar characteristics.[22]

Another useful source of information for risk managers about these rare events is the *ex ante* risk cost that is implied by the market pricing of derivatives. A **credit default swap (CDS)** on an issuing company has an observable price that acts as a signal to a bondholder of the risk cost of a default. Put options, exotic options, insurance contracts, and other financial instruments may contain valuable signals of the cost of rare adverse events, or at least the price of hedging them.

Operational risk is one of the most difficult risks to measure. Consider the operational risk event reported in 2014 in which hackers broke into Home Depot's credit card data base. Assessing the likelihood of such an event and estimating the potential losses would be almost impossible. The threat of litigation alone for years afterward is difficult to quantify. As with credit risk, significant operational risk events are rare but usually quite costly if they do occur. Hence, attempts to quantify the risk usually involve a third party aggregating operational risk events across numerous companies and publishing the statistics.

As mentioned, there are numerous other risks that would likewise be difficult to measure. For example, there is always the possibility of changes in accounting rules, laws, tax rates, and regulatory requirements that can result in significant costs as companies adapt their policies and actions from one regulatory environment to a new one. How would one measure such risks? Moreover, the time period spanned by these risks is extremely long, and in fact, theoretically infinite. Changes in these rules and laws are often motivated by politics. How does one quantify such risks when there are no real numeric measures? Analysis invariably reverts to subjective evaluation of the likelihood of such threats and their potential losses.

---

22 In some sense, aggregating companies with similar characteristics is what credit ratings do. Companies rated BAA/Baa+ can be quite diverse but all are considered similar with respect to their ability to pay their debts.

As we have described, many risks are measurable, at least on an *ex post* basis. Market-related risks are blessed with large quantities of data, so they are relatively measurable. Credit, operational, and other risks are somewhat rare events. Although it is probably a good thing that such events are indeed rare, their infrequency makes measurement more difficult. Nonetheless, virtually any risk manager will attempt to obtain at least a subjective sense of the expected frequency, likelihood, and cost of these events. With either objective or subjective measurements in mind, risk managers can then proceed to modify these risks accordingly.

10 RISK MODIFICATION: PREVENTION, AVOIDANCE, AND ACCEPTANCE

☐ describe methods for measuring and modifying risk exposures and factors to consider in choosing among the methods

The notion of risk modification presumes that an analysis has been conducted in the risk governance stage that defines how much risk is acceptable. Coupled with measurements of the actual risk, as discussed in the previous section, the risk manager then proceeds to align the actual risk with the acceptable risk.

It is important to understand, however, that risk modification is not strictly risk reduction. For example, a portfolio with the strategic objective of maintaining a 50/50 split between equity and cash will naturally find that in a market in which cash outperforms equity, the split between equity and cash will tilt toward cash. Thus, the portfolio becomes less risky. Beyond a certain point, the risk of the portfolio is unacceptably low given the return target. Thus, risk modification would take the form of rebalancing by increasing the risk. For the most part, however, risk management focuses more on reducing the risk. Risk reduction is commonly referred to as hedging. A hedge is a transaction put in place to reduce risk. Some hedges are designed to lead to the ultimate in risk reduction—the complete elimination of risk. Others are simply designed to lower the risk to an acceptable level. For some companies, risk management is primarily concerned with keeping the organization solvent. Regardless of the focus, much of what is done to manage risk is the same. In this section, we will examine four broad categories of risk modification: risk prevention and avoidance, risk acceptance, risk transfer, and risk shifting.

Risk Prevention and Avoidance

One method of managing risk is taking steps to avoid it altogether; however, avoiding risk may not be as simple as it appears. It is difficult to completely avoid risk, but more importantly, it is unclear that every risk should be completely avoided particularly if there are high costs associated with eliminating the risk. Instead we choose a trade-off between cost and benefits. The actual trade-off may be subject to debate because risk assessment and risk management are subject to variation from one person to another.

We could nearly eliminate the risk of being injured or killed in an automobile accident if we choose to never drive or ride in a car. Like any risk-avoidance strategy, however, there would more than likely be a trade-off in terms of the loss of the benefits provided by the activity. We could try to protect our children from all harm, but that may come at the expense of preparing them poorly for adult life. We could invest our entire retirement savings in cash, but would most likely give up protection against inflation and lose out on the opportunity to benefit from long-term economic growth and the performance of investable assets that benefit from that growth.

Insurance companies rely heavily on the techniques of risk prevention and avoidance. An automobile insurance company would prefer that their policyholders never drive their cars. Although it cannot prohibit them from doing so, it can reward them with lower premiums if they drive less and have safe driving records. A life insurance company would prefer that their policyholders do not smoke, and it can reward non-smokers with lower rates.

Nearly every risk we take has an upside, at least as perceived by the person taking the risk. Some counterexamples might seem to belie this point, but not if viewed from the point of view of the risk taker. One could argue that there are no benefits from smoking, but people who smoke may have the opinion that the pleasure they receive exceeds the costs. Casino gambling incurs the risk of significant financial loss and addiction, but it is risk that is acceptable to the consumers who incur it relative to the perceived benefits they receive. The risks of extreme sports, such as skydiving, would seem to be exceeded by the benefits obtained by participants, and yet participants engage in them with apparently much enjoyment. People undertake all types of risky behaviors because they obtain commensurate benefits. These examples are simply cases in which the decision maker chooses to bear a certain degree of risk. They are conceptually the same as an investor who chooses to accept a relatively high degree of risk. Likewise, those who live their lives engaging in very few risky activities are conceptually the same as the investor who keeps only a modest exposure to risky assets.

In organizations, the decision to avoid risk is generally made at the governance level as a part of setting the risk tolerance. Boards will often decide that there are some business or investment activities simply not worth pursuing based on either the goals of the organization or the perceived risk–return trade-off. These are strategic decisions. Boards may exclude some areas or activities to allow management to focus on choosing risks in other areas where they presumably have a better chance of adding value.

We recap this section by noting that risk prevention and avoidance is simply an element of the decision of how much risk to accept, given the trade-off between the risk of loss and the benefit of gain. This could be a direct benefit or an indirect benefit of avoiding or eliminating a risk. Most decisions in life involve a trade-off between benefits and costs, neither of which is necessarily easy to measure. Thus, risk management is an ongoing process of fine-tuning exposure to achieve the level of risk that is desired in relation to the benefits.

If the risk measurement process shows that the risk exceeds the acceptable level, there are three approaches to managing the risk: self-insuring, risk transfer, and risk shifting.

Risk Acceptance: Self-Insurance and Diversification

In many cases, from both a risk tolerance and a strategic standpoint, it makes sense to keep a risk exposure—but to do so in the most efficient manner possible. Self-insurance is the notion of bearing a risk that is considered undesirable but too costly to eliminate by external means. In some cases, self-insuring means simply to bear the risk. In other cases, it may involve the establishment of a reserve to cover losses. Choosing to not have health insurance can be an optimal choice for some young, healthy adults without responsibility for children. Setting aside some money to cover potential health costs completes the picture of an individual who completely self-insures. Similarly, a young healthy individual who does not buy life insurance but engages in a systematic, well-conceived savings and investment plan is engaging in self-insurance.

One must be careful with this approach, however, because there is a fine line between self-insurance and denial. To the extent that self-insurance results in risks that are completely in line with the enterprise's risk tolerance, it would be an example of good governance. But if there is a risk that is outside the enterprise's risk tolerance, and management decides to bear that risk anyway, saying it is self-insuring, management is basically ignoring that risk, disregarding and violating its risk tolerance, and practicing bad risk governance. For example, an investment management firm, via its risk tolerance decision, may decide that it cannot bear any investment loss exceeding €1 billion and may apply a variety of risk management tools to limit its market and credit risk accordingly. But suppose that the firm makes no move to limit or insure its risks from fraud or a rogue trader on the grounds that it is "self-insuring" this risk, which could result in a loss as high as €3 billion. By leaving itself open to a loss that far exceeds its stated risk tolerance, management is violating the firm's risk governance.

From the perspective of a business organization, self-insurance is obtained by setting aside sufficient capital to cover losses. The banking industry is a classic example of self-insurance. Although in many countries government insurance may protect depositors, banks self-insure to some extent by maintaining capital and loan loss reserves.

Another form of accepting risk, but doing so in the most efficient manner possible, is diversification. Technically, it is a risk-mitigation technique. But diversification and "the efficient frontier" are so central to modern portfolio analysis that capturing the full benefits of diversification seems the obvious thing for all organizations to pursue—a starting point at which other risk modification could be appended. Although diversification is one form of risk management, it is usually not effective if used in isolation.

In the next two subsections, we discuss how undesired risk can be modified or eliminated by selling the risk to another party. We make two subtle classifications of these methods: risk transfer and risk shifting.

11. RISK MODIFICATION: TRANSFERRING, SHIFTING, AND HOW TO CHOOSE

> ☐ describe methods for measuring and modifying risk exposures and factors to consider in choosing among the methods

Risk transfer is the process of passing on a risk to another party, often, but not always, in the form of an insurance policy. Insurance is a legal contract in which one party, the insurer, agrees to cover some percentage of a loss incurred by another party, the insured, from a specific event in return for the payment of a premium by the insured. Insurance as a method of risk modification has been in existence for very long time, and in fact, is even mentioned in the Code of Hammurabi almost 4,000 years ago. Insurance has been widely used in the commercial shipping and farming industries going back hundreds of years. Insurance is almost as old as commerce itself.[23]

From the point of view of the insurer, insurance almost always works on the basis of diversification or pooling of risks. An insurer attempts to sell many policies with risks that have low correlations. The insurer assesses the pooled risks and charges a premium that covers the expected aggregate losses and the insurer's operating costs

---

23 It is worth noting that the insurance industry has for a long time referred to itself using the term "risk management." A department of risk management in a large organization is often the group that manages the organization's insurance policies. But since around 1990 or so, the term "risk management" has increasingly come to refer to far more than insurance.

as well as leaves a profit. Insurers need accurate statistics on aggregate risks, but these are often not difficult to obtain. These actuarial data are widely available on accidents, illnesses, property and casualty damage, and death. In principle, a well-diversified insurer does not care if a single insured party has significantly larger-than-average claims as long as there is no reason to believe that the claims are correlated. There will be other parties that have smaller-than-average claims.

Insurers do have to manage their risks carefully. Some risks can be correlated. In the US Gulf Coast region, property insurance, which includes coverage for loss by hurricanes, is typically more expensive than property insurance in other regions. Even with a higher premium, an insurer has to avoid providing too much property coverage in an area where a systemic event, such as a hurricane, can occur in order to diversify its risk exposure.

Although insurers carefully assess their risk and charge premiums that they believe accurately reflect expected losses, they nonetheless remain responsible for potentially large claims. Insurers also manage their risk by avoiding writing too many policies with similar and potentially correlated risks and by selling some of the risk to another insurer, a practice known as reinsurance. A company that primarily insures property in the US Midwest, which is highly subject to tornado risk, might be willing to accept some Gulf Coast hurricane risk for a reasonable premium. Insurers often write provisions into contracts to exclude coverage of special cases. For example, a war might nullify insurance coverage in an area. Most insurance policies also contain provisions to guard against moral hazards, such as suicide or destroying one's own property. In the last 20 years or so, some insurance companies have issued bonds that permit them to legally avoid paying principal and/or interest if insurance claims exceed a certain amount. These instruments, known as catastrophe bonds, essentially pass some of the insurance risk on to the investors who buy the bonds.

Most insurance policies do not cover *all* of the risk that is insured. It is common for policies to contain a provision known as a deductible. A deductible is a monetary amount of the loss that will be covered by the insured before any claims are paid. Thus, both the insured and the insurer bear some of the risk, although the insurer usually bears the greater amount. Deductibles serve several purposes. Because insurers incur fixed costs for each claim, deductibles reduce the number of small claims. Deductibles also encourage good risk management by the insured parties. Finally, deductibles offer the insured the opportunity to combine risk transfer with self-insurance and thereby achieve a potentially better trade-off of risk and reward.

As noted, the concept of insurance relies on the diversification or pooling of risks. In a few cases, however, the risks are not easy to pool. For example, suppose a volatile but extremely successful actor is signed to star in a movie. The production company knows that it runs the risk that the actor will engage in behavior that damages the ability of the company to finish the movie. The number of volatile and extremely successful actors for whom policies could be written at the same time is somewhat limited. Thus, an insurer would have to bear that risk without the benefit of diversification.

For example, suppose a television network plans to cover the Olympics but is concerned about a possible cancellation or boycott. It might want an insurance policy to cover it against loss. Specialized coverage is possible through such companies as Lloyd's of London. The approximately 350-year old Lloyd's is famous for covering unusual risks. It does so by organizing groups of investors who are willing to bear a risk for a premium. These groups, called syndicates, are subject to the full extent of losses. In many cases, investors in these syndicates have been required to pay substantial amounts of money to cover losses.[24] These examples illustrate how syndicates work.

---

24 NBC insured the 1980 Summer Olympics in Moscow through Lloyd's of London to the extent that if a US boycott occurred, Lloyd's would pay NBC for losses that it incurred by prepaying the Soviet Union for broadcasting rights. The United States did boycott the Olympics and NBC collected on its policy.

Although there is only one Olympics to insure, there may also be only one actor to insure. Because the two risks are uncorrelated, a company could write policies on both risks and would achieve some diversification. Moreover, there are other unusual risks that can be covered such that the aggregate pool would represent a highly diverse set of risks that have low correlations.

A very slight variation of insurance is a surety bond. With a surety bond, an insurer promises to pay an insured a certain amount of money if a third party fails to fulfill its obligation. For example, if a party engages the services of another party, the first party is covered if the party obligated to provide the service fails to perform to a satisfactory degree. Surety bonds are widely used in commercial activity when one party bears the risk of the potentially high cost of non-performance by another party. A slight variation of a surety bond is a fidelity bond, which is often used to cover against losses that result from employee dishonesty. Bonds of this type work very similarly to insurance and rely on the pooling of uncorrelated risks.[25] Other similar arrangements include indemnity clauses and hold harmless arrangements, such as when two parties sign a contract and one party agrees to hold the other harmless and/or indemnify the other in the event of loss.

The use of insurance by so many as a risk management tool suggests that the cost of risk exceeds the actuarial cost to many individuals and enterprises. *Ex ante* consideration of the cost of a risk in terms of the organization's value or utility ties risk mitigation back to the risk tolerance decision and the most fundamental governance decisions on which value-added strategies to pursue. As an alternative to *ignoring* the cost of risk, the impact on enterprise value should be quite positive.

Risk Shifting

Whereas risk transfer refers to actions taken that pass the risk on to other parties, **risk shifting** refers to actions that change the distribution of risk outcomes. Risk transfer is often associated with insurance, whereas risk shifting generally involves derivatives as the risk modification vehicle. Although insurance is a form of risk management based on the pooling or diversification of risks, risk shifting diverts some portion of the risk distribution to another market participant who either bears the risk or intermediates that risk by moving it to yet another party. The organization may want to adjust its probability distribution of returns, essentially adjusting the payoff diagram of its risk exposures. An example is a company that is willing to make slightly less profit than it otherwise would if the stock market is up to prevent it from losing too much money if the stock market is down, for example, more than 20% next year. It is adjusting its potential economic outcomes by shifting the probability distribution of its profits conditional on market performance. Risk shifting represents the bulk of hedging and is the most common form of risk modification for financial organizations.

The principal device through which risk shifting is performed is a derivative. We briefly mentioned derivatives earlier in this reading. By definition, a derivative is a financial instrument that derives its price from the price of an underlying asset or rate. Because the price of the underlying and the price of the derivative are so closely related, derivatives can provide essentially the same exposure as the underlying but can do so at lower cost and capital requirements. As such, derivatives permit the efficient shifting of risk across the probability distribution and from one party to another. One can hold the underlying and take an offsetting position in the derivative or vice versa. Whereas insurance can be designed to perform similarly, insurance functions

---

25 In the context of surety and fidelity bonds, the word "bond" does not mean a debt obligation issued by one party, the borrower, and bought by another, the lender. In this context, the word refers to assuring one party that it bears no risk for the actions of a specific other party.

Risk Modification: Transferring, Shifting, and How To Choose

primarily through the pooling of diverse risks. With derivatives, risks are shifted across probability distributions or payoffs and across parties, to leave specific outcomes of the conditional probability distribution with the parties most willing to bear the risk.

There are several types of derivatives, and the manner in which they provide risk shifting varies by type. Derivatives are classified into two categories: forward commitments or contingent claims. Forward commitments are agreements that obligate two parties to undertake a transaction at a future date at a price or rate agreed on when the commitment is made. Forward commitments include such instruments as forward contracts, futures contracts, and swaps. Forward commitments can be used to lock in a future interest rate for a borrower or lender, the purchase or sale price of an asset, or an exchange rate for a currency. Parties who engage in forward commitments do not pay any money at the initiation of the contract. In lieu of any up-front payment from one party to the other, the two parties agree on the terms of the transaction that will be consummated at the end of the contract. Depending on movements in the price or rate of the underlying, one party will ultimately gain from the transaction while the other will lose or, in the less likely case, both parties could breakeven. For example, a corporate treasurer can use a forward contract to lock in the rate at which a foreign cash flow will be converted into the company's domestic currency. Regardless of movements in the exchange rate during the life of the contract, the foreign cash flow will convert to the domestic currency at a rate that is locked in when the contract is initiated. On the opposite side of the transaction, the party can be a speculator who simply bears the risk, or it can be a dealer who intermediates the risk between the hedger and the speculator. We will discuss dealers in more detail in a few paragraphs.

> **EXAMPLE 4**
>
> ### Risk Shifting: Foreign Exchange Risk and Forward Commitments
>
> You are a UK investor, investing 60% in a UK index fund tracking the FTSE 100, the leading index of the UK equity market, and 40% in US Treasuries. You expect returns in US dollars on the US Treasuries of 1.6%, and because you expect 0% return on the USD/GBP exchange rate, this return expectation equals your return expectation in sterling. You expect a return of 5.5% on the FTSE 100. Hence, the expected return on your portfolio is 3.9%.
>
> $R_P = w_1 \times R_1 + (1 - w_1) \times [(1 + R_{lc}) \times (1 + R_{FX}) - 1]$.
>
> $R_P = 0.6 \times 0.055 + 0.4 \times [(1 + .015) \times (1 + 0.0) - 1] = 0.039 = 3.9\%$.
>
> Risk (standard deviation of returns) for the FTSE 100 is 13.2%, and the risk on US Treasuries in sterling is 11.0%. Correlations between US Treasuries, the FTSE 100, and the USD/GBP exchange rate are shown in the following correlation matrix.
>
> | | FTSE 100 | US Treasuries | USD/GBP |
> | --- | --- | --- | --- |
> | FTSE 100 | 1.00 | −0.32 | −0.06 |
> | US Treasuries | −0.32 | 1.00 | 0.33 |
> | USD/GBP | −0.06 | 0.33 | 1.00 |
>
> Using the information provided above, we can calculate the risk of the portfolio with UK large-capitalization equities and US Treasuries as follows:

$$\sigma_p = \sqrt{w_1^2\sigma_1^2 + w_2^2\sigma_2^2 + w_3^2\sigma_3^2 + 2\rho_{1,2}w_1w_2\sigma_1\sigma_2 + 2\rho_{1,3}w_1w_3\sigma_1\sigma_3 + 2\rho_{1,3}w_1w_3\sigma_1\sigma_3}.$$

$\sigma_p = (0.6^2 \times 0.132^2 + 0.4^2 \times 0.040^2 + 0.4^2 \times 0.090^2 + 2 \times -0.32 \times 0.6 \times 0.4 \times 0.132 \times 0.040 + 2 \times -0.06 \times 0.6 \times 0.4 \times 0.132 \times 0.090 + 2 \times 0.33 \times 0.4 \times 0.4 \times 0.040 \times 0.090)^{1/2}$

$\sigma_p = 0.0841 \approx 8.4\%$.

The risk of this portfolio is 8.4%.

As an investor, you would like to examine possibilities to reduce the risk to this portfolio without giving up too much return, and you suspect that the volatility of the USD/GBP exchange rate contributes to risk while not adding to return. You want to know the impact of hedging the currency exposure of the US Treasury investment by means of entering into a forward contract selling USD into GBP in one year's time. You want to hedge 100% of the currency risk of the US Treasury investment.

You have been told that the forward price of a currency expressed in another currency is equal to the current spot price, corrected for the difference between the deposit rates of the countries involved over the time period ("tenor") of the forward contract. The current spot price of USD in sterling is GBP0.7040. The one-year forward price is 0.7038, as 12-month deposit rates in the United Kingdom and the United States are very close to one another.

1. What would be the impact on the risk of the portfolio if you hedge 100% of your US Treasury investment's value using this one-year forward contract?

   Solution

   In a perfect hedge, the impact is the same as ignoring the currency exposure in the US Treasury investment altogether. Filling out the standard deviations and correlations as above in the following formula gives

   $$\sigma_p = \sqrt{w_1^2\sigma_1^2 + w_2^2\sigma_2^2 + 2w_1w_2\rho_{12}\sigma_1\sigma_2}.$$

   $$\sigma_p = \sqrt{(0.6^2 \times 0.132^2) + (0.4^2 \times 0.040^2) + 2 \times 0.6 \times 0.4 \times (-0.32) \times 0.132 \times 0.040}.$$

   $\sigma_p = 0.0757 \approx 7.6\%$.

   This compares to 8.4% risk in the unhedged portfolio, a substantial reduction of risk.

2. Does the decision to 100% hedge the foreign exchange exposure have any consequences for the expected return on the hedged portfolio relative to the unhedged portfolio?

   Solution

   The forward price of the currency will play a role in the return expected on the hedged portfolio. The forward price of USD in GBP is 0.7038, which is 0.03% lower than the spot price today. Because you hedge 40% of current portfolio value, the impact on your expected return is 40% × −0.03%, reducing the hedged portfolio return to 3.87% = 3.9% − 0.03%.

> 3. Will the proposed transaction eliminate all currency risk associated with the US Treasury investment?
>
> **Solution**
>
> No, unfortunately not. As time progresses, the US Treasury investment will fluctuate in value and by the end of the tenor of the forward contract will be worth less or more in USD than the amount of USD you have sold. You have ended up under- or overhedged. In fact, because you expect the value of your investment to increase with your expected return (minus cash distributions), it is logical to expect to be underhedged. The amount to which you are under- or overhedged is subject to currency risk. The risk of being under- or overhedged can be managed by comparing, at regular intervals, the notional value of the forward position with the value of the investment and correct the hedge as required. The decision on how often to evaluate this is a trade-off between costs (monitoring costs, transaction costs) and risk.

The other type of derivative is a contingent claim, which is commonly known as an option. An option is a contract between two parties that gives one party the right to buy or sell an underlying asset or to pay or receive a known underlying rate. An option takes the form of either a call option, which provides the right to buy the underlying or to pay a known rate, or a put option, which provides the right to sell the underlying or to receive a known rate.

With a forward commitment, both parties are mutually obligated to each other. Because an option grants the right, but not the obligation, to one party, that party has an advantage over the other. Consequently, that party, the buyer of the option, must pay cash, called the premium, to the seller of the option at the start of the contract. Once the premium is paid, the option buyer has no further obligation. He can either exercise the option or he can let the option expire unexercised. In the latter case, the option buyer incurs a loss equal to the premium. If the option is a call and it is exercised, the buyer pays the fixed price or rate and receives the underlying. If the option is a put and it is exercised, the buyer receives the fixed price or rate and delivers the underlying.[26] If the buyer of the option does exercise it, he may achieve a gain that exceeds the premium paid but the gain could also be less than the premium paid, thereby resulting in a net overall loss. An option buyer could be using the option to speculate on an upward move in the underlying if a call or downward move if a put. Alternatively, the option buyer could be hedging. In the example used earlier for forward commitments, the corporate treasurer anticipating an inflow of cash in a foreign currency could buy a put option to sell that currency, thereby converting it into his domestic cash flow at a known fixed rate. The option gives the treasurer the flexibility to not exercise it if the underlying currency rises in value. This flexibility comes at the cost of having to pay a premium at the start of the transaction, thus shifting the financial outcome across the entire probability distribution of that uncertain currency rate. In contrast, with the forward contract, the treasurer does not have to pay cash at the start but is obligated to convert at the agreed-upon rate.

Derivatives can be created in public forums, such as on derivatives exchanges, or privately between two parties. On derivatives exchanges, there are a large number of individual and institutional traders that make markets in derivatives. For private derivatives transactions, there is an extensive market of large bank and non-bank dealers willing to buy and sell derivatives. In both types of markets, these dealers assume the risk of being transferred from parties who originate the transactions. These dealers

---

[26] Instead of one party delivering the underlying, some options call for settlement in cash of an equivalent amount. Some forward commitments also settle in cash.

almost always restructure and transfer some portion, if not all, of the risk by finding other parties that are willing to take on that risk. Ultimately, the risk is assumed by some party willing to accept the risk, producing an economically efficient outcome for all parties.

How to Choose Which Method for Modifying Risk

Choosing which risk mitigation method to use—risk prevention and avoidance, self-insuring, risk transfer, or risk shifting—is a critical part of the risk management process. Fortunately, the methods are not mutually exclusive, and many organizations use all methods to some extent. No single method provides a clear-cut advantage over the others. As with all decisions, the trade-off is one of costs versus benefits that are weighed in light of the risk tolerance of the organization or individual.

For example, many companies that have extensive foreign operations and are, therefore, highly exposed to exchange rate risk, hedge that risk using derivatives. Some companies prefer forwards, some prefer swaps, some prefer options, and some use multiple instruments. Some companies attempt to hedge currency risk by setting up operations in foreign countries rather than manufacturing domestically and shipping the goods to foreign countries.[27] Some companies manage their currency risk by attempting to balance currency assets and liabilities. Some airlines hedge the risk of oil price changes and others do not. Some airlines that do hedge this risk do so to a far greater degree than others. Additionally, some prefer the certainty of forwards and swaps, whereas others prefer the flexibility of options, even with the up-front cost that options require. Most insurance companies rely on their actuarial knowledge but supplement it with proactive measures, such as selling risk to other parties.

To the extent possible, most organizations should avoid risks that provide few benefits and potentially extreme costs. Reasonable, low-cost precautions against risks with few benefits should always be taken. Thus, risk prevention and risk avoidance are probably the first choice of measures, especially for risks that lie outside the core competencies of the organization and have little reasonable expectation of adding value. Nonetheless, avoidance may not be the best value for its cost. Moreover, avoiding risk may mean avoiding opportunity. Thus, an organization often cannot simply decide not to take a risk, at least not for all undesirable risks.

Organizations that have large amounts of free cash flow may choose to self-insure some risks, but few organizations have so much cash that they can afford to self-insure all risks. Some risks can potentially imperil the entire capital base. Most companies would, however, prefer to self-insure to the extent possible because self-insurance reduces the costs associated with external monitoring and gives the organization the greatest flexibility. Self-insurance and avoidance should generally be clearly addressed at the governance level and be consistent with stated risk tolerance.

Risk transfer, or the use of insurance, is a widely used risk management tactic, but it may not be suitable for many types of risks. Some risks simply are not insurable, at least not in a cost-effective way. Insurance works best when risks can be pooled, and that is not the case for many types of risks, particularly those that can affect a large number of parties at the same time. The use of risk shifting tools, such as derivatives, may not be available for all types of risks, thus limiting their use in risk mitigation. For financial risks that exceed risk appetite, risk shifting is a very common choice.

---

27 Here is another example of the interactions of risks. A decision to manufacture products in a foreign country involves trade-offs between exchange rate risk, political risk, and a variety of other risks germane to that country's economy, not to mention a potentially different degree of operational risk, in the pursuit of higher profits.

Risk Modification: Transferring, Shifting, and How To Choose

The various risk management methods are not equal in terms of the risk reduction and the risk profile that remains. For example, contingent claims, such as insurance, provide the flexibility in the form of offering opportunity to profit in one direction and have a loss reduced in the other, but they require payment of cash up front. In contrast, forward commitments lock in an outcome. In other words, they provide little flexibility, but they require no cash payment up front. The risk profile that exists when a contingent claim hedge is put in place differs significantly from the risk profile that exists when a forward commitment hedge is placed. This process requires significant understanding and discussion at all levels of the organization.

To recap, risk takers should identify risks that offer few rewards in light of potential costs and avoid those risks when possible. They should self-insure where it makes sense and diversify to the extent possible. They should consider insurance when risks can be pooled effectively if the cost of the insurance is less than the expected benefit. If derivatives are used, they must consider the trade-off of locking in outcomes with forward commitments versus the flexibility relative to cash cost of contingent claims, which can tailor the desired outcomes or payoffs by shifting the risk. Ultimately, the decision is always one of balancing costs against benefits while producing a risk profile that is consistent with the risk management objectives of the organization.

EXAMPLE 5

Measuring and Modifying Risk

1. From the perspective of an organization, which of the following *best* describes risk drivers?
   - **A.** A. The probabilities of adverse events
   - **B.** B. The statistical methods that measure risk
   - **C.** C. Factors that influence macroeconomies and industries

   Solution

   C is correct. Risks (and risk drivers) arise from fundamental factors in macroeconomies and industries.

2. Which of the following concepts directly measures the risk of derivatives?
   - **A.** A. Probability
   - **B.** B. Delta and gamma
   - **C.** C. Beta and standard deviation

   Solution

   B is correct. Delta and gamma are measures of the movement in an option price, given a movement in the underlying. The other answers can reflect some elements of derivatives risk, but they are not direct measures of the risk.

3. The *best* definition of value at risk is:
   - **A.** A. the expected loss if a counterparty defaults.
   - **B.** B. the maximum loss an organization would expect to incur over a holding period.

C. the minimum loss expected over a holding period a certain percentage of the time.

Solution

C is correct. VaR measures a minimum loss expected over a holding period a certain percentage of the time. It is not an expected loss, nor does it reflect the maximum possible loss, which is the entire equity of the organization.

4. Which of the following are methods commonly used to supplement VaR to measure the risk of extreme events?

   A. A. Standard deviation
   B. B. Loss given default
   C. C. Scenario analysis and stress testing

   Solution

   C is correct. Scenario analysis and stress testing both examine the performance of a portfolio subject to extreme events. The other two answers are metrics used in portfolio analysis but are not typically associated with extreme events.

5. Which of the following is a true statement about insurable risks?

   A. A. Insurable risks are less costly.
   B. B. Insurable risks have smaller loss limits.
   C. C. Insurable risks are typically diversifiable by the insurer.

   Solution

   C is correct. Insurance works by pooling risks. It is not necessarily less costly than derivatives nor does it have lower loss limits.

SUMMARY

Success in business and investing requires the skillful selection and management of risks. A well-developed risk management process ties together an organization's goals, strategic competencies, and tools to create value to help it both thrive and survive. Good risk management results in better decision making and a keener assessment of the many important trade-offs in business and investing, helping managers maximize value.

- Risk and risk management are critical to good business and investing. Risk management is *not* only about avoiding risk.
- Taking risk is an active choice by boards and management, investment managers, and individuals. Risks must be understood and carefully chosen and managed.
- Risk exposure is the extent to which an organization's value may be affected through sensitivity to underlying risks.
- Risk management is a process that defines risk tolerance and measures, monitors, and modifies risks to be in line with that tolerance.

- A risk management framework is the infrastructure, processes, and analytics needed to support effective risk management; it includes risk governance, risk identification and measurement, risk infrastructure, risk policies and processes, risk mitigation and management, communication, and strategic risk analysis and integration.
- Risk governance is the top-level foundation for risk management, including risk oversight and setting risk tolerance for the organization.
- Risk identification and measurement is the quantitative and qualitative assessment of all potential sources of risk and the organization's risk exposures.
- Risk infrastructure comprises the resources and systems required to track and assess the organization's risk profile.
- Risk policies and processes are management's complement to risk governance at the operating level.
- Risk mitigation and management is the active monitoring and adjusting of risk exposures, integrating all the other factors of the risk management framework.
- Communication includes risk reporting and active feedback loops so that the risk process improves decision making.
- Strategic risk analysis and integration involves using these risk tools to rigorously sort out the factors that are and are not adding value as well as incorporating this analysis into the management decision process, with the intent of improving outcomes.
- Employing a risk management committee, along with a chief risk officer (CRO), are hallmarks of a strong risk governance framework.
- Governance and the entire risk process should take an enterprise risk management perspective to ensure that the value of the entire enterprise is maximized.
- Risk tolerance, a key element of good risk governance, delineates which risks are acceptable, which are unacceptable, and how much risk the overall organization can be exposed to.
- Risk budgeting is any means of allocating investments or assets by their risk characteristics.
- Financial risks are those that arise from activity in the financial markets.
- Non-financial risks arise from actions within an organization or from external origins, such as the environment, the community, regulators, politicians, suppliers, and customers.
- Financial risks consist of market risk, credit risk, and liquidity risk.
- Market risk arises from movements in stock prices, interest rates, exchange rates, and commodity prices.
- Credit risk is the risk that a counterparty will not pay an amount owed.
- Liquidity risk is the risk that, as a result of degradation in market conditions or the lack of market participants, one will be unable to sell an asset without lowering the price to less than the fundamental value.
- Non-financial risks consist of a variety of risks, including settlement risk, legal risk, regulatory risk, accounting risk, tax risk, model risk, tail risk, and operational risk.

- Operational risk is the risk that arises either from within the operations of an organization or from external events that are beyond the control of the organization but affect its operations. Operational risk can be caused by employees, the weather and natural disasters, vulnerabilities of IT systems, or terrorism.

- Solvency risk is the risk that the organization does not survive or succeed because it runs out of cash to meet its financial obligations.

- Individuals face many of the same organizational risks outlined here but also face health risk, mortality or longevity risk, and property and casualty risk.

- Risks are not necessarily independent because many risks arise as a result of other risks; risk interactions can be extremely non-linear and harmful.

- Risk drivers are the fundamental global and domestic macroeconomic and industry factors that create risk.

- Common measures of risk include standard deviation or volatility; asset-specific measures, such as beta or duration; derivative measures, such as delta, gamma, vega, and rho; and tail measures such as value at risk, CVaR and expected loss given default.

- Risk can be modified by prevention and avoidance, risk transfer (insurance), or risk shifting (derivatives).

- Risk can be mitigated internally through self-insurance or diversification.

- The primary determinants of which method is best for modifying risk are the benefits weighed against the costs, with consideration for the overall final risk profile and adherence to risk governance objectives.

PRACTICE PROBLEMS

1. Risk management in the case of individuals is *best* described as concerned with:
   A. hedging risk exposures.
   B. maximizing utility while bearing a tolerable level of risk.
   C. maximizing utility while avoiding exposure to undesirable risks.

2. Which of the following may be controlled by an investor?
   A. Risk
   B. Raw returns
   C. Risk-adjusted returns

3. The process of risk management includes:
   A. minimizing risk.
   B. maximizing returns.
   C. defining and measuring risks being taken.

4. The factors a risk management framework should address include all of the following *except*:
   A. communications.
   B. policies and processes.
   C. names of responsible individuals.

5. Which of the following *best* describes activities that are supported by a risk management infrastructure?
   A. Risk tolerance, budgeting, and reporting
   B. Risk tolerance, measurement, and monitoring
   C. Risk identification, measurement, and monitoring

6. Risk governance:
   A. aligns risk management activities with the goals of the overall enterprise.
   B. defines the qualitative assessment and evaluation of potential sources of risk in an organization.
   C. delegates responsibility for risk management to all levels of the organization's hierarchy.

7. Effective risk governance in an enterprise provides guidance on all of the following *except*:
   A. unacceptable risks.
   B. worst losses that may be tolerated.

C. specific methods to mitigate risk for each subsidiary in the enterprise.

8. A firm's risk management committee would be expected to do all of the following *except*:
   A. approving the governing body's proposed risk policies.
   B. deliberating the governing body's risk policies at the operational level.
   C. providing top decision-makers with a forum for considering risk management issues.

9. Once an enterprise's risk tolerance is determined, the role of risk management is to:
   A. analyze risk drivers.
   B. align risk exposures with risk appetite.
   C. identify the extent to which the enterprise is willing to fail in meeting its objectives.

10. Which factor should *most* affect a company's ability to tolerate risk?
    A. A stable market environment
    B. The beliefs of the individual board members
    C. The ability to dynamically respond to adverse events

11. Which of the following is the correct sequence of events for risk governance and management that focuses on the entire enterprise? Establishing:
    A. risk tolerance, then risk budgeting, and then risk exposures.
    B. risk exposures, then risk tolerance, and then risk budgeting.
    C. risk budgeting, then risk exposures, and then risk tolerance.

12. Risk budgeting includes all of the following *except*:
    A. determining the target return.
    B. quantifying tolerable risk by specific metrics.
    C. allocating a portfolio by some risk characteristics of the investments.

13. A benefit of risk budgeting is that it:
    A. considers risk tradeoffs.
    B. establishes a firm's risk tolerance.
    C. reduces uncertainty facing the firm.

14. Which of the following risks is *best* described as a financial risk?
    A. Credit
    B. Solvency
    C. Operational

Practice Problems

15. Liquidity risk is *most* associated with:
    A. the probability of default.
    B. a widening bid–ask spread.
    C. a poorly functioning market.

16. An example of a non-financial risk is:
    A. market risk.
    B. liquidity risk.
    C. settlement risk.

17. If a company has a one-day 5% Value at Risk of $1 million, this means:
    A. 5% of the time the firm is expected to lose at least $1 million in one day.
    B. 95% of the time the firm is expected to lose at least $1 million in one day.
    C. 5% of the time the firm is expected to lose no more than $1 million in one day.

18. An organization choosing to accept a risk exposure may:
    A. buy insurance.
    B. enter into a derivative contract.
    C. establish a reserve fund to cover losses.

19. The choice of risk-modification method is based on:
    A. minimizing risk at the lowest cost.
    B. maximizing returns at the lowest cost.
    C. weighing costs versus benefits in light of the organization's risk tolerance.

SOLUTIONS

1. B is correct. For individuals, risk management concerns maximizing utility while taking risk consistent with individual's level of risk tolerance.

2. A is correct. Many decision makers focus on return, which is not something that is easily controlled, as opposed to risk, or exposure to risk, which may actually be managed or controlled

3. C is correct. Risks need to be defined and measured so as to be consistent with the organization's chosen level of risk tolerance and target for returns or other outcomes.

4. C is correct. While risk infrastructure, which a risk management framework must address, refers to the people and systems required to track risk exposures, there is no requirement to actually name the responsible individuals.

5. C is correct. *Risk infrastructure* refers to the people and systems required to track risk exposures and perform most of the quantitative risk analysis to allow an assessment of the organization's risk profile. The risk management infrastructure identifies, measures, and monitors risks (among other things).

6. A is correct. Risk governance is the top-down process that defines risk tolerance, provides risk oversight and guidance to align risk with enterprise goals.

7. C is correct. Risk governance is not about specifying methods to mitigate risk at the business line level. Rather, it is about establishing an appropriate level of risk for the entire enterprise. Specifics of dealing with risk fall under risk management and the risk infrastructure framework.

8. A is correct. The risk management committee is a part of the risk governance structure at the operational level—as such, it does not approve the governing body's policies.

9. B is correct. When risk tolerance has been determined, the risk framework should be geared toward measuring, managing, and complying with the risk tolerance, or aligning risk exposure with risk tolerance. The risk tolerance decision begins by looking at what shortfalls within an organization would cause it to fail to achieve some critical goals and what are the organization's risk drivers.

10. C is correct. If a company has the ability to adapt quickly to adverse events may allow for a higher risk tolerance. There are other factors, such as beliefs of board members and a stable market environment, which may but should not affect risk tolerance.

11. A is correct. In establishing a risk management system, determining risk tolerance must happen before specific risks can be accepted or reduced. Risk tolerance defines the appetite for risk. Risk budgeting determine how or where the risk is taken and quantifies the tolerable risk by specific metrics. Risk exposures can then be measured and compared against the acceptable risk.

12. A is correct. Risk budgeting does not include determining the target return. Risk budgeting quantifies and allocates the tolerable risk by specific metrics.

13. A is correct. The process of risk budgeting forces the firm to consider risk tradeoffs. As a result, the firm should choose to invest where the return per unit

Solutions

of risk is the highest.

14. A is correct. A financial risk originates from the financial markets. Credit risk is one of three financial risks identified in the reading: Credit risk is the chance of loss due to an outside party defaulting on an obligation. Solvency risk depends at least in part on factors internal to the organization and operational risk is an *internal* risk arising from the people and processes within the organization.

15. B is correct. Liquidity risk is also called transaction cost risk. When the bid–ask spread widens, purchase and sale transactions become increasingly costly. The risk arises from the uncertainty of the spread.

16. C is correct. Settlement risk is related to default risk but deals with the timing of payments rather than the risk of default.

17. A is correct. The VaR measure indicates the probability of a loss of at least a certain level in a time period.

18. C is correct. Risk acceptance is similar to self-insurance. An organization choosing to self-insure may set up a reserve fund to cover losses. Buying insurance is a form of risk transfer and using derivatives is a form of risk-shifting, not risk acceptance.

19. C is correct. Among the risk-modification methods of risk avoidance, risk acceptance, risk transfer, and risk shifting none has a clear advantage. One must weigh benefits and costs in light of the firm's risk tolerance when choosing the method to use.

LEARNING MODULE 4

Technical Analysis

by Aksel Kibar, CMT, Barry M. Sine, and Robert A. Strong, PhD, CFA.

Aksel Kibar, CMT, is at Tech Charts Research & Trading (Bulgaria). Barry M. Sine is at Drexel Hamilton, LLC (USA). Robert A. Strong, PhD, CFA, is at the University of Maine (USA).

LEARNING OUTCOME	
Mastery	The candidate should be able to:
☐	explain principles and assumptions of technical analysis
☐	describe potential links between technical analysis and behavioral finance
☐	compare principles of technical analysis and fundamental analysis
☐	describe and interpret different types of technical analysis charts
☐	explain uses of trend, support, and resistance lines
☐	explain common chart patterns
☐	explain common technical indicators
☐	describe principles of intermarket analysis
☐	explain technical analysis applications to portfolio management

INTRODUCTION

Technical analysis has been used by traders, analysts, and investors for centuries and has achieved broad acceptance among regulators and the academic community—particularly with regard to its behavioral finance aspects. This reading gives a brief overview of the field, compares technical analysis with other schools of analysis, and describes some of the main tools used in technical analysis. Although technical analysis follows predefined rules and principles, the interpretation of results is generally subjective. That is, although certain aspects, such as the calculation of indicators, follow specific rules, the interpretation of findings is often based on a melding of techniques that suit the style and approach of the individual analyst. In this respect, technical analysis is similar to fundamental analysis, which has specific rules for calculating ratios, for example, but introduces increased subjectivity in the evaluation phase.

2. PRINCIPLES, ASSUMPTIONS, AND LINKS TO INVESTMENT ANALYSIS

- [ ] explain principles and assumptions of technical analysis
- [ ] describe potential links between technical analysis and behavioral finance
- [ ] compare principles of technical analysis and fundamental analysis

VIGNETTE

Scene 1

You are a portfolio analyst working at a small sovereign wealth fund (SWF) and reporting to the Deputy Chief Investment Officer (CIO). The SWF has recently implemented an investment in GLD for the purposes of improving the risk-adjusted return of the portfolio. This asset allocation decision was based on extensive analysis and agreed on by the CIO, Head of Risk, Head of Alternative Investments, and other members of the Investment Committee. The benefits of adding gold to the portfolio are due to the low correlation gold has with other asset classes in the portfolio.

The Deputy CIO is on a well-deserved sabbatical for several weeks in Antarctica and left you in charge of monitoring the portfolio. You are looking forward to the opportunity to "be in charge" but also hope that there will be no major decisions to make during this time.

Since the investment in GLD is new, you decide to take a look at gold prices and create a basic graph. You prepare a chart that shows the performance of GLD since the start of the year. The purchase price is the blue point, and the current price is the red point. **You realize that the price of GLD is now below the purchase price.**

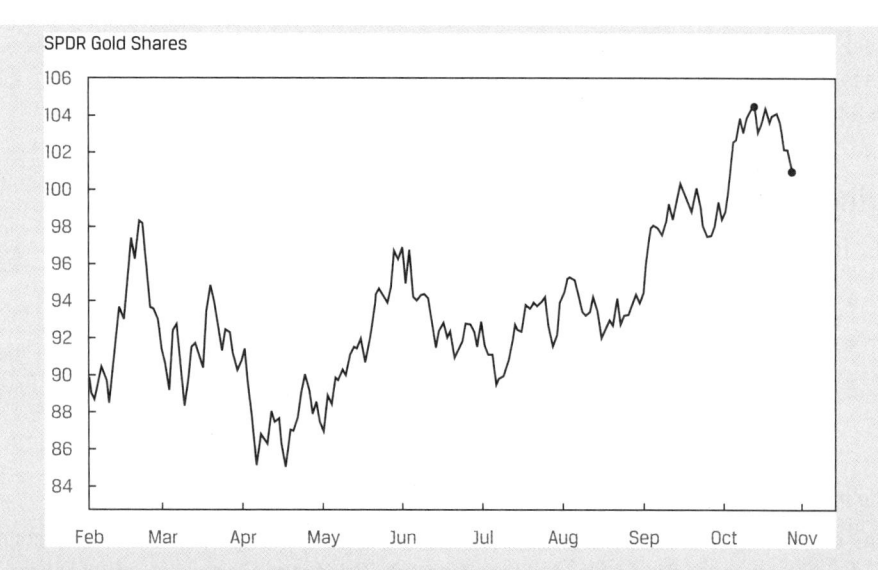

Principles, Assumptions, and links to Investment Analysis

[Chart: SPDR Gold Shares, showing prices from approximately 84 to 106 between Feb and Nov]

There is a knock on the door. The Head of Risk comes into your office and says, *"The price of gold is now below our purchase price. You're in charge of this position, right? Maybe we should sell now to avoid a bigger loss?"*

You respond to the Head of Risk by saying, *"Let's not panic. After all, the decision to invest in gold was not a short-term decision but a long-term asset allocation decision. We should not fall into the behavioral finance trap of letting fear guide our decisions."*

The Head of Risk leaves your office. You look at the chart again, and you begin to worry. *Maybe we should sell?* You decide to ask the Technical Analyst to prepare a chart and share her thoughts.

Technical analysis is a form of security analysis that uses price and volume data, often graphically displayed, in decision making. Technical analysis can be applied to securities in any freely traded market around the globe. A freely traded market is one in which willing buyers trade with willing sellers without external intervention or impediment. Prices are the result of the interaction of supply and demand in real time. Technical analysis allows us to see a battle between buyers and sellers, along with subtle clues as to which side may be winning. Technical analysis is used on a wide range of financial instruments, including equities, bonds, commodity futures, currency futures, and cryptocurrencies.

The underlying logic of technical analysis is simple:

- Supply and demand determine prices.
- Changes in supply and demand—both in price level and volume—cause changes in prices.
- Past price action can be used to anticipate and project potential future prices with charts and other technical tools.

Basic technical analysis of any financial instrument does not require detailed knowledge of that instrument. As long as the chart represents the action in a freely traded market, a technician does not even need to know the name or type of the security to conduct the analysis. Technical analysis can also be applied over any time frame—from short-term price movements to long-term movements of annual closing prices. Trends that are apparent in short-term charts may also appear over longer time frames. While technical analysis is ideal for short-term trading decisions or tactical asset allocation decisions, long-term chart analysis can add value regarding strategic asset allocation or long-term investment decisions. Looking at recurring technical clues on multiple time intervals (monthly, weekly, daily, 60-minute charts, etc.) can be a particularly useful technique.

Principles and Assumptions

The three main principles of technical analysis are as follows:

- The market discounts everything.
- Prices move in trends and countertrends.
- Price action creates certain patterns that tend to reoccur and may be cyclical.

The market discounts everything.

One of the biggest assumptions in technical analysis is that price already reflects all known factors impacting a financial instrument. This form of analysis assumes that at any point in time, a stock's price is a reflection of everything that affects the organization, including fundamental factors, such as the balance sheet, the income statement, the cash flow, and the management team. Technical analysis also considers broader economic factors and market psychology to be reflected in pricing.

Prices move in trends and countertrends.

The second assumption in technical analysis is that prices follow trends, which move directionally—upward, downward, sideways, or in a combination of these directions. Once a trend is recognized, the expectation is that any future movement in the price of the asset will follow that trend rather than go against it. A trend in motion is more likely to continue than to reverse. An important corollary is that a trend in motion will continue until it reverses. Indeed, a common saying among technical analysts is, "The trend is your friend."

Price action is repetitive, and certain patterns tend to reoccur.

The repetition of price movements, according to technical analysts, is due to market psychology. News is constantly bombarding assets, and how markets react depends upon the technical setup of the market at the time such news hits. News is always important, but the value of any news depends upon the initial market psychology. Because the behavior of investors repeats itself, price movements can be charted, allowing technicians to recognize patterns.

Technical Analysis and Behavioral Finance

Technical analysis can be thought of as the study of collective investor psychology or sentiment and thus has a direct connection with behavioral finance. Prices in any freely traded market are set by human beings or their automated proxies (such as computerized trading programs), and a price is set at the equilibrium between supply and demand at any given instant. The role of a good technician is to monitor and evaluate the subtle clues in this battle between supply and demand—much like a doctor looking at a patient for subtle clues to that patient's overall health. Various fundamental theorists have proposed that markets are efficient and rational, but technicians believe that humans are often irrational and emotional and that they tend to behave similarly in similar circumstances. The reason chart patterns have predictive value is that they are graphic representations of human trading activity and human behavior is frequently repeated, especially trading activity that is driven by fear (in market sell-offs) or greed (as evidenced in bubbles—that is, rallies that extend well beyond valuation levels derived from fundamental data). In bubbles, investors, driven by hope and greed, push the price of an asset to irrationally high levels, in the expectation that other buyers will be willing to pay an even higher price for the asset. The resulting chart patterns are analyzed and identified by analysts, traders, and investors for decision-making purposes.

Although fundamental data are key inputs for the determination of value, these data are analyzed by humans, who may be driven, at least partially, by motivations that are not rational. Human behavior is often erratic and driven by emotion in many aspects of one's life, so technicians conclude that it is unreasonable to believe that investing is the one exception where humans always behave rationally. Technicians believe that market trends and patterns reflect this irrational human behavior, which can be seen on price charts in the form of volatile price action, such as major sell-offs or strong buying resulting in parabolic advances. Technical analysis is the study of market trends and patterns. And because trends and patterns tend to repeat themselves, they are potentially identifiable and predictable. So, technicians rely on recognition of patterns that have occurred in the past to project future patterns of security prices.

Another tenet of technical analysis is that the market reflects the collective knowledge and sentiment of the many different participants responsible for the buying and selling activity in a particular security. In a freely traded market, only those market participants who actually buy or sell a security have an impact on its price. And the greater the volume of a participant's trades, the more impact that market participant will tend to have on price. Technical analysis relies on market participants that are taking a directional bet in the market and thereby influencing price and volume. Without trading, there will be no meaningful price fluctuations.

Trades determine volume and price. The impact of a trade occurs instantaneously and frequently anticipates or foreshadows fundamental developments. So, by studying market technical data—price and volume trends—the technician is seeking to understand investor sentiment and to detect any fundamental change that is already transpiring behind the scenes or may shortly transpire. The technician benefits from the wide range of knowledge of market participants and their collective conclusion about a security. In contrast, the fundamental analyst must wait for the release of financial statements to conduct financial statement analysis, so a time lag occurs between the market's activities and the analyst's conclusions. Technicians may therefore be ahead of fundamental analysts in their positioning.

Technical analysts believe that human behavior plays a role in the fluctuation of security prices. Investors with a favorable fundamental view may nonetheless sell a financial instrument for other reasons, including pessimistic investor sentiment, margin calls, and a need for capital. Technicians do not care why market participants are buying or selling, just that they are doing so: These actions move prices, forming trends the technician can profit from. Technical moves happen for both fundamental and behavioral reasons.

Some financial instruments have an associated income stream that contributes to the security's intrinsic value. Bonds have regular coupon payments, and equity shares may have underlying cash flows or dividend streams. A fundamental analyst can adjust these cash flows for risk and use standard time value of money techniques to determine a present value. Other assets, such as bushels of wheat, gallons of crude oil, and ounces of silver, do not have underlying financial statements or an income stream, so valuation models cannot be used to derive their fundamental intrinsic values. For these assets, technical analysis may be particularly valuable. So, whereas fundamental analysis is widely used for fixed-income and equity securities, technical analysis is widely used for commodities, currencies, and futures.

Market participants attempt to anticipate economic developments and enter into trades to profit from them. Technicians believe that security price movements occur before fundamental developments unfold—and certainly before they are reported. This belief may be supported by the fact that stock prices are 1 of the 12 components of the National Bureau of Economic Research's index of leading economic indicators.

Market microstructure

Market microstructure deals with issues of market structure and design, price formation, price discovery, transaction and timing costs, information and disclosure, and investor behavior. It is the process by which buyers find sellers as well as the venues where they meet. The National Bureau of Economic Research (NBER) defines market microstructure as a field of study that is devoted to theoretical, empirical, and experimental research on the economics of security markets. Elements of market microstructure may include minimum tick increments and algorithmic execution interfaces. The field of market microstructure aims to establish connections between activity over the fast-moving short term and the properties that emerge over longer time frames. In this way, market microstructure is a bottom-up approach to understanding financial markets. The recording and analysis of high-quality data that describe the actions and interactions of market participants in the very short term has revealed striking regularities that challenge many theories regarding financial markets.

Market microstructure considers different order types. Every exchange will specify the types of orders that are allowed and how these orders may interact with each other. Some of the important order types are market order, limit order, stop order, good till canceled order, and day order. But hybrid algorithmic orders are also possible and are increasingly prevalent in modern electronic markets (e.g., an order to "participate at 30% of all volume up to a given price limit" or a time-dependent "buy stop close only" order). When placed in the market, orders will have priority depending on such factors as price, time, and size. Buyers with higher bids will have priority over buyers with lower bids. Similarly, sellers with lower asks will have priority over sellers with higher asks. Market orders are executed before limit orders. Orders placed earlier are executed before later orders.

Most trade models assume the presence of both liquidity traders and information traders. Liquidity traders' decisions to buy or sell securities (e.g., for portfolio rebalancing or market making) are assumed to be unrelated to the arrival of new information. Conversely, information traders are cognizant of new information before other market participants during any given trading period. In other words, they have superior knowledge of a security's true equilibrium price. Information traders will buy/sell securities when they can exploit their advantage profitably.

Liquidity traders can be high-frequency traders or market makers on major trading desks. They buy and sell in a tight bid–ask spread with the aim of profiting from small price fluctuations.

Information traders buy and sell because they believe they have sufficient information to predict the next move in a market and thus to beat the market.

Technical Analysis and Fundamental Analysis

Both technical analysis and fundamental analysis are useful and valid, but they approach the market in different ways. Technicians focus solely on analyzing markets and the trading of financial instruments. Fundamental analysis is a much wider field, encompassing financial and economic analysis as well as analysis of societal and political trends. Technicians analyze market prices. A technician's analysis is derived solely from price and volume data, whereas a fundamental analyst studies a company, incorporating data that are external to the market, and then uses this analysis to predict security price movements. Technical analysis assumes that all of the factors considered by a fundamental analyst are reflected in the price of a financial instrument through buying and selling activity.

A key distinction between technical analysis and fundamental analysis is that the technician has more concrete data, primarily price and volume data, to work with. The financial statements analyzed by fundamental analysts do not contain objective data but rather are the result of numerous estimates and assumptions that have been combined to produce the various line items. Even the cash line on a balance sheet is subject to corporate management's opinion about which assets are liquid enough to be considered "cash." This opinion must be agreed to by auditors and, in many countries, regulators (who sometimes differ with the auditors). Financial statements are subject to restatement because of such issues as changes in accounting assumptions and even fraud. But the price and volume data used in technical analysis are objective. When the data are analyzed, both types of analysis become subjective because judgment is exercised when a technician analyzes a price chart and when a fundamental analyst analyzes an income statement. However, by assigning predefined rules and conditions to their techniques, technical analysts can become more objective.

Fundamental analysis can be considered the more theoretical approach because it seeks to determine the underlying long-term (or intrinsic) value of a security. Technical analysis can be considered the more practical approach because a technician studies the markets and financial instruments as they exist, even if trading activity appears, at times, to be irrational. Technicians seek to project the level at which a financial instrument *will* trade, whereas fundamental analysts seek to predict where it *should* trade.

A drawback of technical analysis is that technicians are limited to studying market movements and do not use other predictive analytical methods, such as interviewing the customers of a subject company to determine future demand for a company's products. Technicians study market trends and are mainly concerned with a security's price trend: Is the security trading up, down, or sideways? Trends are driven by collective investor psychology and generally change gradually, so that the trained technician can spot subtle shifts. However, markets can also change without warning. Additionally, it can take some time for a new trend to become evident. Thus, technicians may make wrong calls and have to change their opinions. Technicians are generally better at identifying market moves when the moves are already underway.

Moreover, trends and patterns must be in place for some time before they are recognizable, so a key shortcoming of technical analysis is that, try as it might to identify clues of an impending trend change, it typically still lags actual price data in such identification. This shortcoming mirrors a key shortcoming of fundamental analysis in that securities often overshoot fundamental fair values in an uptrend and undershoot fundamental fair values in a downtrend. Strictly relying on price targets obtained through fundamental analysis can lead to closing profitable investment positions too early because investors may irrationally bid security prices well above or well below intrinsic value.

Technical analysis and fundamental analysis can be seen as opposing approaches to analyzing securities, but in reality, many investors have experienced success by combining the two techniques. For example, an investor may use fundamental analysis to identify an undervalued stock and then use technical analysis to find specific entry and exit points for that position. Using fundamental and technical analysis together works well, for example, when a security is deemed fundamentally cheap but purchasing the security too early could prove costly. In this instance, technical analysis could help identify an attractive risk/reward entry point and moment in time to express the core fundamental view.

Some technical traders will look at fundamentals to support their trades as well. For example, a trader who is monitoring a **breakout** possibility near an earnings report may look at the fundamentals to get an idea of whether the stock is likely to beat earnings. A breakout refers to when the price of an asset moves above a resistance level.

A good example of a context in which technical analysis can be a superior tool to fundamental analysis is securities fraud. In such cases, fundamental analysts can continue to hold favorable views of a company's equity securities even as its share prices decline.

The Differences in Conducting/Interpreting Technical Analysis in Various Types of Markets

In general, technical analysis is a trading tool that requires liquidity, so it is best and most easily applied to liquid and deep markets. In other words, the use of technical analysis is limited in illiquid markets, where even modestly sized trades can have an inordinate impact on prices. For example, in considering a thinly traded American Depositary Receipt (ADR), analyzing the more heavily traded local security frequently yields a better analysis—without any potential currency-related distortions. **Gap openings** are more frequent in thinly traded securities and markets. A gap is an area of a chart where a security's price either rises or falls from the previous day's close with no trading occurring in between. A gap opening is the start of a new trading session with a gap.

Technical analysis can be applied to different asset classes, such as equities, commodities, and currencies. The success rate of technical analysis will depend on the nature of the price action in any asset class. Each market has its own character, and the role of the technician is to interpret—but not force—the technical evidence. With regard to equities, in many less-liquid frontier and emerging markets, local retail investors are active traders, whereas developed markets have a higher percentage of institutional investors.

Market participation (institutional vs. retail) can have an impact on technical analysis. The basic difference between retail and institutional investors is that retail investors tend to have less in-depth information (to be more naive) and to be more momentum-centric than institutional investors. As a result, retail investors may depend upon technical analysis and momentum trading somewhat more than institutional investors. Institutional investors also must have enough float/liquidity in a given stock to participate in scale, so are limited in their interest in micro-cap stocks with minimal liquidity. Strong trend periods are the result of inefficiencies, and inefficiencies can be more easily exploited in emerging and frontier markets.

Question 1

Which one of the statements below cannot be stated as a shortcoming of technical analysis?

- **a.** Technical analysts might be late in identifying a trend or pattern because they will require enough data to make a conclusion.
- **b.** Technical analysts might miss a buying opportunity because the fundamental fair value of a company undershoots in a downtrend.
- **c.** Technical analysis will have limited application in the case of an initial public offering (IPO).

Principles, Assumptions, and links to Investment Analysis

Answer: B. The technical analyst will analyze only the price and volume data. If the stock is in a downtrend, the technical analyst will avoid buying it until a new uptrend is established in the analyzed time frame. For that reason, even though a company is fundamentally cheap, the technical analyst will wait for a buy signal that's confirmed by a chart pattern.
A is not the correct answer because being required to wait for confirmation can be viewed as a shortcoming of technical analysis.
C is not the correct answer because an IPO lacks price data, which are required for conducting technical analysis. Not being able to apply technical analysis to securities with limited price history is a shortcoming of technical analysis.

Question 2

Given the behavioral aspects of financial markets, under which conditions and market environments can an investor/analyst apply technical analysis?

   a. Equity markets with poor liquidity and with limited participation
   b. Pegged currency markets
   c. Blue chip technology stocks trading on the NASDAQ Stock Market

Answer: C. For technical analysis to be applied with good results, a market or a stock should have enough participation. Technical analysis measures crowd psychology. An individual's decision making might be difficult to understand and analyze. However, several individuals acting together produce predictable behavior patterns. Crowd behavior is similar for humans around the world. This is why technical analysis can be applied to different markets as long as there is enough human interaction in the form of buying and selling.
A is not the correct answer because in the case of poor liquidity and limited participation, prices are subject to manipulation. Technical analysis is most effective when prices are determined by demand and supply in free markets.
B is not the correct answer because government intervention is the opposite of what we are looking for in terms of free markets. In such cases, technical analysis will have limited scope.

Question 3

Retail and institutional investors behave differently in the way they invest and trade. Which one of the statements below is NOT one of the basic differences between retail and institutional investors?

   a. Retail investors tend to have less in-depth information when compared to institutional investors.
   b. Retail investors require more float/liquidity in given stocks in order to participate when compared with institutional investors.
   c. Retail investors tends to be more momentum-centric than institutional investors.

Answer: B. Retail traders usually trade with smaller size and can more easily buy and sell shares in less-liquid stocks, such as small-cap and micro-cap stocks.
A is incorrect because it is one of the basic differences between retail and institutional investors. Retail investors typically have limited information, whereas institutional investors typically have dedicated research departments and/or access to significant information.
C is incorrect because it is one of the basic differences between retail and institutional investors. Retail investors are more apt to trade based on market movements and intuition, whereas institutional investors follow a more in-depth investment process.

3 CHART TYPES

- [ ] describe and interpret different types of technical analysis charts
- [ ] explain uses of trend, support, and resistance lines
- [ ] explain common chart patterns

VIGNETTE

Scene 2

The technical analyst tells you that she can happily provide perspective from a technical point of view. **She prepares the following chart:**

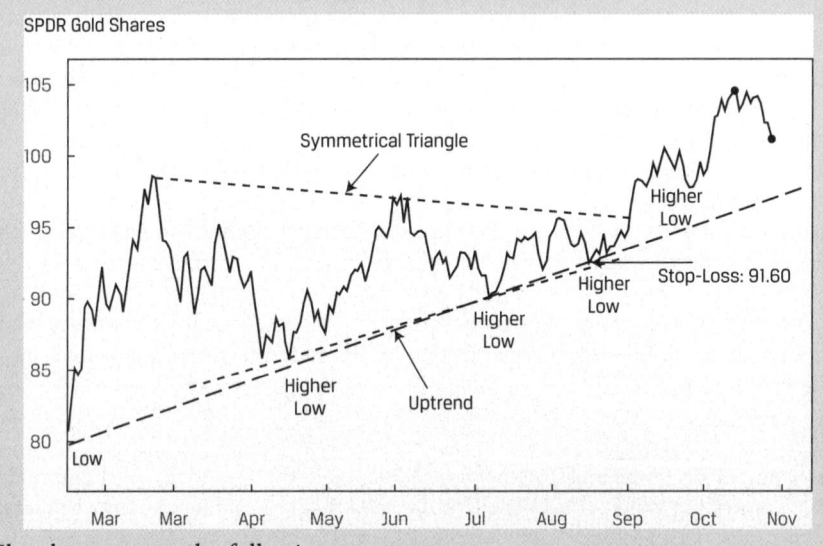

[Chart: SPDR Gold Shares price chart from Mar to Nov showing a Symmetrical Triangle pattern, an Uptrend line connecting Higher Lows, and a Stop-Loss level at 91.60. Price ranges from 80 to 105.]

She also prepares the following comments:

- Between February and September, the GLD price chart formed a symmetrical triangle chart pattern. The breakout took place in the beginning of September. Following the breakout, the price pulled back to the upper boundary of the chart pattern. The pullback offered an entry opportunity for those who missed the initial breakout in the beginning of September. Following the pullback, the GLD price resumed its upward movement in October.

- Since the beginning of the year, GLD has been in a steady uptrend. The uptrend can be seen in the higher lows. When the higher lows are connected with a trendline, a clear uptrend is visible.

- In late October, the price pulled back and put our long GLD position into an unrealized loss. However, the uptrend was not violated, nor was the chart pattern negated. The minor low at the 91.6 level inside the symmetrical triangle served as the protective stop-loss and the level at which the chart pattern would be negated.

Then she summarizes:

"So, even though the position shows an unrealized loss, there is no reason to change the positive outlook at this point in time."

You breathe a sigh of relief now that you have additional perspective.

The primary tools used in technical analysis are charts and indicators. Charts are a graphical display of price and volume data, and the display may be done in a number of ways. Charts are then subjected to various analyses, including the identification of trends and patterns. Before we discuss several concepts regarding charts, it is important to note that not all price data are suitable for technical analysis. Some instruments (whether equities, futures, commodities, FX, or cryptocurrencies) might not have enough interaction between buyers and sellers to produce meaningful price patterns. Other instruments might become illiquid over time, so that the principles of charting might no longer be applicable.

Types of Technical Analysis Charts

Charts are an essential component of the technical analyst's toolkit. Charts present information about past price behavior and provide a basis for inferring likely future price behavior. With the help of technology, we have access to financial data through a variety of charts. MetaStock and TradeStation are examples of technical charting and analysis software. A variety of charts can be useful in studying the markets. The selection of the chart to use in technical analysis is determined by the intended purpose of the analysis.

Advanced charting and trading software, utilizing artificial intelligence (AI), can help in simulating trading ideas or strategies as well as in **backtesting** results on historical price data. Backtesting is a method of assessing the viability of a trading strategy by showing how the strategy would play out using historical data.

Line Chart

Line charts are familiar to all types of analysts and are a simple graphic display of price trends over time. Line charts are typically drawn with closing prices as the data points. The vertical axis (y-axis) reflects price level, and the horizontal axis (x-axis) represents time. Even though the line chart is the simplest kind of chart, an analyst can quickly glean information from this representation of price data. In fact, line charts might be the most effective tool for analyzing price action because they show the closing price of the day, week, or month. The closing price is regarded by traders and investors as the most important data point, as it reflects the final decision for that period's transactions.

Exhibit 1 shows a quarterly chart of the FTSE 100 Index from 1984 through mid-2018. Up years and down years are clearly evident. The strong rally from 1984 through 1999 and the market decline from late 1999 to late 2002 are also clearly visible. The 2003–07 rally did not exceed the high reached in 1999, which suggests that investors were not willing to pay as high a price for stocks on the London Stock Exchange during that rally as they were in the prior rally. The 2007–09 decline didn't reach the lows of 2002, suggesting that investors viewed the prior recessionary period as a support level. From 2009 through mid-2018, the market was in a general uptrend with some pullback in 2015. This visual information in the price chart provides a broad overview of investor sentiment and can lead to further analysis. Importantly, the analyst can access and analyze this information quickly. Collecting and analyzing the full array of data normally incorporated in fundamental analysis would take much longer.

Exhibit 1: Line Chart: FTSE 100 Quarterly Price Data, 1984–mid-2018

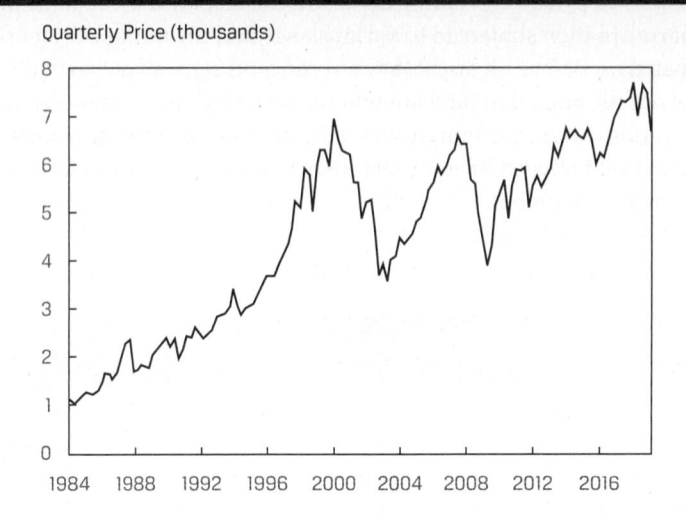

Bar Chart

A line chart has one data point per time interval. A **bar chart**, in contrast, has four bits of data in each entry—the high and low prices encountered during the time interval plus the opening and closing prices. Such charts can be constructed for any time period, but they are customarily constructed from daily data. Traders or investors focusing on longer-term analysis can choose to plot their price data on a weekly or monthly scale. How a chart is interpreted will not depend on its periodicity. However, to get the best results, the analyst/investor or trader should decide on the time frame of operation.

As Exhibit 2 shows, a vertical line connects the high and low prices of the day; a cross-hatch to the right indicates the closing price, and a cross-hatch to the left indicates the opening price. The appeal of this kind of chart is that the analyst immediately gets a sense of the nature of that day's trading. A short bar indicates little price movement during the day; that is, the high, low, and close are near the opening price. A long bar indicates a wide divergence between the high and the low for the day.

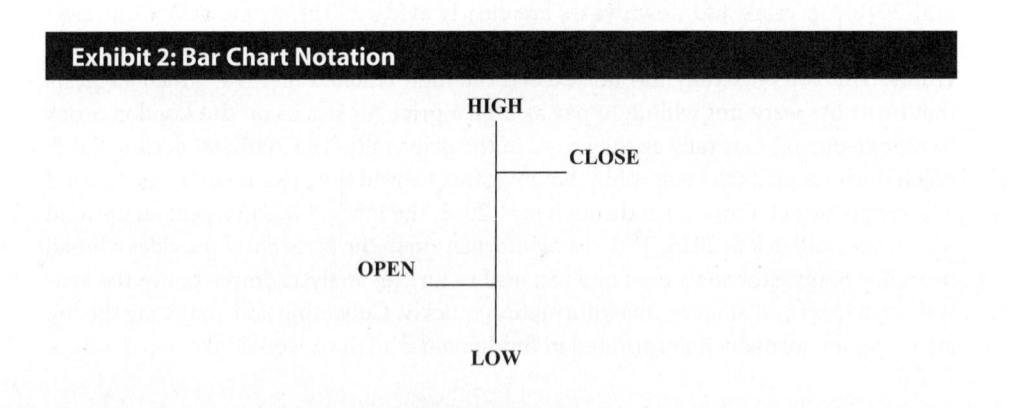

Exhibit 2: Bar Chart Notation

Exhibit 3 shows daily performance of the US dollar (USD) versus the Singapore dollar (SGD) spot FX from early 2018 through late 2018. As we will discuss in the latter sections of this reading, the analyst can identify an orderly, month-long consolidation between the 1.330 and 1.348 levels during the May–June period. Bar charts become

Chart Types

more important in the analysis of short-term price actions, where the identification of support and resistance levels makes a major difference in analysis and trading results. Spikes on the upside and on the downside will form support and resistance levels that can be seen only if the data are plotted as either a bar chart or a candlestick chart (to be discussed shortly). Exhibit 4 shows the same price data plotted as a line chart. With the line chart only, the analyst will not be able to capture the same consolidation period or clearly see the level at which the breakout opportunity will take place. Therefore, it is best to analyze price data that are subject to shorter-term trading by using either bar or candlestick charts.

Exhibit 3: Bar Chart: US Dollar/Singapore Dollar, January 2018–August 2018 (daily data)

Exhibit 4: Line Chart: US Dollar/Singapore Dollar, January 2018–August 2018 (daily data)

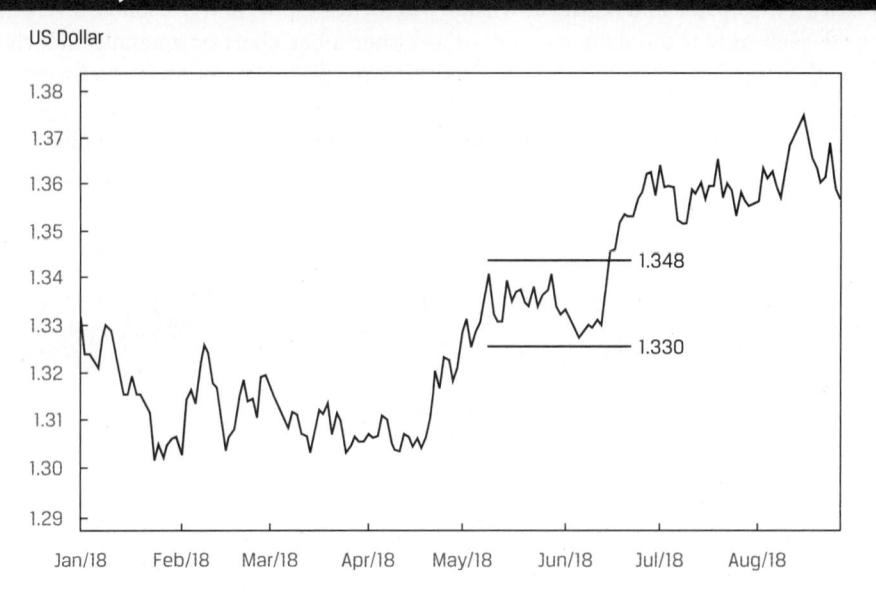

Candlestick Chart

Candlestick charts trace their roots to Japan, where technical analysis has been in use for centuries. Like a bar chart, a **candlestick chart** provides four prices per data point: the opening and closing prices and the high and low prices during the period. As shown in Exhibit 5, a vertical line represents the range through which the security price traveled during the time period. The line is known as the wick or shadow. The body of the candle is white (or clear) if the opening price was lower than the closing price, and the body of the candle is dark if the opening price was higher than the closing price.

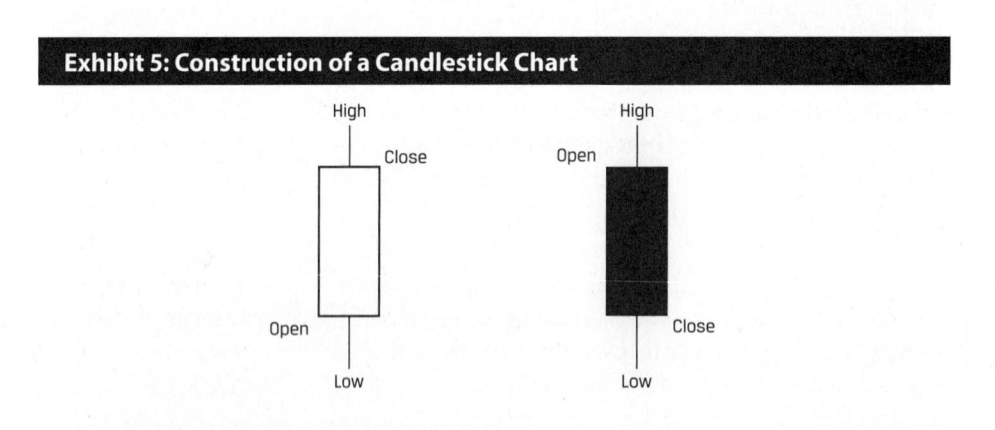

Exhibit 5: Construction of a Candlestick Chart

Exhibit 6 shows the US dollar/Singapore dollar daily price chart on a candlestick graph for the period 1 January through 13 July 2018.

Exhibit 6: Candlestick Chart: US Dollar/Singapore Dollar, 1 January–13 July 2018 (daily data)

The advantage of the candlestick chart over the bar chart is that price fluctuations are much more visible on the candlestick chart, which allows for better analysis. The bar chart indicates market volatility only by the height of each bar, but on candlestick charts, the difference between opening and closing prices and their relationship to the highs and lows of the day are clearly apparent. Long-legged candlesticks usually indicate the price finding support after meeting sellers during the day. We will discuss interpretation of candlestick chart patterns in subsequent sections. For now, we can highlight the importance of long shadows. In the Japanese terminology used in candlestick charting, one of the widely traded and analyzed candlestick patterns is called a **doji**. The doji signifies that after a full day of trading, the positive price influence of buyers and the negative price influence of sellers exactly counteracted each other—with opening and closing prices that are virtually equal—which suggests that the market under analysis is in balance. If a doji occurs at the end of a long uptrend or downtrend, it signals that the trend will probably reverse. The doji in mid-May 2018 not only marked a short-term trend reversal from the 1.33 level but also strengthened that level, which later became a support level during June 2018. The added value of such interpretation can be gained only by using candlestick graphs.

Scale

For any chart—line, bar, or candlestick—the vertical axis can be constructed with either a **linear scale** (also known as an arithmetic scale) or a **logarithmic scale**, depending on how the analyst wants to view the data. With a logarithmic scale, equal vertical distances on the chart correspond to an equal percentage change. With a linear scale, equal vertical distances on the chart correspond to an equal unit change. A logarithmic scale is appropriate when the analyst is working on longer time frames. A linear scale is better suited for shorter-term price charts. In addition, a logarithmic scale is appropriate when the data move through a range of values representing several orders of magnitude (e.g., from 10 to 10,000); a linear scale is better suited for narrower ranges (e.g., prices from $35 to $50). The difference between a logarithmic price chart and an arithmetic (linear) price chart can be small when you are analyzing a short time frame. However, when you look at longer-term charts (more than two years of price data), you will see major differences.

The horizontal axis shows the passage of time. The appropriate time interval depends on the nature of the underlying data and the specific purpose of the chart. An active trader, for instance, may find 10-minute, 5-minute, or even tick-by-tick data useful, but other technical analysts may prefer daily or weekly data. It is important to note that the shorter the time frame, the more random (and thus less meaningful) price action tends to become.

Consider Exhibit 7 and Exhibit 8, which both show the yearly history of the Dow Jones Industrial Average (DJIA) from 1928 to 2018. Plotting the index on a linear scale, as in Exhibit 7, makes it difficult to gather much information from the first 60 years of the data series. Analysts can see a slight uptrend but not much else. The eye is drawn to the bull market of the 1980s, the subsequent dot-com bubble, the subprime crisis, and the sustained recovery. When the index is plotted on a logarithmic scale, as in Exhibit 8, however, the data tell a more comprehensive story. The Great Depression of the 1930s stands out, but over the following 80 years, the data follow a relatively stable upward trend.

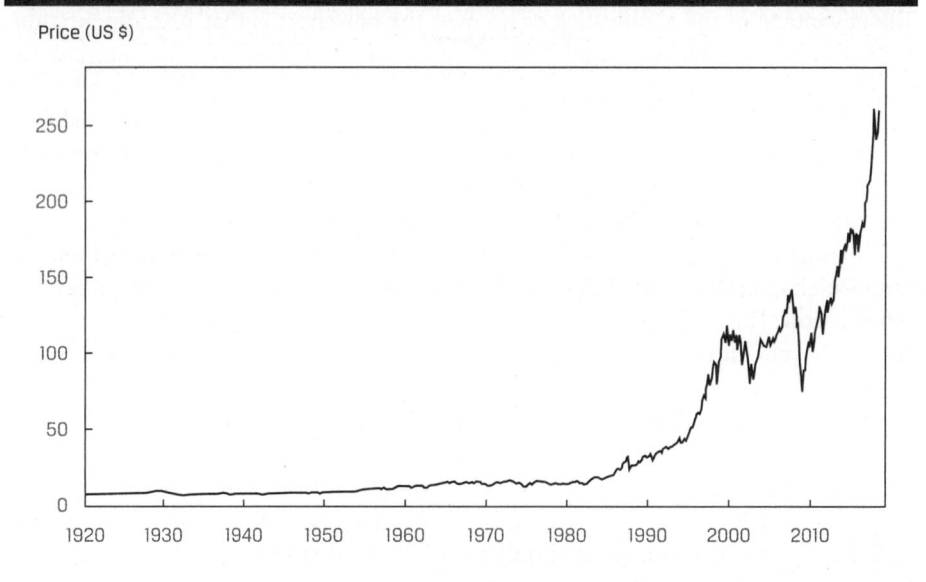

Exhibit 7: Dow Jones Industrial Average on Linear Scale, 1920–2018 (US$)

Chart Types

Exhibit 8: Dow Jones Industrial Average on Logarithmic Scale, 1920–2018 (US$)

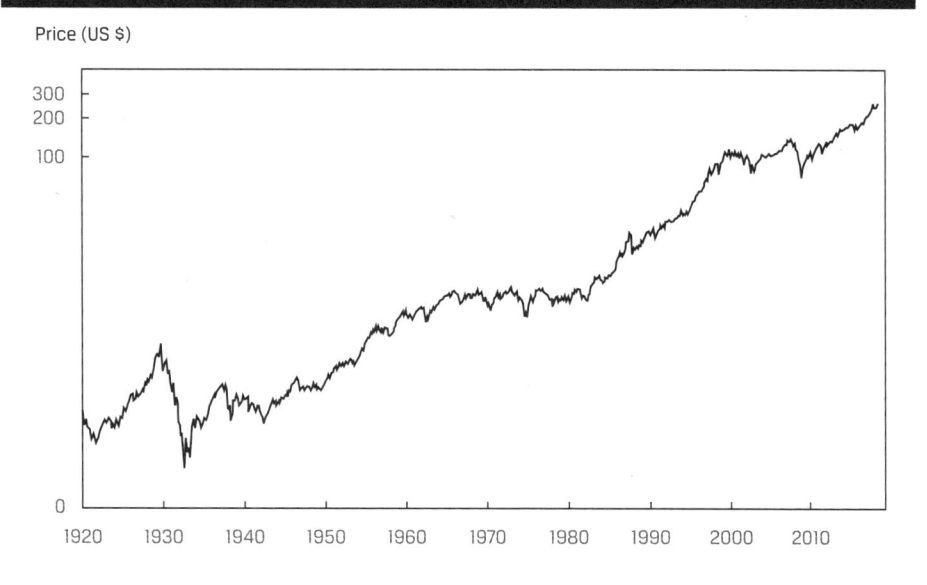

How you construct your scale will impact the trendlines you draw on your price chart. A good example is the price chart of the Russell 2000 Index ETF (IWM). Exhibit 9 shows a price chart of the Russell 2000 Index for the same time period plotted on a linear scale and on a logarithmic scale.

Exhibit 9: Russell 2000 Index Linear and Logarithmic Scales, 2016–2019

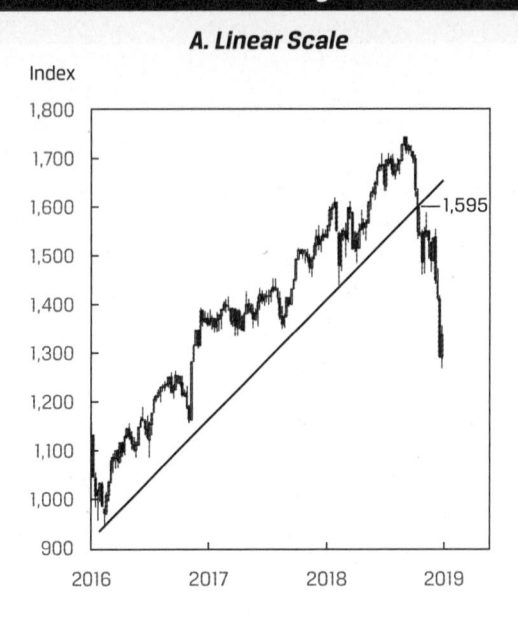

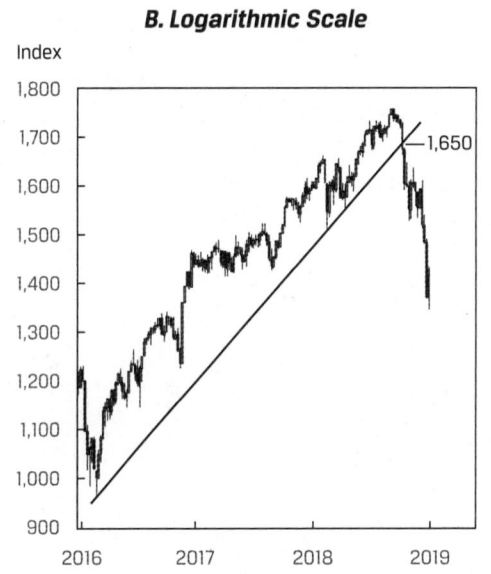

A. Linear Scale

B. Logarithmic Scale

The chart on the left is plotted on a linear scale. The chart on the right is plotted on logarithmic scale. The upward-sloping trendline breaks down earlier on the logarithmic scale than on the linear scale. Upward-sloping logarithmic trendlines are broken sooner than upward-sloping linear trendlines. The opposite is true for downtrends. Downward-sloping trendlines on logarithmic scale charts are broken later than downward-sloping trendlines on linear scale charts. The **breakdown** signal—and the resulting change in trend—takes place at the 1,650 level on the logarithmic scale chart, whereas the same signal occurs much lower—at the 1,595 level—on the linear scale price chart. A breakdown occurs when the price of an asset moves below a support level.

Chart Types

Volume

Volume is an important characteristic that is included at the bottom of many charts. Volume is used to assess the strength or conviction of buyers and sellers in determining a security's price. For example, on a daily price chart, a bar chart below the price section will show the volume traded for that day.

Some technicians consider volume information to be crucial. If volume increases during a time frame in which price is also increasing, that combination is considered positive and the two indicators are said to "confirm" each other. The signal would be interpreted to mean that over time, more and more investors are buying the financial instrument, and they are doing so at higher and higher prices. This pattern is considered a positive technical development.

Conversely, if volume and price diverge—for example, if a stock's price rises while its volume declines—the implication is that fewer and fewer market participants are willing to buy that stock at the new price. If this trend in volume continues, it is expected that the price rally will soon end because demand for the security at higher prices will cease. However, there are cases where a breakout can take place with low volume. Exhibit 10 shows a price chart for Sunac China Holdings with volume displayed separately.

Exhibit 10: Weekly Candlestick Price Chart and Volume Bar Chart: Sunac China Holdings, August 2016–May 2019 (Hong Kong dollars)

Time Intervals

Charts can be constructed using any time interval. The same principles of technical analysis apply irrespective of the time interval. Using longer intervals allows the analyst to chart longer time periods, for the simple reason that longer intervals contain fewer data points, so a longer time frame can be presented on the chart. A useful step for many analysts is to begin the analysis of a security with the chart for a long time frame, such as a weekly or monthly chart, and then construct charts with shorter and shorter time intervals, such as daily or hourly charts. Over the years, an increase in computerized trading and high-frequency trading (HFT) has resulted in more frequent false and distorted signals in shorter-term analysis. Traders, investors, and analysts should bear in mind the randomness involved in very short-term (intraday) analysis and trading.

Relative Strength Analysis

Relative strength analysis is widely used to compare the performance of a particular asset, such as a common stock, with that of some benchmark—such as, in the case of common stocks, the FTSE 100, the Nikkei 225, or the S&P 500 Index—or with the performance of another security. The intent is to show outperformance or underperformance of the individual issue relative to some other index or asset. Typically, the analyst prepares a line chart of the ratio of two prices, with the asset under analysis as the numerator and with the benchmark or other security as the denominator. A rising line shows the asset is performing better than the benchmark or other stock; a declining line shows the opposite. A flat line shows neutral performance.

Suppose a private investor wants to understand changing market trends for two investment ideas she has read about. Amazon Inc. (AMZN) is a well-known technology-enabled retail company, and Walmart Inc. (WMT) is a US-based multinational retail company. The investor wants to determine which of the two companies' stocks has been the stronger performer (relative to the S&P 500) over the roughly seven-year period ending August 2018. Exhibit 11 shows relative strength lines for the two stocks between 2011 and 2018. For ease of comparison, the ratio of each retail company's price data to the S&P 500 is indexed to 1.00 at the beginning of 2011. A move from 1.00 to 1.50 on the chart in Panel A indicates a 50% outperformance for Amazon versus the S&P 500. Likewise, a drop from 1.00 to 0.80 on the chart in Panel B indicates a 20% underperformance for Walmart versus the S&P 500.

Exhibit 11: Relative Strength Analysis of Two Retail Giants: AMZN vs. the S&P 500 and WMT vs. the S&P 500, January 2011–August 2018

A. Amazon.com Inc. vs. S&P 500

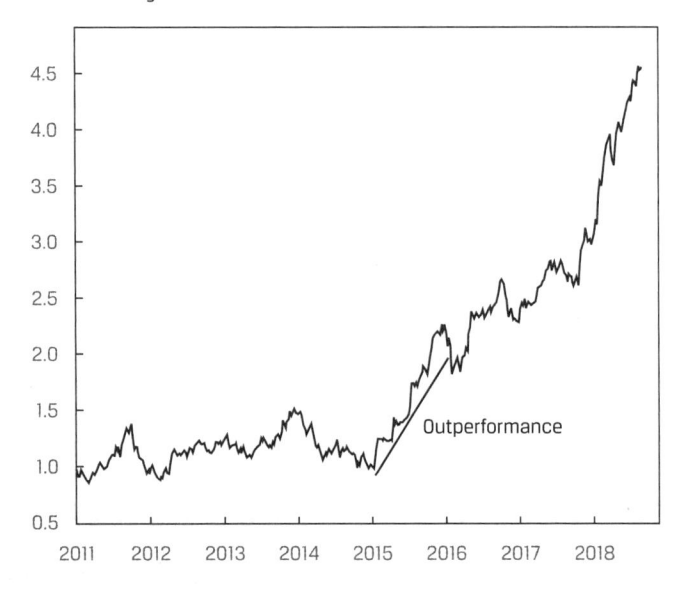

B. Walmart vs. S&P 500

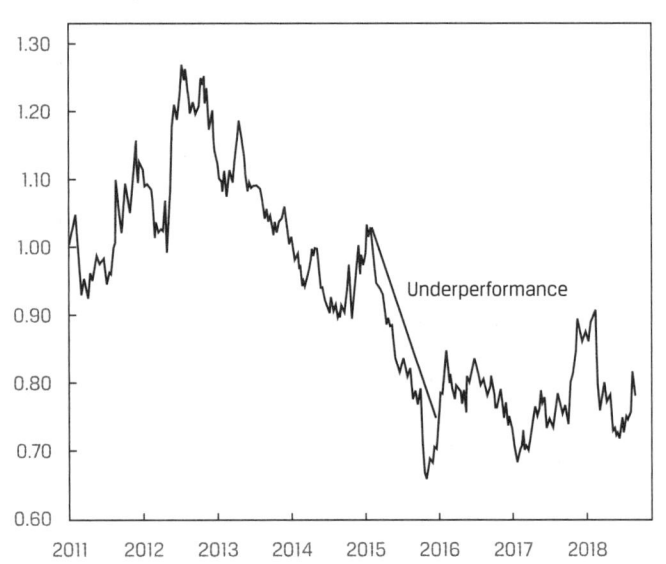

The units on the vertical axis are not significant; the ratio is a function of the relative prices of the assets under consideration. The important information is how the ratio has changed. This type of chart allows an analyst to make a visual determination of that change. As Exhibit 11 illustrates, Amazon was a strong performer starting in 2015, but its relative performance wasn't as strong prior to that year. In contrast, the stock of Walmart lost its leadership in the beginning of 2013, and from that point up to mid-2018, its stock has clearly lagged the performance of the S&P 500.

4. TREND, SUPPORT, AND RESISTANCE

☐ explain uses of trend, support, and resistance lines

The concepts of **trend** and **consolidation** are perhaps the most important aspects of technical analysis. A trend is a long-term pattern of movement in a particular direction. When a security is not trending, it is considered to be in a consolidation. Trend analysis is based on the observations that market participants tend to act in herds and that trends tend to stay in place for some time. A security can be considered to be in an uptrend or a downtrend. The timing of buy and sell decisions will depend on how well we are able to differentiate between a consolidation and a trend phase. Not all securities are in a trend. When a security is not trending, it offers opportunity for traders who buy/sell between well-defined ranges. In the latter part of the reading, we will discuss how to interpret each consolidation period with the help of chart patterns. Not every chart will have obvious or clear implications, so the analyst must avoid the temptation to force a conclusion from every chart, which may lead to a wrong interpretation.

A security is in an **uptrend** when the price goes to higher highs and higher lows. In an uptrend, the forces of demand are greater than the forces of supply. So, traders are willing to pay higher and higher prices for the same asset over time. Presumably, the strong demand indicates that investors believe the intrinsic value of the security is increasing. As the price of the security moves up, each subsequent new high is higher than the prior high, and each time there is a **retracement**, which is a reversal in the movement of the security's price, it must stop at a higher low than the prior lows in the trend period. To draw an uptrend line, a technician draws a line connecting the lows of the price chart. Major breakdowns in price, however, when the price drops through and below the trendline, indicate that the uptrend is over and may signal a further decline in the price. Minor breakthroughs below previous lows simply call for the line to be moderately adjusted over time. Time is also a consideration in trends: The longer the security price stays below the trendline, the more meaningful the breakdown is considered to be.

In a **downtrend**, a security makes lower lows and lower highs. As the price of the security moves down, each subsequent new high must be lower than the prior high, and each time there is a retracement, the price must stop at a lower low than the prior lows in the trend period. To draw a downtrend line, a technician draws a line connecting the highs of the price chart. Major breakouts above the downtrend line indicate that the downtrend is over and a rise in the security's price may occur. And as with an uptrend, the longer the security price stays above the trendline, the more meaningful the breakout is considered to be.

In a downtrend, supply overwhelms demand. Over time, sellers are willing to accept lower and lower prices to exit long positions or enter new short positions. This seller behavior generally indicates deteriorating investor sentiment about the asset. However, selling may be prompted by factors not related to the fundamental or intrinsic value of the stock. For example, investors may be forced to sell to meet margin calls in their portfolios. From a purely technical standpoint, the reason is irrelevant. The downtrend is assumed to continue until contrary technical evidence appears. Combining fundamental analysis with technical analysis in such a case, however, might reveal a security that has attractive fundamentals but a currently negative technical position.

A security may trade in a fairly narrow range, moving sideways on the price chart without much upward or downward movement. This pattern indicates a relative balance between supply and demand. A technical analyst might not expect to profit from

Trend, Support, and Resistance

long or short trades in such securities but might devise profitable option strategies for short-term investors with the ability to accept the risks. For position traders and investors, consolidations are pauses in trends. Such pauses also present an opportunity to assess the strength or weakness of that security. Each consolidation period is eventually followed by a trend period. For buyers of that security, it is important to know how the subsequent trend phase will develop. For sellers of the security, it is important to watch for any change in trend.

Exhibit 12 shows the application of trend and consolidation analysis. It is important to note that each trend period will be followed by a consolidation and each consolidation will give rise to a trend period. Most position traders and investors would like to capture these trend periods. Therefore, differentiation or identification of those consolidation and trend periods becomes an important motive of a **chartist**. A chartist is an individual who uses charts or graphs of a security's historical prices or levels to forecast its future trends.

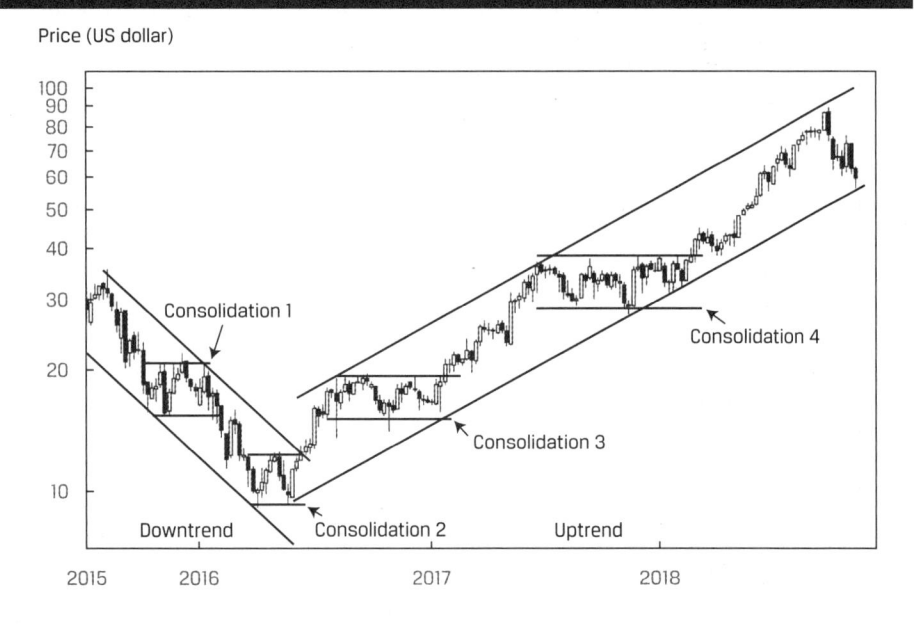

Exhibit 12: Trend and Consolidation Analysis: Teladoc Health Price Chart, 2015–2019 (US$)

The chart in Exhibit 12 covers roughly four years and would most likely be used by investors with a long time horizon. There are four distinct consolidation periods on the price chart. Identification of those consolidation periods would have helped in making investment decisions. Following its IPO, Teladoc Health started trending lower. In the last quarter of 2015, the stock formed its first consolidation (Consolidation 1). Once the boundaries of the consolidation became clear, the chartist should have asked the question, Which way will the consolidation resolve? If it resolved on the downside, this outcome would suggest that the downtrend would resume. If it resolved on the upside, this outcome would suggest a change in trend, a trend reversal. In the last month of 2015, Teladoc broke down its consolidation to resume its downtrend.

Between March 2016 and May 2016, the stock formed another consolidation (Consolidation 2). This time a breakout on the upside followed. The implication of this breakout was a major trend reversal. It offered a long-term opportunity for investors and traders.

Initial upward thrust pushed Teladoc from around the 12 level to around the 19 level. You will remember that each trend period is followed by a consolidation. Consolidation 3, which took six months to complete, offered an opportunity for traders with short horizons. This was also an opportunity to assess the health of the initial positive change in trend. Once the boundaries of the consolidation became clear, the chartist should have asked the question, Which way will the consolidation resolve? Would Teladoc offer a new breakout opportunity and a continuation of the existing uptrend? The new breakout occurred in January 2017. At this point, we had an established uptrend with higher lows and higher highs.

The continuation of the uptrend took Teladoc from around the 19 level to around the 38 level. At that point, the stock entered into another consolidation (Consolidation 4). From May 2017 until February 2018, the stock remained in a tight consolidation range, which acted as another opportunity for traders with short horizons. These types of consolidations, once they are identified and mature, offer traders a chance to sell at the upper boundary and buy back their shares at the lower boundary. For position traders and investors, the consolidation is a time to assess the strength of the stock. Consolidation 4 was completed in March 2018 with a breakout above the 38 level, and the uptrend resumed higher, reaching the 89 level by the last quarter of 2018.

Two concepts related to trend are **support** and **resistance**. Support is defined as a low price range in which buying activity is sufficient to stop the decline in price. It is the opposite of resistance, which is a high price range in which selling activity is sufficient to stop the rise in price. The psychology behind the concepts of support and resistance is that investors have come to a consensus about the price of a security. Support and resistance levels can be sloped lines, as in trendlines or horizontal lines.

A key tenet regarding support and resistance as a part of technical analysis is the **change in polarity principle**, which states that once a support level is breached, it becomes a resistance level. The same holds true for resistance levels; once breached, they become support levels.

Support indicates that at some price level, investors consider a security to be an attractive investment and are willing to buy, even in the wake of a sharp decline. (And resistance indicates that at some level, investors are not willing to buy, even in an uptrend.)

In Exhibit 13, we see an example of support and resistance on a widely followed commodity, WTI Light Crude Oil. For more than two decades, this commodity's price fluctuated between $10 per barrel and $37 per barrel. In 2014, the balance between supply and demand changed and pushed the price above the historical resistance at $37. In four years' time, the commodity was trading as high as the $147 level. High commodity prices had significant impact on global economies. During the subprime crisis and related sell-off, the WTI Light Crude Oil price fell back to the $37 level. Previous resistance acted as a strong support. The second time the WTI price tested the $37 support level was in 2016. Even though the price dipped below the support, the close for the quarter was around the $38 level. The price chart formed a long-legged candlestick, suggesting the strong support was still valid.

Exhibit 13: Support Level: WTI Light Crude Oil Quarterly Price Chart, 1980–2019 (US$ per barrel)

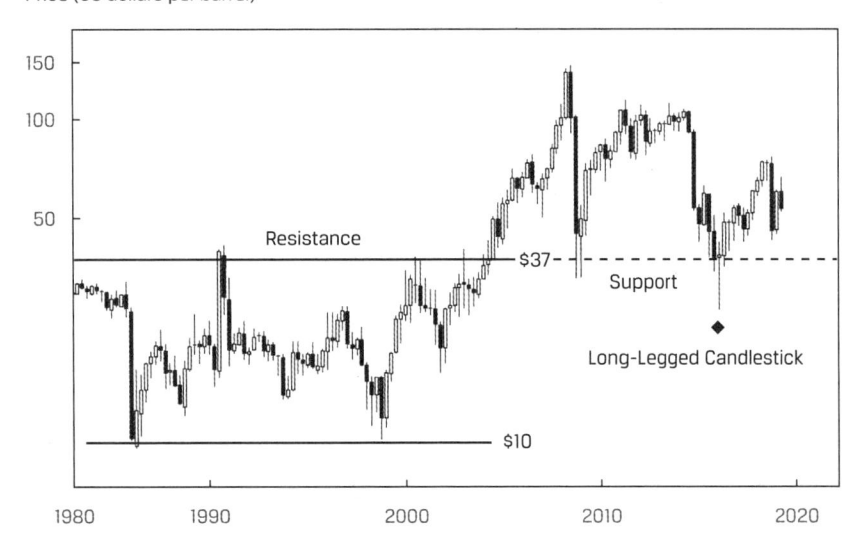

COMMON CHART PATTERNS

☐ explain common chart patterns

Chart patterns are formations that appear in price charts that create some type of recognizable shape over time as the single bar lines accumulate. Common patterns appear repeatedly and often lead to similar subsequent price movements. Thus, the identification and analysis of chart patterns is a basic aspect of how technical analysis is used to predict security prices. An important connection to remember is that because patterns form as a result of the behavior of market participants, these patterns are graphical depictions of the collective psychology of the market at a given time. The recurring patterns that appear in charts can be used as a basis for market analysis.

Chart patterns, while most can be analyzed as a type of consolidation, can be divided into two categories: **reversal patterns** and **continuation patterns**. These terms refer to the trend for the security in question prior to the formation of the pattern (consolidation). The most important concept to understand in using chart patterns is that not every chart will lend itself to easy interpretation. Some charts will be clearer than others, and the analyst should not force an interpretation on any chart. This aspect is frequently forgotten by investors, who are so eager to identify and use patterns that they forget the proper application of charts.

Reversal Patterns

As the name implies, a reversal pattern signals the end of a trend, a change in direction for the financial instrument's price. Evidence that a trend is about to change direction is obviously important, so reversal patterns are noteworthy.

Head and Shoulders

Perhaps the most widely recognized reversal pattern is the **head and shoulders pattern**. This pattern consists of three segments. Volume is an important consideration in interpreting this pattern. Because the head and shoulders pattern indicates a trend reversal, it is important to establish the existence of a prior uptrend. Without a prior uptrend to reverse, there cannot be a head and shoulders reversal pattern. Later, we will discuss the *inverse* head and shoulders pattern (preceded by a downtrend).

Exhibit 14 depicts a head and shoulders pattern for Marriott Vacations.

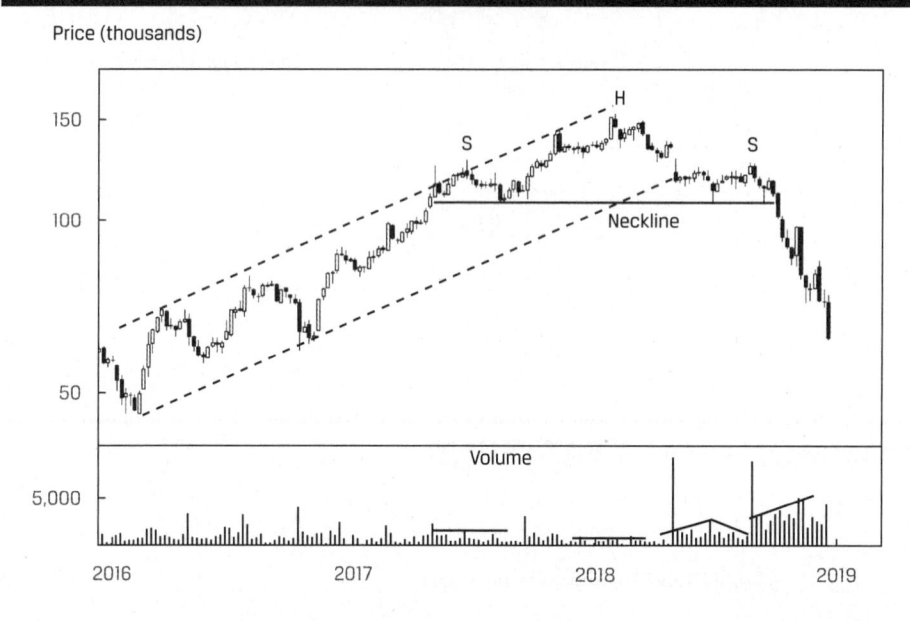

Exhibit 14: Head and Shoulders Pattern: Marriott Vacations Weekly Price Chart, January 2016–December 2018 (US$)

The three parts of the pattern are as follows:

1. Left shoulder: While the security is in an uptrend, the left shoulder forms a peak that marks the high point of the current trend. Often, but not always, this first shoulder may represent the highest volume of the entire pattern. After this peak, a decline ensues to complete the formation of the shoulder.

2. Head: From the low of the left shoulder, an advance begins that exceeds the previous high and marks the top of the head. After this peak, the low of the subsequent decline marks the second point of the neckline. Formation of the head is the first signal that the rally may be coming to an end and that a reversal may be starting. Volume typically will wane a bit into the head high.

3. Right shoulder: The advance from the low of the head forms the right shoulder. This peak is lower than the head (a lower high) and usually in line with the high of the left shoulder. A textbook example should have symmetry between the shoulders in both time and price. The decline from the peak of the right shoulder should break the neckline. It is important that volume be lowest on the second shoulder.

In addition, the following three elements are key for the head and shoulders pattern: neckline, volume, and price target.

- Neckline: The neckline forms by connecting the beginning of the left shoulder and the end of the right shoulder. Depending on the relationship between the two low points, the neckline can slope up, slope down, or be horizontal. A textbook example should have a horizontal chart pattern boundary (neckline) where the lows of both shoulders just touch the horizontal line.
- Volume: As mentioned above, volume plays an important role in the confirmation of a head and shoulders pattern. Ideally, but not always, volume during the advance of the left shoulder should be higher than during the advance of the head. The decrease in volume into the new high of the head then serves as an initial warning sign. The next warning sign comes when volume increases on the decline from the peak of the head, then notably decreases during the advance of the right shoulder. Final confirmation comes when volume increases once again during the decline from the right shoulder.
- Price target: After the price breaks the neckline support, the projected price decline is found by measuring the distance from the neckline to the top of the head. This distance is then subtracted from the neckline to reach a price target. Price targets should be used as guidelines. Price may exceed the chart pattern objective or fall short.

Rarely will an analyst see a perfectly formed head and shoulders pattern; variations include two tops on the shoulders or on the head. The head, however, should rise to a higher price level than either shoulder, whereas the shoulders should be roughly symmetrical. In terms of the neckline price level, the first rally should begin at this level and the left shoulder and head should also decline to roughly this level. But necklines may not always form exactly horizontal lines.

Volume is important in analyzing head and shoulders patterns. A new high in price at the top of the head without a new high in volume signals the presence of fewer bullish market participants. When one indicator is making a new high (or low) but another is not, this situation is called **divergence**.

Once the head and shoulders pattern has formed, the expectation is that the share price will decline through the neckline price. Technicians tend to use filtering rules to make sure that a clear breakdown of the neckline has occurred. These rules may take the form of waiting to trade until the price falls to a meaningful level below the neckline (3% and 5% are commonly used) and/or until the price has remained below the neckline for a specified length of time; when a daily price chart is used, the rule may be several days to a week. Prices commonly rebound to the neckline levels, even after a decline has exceeded the filter levels. Prices generally stop, however, at or around the neckline. The neckline was a support level, and under the change in polarity principle, once a support level is breached, it becomes a resistance level.

Inverse Head and Shoulders

The head and shoulders pattern can also form upside down and act as a reversal pattern for a preceding downtrend. Inverse head and shoulders is also referred to as a head and shoulders bottom.

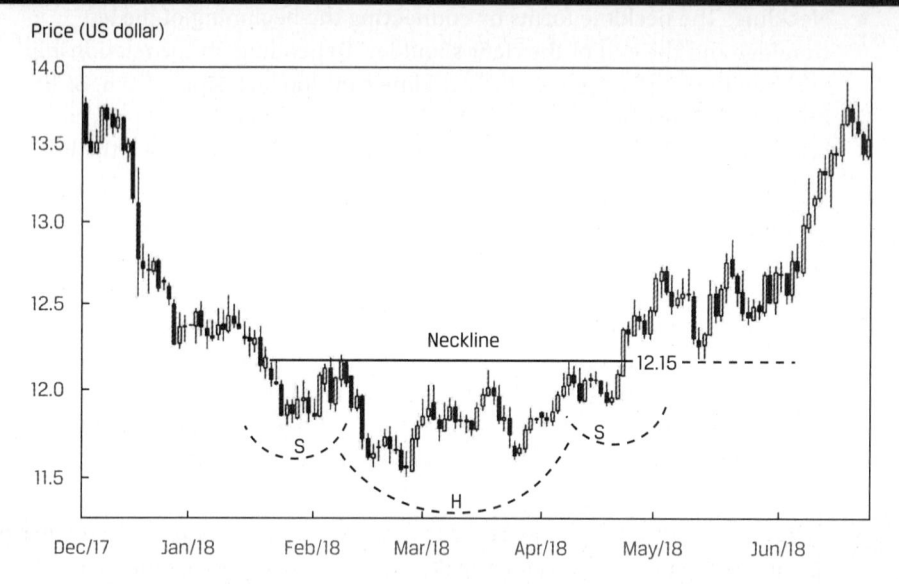

Exhibit 15: Inverse Head and Shoulders Pattern: US Dollar/South African Rand Daily Price Chart, December 2017–July 2018

The three parts of the inverse head and shoulders are as follows:

- Left shoulder: This shoulder appears to show a strong decline, with the slope of the decline greater than that of the prior downtrend. The price movement then reverses back to the level where the rally started, forming a V shape.

- Head: The head is a more pronounced version of the left shoulder. Another decline follows, which takes the price to a lower low than the left shoulder by a significant enough margin that it is clearly evident on the price chart. This second decline also reverses, with price rising to the same level at which the left shoulder began and ended. This price level, the neckline, will also be above the downtrend line formed by connecting the high prices in the downtrend preceding the beginning of the inverse head and shoulders pattern. This pattern is the first signal that the decline may be coming to an end and that a reversal may be near. It is possible for the formation of the head to involve a more complex structure. A head can contain two minor lows, as in the US dollar/South African rand example presented in Exhibit 15.

- Right shoulder: The right shoulder is roughly a mirror image of the left shoulder, signifying less selling enthusiasm. The price declines to roughly the same level as the left shoulder, but the rally reverses at a higher low price than the rally that formed the head.

Volume once again is important to watch and should generally diminish into the final reverse shoulder before ideally exploding higher on the subsequent neckline break.

Setting Price Targets with the Head and Shoulders Pattern

Like all technical patterns, the head and shoulders pattern must be analyzed from the perspective of the security's long-term price trend. The rally before the formation of the pattern must be large enough for there to be something to reverse. The stronger and more pronounced the rally was, the stronger and more pronounced the reversal is likely to be. Similarly, once the neckline is breached, the security is expected to decline by an amount equal to the change in price from the neckline to the top of the head. If

Common Chart Patterns

the preceding rally started at a price higher than the neckline, however, the correction is unlikely to bring the price lower than the level at the start of the rally. Because a head and shoulders formation is a bearish indicator (i.e., a technician would expect the previously established uptrend to end and a downtrend to commence), a technician would seek to profit by shorting the security under analysis. When attempting to profit from the head and shoulders pattern, a technician will often use the price difference between the head and the neckline to set a price target, which is the price at which the technician anticipates closing the investment position. The price target for the head and shoulders pattern is calculated as follows:

Price target = Neckline − (Head − Neckline).

For example, in Exhibit 16, the high price reached at the top of the head is roughly $154 and the neckline formed at roughly $108, for a difference of $46. So a technician would expect the price to decline to a level $46 below the neckline—that is, to $62:

Price target = $108 − ($154 − $108) = $62.

Exhibit 16: Calculating a Price Target: Marriott Vacations Weekly Price Chart, January 2016–December 2018 (US$)

Price targets should be used as guidelines. With stocks in a downtrend and creating bearish chart patterns, a conservative approach to calculating price objectives is warranted. The conservative approach is to take the percentage difference between the high point of the head and the neckline and project it below the breakdown level (the neckline). Note that with a low-priced stock, such as one with a price of $0.50, there is a possibility of projecting price levels below 0. Because negative values for an asset are not possible, measuring price objectives using a percentage decline is more reasonable.

> **EXAMPLE 1**
>
> ### Determining a Price Target from a Head and Shoulders Pattern
>
> 1. Danielle Waterhouse is the technical analyst at Kanektok Securities. One of the companies her firm follows is LPA Petroleum. Waterhouse believes that a graph of LPA's share prices over the past six months reveals a classic head and shoulders pattern. The share price peaked at US$108, and she estimates the neckline at US$79. At today's close, the shares traded at US$78. Based on the head and shoulders pattern, what price target should Waterhouse estimate?
>
> ### Solution:
>
> Waterhouse estimates the neckline at US$79, which is US$108 minus US$79, or US$29, lower than the head. Her price target is thus US$79 minus US$29, which is US$50. Waterhouse would attempt to sell LPA short at today's price of US$78 and anticipate closing the position at US$50 for a profit of US$28 per share (not accounting for transaction costs).

Setting Price Targets with the Inverse Head and Shoulders Pattern

Calculating price targets for inverse head and shoulders patterns is similar to the process for head and shoulders patterns, but because the inverse head and shoulders pattern predicts the end of a downtrend, the technician calculates how high the price is expected to rise once it breaches the neckline. Exhibit 17 illustrates an inverse head and shoulders pattern.

Exhibit 17: Calculating a Price Target for an Inverse Head and Shoulders Pattern: US Dollar/South African Rand Daily Price Chart, December 2017–July 2018

Common Chart Patterns

For an inverse head and shoulders pattern, the formula is similar to that for a head and shoulders pattern:

Price target = Neckline + (Neckline − Head).

For example, in the price chart in Exhibit 17, the low price reached at the bottom of the head is roughly 11.5 and the neckline formed at roughly 12.15. The target can thus be calculated as 12.15 + (12.15 − 11.50) = 12.80. In this case, a technician might have taken a long position on 23 April, with the strong daily breakout above the neckline at the 12.15 level, and projected a possible exit near the 12.80 level.

Double Tops and Bottoms

A **double top** is formed when an uptrend reverses twice at roughly the same high price level. Typically, volume is lower on the second high than on the first high, signaling a diminishing of demand. The longer the time between the two tops and the deeper the sell-off after the first top, the more significant the pattern is considered to be. Price targets can be calculated from this pattern in a manner similar to the calculation for the head and shoulders pattern. For a double top, price is expected to decline below the low of the valley between the two tops by at least the distance from the valley low to the high of the double top.

EXAMPLE 2

Determining a Price Target from a Double Top Pattern

1. Richard Dupuis is a technician who trades Eurodollar futures for his own account. He analyzes charts based on one-minute intervals, looking for short-term trading opportunities. Eurodollar futures contracts have been trending upward most of the morning, but Dupuis now observes what he believes is a double top pattern: After peaking at US$97.00, the futures contract price falls to US$96.42, climbs again to US$97.02, and then starts a decline. Because of the double top, Dupuis anticipates a reversal from the uptrend to a downtrend. Dupuis decides to open a short position to capitalize on the anticipated trend reversal. What price target should Dupuis estimate for closing the position?

Solution:

Dupuis estimates the price target as US$96.42 − (US$97.02 − US$96.42) = US$95.82.

A **double bottom** is formed when the price reaches a low, rebounds, and then declines again to the first low level. Exhibit 18 depicts a double bottom pattern for US 30-year Treasury bond futures (first-month continuation price). Technicians use the double bottom to predict a change from a downtrend to an uptrend in security prices. The neckline for a double bottom is the horizontal line that touches the minor high between the two major troughs. A breakout takes place once the price breaches the neckline. The distance from the resistance breakout to the trough lows can be added to the area above the resistance breakout to estimate a target.

Exhibit 18: Double Bottom Pattern: US 30-Year Treasury Bond Daily Price Chart, August 2018–February 2019 (first-month continuation futures, US$)

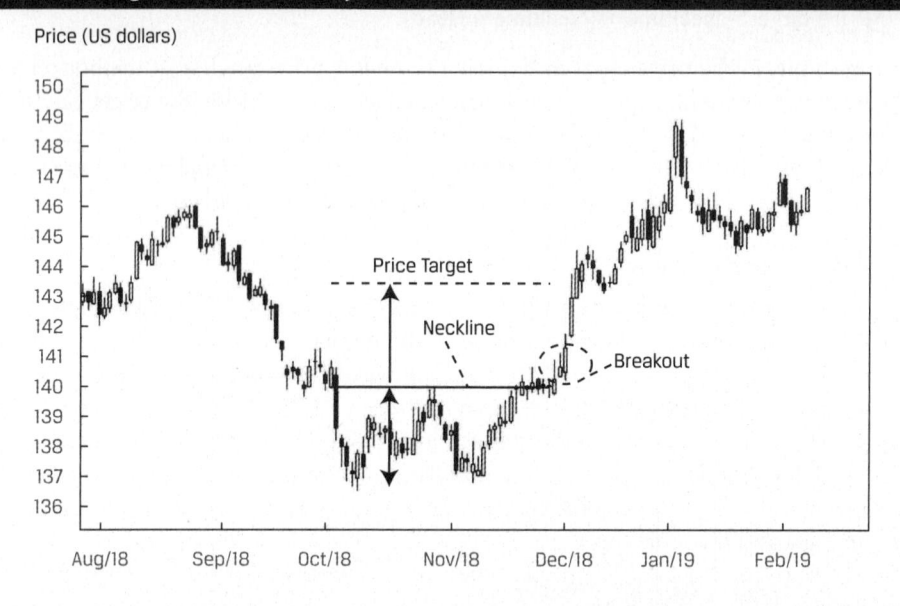

The reason these patterns are significant is that they show that at some price point, investors step in to reverse trends that are underway. For an uptrend, a double top implies that at some price point, enough traders are willing to sell positions (or enter new short positions) that their activities overwhelm and reverse the uptrend created by demand for the shares. A reasonable conclusion is that this price level has been fundamentally derived and that it represents the consensus of investors on the intrinsic value of the security. With double bottoms, if a decline in a security stops at the same price point on two separate occasions, the analyst can conclude that the market consensus is that at that price point, the security is cheap enough to be an attractive investment.

Triple Tops and Bottoms

A **triple top** consists of three peaks at roughly the same price level, and a **triple bottom** consists of three troughs at roughly the same price level. A triple top for Odfjell Drilling during 2018 is shown in Exhibit 19.

Common Chart Patterns 167

Exhibit 19: Triple Top Pattern: Odfjell Drilling Weekly Price Chart, January 2017–January 2019 (Norwegian krone)

One of the challenges with double top and triple top patterns—and one of the valid criticisms of technical analysis in general—is that an analyst cannot know which pattern will result until after the fact. There is no evidence that market corrections must end with a double bottom or that rallies must end with a double top, and there is no generally accepted technical theory that predicts whether a low will be repeated once or even twice before a reversal occurs. A double bottom is considered to be a more significant pattern than a single bottom because traders have stepped in on two occasions to halt declines. However, traders have no way to determine whether a double top or bottom will be followed by a third top or bottom. The goal of a trader, investor, or analyst is not to predict possible price action but to identify well-defined levels for decision making. It is the breach of these levels—the breakout—that matters most because it completes the lengthy consolidation and gives rise to a new trend period. Triple tops and triple bottoms are rare, but when they occur, they are more significant reversal patterns than double tops or double bottoms. On three separate occasions, traders stepped in to sell or buy shares with enough volume to end a rally or decline underway at the time. Nevertheless, the greater the number of times the price reverses at the same level, and the greater the time interval over which this pattern occurs, the greater the significance of the pattern. Note that a bottoming process, whatever the reversal chart pattern, tends to be more predictable than a topping process. This is because in a bottoming process, market forces are capitulating, whereas in a topping process, irrational exuberance can always take prices to higher levels before ultimately reversing.

Some securities, due to either their volatility or their active trader/investor profile, offer similar well-defined chart pattern opportunities. Exhibit 20 shows a triple bottom chart pattern for Odfjell Drilling prior to the strong uptrend that pushed the stock price from around the 3.5 level to the high teens.

Exhibit 20: Triple Bottom Pattern: Odfjell Drilling Weekly Price Chart, January 2017–January 2019 (Norwegian krone)

When identifying chart patterns, we should remind ourselves of the importance of trends and consolidations. Regardless of the chart pattern in question, the formation of a price range is a *consolidation*, which, once completed with a confirmed breakout in either direction, will be expected to give rise to a trend period. For optimal decision making, traders, investors, and analysts should focus on successfully identifying and differentiating those two phases.

Exhibit 21 shows the Odfjell Drilling price chart between September 2013 and January 2019. The downtrend that started in the last quarter of 2013 reached a bottom in the second half of 2015. A yearlong sideways consolidation offered a trading opportunity for short-term traders between well-defined chart pattern boundaries. Traders, investors, and analysts with a slightly longer horizon should be asking: What type of price action can follow after the yearlong consolidation? If the chart pattern acts as a triple bottom with a breakout above the chart pattern boundary, can it reverse the two-year-long downtrend? In the second half of 2016, Odfjell Drilling completed the triple bottom with a strong weekly breakout and started a new uptrend. The triple bottom reversed the existing trend from down to up.

Common Chart Patterns

Exhibit 21: Trend and Consolidation: Odfjell Drilling Weekly Price Chart, September 2013–January 2019 (Norwegian krone)

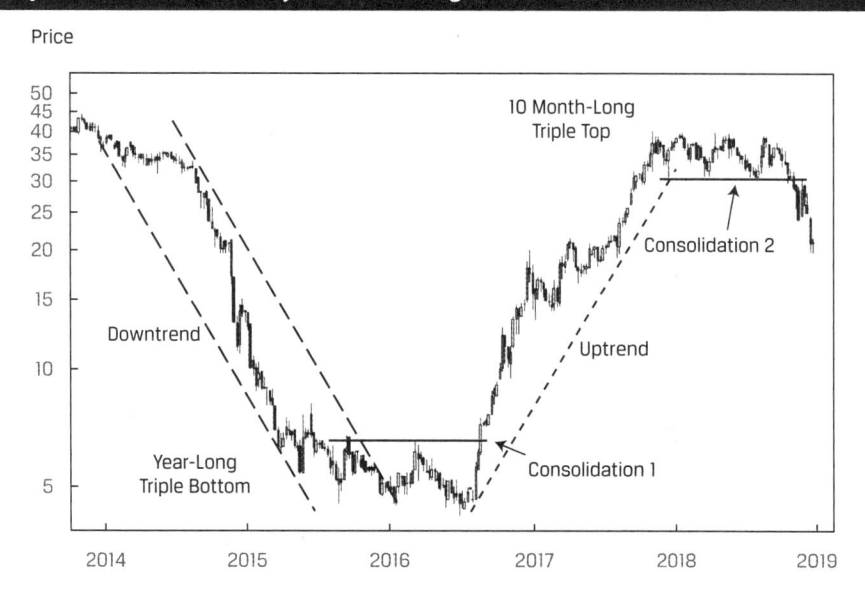

Similar analysis was required from the technician in the last quarter of 2017. Consolidation 2 was a triple top and acted as a top reversal. The uptrend was followed by a consolidation that reversed the existing trend from up to down.

Continuation Patterns

A **continuation pattern** is used to predict the resumption of a market trend that was in place prior to the formation of a pattern. From a supply and demand standpoint, a continuation pattern often indicates a change in ownership from one group of investors to another. For example, if a positive trend was in place prior to a pattern and then one group of investors begins selling, the negative impact on price is quickly offset by other investors buying, so the forces of supply and demand go back and forth in terms of their impact on price. But neither has an overwhelming advantage. This type of pattern is often called "a healthy correction" because the long-term market trend does not change and because while one set of investors is seeking to exit, they are replaced by another set of investors willing to take their positions at roughly the same share price. Continuation patterns can take various forms, including triangles, rectangles, and flags, which are detailed in the rest of this section.

Triangles

Triangle patterns are a type of continuation pattern. They come in three forms: symmetrical triangles, ascending triangles, and descending triangles. A triangle pattern forms as the range between high and low prices narrows, visually forming a triangle. In the older terminology, triangles were referred to as "coils" or "springs" because a triangle was considered analogous to a spring being wound up tighter and tighter, storing energy that would at some point be released. In a triangle, a trendline connects the highs and another trendline connects the lows. As the distance between the highs and lows narrows, the trendlines meet, forming a triangle. In a daily price chart, a triangle pattern usually forms over a period of several weeks. In a weekly price chart, a triangle pattern can extend over several months.

In a symmetrical triangle, the trendline formed by the highs slopes down and the trendline formed by the lows slopes up, both at roughly the same angle, forming a symmetrical pattern.

Exhibit 22 contains a symmetrical triangle formed on the price chart of Diös Fastigheter AB during 2018. This triangle indicates that buyers are becoming more bullish while, simultaneously, sellers are becoming more bearish, so buyers and sellers are moving toward a market-clearing point of consensus. Because the sellers are often dominated by long investors exiting positions (as opposed to short sellers creating new short positions), the pressure to sell diminishes once the sellers have sold the security. Thus, the pattern ends with an ongoing move in the same direction as the trend that preceded it, either up or down.

Exhibit 22: Symmetrical Triangle: Diös Fastigheter AB Weekly Price Chart, March 2017–March 2019 (Swedish krona)

The possible price target is derived by calculating the difference in price from the two trendlines at the start of the triangle. Once the pattern is completed and the price breaches one of the trendlines that forms the triangle, the analyst expects the price to move by at least the amount of the calculated difference in price from the two trendlines at the start of the triangle above or below the trendline. Typically, price breaks out of a triangle pattern between halfway and three-quarters of the way through the pattern. The longer the triangle pattern persists, the more volatile and sustained the subsequent price movement is likely to be.

In an ascending triangle, as shown in Exhibit 23, the trendline connecting the high prices is horizontal and the trendline connecting the low prices forms an uptrend. This pattern means that market participants are selling the stock at the same price level over a period of time and putting a halt to rallies at the same price point, but buyers are getting more and more bullish and stepping in at increasingly higher prices to halt sell-offs instead of waiting for further price declines. An ascending triangle typically forms in an uptrend. However, there are several cases where an ascending triangle can form as a bottom reversal. The bullish implication of the pattern is more important than where the pattern forms on a price chart. The horizontal line represents sellers taking profits at around the same price point. The fact that the breakout pushes

Common Chart Patterns

through the horizontal boundary is usually a bullish signal suggesting that buyers have overcome the selling pressure around the horizontal boundary. Irrespective of where the ascending triangle is identified, occasionally as a reversal chart pattern or more frequently as a continuation chart pattern, it should be considered a *consolidation* with bullish implications, and the breakout above the well-defined horizontal boundary should alert traders, investors, and analysts to act accordingly.

Exhibit 23: Ascending Triangle Pattern

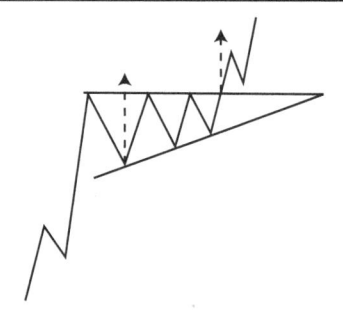

Exhibit 24 contains an ascending triangle formed on the price chart for bitcoin versus the US dollar during 2016. This ascending triangle indicates that buyers are becoming more bullish while sellers are acting around the same price level. The buyers are able to bid the price higher at every correction attempt. Eventually, the sellers lose the battle and the price breaks through the horizontal boundary. The prior trend was up, and the seven-month-long ascending triangle was a consolidation. A breakout above the 470 level completed the consolidation and resulted in a new uptrend. The ascending triangle acted as a bullish continuation chart pattern. The calculation for a chart pattern price target is similar to that for a symmetrical triangle. The possible price target is derived by calculating the difference in price from the two trendlines at the start of the triangle. Once the pattern is broken and the price breaks through one of the trendlines that form the triangle, the analyst will expect the price to move by at least the amount of the breakthrough above or below the trendline.

Exhibit 24: Ascending Triangle: Bitcoin/US Dollar Daily Price Chart, September 2015–June 2016 (US$)

In a descending triangle, as shown in Exhibit 25, the low prices form a horizontal trendline and the high prices form a series of lower and lower highs. Typically, a descending triangle will form in a downtrend. However, there are several situations in which a descending triangle acts as a top reversal. The bearish implication of this pattern is more important than where the pattern forms on a price chart. At some point during the rebounds from the horizontal support, sellers appear with enough supply to halt the countertrend recoveries each time they occur. Sellers push the price to lower levels at each rebound, thereby gaining the upper hand against the buyers who bid the price around the same level. The downward-sloping upper boundary of the descending triangle gives the pattern its bearish bias. Irrespective of where the descending triangle is identified, occasionally as a reversal chart pattern or more frequently as a continuation chart pattern, it should be considered a *consolidation* with bearish implications, and the breakdown below the well-defined horizontal boundary should alert traders, investors, and analysts to act accordingly.

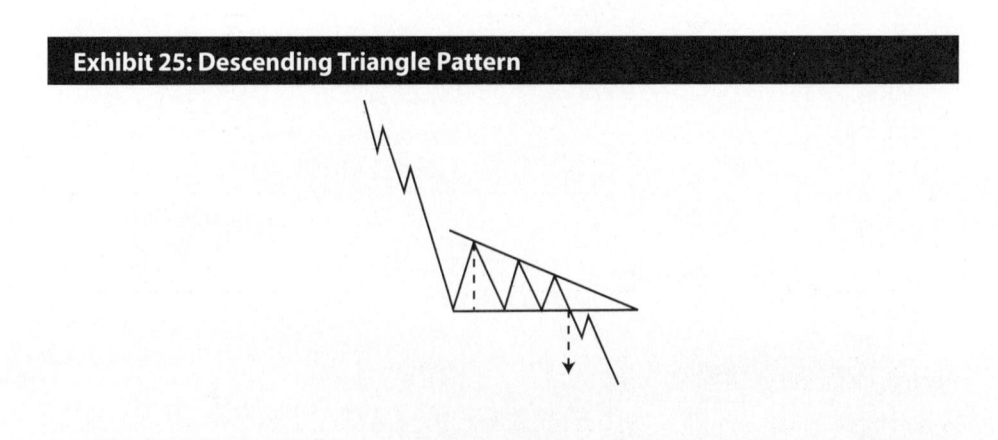

Exhibit 25: Descending Triangle Pattern

Common Chart Patterns

Exhibit 26 shows a descending triangle formed on the price chart of Sibanye Gold Ltd. during 2017. This descending triangle indicates that sellers are becoming more bearish while buyers are acting around the same price level. The sellers are able to push the price lower at every recovery attempt. Eventually, the buyers lose the battle and the price breaks down the horizontal boundary. The prior trend was down, and the yearlong descending triangle was a consolidation. The breakdown below the 1,365 level completed the consolidation and resulted in a downtrend. The descending triangle acted as a bearish continuation pattern. The calculation for a descending triangle pattern price target is slightly different with price charts in a downtrend, partly because of the zero boundary. It is important to note that chart pattern price objectives should be used as guidelines only. Price may reach the projected target, or it may fall short. It is always best to pick the most conservative approach. The possible price target is derived by calculating the percentage change from the two trendlines at the start of the triangle. Sibanye Gold formed a minor high at the 2,200 level. The horizontal boundary was around 1,365. This difference translates roughly into a 38% drop. Once the pattern is completed with a breach of the horizontal support, we can extend the price objective by another 38% on the downside. Please note that we are not taking the absolute price change. A 38% drop from the lower boundary of the descending triangle is equivalent to the 850 level.

Following breakdowns or breakouts, the price can pull back to the chart pattern boundary in an attempt to retest it. Sibanye Gold rebounded to test the previous support at the 1,365 level. The previous support became the new resistance—that is, there was a change in polarity.

Exhibit 26: Descending Triangle: Sibanye Gold Ltd. Weekly Price Chart, March 2016–May 2018 (South African rand)

Rectangle Pattern

A rectangle usually develops as a continuation pattern formed by two parallel trendlines, one connecting the high prices during the pattern and the other connecting the lows. Exhibit 27 shows two rectangle patterns. Like other patterns, the rectangle pattern is a graphical representation of what has been occurring in terms of collective market sentiment. The horizontal resistance line that forms the top of the rectangle shows that investors are repeatedly selling shares at a specific price level, bringing rallies to an end. The horizontal support line forming the bottom of the rectangle indicates that traders are repeatedly making large enough purchases at the same price level to reverse declines. The support level in a bullish rectangle is natural because the long-term trend in the market is bullish. The resistance line may simply represent investors taking profits. Conversely, in a bearish rectangle, the support level may represent investors buying the security. Again, the technician is not concerned with why a pattern has formed, only with the likely next price movement once the price breaks out of the pattern.

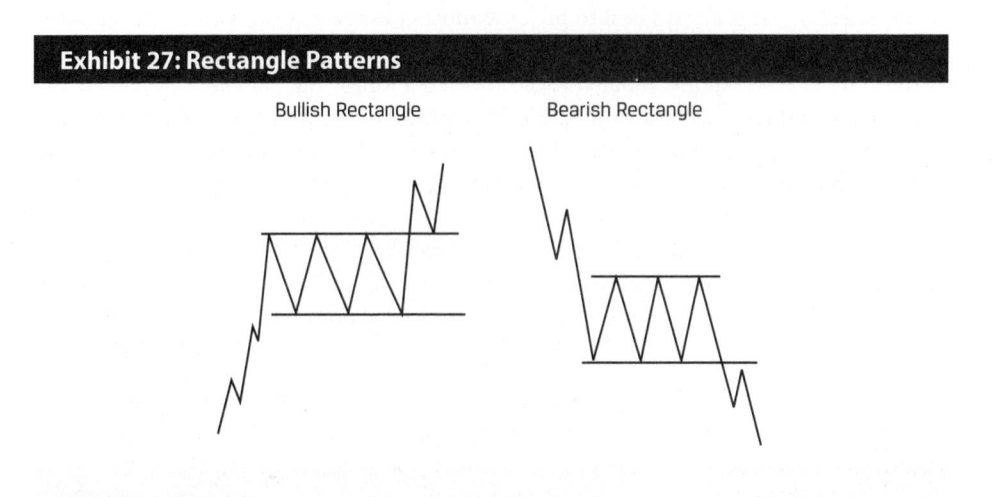

Exhibit 27: Rectangle Patterns

Bullish Rectangle   Bearish Rectangle

Rectangle patterns, due their configuration, are much easier to identify on price charts than other classical chart patterns. Two horizontal boundaries and a clearly visible consolidation period on a price chart allows the analyst to detect the pause in trend periods with ease. This looks similar to a triple top pattern, but a rectangle pattern is a pause in a trend while a triple top pattern is a reversal of a trend.

Exhibit 28 shows a bullish rectangle pattern formed on the price chart of Vitrolife AB between 2017 and 2018. A 15-month-long sideways consolidation formed after a steady uptrend. After several tests of pattern boundaries both on the upside and on the downside, Vitrolife AB cleared the upper boundary that was acting as a strong resistance at the 142 level. The breakout was followed by a pullback, a retesting of the previous resistance. Several weeks of pullback eventually found support at the chart pattern boundary, and the uptrend resumed. The price objective was met in a matter of a few months. It is important to note that Vitrolife AB started a new strong uptrend following the lengthy consolidation. As a result, the price objective was exceeded during the uptrend. The longer the consolidation takes, the stronger the breakout is. The price objective is calculated by taking the width of the rectangle in absolute price terms and adding it to the breakout level.

Common Chart Patterns

Exhibit 28: Bullish Rectangle: Vitrolife AB Weekly Price Chart, December 2016–April 2019 (Swedish krona)

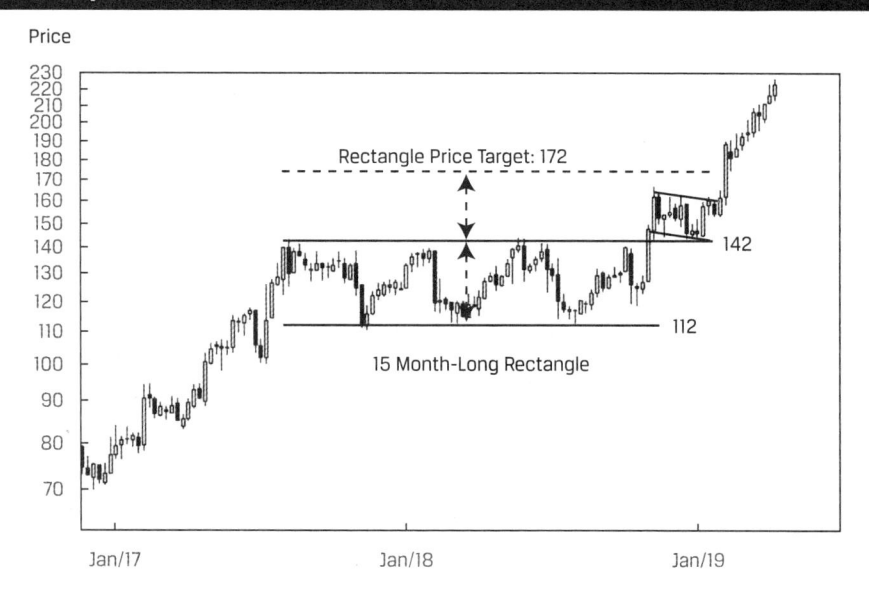

Exhibit 29 shows a bearish rectangle pattern formed on the price chart of Société Générale SA during 2018. A five-month-long sideways consolidation formed after a steady downtrend. After several tests of pattern boundaries, both on the upside and on the downside, Société Générale breached the lower boundary of the rectangle pattern that was acting as a strong support at the 35 level. This breakdown was followed by a pullback, a retesting of the previous support. A short pullback found resistance at the pattern boundary, and the downtrend resumed. The price objective was exceeded during the downtrend. The price objective is calculated by taking the width of the rectangle in percentage terms and projecting it lower from the breakdown level. The difference between the 38.5 and 35 levels translates into a 9% drop. Extending the price objective by 9% from the breakdown level of 35 gives us 31.85.

Exhibit 29: Bearish Rectangle: Société Générale SA Daily Price Chart, April 2018–December 2018 (Price in Euro)

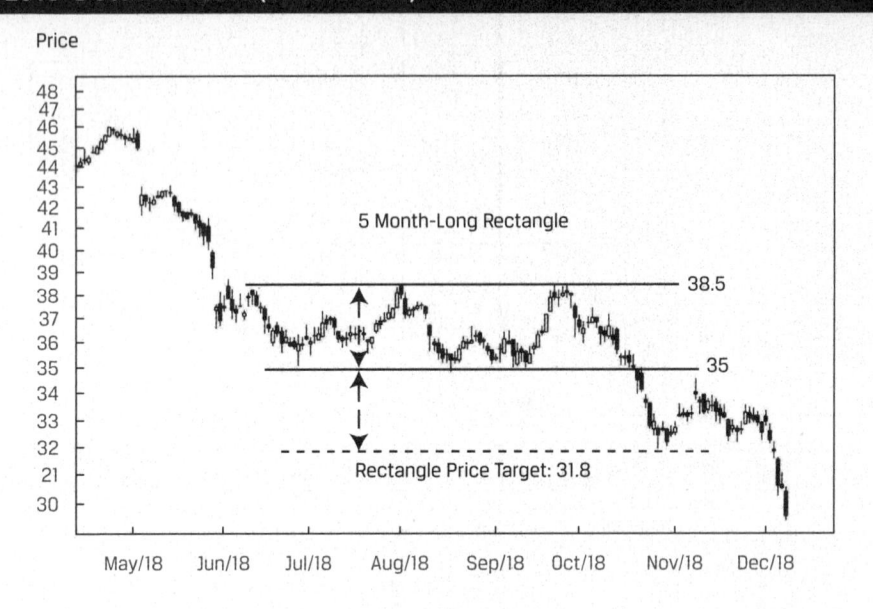

Flags and Pennants

Flags and **pennants** are considered minor continuation patterns because they form over short periods of time—for example, on a daily price chart, typically over a week. However, flags or pennants may form on weekly price charts over slightly longer durations. Flags and pennants are similar and have the same uses. A flag is formed by parallel trendlines, in the same way that most countries' flags are rectangular and create a parallelogram. Typically, the trendlines slope in a direction opposite to the trend up to that time; for example, in an uptrend, the flag's trendlines slope down. A pennant formation is similar except that the trendlines converge to form a triangle. The key difference between a triangle and pennant is that a pennant is a short-term formation whereas a triangle is a long-term formation.

The expectation for both flags and pennants is that the trend will continue after the pattern in the same direction it was going prior to the pattern. The price is expected to change by at least the same amount as the price change from the start of the trend to the formation of the flag or pennant. In Exhibit 30, an uptrend begins at point A, which is €70.5. At point B, which is €111, a flag begins to form. The distance from point A to point B is €40.5. The flag ends at point C, which is €104.5. The price target is €104.5 plus €40.5, which is €145, the line labeled D.

As one added note, volume should ideally be high in the left "flagpole" part of a flag pattern, diminish as the flag forms, and then increase again on the subsequent breakout from the flag pattern. It is not unusual to see chart "gaps" near flag patterns, particularly during the continuation breakout period.

Common Chart Patterns

Exhibit 30: Flag Formation: Nemetschek SE, October 2016–May 2019 (Price in Euro)

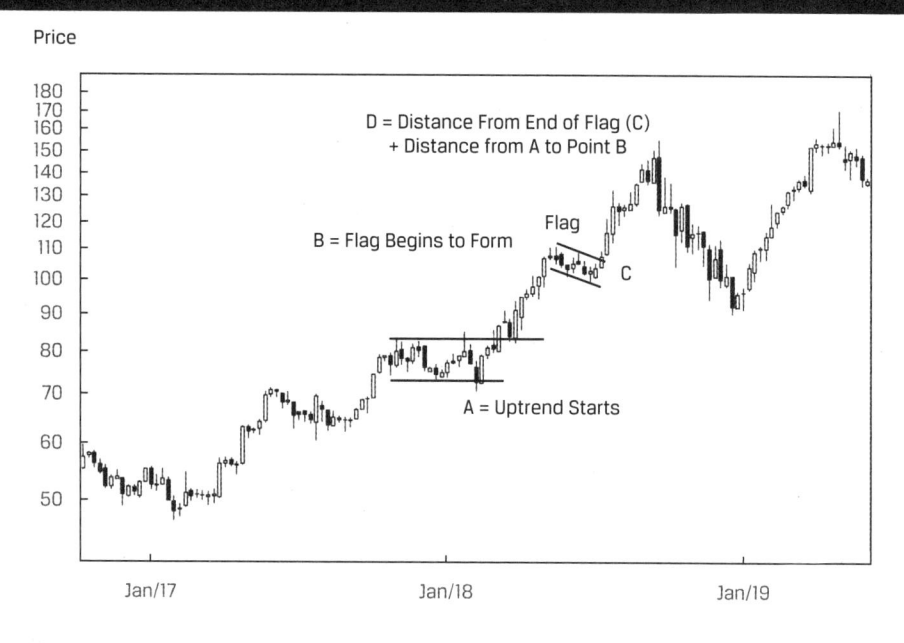

Question 4

Which charting style takes into consideration *only* the closing prices?

- a. Candlestick charts
- b. Line charts
- c. Bar charts

B is correct. Line charts connect the closing prices of each period. Both candlestick charts and bar charts include each period's opening, high, low, and closing prices.
Neither A nor C is the correct answer because both bar charts and candlestick charts take into consideration opening, high, low, and closing values.

Question 5

A trader is looking at long-term charts and wants to exit some of his long positions. In doing so, he wants to confirm major trendline breaks to decide when to exit the positions. Which price scale will generate an earlier breakdown alert?

- a. Linear scale
- b. Logarithmic scale
- c. Scale will not impact this

B is correct. A trendline plotted on a logarithmic scale will be steeper in an uptrend when compared to the same trendline plotted on a linear scale. As a result, a reversal will breach the trendline earlier on a logarithmic scale than on a linear scale.
A is not correct because a trendline plotted on a linear scale will be less steep in an uptrend than the same trendline plotted on a logarithmic scale. As a result, a reversal will breach the trendline later on a linear scale than on a logarithmic scale.
C is not correct because scale will indeed impact the timing of either a breakdown below or a breakout above a trendline.

Question 6

The chart below shows the price of Amana Insurance on Saudi Arabia's Tadawul stock exchange between 2011 and 2015. Over the analyzed period, the stock formed three major classic chart patterns. Each one of those patterns (labeled 1, 2, and 3 on the chart) resulted in a strong trend period following the breakout. Which choice below lists the correct chart patterns in the correct order?

a. Double bottom, rectangle, symmetrical triangle
b. Rectangle, double top, descending triangle
c. Rectangle, head and shoulder top, ascending triangle

B is correct.
The first chart pattern, which formed between 2011 and 2012, is a rectangle. A rectangle is a continuation pattern. Prior to the rectangle, the stock had been in an uptrend. The rectangle acted as a "rest" period in the strong uptrend. A breakout from the rectangle was followed by another strong upward move. In the second half of 2012, the price formed a double top. A double top is a bearish reversal and should come after an advance. The third chart pattern is a descending triangle. A descending triangle is a bearish continuation pattern. Prior to a descending triangle, the price should be in a downtrend. A descending triangle is usually a "rest" period in a steady downtrend. Following the breakdown, the stock resumed its downtrend.
A is incorrect because chart pattern 1 is not a double bottom. For a double bottom, the prior trend should be downward. In this case, the price moved upward prior to the consolidation. A double bottom is a reversal chart pattern that reverses an existing downtrend. Chart pattern 2 is not a rectangle. Chart pattern 3 is not a symmetrical triangle. A symmetrical triangle has two converging boundaries.
C is incorrect because chart pattern 2 is not a head and shoulders top. For a head and shoulders top, there need to be three peaks, with the head being the highest and the two shoulders being lower than the head. Both head and shoulders and double top are reversal chart patterns, but in this case, pattern 2 can be classified as a double top due to its two peaks. Chart pattern 3 is not an ascending triangle. An ascending triangle has a horizontal upper boundary and an upward-sloping lower boundary. Both symmetrical triangles and ascending triangles can act as continuation patterns, but in this case, chart pattern 3 has a downward-sloping upper boundary and a horizontal lower boundary and is clearly a descending triangle.

Question 7

The chart below shows the Ericsson daily price chart between January 2018 and February 2019. The stock is listed on the Stockholm Stock Exchange, and the price is quoted in Swedish krona. Between October 2018 and February 2019, the Ericsson price chart formed a four-month-long symmetrical triangle. The stock is breaking out of a symmetrical triangle chart pattern, and the analyst wants to calculate the price target. Calculate the price target given the reference levels for the chart pattern boundaries.

a. 98.4
b. 94.9
c. 88.3

B is correct.
The price target is calculated by taking the width of the widest point in the symmetrical triangle and adding it to the breakout level at the upper boundary of the symmetrical triangle.

85.6 − 72.8 = 12.8

12.8 + 82.1 = 94.9

A is incorrect because it is not correct to add the width of the widest point (85.6 − 72.8 = 12.8) to the minor high where the symmetrical triangle started forming (12.8 + 85.6 = 98.4). C is incorrect because it is not correct to add the width of the widest point (85.6 − 72.8 = 12.8) to the level of the lower chart pattern boundary (12.8 + 75.5 = 88.3).

TECHNICAL INDICATORS: MOVING AVERAGES AND BOLLINGER BANDS

6

☐ explain common technical indicators

VIGNETTE

Scene 3

A few days pass. You update your basic price chart for GLD and note that the price has been rising. The current price is the yellow point.

[Chart: SPDR Gold Shares ETF – GLD (daily), Feb to Dec, price range 80–110]

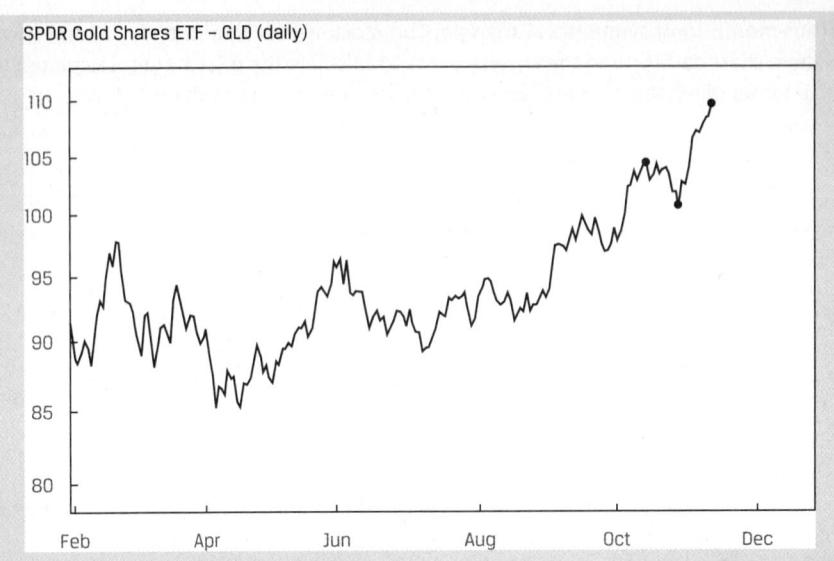

There is a knock on the door. The Head of Alternatives comes into your office and says, *"Hey, gold has rallied and is well above our purchase price. I'm thinking it might be time to sell and take some profits on the investment."*

You respond by saying, *"Remember, this investment in gold is a long-term asset allocation decision. We should not fall into the behavioral finance trap of letting greed guide our decisions."*

You decide to ask the technical analyst to again share her perspective.

The technical analyst prepares the following chart:

[Chart: SPDR Gold Shares ETF – GLD (daily) with Symmetrical Triangle, Symmetrical Triangle Price Target: 109, Stop-Loss: 101.15, Uptrend labeled]

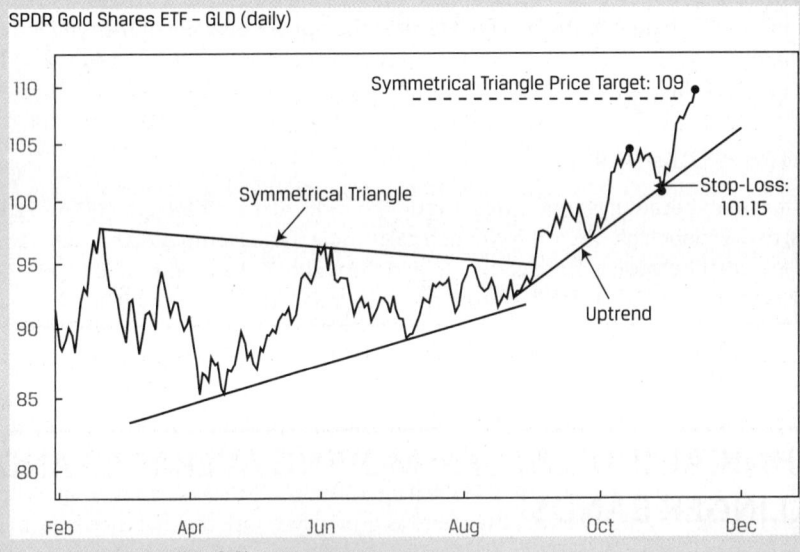

She also prepares the following comments:

- The symmetrical triangle price target has been met at the 109 level. The price target for the symmetrical triangle is calculated by taking the width of the chart pattern at the widest point and adding it to the breakout level.
- However, it is important to note that price can exceed calculated chart pattern price targets. The best way to capture long-term trends is either to use long-term averages to trail the price or to use trendlines to monitor the uptrend for a possible breakdown and a change in trend.

Then, she summarizes:

Technical Indicators: Moving Averages and Bollinger Bands

> *"So, even though the symmetrical triangle chart pattern price objective is met, the uptrend is still strong and is not violated. A new trendline (a steeper one) can be drawn, and the stop-loss can be raised to the most recent minor low of 101.15. In addition, the price continues to record higher lows, which is an indication of a steady uptrend."*
>
> You appreciate the additional perspective.

Technical Indicators

The technical analyst typically uses a variety of other technical indicators to supplement the basic information gleaned from chart patterns. A technical indicator is any measure based on price, market sentiment, or funds flow that can be used to predict changes in price. These mathematically calculated indicators often have a supply and demand underpinning. The moving average is the simplest of these techniques and has been used by statisticians to smooth data since the early 1900s.

Price-Based Indicators

Price-based indicators incorporate information contained in current and historical market prices. Indicators of this type range from simple (e.g., a moving average) to complex (e.g., a stochastic oscillator).

Moving Average

A **moving average** is the average of the closing prices of a security over a specified number of periods. Moving averages smooth out short-term price fluctuations, giving the technician a clearer image of market trends. Technicians commonly use a simple moving average, which weights each price equally in the calculation of the average price. Some technicians prefer to use an exponential moving average (also called an exponentially smoothed moving average), which gives the greatest weight to recent prices while giving exponentially less weight to older prices.

The number of data points included in the moving average depends on the intended use of the moving average. A 20-day moving average is commonly used because a month contains roughly 20 trading days. Also, a 60-day average is commonly used because it represents a quarter year (three months) of trading activity.

Moving averages can be used in conjunction with a price trend or in conjunction with one another. Moving averages are also used to determine support and resistance levels.

Because a moving average is less volatile than price, this tool can be used in several ways. First, whether a price is above or below its moving average is important. As a general guideline, if the price is above a moving average, the trend is up. If the price is below a moving average, the trend is down. Second, the distance between the moving-average line and the price is also significant. Once price begins to move back up toward its moving-average line (in a reversion to the mean), this line can serve as a resistance level. Similarly, when price begins to move down after an upward trend, the moving average can serve as a support level. Even though moving averages for certain time periods (e.g., 200 days) are discussed and widely followed in the financial media, there is no ideal moving-average periodicity. It is important to note that the analyst, trader, or fund manager should pick the time period that is the best fit for the trading/investment horizon.

Two or more moving averages can be used in conjunction. A 5-day moving average is often used as a proxy for short-term momentum, while a 20-day or 60-day moving average can be an indicator of the intermediate trend. The 5-day moving average breaking up through the longer-term moving average can be used as a buy signal, indicating that momentum and trend are changing to the upside, and conversely, the 5-day breaking down through the longer-term moving average can be used as a sell signal.

Longer-horizon investors may want to simply focus on two intermediate-term moving averages. Exhibit 31 shows the price chart of Microsoft Corporation on the NASDAQ stock exchange overlaid with 20-day and 60-day moving averages during 2018–2019. Note that the longer the time frame used in the creation of a moving average, the smoother and less volatile the line will become. Investors often use moving-average crossovers as buy or sell signals. When a short-term moving average (e.g., one month) crosses a longer-term average (e.g., three months) from underneath, this movement is considered bullish. This crossover is called a **bullish crossover**. Conversely, when a short-term moving average crosses a longer-term moving average from above, this movement is considered bearish. This crossover is called a **bearish crossover**. In the case shown in Exhibit 31, a trading strategy of buying on bullish crosses and selling on bearish crosses would have been profitable.

A widely followed moving-average crossover signal is the one that takes place between the 50-day moving average and the 200-day moving average. Financial networks (such as Bloomberg and Reuters) refer this crossover signal as either a **golden cross** or a **death cross**. When the short-term (50-day) moving average crosses above the long-term (200-day) moving average, this movement is called a golden cross and is a bullish signal. Conversely, when the short-term average crosses below the long-term average, this movement is called a death cross and is a bearish signal.

Moving averages, while reducing noise by smoothing out day-to-day fluctuations, are useful for keeping the trader or investor on the right side of the price action and are key to trend-following strategies often used by commodity trading advisers (CTAs). When a short-term moving average is above the long-term average or the price is clearly above the average, traders and investors know that the trend in the given period of analysis is up, and therefore they should remain invested in the overall direction of the trend.

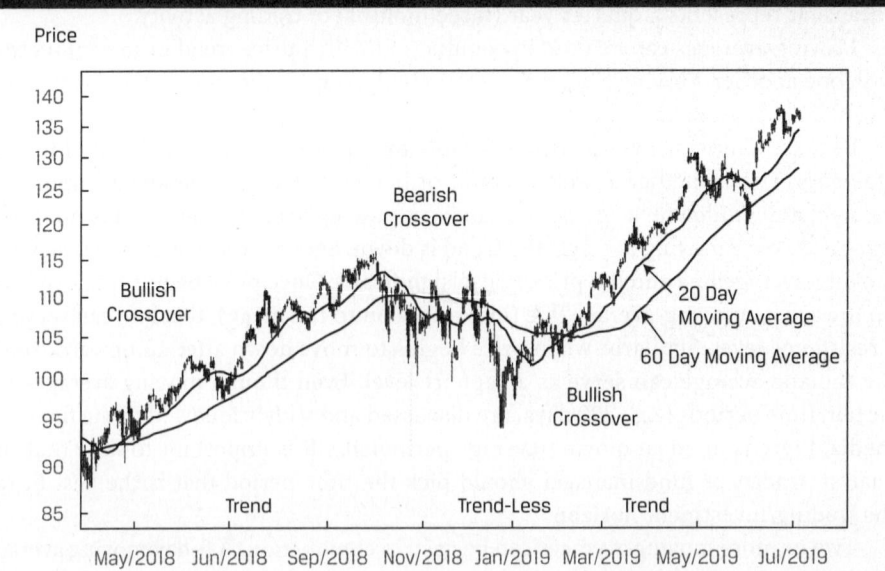

Exhibit 31: Daily Price Chart with 20-Day and 60-Day Moving Averages: Microsoft Corporation, April 2018–April 2019 (US$)

Technical Indicators: Moving Averages and Bollinger Bands

Moving averages are easy to construct, and simple trading rules can be created for using them. Computers can optimize the time lengths to set when using two moving averages. This optimization may take the form of changing the number of days included in each moving average or adding filter rules, such as waiting several days after a trade signal is given, or waiting until a minimum penetration distance is achieved, to make a trade. Reasons for optimization include the desire to minimize false signals and thereby manage capital drawdowns (maximize gains and minimize losses). Once the moving average is optimized, even if a profitable trading system is devised for that security, the strategy is unlikely to work for other securities, especially if they are dissimilar. Also, as market conditions change, a previously optimized trading system may no longer work. For that reason, one should not focus too much on the optimization of moving averages because this practice risks "overfitting" past data that may not necessarily repeat in the future. Moving averages should be used as trend filters.

When the price is above the moving average, this scenario suggests that the trend is upward. When the price is below the average, this scenario should warn the analyst of further weakness. When the short-term moving average is above the long-term moving average, the analyst should be alert for the continuation of that uptrend. When the short-term moving average is below the long-term average, this scenario should signal caution. It may suggest that any initial long exposure should be closed and that the investor should step to the sidelines in expectation of further weakness.

Bollinger Bands

Market veteran John Bollinger combined his knowledge of technical analysis with his knowledge of statistics to create an indicator called **Bollinger Bands**. Bollinger Bands consist of a moving average (middle band), a higher line (upper band) representing the moving average plus a set number of standard deviations from the average price (for the same number of periods used to calculate the moving average), and a lower line (lower band) that is a moving average minus the same number of standard deviations. This indicator can help define a statistically reasonable range that the market is expected to trade within. Exhibit 32 depicts Bollinger Bands for Microsoft Corporation.

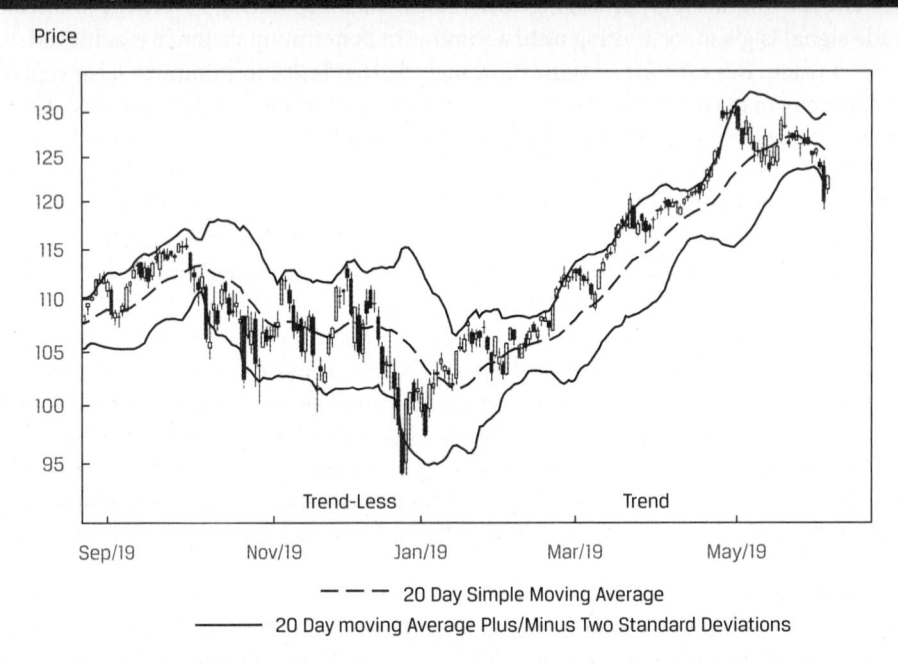

Exhibit 32: Bollinger Bands Using 20-Day Moving Average and Two Standard Deviations: Microsoft Corporation Daily Price Chart, September 2018–April 2019 (US$)

The more volatile the security being analyzed becomes, the wider the range becomes between the two outer lines or bands. Like moving averages, Bollinger Bands can be used to create trading strategies that can be easily computerized and tested. A common use is as a contrarian strategy, in which the investor sells when a security price reaches the upper band and buys the security back when the price reaches either the middle band (if within a perceived uptrend) or the lower band (when within a perceived range). This strategy assumes that the security price will stay within the bands. During trendless periods, this strategy works well. This type of strategy is likely to lead to a large number of trades, but it also limits risk because the trader can quickly exit unprofitable trades. In the event of a sharp price move, investors might instead buy on a significant breakout above the upper band because a major breakout would imply a change in trend that is likely to persist for some time.

The long-term investor would sell on a significant breakdown below the lower band in an attempt to limit downside risk. In this strategy, statistical significance would be defined as breaking above or below the band by a certain percentage (say, 5% or 10%) and/or for a certain period of time (say, a week for a daily price chart). Again, such rules can easily be computerized and tested. In the example of Microsoft, October 2018–February 2019 was a trendless period. A death cross took place in October 2018, and the stock remained choppy within a wide trading range. During this period, a trader could have applied the Bollinger Band strategy to buy at the touch of the lower band and sell at the touch of the upper band. This strategy would have worked well until the stock experienced a change in trend.

In February 2019, Microsoft experienced a bullish moving-average crossover resulting in a golden cross. Following the bullish signal, the price touched the upper Bollinger Band, suggesting a continuation of the uptrend. Selling at the touch of the upper band and waiting for prices to return to the lower band was not the right strategy; buying at the touch of the middle band would have worked better.

Bollinger Band Width Indicator

Technical Indicators: Moving Averages and Bollinger Bands

Bollinger Band width is an indicator derived from Bollinger Bands. Band width measures the percentage difference between the upper band and the lower band. Band width decreases as Bollinger Bands narrow and increases as Bollinger Bands widen. Because Bollinger Bands are based on standard deviation, falling band width reflects decreasing volatility and rising band width reflects increasing volatility.

Bollinger Band width = [(Upper band − Lower band)/Middle band] × 100

When calculating band width, the first step is to subtract the value of the lower band from the value of the upper band. The result is the absolute difference. This difference is then divided by the value of the middle band to normalize the value. This normalized band width can then be compared across different time frames or with the band width values for other securities.

Band width is relative. Band width values should be gauged relative to prior band width values over a period of time. It is important to use an adequate look-back period to define the band width range for a particular ETF, index, or stock.

Bollinger Band width is best known for identifying a "squeeze." A squeeze occurs when volatility falls to a very low level, as evidenced by the narrowing bands.

The theory is that periods of low volatility are followed by periods of high volatility. Relatively narrow band width can foreshadow a significant advance or decline. After a squeeze, a price surge and a subsequent band break signal the start of a new move. A new advance starts with a squeeze and a subsequent break above the upper band. A new decline starts with a squeeze and a subsequent break below the lower band.

Exhibit 33: Bollinger Band Width and Squeeze: Diös Fastigheter AB, March 2017–March 2019 Weekly Scale Price Chart (Swedish krona)

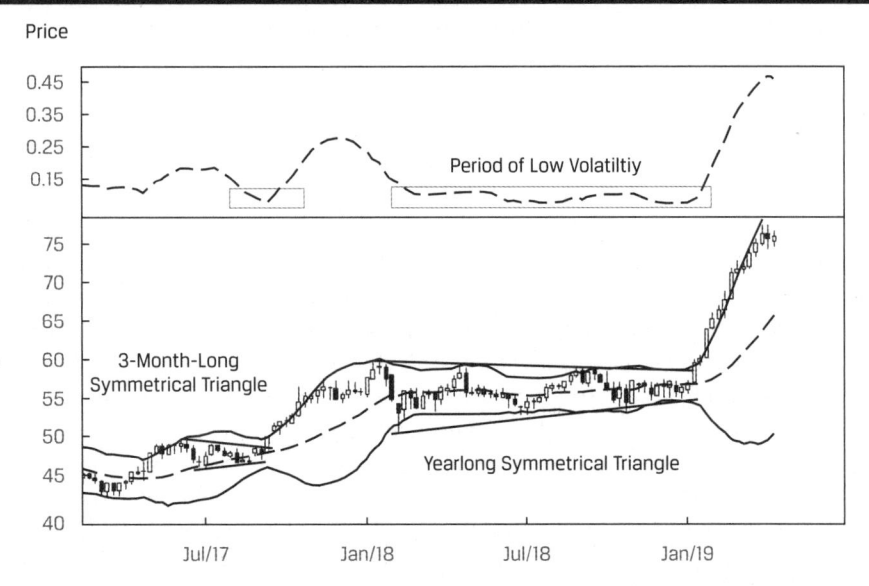

Exhibit 33 shows the Diös Fastigheter AB price chart that was featured earlier in this reading (see Exhibit 22). Every time the stock entered into a consolidation period, the volatility dropped to low levels. Low volatility was an indication of a possible high-volatility period to come. Low volatility begets high volatility, and vice versa. A breakout from low-volatility conditions can be seen on the Bollinger Band width indicator: Bollinger Bands start expanding, and Bollinger Band width starts rising from extremely low levels.

When combined with classical charting tools (such as a breakout above a predefined chart pattern boundary), Bollinger Bands have significant value. A breakout from a consolidation period at a time of historical low volatility suggests that the trend period that follows will have the strength to resume toward much higher levels. The two breakouts shown in Exhibit 33, one from a three-month-long symmetrical triangle and the other from a yearlong symmetrical triangle, both started from extreme low-volatility conditions.

7 TECHNICAL INDICATORS: OSCILLATORS, RELATIVE STRENGTH, AND SENTIMENT

☐ explain common technical indicators

One of the key challenges in using indicators overlaid on a price chart is the difficulty of discerning changes in market movements that are out of the ordinary. **Momentum oscillators** are one tool intended to alleviate this problem. They are constructed from the rate of change in price data, but they are calculated so that they either oscillate between a low and a high (typically 0 and 100) or oscillate around a number (such as 0 or 100). Because of this construction, extreme highs and lows are easily discernible. These extremes can be viewed as graphic representations of market sentiment when selling or buying activity is more aggressive than has been historically typical. Because they are price based, momentum oscillators can be analyzed by using the same tools technicians use to analyze price, such as the concepts of trend, support, and resistance. It is important to note that indicators that are derived from price will lag price. An analyst will be able to calculate the latest value for the indicator only after the relevant day's, week's, or month's price data are recorded.

Technicians also look for **convergence** or **divergence** between oscillators and price. Convergence occurs when the oscillator moves in the same manner as the security being analyzed, and divergence occurs when the oscillator moves differently from the security. For example, when price reaches a new high, this sign is considered bullish, but if the momentum oscillator being used does not also reach a new high at the same time, the result is divergence. Divergence is considered to be an early warning of weakness, an indication that (in this case) the uptrend may soon end because momentum (or the rate of change in prices) is actually waning despite the new highs.

Momentum oscillators should be used in conjunction with an understanding of the existing market (price) trend. Oscillators alert a trader to **overbought** or **oversold** conditions. In overbought conditions, market sentiment is considered unsustainably bullish. In oversold conditions, market sentiment is considered unsustainably bearish. In other words, the oscillator *range* must be judged separately for every security. Some securities may experience wide variations, and others may experience only minor variations.

Oscillators have three main uses:

1. Oscillators can be used to determine the strength of a trend. Extreme overbought levels are warning signals for uptrends, and extreme oversold levels are warning signals for downtrends. We should note, however, that occasionally an indicator can stay overbought or oversold for an extended period of time. As a result, just because the indicator reached an overbought level

doesn't mean we should anticipate a sudden change in trend. Uptrends and downtrends can sometimes resume despite overbought/oversold readings on oscillators.

2. When oscillators reach historically high or low levels, they may be signaling a pending trend reversal. For oscillators that move above and below zero, crossing the zero level signals a change in the direction of the trend. For oscillators that move above and below 100, crossing the 100 level signals a change in the direction of the trend.

3. In a trendless market, oscillators can be used for short-term trading decisions—that is, to sell at overbought levels and to buy at oversold levels.

Rate of Change Oscillator

The rate of change (ROC) oscillator is a pure momentum oscillator and is sometimes referred to as simply the momentum oscillator. The ROC oscillator is calculated by taking the most recent closing price, subtracting the closing price from a date that is a set number of days in the past, and multiplying the result by 100:

$$M = (V - Vx) \times 100,$$

where

M = momentum oscillator value

V = most recent closing price

Vx = closing price x days ago, typically 10 days

When the ROC oscillator crosses zero in the same direction as the direction of the trend, this movement is considered a buy or sell signal. For example, if the ROC oscillator crosses into positive territory during an uptrend, this movement is a buy signal. If it enters into negative territory during a downtrend, the crossover is considered a sell signal. The technician will ignore crossovers in opposition to the trend because when using oscillators, the technician must *alwaysfirst* take into account the general trend.

An alternative method of constructing this oscillator is to set it to oscillate above and below 100, instead of 0, as follows:

$$M = \frac{V}{Vx} \times 100$$

This approach is shown in Exhibit 34 for Microsoft Corporation.

Exhibit 34: ROC Oscillator with 100 as Midpoint: Microsoft Corporation, April 2018–April 2019 (US$)

In Exhibit 34, the ROC oscillator for Microsoft stock, traded on the NASDAQ stock exchange, is set to move around 100, and x is 12 days. An extreme high means that the stock has posted its highest gain in any 12-day period, and an extreme low reading means it has posted its greatest loss over any 12-day period. When investors bid up the price of a security too rapidly, the indication is that sentiment may be unduly bullish and the market may be overbought. Exhibit 34 shows that overbought levels of the ROC oscillator coincide with temporary highs in the stock price. So, those levels would have been signals to sell the stock. We analyzed the moving-average crossovers and the trend and consolidation periods in preceding sections of this reading. It is important to incorporate that information in analyzing the price chart. During trend periods, we can see that the ROC oscillator moves approximately between 100 and 110. So once the uptrend is confirmed with a bullish crossover, we can use the ROC oscillator to time the minor peaks and troughs in the uptrend. A good strategy would be to take profits as the ROC approaches the 110 level and initiate new long positions as it falls back to the 100 level. During a trendless period (consolidation), we can see that the ROC oscillator moves in a wide range between 80 and 110. Following the bearish crossover, we should be aware that the trend period might be over and that we might see choppy price action. The timing of entry and exit might be more difficult in such a market environment.

However, with the help of Bollinger Bands and ROC oscillators, the analyst can capture overbought/oversold levels in the consolidation range. In the beginning of 2019, the ROC oscillator once again climbed above the 100 level, and the trend was confirmed with a bullish crossover, suggesting a new uptrend. In February 2019, the ROC oscillator found support around 100, the low level for the indicator during an uptrend. It was a good time to initiate a long position as the stock was entering a new uptrend period. In previous sections, we have seen that the Microsoft price also touchedthe upper Bollinger Band following the bullish crossover signal and generated a buy signal based on the Bollinger Band strategy. The other notable aspect of Exhibit 34 is the divergence when the share price hit a new high in October 2018 but the ROC oscillator did not reach its July high. This divergence would have been a bearish signal and would have been interpreted to mean that, although the share price hit a new high, market momentum was actually lower than it had been previously. In itself, this information would not have been enough to warrant selling the shares because an uptrend in price was still in place, but it alerted the technician to the fact that the trend might end soon. The technician could then look for further indications of the trend's end—such as a moving-average crossover to the downside—and with such confirmation, decide to sell the stock.

Relative Strength Index

Another tool often used to measure momentum is a **relative strength index (RSI)**, which is computed over a rolling time period. The RSI graphically compares a security's gains with its losses over the set period. The creator of the RSI, Welles Wilder, proposed a 14-day time period, and this is the period used by most technical analysis software. The technician should understand that this variable can be changed and that the optimal time range should be determined by how the technician intends to use the RSI information. Factors that influence the selection of a time period for the RSI are similar to those that influence the selection of a time period for moving averages.

The RSI is a momentum oscillator and provides information on whether or not an asset is overbought—in other words, whether an asset has advanced too quickly relative to a chance to digest recent advances. The formula is as follows:

$$RSI = 100 - \frac{100}{1 + RS},$$

where

$$RS = \frac{\sum (\text{Up changes for the period under consideration})}{\sum (\text{Down changes for the period under consideration})}.$$

The RSI indicator is primarily used to analyze the inner momentum of a security. The analysis is performed by identifying divergences. A positive divergence takes place when the security price records a new low but the RSI records a higher low. This scenario suggests that while the price is reaching a new low, the inner momentum is improving; in other words, the selling pressure is decreasing.

A negative divergence takes place when the security price reaches a new high but the RSI fails to reach a new high. This scenario suggests that while the price is reaching a new high, the inner momentum is deteriorating; in other words, buying pressure is decreasing. Divergences are early signs of reversal that may foreshadow and anticipate a subsequent moving-average crossover reversal.

Note: The RSI is not to be confused with the "relative strength analysis" charting method. The RSI measures the internal strength of a single asset in terms of a ratio of the magnitude of "up days" to the magnitude of "down days" of that asset across a given period, whereas relative strength analysis compares the ratio of two security prices plotted over time or the relative performance of two assets.

Exhibit 35: Candlestick Chart with RSI: WTI Light Crude Oil First-Month Continuation Futures Price, June 2014–April 2019 (US$)

The candlestick chart of the WTI Light Crude Oil futures price in Exhibit 35 illustrates several aspects of the use of an RSI. For example, because the RSI oscillator was lower than 30 in the beginning of 2015, so the commodity was oversold at that time, a simple reading of the chart might have led to the conclusion that the trader should buy the commodity because an "oversold" indicator reading suggests the price is likely to rebound in the near term. However, this decision would have resulted in further losses as the price slid to new lows. A more careful technical interpretation that took the general trend into account would have indicated that the commodity was in a downtrend, as can be seen by the trendline and the fact that the price was trading below its long-term average, so further RSI readings below 30 could be expected. In other words, using the RSI alone may identify short-term reversal levels but risk early bottom-picking or top-picking that can still prove problematic. Buying at the time of an oversold condition might not be the best timing tool for trend reversals. Likewise, an overbought reading above the 80 level alone is not sufficient to conclude that price will reverse. It is best to combine the momentum indicator with elements of trend analysis, such as a trendline break.

Even if a stock, commodity, or currency is showing an oversold reading on the RSI, there is often not enough information to conclude that it is a good time to buy that security. In the second half of 2015, WTI reached a new low, but this time the RSI didn't reach a new low. Again, just because we have seen the first positive divergence (RSI lows labeled 1 and 2 in Exhibit 35) doesn't mean that a trend reversal is taking place. We need to see confirmation of the change in trend in the form of a breach of a trendline or a long-term average (confirmation by price action). In the beginning of 2016, the WTI price reached a new low but the RSI generated its second positive divergence. It was after this low that the price managed to breach the downtrend line and the long-term moving average on the upside, confirming a change in trend. A technician should be patient enough to wait for such periods of clear divergence late in the trend of a given asset.

Similarly, the top that formed during 2018 on the WTI price chart followed the same sequence of divergences. This time, the price continued to reach new highs but the RSI warned of a possible eventual change in trend direction. Only after the second negative divergence (RSI peaks labeled 2 and 3 in Exhibit 35) did the price of WTI break down the trendline (confirmation by price action) and the long-term average, resulting in a change in trend.

Stochastic Oscillator

The **stochastic oscillator** is a momentum indicator that compares a particular closing price of a security to a range of its prices over a certain period of time. The stochastic oscillator is based on the observation that in uptrends, prices tend to close at or near the high end of their recent range and in downtrends, they tend to close near the low end. The logic behind these patterns is that if the shares of a stock are constantly being bid up during the day but then lose value by the close, continuation of the rally is doubtful. If sellers have enough supply to overwhelm buyers, the rally is suspect. If a stock rallies during the day and is able to hold on to some or most of those gains by the close, that sign is bullish.

The stochastic oscillator oscillates between 0 and 100 and has a default 14-day period, which may be adjusted for the situation, as we discussed for the RSI. The oscillator is composed of two lines, called %K and %D, that are calculated as follows:

$$\%K = 100\left(\frac{C - L14}{H14 - L14}\right),$$

where

C = the latest closing price

$L14$ = the lowest price in the past 14 days

$H14$ = the highest price in the past 14 daysand where

$\%D$ = the average of the last three %K values calculated daily

Analysts should think about %D in the same way they would a long-term moving-average line in conjunction with a short-term line. That is, %D, because it is the average of three %K values, is the slower-moving, smoother line and is called the signal line. And %K is the faster-moving line. The %K value means that the latest closing price (C) was in the %K percentile of the low–high range ($L14$ to $H14$).

The default oversold–overbought range for the stochastic oscillator is based on reading the signal line relative to readings of 20 and 80. The shorter the time frame is, the more volatile the oscillator becomes and the more false signals it generates.

The stochastic oscillator should be used with other technical tools, such as trend analysis, pattern analysis, and RSI analysis. If several methods suggest the same conclusion, the trader has convergence (or confirmation), but if they give conflicting signals, the trader has divergence, which is a warning signal suggesting that further analysis is necessary.

The absolute level of the two lines should be considered in light of their normal range. Movements or changes in trend in the middle of an 80–20 indexed range can most often be deemed short-term noise. To a technician, movements above this range indicate an overbought security and are considered bearish; movements below this range indicate an oversold security and are considered bullish. But it is important to note that an overbought indicator doesn't warrant selling the security. Likewise, an oversold reading is not an indication to buy. One should generally look for changes in trend with the help of the %K line changing direction or a trendline break or a breach of moving average.

Crossovers of the two lines can also give trading signals, the same way crossovers of two moving averages give signals. When %K moves from below the %D line to above it, this move is considered a bullish short-term trading signal; conversely, when %K moves from above the %D line to below it, this movement is considered bearish. In practice, a trader can use technical analysis software to adjust trading rules and optimize the calculation of the stochastic oscillator for a particular security and investment purpose (e.g., short-term trading or long-term investing). While optimization can help to achieve better results for a certain period, as conditions change, the parameters might need to be revised.

The reason technicians use historical data to test their trading rules and find the optimal parameters for each security is that each security is different and may have its own natural rhythm. The group of market participants actively trading also differs from security to security. Just as each person has a different personality, so do groups of people. In effect, the group of active market participants trading each security is imparting its personality on the trading activity for that security. As this group changes over time, the ideal parameters for a particular security may change. The choice of either optimizing the indicator or following the default set of parameters is a continuous trade-off.

There are benefits as well as disadvantages to optimization. Exhibit 36 provides a good example of how the stochastic oscillator can be used together with trend analysis. The exhibit provides the daily price chart and stochastic oscillator for Total SA, which is traded on the Paris stock exchange, from July 2018 through April 2019. Note that during the sideways movement between July and October, the stochastic oscillator moved between 20 and 80 from one boundary to the other. It was one of the best times to trade the stock with the help of overbought/oversold conditions identified by the oscillator. Each time the oscillator reversed from the 80 level, it provided a valid sell signal, and each time it reversed from the 20 level, it provided a valid buy signal. These reversals coincided with reversals from horizontal support/resistance levels on the price chart. When the downtrend started in October, the stochastic oscillator reached oversold levels and hardly recovered above 50. Technicians should be able to identify the trend period (sideways, upward, or downward) and then adjust their expectations as to the levels the indicator can reach. During the downtrend, the oversold level remained around 20 but the overbought level shifted down to 50. Selling the rally around the 50 level in the established downtrend proved to be a good strategy. When the uptrend started at the beginning of January, the stochastic oscillator reached overbought levels. However, during the uptrend, the oscillator didn't reach oversold levels. While the overbought level remained around 80, the oversold level during the uptrend shifted up to 50. Buying the pullback when the indicator reached the 50 level proved to be a good strategy.

Technical Indicators: Oscillators, Relative Strength, and Sentiment

Exhibit 36: Daily Price Chart and Stochastic Oscillator: Total SA, July 2018–April 2019 (€)

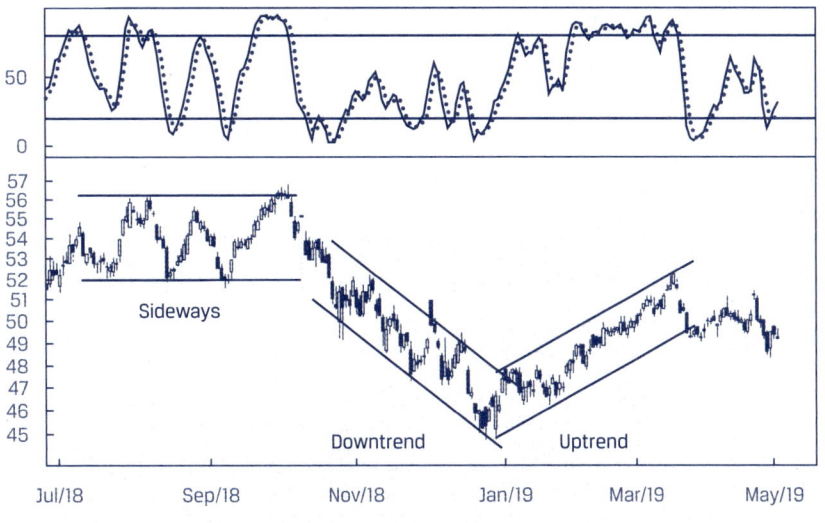

Moving-Average Convergence/Divergence Oscillator (MACD)

The **moving-average convergence/divergence oscillator** is commonly referred to as the MACD. The MACD is the difference between short-term and long-term moving averages of the security's price. The MACD is constructed by calculating two lines, the MACD line and the signal line:

- The MACD line is the difference between two exponentially smoothed moving averages, generally over periods of 12 and 26 days.
- The signal line is the exponentially smoothed average of the MACD line, generally over 9 days.

The indicator oscillates around zero and has no upper or lower limit. Rather than using a set overbought–oversold range for the MACD, the analyst compares the current level with the historical performance of the oscillator for a particular security to determine when a security is out of its normal sentiment range.

The MACD is used in technical analysis in three ways:

1. to note crossovers of the MACD line and the signal line, as discussed for moving averages and the stochastic oscillator. Crossovers of the two lines may indicate a change in trend.
2. to look for times when the MACD is outside its normal range for a given security.
3. to use trendlines on the MACD itself. When the MACD is trending in the same direction as price, this pattern is in convergence, and when the two are trending in opposite directions, the pattern is in divergence.

Exhibit 37 shows a weekly price chart for Palladium (at the top) with the MACD oscillator for August 2016 through April of 2019. The chart shows the effectiveness of MACD crossover signals when used in conjunction with trendline breakouts. This example highlights once again the importance of confirming any indicator signal with price action. During the uptrend between October 2016 and December 2018, the MACD generated several crossover signals. The early 2018 crossover signal was confirmed by a breakdown of the uptrend channel. Similarly, the trend reversal that took place in the last quarter of 2018 was confirmed by both the MACD crossover signal and a trend channel breakout. In August 2018, we can also identify the long-legged doji candlestick that marked the bottom. The uptrend that started in the last quarter of 2018 pushed the MACD to historical high levels when compared with previous readings. The reversal not only generated a MACD crossover but also broke down the upward trend channel.

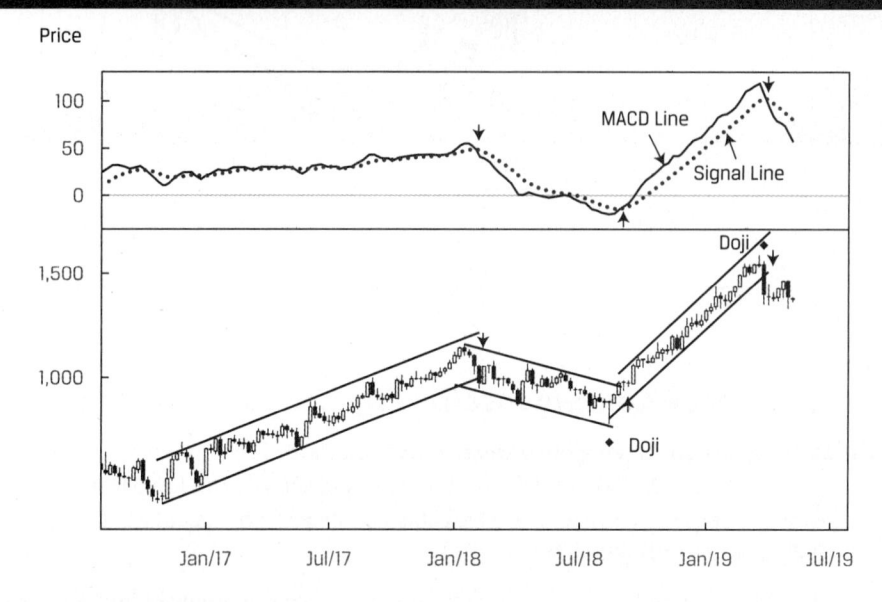

Exhibit 37: MACD and Weekly Price Chart: Palladium, August 2016–April 2019 (US$)

Sentiment Indicators

Sentiment indicators attempt to gauge investor activity for signs of increasing bullishness or bearishness. Sentiment indicators come in two forms—investor polls and calculated statistical indexes.

Calculated Statistical Indexes

Statistical indexes are sentiment indicators that are calculated from market data, such as security prices. The two most commonly used are derived from the options market; they are the put/call ratio and the volatility index. Additionally, many analysts look at margin debt and short interest.

The **put/call ratio** is the volume of put options traded divided by the volume of call options traded for a particular financial instrument. Investors who buy put options on a security are presumably bearish, and investors who buy call options are presumably bullish. The volume of call options traded is greater than the volume of put options over time, so the put/call ratio is normally below 1.0. The ratio is considered to be a contrarian indicator, meaning that higher values of put volume relative to call volume are considered bullish and lower values are considered bearish. But the ratio's usefulness as a contrarian indicator is limited, except at extreme low or high levels (relative to the historical trading level) of the put/call ratio for a particular financial instrument. The actual value of the put/call ratio and its normal range will be different for each security or market, so no standard definitions of overbought and oversold levels exist.

The **CBOE Volatility Index (VIX)** is a measure of near-term market volatility calculated by the Chicago Board Options Exchange. Since 2003, the VIX has been calculated from option prices on the stocks in the S&P 500. The VIX rises when market participants become fearful of an impending market decline. These participants bid up the price of puts, and the result is an increase in the VIX level. Technicians use the VIX in conjunction with trend, pattern, and oscillator tools, and it is interpreted from a contrarian perspective. When other indicators suggest that the market is oversold and the VIX is at an extreme high, this combination is considered bullish. Exhibit 38 shows the VIX from March 2005 to April 2019.

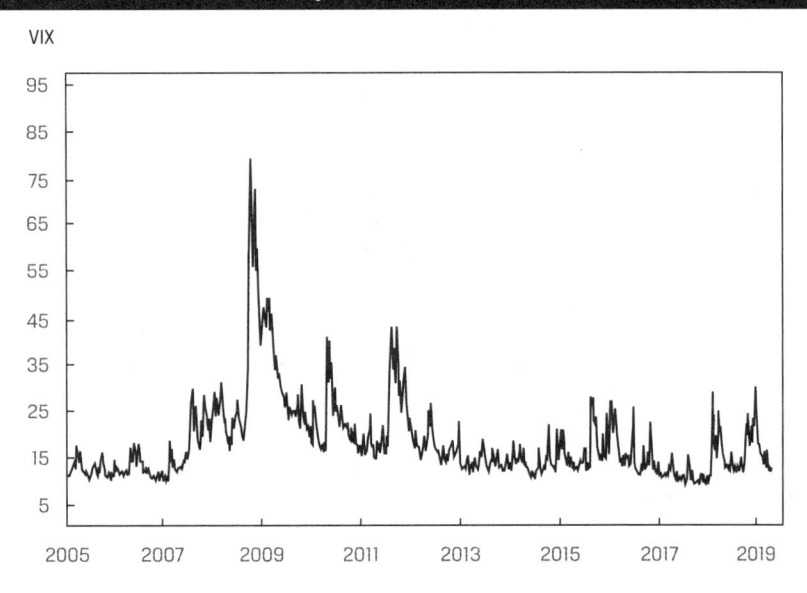

Exhibit 38: VIX, March 2005–April 2019

Margin debt is also often used as an intermediate- to long-term indication of sentiment. As a group, investors have a history of buying near market tops and selling at the bottom. When the market is rising and indexes reach new highs, investors are motivated to buy more equities in the hope of participating in the market rally. A margin account permits an investor to borrow part of the investment cost from the brokerage firm. This debt magnifies the gains or losses resulting from the investment.

Investor psychology plays an important role in the concept of margin debt as an indicator. When stock margin debt is increasing, investors are aggressively buying, and stock prices will move higher because of increased demand. Eventually, the margin traders use all of their available credit, so their buying power (and, therefore, demand) decreases, which fuels a price decline. Falling prices may trigger margin calls and forced selling, which drive prices even lower.

Brokerage firms must report activity in their customers' margin accounts, so keeping track of borrowing behavior is relatively easy. Exhibit 39 provides a 22-year comparison of margin debt with the S&P 500. The correlation is striking: Rising margin debt is generally associated with a rising index level, and falling margin debt is associated with a falling index level. In fact, for the two decades shown in Exhibit 39, the correlation coefficient between the level of margin debt and the S&P 500 is 80.2%. When margin debt peaked in the summer of 2007, the market also topped out. Margin debt dropped sharply during the latter part of 2008 as the subprime crisis took the market down. Investors began to use borrowed funds again in the first half of 2009, when heavily discounted shares became increasingly attractive. Margin debt was still well below the average of the last decade, but in this instance, the upturn would be viewed as a bullish sign by advocates of this indicator. Over the past decade, both margin debt and the S&P 500 have climbed to new highs. This outcome has been bullish for the market in the short term but is concerning in the longer term.

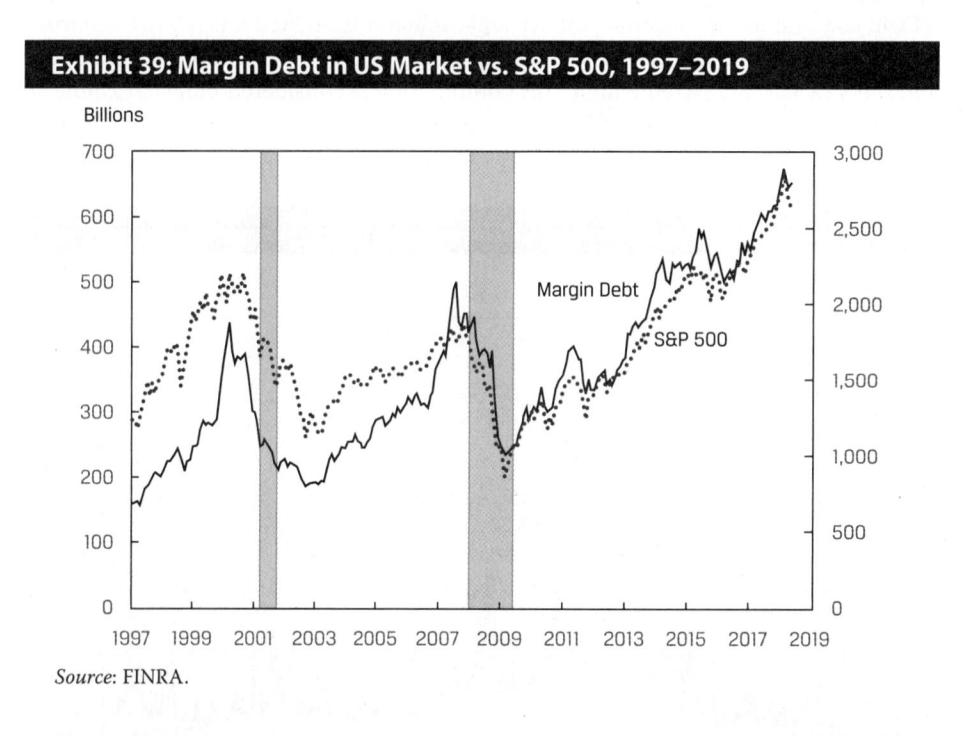

Exhibit 39: Margin Debt in US Market vs. S&P 500, 1997–2019

Source: FINRA.

Question 8

A trader wants to buy WTI Crude Oil futures. She wants to build a sizable position and is willing to enter a long position after the uptrend is underway. In other words, the trader aims to invest once the uptrend is established. For this reason, the trader wants to utilize moving-average crossovers as a trend filter and wants to buy after the bullish crossover. In addition to utilizing moving averages, she wants to utilize momentum as a timing tool to enter long positions. The trader knows that in uptrends, a pullback to the 100 level on the momentum indicator offers a buying opportunity. Find three points on the chart that meet those two criteria for a buying opportunity: an uptrend and a pullback to the 100 level.

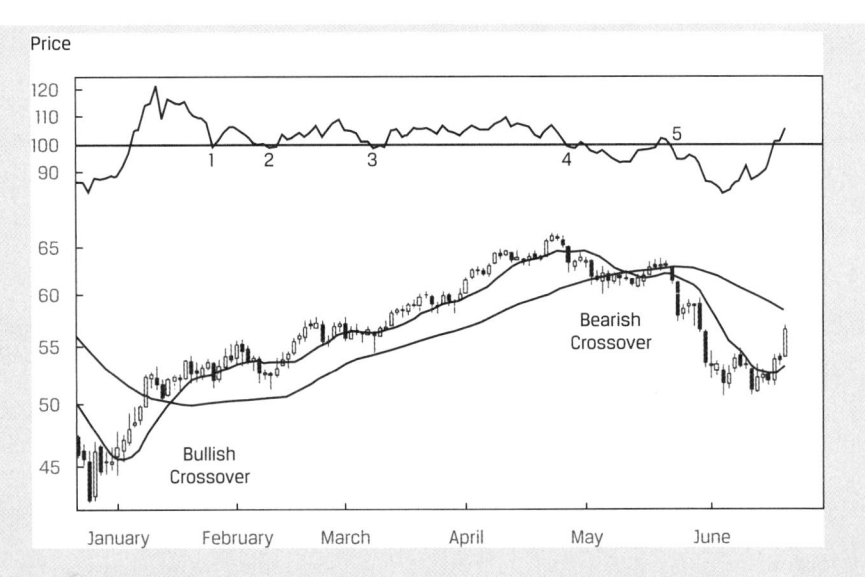

Technical Indicators: Oscillators, Relative Strength, and Sentiment

[Chart showing price with momentum indicator above and candlesticks with moving averages below, labeled points 1-5, Bullish Crossover in January and Bearish Crossover in May/June]

- a. 3, 4, and 5
- b. 1, 4, and 5
- c. 1, 3, and 4

Answer: C. The bullish crossover took place in the middle of January 2019. At the time, the momentum indicator was above 110—an overbought level. Later, the indicator pulled back to the 100 level. The points labeled 1, 2, 3, and 4 were all buying opportunities in a steady uptrend. Even though point 4 met both criteria, the move failed to materialize into a new uptrend, and the indicator fell below the 100 level, indicating a change in trend. Weakness in momentum was followed by a bearish crossover on the moving averages. Neither A nor B is the correct answer because at point 5, the momentum indicator was pulling back to the 100 level but the moving averages had already had a bearish crossover, suggesting a downtrend. All points except 5 were buying opportunities in an uptrend.

Question 9

When a stock price moves to a new high but the momentum indicator records a lower high, the analyst labels the divergence as a:

- a. positive divergence.
- b. negative divergence.
- c. positive reversal divergence.

Answer: B. A negative divergence takes place when a stock price moves to a new high but the momentum indicator fails to keep up with the price and records a lower high.
A is not the correct answer because a positive divergence takes place when a stock moves to a new low but the indicator records a higher low.
C is not the correct answer because a positive reversal divergence takes place when the indicator reaches a new low but the price fails to record a new low.

Question 10

A trader wants to take a long position in WTI Crude Oil. He wants to utilize the RSI indicator to check for positive divergence as an early trend reversal signal but also wants to time his entry with a chart pattern breakout signal. Which number on the chart below is sufficient to make a trade decision based on the above requirements?

a. 1
b. 2
c. 3

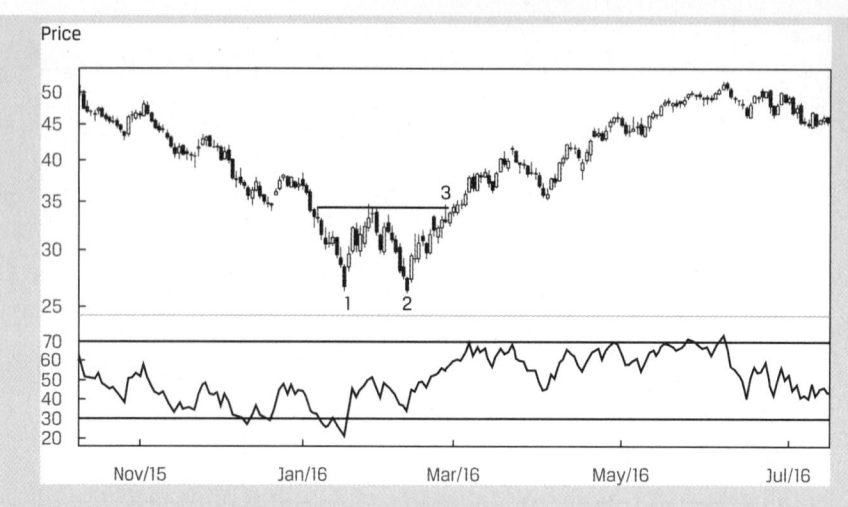

Answer: C. At point 3, the RSI has already reached an oversold level, rebounded, and formed a positive divergence. Meanwhile, the price holds at its previous low, forming a double bottom. Double bottom breakout confirmation takes place when the price breaches the neckline at point 3.

A is not the correct answer because at point 1, the price is in a steady downtrend and the indicator is at an oversold level. The price can continue to fall, and the indicator can remain in oversold territory.

B is not the correct answer because at point 2, the price is testing a support (previous low) and the indicator is showing a positive divergence. However, we don't have confirmation on the price chart in the form of a reversal chart pattern completion or a downtrend breakout. The trend reversal confirmation takes place at point 3.

Question 11

The chart below shows the price of bitcoin versus the US dollar between August 2015 and December 2015. In November 2015, bitcoin had a sharp advance, which turned into a buying frenzy and reached the 500 level. After the sharp advance, the price of bitcoin sold off to test 295. In late 2015, the bitcoin/US dollar price chart tested the November 2015 highs. During the uptrend between November and December, the stochastic oscillator reached overbought levels. An overbought indicator can remain overbought while price continues to move higher. Based on support/resistance levels and the stochastic oscillator, what would be your strategy at point 3?

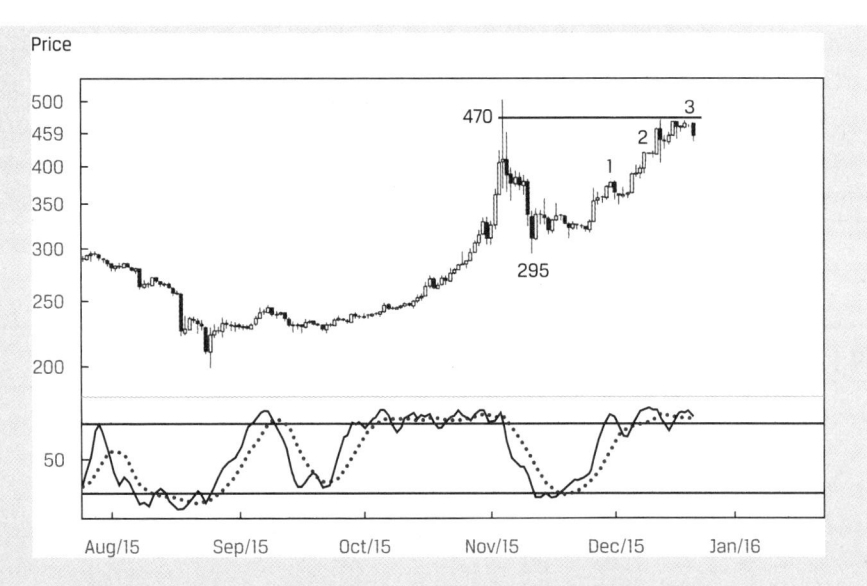

Technical Indicators: Oscillators, Relative Strength, and Sentiment

a. Buy more, because the price is in an uptrend and the indicator is overbought.

b. Sell, because the price has reached an important resistance-level overbought reading on the stochastic oscillator.

c. Sell, because the indicator has formed its fifth negative divergence.

Answer: B. The stochastic oscillator can reach overbought levels and stay in the overbought range (above 80). This scenario doesn't mean one should sell because of the overbought reading. Point 1 is an overbought reading on the stochastic oscillator, but the price is still far from the strong resistance area. Point 2 is similar. The stochastic oscillator is at an overbought level once again, but the price is below the strong resistance. At point 3, price meets both conditions: an overbought reading on the oscillator and a test of the strong resistance level. From a risk/reward perspective, it is a better decision to sell at the resistance with overbought conditions.

A is not the correct answer because the price of bitcoin is reaching the resistance level formed by the minor high at the 470 level. The test of the resistance takes place after the stochastic oscillator reaches an overbought level. The probability of a reversal is higher at point 3 than at 1 and 2. As a result, buying more bitcoin at the resistance is not the best strategy.

C is not the correct answer because the indicator hasn't formed its fifth negative divergence. Between the minor highs of points 2 and 3, the indicator forms its first negative divergence.

Question 12

A trader is looking to trade breakout opportunities as she thinks the cyclical nature of the markets suggests a strong trend period approaching. She knows that volatility is cyclical and that low volatility begets high volatility and vice versa. She opens charts with three different indicators: Bollinger Band width, the MACD, and the RSI. Which indicator and condition will guide her in identifying breakout opportunities by capturing low-volatility conditions?

a. The MACD line crossing over the signal line when the indicator is below the zero level

b. The RSI crossing above the 30 level after generating a positive divergence

c. The Bollinger Band width indicator reaching its lowest level over a three-year look-back period

Answer: C. Bollinger Band width measures volatility with the help of Bollinger Bands. Band width is narrow and the indicator reaches low levels when price goes through a low-volatility condition. Low-volatility periods are usually followed by high-volatility periods, and these are usually trend periods that emerge from lengthy consolidations. Neither A nor B is the correct answer because both the MACD and the RSI are price-based trend indicators. They don't have a volatility component in their calculation.

8. INTERMARKET ANALYSIS

☐ describe principles of intermarket analysis
☐ explain technical analysis applications to portfolio management

VIGNETTE

Scene 4

A few days pass, and the Deputy CIO is back from her Antarctic vacation. She thanks you for your efforts while she was away. She mentions that while viewing the penguins in Antarctica, she was thinking that although the gold investment was put in place for long-term asset allocation, she should find out about any tactical asset allocation opportunities. She asks you to look at gold versus oil. Before doing an in-depth analysis, you ask the technical analyst to provide perspective using intermarket analysis.

The technical analyst prepares the following chart:

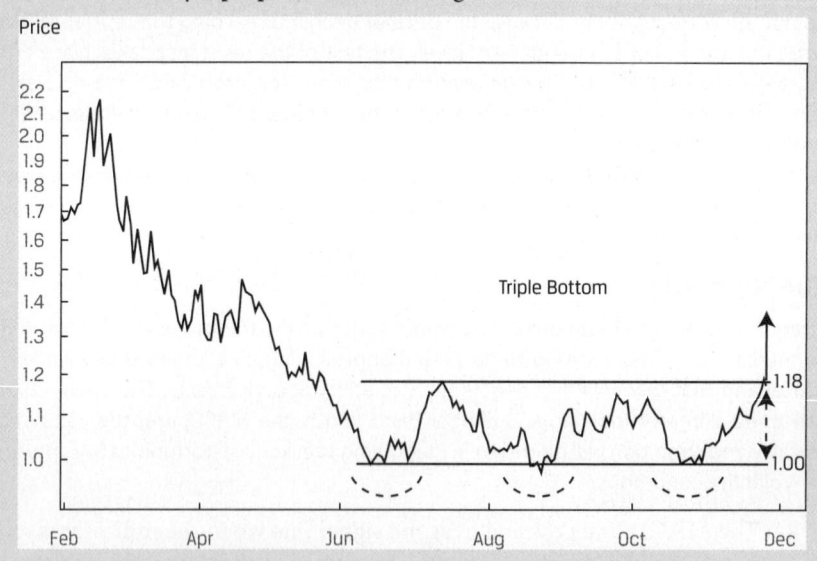

She also prepares the following comments:

- For ease of understanding, the GLD/WTI ratio is indexed to 1.0 at the low in June 2009.
- Between February and June, GLD underperformed WTI. However, since June 2009, the GLD/WTI ratio has started forming a bottom. The GLD/WTI ratio has fluctuated between the 1.0 level and the 1.18 level.

> - The sideways consolidation of the GLD/WTI ratio formed a triple bottom. A triple bottom can act as a major reversal and could result in a strong outperformance period for GLD.
>
> Then, she summarizes:
>
> "So, now is not the time to allocate from GLD to WTI because GLD could start outperforming WTI. In addition, a breakout on the relative performance chart of GLD/WTI would put the gold price on the radar of many investors."
>
> You thank the technical analyst for her support. You are also glad that you had a chance to work with the technical analyst and feel that you better understand the role technical analysis can play in investment management. You are also happy that the Deputy CIO is back in the office! Well, mostly…

Principles of Intermarket Analysis

Intermarket analysis is a field within technical analysis that combines analyses of major categories of securities—namely, equities, bonds, currencies, and commodities—to identify market trends and possible inflections in a trend. Intermarket analysis also looks at industry subsectors and their relationship to sectors and industries. In addition, it measures the relative performance of major equity benchmarks around the globe.

In intermarket analysis, technicians often look for inflection points in one market as a sign or clue to start looking for a change in trend in a related market. To identify these intermarket relationships, a commonly used tool is relative strength analysis, which charts the price of one security divided by the price of another or the ratio of the values of two assets. A subtle shift may show up first in this kind of ratio analysis, where it may be clearer than in either individual chart pattern. Compared to traditional global macro analysis, using technical analysis to conduct intermarket analysis is considerably less time-consuming.

Exhibit 40 shows the price of 10-year US Treasury bonds compared with the S&P 500. Major trends can be clearly seen in periods of both outperformance and underperformance of the T-bond price relative to the S&P 500. The inflection points in this chart occur in 2000, 2003, 2007, and 2009. At each of these points, the relative performance ratio signaled that the time had come to move investments between these asset classes.

Exhibit 40: Relative Strength of 10-Year T-Bonds vs. S&P 500, 1999–2018

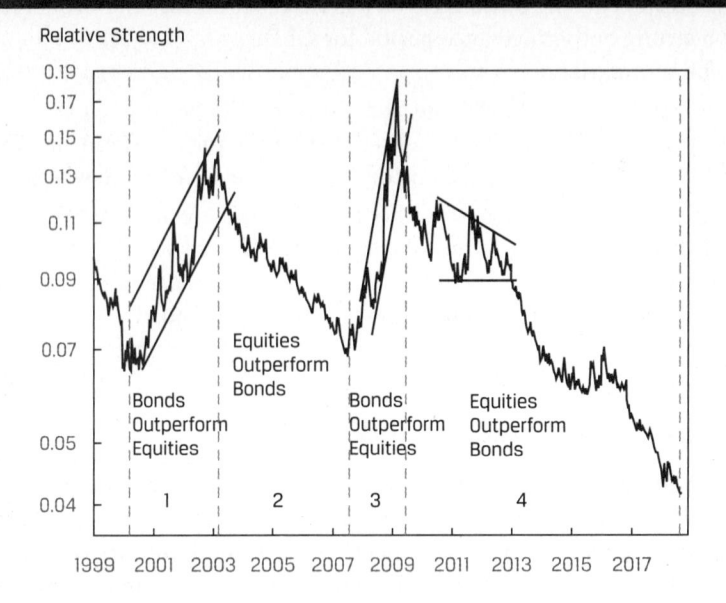

Exhibit 41 is a relative strength chart depicting the ratio of the S&P 500 to commodity prices. The chart shows a clear reversal of trend in mid-2008 from outperformance by commodities to outperformance by equities. This inflection point shows US stocks strengthening relative to commodities and indicates that moving funds away from commodities and into US equities might be appropriate. Of course, promptly interpreting such a sudden "V-reversal" in trend is still difficult to do, but a ratio chart may still help in the identification of a macro inflection point.

Exhibit 41: Historical Example: S&P 500 Index vs. Commodity Prices, 2007–2010

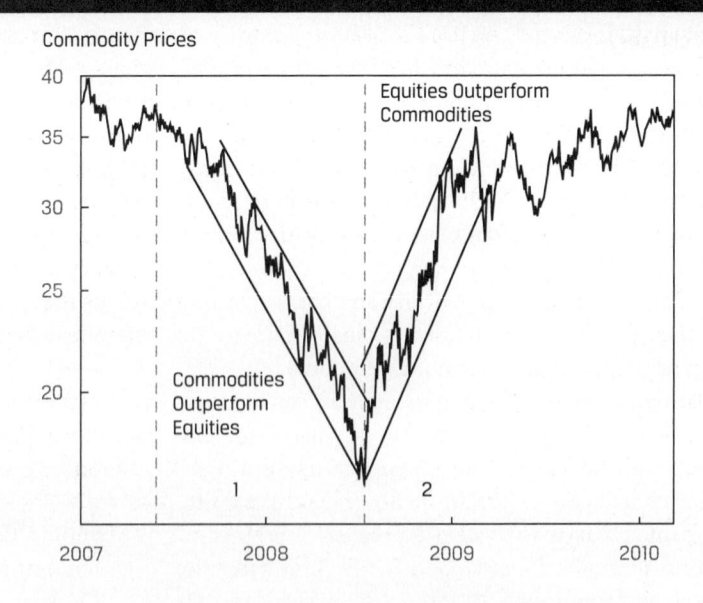

Intermarket Analysis

In addition to the preceding comparisons, once an asset category has been identified, relative strength analysis can be used to identify the best-performing securities in a sector. For example, if commodities look promising, an investor can analyze each of the major commodities relative to a broad commodity index in order to find the strongest commodities.

Exhibit 41 shows the relative price performance of Palladium versus commodities from 2009 to 2019. The ratio is constructed and indexed to 1.0 at the beginning of 2019. As of May 2019, the ratio is at the 13 level, meaning that Palladium outperformed commodities by a factor of 13. The year 2015 marked the acceleration of Palladium's outperformance versus the commodity index.

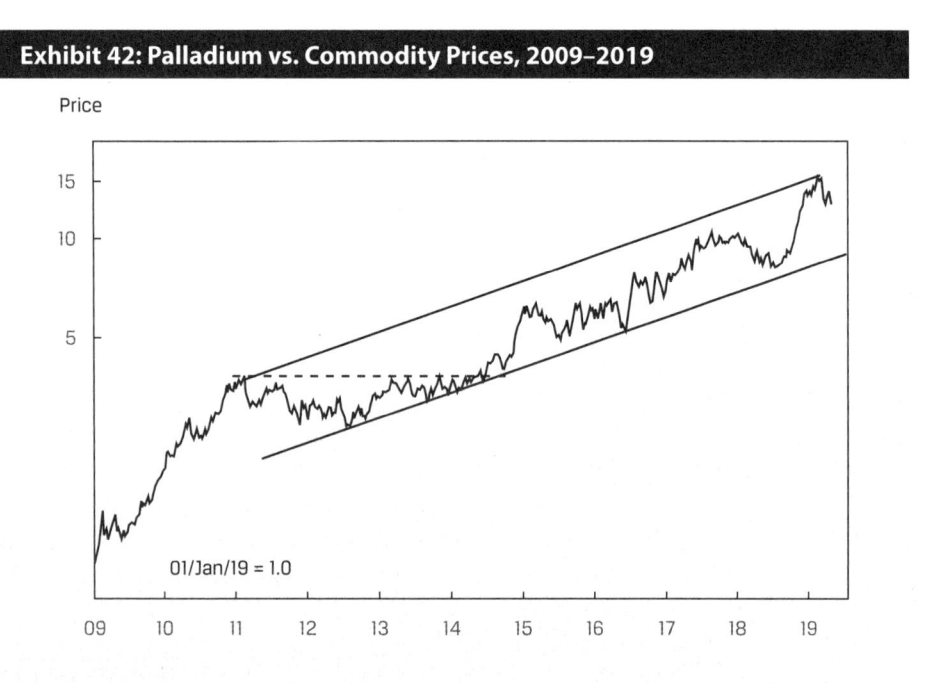

Exhibit 42: Palladium vs. Commodity Prices, 2009–2019

Intermarket analysis can also be used to identify sectors of the equity market to invest in—often in connection with technical observations of the business cycle at any given time. The equities of certain industry sectors tend to perform best at the beginning of an economic cycle. These sectors include financials, consumer non-durables, and transportation. As an economic recovery gets underway, retailers, manufacturers, health care, and consumer durables tend to outperform. Lagging sectors sometimes include those tied to commodity prices, such as energy and basic industrial commodities, which may catch up only in late-cycle, increasingly inflationary periods. In the final stage of a waning expansion, utility and consumer staple stocks may outperform because of their perceived safety, while transportation stocks often lead early market weakness in anticipation of a softening economy.

Observations based on intermarket analysis can also help in allocating funds across national markets. Certain countries' economies—for example, those of Australia, Canada, and South Africa—are closely tied to commodities. As economies evolve, these relationships change. So, the relationships must be monitored closely. For instance, a strong performance in industrial and precious metals can benefit mining stocks. The economies of Australia, Canada, and South Africa depend on the mining industry's performance, and as a result, strong metal prices can have a positive impact on the performance of these countries' equity markets.

Technical Analysis Applications to Portfolio Management

A technician acts very much like a doctor, who analyzes a patient for signs of wellness or sickness and then uses the clues discovered to formulate a composite opinion about fundamental changes in that patient's health. In this way, technical analysis complements fundamental analysis, whether the approach is top-down or bottom-up.

The top-down approach focuses on how the overall economy is affecting different sectors or industries. Analysts who apply a top-down approach believe that if a sector is doing well, stocks in that sector should also perform well.

Intermarket analysis is a key technical analysis tool that helps put the "big picture" into perspective. Intermarket analysis and relative strength analysis help the technician identify trends in countries, sectors, and industries and even among stocks within the same industry.

The bottom-up approach to identifying investment opportunities depends on rules and conditions. The analyst, trader, or investor starts his or her research with an *opportunity set* and tries to pick stocks that meet the *predefined criteria* irrespective of country, sector, or industry trends, which are sometimes considered as extraneous unknowable factors most easily considered as "All else being equal." Sometimes several opportunities in the same sector or industry will point to a developing overall *theme*. For example, finding several investment opportunities in mining stocks will alert the analyst, trader, or investor that metals (precious or industrial) might have strong performance. Or breakdowns in small-cap stocks might alert the analyst, trader, or investor that a possible "risk-off" environment is around the corner for the major equity benchmarks.

Technical Analysis Applications to Portfolio Management: Top-Down Approach

Analysts, traders, or investors whose focus is global equity markets often start their top-down approach by analyzing global benchmarks, such as MSCI and FTSE. The relative performance of major indexes will reveal important investment themes for investors with a long-term focus.

The same principles of charting and technical analysis discussed in the earlier sections of this reading can be applied to relative strength analysis. The aim is to identify consolidation periods and then participate in major trends once these consolidations are completed, whether on the upside or on the downside. In other words, the technician attempts to capture trend periods by focusing on major inflection points on price charts.

Exhibit 43 shows the relative strength of the MSCI Emerging Markets Index and the MSCI All Country World Index between 1997 and 2019. The highest point reached in 2010 is indexed to 1.0 for ease of analysis. Starting in July 1997, the Asian financial crisis was a period of turmoil in currency and equity markets that gripped much of East Asia and Southeast Asia and raised fears of a worldwide economic meltdown through financial contagion.

The relative strength chart for the Emerging Markets Index and the All Country World Index shows that 1997–1999 was a period of strong underperformance for the Emerging Markets Index. Indonesia, South Korea, and Thailand were the countries most affected by the crisis. Hong Kong SAR, Malaysia, and the Philippines were also hurt by the slump. These were all countries classified as emerging markets.

However, in 2001–2002, the performance ratio tested the 1998–99 lows and formed a double bottom chart pattern. Retesting of the previous lows and a reversal from the support area were the first signs of a change in trend. The actual change took place in 2003, when the ratio cleared its long-term average and the horizontal boundary (resistance) of the double bottom chart pattern. This movement signaled the beginning of a period of outperformance for the Emerging Markets Index against the All Country World Index. For investors, it was a time to focus on emerging market opportunities.

Intermarket Analysis

Strong outperformance for the Emerging Markets Index continued until 2012, when the ratio started challenging its long-term average and the upward-sloping trendline. A new trend was established: Since 2012, the developed markets have been outperforming the emerging markets. Global asset allocators would have captured much better performance by investing in developed market equities over the past six years.

In Exhibit 43, the two major inflection points are the breakout from the double bottom chart pattern with the breach of the long-term average in 2003 and the breakdown of the trendline and long-term average in 2012. These inflection points are labeled as "trend change" on the price chart.

Exhibit 43: MSCI Emerging Markets Index vs. MSCI ACWI, 1997–2019

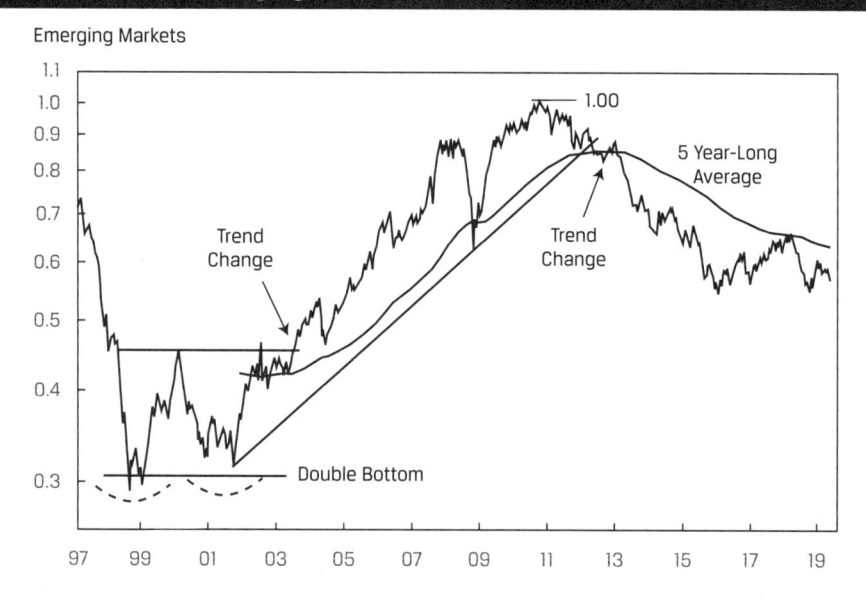

Exhibit 44 shows the relative strength of the MSCI Frontier Markets Index and the MSCI All Country World Index between 2002 and 2019. The highest point reached in 2005 is indexed to 1.0 for ease of analysis.

The charted ratio shows a strong outperformance for frontier market equities between 2002 and 2005. The ratio moved from the 0.35 level to as high as 1.00. This is almost 3 times outperformance during the three-year period. However, 2005 marked the highest point for the ratio over the analyzed period. In 2008, the ratio reached the previous highs and formed a double top. This chart pattern is the exact opposite of the one identified on the MSCI Emerging Markets versus MSCI ACWI chart during the 1998–2002 period.

A double top warns of a change in trend from up to down. At the beginning of 2009, the ratio not only breached the long-term average but also broke down the horizontal support formed by the neckline of the double top chart pattern.

Investors who had benefited from the outperformance of frontier market equities during 2002–2008 started allocating their funds out of frontier markets due to a change in trend. The following decade was a period of underperformance for the Frontier Markets Index. The ratio dropped from 0.7 to 0.35.

Exhibit 44: MSCI Frontier Markets Index vs. MSCI ACWI, 2002–2019

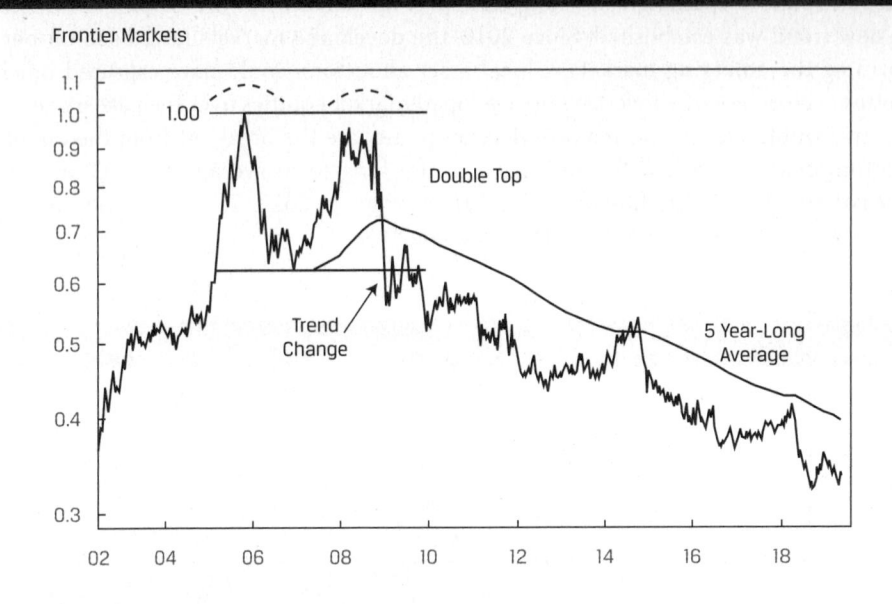

Out of the three major MSCI benchmarks—the developed, emerging, and frontier market indexes—both the Emerging Markets Index and the Frontier Markets Index started underperforming the All Country World Index after 2009–2010. At the same time, developed markets started outperforming the All Country World Index. The intermarket analysis suggested an allocation to developed markets.

However, not all developed markets performed well after the 2009–10 period. The analyst or investor should also have been selective in picking the outperforming countries.

Intermarket analysis can be used to advantage in asset allocation decisions. **Tactical asset allocation (TAA)** is a portfolio strategy that shifts the percentages of assets held in various asset classes (or categories) to take advantage of market opportunities. Allocation shifts can occur within an asset class or across asset classes. This strategy allows portfolio managers to add value by taking advantage of certain situations in the marketplace.

Technical analysis and intermarket analysis help the portfolio manager make discretionary TAA decisions. In preparing to make these decisions, the portfolio manager studies trends and possible changes in the relationships on relative strength charts.

Exhibit 45 shows the relative strength of the S&P 500 Index and the Goldman Sachs Commodity Index on a daily scale. The ratio of these indexes was trending down between May 2007 and July 2008. The downtrend in the ratio signaled an outperformance for commodities. The ratio formed a head and shoulders bottom reversal during 2008. Completion of the head and shoulders bottom took place at the same time as a breach above the 200-day average. These two signals confirmed the change in trend, which favored equities over commodities. From a TAA perspective, intermarket analysis suggested shifting assets from commodities to equities.

Intermarket Analysis

Exhibit 45: S&P 500 Index vs. GSCI (Equities vs. Commodities), May 2007–August 2010

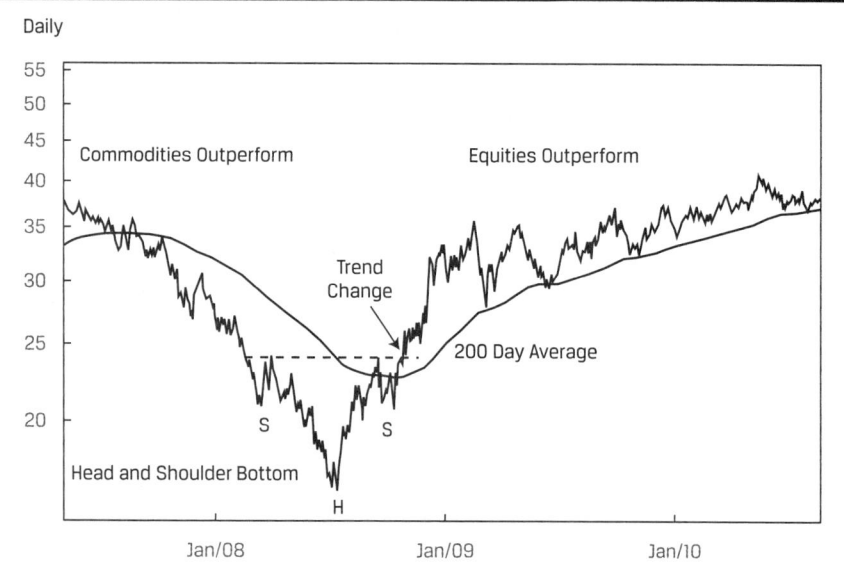

Short-term charts such as the daily scale help us identify changes in trends at the early stages. Longer time frames will alert us to major shifts in demand and supply.

Exhibit 46 shows the relative performance of the S&P 500 Index and the Goldman Sachs Commodity Index on a weekly scale. Following the initial trend change in the last quarter of 2008, equities outperformed commodities until 2010. The ratio moved sideways between 2010 and 2012. In the first half of 2012, the S&P 500 to GSCI ratio cleared the horizontal resistance, suggesting a new phase of outperformance. Asset allocators would have higher conviction for increasing equity allocations following the renewed strength and breakout in the second half of 2012.

Exhibit 46: S&P 500 Index vs. GSCI (Equities vs. Commodities), 2007–2019

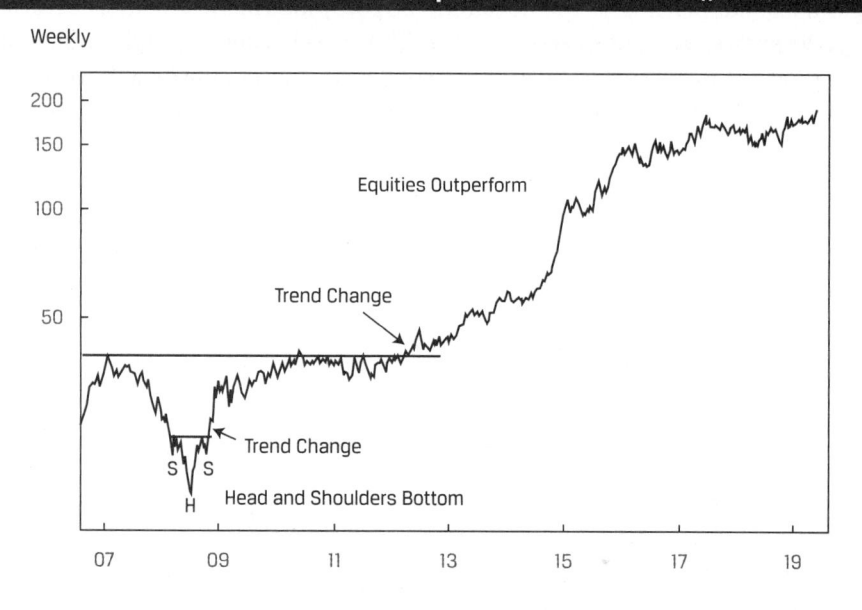

A similar relative strength chart can be drawn to compare bonds and commodities. Exhibit 47 shows the ratio of the 30-year US Treasury bond to the Goldman Sachs Commodity Index. Bonds started outperforming commodities in the second half of 2008. From the first quarter of 2009 till the last quarter of 2014, the ratio remained sideways and formed a symmetrical triangle. Consolidation periods are usually followed by trends. The breakout and trend change took place in the last quarter of 2014. Renewed strength in the ratio suggested outperformance for bonds versus commodities. From a TAA perspective, the intermarket analysis suggested shifting allocations from commodities to bonds.

Exhibit 47: 30-Year US Treasury Bond vs. GSCI (Bonds vs. Commodities), 2006–2019

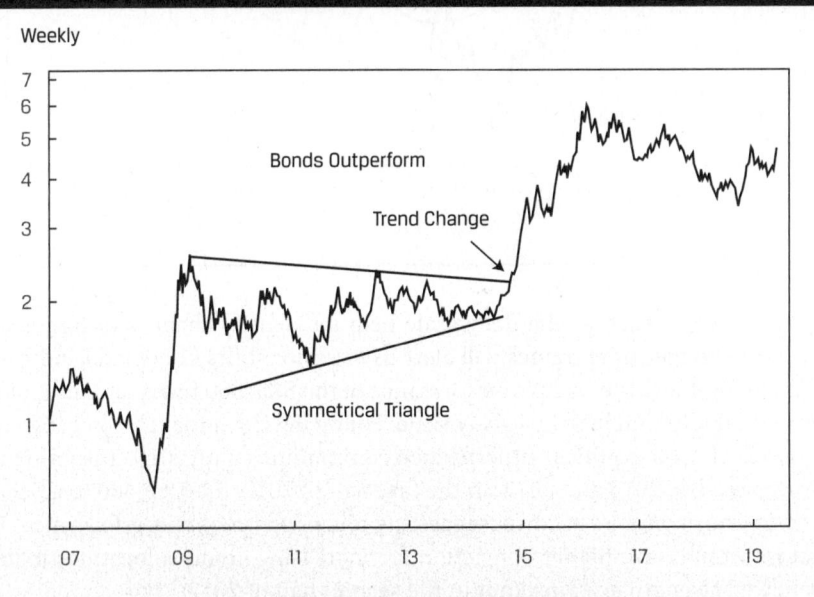

Exhibit 48 shows the relative strength of the S&P 500 Index and the 30-year US Treasury bond. Starting at the beginning of 2009, intermarket analysis suggested outperformance for equities versus bonds. Classical charting principles would have helped the asset allocator to identify the change in trend at the beginning of 2013, when the ratio completed a symmetrical triangle.

Intermarket Analysis

Exhibit 48: S&P 500 Index vs. 30-Year US Treasury Bond (Equities vs. Bonds), 2006–2019

We started our intermarket analysis with global equity markets. With the help of relative strength analysis and classical charting principles, we have identified trends favoring emerging and frontier markets and then developed markets.

As another example, Exhibit 49 shows the relative strength of Microsoft Corporation and the MSCI USA Index. Microsoft is a large holding in this benchmark. It is important for fund managers and portfolio managers to have a view on large holdings in the index. The only significant technical analysis signal was triggered when the ratio completed a multi-year-long symmetrical triangle consolidation at the beginning of 2016. The inflection point is labeled "trend change" on the chart and is indexed to 1.0. After the breakout, the ratio pulled back to test the previous support/resistance area formed by the apex of the symmetrical triangle. Microsoft entered a period of strong outperformance between 2016 and 2019. The ratio moved from 1.00 to 1.90 over the three-year period. The intermarket analysis suggested an overweight position for Microsoft.

Exhibit 49: Microsoft Corporation vs. MSCI USA Index, 2000–2019

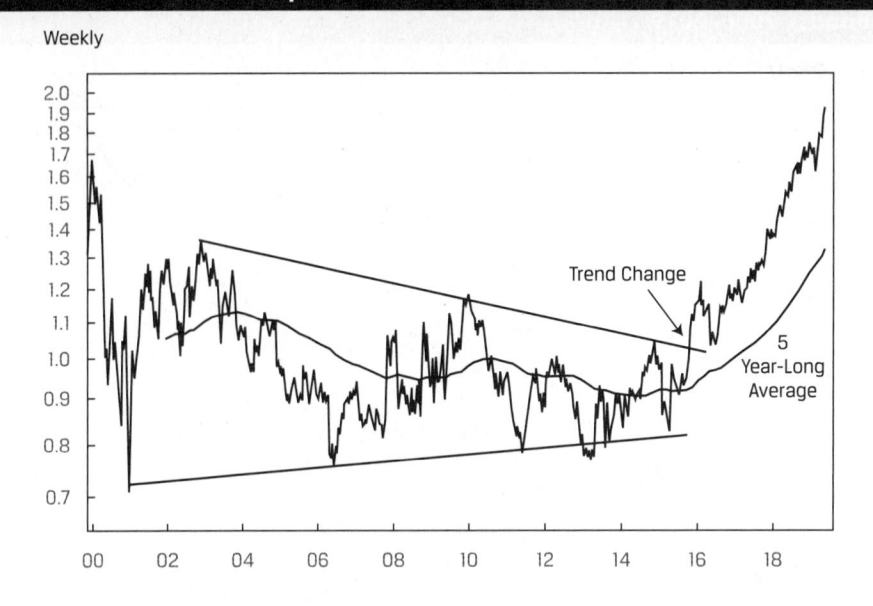

While the price ratio was generating a positive technical signal in favor of Microsoft, one would have questioned how to build positions in the stock. At this point, the analyst or investor would refer to the company's price chart to see trend and consolidation periods and the possibility to capture one of those well-defined breakout opportunities.

Exhibit 50 shows the price chart for Microsoft between October 2014 and May 2019. At the time when Microsoft started outperforming the MSCI USA Index, the price chart was trying to complete the yearlong rectangle labeled "Consolidation 1." The upper boundary of this yearlong consolidation acted as resistance at the 49.5 level. In the last quarter of 2015, Microsoft broke out of its rectangle chart pattern with a strong weekly candlestick. At the same time, the ratio of Microsoft to the MSCI USA (Exhibit 49) broke out of its multi-year-long symmetrical triangle consolidation.

The breakout on the Microsoft price chart was followed by a pullback and another multi-month-long consolidation. During this new consolidation, labeled "Consolidation 2" in Exhibit 50, previous resistance acted as support at the 49.5 level. Consolidation periods are price ranges in which investors with a longer-term focus assess the strength of the company and accumulate shares. If demand overcomes the supply, price eventually breaks out of the consolidation, and the trend resumes. Microsoft completed the second rectangle chart pattern in the second half of 2016 and resumed its uptrend. "Breakout 1" and "Breakout 2" are two inflection points on the price chart where Microsoft generated technical buy signals.

Exhibit 50: Microsoft Corporation, October 2014–May 2019 (US$)

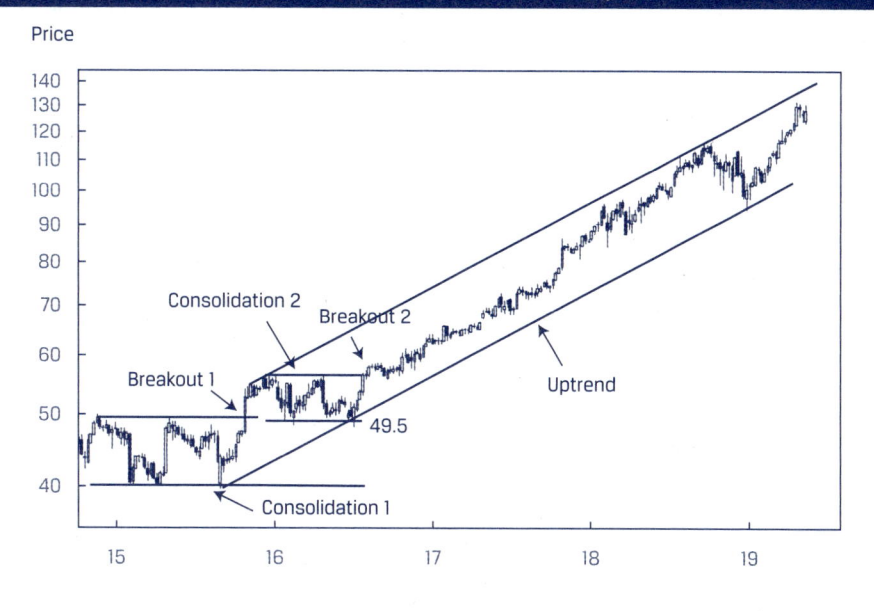

Technical Analysis Applications to Portfolio Management: Bottom-Up Approach

A bottom-up investing approach focuses on the analysis of individual stocks. In bottom-up investing, the investor focuses his or her attention on a specific company's technicals rather than on the industry or index in which that company is classified. A bottom-up approach focuses on stock picking irrespective of market, industry, or more macro trends. It is possible that a thorough analysis of individual stocks will reveal investment themes in different sectors and industries. For example, several bottom reversals on individual health care stocks might suggest a turnaround in that sector due to anticipated news or a change in fundamentals.

To use the bottom-up approach, first, the investor or analyst needs an investment universe—a group of instruments to make a selection from. Second, the investor or analyst needs a method for selecting instruments using predefined criteria.

We will focus on momentum and breakout strategies. A breakout trader enters a long position after the stock price breaks above resistance or enters a short position after the stock breaks below support.

In our analysis, we will follow the following criteria, or trading rules, for stock selection:

1. The breakout should take place above the 200-day exponential moving average (long-only strategy).
2. Price should be in a low-volatility condition prior to the breakout.
3. The breakout should take place from a well-defined classical chart pattern between 3 and 24 months in duration.
4. Breakout confirmation should be a weekly close above the chart pattern boundary.

Our opportunity set will be developed market equities.

The examples below highlight breakout opportunities that were possible to identify during 2016. These breakouts not only captured directional movements on price charts but also pointed analysts and investors to a specific theme.

Our initial requirement for a stock is that it be going through a low-volatility period. We would like to capture those stocks that are in consolidation periods. If the opportunity set is large, the analyst can use filtering criteria to identify stocks with low Bollinger Band readings, as discussed in preceding sections. Following the initial screening, the analyst will use the **visual technique** to select one of the well-defined classical chart patterns.

Before we proceed to the examples below, we should clarify one important point. To use a bottom-up approach to stock selection, an analyst should have a method for identifying potential trades. Focusing on breakout and momentum is one of many different approaches to stock selection and investment decision making. Each analyst, investor, or trader can implement his or her own approach to identifying opportunities.

In our simplified scenario, these are the commonsense technical rules that we choose to apply:

- The breakout should take place above the 200-day exponential moving average (long-only strategy).

It is important to identify stocks that are already in a steady uptrend or are entering into an uptrend. Breakouts from consolidation periods in or preceding an uptrend are usually followed by a continuation of the existing trend. Investing in the overall direction of the trend is the *path of least resistance.*

- Price should be in a low-volatility condition.

Low-volatility conditions are usually followed by high volatility, and vice versa. Stocks that break out from low-volatility conditions are likely to experience high volatility, and high volatility in the direction of the existing trend will usually help the trend to pick up momentum.

- The breakout should take place from a well-defined classical chart pattern between 3 and 24 months in duration.

The longer the consolidation, the stronger the breakout and the subsequent trend period will be.

- Breakout confirmation should be a weekly close above the chart pattern boundary.

In an attempt to avoid premature breakout decisions, we will wait for a decisive weekly close above the chart pattern boundary.

Exhibit 51 shows the price chart for Belo Sun Mining Company from July 2013 to February 2017. The stock is listed on the Toronto Stock Exchange. The price chart formed a multi-month-long ascending triangle between 2014 and 2015. An ascending triangle is a bullish chart pattern. Its upward-sloping boundary gives this triangle its bullish bias. This pattern suggests that buyers are able to bid the price to higher levels after each correction.

Prior to the formation of an ascending triangle, the stock was in a steady downtrend. The ascending triangle acted as a consolidation and represented a period of low volatility. The breakout above the chart pattern boundary at 0.28 took place at the beginning of 2016. At this point, the stock was above its long-term average and ready for a new trend period. The breakout took place with a strong weekly candlestick. The bullish ascending triangle acted as a bottom reversal for the silver mining company, and a strong trend period followed. According to the bottom-up approach, in the last quarter of 2015, Belo Sun Mining should have been on our watch list for a possible breakout opportunity.

Intermarket Analysis

Exhibit 51: Belo Sun Mining Company, July 2013–February 2017 (Price in Canadian Dollars)

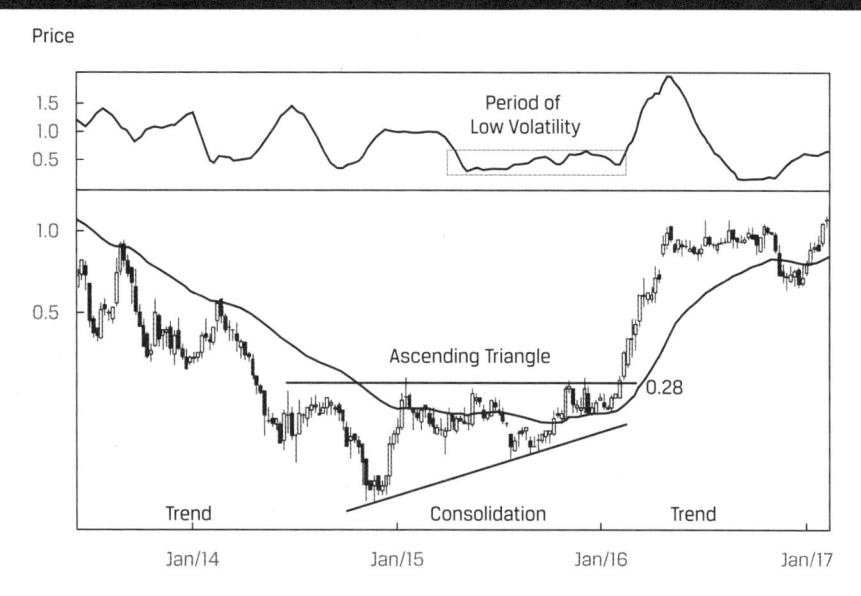

Exhibit 52 shows the price chart for Pan American Silver Corporation between January 2014 and September 2016. The stock is listed on the Toronto Stock Exchange. Pan American Silver formed a double bottom chart pattern, a bullish reversal, around the same time some of the silver mining companies formed consolidations. The double bottom formed in the second half of 2015. At the beginning of 2016, a breakout from the bullish reversal chart pattern above the 11.2 levels took place with a strong weekly candlestick.

Because these two stocks were going through low-volatility conditions and forming one of the well-defined chart patterns, they would have been on our watch list. Bullish bias in all the chart pattern developments would have alerted us to a possible reversal on silver prices and possibly other precious/industrial metal prices. This example shows how one can start with individual stocks and end up finding an investment theme.

Exhibit 52: Pan American Silver Corporation, January 2014–September 2016 (Price in Canadian Dollars)

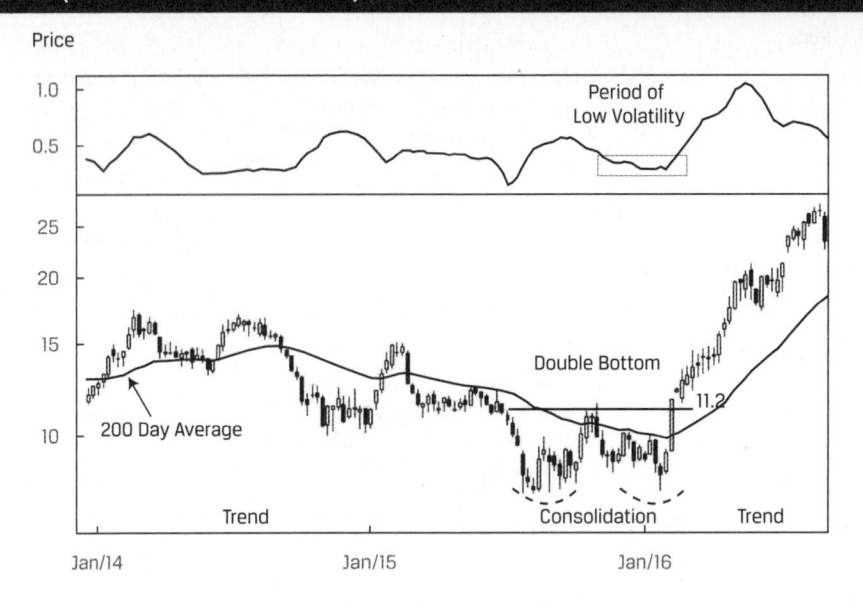

In this instance, strength in silver mining equities happened to lead the breakout in commodity prices.

Exhibit 53 shows the silver (per ounce) price between April 2014 and August 2016. Silver mining equities bottomed or completed bullish continuation chart patterns in the beginning of 2016. Silver prices formed an inverse head and shoulders chart pattern from the second half of 2015 to the first quarter of 2016. A breakout from the inverse head and shoulders chart pattern took place in April 2016, when price cleared the horizontal resistance at the 16 level. Following the breakout, price pulled back to the chart pattern boundary and resumed the uptrend.

Exhibit 53: Silver (per Ounce) Price, April 2014–August 2016 (US$)

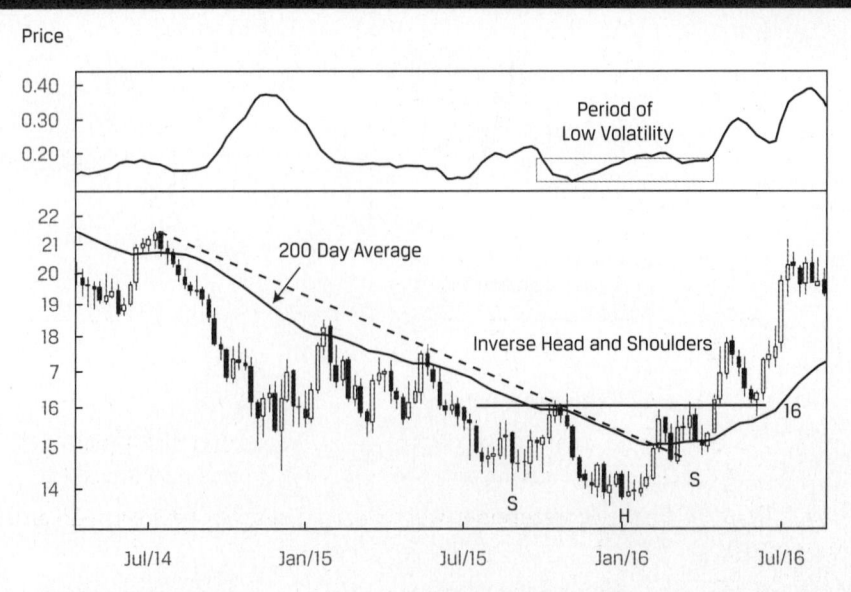

The Role of the Technical Analyst in Fundamental Portfolio Management

A technical analyst can serve a supporting role in a team of investors. The technician can conduct research and find investment opportunities by applying different strategies. As mentioned in the examples above, the technical analyst goes through the opportunity set and provides trade and investment ideas to the portfolio/fund managers.

The key value-added input would be in the form of timing of the purchase or sale of that security. The technical analyst should provide the rationale as well as potential price targets for the expected move and the price level at which the analysis would be invalidated. The technical analyst should follow a purist approach and follow the results of the research without being influenced by other inputs, such as news and fundamental data on the specific company—though news confirming the development of a technical trend is always welcome.

The technical analyst will typically not be directly involved in position sizing decisions, such as how much of the portfolio to allocate to a certain idea or by what margin the fund should overweight or underweight the specific stock. However, the portfolio manager may well use high-conviction inputs from the technical analyst in weighting decisions.

Question 13

A trader identifies an inverse head and shoulders chart pattern on the commodity XYZ. He plans to buy 100 units of the commodity at the time of the breakout. However, he only manages to get filled for 20 units because the price moves quickly. Over the next few weeks, the price moves close to the chart pattern price target at the 18.6 level but then reverses back to the breakout level. What should the trader do, given the price movement, assuming the chart pattern will hold?

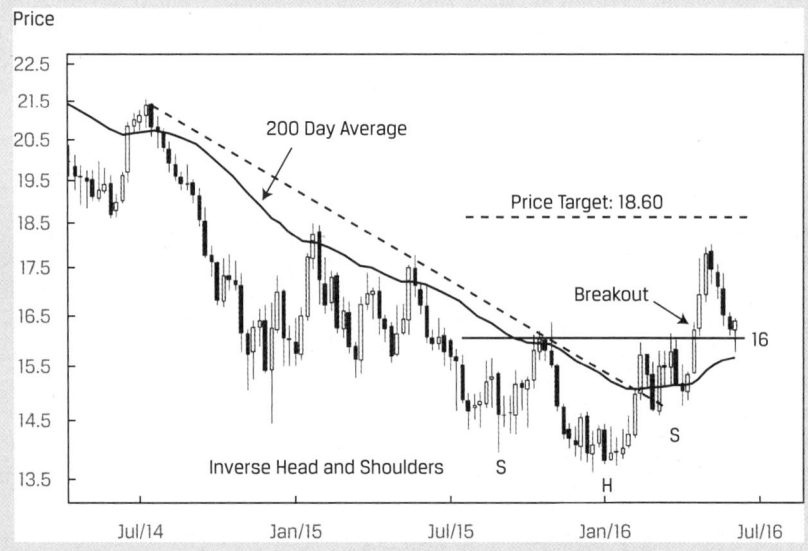

a. Sell the existing 20 units because the breakout failed.
b. Buy the remaining 80 units (of the initial 100-unit purchase plan) because the price is giving another opportunity with a pullback.
c. Wait for further correction toward the next support between 14.5 and 15.0.

Answer: B. The price pullback to the chart pattern boundary provides an opportunity to complete the purchase of the planned quantity.

A is not the correct answer because the breakout didn't fail: The price held above the chart pattern boundary.

C is not the correct answer because a correction toward the 14.5–15.0 area would put the bullish interpretation in question and the chart pattern might lose its validity.

Question 14

A fund manager has been trading ABC stock between the horizontal chart pattern boundaries throughout 2018. Every time the price reached the 60 level (support), she was overweighting the stock, and every time it reached the 70 level (resistance), she was underweighting it. This strategy worked well until October 2018, when the stock price slipped below the horizontal support at the 60 level. The fund manager's mandate is to beat a benchmark, and the stock is one of the blue chips in the index with a high weighting. What should the fund manager do?

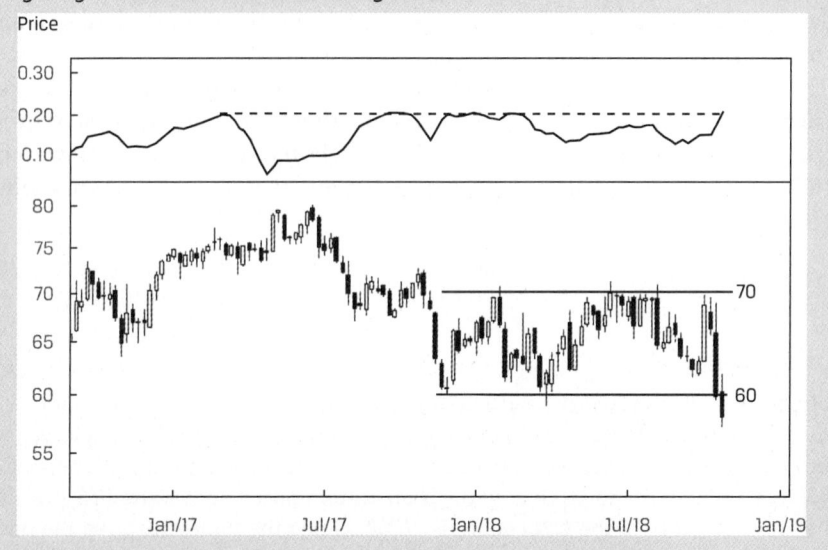

a. Buy more of the ABC stock and remain overweight because the stock is now cheaper.

b. Sell part of the exposure and remain underweight because the stock might be breaking down a lengthy consolidation.

c. Expect the stock to remain sideways and maintain a market-weight position.

Answer: B.

The stock is completing a yearlong rectangle pattern, and the volatility measured by the Bollinger Band width is about to break out from a two-year-long consolidation. Therefore, there is a high probability that a trend period will follow and the stock will underperform. Selling part of the exposure and going underweight the benchmark at a time when the stock is likely to trend downward would result in outperformance versus the benchmark, adding value to the portfolio.

A is not the correct answer because buying more of the stock and overweighting the position at a time when the stock is likely to trend downward would result in underperformance versus the benchmark.

C is not the correct answer because maintaining a market-weight position at a time when the stock is likely to trend downward would result in a lost opportunity to outperform the benchmark by underweighting the position.

SUMMARY

- Technical analysis is a form of security analysis that uses price data and volume data, typically displayed graphically in charts. The charts are analyzed using various indicators in order to make investment recommendations.

- Technical analysis has three main principles and assumptions: (1) The market discounts everything, (2) prices move in trends and countertrends, and (3) price action is repetitive, with certain patterns reoccurring.

- Increasingly, analysts, fund managers, and individual investors are studying the basic principles of technical analysis to support their decision making in financial markets. Behavioral finance, which is the study of the influence of psychology on the behavior of investors, focuses on the fact that investors are not always rational, have limits to their self-control, and are influenced by their own biases. This relatively new field of finance is motivating more practitioners to consider technical analysis as a tool for understanding and explaining irrationalities in financial markets.

- Technical analysis can be used on any freely traded security in the global market and is used on a wide range of financial instruments, such as equities, bonds, commodities, currencies, and futures. However, in general, technical analysis is most effectively applied to liquid markets. Therefore, technical analysis has limited usefulness for illiquid securities, where a small trade can have a large impact on prices.

- The primary tools used in technical analysis are charts and indicators. Charts are graphical displays of price and volume data. Indicators are approaches to analyzing the charts. While the tools can be used on a stand-alone basis, many analysts, fund managers, and investors will find added value in combining the techniques of chart analysis with their own research and investment approach.

- Charts provide information about past price behavior and provide a basis for inferences about likely future price behavior. Basic charts include line charts, bar charts, and candlestick charts.

- Charts can be drawn either to a linear scale or to a logarithmic scale. A logarithmic scale is appropriate when the data move through a range of values representing several orders of magnitude (e.g., from 10 to 10,000), whereas a linear scale is better suited to narrower ranges (e.g., $35 to $50).

- Volume is an important element of technical analysis and is often included on charts. Volume can be viewed as a confirmation in that it indicates the strength or conviction of buyers and sellers in determining a security's price.

- One of the most important steps in successfully applying technical analysis is to define the time period being analyzed. Technical analysis and charting become more reliable as the time scale increases from intraday to daily, weekly, and even monthly. Analysts and investors whose primary research method is fundamental analysis will find more value in charting instruments on a weekly and/or a monthly scale. Longer time frames will allow analysts and investors to better identify the consolidation and trend periods and time their purchases or sales of securities.

- Several basic concepts can be applied to charts. These include relative strength analysis, trend, consolidation, support, resistance, and change in polarity.

- Relative strength analysis is based on the ratio of the prices of a security and a benchmark and is used to compare the performance of one asset with the performance of another asset.
- The concept of trend is an important aspect of technical analysis. An uptrend is defined as a sequence of higher highs and higher lows. To draw an uptrend line, a technician draws a line connecting the lows on the price chart. A downtrend is defined as a sequence of lower highs and lower lows. To draw a downtrend line, a technician draws a line connecting the highs on the price chart.
- Support is defined as a low price range in which the price stops declining because of buying activity. It is the opposite of resistance, which is a price range in which price stops rising because of selling activity.
- Chart patterns are formations appearing on price charts that create some type of recognizable shape. There are two major types of chart patterns: reversal patterns and continuation patterns.
- Reversal patterns signal the end of a trend. Common reversal patterns are head and shoulders (H&S), inverse H&S, double top, double bottom, triple top, and triple bottom.
- Continuation patterns indicate that a market trend that was in place prior to the pattern formation will continue once the pattern is completed. Common continuation patterns are triangles (symmetrical, ascending, and descending), rectangles (bullish and bearish), flags, and pennants.
- Technical indicators are used to derive additional information from basic chart patterns. An indicator is any measure based on price, market sentiment, or fund flows that can be used to predict changes in price. Mathematically calculated indicators usually have a supply and demand underpinning. Basic types of indicators include price-based indicators, momentum oscillators, and sentiment indicators.
- Price-based indicators incorporate information contained in market prices. Common price-based indicators include the moving average and Bollinger Bands.
- The moving average is the average of the closing prices of a security over a specified number of periods. Moving averages are a smoothing technique that gives the technical analyst a view of market trends. So, a moving average can be viewed as a trend filter. Long-term moving averages can provide important signals. A price move above the long-term moving average is a sign of an uptrend. A price move below the long-term moving average is a sign of a downtrend.
- When a short-term moving average crosses over a longer-term moving average from underneath, this movement is considered a bullish indicator and is called a "bullish crossover." When a short-term moving-average crosses over a longer-term moving average from above, this movement is a bearish indicator and is called a "bearish crossover."
- Bollinger Bands combine the concept of a moving average with standard deviations around the moving average. This tool is useful in defining a trading range for the security being analyzed. The Bollinger Band width indicator provides an indication of volatility. The idea is that periods of low volatility are followed by periods of high volatility, so that relatively narrow band width can foreshadow an advance or decline in the security under analysis.

- Momentum oscillators are constructed from price data, but they are calculated so that they fluctuate between a low and a high, typically between 0 and 100. Some examples of momentum oscillators include rate of change (ROC) oscillators, the relative strength index (RSI), stochastic oscillators, and the MACD (moving-average convergence/divergence oscillator).

- Momentum oscillators can be viewed as graphical representations of market sentiment that show when selling or buying activity is more aggressive than usual. Technical analysts also look for convergence or divergence between oscillators and price. For example, when the price reaches a new high, this outcome is usually considered "bullish." But if the momentum oscillator does not also reach a new high, this scenario is considered divergence and an early warning sign of weakness.

- Momentum oscillators also alert the technical analyst to overbought or oversold conditions. For example, in an oversold condition, market sentiment is considered unsustainably bearish.

- Sentiment indicators attempt to gauge investor activity for signs of increasing bullishness or bearishness. Commonly used calculated statistical indexes are the put/call ratio, the VIX, and margin debt.

- Intermarket analysis combines technical analysis of the major categories of securities—namely, equities, bonds, currencies, and commodities—to identify market trends and possible inflections in trends. Intermarket analysis also looks at industry subsectors and their relationship to sectors and industries. In addition, it measures the relative performance of major equity benchmarks around the globe.

- Technical analysis can use either a top-down approach or a bottom-up approach to analyze securities. The top-down method is useful for identifying outperforming asset classes, countries, or sectors. This approach can add value to asset allocation decisions. Allocation shifts can occur within an asset class or across asset classes. The bottom-up method is useful for identifying individual stocks, commodities, or currencies that are outperforming, irrespective of market, industry, or macro trends.

- The technical analyst can add value to an investment team by providing trading/investment ideas through either top-down or bottom-up analysis, depending on the nature of the investment firm or fund. In addition, technical analysis can add value to a fundamental portfolio approach by providing input on the timing of the purchase or sale of a security.

PRACTICE PROBLEMS

1. Technical analysis relies most importantly on:
   A. price and volume data.
   B. accurate financial statements.
   C. fundamental analysis to confirm conclusions.

2. Which of the following is *not* an assumption of technical analysis?
   A. Security markets are efficient.
   B. The security under analysis is freely traded.
   C. Market trends and patterns tend to repeat themselves.

3. Drawbacks of technical analysis include which of the following?
   A. It identifies changes in trends only after the fact.
   B. Deviations from intrinsic value can persist for long periods.
   C. It usually requires detailed knowledge of the financial instrument under analysis.

4. Why is technical analysis especially useful in the analysis of commodities and currencies?
   A. Valuation models cannot be used to determine fundamental intrinsic value for these securities.
   B. Government regulators are more likely to intervene in these markets.
   C. These types of securities display clearer trends than equities and bonds do.

5. Technical analysis is a form of security analysis that:
   A. assesses past price action to project future prices.
   B. requires in-depth knowledge of financial instruments.
   C. is ineffective when evaluating long-term price movements.

6. One principle of technical analysis is that a security's price:
   A. tends to move in a random fashion.
   B. moves in patterns that tend to reoccur.
   C. does not reflect all known factor information relating to the security.

7. A daily bar chart provides:
   A. a logarithmically scaled horizontal axis.
   B. a horizontal axis that represents changes in price.
   C. high and low prices during the day and the day's opening and closing prices.

Practice Problems

8. A candlestick chart is similar to a bar chart *except* that the candlestick chart:
   A. represents upward movements in price with X's.
   B. also graphically shows the range of the period's highs and lows.
   C. has a body that is light or dark depending on whether the security closed higher or lower than its open.

9. In a candlestick chart, a shaded candlestick body indicates that the opening price was:
   A. equal to the closing price.
   B. lower than the closing price.
   C. higher than the closing price.

10. A chart constructed with a single data point per time interval is a:
    A. bar chart.
    B. line chart.
    C. candlestick chart.

11. In constructing a chart, using a logarithmic scale on the vertical axis is likely to be *most useful* for which of the following applications?
    A. The price of gold for the past 100 years.
    B. The share price of a company over the past month.
    C. Yields on 10-year US Treasuries for the past 5 years.

12. A linear price scale is:
    A. inappropriate for a candlestick chart.
    B. better suited for analysis of short-term price movements.
    C. constructed with equal vertical distances corresponding to an equal percentage price change.

13. Relative strength analysis typically compares the performance of an asset with that of a benchmark or other security using a:
    A. bar chart that reflects the two assets' price history.
    B. line chart that reflects the ratio of the two assets' prices.
    C. candlestick chart that reflects ratios measuring the magnitude of each asset's up days versus down days.

14. In analyzing a price chart, high or increasing volume *most likely* indicates which of the following?
    A. Predicts a reversal in the price trend.
    B. Predicts that a trendless period will follow.
    C. Confirms a rising or declining trend in prices.

15. A downtrend line is constructed by drawing a line connecting:
    A. the lows of the price chart.
    B. the highs of the price chart.
    C. the highest high to the lowest low of the price chart.

16. Exhibit 1 depicts ABC Co., Ltd., ordinary shares, traded on the Shenzhen Stock Exchange, for the months of November through September in renminbi (RMB).

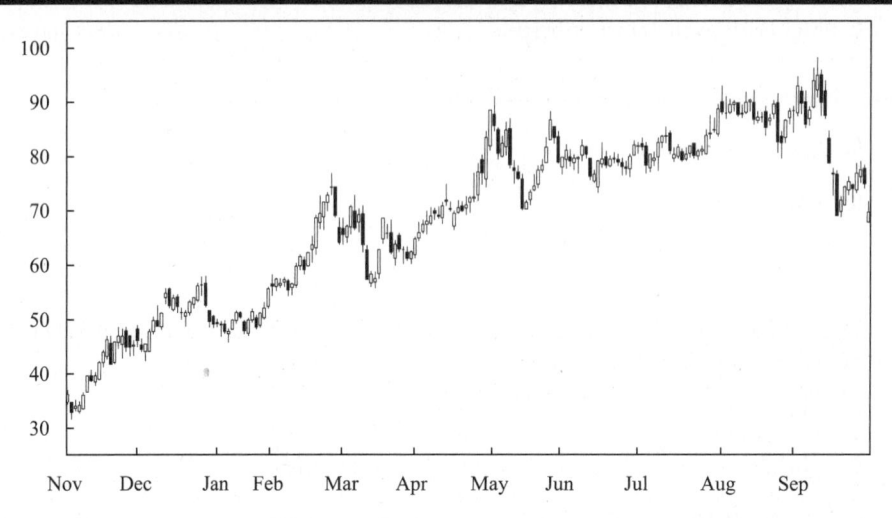

Exhibit 1: Candlestick Chart: ABC Co., Ltd. Price Data, November–September (Price Measured in RMB × 10)

Based on Exhibit 1, the uptrend was *most likely* broken at a price level nearest to:
    A. 7 RMB.
    B. 8.5 RMB.
    C. 10 RMB.

17. The "change in polarity" principle states which of the following?
    A. Once an uptrend is broken, it becomes a downtrend.
    B. Once a resistance level is breached, it becomes a support level.
    C. The short-term moving average has crossed over the longer-term moving average.

18. Exhibit 2 depicts XYZ Co. ordinary shares, traded on the London Stock Ex-

Practice Problems

change, in British pence.

Exhibit 2: Candlestick Chart: XYZ Co. Price Data, January–January (Price Measured in British Pence)

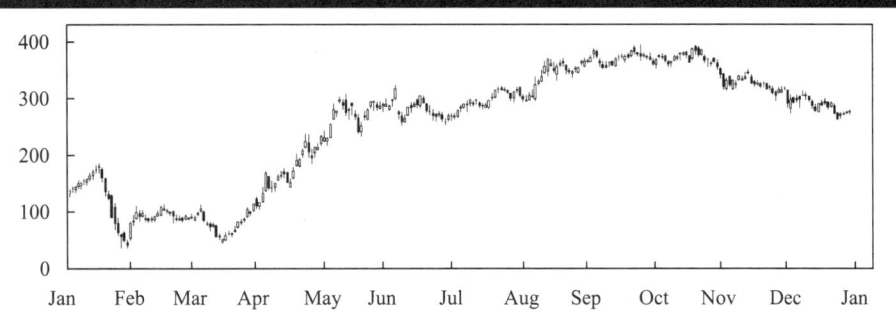

Based on Exhibit 2, Barclays appears to show resistance at a level nearest to:

A. 50p.

B. 275p.

C. 390p.

19. When a security is not trending, it is considered to be in a:

    A. breakout.

    B. retracement.

    C. consolidation.

20. A technical analyst who observes a downtrending security break out of a consolidation range on the downside will *most likely* predict that the downtrend will:

    A. resume.

    B. reverse trend with an upside breakout.

    C. retrace back to the consolidation range.

21. Which of the following statements regarding technical support and resistance is correct?

    A. A breached support level becomes a new level of resistance.

    B. Support is a price range where selling activity is sufficient to stop a rise in price.

    C. Resistance is a price range where buying activity is sufficient to stop a decline in price.

22. Exhibit 3 depicts DGF Company common shares, traded on the New York Stock

Exchange, for five years in US dollars.

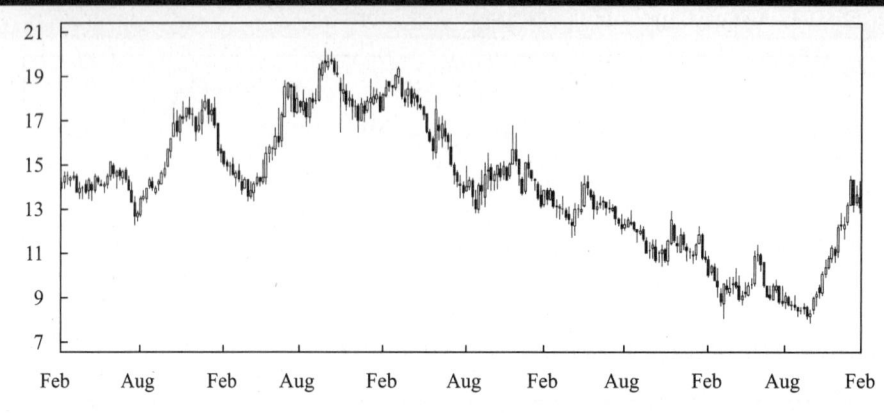

Exhibit 3: Candlestick Chart: DGF Company, five years, February–February

Exhibit 3 illustrates *most* clearly which type of pattern?

A. Triangle.

B. Triple top.

C. Head and shoulders.

23. A triangle chart pattern that indicates a consolidation period and has bullish trading implications would *most likely* be classified as a(n):

A. ascending triangle.

B. descending triangle.

C. symmetrical triangle.

24. In an inverted head and shoulders pattern, if the neckline is at €100, the shoulders at €90, and the head at €75, the price target is *closest* to which of the following?

A. €50.

B. €110.

C. €125.

25. Which of the following chart patterns signals the end of an uptrend in price?

A. Bearish rectangle

B. Head and shoulders

C. Symmetrical triangle

26. An inverse head and shoulders acts as a reversal pattern for a preceding:

A. uptrend.

B. downtrend.

Practice Problems

    C. consolidation.

27. A fully formed head and shoulders pattern is *most likely* an indicator to:

    A. buy.

    B. sell.

    C. hold.

28. To profit from a head and shoulders formation, a technician often sets a price target below the neckline price by an increment equal to the:

    A. head minus neckline.

    B. head minus top of right shoulder.

    C. top of right shoulder minus neckline.

29. A "healthy correction" chart pattern:

    A. is classified as a type of reversal pattern.

    B. does not change long-term price trends since supply and demand remain in balance.

    C. is formed when the price reaches a low, rebounds, and then sells off back to the first low level.

30. Which of the following is a continuation pattern?

    A. Triangle.

    B. Triple top.

    C. Head and shoulders.

31. Which of the following is a reversal pattern?

    A. Pennant.

    B. Rectangle.

    C. Double bottom.

32. Which of the following is generally true of the head and shoulders pattern?

    A. Volume is important in interpreting the data.

    B. The neckline, once breached, becomes a support level.

    C. Head and shoulders patterns are generally followed by an uptrend in the security's price.

33. If the 5-day moving average for AZB Company crossed over its 60-day moving average from underneath, it would be considered a:

    A. bullish indicator.

    B. bearish indicator.

    C. new level of resistance.

34. A trader observes that the 50-day moving average for the S&P 500 Index recently crossed below its long-term 200-day moving average. This situation is referred to as a:

    A. death cross.

    B. golden cross.

    C. Bollinger Band.

35. Bollinger Bands are constructed by plotting:

    A. a MACD line and a signal line.

    B. a moving-average line with an uptrend line above and downtrend line below.

    C. a moving-average line with upper and lower lines that are at a set number of standard deviations apart.

36. A Bollinger Band "squeeze" occurs when volatility:

    A. falls to low levels as the Bollinger Band widens.

    B. falls to low levels as the Bollinger Band narrows.

    C. rises to high levels as the Bollinger Band narrows.

37. Which of the following is *not* a momentum oscillator?

    A. MACD.

    B. Stochastic oscillator.

    C. Bollinger Bands.

38. Intermarket analysis focuses on the:

    A. valuation drivers of intermarket asset price relationships.

    B. bottom-up economic fundamentals of intermarket relationships.

    C. identification of inflection points in intermarket relationships using relative strength indicators.

39. A technical analyst following a bottom-up investing approach focusing on momentum and breakout strategies should favor long positions in stocks with:

    A. shorter consolidation periods.

    B. high Bollinger Band readings.

    C. low volatility prior to an upside breakout.

SOLUTIONS

1. A is correct. Almost all technical analysis relies on these data inputs.

2. A is correct. Technical analysis works because markets are *not* efficient and rational and because human beings tend to behave similarly in similar circumstances. The result is market trends and patterns that repeat themselves and are somewhat predictable.

3. A is correct. Trends generally must be in place for some time before they are recognizable. Thus, some time may be needed for a change in trend to be identified.

4. A is correct. Commodities and currencies do not have underlying financial statements or an income stream; thus, fundamental analysis is useless in determining theoretical values for them or whether they are over- or undervalued.

5. A is correct. The underlying logic of technical analysis is that past price action can be useful to anticipate and project potential future prices with charts and other technical tools

6. B is correct. According to technical analysts, market psychology leads to repetition of price movements. Because investor behavior repeats itself, price movement patterns can be charted out, allowing technicians to recognize patterns.

7. C is correct. The top and bottom of the bars indicate the highs and lows for the day; the line on the left indicates the opening price and the line on the right indicates the closing price.

8. C is correct. Dark and light shading is a unique feature of candlestick charts.

9. C is correct. A shaded candlestick body indicates that the price of the security closed down from its opening price, whereas a clear body indicates that the price closed up from its opening price. Thus, a shaded candlestick body indicates that the opening price was higher than the closing price.

10. B is correct. A line chart has one data point per time interval, with price on the vertical axis and unit of time on the horizontal axis.

11. A is correct. The price of gold in nominal dollars was several orders of magnitude cheaper 100 years ago than it is today (roughly US$20 then versus US$1,100 today). Such a wide range of prices lends itself well to being graphically displayed on a logarithmic scale.

12. B is correct. A linearly scaled (rather than a logarithmically scaled) chart is better suited for analysis of short-term price movements. A linear scale plots price against a vertical axis with an equal distance between prices, whereas with a logarithmic scale, equal vertical distances correspond to an equal percentage change. The difference between a logarithmic price chart and an arithmetic (linear) price chart can be small when analyzing a chart in the short term. However, major differences are apparent when analyzing longer-term charts (more than two years of price data).

13. B is correct. In relative strength analysis, the analyst typically prepares a line chart of the ratio of the two assets' prices, with the asset under analysis as the numerator and with the benchmark or other security as the denominator. With

this single line chart, the analyst can readily visualize relative performance by the positive or negative slope of the line. A rising line shows the asset is performing better than the index or other stock; a declining line shows the opposite.

14. C is correct. Rising volume shows conviction by many market participants, which is likely to lead to a continuation of the trend.

15. B is correct. A downtrend line is constructed by drawing a line connecting the highs of the price chart.

16. B is correct. It is demonstrated in the following chart:

Exhibit 1: Candlestick Chart: ABC Co., Ltd. Price Data, November–September (Price Measured in RMB × 10)

Share price breaks through trend line at approximately RMB 8.5

17. B is correct.

18. C is correct. As shown in the following chart, XYZ Co. shares traded up to 390p on three occasions, each several weeks apart, and declined thereafter each time.

Solutions

Exhibit 2: Candlestick Chart: XYZ Co. Price Data, January–January (Price Measured in British Pence)

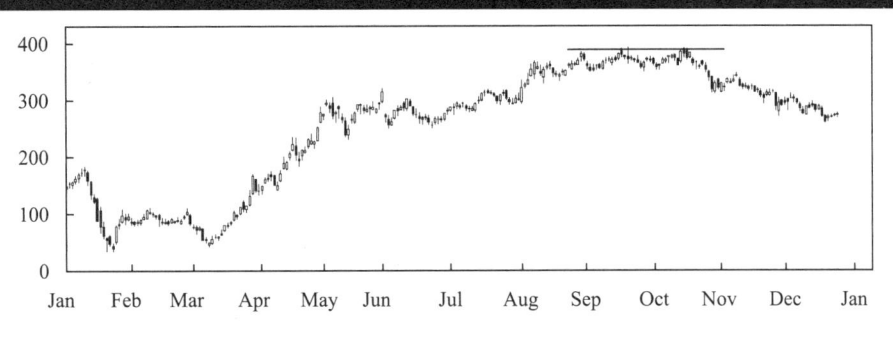

19. C is correct. In technical analysis, when a security is not trending, it is considered to be in consolidation. A consolidation phase is characterized by a fairly narrow trading range in which the price moves sideways (indicative of relative supply/demand balance) without much upward or downward movement. The key to technical analysis is the ability to differentiate between a consolidation and a trend phase.

20. A is correct. When a previously downtrending price breaks out of its consolidation range on the downside, it suggests that the price will enter a new downtrend phase.

21. A is correct. According to the change in polarity principle, once a support level is breached, it becomes a level of resistance. Likewise, when a resistance level is breached, it becomes a level of support.

22. C is correct. The left shoulder formed at around US$18.50, the head formed at around US$20.50, and the second shoulder formed at around US$19.

Exhibit 3: Candlestick Chart: DGF Company, five years, February–February

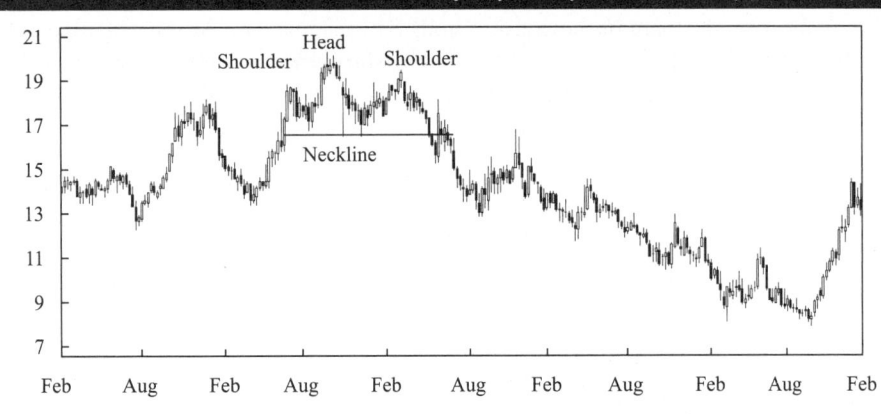

23. A is correct. In the ascending triangle pattern, irrespective of where the ascending triangle is identified, it should be considered as a consolidation with bullish

24. C is correct. Target = Neckline + (Neckline − Head): €100 + (€100 − €75) = €125

25. B is correct. A head and shoulders pattern is a reversal pattern that signals the end of an uptrend in price. Once a head and shoulders pattern has been formed, the expectation is that the price will decline through the neckline price of the formation.

26. B is correct. An inverse head and shoulders is a reversal pattern for a downtrend that preceded the formation of the pattern. An inverse head and shoulders is also referred to as a head and shoulders bottom and signals a potential reversal from the preceding downtrend to an uptrend. An inverse head and shoulders is the opposite of a head and shoulders pattern that signals a reversal from a preceding uptrend to a downtrend.

27. B is correct. A head and shoulders formation is a sell indicator that signals a reversal of a preceding uptrend. Once the head and shoulders pattern forms, the expectation is that the price will decline through the neckline price, setting the stage for a downtrend phase.

28. A is correct. When attempting to profit from a head and shoulders formation, a technician will often use the price difference between the head and neckline to set a price target below the neckline. The price target is therefore set as follows: Price target = Neckline − (Head − Neckline).

29. B is correct. With a "healthy correction," a type of continuation pattern, the long-term price trend does not change as supply and demand remains in balance while ownership transitions from one investor group to another.

30. A is correct. Triangles are one of several continuation patterns.

31. C is correct. It is one of several reversal patterns.

32. A is correct. Volume is necessary to confirm the various market rallies and reversals during the formation of the head and shoulders pattern.

33. A is correct. When the short-term moving average crosses above the long-term moving average, it can be viewed as a bullish buy signal. For example, a 5-day short-term moving average (a proxy for short-term momentum) breaking up through a 60-day longer-term moving average (an indicator of intermediate trend) can be used as a buy signal.

34. A is correct. A widely followed moving average crossover signal is the one that takes place between the 50-day moving average and the 200-day moving average. When the short-term (50-day) moving average crosses below the long-term (200-day) moving average, it is called a death cross and is a bearish signal.

35. C is correct. Bollinger Bands consist of a moving average and a higher line representing the moving average plus a set number of standard deviations from average price (for the same number of periods as used to calculate the moving average) and a lower line that is a moving average minus the same number of standard deviations.

36. B is correct. A Bollinger Band "squeeze" occurs when volatility falls to a very low level, as evidenced by the narrowing bands.

37. C is correct. Bollinger Bands are price-based indicators, *not* momentum oscil-

lators, which are constructed so that they oscillate between a high and a low or around 0 or 100.

38. C is correct. Intermarket analysis is a field within technical analysis that combines analysis of major categories of securities, industries, benchmarks, and geographies to identify intermarket relationships, trends, and possible inflections in a trend. To identify these intermarket relationships and trends, a commonly used tool is relative strength analysis, which charts the ratio of the price of two assets.

39. C is correct. Securities that break out from low-volatility conditions are likely to experience high volatility, and high volatility in the direction of an existing trend will usually help the trend pick up momentum. Breakouts from consolidation periods in an uptrend or entering an uptrend are usually followed by a continuation of the existing trend.

LEARNING MODULE

5

Fintech in Investment Management

by Robert Kissell, PhD, and Barbara J. Mack.

Robert Kissell, PhD, is at Molloy College and Kissell Research Group (USA). Barbara J. Mack is at Pingry Hill Enterprises, Inc. (USA).

LEARNING OUTCOME	
Mastery	The candidate should be able to:
☐	describe "fintech"
☐	describe Big Data, artificial intelligence, and machine learning
☐	describe fintech applications to investment management
☐	describe financial applications of distributed ledger technology

INTRODUCTION

1

☐ describe "fintech"

The meeting of finance and technology, commonly known as *fintech*, is changing the landscape of investment management. Advancements include the use of Big Data, artificial intelligence, and machine learning to evaluate investment opportunities, optimize portfolios, and mitigate risks. These developments are affecting not only quantitative asset managers but also fundamental asset managers who make use of these tools and technologies to engage in hybrid forms of investment decision making.

Investment advisory services are undergoing changes with the growth of automated wealth advisers or "robo-advisers." Robo-advisers might assist investors without the intervention of a human adviser, or they might be used in combination with a human adviser. The desired outcome is the ability to provide tailored, actionable advice to investors with greater ease of access and at lower cost.

In the area of financial record keeping, blockchain and distributed ledger technology (DLT) are creating new ways to record, track, and store transactions for financial assets. An early example of this trend is the cryptocurrency bitcoin, but the technology is being considered in a broader set of applications.

This reading is divided into seven main sections, which together define fintech and outline some of its key areas of impact in the field of investment management. Section 1 explains the concept and areas of fintech. Sections 2 and 3 discuss Big Data, artificial intelligence, and machine learning. Section 4 discusses data science, and Sections 5–8 provide applications of fintech to investment management. Sections 9 and 10 examine DLT. A summary of key points completes the reading.

What Is Fintech?

In its broadest sense, the term "fintech" generally refers to technology-driven innovation occurring in the financial services industry. For the purposes of this reading, **fintech** refers to technological innovation in the design and delivery of financial services and products. Note, however, that in common usage, fintech can also refer to companies (often new, startup companies) involved in developing the new technologies and their applications, as well as the business sector that comprises such companies. Many of these innovations are challenging the traditional business models of incumbent financial services providers.

Early forms of fintech included data processing and the automation of routine tasks. Then followed systems that provided execution of decisions according to specified rules and instructions. Fintech has since advanced into decision-making applications based on complex machine-learning logic, where computer programs are able to "learn" how to complete tasks over time. In some applications, advanced computer systems are performing tasks at levels far surpassing human capabilities. Fintech has changed the financial services industry in many ways, giving rise to new systems for investment advice, financial planning, business lending, and payments.

Whereas fintech covers a broad range of services and applications, areas of fintech development that are more directly relevant to the investment industry include the following:

- **Analysis of large datasets.** In addition to growing amounts of traditional data, such as security prices, corporate financial statements, and economic indicators, massive amounts of **alternative data** generated from non-traditional data sources, such as social media and sensor networks, can now be integrated into a portfolio manager's investment decision-making process and used to help generate alpha and reduce losses.

- **Analytical tools.** For extremely large datasets, techniques involving **artificial intelligence** (AI)—computer systems capable of performing tasks that previously required human intelligence—might be better suited to identify complex, non-linear relationships than traditional quantitative methods and statistical analysis. Advances in AI-based techniques are enabling different data analysis approaches. For example, analysts are turning to AI to sort through the enormous amounts of data from company filings, annual reports, and earnings calls to determine which data are most important and to help uncover trends and generate insights relating to human sentiment and behavior.

- **Automated trading.** Executing investment decisions through computer algorithms or automated trading applications could provide a number of benefits to investors, including more efficient trading, lower transaction costs, anonymity, and greater access to market liquidity.

- **Automated advice. Robo-advisers** or automated personal wealth management services provide investment services to a larger number of retail investors at lower cost than traditional adviser models can provide.

Introduction

- **Financial record keeping.** New technology, such as DLT, could provide secure ways to track ownership of financial assets on a peer-to-peer (P2P) basis. By allowing P2P interactions—in which individuals or firms transact directly with each other without mediation by a third party—DLT reduces the need for financial intermediaries.

Fintechs in Financial Services

Over the past several years, fintechs have evolved rapidly and include everything from mobile payment apps to robo-advisors. Fintechs reduce costs to customers while increasing the Tcustomer interactions. Their rapid growth threatens established brick-and-mortar banks, financial institutions, insurance companies, and asset managers. The following offers a brief overview of the main fintech types.

- In lending, LendTech and CreditTech companies such as Lendio and Affirm offer loans directly to both consumers and businesses. Their advantage comes from the automation of the time-consuming loan documentation and loan review processes and their ability to assess a borrower's creditworthiness quickly. ClearScore specializes in online credit scoring services. By streamlining all the steps in the underwriting process, these companies serve retail and corporate borrowers alike. Some of these fintechs are cost-efficient marketing and distribution platforms for banks, but increasingly, fintechs lend their own capital directly to borrowers.
- In payments, PayTech companies simplify the payment process by bypassing banks, reduce transaction fees for payments, and increase both the ease and the speed with which payments are made. Their main areas of focus are as follows:
  - *Online payment gateways* such as Razorpay, Shopify, and Checkout.com give customers convenient online payment access for products or services on a website by integrating debit cards, credit cards, digital wallets, and bank accounts.
  - *Mobile payments* such as Apple Pay facilitate everyday financial transactions using apps or mobile wallets andcontactless point of sale payments using smartphones, mobile card readers, and P2P payments.
  - *Remittances* have been quite expensive historically and slow to process. But technological advances, such as those offered by Wise, provide low-cost service to quickly send and collect money from anywhere in the world.
- In personal finance, WealthTech companies provide convenient access to personal finance tools. Algorithmic tools have increased efficiency in offering these services and pass on the lower costs directly to consumers.
  - *Financial planning and budgeting* tools such those offered by SoFi and Stash provide simple and efficient ways to monitor income and expenses, manage payments, conduct price comparison, and provide spending advice.
  - *Saving, investment, and retirement* advice and services, provided by firms such as Betterment, range from online banks to robo-advisors and provide algorithm-based asset recommendations and customizable portfolio management solutions to a large number of customers.

- *Trading on the financial markets* is facilitated by companies such as eToro and Kraken, which use online access to offer low- or no-cost trade execution by routing trades through specific venues. They also provide access to financial market commentary, research, financial information, and analysis.
- In consumer banking, fintechs such as Revolut, Monzo, and Varo provide low-cost, online access to banking services, specifically deposits, loans, and payments. Most fintech consumer banks, such as Chime and Marcus, serve as the online distribution platforms for traditional brick-and-mortar banks. An increasing number are entirely online, with no physical branch network. Many online consumer banking solutions build on digital wallets that are linked to smartphones.
- In insurance, InsurTech fintechs, such as Ethos and Health IQ, provide cost-efficient, large-scale distribution, underwriting, and claims management for various insurance products. Several traditional insurance companies rely on these online platforms to reach new customers and offer them lower prices.
- P2P financing simplifies the capital-raising process by collecting money from investors. These fintechs rely on scale and digital distribution and often provide up-to-date financial and other performance information for investors, allowing them convenient access when monitoring the performance of a company they have invested in.
- *P2P lending firms*, such as LendingClub, Prosper, and Zopa, allow businesses and individuals to bypass banks to raise debt capital and pool funds through an online platform.
- *Crowdfunding platforms*, such as AngelList, can connect accredited investors with startups that meet certain requirements to raise equity capital.
- Fintech companies specializing in regulatory or supervisory solutions, RegTech or SupTech, focus on technologies that simplify the monitoring of regulatory requirements, making regulatory reporting more efficient, transparent, and effective. The high cost of regulatory compliance drove the emergence of RegTech. XBRL, an open data exchange standard for business reporting, facilitates financial reporting and simplifies supervisory compliance. Besides automated regulatory reporting, other uses include compliance (CompTech), specifically anti–money laundering, anti–terrorist financing, and customer identification (Know Your Customer, or KYC). The real-time monitoring of financial transactions can identify and prevent potentially criminal or unsanctioned activities for banks and financial services. Many companies offer these services, including ComplyAdvantage, SteelEye, and Quantexa.

Drivers underlying fintech development in these areas include extremely rapid growth in data—including their quantity, types, sources, and quality—and technological advances that enable the capture and extraction of information from them. The data explosion is addressed in Section 2, and selected technological advances and data science are addressed in Sections 3 and 4, respectively.

BIG DATA

2

☐ describe Big Data, artificial intelligence, and machine learning

As noted, datasets are growing rapidly in terms of the size and diversity of data types that are available for analysis. The term **Big Data** has been in use since the late 1990s and refers to the vast amount of data being generated by industry, governments, individuals, and electronic devices. Big Data includes data generated from traditional sources—such as stock exchanges, companies, and governments—as well as non-traditional data types, also known as **alternative data**, arising from the use of electronic devices, social media, sensor networks, and company exhaust (data generated in the normal course of doing business).

Traditional data sources include corporate data in the form of annual reports, regulatory filings, sales and earnings figures, and conference calls with analysts. Traditional data also include data that are generated in the financial markets, including trade prices and volumes. Because the world has become increasingly connected, we can now obtain data from a wide range of devices, including smart phones, cameras, microphones, radio-frequency identification (RFID) readers, wireless sensors, and satellites that are now in use all over the world. As the internet and the presence of such networked devices have grown, the use of non-traditional data sources, or alternative data sources—including social media (posts, tweets, and blogs), email and text communications, web traffic, online news sites, and other electronic information sources—has risen.

The term *Big Data* typically refers to datasets having the following characteristics:

- **Volume**: The amount of data collected in files, records, and tables is very large, representing many millions, or even billions, of data points.
- **Velocity**: The speed with which the data are communicated is extremely great. Real-time or near-real-time data have become the norm in many areas.
- **Variety**: The data are collected from many different sources and in a variety of formats, including structured data (e.g., SQL tables or CSV files), semi-structured data (e.g., HTML code), and unstructured data (e.g., video messages).

Features relating to Big Data's volume, velocity, and variety are shown in Exhibit 1.

Exhibit 1: Big Data Characteristics: Volume, Velocity, and Variety

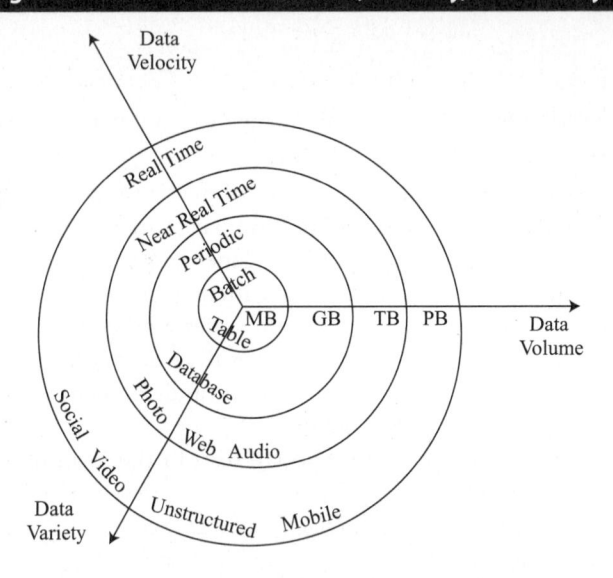

Data	Volume Key	Bytes of Information
MB	Megabyte	One Million
GB	Gigabyte	One Billion
TB	Terabyte	One Trillion
PB	Petabyte	One Quadrillion

Source: http://whatis.techtarget.com/definition/3Vs.

Exhibit 1 shows that data volumes are growing from megabytes and gigabytes to far larger sizes, such as terabytes and petabytes, as more data are being generated, captured, and stored. At the same time, more data, traditional and non-traditional, are available on a real-time or near-real-time basis with far greater variety in data types than ever before.

When Big Data is used for inference or prediction, a "fourth V" comes into play: Veracity relates to the credibility and reliability of different data sources. Determining the credibility and reliability of data sources is an important part of any empirical investigation. The issue of veracity becomes critically important for Big Data, however, because of the varied sources of these large datasets. Big Data amplifies the age-old challenge of disentangling quality from quantity.

Big Data can be structured, semi-structured, or unstructured data. Structured data items can be organized in tables and are commonly stored in a database where each field represents the same type of information. Unstructured data can be disparate, unorganized data that cannot be represented in tabular form. Unstructured data, such as those generated by social media, email, text messages, voice recordings, pictures, blogs, scanners, and sensors, often require different, specialized applications or custom programs before they can be useful to investment professionals. For example, to analyze data contained in emails or texts, specially developed or customized computer code might be required to first process these files. Semi-structured data can have attributes of both structured and unstructured data.

Sources of Big Data

Big Data, therefore, encompasses data generated by

- financial markets (e.g., equity, fixed income, futures, options, and other derivatives),
- businesses (e.g., corporate financials, commercial transactions, and credit card purchases),
- governments (e.g., trade, economic, employment, and payroll data),
- individuals (e.g., credit card purchases, product reviews, internet search logs, and social media posts),
- sensors (e.g., satellite imagery, shipping cargo information, and traffic patterns), and, in particular,
- the Internet of Things, or IoT (e.g., data generated by "smart" buildings, where the building is providing a steady stream of information about climate control, energy consumption, security, and other operational details).

In gathering business intelligence, historically, analysts have tended to draw on traditional data sources, using statistical methods to measure performance, predict future growth, and analyze sector and market trends. In contrast, the analysis of Big Data incorporates the use of alternative data sources.

From retail sales data to social media sentiment to satellite imagery that might reveal information about agriculture, shipping, and oil rigs, alternative datasets can provide additional insights about consumer behavior, firm performance, trends, and other factors important for investment-related activities. Such information is having a significant effect on the way that professional investors, particularly quantitative investors, approach financial analysis and decision-making processes.

The three main sources of alternative data are

- data generated by individuals,
- data generated by business processes, and
- data generated by sensors.

Data generated by individuals are often produced in text, video, photo, and audio formats and can also be generated through such means as website clicks or time spent on a webpage. This type of data tends to be unstructured. The volume of this type of data is growing dramatically as people participate in greater numbers and more frequently in online activities, such as social media and e-commerce, including online reviews of products, services, and entire companies, and as they make personal data available through web searches, email, and other electronic trails.

Business process data include information flows from corporations and other public entities. These data tend to be structured data and include direct sales information, such as credit card data, as well as corporate exhaust. Corporate exhaust includes corporate supply chain information, banking records, and retail point-of-sale scanner data. Business process data can be leading or real-time indicators of business performance, whereas traditional corporate metrics might be reported only on a quarterly or even yearly basis and are typically lagging indicators of performance.

Sensor data are collected from such devices as smart phones, cameras, RFID chips, and satellites that are usually connected to computers via wireless networks. Sensor data can be unstructured, and the volume of data is many orders of magnitude greater than that of individual or business process datastreams. This form of data is growing exponentially because microprocessors and networking technology are increasingly present in a wide array of personal and commercial electronic devices. Extended to office buildings, homes, vehicles, and many other physical forms, this culminates in a network arrangement, known as the **Internet of Things**, that is formed by the vast array of physical devices, home appliances, smart buildings, vehicles, and other items that are embedded with electronics, sensors, software, and network connections that enable the objects in the system to interact and share information.

Exhibit 2 shows a classification of alternative data sources and includes examples for each.

Exhibit 2: Classification of Alternative Data Sources

Individuals	Business Processes	Sensors
Social media	Transaction data	Satellites
News, reviews	Corporate data	Geolocation
Web searches, personal data		Internet of Things
		Other sensors

In the search to identify new factors that could affect security prices, enhance asset selection, improve trade execution, and uncover trends, alternative data are being used to support data-driven investment models and decisions. As interest in alternative data has risen, the number of specialized firms that collect, aggregate, and sell alternative datasets has grown.

While the marketplace for alternative data is expanding, investment professionals should understand potential legal and ethical issues related to information that is not in the public domain. For example, the scraping of web data could potentially capture personal information that is protected by regulations or that might have been published or provided without the explicit knowledge and consent of the individuals involved. Best practices are still in development in many jurisdictions, and because of varying approaches taken by national regulators, the different forms of guidance could conflict.

Big Data Challenges

Big Data poses several challenges when it is used in investment analysis, including the quality, volume, and appropriateness of the data. Key issues revolve around the following questions, among others: Does the dataset have selection bias, missing data, or data outliers? Is the volume of collected data sufficient? Is the dataset well suited for the type of analysis? In most instances, the data must be sourced, cleansed, and organized before analysis can occur. This process can be extremely difficult with alternative data owing to the unstructured characteristics of the data involved, which are more often qualitative (e.g., texts, photos, and videos) than quantitative in nature.

Given the size and complexity of alternative datasets, traditional analytical methods cannot always be used to interpret and evaluate these datasets. To address this challenge, AI and machine learning techniques have emerged that support work on such large and complex sources of information.

3   ADVANCED ANALYTICAL TOOLS: AI AND MACHINE LEARNING

describe Big Data, artificial intelligence, and machine learning

Advanced Analytical Tools: AI and Machine Learning

AI computer systems are capable of performing tasks that have traditionally required human intelligence. AI technology has enabled the development of computer systems that exhibit cognitive and decision-making ability comparable or superior to that of human beings.

An early example of AI was the "expert system," a type of computer programming that attempted to simulate the knowledge base and analytical abilities of human experts in specific problem-solving contexts. This was often accomplished through the use of "if-then" rules. By the late 1990s, faster networks and more powerful processors enabled AI to be deployed in logistics, data mining, financial analysis, medical diagnosis, and other areas. Since the 1980s, financial institutions have made use of AI—particularly, **neural networks**, programming based on how our brain learns and processes information—to detect abnormal charges or claims in credit card fraud detection systems.

Machine learning (ML) involves computer-based techniques that seek to extract knowledge from large amounts of data without making any assumptions on the data's underlying probability distribution. The goal of ML algorithms is to automate decision-making processes by generalizing, or "learning," from known examples to determine an underlying structure in the data. The emphasis is on the ability of the algorithm to generate structure or predictions without any help from a human. Simply put, ML algorithms aim to "find the pattern, apply the pattern."

As it is currently used in the investing context, ML requires massive amounts of data for "training," so although some ML techniques have existed for years, insufficient data have historically limited broader application. Previously, these algorithms lacked access to the large amounts of data needed to model relationships successfully. The growth in Big Data has provided ML algorithms, such as neural networks, with sufficient data to improve modeling and predictive accuracy, and greater use of ML techniques is now possible.

In ML, the computer algorithm is given "inputs" (a set of variables or datasets) and might be given "outputs" (the target data). The algorithm "learns" from the data provided how best to model inputs to outputs (if provided) or how to identify or describe underlying data structure if no outputs are given. Training occurs as the algorithm identifies relationships in the data and uses that information to refine its learning process.

ML involves splitting the dataset into three distinct subsets: a training dataset, a validation dataset, and a test dataset. The training dataset allows the algorithm to identify relationships between inputs and outputs based on historical patterns in the data. These relationships are then validated, and the model tuned, using the validation dataset. The test dataset is used to test the model's ability to predict well on new data. Once an algorithm has been trained, validated, and tested, the ML model can be used to predict outcomes based on other datasets.

ML still requires human judgement in understanding the underlying data and selecting the appropriate techniques for data analysis. Before they can be used, the data must be clean and free of biases and spurious data. As noted, ML models also require sufficiently large amounts of data and might not perform well when not enough available data are available to train and validate the model.

Analysts must also be cognizant of errors that could arise from **overfitting** the data, because models that overfit the data might discover "false" relationships or "unsubstantiated" patterns that will lead to prediction errors and incorrect output forecasts. Overfitting occurs when the ML model learns the input and target dataset too precisely. In such cases, the model has been "over-trained" on the data and treats noise in the data as true parameters. An ML model that has been overfitted is not able to accurately predict outcomes using a different dataset and might be too complex. When a model has been underfitted, the ML model treats true parameters as if they are noise and is not able to recognize relationships within the training data. In such cases, the model could be too simplistic. Underfitted models will typically fail to fully discover patterns that underlie the data.

In addition, because they are not explicitly programmed, ML techniques can appear to be opaque or "black box" approaches, which arrive at outcomes that might not be entirely understood or explainable.

Types of ML

ML approaches can help identify relationships between variables, detect patterns or trends, and create structure from data, including data classification. ML can be broadly divided into three distinct classes of techniques: supervised learning, unsupervised learning, and deep learning.

In **supervised learning**, computers learn to model relationships based on labeled training data. In supervised learning, inputs and outputs are labeled, or identified, for the algorithm. After learning how best to model relationships for the labeled data, the trained algorithms are used to model or predict outcomes for new datasets. Trying to identify the best signal, or variable, to forecast future returns on a stock or trying to predict whether local stock market performance will be up, down, or flat during the next business day are problems that could be approached using supervised learning techniques.

In **unsupervised learning**, computers are not given labeled data but instead are given only data from which the algorithm seeks to describe the data and their structure. Trying to group companies into peer groups based on their characteristics rather than using standard sector or country groupings is a problem that could be approached using unsupervised learning techniques.

Underlying AI advances have been key developments relating to neural networks. In **deep learning** (or **deep learning nets**), computers use neural networks, often with many hidden layers, to perform multistage, non-linear data processing to identify patterns. Deep learning can use supervised or unsupervised ML approaches. By taking a layered or multistage approach to data analysis, deep learning develops an understanding of simple concepts that informs analysis of more complex concepts. Neural networks have existed since 1958 and have been used for many applications, such as forecasting and pattern recognition, since the early 1990s. Improvements in the algorithms underlying neural networks are providing more accurate models that better incorporate and learn from data. As a result, these algorithms are now far better at such activities as image, pattern, and speech recognition. In many cases, the advanced algorithms require less computing power than the earlier neural networks, and their improved solution enables analysts to discover insights and identify relationships that were previously too difficult or too time consuming to uncover.

Advances in AI outside Finance

Non-finance-related AI breakthroughs include victories in the general knowledge game-show *Jeopardy* (by IBM's Watson in 2011) and in the ancient Chinese board game Go (by Google's DeepMind in 2016). Not only is AI providing solutions where perfect information exists (all players have equal access to the same information), such as checkers, chess, and Go, but AI is also providing insight in cases where information might be imperfect and players have hidden information; AI successes at the game of poker (by DeepStack) are an example. AI has also been behind the rise of virtual assistants, such as Siri (from Apple), Google's Translate app, and Amazon's product recommendation engine.

The ability to analyze Big Data using ML techniques, alongside more traditional statistical methods, represents a significant development in investment research, supported by the presence of greater data availability and advances in the algorithms themselves. Improvements in computing power and software processing speeds and falling storage costs have further supported this evolution.

ML techniques are being used for Big Data analysis to help predict trends or market events, such as the likelihood of a successful merger or an outcome to a political election. Image recognition algorithms can now analyze data from satellite-imaging systems to provide intelligence on the number of consumers in retail store parking lots, shipping activity and manufacturing facilities, and yields on agricultural crops, to name just a few examples.

Such information could provide insights into individual firms or at national or global levels and might be used as inputs into valuation or economic models.

DATA SCIENCE: EXTRACTING INFORMATION FROM BIG DATA

4

☐ describe fintech applications to investment management

Data science can be defined as an interdisciplinary field that harnesses advances in computer science (including ML), statistics, and other disciplines for the purpose of extracting information from Big Data (or data in general). Companies rely on the expertise of data scientists/analysts to extract information and insights from Big Data for a wide variety of business and investment purposes.

An important consideration for the data scientist is the structure of the data. As noted in the discussion on Big Data, because of their unstructured nature, alternative data often require specialized treatment before they can be used for analysis.

Data Processing Methods

To help determine the best data management technique needed for Big Data analysis, data scientists use various data processing methods, including capture, curation, storage, search, and transfer.

- Capture—Data capture refers to how the data are collected and transformed into a format that can be used by the analytical process. Low-latency systems—systems that operate on networks that communicate high volumes of data with minimal delay (latency)—are essential for automated trading applications that make decisions based on real-time prices and market events. In contrast, high-latency systems do not require access to real-time data and calculations.
- Curation—Data curation refers to the process of ensuring data quality and accuracy through a data cleaning exercise. This process consists of reviewing all data to detect and uncover data errors—bad or inaccurate data—and making adjustments for missing data when appropriate.
- Storage—Data storage refers to how the data will be recorded, archived, and accessed and the underlying database design. An important consideration for data storage is whether the data are structured or unstructured and whether analytical needs require low-latency solutions.

- Search—Search refers to how to query data. Big Data has created the need for advanced applications capable of examining and reviewing large quantities of data to locate requested data content.
- Transfer—Transfer refers to how the data will move from the underlying data source or storage location to the underlying analytical tool. This could be through a direct data feed, such as a stock exchange's price feed.

Data Visualization

Data visualization is an important tool for understanding Big Data. Visualization refers to how the data will be formatted, displayed, and summarized in graphical form. Traditional structured data can be visualized using tables, charts, and trends, whereas non-traditional unstructured data require new techniques of data visualization. These visualization tools include, for example, interactive three-dimensional (3D) graphics, where users can focus in on specified data ranges and rotate the data across 3D axes to help identify trends and uncover relationships. Multidimensional data analysis consisting of more than three variables requires additional data visualization techniques—for example, adding color, shapes, and sizes to the 3D charts. Further, a wide variety of solutions exists to reflect the structure of the data through the geometry of the visualization, with interactive graphics allowing for especially rich possibilities. Examples include heat maps, tree diagrams, and network graphs.

Another valuable Big Data visualization technique that is applicable to textual data is a "tag cloud," where words are sized and displayed on the basis of the frequency of the word in the data file. For example, words that appear more often are shown with a larger font, and words that appear less often are shown with a smaller font. A "mind map" is another data visualization technique; it is a variation of the tag cloud, but rather than displaying the frequency of words, a mind map shows how different concepts are related to each other.

Exhibit 3 shows an example of a "tag cloud" based on a section of this reading. The more frequently a word is found within the text, the larger it becomes in the tag cloud. As shown in the tag cloud, the words appearing most frequently in the section include "data," "ML," "learning," "AI," "techniques," "model," and "relationships."

Data Science: Extracting Information from Big Data

Exhibit 3: Data Visualization Tag Cloud: Section 3, Advanced Analytical Tools

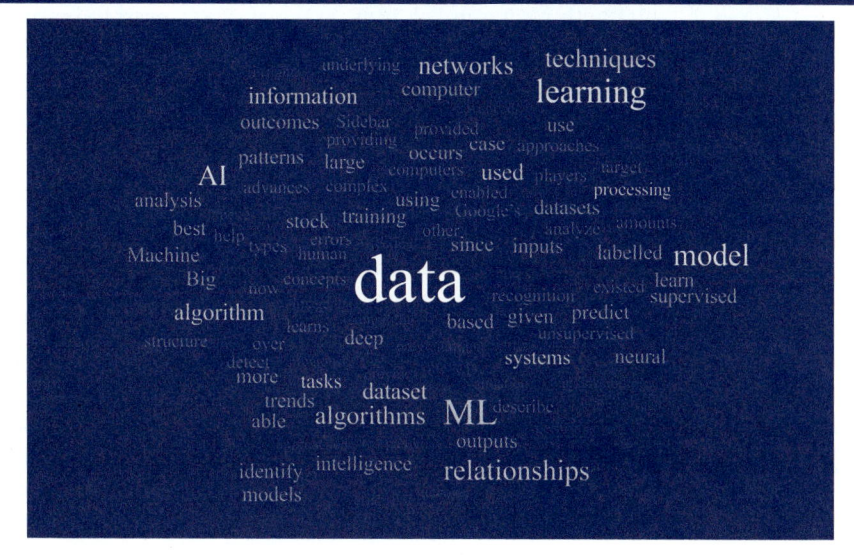

Source: https://worditout.com/word-cloud/create.

Programming Languages and Databases

Some of the more common programming languages used in data science include the following:

- **Python:** Python is an open source, free programming language that does not require an in-depth understanding of computer programming. Python allows individuals with little or no programming experience to develop computer applications for advanced analytical use and is the basis for many fintech applications.
- **R:** R is an open source, free programming language traditionally used for statistical analysis. R has mathematical packages for statistical analysis, ML, optimization, econometrics, and financial analysis.
- **Java:** Java is a programming language that can run on different computers, servers, and operating systems. Java is the underlying program language used in many internet applications.
- **C/C++:** C/C++ is a specialized programming language that provides the ability to optimize source code to achieve superior calculation speed and processing performance. C/C++ is used in applications for algorithmic and high-frequency trading.
- **Excel VBA:** Excel VBA helps bridge the gap between programming and manual data processing by allowing users to run macros to automate tasks, such as updating data tables and formulas, running data queries and collecting data from different web locations, and performing calculations. Excel VBA allows users to develop customized reports and analyses that rely on data that are updated from different applications and databases.

> Some of the more common databases in use include the following:
>
> - **SQL:** SQL is a database for structured data where the data can be stored in tables with rows and columns. SQL databases need to be run on a server that is accessed by users.
> - **SQLite:** SQLite is a database for structured data. SQLite databases are embedded into the program and do not need to be run on a server. It is the most common database for mobile apps that require access to data.
> - **NoSQL:** NoSQL is a database used for unstructured data where the data cannot be summarized in traditional tables with rows and columns.

5. APPLYING FINTECH TO INVESTMENT MANAGEMENT

> describe fintech applications to investment management

Fintech is being used in numerous areas of investment management. Applications for investment management include text analytics and natural language processing, robo-advisory services, risk analysis, and algorithmic trading.

Text Analytics and Natural Language Processing

Text analytics involves the use of computer programs to analyze and derive meaning typically from large, unstructured text- or voice-based datasets, such as company filings, written reports, quarterly earnings calls, social media, email, internet postings, and surveys. Text analytics includes using computer programs to perform automated information retrieval from different, unrelated sources to aid the decision-making process. More analytical usage includes lexical analysis, or the analysis of word frequency in a document and pattern recognition based on key words and phrases. Text analytics could be used in predictive analysis to help identify indicators of future performance, such as consumer sentiment.

Natural language processing (NLP) is a field of research at the intersection of computer science, AI, and linguistics that focuses on developing computer programs to analyze and interpret human language. Within the larger field of text analytics, NLP is an important application. Automated tasks using NLP include translation, speech recognition, text mining, sentiment analysis, and topic analysis. NLP might also be used in compliance functions to review employee voice and electronic communications for adherence to company or regulatory policy, inappropriate conduct, or fraud or for ensuring private or customer information is kept confidential.

Consider that all the public corporations worldwide generate millions of pages of annual reports and tens of thousands of hours of earnings calls each year. This is more information than any individual analyst or team of researchers can assess. NLP, especially when aided by ML algorithms, can analyze annual reports, call transcripts, news articles, social media posts, and other text- and audio-based data to identify trends in shorter timespans and with greater scale and accuracy than is humanly possible.

For example, NLP can be used to monitor analyst commentary to aid investment decision making. Financial analysts might generate earnings-per-share (EPS) forecasts reflecting their views on a company's near-term prospects. Focusing on forecasted EPS numbers could mean investors miss subtleties contained in an analyst's written research report. Because analysts tend not to change their buy, hold, and sell recommendations for a company frequently, they might instead offer nuanced commentary without making a change in their investment recommendation. After analyzing analyst commentary, NLP can assign sentiment ratings ranging from very negative to very positive for each. NLP can, therefore, be used to detect, monitor, and tag shifts in sentiment, potentially ahead of an analyst's recommendation change. Machine capabilities enable this analysis to scale across thousands of companies worldwide, performing work previously done by humans.

Similarly, communications and transcripts from policymakers, such as the European Central Bank or the US Federal Reserve, offer an opportunity for NLP-based analysis because officials at these institutions might send subtle messages through their choice of topics, words, and inferred tone. NLP can help analyze nuances within text to provide insights around trending or waning topics of interest, such as interest rate policy, aggregate output, or inflation expectations.

Models using NLP analysis might incorporate non-traditional information to evaluate what people are saying—via their preferences, opinions, likes, or dislikes—in an attempt to identify trends and short-term indicators about a company, a stock, or an economic event that might have a bearing on future performance. Past research has evaluated the predictive power of Twitter sentiment regarding IPO performance, for example.[1] The effect of positive and negative news sentiment on stock returns has also been researched.[2]

ROBO-ADVISORY SERVICES

☐ describe fintech applications to investment management

Since their emergence in 2008, a number of startup firms, as well as large asset managers, have introduced robo-advisory services, which provide investment solutions through online platforms, reducing the need for direct interaction with financial advisers.

As robo-advisers have been incorporated into the investment landscape, they have drawn the attention of regulatory authorities. In the United States, robo-advisers must be established as registered investment advisers, and they are regulated by the Securities and Exchange Commission. In the United Kingdom, they are regulated by the Financial Conduct Authority. In Australia, all financial advisers must obtain an Australian Financial Services license, with guidance on digital advisers coming from the Australian Securities and Investments Commission. Robo-advisers are also on the rise in parts of Asia and the rest of the world. Although regulatory conditions vary, robo-advisers are likely to be held to a similar level of scrutiny and code of conduct as other investment professionals in the given region.

---

1 Jim Kyung-Soo Liew and Garrett Zhengyuan Wang, "Twitter Sentiment and IPO Performance: A Cross-Sectional Examination," *Journal of Portfolio Management*, vol. 42, no. 4 (Summer 2016): 129–135.
2 Steven L. Heston and Nitish Ranjan Sinha, "News vs. Sentiment: Predicting Stock Returns from News Stories," *Financial Analysts Journal*, vol. 73, no. 3 (Third Quarter 2017): 67–83. (https://www.tandfonline.com/doi/abs/10.2469/faj.v73.n3.3).

Robo-advice tends to start with an investor questionnaire, which could include many of the categories and subcategories shown in Exhibit 4. Exhibit 4 is a synthesis of questionnaires created by the researchers attributed in the source note. Once assets, liabilities, risk preferences, and target investment returns have been digitally entered by a client, the robo-adviser software produces recommendations, based on algorithmic rules and historical market data, that incorporate the client's stated investment parameters. According to research by Michael Tertilt and Peter Scholz, robo-advisers do not seem to incorporate the full range of available information into their recommendations;[3] further research will be necessary over time to see how this might affect performance and the evolution of digital advisory services. Nevertheless, current robo-advisory services include automated asset allocation, trade execution, portfolio optimization, tax-loss harvesting, and rebalancing for investor portfolios.

Exhibit 4: Categories and Subcategories for Investor Questionnaires

General Information	Risk Tolerance
Income	Age
Investment Amount	Association with Investing
Job Description	Association with Risk
Other	Choose Portfolio Risk Level
Source of Income	Comfort Investing in Stock
Spendings	Credit Based Investments
Time to Retirement	Dealing with Financial Decisions
Type of Account	Degree of Financial Risk Taken
Working Status	Education
Risk Capacity	Ever Interested in Risky Asset for Thrill
Dependence on Withdrawal of Investment Amount	Experience of Drop/Reaction on Drop/Max Drop before Selling
Income Prediction	Family and Household Status
Investment Amount/Savings Rate Ratio	Financial Knowledge
Investment Amount/Total Capital Ratio	Gender
Investment Horizon	Investment Experience
Liabilities	Investment Goal
Savings Rate	Investor Type/Self-Assessment Risk Tolerance
Total Capital	Preference Return vs. Risk

Source: Michael Tertilt and Peter Scholz, 2017, "To Advise, or Not to Advise—How Robo-Advisors Evaluate the Risk Preferences of Private Investors," working paper (13 June): Table 1: Categories and Subcategories for Questionnaires.

Although their analyses and recommendations can cover both active and passive management styles, most robo-advisers follow a passive investment approach. These robo-advisers typically have low fees and low account minimums, implementing their recommendations with low-cost, diversified index mutual funds or exchange-traded funds (ETFs). A diverse range of asset classes can be managed in this manner, including

---

[3] Michael Tertilt and Peter Scholz, To Advise, or Not to Advise — How Robo-Advisors Evaluate the Risk Preferences of Private Investors (June 12, 2017). Available at SSRN: https://ssrn.com/abstract=2913178 or http://dx.doi.org/10.2139/ssrn.2913178

stocks, bonds, commodities, futures, and real estate. Because of their low-cost structure, robo-advisers can reach underserved populations, such as the mass affluent or mass market segments, which are less able to afford a traditional financial adviser.

Two types of wealth management services dominate the robo-advice sector: fully automated digital wealth managers and adviser-assisted digital wealth managers.

- **Fully Automated Digital Wealth Managers**

    The fully automated model does not rely on assistance from a human financial adviser. These services seek to offer a low-cost solution to investing and recommend an investment portfolio, which is often composed of ETFs. The service package can include direct deposits, periodic rebalancing, and dividend reinvestment options.

- **Adviser-Assisted Digital Wealth Managers**

    Adviser-assisted digital wealth managers provide automated investment services along with a virtual financial adviser, who is available to offer basic financial planning advice and periodic reviews by phone. Adviser-assisted digital wealth managers are capable of providing additional services that might involve a more holistic analysis of a client's assets and liabilities.

Wealthy and ultra-wealthy individuals typically have had access to human advisory teams, but a gap has existed in the availability and quality of advisers to serve investors with less wealth. The advent of robo-advisers offers a cost-effective and easily accessible form of financial guidance. In following a typically passive investment approach, research suggests that robo-advisers tend to offer fairly conservative advice.

However, critics of robo-advisers have wondered what would happen in a time of crisis, when people most tend to look to human expertise for guidance. Why a robo-adviser chooses to make a certain recommendation or take a certain trading action might not always be completely transparent, whereas a human adviser can provide his or her rationale. And finally, trust issues could arise in allowing computers to make these decisions, including worries of instances when robo-advisers might recommend inappropriate investments.

As the complexity and size of an investor's portfolio grows, robo-advisers might not be able to sufficiently address the particular preferences and needs of the investor. In the case of extremely affluent investors who might own a greater number of asset types—including alternative investments (e.g., venture capital, private equity, hedge funds, and real estate)—in addition to global stocks and bonds and have greater demands for customization, the need for a team of human advisers, each with particular areas of investment or wealth-management expertise, is likely to endure.

RISK ANALYSIS

☐ describe fintech applications to investment management

As mandated by regulators worldwide, the global investment industry has undertaken major steps in stress testing and risk assessment that involve the analysis of vast amounts of quantitative and qualitative risk data. Required data include information on the liquidity of the firm and its trading partners, balance sheet positions, credit exposures, risk-weighted assets, and risk parameters. Stress tests might also take qualitative information into consideration, such as capital planning procedures, expected business plan changes, business model sustainability, and operational risk.

Interest is increasing in monitoring risk in real time. To do so, relevant data must be taken by a firm, mapped to known risks, and identified as it moves within the firm. Data might be aggregated for reporting purposes or used as inputs to risk models. Big Data could provide insights into real-time and changing market circumstances to help identify weakening market conditions and adverse trends in advance, allowing managers to use risk management techniques and hedging practices sooner to help preserve asset value. For example, evaluation of alternative data using ML techniques could help foreshadow declining company earnings and future stock performance. Furthermore, analysis of real-time market data and trading patterns might help analysts detect buying or selling pressure in the stock.

ML techniques might be used to help assess data quality. To help ensure accurate and reliable data that might originate from numerous alternative data sources, ML techniques can help validate data quality by identifying questionable data, potential errors, and data outliers before integration with traditional data for use in risk models and in risk management applications.

Portfolio risk management often makes use of scenario analysis—analyzing the likely performance of the portfolio and liquidation costs under a hypothetical stress scenario or the repeat of a historical stress event. For example, to understand the implications of holding or liquidating positions during adverse or extreme market periods, such as the financial crisis, fund managers might perform "what-if" scenario analysis and portfolio backtesting using point-in-time data to understand liquidation costs and portfolio consequences under differing market conditions. These backtesting simulations are often computationally intense and could be facilitated through the use of advanced AI-based techniques.

8 ALGORITHMIC TRADING

☐ describe fintech applications to investment management

Algorithmic trading is the computerized buying and selling of financial instruments, in accordance with pre-specified rules and guidelines. Algorithmic trading is often used to execute large institutional orders, slicing orders into smaller pieces and executing across different exchanges and trading venues. Algorithmic trading provides investors with many benefits, including speed of execution, anonymity, and lower transaction costs. Over the course of a day, algorithms might continuously update and revise their execution strategy on the basis of changing prices, volumes, and market volatility. Algorithms could also determine the best way to price the order (e.g., limit or market order) and the most appropriate trading venue (e.g., exchange or dark pool) to route for execution.

High-frequency trading is a form of algorithmic trading that makes use of vast quantities of granular financial data (tick data, for example) to automatically place trades when certain conditions are met. Trades are executed on ultra-high-speed, low-latency networks in fractions of a second. HFT algorithms decide what to buy or sell and where to execute on the basis of real-time prices and market conditions, seeking to earn a profit from intraday market mispricings.

Global financial markets have undergone substantial change as markets have fragmented into multiple trading destinations consisting of electronic exchanges, alternative trading systems, and so-called dark pools, and average trade sizes have fallen. In this environment, and with markets continuously reflecting real-time information, algorithmic trading has been viewed as an important tool.

DLT AND PERMISSIONED AND PERMISSIONLESS NETWORKS

9

☐ describe financial applications of distributed ledger technology

DLT (**distributed ledger technology**)—technology based on a distributed ledger (defined later)—represents a fintech development that offers potential improvements in the area of financial record keeping. DLT networks are being considered as an efficient means to create, exchange, and track ownership of financial assets on a P2P basis. Potential benefits include greater accuracy, transparency, and security in record keeping; faster transfer of ownership; and P2P interactions. However, the technology is not fully secure, and breaches in privacy and data protection are possible. In addition, the processes underlying DLT generally require massive amounts of energy to verify transaction activity.

A **distributed ledger** is a type of database that can be shared among entities in a network. In a distributed ledger, entries are recorded, stored, and distributed across a network of participants so that each participant has a matching copy of the digital database. Basic elements of a DLT network include a digital ledger, a consensus mechanism used to confirm new entries, and a participant network.

The consensus mechanism is the process by which the computer entities (or nodes) in a network agree on a common state of the ledger. Consensus generally involves two steps: transaction validation and agreement on ledger update by network parties. These features enable the creation of records that are, for the most part, considered immutable, or unchangeable, yet they are transparent and accessible to network participants on a near-real-time basis.

Features of DLT include the use of **cryptography**—an algorithmic process to encrypt data, making the data unusable if received by unauthorized parties—which enables a high level of network security and database integrity. For example, DLT uses cryptographic methods of proof to verify network participant identity and for data encryption.

DLT has the potential to accommodate "**smart contracts**," which are computer programs that self-execute on the basis of pre-specified terms and conditions agreed to by the parties to a contract. Examples of smart contract use are the automatic execution of contingent claims for derivatives and the instantaneous transfer of collateral in the event of default.

Exhibit 5 illustrates a distributed ledger network in which all nodes are connected to one another, each having a copy of the distributed ledger. The term "Consensus" is shown in the center of the network and represents the consensus mechanism in which the nodes agree on new transactions and ledger updates.

Exhibit 5: Distributed Ledger Network Setup

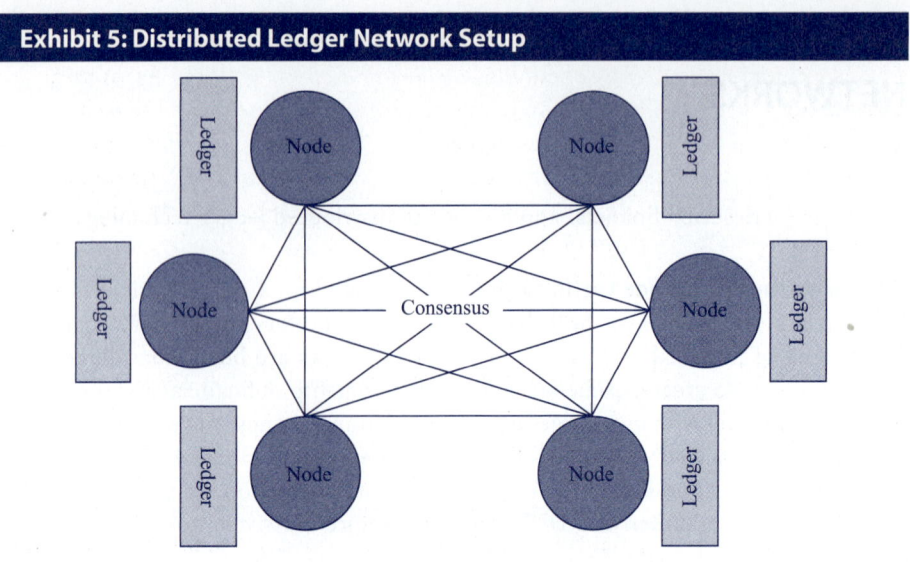

Source: https://blockgeeks.com/guides/what-is-hyperledger/.

Blockchain is a type of digital ledger in which information, such as changes in ownership, is recorded sequentially within blocks that are then linked or "chained" together and secured using cryptographic methods. Each block contains a grouping of transactions (or entries) and a secure link (known as a hash) to the previous block. New transactions are inserted into the chain only after validation via a consensus mechanism in which authorized members agree on the transaction and the preceding order, or history, in which previous transactions have occurred.

The consensus mechanism used to verify a transaction includes a cryptographic problem that must be solved by some computers on the network (known as miners) each time a transaction takes place. The process to update the blockchain can require substantial amounts of computing power, making it very difficult and extremely expensive for an individual third party to manipulate historical data. To manipulate historical data, an individual or entity would have to control the majority of nodes in the network. The success of the network, therefore, relies on broad network participation.

Blockchain (Distributed Ledger) Network—How Do Transactions Get Added?

Outlined below are the steps involved in adding a transaction to a blockchain distributed ledger.

1. Transaction takes place between buyer and seller.
2. Transaction is broadcast to the network of computers (nodes).
3. Nodes validate the transaction details and parties to the transaction.
4. Once verified, the transaction is combined with other transactions to form a new block (of predetermined size) of data for the ledger.
5. This block of data is then added or linked (using a cryptographic process) to the previous block(s) containing data.
6. Transaction is considered complete and ledger has been updated.

Permissioned and Permissionless Networks

DLT can take the form of permissionless or permissioned networks. **Permissionless networks** are open to any user who wishes to make a transaction, and all users within the network can see all transactions that exist on the blockchain. In a permissionless, or open, DLT system, network participants can perform all network functions.

The main benefit of a permissionless network is that it does not depend on a centralized authority to confirm or deny the validity of transactions, because this takes place through the consensus mechanism. This means no single point of failure exists because all transactions are recorded on a single distributed database and every node stores a copy of the database. Once a transaction has been added to the blockchain, it cannot be changed, barring manipulation; the distributed ledger becomes a permanent and immutable record of all previous transactions. In a permissionless network, trust is not a requirement between transacting parties.

Bitcoin is a well-known use of an open permissionless network. Using blockchain technology, Bitcoin was created in 2009 to serve as the public ledger for all transactions occurring on its virtual currency. Since the introduction of bitcoin, many more cryptocurrencies, or digital currencies, which use permissionless DLT networks, have been created.

In **permissioned networks**, network members might be restricted from participating in certain network activities. Controls, or permissions, can be used to allow varying levels of access to the ledger, from adding transactions (e.g., a participant) to viewing transactions only (e.g., a regulator) to viewing selective details of the transactions but not the full record.

APPLICATIONS OF DLT TO INVESTMENT MANAGEMENT

☐ describe financial applications of distributed ledger technology

Potential applications of DLT to investment management include cryptocurrencies, tokenization, post-trade clearing and settlement, and compliance.

Cryptocurrencies

A **cryptocurrency**, also known as a digital currency, operates as electronic currency and allows near-real-time transactions between parties without the need for an intermediary, such as a bank. As electronic mediums of exchange, cryptocurrencies lack physical form and are issued privately by individuals, companies, and other organizations. Most issued cryptocurrencies utilize open DLT systems in which a decentralized distributed ledger is used to record and verify all digital currency transactions. Cryptocurrencies have not traditionally been government backed or regulated. Central banks around the world, however, are recognizing potential benefits and examining use cases for their own cryptocurrency versions.

Many cryptocurrencies have a self-imposed limit on the total amount of currency they may issue. Although such limits could help maintain their store of value, it is important to note that many cryptocurrencies have experienced high levels of price volatility. A lack of clear fundamentals underlying these currencies has contributed to their volatility.

Cryptocurrencies have proven to be an attractive means for companies looking to raise capital. An **initial coin offering** (ICO) is an unregulated process whereby companies sell their crypto tokens to investors in exchange for fiat money or for another agreed upon cryptocurrency. An ICO is typically structured to issue digital tokens to investors that can be used to purchase future products or services being developed by the issuer. ICOs provide an alternative to traditional, regulated capital-raising processes, such as IPOs. Compared to the regulated IPO market, ICOs might have lower associated issuance costs and shorter capital raising time frames. However, most ICOs do not typically have attached voting rights. Regulation for ICOs is under consideration in a number of jurisdictions, and numerous instances of investor loss have resulted from fraudulent schemes.

Tokenization

Transactions involving physical assets, such as real estate, luxury goods, and commodities, often require substantial efforts in ownership verification and examination each time a transfer in ownership takes place. Through **tokenization**, the process of representing ownership rights to physical assets on a blockchain or distributed ledger, DLT has the potential to streamline this process by creating a single, digital record of ownership with which to verify ownership title and authenticity, including all historical activity. Real estate transactions that require ownership and identify verification might be one area to benefit from tokenization, because these transactions are typically labor intensive and costly, involving decentralized, paper-based records and multiple parties.

Post-Trade Clearing and Settlement

In the financial securities markets, post-trade processes to confirm, clear, and settle transactions are often complex and labor intensive, requiring multiple interactions between counterparties and financial intermediaries. DLT has the ability to streamline existing post-trade processes by providing near-real-time trade verification, reconciliation, and settlement, thereby reducing the complexity, time, and costs associated with processing transactions. A single distributed record of ownership between network peers would eliminate the need for independent and duplicative reconciliation efforts between parties and reduce the need for third-party facilitation. A shortened settlement time frame could lessen the time exposed to counterparty risk and associated collateral requirements while increasing the potential liquidity of assets and funds. Additionally, the use of automated contracts could also help to reduce post-trade time frames, lowering exposure to counterparty credit risk and trade fails.

Compliance

Regulators worldwide have imposed more stringent reporting requirements and demand greater transparency and access to data. To meet these requirements, many firms have added staff to their post-trade and compliance groups. But these functions remain predominantly manual. To comply with regulations, firms need to maintain and process large amounts of risk-related data. DLT could allow regulators and firms to maintain near-real-time review over transactions and other compliance-related processes. Improved post-trade reconciliation and automation through DLT could lead to more accurate record keeping and create operational efficiencies for a firm's compliance and regulatory reporting processes, while providing greater transparency and auditability for external authorities and regulators.

DLT-based compliance might better support shared information, communications, and transparency within and between firms, exchanges, custodians, and regulators. Closed or permissioned networks could offer advantages in security and privacy. These platforms could store highly sensitive information in a way that is secure but easily accessible to internal and external authorities. DLT could help uncover fraudulent activity and reduce compliance costs associated with know-your-customer and anti-money-laundering regulations, which entail verifying the identity of clients and business partners.

DLT Challenges

A number of challenges exist before DLT can be successfully adopted by the investment industry. These include the following:

- DLT network standardization is lacking, and integrating with legacy systems is difficult.
- DLT processing capabilities might not be financially competitive with existing solutions.
- Increasing the scale of DLT systems requires substantial (storage) resources.
- Immutability of transactions means accidental or "canceled" trades can be undone only by submitting an equal and offsetting trade.
- DLT requires huge amounts of computer power normally associated with high electricity usage.
- Regulatory approaches could differ by jurisdiction.

SUMMARY

- The term "fintech" refers to technological innovation in the design and delivery of financial services and products.
- Areas of fintech development include the analysis of large datasets, analytical techniques, automated trading, automated advice, and financial record keeping.
- Big Data is characterized by the three Vs—volume, velocity, and variety—and includes both traditional and non-traditional (or alternative) datasets.
- Among the main sources of alternative data are data generated by individuals, business processes, and sensors.
- AI computer systems are capable of performing tasks that traditionally required human intelligence at levels comparable (or superior) to those of human beings.
- ML seeks to extract knowledge from large amounts of data by "learning" from known examples and then generating structure or predictions. Simply put, ML algorithms aim to "find the pattern, apply the pattern." Main types of ML include supervised learning, unsupervised learning, and deep learning.
- NLP is an application of text analytics that uses insight into the structure of human language to analyze and interpret text- and voice-based data.

- Robo-advisory services are providing automated advisory services to increasing numbers of retail investors. Services include asset allocation, portfolio optimization, trade execution, rebalancing, and tax strategies.
- Big Data and ML techniques could provide insights into real-time and changing market circumstances to help identify weakening or adverse trends in advance, allowing for improved risk management and investment decision making.
- Algorithmic traders use automated trading programs to determine when, where, and how to trade an order on the basis of pre-specified rules and market conditions. Benefits include speed of executions, lower trading costs, and anonymity.
- Blockchain and DLT might offer a new way to store, record, and track financial assets on a secure, distributed basis. Applications include cryptocurrencies and tokenization. Additionally, DLT could bring efficiencies to post-trade and compliance processes through automation, smart contracts, and identity verification.

PRACTICE PROBLEMS

1. A correct description of fintech is that it:
   A. is driven by rapid growth in data and related technological advances.
   B. increases the need for intermediaries.
   C. is at its most advanced state using systems that follow specified rules and instructions.

2. A characteristic of Big Data is that:
   A. one of its traditional sources is business processes.
   B. it involves formats with diverse structures.
   C. real-time communication of it is uncommon due to vast content.

3. In the use of ML:
   A. some techniques are termed "black box" due to data biases.
   B. human judgment is not needed because algorithms continuously learn from data.
   C. training data can be learned too precisely, resulting in inaccurate predictions when used with different datasets.

4. Text analytics is appropriate for application to:
   A. economic trend analysis.
   B. large, structured datasets.
   C. public but not private information.

5. In providing investment services, robo-advisers are *most likely* to:
   A. rely on their cost effectiveness to pursue active strategies.
   B. offer fairly conservative advice as easily accessible guidance.
   C. be free from regulation when acting as fully automated wealth managers.

6. Which of the following statements on fintech's use of data as part of risk analysis is correct?
   A. Stress testing requires precise inputs and excludes qualitative data.
   B. ML ensures that traditional and alternative data are fully segregated.
   C. For real-time risk monitoring, data can be aggregated for reporting and used as model inputs.

7. A factor associated with the widespread adoption of algorithmic trading is increased:
   A. market efficiency.

B. average trade sizes.

C. trading destinations.

8. A benefit of DLT favoring its use by the investment industry is its:
   A. scalability of underlying systems.
   B. ease of integration with existing systems.
   C. streamlining of current post-trade processes.

9. What is a DLT application suited for physical assets?
   A. Tokenization
   B. Cryptocurrencies
   C. Permissioned networks

SOLUTIONS

1. A is correct. Drivers of fintech include extremely rapid growth in data (including their quantity, types, sources, and quality) and technological advances enabling the capture and extraction of information from it.

2. B is correct. Big Data is collected from many different sources and is in a variety of formats, including structured data (e.g., SQL tables or CSV files), semi-structured data (e.g., HTML code), and unstructured data (e.g., video messages).

3. C is correct. Overfitting occurs when the ML model learns the input and target dataset too precisely. In this case, the model has been "over trained" on the data and is treating noise in the data as true parameters. An ML model that has been overfitted is not able to accurately predict outcomes using a different dataset and might be too complex.

4. A is correct. Through the text analytics application of NLP, models using NLP analysis might incorporate non-traditional information to evaluate what people are saying—via their preferences, opinions, likes, or dislikes—in the attempt to identify trends and short-term indicators about a company, a stock, or an economic event that might have a bearing on future performance.

5. B is correct. Research suggests that robo-advisers tend to offer fairly conservative advice, providing a cost-effective and easily accessible form of financial guidance to underserved populations, such as the mass affluent and mass market segments.

6. C is correct. Interest is increasing in monitoring risk in real time. To do so, relevant data must be taken by a firm, mapped to known risks, and identified while moving within the firm. Data could be aggregated for reporting purposes or used as inputs to risk models.

7. C is correct. Global financial markets have undergone substantial change as markets have fragmented into multiple trading destinations consisting of electronic exchanges, alternative trading systems, and so-called dark pools. In such an environment, when markets are continuously reflecting real-time information and continuously changing conditions, algorithmic trading has been viewed as an important tool.

8. C is correct. DLT has the potential to streamline the existing, often complex and labor-intensive post-trade processes in securities markets by providing close to real-time trade verification, reconciliation, and settlement, thereby reducing related complexity, time, and costs.

9. A is correct. Through tokenization—the process of representing ownership rights to physical assets on a blockchain or distributed ledger—DLT has the potential to streamline this rights process by creating a single, digital record of ownership with which to verify ownership title and authenticity, including all historical activity.

Ethical and Professional Standards

LEARNING MODULE
1

Ethics and Trust in the Investment Profession

by Bidhan L. Parmar, PhD, Dorothy C. Kelly, CFA, Colin McLean, MBA, FIA, FSIP, Nitin Mehta, CFA, FSIP, and David B. Stevens, CIMC, CFA.

Bidhan L. Parmar, PhD, is at the University of Virginia (USA). Dorothy C. Kelly, CFA, is at McIntire School of Commerce, University of Virginia (USA). Colin McLean, MBA, FIA, FSIP, is at SVM Asset Management (United Kingdom). Nitin Mehta, CFA, FSIP (United Kingdom). David B. Stevens, CIMC, CFA, is at Wells Fargo Wealth Management (USA).

LEARNING OUTCOME	
Mastery	The candidate should be able to:
☐	explain ethics
☐	describe the role of a code of ethics in defining a profession
☐	describe professions and how they establish trust
☐	describe the need for high ethical standards in investment management
☐	explain professionalism in investment management
☐	identify challenges to ethical behavior
☐	compare and contrast ethical standards with legal standards
☐	describe a framework for ethical decision making

INTRODUCTION

As a candidate in the CFA Program, you are both expected and required to meet high ethical standards. This reading introduces ideas and concepts that will help you understand the importance of ethical behavior in the investment industry. You will be introduced to various types of ethical issues within the investment profession and learn about the CFA Institute Code of Ethics.

The readings covering ethics and professional standards demonstrate that ethical behavior is central to creating trust. Professional behavior is equally important. Professions help maintain trust in an industry by establishing codes and setting standards that put a framework around ethical behavior and technical competence. Professions also set the wider goal of gaining and maintaining the trust of society as a whole. In this regard, professions have a sense of purpose that society values.

Imagine that you are employed in the research department of a large financial services firm. You and your colleagues spend your days researching, analyzing, and valuing the shares of publicly traded companies and sharing your investment recommendations with clients. You love your work and take great satisfaction in knowing that your recommendations can help the firm's investing clients make informed investment decisions that will help them meet their financial goals and improve their lives.

Several months after starting at the firm, you learn that an analyst at the firm has been terminated for writing and publishing research reports that misrepresented the fundamental risks of some companies to investors. You learn that the analyst wrote the reports with the goal of pleasing the management of the companies that were the subjects of the research reports. He hoped that these companies would hire your firm's investment banking division for its services and he would be rewarded with large bonuses for helping the firm increase its investment banking fees. Some clients bought shares based on the analyst's reports and suffered losses. They posted stories on the internet about their losses and the misleading nature of the reports. When the media investigated and published the story, the firm's reputation for investment research suffered. Investors began to question the firm's motives and the objectivity of its research recommendations. The firm's investment clients started to look elsewhere for investment advice, and company clients begin to transfer their business to firms with untarnished reputations. With business declining, management is forced to trim staff. Along with many other hard-working colleagues, you lose your job—through no fault of your own.

Imagine how you would feel in this situation. Most people would feel upset and resentful that their hard and honest work was derailed by someone else's unethical behavior. Yet, this type of scenario is not uncommon. Around the world, unsuspecting employees at such companies as SAC Capital, Stanford Financial Group, Everbright Securities, Enron, Satyam Computer Services, Arthur Andersen, and other large companies have experienced such career setbacks when someone else's actions destroyed trust in their companies and industries.

Businesses and financial markets thrive on trust—defined as a strong belief in the reliability of a person or institution. In a 2016 study on trust, investors indicated that to earn their trust, the top two attributes of an investment manager should be that it (1) has transparent and open business practices, and (2) has ethical business practices.[1] Although these attributes are valued by customers and clients in any industry, this reading will explore why they are of particular importance to the investment industry.

People may think that ethical behavior is simply about following laws, regulations, and other rules, but throughout our lives and careers we will encounter situations in which there is no definitive rule that specifies how to act, or the rules that exist may be unclear or even in conflict with each other. Responsible people, including investment professionals, must be willing and able to identify potential ethical issues and create solutions to them even in the absence of clearly stated rules.

---

[1] CFA Institute From Trust to Loyalty: A Global Survey of What Investors Want (2013): http://www.cfa-pubs.org/doi/pdf/10.2469/ccb.v2013.n14.1.(2016): https://www.cfainstitute.org/research/survey-reports/from-trust-to-loyalty

ETHICS

☐ explain ethics

Through our individual actions, each of us can affect the lives of others. Our decisions and behavior can harm or benefit a variety of **stakeholders**—individuals or groups of individuals who could be affected either directly or indirectly by a decision and thus have an interest, or stake, in the decision. Examples of stakeholders in decisions made by investment industry professionals include our colleagues, our clients, our employers, the communities in which we live and work, the investment profession, trade associations, regulators, and other financial market participants. In some cases, our actions may benefit all of these stakeholder groups; in other cases, our actions may benefit only some stakeholder groups; and in still other cases, our actions may benefit some stakeholder groups and harm others. For example, recall the research analyst in the introduction who wrote misleading research reports with the aim of increasing the financial benefit to himself and his employer. In the very short term, his conduct seemed to directly benefit some stakeholders (certain clients, himself, and his employer) and to harm other stakeholders (clients who invested based on his reports). Over a longer time period, his conduct resulted in harm to himself and many other stakeholders—his employer, his employer's clients, his colleagues, investors, and through loss of trust when the story was published, the larger financial market.

Ethics encompasses a set of moral principles and rules of conduct that provide guidance for our behavior. The word "ethics" comes from the Greek word "ethos," meaning character, used to describe the guiding beliefs or ideals characterizing a society or societal group. Beliefs are assumptions or thoughts we hold to be true. A principle is defined as a belief or fundamental truth that serves as the foundation for a system of belief or behavior or a chain of reasoning. Our beliefs form our values—those things we deem to have worth or merit.

Moral principles or **ethical principles** are beliefs regarding what is good, acceptable, or obligatory behavior and what is bad, unacceptable, or forbidden behavior. Ethical principles may refer to beliefs regarding behavior that an individual expects of himself or herself, as well as shared beliefs regarding standards of behavior expected or required by a community or societal group.

The study of ethics examines the role of consequences and personal character in defining what is considered good, or ethical, conduct.

Ethical conduct is behavior that follows moral principles and balances self-interest with both the direct and the indirect consequences of the behavior on others. Ethical actions are those actions that are perceived as beneficial and conforming to the ethical expectations of society. An action may be considered beneficial if it improves the outcomes or consequences for stakeholders affected by the action. Telling the truth about the risks or costs associated with a recommended investment, for example, is an ethical action—that is, one that conforms to the ethical expectations of society in general and clients in particular. Telling the truth is also beneficial; telling the truth builds trust with customers and clients and enables them to make more informed decisions, which should lead to better outcomes for them and higher levels of client/customer satisfaction for you and your employer.

Widely acknowledged ethical principles include honesty, transparency, fairness or justice, diligence, and respect for the rights of others. Most societal groups share these fundamental ethical principles and build on them, establishing a shared set of rules regarding how members should behave in certain situations. The principles or rules may take different forms depending on the community establishing them.

Governments and related entities, for example, may establish laws and/or regulations to reflect widely shared beliefs about obligatory and forbidden conduct. Laws and regulations are rules of conduct specified by a governing body, such as a legislature or a regulator, identifying how individuals and entities under its jurisdiction should behave in certain situations. Most countries have laws and regulations governing the investment industry and the conduct of its participants. Differences in laws may reflect differences in beliefs and values.

In some countries, for example, the law requires that an investment adviser act in the best interests of his or her clients. Other countries require that investment professionals recommend investments that are suitable for their clients. These differing requirements can also hold true within one country where some advisers are held to a suitability standard and others to the fiduciary standard of the client's best interests. Investment advisers and portfolio managers who are required by law to act in their clients' best interests must always put their clients' interests ahead of their own or their employers' interests. An investment adviser who is required by law to act in a client's best interest must understand the client's financial objectives and risk tolerance, research and investigate multiple investment opportunities, and recommend the investment or investment portfolio that is *most* suitable for the client in terms of meeting his or her long-term financial objectives. In addition, the investment adviser would be expected to monitor the client's financial situation and investments to ensure that the investments recommended remain the *best* overall option for meeting the client's long-term financial objectives. In countries with only a suitability requirement, it is legal for investment professionals to recommend a suitable investment to a client even if other, similar suitable investments with lower fees are available. These differences in laws reflect differences in beliefs and values.

Specific communities or societal groups in which we live and work sometimes codify their beliefs about obligatory and forbidden conduct in a written set of principles, often called a **code of ethics**. Universities, employers, and professional associations often adopt a code of ethics to communicate the organization's values and overall expectations regarding member behavior. The code of ethics serves as a general guide for how community members should act. Some communities will also expand on their codes of ethics and adopt explicit rules or standards that identify specific behaviors required of community members. These **standards of conduct** serve as benchmarks for the minimally acceptable behavior of community members and can help clarify the code of ethics. Members can choose behaviors that demonstrate even higher standards. By joining the community, members are agreeing to adhere to the community's code of ethics and standards of conduct. To promote their code of ethics and reduce the incidence of violations, communities frequently display their codes in prominent locations and in written materials. In addition, most communities require that members commit to their codes in writing on an annual or more frequent basis.

Violations of a community's established code of ethics and/or standards of conduct can harm the community in a variety of ways. Violations have the potential to damage the community's reputation among external stakeholders and the general public. Violations can also damage the community's reputation internally and lead to reduced trust among community members and can cause the organization to fracture or splinter from within. To protect the reputation of its membership and limit potential harm to innocent members, the community may take corrective actions to investigate possible violations, repair any damages, and attempt to discipline the violator or, in severe cases, revoke the violator's membership in the community.

EXAMPLE 1

Ethics

1. Which of the following statements is *most* accurate? Ethics can be described as:

   A. a commitment to upholding the law.

   B. an individual's personal opinion about right and wrong.

   C. a set of moral principles that provide guidance for our behavior.

Solution:

C is correct. Ethics can be described as a set of moral principles that provide guidance for our behavior; these may be moral principles shared by a community or societal group.

2. Which of the following statements is *most* accurate? Standards of conduct:

   A. are a necessary component of any code of ethics.

   B. serve as a general guide regarding proper conduct by members of a group.

   C. serve as benchmarks for the minimally acceptable behavior required of members of a group.

Solution:

C is correct. Standards of conduct serve as benchmarks for the minimally acceptable behavior required of members of a group. Some organizations will adopt only a code of ethics, which communicates the organization's values and overall expectations regarding member behavior. Others may adopt both a code of ethics and standards of conduct. Standards of conduct identify specific behavior required of community members and serve as benchmarks for the minimally acceptable behavior of community members.

ETHICS AND PROFESSIONALISM

3

- ☐ describe the role of a code of ethics in defining a profession
- ☐ describe professions and how they establish trust
- ☐ describe the need for high ethical standards in investment management
- ☐ explain professionalism in investment management

A **profession** is an occupational community that has specific education, expert knowledge, and a framework of practice and behavior that underpins community trust, respect, and recognition. Most professions emphasize an ethical approach, the importance of good service, and empathy with the client.

Professions have grown in size and number over the last century: the rise of new specialist areas of expertise has created new professions. Driving forces of a new profession include governments and regulators, which encourage the formation of an ethical relationship between professionals and society at large. There is also demand for professions from individuals who see an advantage in working as a professional and from clients who desire to work with professionals.

Professions have not developed in every country. But in most countries, those who work in specialized areas—such as doctors, lawyers, actuaries, accountants, architects, and engineers—are subject to some combination of licensed status and technical standards. These standards distinguish professions from the craft guilds and trade bodies that were established in many countries. In particular, the requirement for members of professions to uphold high ethical standards is one clear difference. Another difference is that trade bodies do not normally have a mission to serve society or to set and enforce professional conduct rules for practitioners.

How Professions Establish Trust

For a profession to be credible, a primary goal is to establish trust among clients and among society in general. In doing so, professions have a number of common characteristics that, when combined, greatly increase confidence and credibility in professionals and their organizations.

Professions normalize practitioner behavior.

Professionalism is underpinned by codes and standards developed by professional bodies. Regulators typically support professional ethics and recognize the framework for ethics that professions can provide. Many regulators around the world have engaged closely with professional bodies to understand their codes and standards, as well as how they are enforced. Codes and standards developed by practitioners can be complementary to regulations, codifying many more individual practices than the high-level principles set by regulation.

Many governments have recognized that a profession can develop a more sophisticated system of standards than a regulator can, via continuous practitioner input and a strong mutual interest within the profession to maintain good standards and adopt best practices. Government support of professions is attributable to the role of professions in helping the public and ensuring expert and principled performance of complex services.

Professions provide a service to society.

There is an obligation for professionals to go beyond codes and standards. Professionals should advocate for higher educational and ethical standards in the industry, individually and through their companies. Professions can widen access to services and support economic activity by encouraging trust in the industries they serve. Professions have realized that earning community trust not only creates professional pride and acceptance but also delivers commercial benefits. A profession that earns trust may ultimately have greater flexibility and independence from government regulators to manage its own affairs, which allows members of the profession to develop service models that are both useful to clients and beneficial to members.

Professions are client focused.

An integral part of a profession's mission is to develop and administer codes, best practice guidelines, and standards that guide an industry. These codes, standards, and guidelines help ensure that all professionals place the integrity of their profession and the interests of clients above their own personal interests. At a minimum, professionals must act in the best interest of the client, exercising a reasonable level of care, skill, and diligence. The obligation to deliver a high standard of care when acting for the benefit of another party is called *fiduciary duty*. Other entities, including employers, regulators, trade associations, and not-for-profit organizations, may also support an industry but are not the same as professional bodies. Unlike professions, these other entities generally do not exist to set and maintain professional standards. Most employers encourage employees to be members of relevant professions, and many give financial support for this membership to ideally improve the quality of client service and reinforce ethical awareness.

Professions have high entry standards.
Membership in a profession is a signal to the market that the professional will deliver high-quality service of a promised standard, going beyond simply academic credentials. Professions develop curricula that equip future professionals with competence, including technical skills, knowledge, and ethics.

Professions possess a body of expert knowledge.
A repository of knowledge, developed by experienced and skilled practitioners, is made available to all members of a profession. This knowledge helps members work effectively and ethically and is based on best practice.

Professions encourage and facilitate continuing education.
Entry into a profession does not, on its own, guarantee that an individual will maintain competency and continue to uphold professional standards. After qualification and throughout the working life of a professional, there will be changes in knowledge and technical skills to perform certain jobs, in technology and standards of ethical behavior, in services that can be offered, and in the legal and business environment in which professional services are delivered. These all require the development of competence and ethical awareness. Most professional bodies make it a condition of membership that a specific amount of new learning is undertaken each year. Typically, such conditions specify a time commitment, which may be separated into different competencies and types of learning activity. This is often referred to as *continuing professional development* and is seen as an important part of maintaining professional standards. The training and education that professionals undertake increase the value of human capital, which can contribute to economic growth and social mobility.

Professions monitor professional conduct.
Members of a profession must be held accountable for their conduct to maintain the integrity and reputation of an industry. Doing so often involves self-regulation by professional bodies through monitoring and imposition of sanctions on members.

Professions are collegial.
Professionals should be respectful to each other, even when they are competing. At the very least, they must respect the rights, dignity, and autonomy of others.

Professions are recognized oversight bodies.
Many professional bodies are not-for-profit organizations with a mission emphasizing excellence, integrity, and public service. Although it is the responsibility of individual professionals to remain competent, an oversight body typically monitors this responsibility. Such bodies provide individuals with ongoing educational resources and access to information about changes in standards and imposes a framework of discipline. Continuing membership indicates sustained competence in (and updating of) practical skills while maintaining ongoing compliance with an ethical code of conduct.

Professions encourage the engagement of members.
Participation by members as volunteers is part of the essence of a profession. Professionals are more likely to refer to, use, and adhere to values that they have helped develop, and they typically have the power as members to revise these values.

A good professional will want to mentor and inspire others who recently entered or wish to enter the profession. Professionals should be willing to volunteer to advance the profession and engage with peers to develop expertise and ethics. Professionals should volunteer to help educate new generations in ethical knowledge and ethical decision making and to foster a productive debate about new areas of ethics. Most professionals find that the experience of volunteering within the profession enhances their skills and widens their contacts within the industry. Membership in a professional body allows the necessary engagement with other professionals.

Professions Are Evolving

No profession stands still. Such trends as greater transparency and public accountability force professions to adapt to change. Meanwhile, technology opens up possibilities for new services and different ways of working. In addition, key processes of a profession's responsibilities may need to be reviewed by a government agency or independent public body. In general, professions often engage with non-member individuals. This can help a profession evaluate the viewpoints of the public, clients, or other stakeholders when determining policy and practice and can encourage public trust for a profession's conduct and disciplinary process.

Effective professions continue to develop their role to account for changing best practices. Some medical professional bodies, for instance, have been established for more than 500 years but may now have the same need to adapt as the much younger investment management profession. This means that at any point in time, society may recognize an area of work as a profession even if it has not fully or universally implemented all the expectations. As the requirements for a profession evolve, gaps open up that may take time to remedy. Effective professions also actively learn from other professions, particularly in the area of ethics. New standards of conduct in the accounting profession might be an influence on standards considered in investment management, for example.

Professionalism in Investment Management

> Successful investing professionals are disciplined and consistent and they think a great deal about what they do and how they do it.
>
> —Benjamin Graham, *The Intelligent Investor* (1949)

Investment management is a relatively young profession, which means that public understanding of its practice and codes is still developing. Recognition by regulators and employers also lags established professions. Not everyone engaged in investment management is a professional; some practitioners have not undertaken specific investment training or are not members of a professional body. That creates a challenge for the investment management profession to gain trust, because not all practitioners need to be committed to high ethical standards. However, key elements of the profession have been steadily established over several decades. For example, the publication of Graham and Dodd's *Security Analysis* in 1934 was an important step in establishing a body of knowledge for investment.

The investment management profession meets most, but currently not all, of the expectations of a profession. In most countries, some form of certification or licensing is needed to practice, but there may not be a requirement to join a professional body. Globally, the trend is to require examined entry to practice investment management and to maintain competence. But few professions have perfect implementation of all the expected attributes. The investment management profession, similar to other professions, is on a journey to improve implementation and keep up with changing demands.

The investment management profession has become increasingly global as capital markets have opened up around the world. Investment management professionals may seek cross-border opportunities or may need to relocate between offices within multinational asset management firms. Regulatory coordination across borders and the emergence of technology are contributing factors to this globalization of investment management. Various investment management professional bodies have developed in individual countries, and several of these bodies have expanded internationally. In addition, several other professional bodies, including those focused on actuarial and accountancy services, have investment management professionals as members.

Trust in Investment Management

The investment management professional today has similarities with professionals in longer-established professions, such as medicine and law. Like doctors and lawyers, investment management professionals are trusted to draw on a body of formal knowledge and apply that knowledge with care and judgement. In comparison to clients, investment professionals are also expected to have superior financial expertise, technical knowledge, and knowledge of the applicable laws and regulations. There is a risk that clients may not be fully aware of the conflicts, risks, and fees involved, so investment management professionals must always handle and fully disclose these issues in a way that serves the best interests of clients. Compliance with codes of ethics and professional standards is essential, and practice must be guided by care, transparency, and integrity.

The investment management profession and investment firms must be interdependent to maintain trust. Employers and regulators have their own standards and practices that may differ from regulations and standards set by professional bodies. The investment management professional bodies typically direct professionals in how to resolve these differences.

In many developed economies, the investment management profession affects many key aspects of the economy, including savings, retirement planning, and the pricing and allocation of capital. In most countries, skilled evaluation of securities leads to more efficient capital allocation and, combined with ethical corporate governance, can assist in attracting investment from international investors. The investment management profession can deliver more value to society when higher levels of trust and better capital allocation reduce transaction costs and help meet client objectives. These reasons explain why practitioners, clients, regulators, and governments have supported the development of an investment management profession.

CFA Institute as an Investment Management Professional Body

CFA Institute is the largest body for investment management professionals.[2] Reflecting the globalization of investment management, CFA Institute moved beyond North America in the 1980s. CFA Institute initiated a number of other changes in line with the growth of investment management. One significant change occurred in 2015, when CFA Institute decided to implement the highest standards of governance in the

---

[2] Eligibility and requirements for becoming a member of CFA Institute vary by jurisdiction. Please consult www.cfainstitute.org for further details.

US not-for-profit sector. The Board of Governors resolved "to implement US Public Company Standards and US not-for-profit leading practices, unless the Board determines that it is not in the best interest of the membership or organization to do so."

The mission of CFA Institute is "to lead the investment profession globally, by promoting the highest standards of ethics, education, and professional excellence for the ultimate benefit of society." The CFA Institute Code of Ethics and Standards of Professional Conduct (Code and Standards) promote the integrity of charterholders and establish a model for ethical behavior. CFA Institute candidates and charterholders must meet the highest standards among those established by CFA Institute, regulators, or the employer. If candidates and charterholders do not meet these standards, there are negative consequences. Where client interests and market interests conflict, the Code and Standards set an investment management professional's duty to market integrity as the overriding obligation. The advocacy efforts of CFA Institute aim to build market integrity by calling for regulations that align the interests of firms and clients.

As a professional body, CFA Institute gathers knowledge from practicing investment professionals, conducts rigorous examinations, and ensures practitioner involvement in developing its codes and values. The CFA Institute Global Body of Investment Knowledge (GBIK) and Candidate Body of Knowledge (CBOK) are updated on an ongoing basis through a process known as *practice analysis*. Through interactions with practicing investment management professionals, practice analysis helps ensure that the body of knowledge for the investment management profession remains current and globally relevant. The CFA Program ensures that candidates have sufficiently mastered the core knowledge, skills, and abilities (competencies) necessary that are generally accepted and applied by investment professionals. CFA Institute also contributes to the dissemination of new research and ideas in finance with the publication of the *Financial Analysts Journal*; CFA Institute Research Foundation books, research briefs, and reviews; and *CFA Institute Magazine*.

CFA Institute encourages charterholders to engage in their professional communities and involves charterholders in its initiatives. CFA Institute local societies keep charterholders connected and engaged in their communities. CFA Institute assists local societies with providing continuing education programs and events that facilitate charterholders engagement. For CFA charterholders, a local CFA society is an important route to maintaining professionalism, particularly for continuing professional development.

CFA charterholders and CFA Program candidates are required to adhere to the Code and Standards and to sign annually a statement attesting to that continued adherence. Charterholders and candidates must maintain and improve their professional competence and strive to maintain and improve the competence of other investment professionals.

EXAMPLE 2

Ethics and Professionalism

1. Which of the following statements is *most* accurate? Investment professionals have a special responsibility to act ethically because:

    A. the industry is heavily regulated.

    B. they are entrusted to protect clients' assets.

    C. the profession requires compliance with its code of ethics.

Solution:

B is correct. Investment professionals have a special responsibility because clients entrust them to protect the clients' assets.

2. Which of the following statements *best* completes the following sentence? Professionals use their specialized knowledge and skills:

   A. in service to others.
   B. to advance their career.
   C. for the exclusive benefit of their employers.

Solution:

A is correct. Professionals use specialized knowledge and skills in service to others. Their career and employer may benefit, but those results are not the primary focus of a professional's use of his or her specialized knowledge and skills.

3. Which of the following statements is *most* accurate? A profession's code of ethics:

   A. includes standards of conduct or specific benchmarks for behavior.
   B. ensures that all members of a profession will act ethically at all times.
   C. publicly communicates the shared principles and expected behaviors of a profession's members.

Solution:

C is correct. A profession's code of ethics publicly communicates the shared principles and expected behaviors of a profession's members. The existence of a code of ethics does not ensure that all members will behave in a manner consistent with the code and act ethically at all times. A profession will often establish a disciplinary process to address alleged violations of the code of ethics. A profession may adopt standards of conduct to enhance and clarify the code of ethics.

CHALLENGES TO ETHICAL CONDUCT

4

☐ identify challenges to ethical behavior

Professionals generally aim to be responsible and to adhere to high moral standards, so what is the benefit of studying ethics? Throughout our careers, we may find ourselves in difficult or at least unfamiliar situations in which an appropriate course of action is not immediately clear and/or there may be more than one seemingly acceptable choice; studying ethics helps us prepare for such situations. This section addresses challenges to engaging in ethical conduct. Failure to acknowledge, understand, or consider these challenges can lead to poor decision making, resulting in unintentional consequences, such as unethical conduct and potential violations of the Code and Standards.

Several challenges can make adherence to ethical conduct difficult. First, people tend to believe that they are ethical people and that their ethical standards are higher than average. Of course, everyone cannot be above average. However, surveys show this belief in above averageness remains.

These survey results illustrate overconfidence, a common behavioral bias that can lead to faulty decision making. Studies have shown that our beliefs and emotions frequently interfere with our cognitive reasoning and result in behavioral bias, a tendency to behave in a way that is not strictly rational. As a result of the overconfidence bias, we are more likely to overestimate the morality of our own behavior, particularly in situations that we have not faced before. The overconfidence bias can result in a failure to consider, explicitly or implicitly, important inputs and variables needed to form the best decision from an ethical perspective. In general, the overconfidence bias leads us to place too much importance on internal traits and intrinsic motivations, such as "I'm honest and would not lie," even though studies have shown that internal traits are generally not the main determinant of whether or not someone will behave ethically in a given situation.

A second challenge is that decision makers often fail to recognize and/or significantly underestimate the effect of situational influences, such as what other people around them are doing. **Situational influences** are external factors, such as environmental or cultural elements, that shape our thinking, decision making, and behavior. Social psychologists have studied how much situational influences affect our behavior and have found that even good people with honorable motives can and often will be influenced to do unethical things when put into difficult situations. Experiments have shown that even people who consider themselves strong, independent, free thinkers will conform to social pressures in many situations. The bystander effect, for example, demonstrates that people are less likely to intervene in an emergency when others are present. Fortunately, experiments have also shown that situational influences can induce people to act more ethically. For example, people tend to behave more ethically when they think someone else is watching or when there is a mirror placed close to them. The important concept to understand is that situational influences have a very powerful and often unrecognized effect on our thinking and behavior. Thus, learning to recognize situational influences is critical to making good decisions.

Common situational influences in the investment industry that can shape thinking and behavior include money and prestige. One experiment found that simply mentioning money can reduce ethical behavior. In the experiment, participants were less likely to cooperate when playing a game if the game was called the Wall Street Game, rather than the Community Game. In the investment industry, large financial rewards—including individual salaries, bonuses, and/or investment gains—can induce honest and well-intentioned individuals to act in ways that others might not consider ethical. Large financial rewards and/or prestige can motivate individuals to act in their own short-term self-interests, ignoring possible short-term risks or consequences to themselves and others as well as long-term risks or consequences for both themselves and others. Another extremely powerful situational influence is loyalty. Loyalty to supervisors or organizations, fellow employees, and other colleagues can tempt individuals to make compromises and take actions that they would reject under different situational influences or judge harshly when taken by others.

Situational influences often blind people to other important considerations. Bonuses, promotions, prestige, and loyalty to employer and colleagues are examples of situational influences that frequently have a disproportionate weight in our decision making. Our brains more easily and quickly identify, recognize, and consider these short-term situational influences than longer-term considerations, such as a commitment to maintaining our integrity and contributing to the integrity of the financial markets. Although absolutely important, these long-term considerations often have less immediate consequences than situational influences, making them less obvious as factors to consider in a decision and, therefore, less likely to influence our overall decision making. Situational influences shift our brain's focus from the long term to the short or immediate term. When our decision making is too narrowly focused on short-term factors and/or self-interest, we tend to ignore and/or minimize the longer-term risks and/or costs and consequences to ourselves and others, and the likelihood of suffering ethical lapses and making poor decisions increases.

Challenges to Ethical Conduct

Loyalty to employer and/or colleagues is an extremely powerful situational influence. Our colleagues can influence our thinking and behavior in both positive and negative ways. For example, colleagues may have encouraged you to signal your commitment to your career and high ethical standards by enrolling in the CFA Program. If you work for or with people who are not bound by the Code and Standards, they might encourage you to take actions that are consistent with local law, unaware that the recommended conduct falls short of the Code and Standards.

Well-intentioned firms may adopt or develop strong compliance programs to encourage adherence to rules, regulations, and policies. A strong compliance policy is a good start to developing an ethical culture, but a focus on adherence to rules may not be sufficient. A compliance approach may not encourage decision makers to consider the larger picture and can oversimplify decision making. Taken to the extreme, a strong compliance culture can become another situational influence that blinds employees to other important considerations. In a firm focused primarily on compliance, employees may adopt a "check the box" mentality rather than an ethical decision-making approach. Employees may ask the question "What *can* I do?" rather than "What *should* I do?"

EXAMPLE 3

Challenges to Ethical Conduct

1. Which of the following will *most likely* determine whether an individual will behave unethically?

    A. The person's character
    B. The person's internal traits and intrinsic motivation
    C. External factors, such as environmental or cultural elements

    ### Solution:

    C is correct. Social psychologists have shown that even good people may behave unethically in difficult situations. Situational influences, which are external factors (e.g., environmental or cultural elements), can shape our thinking, decision making, and behavior and are more likely to lead to unethical behavior than internal traits or character.

2. Which of the following statements is *most* accurate?

    A. Large financial rewards, such as bonuses, are the most powerful situational influences.
    B. When decision making focuses on short-term factors, the likelihood of ethical conduct increases.
    C. Situational influences can motivate individuals to act in their short-term self-interests without recognizing the long-term risks or consequences for themselves and others.

    ### Solution:

    C is correct. Situational influences can motivate individuals to act in their short-term self-interests without recognizing the long-term risks or consequences for themselves and others. Large financial rewards are powerful situational influences, but in some situations, other situational influences, such as loyalty to colleagues, may be even more powerful.

5. ETHICAL VS. LEGAL STANDARDS

☐ compare and contrast ethical standards with legal standards

Many times, stakeholders have common ethical expectations. Other times, different stakeholders will have different perceptions and perspectives and use different criteria to decide whether something is beneficial and/or ethical.

Laws and regulations often codify ethical actions that lead to better outcomes for society or specific groups of stakeholders. For example, some laws and regulations require businesses and their representatives to tell the truth. They require specific written disclosures in marketing and other materials. Complying with such rules is considered an ethical action; it creates a more satisfactory outcome that conforms to stakeholders' ethical expectations. As an example, consider disclosure requirements mandated by securities regulators regarding the risks of investing. Complying with such rules creates better outcomes for you, your clients, and your employer. First, compliance with the rule reduces the risk that clients will invest in securities without understanding the risks involved, which, in turn, reduces the risk that clients will file complaints and/or take legal action if their investments decline in value. Complying with the rules also reduces the risk that regulators will initiate an investigation, file charges, or/and discipline or sanction you and/or your employer. Any of these actions could jeopardize the reputation and future prospects of you and your employer. Conduct that reduces these risks (e.g., following disclosure rules) would be considered ethical; it leads to better outcomes for you, your clients, and your employer and conforms to the ethical expectations of various stakeholders.

Although laws frequently codify ethical actions, legal and ethical conduct are not always the same. Think about the diagram in Exhibit 1. Many types of conduct are both legal and ethical, but some conduct may be one and not the other. Some legal behaviors or activities may be considered unethical, and some behaviors or activities considered ethical may be deemed illegal in certain jurisdictions. Acts of civil disobedience, such as peaceful protests, may be in response to laws that individuals consider unethical. The act of civil disobedience may itself be considered ethical, and yet it violates existing local laws.

The investment industry has examples of conduct that may be legal but considered by some to be unethical. Some countries, for example, do not have laws prohibiting trading while in possession of material nonpublic information, but many investment professionals and CFA Institute consider such trading unethical.

Another area in which ethics and laws may conflict is the area of "whistleblowing." Whistleblowing refers to the disclosure by an individual of dishonest, corrupt, or illegal activity by an organization or government. Depending on the circumstances, a whistleblower may violate organizational policies and even local laws with the disclosure; thus, a whistleblower's actions may be deemed illegal and yet considered by some to be ethical.

Exhibit 1: Types of Conduct

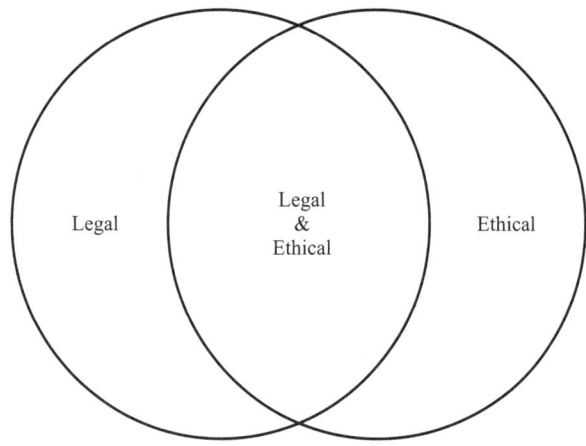

A Venn diagram with two overlapping circles labeled "Legal" (left) and "Ethical" (right), with the overlap labeled "Legal & Ethical".

Some people advocate that increased regulation and monitoring of the behavior of participants in the investment industry will increase trust in the financial markets. Although this approach may work in some circumstances, the law is not always the best mechanism to reduce unethical behavior for several reasons. First, laws typically follow market practices; regulators may proactively design laws and regulations to address existing or anticipated practices that may adversely affect the fairness and efficiency of markets or reactively design laws and regulations in response to a crisis or an event that resulted in significant monetary losses and loss of confidence/trust in the financial system. Regulators' responses typically take significant time, during which the problematic practice may continue or even grow. Once enacted, a new law may be vague, conflicting, and/or too narrow in scope. A new law may reduce or even eliminate the existing activity while simultaneously creating an opportunity for a different, but similarly problematic, activity. Additionally, laws vary across countries or jurisdictions, allowing questionable practices to move to places that lack laws relevant to the questionable practice. Laws are also subject to interpretation and compliance by market participants, who may choose to interpret the law in the most advantageous way possible or delay compliance until a later date. For these reasons, laws and regulations are insufficient to ensure the ethical behavior of investment professionals and market participants.

Ethical conduct goes beyond what is legally required and encompasses what different societal groups or communities, including professional associations, consider to be ethically correct behavior. To act ethically, individuals need to be able to think through the facts of the situation and make good choices even in the absence of clear laws or rules. In many cases, there is no simple algorithm or formula that will always lead to an ethical course of action. Ethics requires judgment—the ability to make considered decisions and reach sensible conclusions. Good ethical judgment requires actively considering the interests of stakeholders and trying to benefit multiple stakeholders—clients, family, colleagues, employers, market participants, and so forth—and minimize risks, including reputational risk.

> **EXAMPLE 4**
>
> ### Ethical vs. Legal Standards
>
> 1. Which of the following statements is *most* accurate?
>   - **A.** All legal behavior is ethical behavior.
>   - **B.** Some ethical behavior may be illegal.
>   - **C.** Legal standards represent the highest standard.
>
> **Solution:**
>
> B is correct. Some ethical behavior may be illegal. Civil disobedience is an example of what may be illegal behavior that some consider to be ethical. Legal and ethical behavior often coincide but not always. Standards of conduct based on ethical principles may represent a higher standard of behavior than the behavior required by law.
>
> 2. Which of the following statements is *most* accurate?
>   - **A.** Increased regulations are the most useful means to reduce unethical behavior by market participants.
>   - **B.** Regulators quickly design and implement laws and regulations to address practices that adversely affect the fairness and efficiency of markets.
>   - **C.** New laws designed to reduce or eliminate conduct that adversely affects the markets can create opportunities for different, but similarly problematic, conduct.
>
> **Solution:**
>
> C is correct. New laws designed to reduce or eliminate conduct that adversely affects the markets can create opportunities for different, but similarly problematic, conduct.

6. ETHICAL DECISION-MAKING FRAMEWORKS

> describe a framework for ethical decision making

Laws, regulations, professional standards, and codes of ethics can guide ethical behavior, but individual judgment is a critical ingredient in making principled choices and engaging in appropriate conduct. One strategy to increase trust in the investment industry is to increase the ability and motivation of market participants to act ethically and help them minimize the likelihood of unethical actions. By integrating ethics into the decision-making activities of employees, firms can enhance the ability and the motivation of employees to act ethically, thereby reducing the likelihood of unethical actions. The ability to relate an ethical decision-making framework to a firm's or profession's code of ethics allows investment professionals to bring the principles of the code of ethics to life. An investment professional's natural desire to "do the right thing" can be reinforced by building a culture of integrity and accountability in the workplace. Development, maintenance, and demonstration of a strong culture of integrity within the firm by senior management may be the single most important factor in promoting ethical behavior among the firm's employees.

Adopting a code that clearly lays out the ethical principles that guide the thought processes and conduct the firm expects from its employees is a critical first step. But a code of ethics, although necessary, is insufficient. Simply nurturing an inclination to do right is no match for the multitude of daily decisions that investment professionals make. We need to exercise ethical decision-making skills to develop the muscle memory necessary for fundamentally ethical people to make good decisions despite the reality of conflicts and our natural instinct for self-preservation. Just as coaching and practice transform our natural ability to run across a field into the technique and endurance required to run a race, teaching, reinforcing, and practicing ethical decision-making skills prepare us to confront the hard issues effectively. It is good for business, individuals, firms, the industry, and the markets, as well as society as a whole, to engage in the investment management profession in a highly ethical manner. A strong ethical culture, built on a defined set of principles, that helps honest, ethical people engage in ethical behavior will foster the trust of investors, lead to robust global financial markets, and ultimately benefit society. That is why ethics matter.

The Framework for Ethical Decision-Making

When faced with decisions that can affect multiple stakeholders, investment professionals must have a well-developed set of principles; otherwise, their thought processes can lead to, at best, indecision and, at worst, fraudulent conduct and destruction of the public trust. Establishing an ethical framework to guide your internal thought process regarding how to act is a crucial step to engaging in ethical conduct. Investment professionals are generally comfortable analyzing and making decisions from an economic (profit/loss) perspective. Given the importance of ethical behavior in carrying out professional responsibilities, it is also important to analyze decisions and their potential consequences from an ethical perspective. Using a framework for ethical decision making will help investment professionals to effectively examine their choices in the context of conflicting interests common to their professional obligations (e.g., researching and gathering information, developing investment recommendations, and managing money for others). Such a framework will allow investment professionals to analyze and choose options in a way that allows them to meet high standards of ethical behavior. An ethical decision-making framework provides investment professionals with a tool to help them adhere to a code of ethics. By applying the framework and analyzing the particular circumstances of each available alternative, investment professionals are able to determine the best course of action to fulfill their responsibilities in an ethical manner.

An ethical decision-making framework will help a decision maker see the situation from multiple perspectives and pay attention to aspects of the situation that may be less evident with a short-term, self-focused perspective. The goal of getting a broader picture of a situation is to be able to create a plan of action that is less likely to harm stakeholders and more likely to benefit them. If a decision maker does not know or understand the effects of his or her actions on stakeholders, the likelihood of making a decision and taking action that harms stakeholders is more likely to occur, even if unintentionally. Finally, an ethical decision-making framework helps decision makers explain and justify their actions to a broader audience of stakeholders.

Ethical decision-making frameworks are designed to facilitate the decision-making process for all decisions. They help people look at and evaluate a decision from multiple perspectives, enabling them to identify important issues they might not otherwise consider. Using an ethical decision-making framework consistently will help you develop sound judgment and decision-making skills and avoid making decisions that have unanticipated ethical consequences. Ethical decision-making frameworks come in many forms with varying degrees of detail. A general ethical decision-making framework is shown in Exhibit 2.

Exhibit 2: Ethical Decision-Making Framework

- Identify: Relevant facts, stakeholders and duties owed, ethical principles, conflicts of interest
- Consider: Situational influences, additional guidance, alternative actions
- Decide and act
- Reflect: Was the outcome as anticipated? Why or why not?

The ethical decision-making process includes multiple phases, each of which has multiple components. The process is often iterative, and you, the decision maker, may move between phases in an order different from what is presented. For simplicity, we will discuss the phases sequentially. In the initial phase, you will want to identify the important facts that you have available to you, as well as information that you may not have but would like to have to give yourself a more complete understanding of the situation. It is helpful to distinguish between facts and personal opinion, judgements, and biases. You will also want to identify the stakeholders—clients, family, colleagues, your employer, market participants, and so forth—and the duties you have to each of them. You will then want to identify relevant ethical principles and/or legal requirements that might apply to the situation. You should also identify any potential conflicts of interest inherent in the situation or conflicts in the duties you hold to others. For example, your duty to your client may conflict with your duty to your employer.

In the second phase of ethical decision making, you will take time to consider the situational influences as well as personal behavioral biases that could affect your thinking and thus decision making. These situational influences and biases could include a desire to please your boss, to be seen as successful by your peers and family, to gain acceptance, to earn a large bonus, and so on. During this phase, you may seek additional guidance from trusted sources—perhaps a family member, colleague, or mentor who can help you think through the situation and help you identify and evaluate alternative actions. You may turn to your compliance department for assistance or you may even consult outside legal counsel. Seeking additional guidance is a critical step in viewing the situation from different perspectives. You should seek guidance from someone, possibly external to the firm, who is not affected by the same situational influences and behavioral biases as you are and can, therefore, provide a fresh perspective. You should also seek guidance from your firm's policies and procedures and the CFA Institute Code and Standards. A helpful technique might be to imagine how an ethical peer or role model might act in the situation.

The next phase of the framework is to make a decision and act. After you have acted on your decision, you should take the time to reflect on and assess your decision and its outcome. Was the outcome what you anticipated? Why or why not? Had you properly identified all the important facts, stakeholders, duties to stakeholders, conflicts of interest, and relevant ethical principles? Had you considered the situational influences? Did you identify personal behavioral biases that might affect your thinking? Had you sought sufficient guidance? Had you considered and properly evaluated a variety of alternative actions? You may want to reflect on the decision multiple times as the immediate and longer-term consequences of your decision and actions become apparent.

The process is often iterative. After identifying the relevant facts and considering situational influences, you may, for example, decide that you cannot make a decision without more information. You may seek additional guidance on how to obtain the information you need. You may also begin considering alternative actions regarding how to proceed based on expectations of what the additional information will reveal, or you may wait until you have more information, reflect on what you have done and learned so far, and start the process over again. Sometimes cases can be complicated and multiple iterations may reveal that no totally acceptable solution can be created. Applying an ethical decision-making framework can help you evaluate the situation so you can make the best possible decision. The next section shows applications of the framework shown in Exhibit 2.

Applying the Framework

To illustrate how the framework could be applied in your career, consider the scenario in Example 5.

EXAMPLE 5

Applying an Ethical Decision-Making Framework I

1. You have been hired as a junior analyst with a major investment bank. When you join the bank, you receive a copy of the firm's policies as well as training on the policies. Your supervisor is the senior technology analyst for the investment bank. As part of your duties, you gather information, draft documents, conduct analysis, and perform other support functions for the senior analyst.

   Your employer is one of several investment banks working on the initial public offering (IPO) of a well-known technology company. The IPO is expected to generate significant revenues for the investment banks participating in the offering. The IPO has been highly anticipated and is in the news every day.

   You are thrilled when your supervisor asks you to work on several research projects related to analyzing and valuing the upcoming IPO for investors. You eagerly compile information and draft a one-page outline. You stop to consider what other information you could add to improve the report before proceeding. You realize that you have two excellent contacts in the technology industry who could review your work and provide some additional and potentially valuable perspectives. You draft an email to your contacts reading:

   > I am working on an analysis and valuation of Big Tech Company for investors. My employer is one of the banks participating in the IPO, and I want to make sure I have considered everything. I was hoping you could give me feedback on the prospects and risks facing Big Tech. Please treat all the attached material as confidential.

   Before hitting the send button, you stop and think about the ethical decision-making framework you have studied. You decide to apply the framework and jot down some notes as you work through the process: On the first page, you work through the identification phase and make a list of the relevant facts, stakeholders to whom you owe a duty, potential conflicts of interest, and ethical principles. This list is shown is Exhibit 3.

Exhibit 3: Identification Phase

1. Relevant facts:
   - *Working on the deal/IPO of the decade*
   - *Employer is one of several investment banks working on IPO*
   - *The IPO is highly anticipated*
   - *A successful IPO could lead to additional investment banking deals and revenues for the firm*
   - *Supervisor is relying on me*
   - *Employer has documented policies and procedures*
   - *Industry is regulated, with many rules and regulations in place*

2. Stakeholders and duties owed. I have a duty to the following:
   - *Supervisor*
   - *Employer*
   - *Employer's corporate client, the technology company*
   - *Employer's asset management and other investing clients*
   - *Employer's partners in the IPO*
   - *Investors and market participants interested in the IPO*
   - *All capital market participants*
   - *Profession*
   - *Society as a whole*

3. Conflicts or potential conflicts of interest include the following:
   - *Gathering additional research from external sources versus maintaining confidentiality*
   - *Duty to supervisor versus desire to impress*
   - *Duty to corporate client versus duty to other clients of the firm*
   - *The firm's corporate client benefits from a high IPO price whereas the firm's asset management clients would benefit from a low IPO price*
   - *Making the IPO look attractive to the market (sell-side marketing) versus objective analysis of the investment potential of this deal (buy-side analysis)*
   - *My bonus, compensation, and career prospects are tied to my supervisor's and the IPO's success; duty to employer, employer's investing clients, profession*

4. Ethical principles that are relevant to this situation include the following:
   - *Duty of loyalty to employer*
   - *Client interests come first*
   - *Maintain confidences and confidentiality of information*
   - *Objectivity of analysis*

Ethical Decision-Making Frameworks

- *Fairness to market participants*

On the next page, you write notes relating to the second phase of the framework, considering the various situational factors and the guidance available to you before considering alternative actions. These notes are shown in Exhibit 4.

Exhibit 4: Consideration Phase

1. Situational influences:
   - *The firm's written policies*
   - *The bank will earn big fees from the IPO*
   - *I want to impress my boss—and potential future bosses*
   - *My bonus, compensation, and career prospects will be influenced by my contribution to the success of this deal and other deals*
   - *I am one of very few people working on this deal; it is a real honor, and others would be impressed that I am working on this deal*
   - *My employer is filled with successful and wealthy people who are go-getters; I want to be successful and wealthy like them*
2. Additional guidance. I could seek guidance from the following:
   - *The firm's code of ethics*
   - *The firm's written policies*
   - *A peer in my firm*
   - *My supervisor, the senior analyst*
   - *The compliance department*
   - *A mentor either at the firm or perhaps from university or industry*
   - *The CFA Institute Code and Standards*
   - *Outside legal counsel*
3. Alternative actions. I could consider the following:
   - *Asking contacts what they have heard*
   - *Submitting the report as a draft and suggesting that contacts in the industry might be able to provide more perspective*
   - *Sending a survey to various technology industry veterans soliciting their viewpoints on developments*

After completing these steps, you decide to check the firm's policies. Under a section entitled "Research Analyst Role in Securities Offerings," the manual states, "You may not distribute any written (which include email, fax, electronic, and other means) material related to companies and/or their offerings . . . during the course of any offering and the related quiet period."

You read further and note a section entitled "Wall Crossing Policy and Procedures" that states that "employees with confidential information may not communicate the information to anyone who does not have a valid need to know" without first obtaining clearance from the legal and compliance department.

> You decide that your contacts do not have a "valid need to know" and that it is unlikely the firm's legal and compliance professionals would approve sharing the information. You then decide to mention your contacts to the senior research analyst. He suggests that they may have some useful perspective and that you might talk to them to hear their perspective and cautions you not to disclose any information about any of the firm's clients, pending deals, or research. You return to your desk, delete the email, and following the senior research analyst's advice, call your contacts on the telephone to discuss the technology sector, its prospects, and its challenges. During the calls, you take care not to reveal any details about Big Tech Company or its offering.
>
> Whatever action you take, you should take time afterward to reflect on the decision and the outcome. Was the outcome as anticipated? Why or why not?

The initial facts presented in the example are based on the real-life experience of a young junior analyst working on a highly anticipated IPO. The junior analyst may or may not have used an ethical decision-making framework to evaluate his situation. Without seeking additional guidance, the junior analyst sent an email similar to the one in the example with an attachment that included confidential, proprietary information, including the senior analyst's analysis and forecasts. Months later, long after the IPO offering, the junior analyst's email was discovered by his employer. When questioned, he admitted that he had received training regarding the firm's policies and that he did not discuss or seek approval from anyone before sending the email. Two days later, the firm terminated the junior analyst's employment and reported to regulatory authorities that he had been terminated for distributing written materials, by email, during a securities offering in violation of firm policies that prohibit the dissemination of any written materials during the course of a securities offering and related periods. The junior analyst's supervisor also lost his job for failing to properly supervise the analyst. Multiple regulators investigated the matter, and the firm was fined millions of dollars for failing to supervise its employees properly. The information regarding the junior analyst's termination was posted and remains available on the regulator's website for all to see. Future employers conducting routine background checks will know that the analyst was terminated for violating firm policies relating to a securities offering.

The example presented is similar to situations faced by many analysts. Using an ethical decision-making framework will help you evaluate situations from multiple perspectives, avoid poor decision making, and avoid the consequences that can result from taking an ill-conceived course of action. Using an ethical decision-making framework is no guarantee of a positive outcome but may help you avoid making unethical decisions.

EXAMPLE 6

Applying an Ethical Decision-Making Framework II

A financial adviser has been saving a portion of his salary to purchase a new vehicle. He is on track to have enough saved within the next three months. His employer has offered a special bonus for this quarter, which will go to the team that attracts the most new investors into the firm's investment funds. In addition to the potential bonus, the firm pays a 5% commission to employees who sell shares in the firm's investment funds. Several of the funds are highly rated, including one designed to provide steady income to investors.

Ethical Decision-Making Frameworks

The financial adviser has added only a few new investors to the firm's funds, but his teammates have been very successful in their efforts. The end of the quarter is one week away, and his team is competing closely with another team for the bonus. One of his teammates informs the financial adviser that he really needs the bonus so his elderly mother can receive medical treatment.

Later that day, the financial adviser meets with an elderly client on a limited income who is seeking more income from his investment portfolio. The client is 89 years old and in poor health. According to the client's will, the client's investment portfolio will go to his favorite charity upon his death.

1. Which of the following situational influences is likely to have the *most* effect on the financial adviser's efforts to get new clients to invest in the funds? His relationship with his:

    A. client.
    B. employer.
    C. teammates.

Solution:

C is correct. The financial adviser's relationship with his teammates is likely to have the most effect on the financial adviser's efforts. The teammates share in earning the bonus from the employer. In addition, the team works with each other on a regular basis where there is a likelihood that social influences of working together play a role in decision making and effort.

2. Which of the following statements is *most* accurate? An ethical decision-making framework:

    A. is only beneficial when a firm lacks a code of ethics.
    B. is used to improve compliance with laws and regulations.
    C. is a tool for analyzing the potential alternative actions and consequences of a decision.

Solution:

C is correct. An ethical decision-making framework is a tool for analyzing the potential alternative actions and consequences of a decision.

3. Which of the following is *most* accurate? Ethical decision-making frameworks:

    A. raise awareness of different perspectives.
    B. focus attention on short-term consequences.
    C. allocate more weight to those who will directly benefit from the decision.

Solution:

A is correct. Ethical decision-making frameworks raise awareness of different perspectives. The framework should consider short-term consequences, but they are not the focus of the framework. Similarly, the framework may allocate more weight to those who directly benefit from decisions, but this is not the primary goal of an ethical decision-making framework.

4. Which of the following is *most* accurate? Ethical decision-making frameworks:

   A. are not needed if behavior is legal.

   B. identify who gains the most from a decision.

   C. can help reduce unanticipated ethical lapses and unexpected consequences.

   ## Solution:

   C is correct. Ethical decision-making frameworks can help avoid unanticipated ethical consequences. As it relates to A, ethics standards are often higher than legal standards so an ethical decision-making framework would be needed. Although B is accurate, identifying who gains most from the decision is a small component of the framework.

5. Using an ethical decision-making framework, which of the following duties would *most likely* take precedence in the scenario described? The financial adviser's duty to his:

   A. client.

   B. employer.

   C. colleagues.

   ## Solution:

   A is correct. Using an ethical decision-making framework, the financial adviser's relationship with his client would most likely take precedence in this scenario. The adviser should put his client's interests first. The exception to client interests taking precedence occurs when market integrity effects take precedence.

6. Using an ethical decision-making framework, the financial adviser would *most likely*:

   A. recommend that the elderly client invest at least some of his assets in the highly rated fund.

   B. research other investments that can provide steady income before making a recommendation to his elderly client.

   C. disclose the commission he would earn before recommending that the elderly client invest at least some of his assets in the highly rated fund.

   ## Solution:

   B is correct. Using an ethical decision-making framework, the financial adviser would identify the relevant facts, stakeholders, duties owed, and potential conflicts. In this scenario, the financial adviser owes a duty to his client as well as his employer. His client's interests take precedence over all other interests. The bonus and his colleague's desire to help his mother are situational influences. To navigate this situation, the financial adviser should seek additional information; he should research the risk and return parameters and fee structures of other investments that can provide steady income before making a recommendation to his client.

CONCLUSION

This reading introduced ideas and concepts that will help you understand the importance of ethical behavior in the investment industry as well as the challenges to adhering to high ethical standards. A code of ethics will communicate an organization's values and the expected behavior of its members as well as provide guidance for decision making. A code of ethics may be further enhanced and clarified by the adoption of standards of conduct. Professions and professional organizations, such as the CFA Institute, can help to establish codes and standards that provide a framework and technical competence for practitioners. An ethical decision-making framework combined with a code of ethics may help investment professionals analyze their decisions in a way that identifies potential conflicts and negative consequences.

Knowing the rules to apply in a particular situation, although important, may not be sufficient to ensure ethical conduct if used alone. Responsible professionals in the investment industry must be able both to recognize areas that are prone to ethical pitfalls and to identify and process those circumstances and influences that can impair judgment and lead to ethical lapses.

SUMMARY

- Ethics refers to the study of making good choices. Ethics encompasses a set of moral principles and rules of conduct that provide guidance for our behavior.
- Situational influences are external factors that may shape our behavior.
- Challenges to ethical behavior include being overconfident in our own morality, underestimating the effect of situational influences, and focusing on the immediate rather than long-term outcomes or consequences of a decision.
- In any given profession, the code of ethics publicly communicates the established principles and expected behavior of its members.
- Members of a profession use specialized knowledge and skills to serve others; they share and agree to adhere to a common code of ethics to serve others and advance the profession.
- A code of ethics helps foster public confidence that members of the profession will use their specialized skills and knowledge to serve their clients and others.
- A profession is an occupational group that has specific education, expert knowledge, and a framework of practice and behavior that underpins community trust, respect, and recognition.
- The requirement to uphold high ethical standards is one clear difference between professions and craft guilds or trade bodies.
- A primary goal of professions is to establish trust among clients and among society in general.
- Common characteristics of professions include normalization of practitioner behavior, service to society, client focus, high entry standards, a body of expert knowledge, encouragement and facilitation of continuing education, monitoring of professional conduct, collegiality, recognized overseeing bodies, and encouragement of member engagement.

- The investment management profession has become increasingly global, driven by the opening of capital markets, coordination of regulation across borders, and the emergence of technology.
- Investment management professionals are trusted to draw on a body of formal knowledge and apply that knowledge with care and judgement. In comparison to clients, investment professionals are also expected to have superior financial expertise, technical knowledge, and knowledge of the applicable laws and regulations.
- As a professional body, CFA Institute gathers knowledge from practicing investment professionals, conducts rigorous examinations, and ensures practitioner involvement in developing its codes and values.
- Investment management professionals are likely to encounter dilemmas, including those with ethical implications. Professionals should consider carefully how to determine the facts of the issue and assess the implications.
- High ethical standards always matter and are of particular importance in the investment management profession, which is based almost entirely on trust. Clients trust investment professionals to use their specialized skills and knowledge to serve clients and protect client assets. All stakeholders gain long-term benefits when investment professionals adhere to high ethical standards.
- Legal standards are often rule based. Ethical conduct goes beyond legal standards, balancing self-interest with the direct and indirect consequences of behavior on others.
- A framework for ethical decision making can help people look at and evaluate a decision from different perspectives, enabling them to identify important issues, make wise decisions, and limit unintended consequences.

PRACTICE PROBLEMS

1. Benchmarks for minimally acceptable behaviors of community members are:
   A. a code of ethics.
   B. laws and regulations.
   C. standards of conduct.

2. Specialized knowledge and skills, a commitment to serve others, and a shared code of ethics *best* characterize a(n):
   A. vocation.
   B. profession.
   C. occupation.

3. When unethical behavior erodes trust in an investment firm, that firm is *more-likely* to experience:
   A. lower revenues only.
   B. higher expenses only.
   C. lower revenues and higher expenses.

4. High ethical standards are distinguishing features of which of the following bodies?
   A. Craft guilds
   B. Trade bodies
   C. Professional bodies

5. Fiduciary duty is a standard *most likely* to be upheld by members of a(n):
   A. employer.
   B. profession.
   C. not-for-profit body.

6. Which of the following *best* identifies an internal trait that may lead to poor ethical decision making?
   A. Overconfidence
   B. Loyalty to employer
   C. Promise of money or prestige

7. Situational influences in decision making will *mostlikely* be minimized if:
   A. strong compliance programs are in place.
   B. longer-term consequences are considered.

C. individuals believe they are truthful and honest.

8. Decision makers who use a compliance approach are *mostlikely* to:
   A. avoid situational influences.
   B. oversimplify decision making.
   C. consider more factors than when using an ethical decision-making approach.

9. To maintain trust, the investment management profession must be interdependent with:
   A. regulators.
   B. employers.
   C. investment firms.

10. Which is an example of an activity that may be legal but that CFA Institute considers unethical?
    A. Making legally required disclosures in marketing materials
    B. Trading while in possession of material nonpublic information
    C. Disclosure by an employee of his or her own company's dishonest activity

11. An ethical decision-making framework will *mostlikely*:
    A. include a pre-determined, uniform sequence.
    B. focus exclusively on confirmable facts and relationships.
    C. help avoid a decision that has unanticipated ethical consequences.

12. When an ethical dilemma occurs, an investment professional should *most likely* first raise the issue with a:
    A. mentor outside the firm.
    B. professional body's hotline.
    C. senior individual in the firm.

SOLUTIONS

1. C is correct. Standards of conduct are applied to specific communities or societal groups and identify specific behaviors required of community members. These standards of conduct serve as benchmarks for the minimally acceptable behavior of community members. Codes of ethics serve as a general guide for how community members should act; they communicate the organization's values and overall expectations regarding member behavior, but they do not identify specific behaviors required of community members. Laws and regulations are rules of conduct defined by governments and related entities about obligatory and forbidden conduct broadly applicable for individuals and entities under their jurisdiction.

2. B is correct. A profession has several characteristics that distinguish it from an occupation or vocation, such as specialized knowledge and skills, service to others, and a code of ethics shared by its members. A profession is the ultimate evolution of an occupation, resulting from excellence in practice, a mastery mindset, and expected adherence to a code of ethics and standards of practice.

3. C is correct. Unethical behavior ultimately harms investment firms. Clients are not attracted if they suspect unethical behavior, leading to less business and lower revenues. Investment firms may also experience higher relative costs because regulators are more likely to have cause to initiate costly investigations.

4. C is correct. High ethical standards distinguish professions from the craft guilds or trade bodies. Unlike trade bodies, professional bodies also typically have a mission to serve society and enforce professional conduct rules for practitioners.

5. B is correct. Fiduciary duty is an obligation to deliver a high standard of care when acting for the benefit of another party. Professionals must act in the best interest of the client, exercising a reasonable level of care, skill, and diligence. Other entities—including employers, regulators, trade associations, and not-for-profit bodies—may also support an industry but are not the same as professional bodies. Unlike professions, these other entities generally do not exist to set and maintain professional standards.

6. A is correct. An overconfidence bias can lead individuals to put too much importance on internal traits and intrinsic motivations, such as their own perceptions of personal honesty, that can lead to faulty decision making. Loyalty to an employer and promise of money or prestige are situational influences that can lead to faulty decision making.

7. B is correct. Consciously considering long-term consequences will help offset situational influences. We more easily recognize and consider short-term situational influences than longer-term considerations because longer-term considerations have fewer immediate consequences than situational influences do. When decision making is too narrowly focused on short-term factors, we tend to ignore longer-term risks and consequences, and the likelihood of poor ethical decision making increases. A strong compliance policy is a good first step toward developing an ethical culture; a focus on rules adherence may not be sufficient. Emphasis on compliance may not encourage decision makers to consider the larger picture and can oversimplify decision making. Taken to the extreme, a strong compliance culture can become another situational influence that blinds employees to other important considerations. An overconfidence bias can place too much importance on internal traits and intrinsic motivations, such as "I'm honest and would

not lie," even though studies have shown that internal traits are generally not the main determinant of whether or not someone will behave ethically in a given situation.

8. B is correct. A compliance approach can oversimplify decision making and may not encourage decision makers to consider the larger picture. A strong compliance culture may be a good start in developing an ethical culture but can become another situational influence that may result in employees failing to consider other important factors.

9. C is correct. The investment management profession and investment firms must be interdependent to maintain trust. Employers and regulators have their own standards and practices, which may differ from regulations and standards set by professional bodies.

10. B is correct. The investment industry has examples of conduct that may be legal but that CFA Institute considers unethical. Trading while in possession of material nonpublic information is not prohibited by law worldwide and can, therefore, be legal, but CFA Institute considers such trading unethical.

11. C is correct. Using an ethical decision-making framework consistently will help you develop sound judgment and decision-making skills and avoid making decisions that have unanticipated ethical consequences. The decision-making process is often iterative, and the decision maker may move between phases of the framework. A decision maker should consider more than confirmable facts and relationships; for example, the decision maker should consider situational influences and personal biases.

12. C is correct. When a dilemma occurs, raising an issue internally with a senior employee is often a good starting place and creates an opportunity for an independent internal review. Protecting the client and the firm may take priority over the position of an individual professional raising a concern.

LEARNING MODULE 2

Code of Ethics and Standards of Professional Conduct

LEARNING OUTCOME	
Mastery	The candidate should be able to:
☐	describe the structure of the CFA Institute Professional Conduct Program and the process for the enforcement of the Code and Standards
☐	identify the six components of the Code of Ethics and the seven Standards of Professional Conduct
☐	explain the ethical responsibilities required by the Code and Standards, including the sub-sections of each Standard

PREFACE

☐	describe the structure of the CFA Institute Professional Conduct Program and the process for the enforcement of the Code and Standards

The *Standards of Practice Handbook* (*Handbook*) provides guidance to the people who grapple with real ethical dilemmas in the investment profession on a daily basis; the *Handbook* addresses the professional intersection where theory meets practice and where the concept of ethical behavior crosses from the abstract to the concrete. The *Handbook* is intended for a diverse and global audience: CFA Institute members navigating ambiguous ethical situations; supervisors and direct/indirect reports determining the nature of their responsibilities to each other, to existing and potential clients, and to the broader financial markets; and candidates preparing for the Chartered Financial Analyst (CFA) examinations.

Recent events in the global financial markets have tested the ethical mettle of financial market participants, including CFA Institute members. The standards taught in the CFA Program and by which CFA Institute members and candidates must abide represent timeless ethical principles and professional conduct for all market conditions. Through adherence to these standards, which continue to serve as the model for ethical behavior in the investment profession globally, each market participant does his or her part to improve the integrity and efficient operations of the financial markets.

The *Handbook* provides guidance in understanding the interconnectedness of the aspirational and practical principles and provisions of the Code of Ethics and Standards of Professional Conduct (Code and Standards). The Code contains high-level aspirational ethical principles that drive members and candidates to create a positive and reputable investment profession. The Standards contain practical ethical principles of conduct that members and candidates must follow to achieve the broader industry expectations. However, applying the principles individually may not capture the complexity of ethical requirements related to the investment industry. The Code and Standards should be viewed and interpreted as an interwoven tapestry of ethical requirements. Through members' and candidates' adherence to these principles as a whole, the integrity of and trust in the capital markets are improved.

Evolution of the CFA Institute Code of Ethics and Standards of Professional Conduct

Generally, changes to the Code and Standards over the years have been minor. CFA Institute has revised the language of the Code and Standards and occasionally added a new standard to address a prominent issue of the day. For instance, in 1992, CFA Institute added the standard addressing performance presentation to the existing list of standards.

Major changes came in 2005 with the ninth edition of the *Handbook*. CFA Institute adopted new standards, revised some existing standards, and reorganized the standards. The revisions were intended to clarify the requirements of the Code and Standards and effectively convey to its global membership what constitutes "best practice" in a number of areas relating to the investment profession.

The Code and Standards must be regularly reviewed and updated if they are to remain effective and continue to represent the highest ethical standards in the global investment industry. CFA Institute strongly believes that revisions of the Code and Standards are not undertaken for cosmetic purposes but to add value by addressing legitimate concerns and improving comprehension.

Changes to the Code and Standards have far-reaching implications for the CFA Institute membership, the CFA Program, and the investment industry as a whole. CFA Institute members and candidates are *required* to adhere to the Code and Standards. In addition, the Code and Standards are increasingly being adopted, in whole or in part, by firms and regulatory authorities. Their relevance goes well beyond CFA Institute members and candidates.

Standards of Practice Handbook

The periodic revisions of the Code and Standards have come in conjunction with updates of the *Standards of Practice Handbook*. The *Handbook* is the fundamental element of the ethics education effort of CFA Institute and the primary resource for guidance in interpreting and implementing the Code and Standards. The *Handbook* seeks to educate members and candidates on how to apply the Code and Standards to their professional lives and thereby benefit their clients, employers, and the investing public in general. The *Handbook* explains the purpose of the Code and Standards and how they apply in a variety of situations. The sections discuss and amplify each standard and suggest procedures to prevent violations.

Examples in the "Application of the Standard" sections are meant to illustrate how the standard applies to hypothetical but factual situations. The names contained in the examples are fictional and are not meant to refer to any actual person or entity. Unless otherwise stated (e.g., one or more people specifically identified), individuals in each example are CFA Institute members and holders of the CFA designation. Because

Preface

factual circumstances vary so widely and often involve gray areas, the explanatory material and examples are not intended to be all inclusive. Many examples set forth in the application sections involve standards that have legal counterparts; ***members are strongly urged to discuss with their supervisors and legal and compliance departments the content of the Code and Standards and the members' general obligations under the Code and Standards***.

CFA Institute recognizes that the presence of any set of ethical standards may create a false sense of security unless the documents are fully understood, enforced, and made a meaningful part of everyday professional activities. The *Handbook* is intended to provide a useful frame of reference that suggests ethical professional behavior in the investment decision-making process. This book cannot cover every contingency or circumstance, however, and it does not attempt to do so. The development and interpretation of the Code and Standards are evolving processes; the Code and Standards will be subject to continuing refinement.

Summary of Changes in the Eleventh Edition

The comprehensive review of the Code and Standards in 2005 resulted in principle requirements that remain applicable today. The review carried out for the eleventh edition focused on market practices that have evolved since the tenth edition. Along with updates to the guidance and examples within the *Handbook*, the eleventh edition includes an update to the Code of Ethics that embraces the members' role of maintaining the social contract between the industry and investors. Additionally, there are three changes to the Standards of Professional Conduct, which recognize the importance of proper supervision, clear communications with clients, and the expanding educational programs of CFA Institute.

Inclusion of Updated CFA Institute Mission

The CFA Institute Board of Governors approved an updated mission for the organization that is included in the Preamble to the Code and Standards. The new mission conveys the organization's conviction in the investment industry's role in the betterment of society at large.

> *Mission:*
>
> To lead the investment profession globally by promoting the highest standards of ethics, education, and professional excellence for the ultimate benefit of society.

Updated Code of Ethics Principle

One of the bullets in the Code of Ethics was updated to reflect the role that the capital markets have in the greater society. As members work to promote and maintain the integrity of the markets, their actions should also help maintain the social contract with investors.

> *Old:*
>
> Promote the integrity of and uphold the rules governing capital markets.

> *New:*
>
> Promote the integrity and viability of the global capital markets for the ultimate benefit of society.

New Standard Regarding Responsibilities of Supervisors [IV(C)]

The standard for members and candidates with supervision or authority over others within their firms was updated to bring about improvements in preventing illegal and unethical actions from occurring. The prior version of Standard IV(C) focused on the detection and prevention of violations. The updated version stresses broader compliance expectations, which include the detection and prevention aspects of the original version.

> *Old:*
>
> Members and Candidates must make reasonable efforts to detect and prevent violations of applicable laws, rules, regulations, and the Code and Standards by anyone subject to their supervision or authority.

> *New:*
>
> Members and Candidates must make reasonable efforts to ensure that anyone subject to their supervision or authority complies with applicable laws, rules, regulations, and the Code and Standards.

Additional Requirement under the Standard for Communication with Clients and Prospective Clients [V(B)]

Given the constant development of new and exotic financial instruments and strategies, the standard regarding communicating with clients now includes an implicit requirement to discuss the risks and limitations of recommendations being made to clients. The new principle and related guidance take into account the fact that levels of disclosure will differ between products and services. Members and candidates, along with their firms, must determine the specific disclosures their clients should receive while ensuring appropriate transparency of the individual firms' investment processes.

> *Addition:*
>
> Disclose to clients and prospective clients significant limitations and risks associated with the investment process.

Modification to Standard VII(A)

Since this standard was developed, CFA Institute has launched additional educational programs. The updated standard not only maintains the integrity of the CFA Program but also expands the same ethical considerations when members or candidates participate in such programs as the CIPM Program and the CFA Institute Investment Foundations certificate program. Whether participating as a member assisting with the curriculum or an examination or as a sitting candidate within a program, we expect them to engage in these programs as they would participate in the CFA Program.

> *Old:*
>
> Conduct as Members and Candidates in the CFA Program
>
> Members and Candidates must not engage in any conduct that compromises the reputation or integrity of CFA Institute or the CFA designation or the integrity, validity, or security of the CFA examinations.

> *New:*
>
> Conduct as Participants in CFA Institute Programs

Preface

> Members and Candidates must not engage in any conduct that compromises the reputation or integrity of CFA Institute or the CFA designation or the integrity, validity, or security of CFA Institute programs.

General Guidance and Example Revision

The guidance and examples were updated to reflect practices and scenarios applicable to today's investment industry. Two concepts that appear frequently in the updates in this edition relate to the increased use of social media for business communications and the use of and reliance on the output of quantitative models. The use of social media platforms has increased significantly since the publication of the tenth edition. And although financial modeling is not new to the industry, this update reflects upon actions that are viewed as possible contributing factors to the financial crises of the past decade.

CFA Institute Professional Conduct Program

All CFA Institute members and candidates enrolled in the CFA Program are required to comply with the Code and Standards. The CFA Institute Board of Governors maintains oversight and responsibility for the Professional Conduct Program (PCP), which, in conjunction with the Disciplinary Review Committee (DRC), is responsible for enforcement of the Code and Standards. The DRC is a volunteer committee of CFA charterholders who serve on panels to review conduct and partner with Professional Conduct staff to establish and review professional conduct policies. The CFA Institute Bylaws and Rules of Procedure for Professional Conduct (Rules of Procedure) form the basic structure for enforcing the Code and Standards. The Professional Conduct division is also responsible for enforcing testing policies of other CFA Institute education programs as well as the professional conduct of Certificate in Investment Performance Measurement (CIPM) certificants.

Professional Conduct inquiries come from a number of sources. First, members and candidates must self-disclose on the annual Professional Conduct Statement all matters that question their professional conduct, such as involvement in civil litigation or a criminal investigation or being the subject of a written complaint. Second, written complaints received by Professional Conduct staff can bring about an investigation. Third, CFA Institute staff may become aware of questionable conduct by a member or candidate through the media, regulatory notices, or another public source. Fourth, candidate conduct is monitored by proctors who complete reports on candidates suspected to have violated testing rules on exam day. Lastly, CFA Institute may also conduct analyses of scores and exam materials after the exam, as well as monitor online and social media to detect disclosure of confidential exam information.

When an inquiry is initiated, the Professional Conduct staff conducts an investigation that may include requesting a written explanation from the member or candidate; interviewing the member or candidate, complaining parties, and third parties; and collecting documents and records relevant to the investigation. Upon reviewing the material obtained during the investigation, the Professional Conduct staff may conclude the inquiry with no disciplinary sanction, issue a cautionary letter, or continue proceedings to discipline the member or candidate. If the Professional Conduct staff believes a violation of the Code and Standards or testing policies has occurred, the member or candidate has the opportunity to reject or accept any charges and the proposed sanctions.

If the member or candidate does not accept the charges and proposed sanction, the matter is referred to a panel composed of DRC members. Panels review materials and presentations from Professional Conduct staff and from the member or candidate. The panel's task is to determine whether a violation of the Code and Standards or testing policies occurred and, if so, what sanction should be imposed.

Sanctions imposed by CFA Institute may have significant consequences; they include public censure, suspension of membership and use of the CFA designation, and revocation of the CFA charter. Candidates enrolled in the CFA Program who have violated the Code and Standards or testing policies may be suspended or prohibited from further participation in the CFA Program.

Adoption of the Code and Standards

The Code and Standards apply to individual members of CFA Institute and candidates in the CFA Program. CFA Institute does encourage firms to adopt the Code and Standards, however, as part of their code of ethics. Those who claim compliance should fully understand the requirements of each of the principles of the Code and Standards.

Once a party—nonmember or firm—ensures its code of ethics meets the principles of the Code and Standards, that party should make the following statement whenever claiming compliance:

> "[Insert name of party] claims compliance with the CFA Institute Code of Ethics and Standards of Professional Conduct. This claim has not been verified by CFA Institute."

CFA Institute welcomes public acknowledgement, when appropriate, that firms are complying with the CFA Institute Code of Ethics and Standards of Professional Conduct and encourages firms to notify us of the adoption plans. For firms that would like to distribute the Code and Standards to clients and potential clients, attractive one-page copies of the Code and Standards, including translations, are available on the CFA Institute website (www.cfainstitute.org).

CFA Institute has also published the Asset Manager Code of Professional Conduct, which is designed, in part, to help asset managers comply with the regulations mandating codes of ethics for investment advisers. Whereas the Code and Standards are aimed at individual investment professionals who are members of CFA Institute or candidates in the CFA Program, the Asset Manager Code was drafted specifically for firms. The Asset Manager Code provides specific, practical guidelines for asset managers in six areas: loyalty to clients, the investment process, trading, compliance, performance evaluation, and disclosure. The Asset Manager Code and the appropriate steps to acknowledge adoption or compliance can be found on the CFA Institute website (www.cfainstitute.org).

Acknowledgments

CFA Institute is a not-for-profit organization that is heavily dependent on the expertise and intellectual contributions of member volunteers. Members devote their time because they share a mutual interest in the organization's mission to promote and achieve ethical practice in the investment profession. CFA Institute owes much to the volunteers' abundant generosity and energy in extending ethical integrity.

The CFA Institute Standards of Practice Council (SPC), a group consisting of CFA charterholder volunteers from many different countries, is charged with maintaining and interpreting the Code and Standards and ensuring that they are effective. The SPC draws its membership from a broad spectrum of organizations in the securities field, including brokers, investment advisers, banks, and insurance companies. In most instances, the SPC members have important supervisory responsibilities within their firms.

The SPC continually evaluates the Code and Standards, as well as the guidance in the *Handbook*, to ensure that they are

- representative of high standards of professional conduct,
- relevant to the changing nature of the investment profession,
- globally applicable,
- sufficiently comprehensive, practical, and specific,
- enforceable, and
- testable for the CFA Program.

The SPC has spent countless hours reviewing and discussing revisions to the Code and Standards and updates to the guidance that make up the eleventh edition of the *Handbook*. Following is a list of the current and former members of the SPC who generously donated their time and energy to this effort.

James E. Hollis III, CFA, Chair	Christopher C. Loop, CFA,
Rik Albrecht, CFA	James M. Meeth, CFA
Terence E. Burns, CFA	Guy G. Rutherfurd, Jr., CFA
Laura Dagan, CFA	Edouard Senechal, CFA
Samuel B. Jones, Jr., CFA	Wenliang (Richard) Wang, CFA
Ulrike Kaiser-Boeing, CFA	Peng Lian Wee, CFA
Jinliang (Jack) Li, CFA	

ETHICS AND THE INVESTMENT INDUSTRY

Society ultimately benefits from efficient markets where capital can freely flow to the most productive or innovative destination. Well-functioning capital markets efficiently match those needing capital with those seeking to invest their assets in revenue-generating ventures. In order for capital markets to be efficient, investors must be able to trust that the markets are fair and transparent and offer them the opportunity to be rewarded for the risk they choose to take. Laws, regulations, and enforcement play a vital role but are insufficient alone to guarantee fair and transparent markets. The markets depend on an ethical foundation to guide participants' judgment and behavior. CFA Institute maintains and promotes the Code of Ethics and Standards of Professional Conduct in order to create a culture of ethics for the ultimate benefit of society.

Why Ethics Matters

Ethics can be defined as a set of moral principles or rules of conduct that provide guidance for our behavior when it affects others. Widely acknowledged fundamental ethical principles include honesty, fairness, diligence, and care and respect for others. Ethical conduct follows those principles and balances self-interest with both the direct and the indirect consequences of that behavior for other people.

Not only does unethical behavior by individuals have serious personal consequences—ranging from job loss and reputational damage to fines and even jail—but unethical conduct from market participants, investment professionals, and those who service investors can damage investor trust and thereby impair the sustainability of the global capital markets as a whole. Unfortunately, there seems to be an unending parade of stories bringing to light accounting frauds and manipulations, Ponzi schemes, insider-trading scandals, and other misdeeds. Not surprisingly, this has led to erosion in public confidence in investment professionals. Empirical evidence from numerous surveys documents the low standing in the eyes of the investing public of banks and financial services firms—the very institutions that are entrusted with the economic well-being and retirement security of society.

Governments and regulators have historically tried to combat misconduct in the industry through regulatory reform, with various levels of success. Global capital markets are highly regulated to protect investors and other market participants. However, compliance with regulation alone is insufficient to fully earn investor trust. Individuals and firms must develop a "culture of integrity" that permeates all levels of operations and promotes the ethical principles of stewardship of investor assets and working in the best interests of clients, above and beyond strict compliance with the law. A strong ethical culture that helps honest, ethical people engage in ethical behavior will foster the trust of investors, lead to robust global capital markets, and ultimately benefit society. That is why ethics matters.

Ethics, Society, and the Capital Markets

CFA Institute recently added the concept "for the ultimate benefit of society" to its mission. The premise is that we want to live in a socially, politically, and financially stable society that fosters individual well-being and welfare of the public. A key ingredient for this goal is global capital markets that facilitate the efficient allocation of resources so that the available capital finds its way to places where it most benefits that society. These investments are then used to produce goods and services, to fund innovation and jobs, and to promote improvements in standards of living. Indeed, such a function serves the interests of the society. Efficient capital markets, in turn, provide a host of benefits to those providing the investment capital. Investors are provided the opportunity to transfer and transform risk because the capital markets serve as an information exchange, create investment products, provide liquidity, and limit transaction costs.

However, a well-functioning and efficient capital market system is dependent on trust of the participants. If investors believe that capital market participants—investment professionals and firms—cannot be trusted with their financial assets or that the capital markets are unfair such that only insiders can be successful, they will be unlikely to invest or, at the very least, will require a higher risk premium. Decreased investment capital can reduce innovation and job creation and hurt the economy and society as a whole. Reduced trust in capital markets can also result in a less vibrant, if not smaller, investment industry.

Ethics for a global investment industry should be universal and ultimately support trust and integrity above acceptable local or regional customs and culture. Universal ethics for a global industry strongly supports the efficiency, values, and mission of the industry as a whole. Different countries may be at different stages of development in establishing standards of practice, but the end goal must be to achieve rules, regulations, and standards that support and promote fundamental ethical principles on a global basis.

Capital Market Sustainability and the Actions of One

Individuals and firms also have to look at the indirect impacts of their actions on the broader investment community. The increasingly interconnected nature of global finance brings to the fore an added consideration of market sustainability that was,

Ethics and the Investment Industry

perhaps, less appreciated in years past. In addition to committing to the highest levels of ethical behavior, today's investment professionals and their employers should consider the long-term health of the market as a whole.

As recent events have demonstrated, apparently isolated and unrelated decisions, however innocuous when considered on an individual basis, in aggregate can precipitate a market crisis. In an interconnected global economy and marketplace, each participant should strive to be aware of how his or her actions or the products he or she distributes may have an impact on capital market participants in other regions or countries.

Investment professionals should consider how their investment decision-making processes affect the global financial markets in the broader context of how they apply their ethical and professional obligations. Those in positions of authority have a special responsibility to consider the broader context of market sustainability in their development and approval of corporate policies, particularly those involving risk management and product development. In addition, corporate compensation strategies should not encourage otherwise ethically sound individuals to engage in unethical or questionable conduct for financial gain. Ethics, sustainability, and properly functioning capital markets are components of the same concept of protecting the best interests of all. To always place the interests of clients ahead of both investment professionals' own interests and those of their employer remains a key ethos.

The Relationship between Ethics and Regulations

Some equate ethical behavior with legal behavior: If you are following the law, you must be acting appropriately. Ethical principles, like laws and regulations, prescribe appropriate constraints on our natural tendency to pursue self-interest that could harm the interests of others. Laws and regulations often attempt to guide people toward ethical behavior, but they do not cover all unethical behavior. Ethical behavior is often distinguished from legal conduct by describing legal behavior as what is required and ethical behavior as conduct that is morally correct. Ethical principles go beyond that which is legally sufficient and encompass what is the right thing to do.

Given many regulators' lack of sufficient resources to enforce well-conceived rules and regulations, relying on a regulatory framework to lead the charge in establishing ethical behavior has its challenges. Therefore, reliance on compliance with laws and regulation alone is insufficient to ensure ethical behavior of investment professionals or to create a truly ethical culture in the industry.

The recent past has shown us that some individuals will succeed at circumventing the regulatory rules for their personal gain. Only the application of strong ethical principles, at both the individual level and the firm level, will limit abuses. Knowing the rules or regulations to apply in a particular situation, although important, may not be sufficient to ensure ethical conduct. Individuals must be able both to recognize areas that are prone to ethical pitfalls and to identify and process those circumstances and influences that can impair ethical judgment.

Applying an Ethical Framework

Laws, regulations, professional standards, and codes of ethics can guide ethical behavior, but individual judgment is a critical ingredient in making principled choices and engaging in appropriate conduct. When faced with an ethical dilemma, individuals must have a well-developed set of principles; otherwise, their thought processes can lead to, at best, equivocation and indecision and, at worst, fraudulent conduct and destruction of the public trust. Establishing an ethical framework for an internal thought process prior to deciding to act is a crucial step in engaging in ethical conduct.

Most investment professionals are used to making decisions from a business (profit/loss) outlook. But given the importance of ethical behavior in carrying out professional responsibilities, it is critical to also analyze decisions and potential conduct from an ethical perspective. Utilizing a framework for ethical decision making will help investment professionals effectively examine their conduct in the context of conflicting interests common to their professional obligations (e.g., researching and gathering information, developing investment recommendations, and managing money for others). Such a framework will allow investment professionals to analyze their conduct in a way that meets high standards of ethical behavior.

An ethical decision-making framework can come in many forms but should provide investment professionals with a tool for following the principles of the firm's code of ethics. Through analyzing the particular circumstances of each decision, investment professionals are able to determine the best course of action to fulfill their responsibilities in an ethical manner.

Commitment to Ethics by Firms

A firm's code of ethics risks becoming a largely ignored, dusty compilation if it is not truly integrated into the fabric of the business. The ability to relate an ethical decision-making framework to a firm's code of ethics allows investment professionals to bring the aspirations and principles of the code of ethics to life—transforming it from a compliance exercise to something that is at the heart of a firm's culture.

An investment professional's natural desire to "do the right thing" must be reinforced by building a culture of integrity in the workplace. Development, maintenance, and demonstration of a strong culture of integrity within the firm by senior management may be the single most important factor in promoting ethical behavior among the firm's employees. Adopting a code that clearly lays out the ethical principles that guide the thought processes and conduct the firm expects from its employees is a critical first step. But a code of ethics, while necessary, is insufficient.

Simply nurturing an inclination to do right is no match for the multitude of daily decisions that investment managers make. We need to exercise ethical decision-making skills to develop the muscle memory necessary for fundamentally ethical people to make good decisions despite the reality of agent conflicts. Just as coaching and practice transform our natural ability to run across a field into the technique and endurance required to run a race, teaching, reinforcing, and practicing ethical decision-making skills prepare us to confront the hard issues effectively. It is good for business, individuals, firms, the industry, and the markets, as well as society as a whole, to engage in the investment management profession in a highly ethical manner.

Ethical Commitment of CFA Institute

An important goal of CFA Institute is to ensure that the organization and its members and candidates develop, promote, and follow the highest ethical standards in the investment industry. The CFA Institute Code of Ethics (Code) and Standards of Professional Conduct (Standards) are the foundation supporting the organization's quest to uphold the industry's highest standards of individual and corporate practice and to help serve the greater good. The Code is a set of principles that define the overarching conduct CFA Institute expects from its members and CFA Program candidates. The Code works in tandem with the Standards, which outline professional conduct that constitutes fair and ethical business practices.

For more than 50 years, CFA Institute members and candidates have been required to abide by the organization's Code and Standards. Periodically, CFA Institute has revised and updated its Code and Standards to ensure that they remain relevant to the changing nature of the investment profession and representative of the highest standard of professional conduct. Within this *Handbook*, CFA Institute addresses ethical principles for the profession, including individual professionalism; responsibilities to capital markets, clients, and employers; ethics involved in investment analysis, recommendations, and actions; and possible conflicts of interest. Although the investment world has become a far more complex place since the first publication of the *Standard of Practice Handbook*, distinguishing right from wrong remains the paramount principle of the Code and Standards.

New challenges will continually arise for members and candidates in applying the Code and Standards because many decisions are not unambiguously right or wrong. The dilemma exists because the choice between right and wrong is not always clear. Even well-intentioned investment professionals can find themselves in circumstances that may tempt them to cut corners. Situational influences can overpower the best of intentions.

CFA Institute has made a significant commitment to providing members and candidates with the resources to extend and deepen their understanding of how to appropriately apply the principles of the Code and Standards. The product offerings from CFA Institute offer a wealth of material. Through publications, conferences, webcasts, and podcasts, the ethical challenges of investment professionals are brought to light. Archived issues of these items are available on the CFA Institute website (www.cfainstitute.org).

By reviewing these resources and discussing with their peers, market participants can further enhance their abilities to apply an effective ethical decision-making framework. In time, this should help restore some of the trust recently lost by investors.

Markets function to an important extent on trust. Recent events have shown the fragility of this foundation and the devastating consequences that can ensue when it is fundamentally questioned. Investment professionals should remain mindful of the long-term health of financial markets and incorporate this concern for the market's sustainability in their investment decision making. CFA Institute and the Standards of Practice Council hope this edition of the *Handbook* will assist and guide investment professionals in meeting the ethical demands of the highly interconnected global capital markets for the ultimate benefit of society.

CFA INSTITUTE CODE OF ETHICS AND STANDARDS OF PROFESSIONAL CONDUCT

3

- ☐ identify the six components of the Code of Ethics and the seven Standards of Professional Conduct
- ☐ explain the ethical responsibilities required by the Code and Standards, including the sub-sections of each Standard

Preamble

The CFA Institute Code of Ethics and Standards of Professional Conduct are fundamental to the values of CFA Institute and essential to achieving its mission to lead the investment profession globally by promoting the highest standards of ethics, education, and professional excellence for the ultimate benefit of society. High ethical standards are critical to maintaining the public's trust in financial markets and in the investment profession. Since their creation in the 1960s, the Code and Standards have promoted the integrity of CFA Institute members and served as a model for measuring the ethics of investment professionals globally, regardless of job function, cultural differences, or local laws and regulations. All CFA Institute members (including holders of the Chartered Financial Analyst [CFA] designation) and CFA candidates have the personal responsibility to embrace and uphold the provisions of the Code and Standards and are encouraged to notify their employer of this responsibility. Violations may result in disciplinary sanctions by CFA Institute. Sanctions can include revocation of membership, revocation of candidacy in the CFA Program, and revocation of the right to use the CFA designation.

The Code of Ethics

Members of CFA Institute (including CFA charterholders) and candidates for the CFA designation ("Members and Candidates") must:

- Act with integrity, competence, diligence, and respect and in an ethical manner with the public, clients, prospective clients, employers, employees, colleagues in the investment profession, and other participants in the global capital markets.
- Place the integrity of the investment profession and the interests of clients above their own personal interests.
- Use reasonable care and exercise independent professional judgment when conducting investment analysis, making investment recommendations, taking investment actions, and engaging in other professional activities.
- Practice and encourage others to practice in a professional and ethical manner that will reflect credit on themselves and the profession.
- Promote the integrity and viability of the global capital markets for the ultimate benefit of society.
- Maintain and improve their professional competence and strive to maintain and improve the competence of other investment professionals.

Standards of Professional Conduct

i. PROFESSIONALISM

   A. Knowledge of the Law

   Members and Candidates must understand and comply with all applicable laws, rules, and regulations (including the CFA Institute Code of Ethics and Standards of Professional Conduct) of any government, regulatory organization, licensing agency, or professional association governing their professional activities. In the event of conflict, Members and Candidates must comply with the more strict law, rule, or regulation. Members and Candidates must not knowingly participate or assist in and must dissociate from any violation of such laws, rules, or regulations.

   B. Independence and Objectivity

   Members and Candidates must use reasonable care and judgment to achieve and maintain independence and objectivity in their professional activities. Members and Candidates must not offer, solicit, or accept any gift, benefit, compensation, or consideration that reasonably could be expected to compromise their own or another's independence and objectivity.

   C. Misrepresentation

Members and Candidates must not knowingly make any misrepresentations relating to investment analysis, recommendations, actions, or other professional activities.

D. Misconduct

Members and Candidates must not engage in any professional conduct involving dishonesty, fraud, or deceit or commit any act that reflects adversely on their professional reputation, integrity, or competence.

ii. INTEGRITY OF CAPITAL MARKETS

A. Material Nonpublic Information

Members and Candidates who possess material nonpublic information that could affect the value of an investment must not act or cause others to act on the information.

B. Market Manipulation

Members and Candidates must not engage in practices that distort prices or artificially inflate trading volume with the intent to mislead market participants.

iii. DUTIES TO CLIENTS

A. Loyalty, Prudence, and Care

Members and Candidates have a duty of loyalty to their clients and must act with reasonable care and exercise prudent judgment. Members and Candidates must act for the benefit of their clients and place their clients' interests before their employer's or their own interests.

B. Fair Dealing

Members and Candidates must deal fairly and objectively with all clients when providing investment analysis, making investment recommendations, taking investment action, or engaging in other professional activities.

C. Suitability

1. When Members and Candidates are in an advisory relationship with a client, they must:

   a. Make a reasonable inquiry into a client's or prospective client's investment experience, risk and return objectives, and financial constraints prior to making any investment recommendation or taking investment action and must reassess and update this information regularly.

   b. Determine that an investment is suitable to the client's financial situation and consistent with the client's written objectives, mandates, and constraints before making an investment recommendation or taking investment action.

   c. Judge the suitability of investments in the context of the client's total portfolio.

2. When Members and Candidates are responsible for managing a portfolio to a specific mandate, strategy, or style, they must make only investment recommendations or take only investment actions that are consistent with the stated objectives and constraints of the portfolio.

D. Performance Presentation

When communicating investment performance information, Members and Candidates must make reasonable efforts to ensure that it is fair, accurate, and complete.

E. Preservation of Confidentiality

Members and Candidates must keep information about current, former, and prospective clients confidential unless:

1. The information concerns illegal activities on the part of the client or prospective client,

2. Disclosure is required by law, or

3. The client or prospective client permits disclosure of the information.

iv. DUTIES TO EMPLOYERS

A. Loyalty

In matters related to their employment, Members and Candidates must act for the benefit of their employer and not deprive their employer of the advantage of their skills and abilities, divulge confidential information, or otherwise cause harm to their employer.

B. Additional Compensation Arrangements

Members and Candidates must not accept gifts, benefits, compensation, or consideration that competes with or might reasonably be expected to create a conflict of interest with their employer's interest unless they obtain written consent from all parties involved.

C. Responsibilities of Supervisors

Members and Candidates must make reasonable efforts to ensure that anyone subject to their supervision or authority complies with applicable laws, rules, regulations, and the Code and Standards.

v. INVESTMENT ANALYSIS, RECOMMENDATIONS, AND ACTIONS

A. Diligence and Reasonable Basis

Members and Candidates must:

1. Exercise diligence, independence, and thoroughness in analyzing investments, making investment recommendations, and taking investment actions.

2. Have a reasonable and adequate basis, supported by appropriate research and investigation, for any investment analysis, recommendation, or action.

B. Communication with Clients and Prospective Clients

Members and Candidates must:

1. Disclose to clients and prospective clients the basic format and general principles of the investment processes they use to analyze investments, select securities, and construct portfolios and must promptly disclose any changes that might materially affect those processes.

2. Disclose to clients and prospective clients significant limitations and risks associated with the investment process.

3. Use reasonable judgment in identifying which factors are important to their investment analyses, recommendations, or actions and include those factors in communications with clients and prospective clients.

4. Distinguish between fact and opinion in the presentation of investment analysis and recommendations.

C. Record Retention

Members and Candidates must develop and maintain appropriate records to support their investment analyses, recommendations, actions, and other investment-related communications with clients and prospective clients.

vi. CONFLICTS OF INTEREST

A. Disclosure of Conflicts

Members and Candidates must make full and fair disclosure of all matters that could reasonably be expected to impair their independence and objectivity or interfere with respective duties to their clients, prospective clients, and employer. Members and Candidates must ensure that such disclosures are prominent, are delivered in plain language, and communicate the relevant information effectively.

B. Priority of Transactions

Investment transactions for clients and employers must have priority over investment transactions in which a Member or Candidate is the beneficial owner.

C. Referral Fees

Members and Candidates must disclose to their employer, clients, and prospective clients, as appropriate, any compensation, consideration, or benefit received from or paid to others for the recommendation of products or services.

vii. RESPONSIBILITIES AS A CFA INSTITUTE MEMBER OR CFA CANDIDATE

A. Conduct as Participants in CFA Institute Programs

Members and Candidates must not engage in any conduct that compromises the reputation or integrity of CFA Institute or the CFA designation or the integrity, validity, or security of CFA Institute programs.

B. Reference to CFA Institute, the CFA Designation, and the CFA Program

When referring to CFA Institute, CFA Institute membership, the CFA designation, or candidacy in the CFA Program, Members and Candidates must not misrepresent or exaggerate the meaning or implications of membership in CFA Institute, holding the CFA designation, or candidacy in the CFA Program.

PRACTICE PROBLEMS

1. The Standards of Practice Handbook provides guidance:
   A. regarding the penalties incurred as a result of ethical violations.
   B. to which all CFA Institute members and candidates must adhere.
   C. through explanatory material and examples intended to be all inclusive.

2. Which of the following statements *best* describes an aspect of the Professional Conduct Program process?
   A. Inquiries are not initiated in response to information provided by the media.
   B. Investigations result in Disciplinary Review Committee panels for each case.
   C. Investigations may include requesting a written explanation from the member or candidate.

3. A current Code of Ethics principle reads in full, "Promote the integrity:
   A. and viability of the global capital markets."
   B. of and uphold the rules governing capital markets."
   C. and viability of the global capital markets for the ultimate benefit of society."

4. As stated in the revised 11th edition, the Standards of Professional Conduct:
   A. require supervisors to focus on the detection and prevention of violations.
   B. adopt separate ethical considerations for programs such as CIPM and Investment Foundations.
   C. address the risks and limitations of recommendations being made to clients.

5. According to the Code of Ethics, members of CFA Institute and candidates for the CFA designation must:
   A. maintain their professional competence to exercise independent professional judgment.
   B. place the integrity of the investment profession and the interests of clients above their own personal interests.
   C. practice in a professional and ethical manner with the public, clients, and others in the global capital markets.

6. Which of the following statements *best* describes an aspect of the Standards of Professional Conduct? Members and candidates are required to:
   A. ensure any portfolio mandate followed is fair, accurate, and complete.
   B. promptly disclose changes that might materially affect investment processes.
   C. have a reasonable and adequate basis for decisions about client confidentiality.

Practice Problems

7. Which of the following responses most completely represents an ethical principle of CFA Institute as outlined in the *Standards of Practice Handbook*?

    A. Individual professionalism

    B. Responsibilities to clients and employers

    C. Ethics involved in investment analysis and recommendations

8. A CFA Institute member would violate the standard for material nonpublic information by:

    A. conducting price distortion practices.

    B. inappropriately causing others to act.

    C. inadequately maintaining investment records.

9. According to the Duties to Clients standard, suitability requires members and candidates in an advisory relationship with a client to:

    A. place their clients' interests before their own interests.

    B. consider investments in the context of the client's total portfolio.

    C. not knowingly make misrepresentations relating to recommendations.

10. As part of the Duties to Clients standard, members and candidates must:

    A. document client financial constraints after an initial investment action.

    B. maintain an equal balance of interests owed to their clients and employers.

    C. deal fairly and objectively with all clients when engaging in professional activities.

11. The Duties to Employers standard states that members and candidates must not:

    A. accept any gifts that might compromise their independence and objectivity.

    B. deprive their employer of their skills and abilities as related to their employment.

    C. accept compensation competing with their employer's interest and with the written consent of all parties involved.

12. The Investment Analysis, Recommendations, and Actions standard states that members and candidates must:

    A. find an investment suitable for their client before making a recommendation.

    B. make reasonable efforts to ensure that performance presentation is fair, accurate, and complete.

    C. distinguish between fact and opinion in the presentation of investment analysis and recommendations.

13. Based on the Conflicts of Interest standard, members and candidates must:

    A. disclose, as required by law, those conflicts interfering with their professional duties.

    B. disclose, as appropriate, any benefit paid to others for the recommendation of products.

    C. seek employer approval before prioritizing their investment transactions over those clients.

14. The Responsibilities as a CFA Institute Member or CFA Candidate Standard explicitly states a requirement regarding:

    A. loyalty.

    B. responsibility of supervisors.

    C. reference to the CFA Program.

SOLUTIONS

1. B is correct. The *Standards of Practice Handbook* provides guidance to which CFA Institute members and candidates are required to adhere.

    A is incorrect because the *Handbook* provides guidance in understanding the interconnectedness of the aspirational and practical principles (not regarding penalties for violations) of the Code of Ethics and Standards of Conduct.

    C is incorrect because although the *Standards of Practice Handbook* provides hypothetical but factual situations, the explanatory material and examples are not intended to be all inclusive.

2. C is correct. When an inquiry is initiated, the Professional Conduct staff conducts an investigation that may include requesting a written explanation from the member or candidate.

    A is incorrect because Professional Conduct inquiries can be initiated in response to information provided by the media. CFA Institute staff may become aware of questionable conduct by a member or candidate through the media, regulatory notices, or another public source.

    B is incorrect because although the Disciplinary Review Committee (DRC) is responsible for enforcement of the Code and Standards in conjunction with the Professional Conduct Program (PCP), only in the event that a member or candidate does not accept the charges and proposed sanction is the matter referred to a panel composed of DRC members.

3. C is correct. One of the principles in the Code of Ethics was updated to reflect the role that the capital markets have in society as a whole.

    A is incorrect because it is incomplete, missing the additional language to reflect the role that the capital markets have in society as a whole.

    B is incorrect because this is the old principle as written in the Code of Ethics, which was recently updated to reflect the role of the capital markets in society as a whole.

4. C is correct. Given the constant development of new and exotic financial instruments and strategies, the standard regarding communicating with clients now includes an implicit requirement to discuss the risks and limitations of recommendations being made to clients.

    A is incorrect because the updated standard for members and candidates with supervision or authority over others within their firms stresses broader compliance expectations, which include the detection and prevention aspects of the original version that was the prior focus.

    B is incorrect because the updated standard not only maintains the integrity of the CFA Program but also expands the same (not separate) ethical considerations when members or candidates participate in such programs as the CIPM Program and the Investment Foundations Certificate.

5. B is correct. Members of CFA Institute and candidates for the CFA designation must place the integrity of the investment profession and the interests of clients above their own personal interests.

    A is incorrect because members of CFA Institute and candidates for the CFA designation must maintain and improve their professional competence and strive to maintain and improve the competence of other investment professionals. The exercise of independent professional judgment is associated with using reasonable care.

C is incorrect because members of CFA Institute and candidates for the CFA designation must practice and encourage others to practice in a professional and ethical manner that will reflect credibly on themselves and the profession. Members are supposed to act with integrity, competence, diligence, and respect and in an ethical manner with the public, clients, and other market participants.

6. B is correct. The current Standards of Professional Conduct requires members and candidates to promptly disclose any changes that might materially affect investment processes.

    A is incorrect because under Standard III.C.2 Suitability, when members and candidates are responsible for managing a portfolio according to a specific mandate, they must take only investment actions that are consistent with the stated objectives of the portfolio. The "fair, accurate, and complete" criterion relates to the Standard III D Performance Presentation.

    C is incorrect because under Standard III.E.1, 2, 3 Preservation of Confidentiality, members and candidates must keep information about current clients confidential unless the information concerns illegal activities on the part of the client, disclosure is required by law, or the client permits disclosure. No decisions on confidentiality are required, with the "reasonable and adequate basis" criterion related to Standard V.A.2 Diligence and Reasonable Basis.

7. A is correct. Within the Standards of Practice Handbook, CFA Institute addresses ethical principles for the profession in the following Standards: individual professionalism; integrity in capital markets; responsibilities to clients, responsibilities to employers; ethics involved in investment analysis, recommendations, and actions; and possible conflicts of interest. B is incorrect because it represents, and combines, two ethical principles, those relating to the Standards "Duties to Clients" and "Duties to Employers." C is incorrect because the ethical principle (and Standard) relating to ethics in investment analysis and recommendations also includes actions.

8. B is correct. Under Standard II.A Material Nonpublic Information, members having material nonpublic information that could affect the value of an investment must not cause others to act on the information.

    A is incorrect because price distortion is mentioned in the Standard II.B Market Manipulation, not Standard II.A Material Nonpublic Information.

    C is incorrect because the maintenance of appropriate records to support investment analyses is noted in Standard V.C Record Retention, not Standard II.A Material Nonpublic Information.

9. B is correct. Standard III.C.1c Suitability states that when members and candidates are in an advisory relationship with a client, they must judge the suitability of investments in the context of the client's total portfolio.

    A is incorrect because this is a requirement addressed under Standard III.A Loyalty, Prudence, and Care, not Standard III.C.1c Suitability.

    C is incorrect because this is a requirement addressed under Standard I.C Misrepresentation, not Standard III.C.1c Suitability.

10. C is correct. Under the III.B Fair Dealing section of the Duty to Clients standard, members and candidates must deal fairly and objectively with all clients when providing investment analysis, making investment recommendations, taking investment action, or engaging in other professional activities.

    A is incorrect because under Standard III.C.1a Suitability, a section of Duties to Clients, members and candidates in an advisory relationship must make a reasonable inquiry into a client's financial constraints prior to (not after) taking investment action and must reassess and update this regularly.

B is incorrect because under Standard III.A Loyalty, Prudence, and Care, members and candidates must act for the benefit of their clients and place their clients' interests before (not maintain an equal balance with) their employer's or their own interests.

11. B is correct. The IV.A Loyalty section of the Duties to Employers standard states that members and candidates cannot deprive their employer of the advantage of their skills and abilities in matters related to their employment.

    A is incorrect because accepting gifts that might compromise a member or candidate's independence and objectivity is addressed by Standard I.B Independence and Objectivity, a section of Professionalism, not under Standard IV Duties to Employers.

    C is incorrect because IV.B Additional Compensation Arrangements, part of the Duties to Employers standard, permits members and candidates to accept compensation that competes with their employer's interest if they obtain written consent from all parties involved.

12. C is correct. The V.B.4 Communications with Clients and Prospective Clients section of the Investment Analysis, Recommendations, and Actions standard states that members and candidates must distinguish between fact and opinion in the presentation of investment analysis and recommendations.

    A is incorrect because this standard is discussed in the III.C.1b Suitability section of the Duties to Clients standard.

    B is incorrect because performance presentation is discussed in the III.D Performance Presentation section of the Duties to Clients standard.

13. B is correct. The VI.C Referral Fees section of the Conflicts of Interest standard requires members and candidates to disclose to their employer, clients, and prospective clients, as appropriate, any compensation, consideration, or benefit received from or paid to others for the recommendation of products or services.

    A is incorrect because the VI.A Disclosure of Conflicts section of the Conflicts of Interest standard requires members and candidates to make full and fair disclosure of all matters (not limited to legal requirements) that could reasonably be expected to impair their independence and objectivity or interfere with respective duties to their clients, prospective clients, and employer.

    C is incorrect because the VI.B Priority of Transactions section of the Conflicts of Interest standard requires members and candidates to give priority to investment transactions for clients and employers versus those in which a member or candidate is the beneficial owner. This requirement is not waived by an employer's approval.

14. C is correct. The VII.B Reference to CFA Institute, the CFA Designation, and the CFA Program section of the Responsibilities as a CFA Institute Member or CFA Candidate standard explicitly states the appropriate manner to make reference to CFA Institute, CFA Institute membership, the CFA designation, or candidacy in the CFA Program.

    A is incorrect because Standard VII Responsibilities as a CFA Institute Member or CFA Candidate standard does not refer to loyalty. Loyalty is addressed in two other standards, Standard III.A Loyalty, Prudence, and Care and Standard IV.A Loyalty.

    B is incorrect because Standard VII Responsibilities as a CFA Institute Member or CFA Candidate standard does not refer to the responsibility of supervisors. The responsibility of supervisors is addressed in Standard IV.C Responsibility of Supervisors.

LEARNING MODULE 3

Guidance for Standards I–VII

LEARNING OUTCOME

Mastery	The candidate should be able to:
☐	demonstrate the application of the Code of Ethics and Standards of Professional Conduct to situations involving issues of professional integrity
☐	recommend practices and procedures designed to prevent violations of the Code of Ethics and Standards of Professional Conduct
☐	identify conduct that conforms to the Code and Standards and conduct that violates the Code and Standards

STANDARD I(A): PROFESSIONALISM - KNOWLEDGE OF THE LAW

☐ demonstrate the application of the Code of Ethics and Standards of Professional Conduct to situations involving issues of professional integrity

Standard I(A) Knowledge of the Law

> Members and Candidates must understand and comply with all applicable laws, rules, and regulations (including the CFA Institute Code of Ethics and Standards of Professional Conduct) of any government, regulatory organization, licensing agency, or professional association governing their professional activities. In the event of conflict, Members and Candidates must comply with the more strict law, rule, or regulation. Members and Candidates must not knowingly participate or assist in and must dissociate from any violation of such laws, rules, or regulations.

Guidance

Highlights:

- *Relationship between the Code and Standards and Applicable Law*
- *Participation in or Association with Violations by Others*
- *Investment Products and Applicable Laws*

Members and candidates must understand the applicable laws and regulations of the countries and jurisdictions where they engage in professional activities. These activities may include, but are not limited to, trading of securities or other financial instruments, providing investment advice, conducting research, or performing other investment services. On the basis of their reasonable and good faith understanding, members and candidates must comply with the laws and regulations that directly govern their professional activities and resulting outcomes and that protect the interests of the clients.

When questions arise, members and candidates should know their firm's policies and procedures for accessing compliance guidance. This standard does not require members and candidates to become experts, however, in compliance. Additionally, members and candidates are not required to have detailed knowledge of or be experts on all the laws that could potentially govern their activities.

During times of changing regulations, members and candidates must remain vigilant in maintaining their knowledge of the requirements for their professional activities. New financial products and processes, along with uncovered ethical missteps, create an environment for recurring and potentially wide-ranging regulatory changes. Members and candidates are also continually provided improved and enhanced methods of communicating with both clients and potential clients, such as mobile applications and web-based social networking platforms. As new local, regional, and global requirements are updated to address these and other changes, members, candidates, and their firms must adjust their procedures and practices to remain in compliance.

Relationship between the Code and Standards and Applicable Law

Some members or candidates may live, work, or provide investment services to clients living in a country that has no law or regulation governing a particular action or that has laws or regulations that differ from the requirements of the Code and Standards. When applicable law and the Code and Standards require different conduct, members and candidates must follow the more strict of the applicable law or the Code and Standards.

"Applicable law" is the law that governs the member's or candidate's conduct. Which law applies will depend on the particular facts and circumstances of each case. The "more strict" law or regulation is the law or regulation that imposes greater restrictions on the action of the member or candidate or calls for the member or candidate to exert a greater degree of action that protects the interests of investors. For example, applicable law or regulation may not require members and candidates to disclose referral fees received from or paid to others for the recommendation of investment products or services. Because the Code and Standards impose this obligation, however, members and candidates must disclose the existence of such fees.

Members and candidates must adhere to the following principles:

- Members and candidates must comply with applicable laws or regulations related to their professional activities.
- Members and candidates must not engage in conduct that constitutes a violation of the Code and Standards, even though it may otherwise be legal.

- In the absence of any applicable law or regulation or when the Code and Standards impose a higher degree of responsibility than applicable laws and regulations, members and candidates must adhere to the Code and Standards. Applications of these principles are outlined in Exhibit 1.

The applicable laws governing the responsibilities of a member or candidate should be viewed as the minimal threshold of acceptable actions. When members and candidates take actions that exceed the minimal requirements, they further support the conduct required of Standard I(A).

CFA Institute members are obligated to abide by the CFA Institute Articles of Incorporation, Bylaws, Code of Ethics, Standards of Professional Conduct, Rules of Procedure, Membership Agreement, and other applicable rules promulgated by CFA Institute, all as amended periodically. CFA candidates who are not members must also abide by these documents (except for the Membership Agreement) as well as rules and regulations related to the administration of the CFA examination, the Candidate Responsibility Statement, and the Candidate Pledge.

Participation in or Association with Violations by Others

Members and candidates are responsible for violations in which they *knowingly* participate or assist. Although members and candidates are presumed to have knowledge of all applicable laws, rules, and regulations, CFA Institute acknowledges that members may not recognize violations if they are not aware of all the facts giving rise to the violations. Standard I(A) applies when members and candidates know or should know that their conduct may contribute to a violation of applicable laws, rules, or regulations or the Code and Standards.

If a member or candidate has reasonable grounds to believe that imminent or ongoing client or employer activities are illegal or unethical, the member or candidate must dissociate, or separate, from the activity. In extreme cases, dissociation may require a member or candidate to leave his or her employment. Members and candidates may take the following intermediate steps to dissociate from ethical violations of others when direct discussions with the person or persons committing the violation are unsuccessful. The first step should be to attempt to stop the behavior by bringing it to the attention of the employer through a supervisor or the firm's compliance department. If this attempt is unsuccessful, then members and candidates have a responsibility to step away and dissociate from the activity. Dissociation practices will differ on the basis of the member's or candidate's role in the investment industry. It may include removing one's name from written reports or recommendations, asking for a different assignment, or refusing to accept a new client or continue to advise a current client. Inaction combined with continuing association with those involved in illegal or unethical conduct may be construed as participation or assistance in the illegal or unethical conduct.

CFA Institute strongly encourages members and candidates to report potential violations of the Code and Standards committed by fellow members and candidates. Although a failure to report is less likely to be construed as a violation than a failure to dissociate from unethical conduct, the impact of inactivity on the integrity of capital markets can be significant. Although the Code and Standards do not compel members and candidates to report violations to their governmental or regulatory organizations unless such disclosure is mandatory under applicable law (voluntary reporting is often referred to as whistleblowing), such disclosure may be prudent under certain circumstances. Members and candidates should consult their legal and compliance advisers for guidance.

Additionally, CFA Institute encourages members, nonmembers, clients, and the investing public to report violations of the Code and Standards by CFA Institute members or CFA candidates by submitting a complaint in writing to the CFA Institute Professional Conduct Program via e-mail (pcprogram@cfainstitute.org) or the CFA Institute website (www.cfainstitute.org).

Investment Products and Applicable Laws

Members and candidates involved in creating or maintaining investment services or investment products or packages of securities and/or derivatives should be mindful of where these products or packages will be sold as well as their places of origination. The applicable laws and regulations of the countries or regions of origination and expected sale should be understood by those responsible for the supervision of the services or creation and maintenance of the products or packages. Members or candidates should make reasonable efforts to review whether associated firms that are distributing products or services developed by their employing firm also abide by the laws and regulations of the countries and regions of distribution. Members and candidates should undertake the necessary due diligence when transacting cross-border business to understand the multiple applicable laws and regulations in order to protect the reputation of their firm and themselves.

Given the complexity that can arise with business transactions in today's market, there may be some uncertainty surrounding which laws or regulations are considered applicable when activities are being conducted in multiple jurisdictions. Members and candidates should seek the appropriate guidance, potentially including the firm's compliance or legal departments and legal counsel outside the organization, to gain a reasonable understanding of their responsibilities and how to implement them appropriately.

> **Exhibit 1: Global Application of the Code and Standards**
>
> Members and candidates who practice in multiple jurisdictions may be subject to varied securities laws and regulations. If applicable law is stricter than the requirements of the Code and Standards, members and candidates must adhere to applicable law; otherwise, they must adhere to the Code and Standards. The following chart provides illustrations involving a member who may be subject to the securities laws and regulations of three different types of countries:
>
> NS: country with no securities laws or regulations
>
> LS: country with *less* strict securities laws and regulations than the Code and Standards
>
> MS: country with *more* strict securities laws and regulations than the Code and Standards
>
> | Applicable Law | Duties | Explanation |
> | --- | --- | --- |
> | Member resides in NS country, does business in LS country; LS law applies. | Member must adhere to the Code and Standards. | Because applicable law is less strict than the Code and Standards, the member must adhere to the Code and Standards. |
> | Member resides in NS country, does business in MS country; MS law applies. | Member must adhere to the law of MS country. | Because applicable law is stricter than the Code and Standards, member must adhere to the more strict applicable law. |

Standard I(A): Professionalism - Knowledge of the Law

Applicable Law	Duties	Explanation
Member resides in LS country, does business in NS country; LS law applies.	Member must adhere to the Code and Standards.	Because applicable law is less strict than the Code and Standards, member must adhere to the Code and Standards.
Member resides in LS country, does business in MS country; MS law applies.	Member must adhere to the law of MS country.	Because applicable law is stricter than the Code and Standards, member must adhere to the more strict applicable law.
Member resides in LS country, does business in NS country; LS law applies, but it states that law of locality where business is conducted governs.	Member must adhere to the Code and Standards.	Because applicable law states that the law of the locality where the business is conducted governs and there is no local law, the member must adhere to the Code and Standards.
Member resides in LS country, does business in MS country; LS law applies, but it states that law of locality where business is conducted governs.	Member must adhere to the law of MS country.	Because applicable law of the locality where the business is conducted governs and local law is stricter than the Code and Standards, member must adhere to the more strict applicable law.
Member resides in MS country, does business in LS country; MS law applies.	Member must adhere to the law of MS country.	Because applicable law is stricter than the Code and Standards, member must adhere to the more strict applicable law.
Member resides in MS country, does business in LS country; MS law applies, but it states that law of locality where business is conducted governs.	Member must adhere to the Code and Standards.	Because applicable law states that the law of the locality where the business is conducted governs and local law is less strict than the Code and Standards, member must adhere to the Code and Standards.
Member resides in MS country, does business in LS country with a client who is a citizen of LS country; MS law applies, but it states that the law of the client's home country governs.	Member must adhere to the Code and Standards.	Because applicable law states that the law of the client's home country governs (which is less strict than the Code and Standards), member must adhere to the Code and Standards.
Member resides in MS country, does business in LS country with a client who is a citizen of MS country; MS law applies, but it states that the law of the client's home country governs.	Member must adhere to the law of MS country.	Because applicable law states that the law of the client's home country governs and the law of the client's home country is stricter than the Code and Standards, the member must adhere to the more strict applicable law.

2 STANDARD I(A): RECOMMENDED PROCEDURES

☐ recommend practices and procedures designed to prevent violations of the Code of Ethics and Standards of Professional Conduct

Members and Candidates

Suggested methods by which members and candidates can acquire and maintain understanding of applicable laws, rules, and regulations include the following:

- *Stay informed*: Members and candidates should establish or encourage their employers to establish a procedure by which employees are regularly informed about changes in applicable laws, rules, regulations, and case law. In many instances, the employer's compliance department or legal counsel can provide such information in the form of memorandums distributed to employees in the organization. Also, participation in an internal or external continuing education program is a practical method of staying current.

- *Review procedures*: Members and candidates should review, or encourage their employers to review, the firm's written compliance procedures on a regular basis to ensure that the procedures reflect current law and provide adequate guidance to employees about what is permissible conduct under the law and/or the Code and Standards. Recommended compliance procedures for specific items of the Code and Standards are discussed in this *Handbook* in the "Guidance" sections associated with each standard.

- *Maintain current files*: Members and candidates should maintain or encourage their employers to maintain readily accessible current reference copies of applicable statutes, rules, regulations, and important cases.

Distribution Area Laws

Members and candidates should make reasonable efforts to understand the applicable laws—both country and regional—for the countries and regions where their investment products are developed and are most likely to be distributed to clients.

Legal Counsel

When in doubt about the appropriate action to undertake, it is recommended that a member or candidate seek the advice of compliance personnel or legal counsel concerning legal requirements. If a potential violation is being committed by a fellow employee, it may also be prudent for the member or candidate to seek the advice of the firm's compliance department or legal counsel.

Dissociation

When dissociating from an activity that violates the Code and Standards, members and candidates should document the violation and urge their firms to attempt to persuade the perpetrator(s) to cease such conduct. To dissociate from the conduct, a member or candidate may have to resign his or her employment.

Firms

The formality and complexity of compliance procedures for firms depend on the nature and size of the organization and the nature of its investment operations. Members and candidates should encourage their firms to consider the following policies and procedures to support the principles of Standard I(A):

- *Develop and/or adopt a code of ethics*: The ethical culture of an organization starts at the top. Members and candidates should encourage their supervisors or managers to adopt a code of ethics. Adhering to a code of ethics facilitates solutions when people face ethical dilemmas and can prevent the need for employees to resort to a "whistleblowing" solution publicly alleging concealed misconduct. CFA Institute has published the *Asset Manager Code of Professional Conduct*, which firms may adopt or use as the basis for their codes (visit www.cfainstitute.org).

- *Provide information on applicable laws*: Pertinent information that highlights applicable laws and regulations might be distributed to employees or made available in a central location. Information sources might include primary information developed by the relevant government, governmental agencies, regulatory organizations, licensing agencies, and professional associations (e.g., from their websites); law firm memorandums or newsletters; and association memorandums or publications (e.g., *CFA Institute Magazine*).

- *Establish procedures for reporting violations*: Firms might provide written protocols for reporting suspected violations of laws, regulations, or company policies.

STANDARD I(A): APPLICATION OF THE STANDARD 3

- ☐ demonstrate the application of the Code of Ethics and Standards of Professional Conduct to situations involving issues of professional integrity
- ☐ recommend practices and procedures designed to prevent violations of the Code of Ethics and Standards of Professional Conduct

Example 1 (Notification of Known Violations):

Michael Allen works for a brokerage firm and is responsible for an underwriting of securities. A company official gives Allen information indicating that the financial statements Allen filed with the regulator overstate the issuer's earnings. Allen seeks the advice of the brokerage firm's general counsel, who states that it would be difficult for the regulator to prove that Allen has been involved in any wrongdoing.

> *Comment*: Although it is recommended that members and candidates seek the advice of legal counsel, the reliance on such advice does not absolve a member or candidate from the requirement to comply with the law or regulation. Allen should report this situation to his supervisor, seek an independent legal opinion, and determine whether the regulator should be notified of the error.

Example 2 (Dissociating from a Violation):

Lawrence Brown's employer, an investment banking firm, is the principal underwriter for an issue of convertible debentures by the Courtney Company. Brown discovers that the Courtney Company has concealed severe third-quarter losses in its foreign operations. The preliminary prospectus has already been distributed.

> *Comment*: Knowing that the preliminary prospectus is misleading, Brown should report his findings to the appropriate supervisory persons in his firm. If the matter is not remedied and Brown's employer does not dissociate from the underwriting, Brown should sever all his connections with the underwriting. Brown should also seek legal advice to determine whether additional reporting or other action should be taken.

Example 3 (Dissociating from a Violation):

Kamisha Washington's firm advertises its past performance record by showing the 10-year return of a composite of its client accounts. Washington discovers, however, that the composite omits the performance of accounts that have left the firm during the 10-year period, whereas the description of the composite indicates the inclusion of all firm accounts. This omission has led to an inflated performance figure. Washington is asked to use promotional material that includes the erroneous performance number when soliciting business for the firm.

> *Comment*: Misrepresenting performance is a violation of the Code and Standards. Although she did not calculate the performance herself, Washington would be assisting in violating Standard I(A) if she were to use the inflated performance number when soliciting clients. She must dissociate herself from the activity. If discussing the misleading number with the person responsible is not an option for correcting the problem, she can bring the situation to the attention of her supervisor or the compliance department at her firm. If her firm is unwilling to recalculate performance, she must refrain from using the misleading promotional material and should notify the firm of her reasons. If the firm insists that she use the material, she should consider whether her obligation to dissociate from the activity requires her to seek other employment.

Example 4 (Following the Highest Requirements):

James Collins is an investment analyst for a major Wall Street brokerage firm. He works in a developing country with a rapidly modernizing economy and a growing capital market. Local securities laws are minimal—in form and content—and include no punitive prohibitions against insider trading.

> *Comment*: Collins must abide by the requirements of the Code and Standards, which might be more strict than the rules of the developing country. He should be aware of the risks that a small market and the absence of a fairly regulated flow of information to the market represent to his ability to obtain information and make timely judgments. He should include this factor in formulating his advice to clients. In handling material nonpublic information that accidentally comes into his possession, he must follow Standard II(A)–Material Nonpublic Information.

Example 5 (Following the Highest Requirements):

Laura Jameson works for a multinational investment adviser based in the United States. Jameson lives and works as a registered investment adviser in the tiny, but wealthy, island nation of Karramba. Karramba's securities laws state that no investment adviser registered and working in that country can participate in initial public offerings (IPOs) for the adviser's personal account. Jameson, believing that, as a US citizen working for a US-based company, she should comply only with US law, has ignored this Karrambian law. In addition, Jameson believes that as a charterholder, as long as she adheres to the Code and Standards requirement that she disclose her participation in any IPO to her employer and clients when such ownership creates a conflict of interest, she is meeting the highest ethical requirements.

> *Comment*: Jameson is in violation of Standard I(A). As a registered investment adviser in Karramba, Jameson is prevented by Karrambian securities law from participating in IPOs regardless of the law of her home country. In addition, because the law of the country where she is working is stricter than the Code and Standards, she must follow the stricter requirements of the local law rather than the requirements of the Code and Standards.

Example 6 (Laws and Regulations Based on Religious Tenets):

Amanda Janney is employed as a fixed-income portfolio manager for a large international firm. She is on a team within her firm that is responsible for creating and managing a fixed-income hedge fund to be sold throughout the firm's distribution centers to high-net-worth clients. Her firm receives expressions of interest from potential clients from the Middle East who are seeking investments that comply with Islamic law. The marketing and promotional materials for the fixed-income hedge fund do not specify whether or not the fund is a suitable investment for an investor seeking compliance with Islamic law. Because the fund is being distributed globally, Janney is concerned about the reputation of the fund and the firm and believes disclosure of whether or not the fund complies with Islamic law could help minimize potential mistakes with placing this investment.

> *Comment*: As the financial market continues to become globalized, members and candidates will need to be aware of the differences between cultural and religious laws and requirements as well as the different governmental laws and regulations. Janney and the firm could be proactive in their efforts to acknowledge areas where the new fund may not be suitable for clients.

Example 7 (Reporting Potential Unethical Actions):

Krista Blume is a junior portfolio manager for high-net-worth portfolios at a large global investment manager. She observes a number of new portfolios and relationships coming from a country in Europe where the firm did not have previous business and is told that a broker in that country is responsible for this new business. At a meeting on allocation of research resources to third-party research firms, Blume notes that this broker has been added to the list and is allocated payments for research. However, she knows the portfolios do not invest in securities in the broker's country, and she has not seen any research come from this broker. Blume asks her supervisor about the name being on the list and is told that someone in marketing is receiving the research and that the name being on the list is OK. She believes that what may be going on is that the broker is being paid for new business through the inappropriate research payments, and she wishes to dissociate from the misconduct.

Comment: Blume should follow the firm's policies and procedures for reporting potential unethical activity, which may include discussions with her supervisor or someone in a designated compliance department. She should communicate her concerns appropriately while advocating for disclosure between the new broker relationship and the research payments.

Example 8 (Failure to Maintain Knowledge of the Law):

Colleen White is excited to use new technology to communicate with clients and potential clients. She recently began posting investment information, including performance reports and investment opinions and recommendations, to her Facebook page. In addition, she sends out brief announcements, opinions, and thoughts via her Twitter account (for example, "Prospects for future growth of XYZ company look good! #makingmoney4U"). Prior to White's use of these social media platforms, the local regulator had issued new requirements and guidance governing online electronic communication. White's communications appear to conflict with the recent regulatory announcements.

Comment: White is in violation of Standard I(A) because her communications do not comply with the existing guidance and regulation governing use of social media. White must be aware of the evolving legal requirements pertaining to new and dynamic areas of the financial services industry that are applicable to her. She should seek guidance from appropriate, knowledgeable, and reliable sources, such as her firm's compliance department, external service providers, or outside counsel, unless she diligently follows legal and regulatory trends affecting her professional responsibilities.

4. STANDARD I(B): PROFESSIONALISM - INDEPENDENCE AND OBJECTIVITY

☐ demonstrate the application of the Code of Ethics and Standards of Professional Conduct to situations involving issues of professional integrity

> Members and Candidates must use reasonable care and judgment to achieve and maintain independence and objectivity in their professional activities. Members and Candidates must not offer, solicit, or accept any gift, benefit, compensation, or consideration that reasonably could be expected to compromise their own or another's independence and objectivity.

Guidance

Highlights:

- *Buy-Side Clients*
- *Fund Manager and Custodial Relationships*
- *Investment Banking Relationships*

Standard I(B): Professionalism - Independence and Objectivity

- *Performance Measurement and Attribution*
- *Public Companies*
- *Credit Rating Agency Opinions*
- *Influence during the Manager Selection/Procurement Process*
- *Issuer-Paid Research*
- *Travel Funding*

Standard I(B) states the responsibility of CFA Institute members and candidates in the CFA Program to maintain independence and objectivity so that their clients will have the benefit of their work and opinions unaffected by any potential conflict of interest or other circumstance adversely affecting their judgment. Every member and candidate should endeavor to avoid situations that could cause or be perceived to cause a loss of independence or objectivity in recommending investments or taking investment action.

External sources may try to influence the investment process by offering analysts and portfolio managers a variety of benefits. Corporations may seek expanded research coverage, issuers and underwriters may wish to promote new securities offerings, brokers may want to increase commission business, and independent rating agencies may be influenced by the company requesting the rating. Benefits may include gifts, invitations to lavish functions, tickets, favors, or job referrals. One type of benefit is the allocation of shares in oversubscribed IPOs to investment managers for their personal accounts. This practice affords managers the opportunity to make quick profits that may not be available to their clients. Such a practice is prohibited under Standard I(B). Modest gifts and entertainment are acceptable, but special care must be taken by members and candidates to resist subtle and not-so-subtle pressures to act in conflict with the interests of their clients. Best practice dictates that members and candidates reject any offer of gift or entertainment that could be expected to threaten their independence and objectivity.

Receiving a gift, benefit, or consideration from a *client* can be distinguished from gifts given by entities seeking to influence a member or candidate to the detriment of other clients. In a client relationship, the client has already entered some type of compensation arrangement with the member, candidate, or his or her firm. A gift from a client could be considered supplementary compensation. The potential for obtaining influence to the detriment of other clients, although present, is not as great as in situations where no compensation arrangement exists. When possible, prior to accepting "bonuses" or gifts from clients, members and candidates should disclose to their employers such benefits offered by clients. If notification is not possible prior to acceptance, members and candidates must disclose to their employer benefits previously accepted from clients. Disclosure allows the employer of a member or candidate to make an independent determination about the extent to which the gift may affect the member's or candidate's independence and objectivity.

Members and candidates may also come under pressure from their own firms to, for example, issue favorable research reports or recommendations for certain companies with potential or continuing business relationships with the firm. The situation may be aggravated if an executive of the company sits on the bank or investment firm's board and attempts to interfere in investment decision making. Members and candidates acting in a sales or marketing capacity must be especially mindful of their objectivity in promoting appropriate investments for their clients.

Left unmanaged, pressures that threaten independence place research analysts in a difficult position and may jeopardize their ability to act independently and objectively. One of the ways that research analysts have coped with these pressures in the past is to use subtle and ambiguous language in their recommendations or to temper the tone of their research reports. Such subtleties are lost on some investors, however, who reasonably expect research reports and recommendations to be straightforward and transparent and to communicate clearly an analyst's views based on unbiased analysis and independent judgment.

Members and candidates are personally responsible for maintaining independence and objectivity when preparing research reports, making investment recommendations, and taking investment action on behalf of clients. Recommendations must convey the member's or candidate's true opinions, free of bias from internal or external pressures, and be stated in clear and unambiguous language.

Members and candidates also should be aware that some of their professional or social activities within CFA Institute or its member societies may subtly threaten their independence or objectivity. When seeking corporate financial support for conventions, seminars, or even weekly society luncheons, the members or candidates responsible for the activities should evaluate both the actual effect of such solicitations on their independence and whether their objectivity might be perceived to be compromised in the eyes of their clients.

Buy-Side Clients

One source of pressure on sell-side analysts is buy-side clients. Institutional clients are traditionally the primary users of sell-side research, either directly or with soft dollar brokerage. Portfolio managers may have significant positions in the security of a company under review. A rating downgrade may adversely affect the portfolio's performance, particularly in the short term, because the sensitivity of stock prices to ratings changes has increased in recent years. A downgrade may also affect the manager's compensation, which is usually tied to portfolio performance. Moreover, portfolio performance is subject to media and public scrutiny, which may affect the manager's professional reputation. Consequently, some portfolio managers implicitly or explicitly support sell-side ratings inflation.

Portfolio managers have a responsibility to respect and foster the intellectual honesty of sell-side research. Therefore, it is improper for portfolio managers to threaten or engage in retaliatory practices, such as reporting sell-side analysts to the covered company in order to instigate negative corporate reactions. Although most portfolio managers do not engage in such practices, the perception by the research analyst that a reprisal is possible may cause concern and make it difficult for the analyst to maintain independence and objectivity.

Fund Manager and Custodial Relationships

Research analysts are not the only people who must be concerned with maintaining their independence. Members and candidates who are responsible for hiring and retaining outside managers and third-party custodians should not accepts gifts, entertainment, or travel funding that may be perceived as impairing their decisions. The use of secondary fund managers has evolved into a common practice to manage specific asset allocations. The use of third-party custodians is common practice for independent investment advisory firms and helps them with trading capabilities and reporting requirements. Primary and secondary fund managers, as well as third-party custodians, often arrange educational and marketing events to inform others about their business strategies, investment process, or custodial services. Members and candidates must review the merits of each offer individually in determining whether they may attend yet maintain their independence.

Investment Banking Relationships

Some sell-side firms may exert pressure on their analysts to issue favorable research reports on current or prospective investment banking clients. For many of these firms, income from investment banking has become increasingly important to overall firm profitability because brokerage income has declined as a result of price competition. Consequently, firms offering investment banking services work hard to develop and maintain relationships with investment banking clients and prospects. These companies are often covered by the firm's research analysts because companies often select their investment banks on the basis of the reputation of their research analysts, the quality of their work, and their standing in the industry.

In some countries, research analysts frequently work closely with their investment banking colleagues to help evaluate prospective investment banking clients. In other countries, because of past abuses in managing the obvious conflicts of interest, regulators have established clear rules prohibiting the interaction of these groups. Although collaboration between research analysts and investment banking colleagues may benefit the firm and enhance market efficiency (e.g., by allowing firms to assess risks more accurately and make better pricing assumptions), it requires firms to carefully balance the conflicts of interest inherent in the collaboration. Having analysts work with investment bankers is appropriate only when the conflicts are adequately and effectively managed and disclosed. Firm managers have a responsibility to provide an environment in which analysts are neither coerced nor enticed into issuing research that does not reflect their true opinions. Firms should require public disclosure of actual conflicts of interest to investors.

Members, candidates, and their firms must adopt and follow perceived best practices in maintaining independence and objectivity in the corporate culture and protecting analysts from undue pressure by their investment banking colleagues. The "firewalls" traditionally built between these two functions must be managed to minimize conflicts of interest; indeed, enhanced firewall policies may go as far as prohibiting all communications between these groups. A key element of an enhanced firewall is separate reporting structures for personnel on the research side and personnel on the investment banking side. For example, investment banking personnel should not have any authority to approve, disapprove, or make changes to research reports or recommendations. Another element should be a compensation arrangement that minimizes the pressures on research analysts and rewards objectivity and accuracy. Compensation arrangements should not link analyst remuneration directly to investment banking assignments in which the analyst may participate as a team member. Firms should also regularly review their policies and procedures to determine whether analysts are adequately safeguarded and to improve the transparency of disclosures relating to conflicts of interest. The highest level of transparency is achieved when disclosures are prominent and specific rather than marginalized and generic.

Performance Measurement and Attribution

Members and candidates working within a firm's investment performance measurement department may also be presented with situations that challenge their independence and objectivity. As performance analysts, their analyses may reveal instances where managers may appear to have strayed from their mandate. Additionally, the performance analyst may receive requests to alter the construction of composite indexes owing to negative results for a selected account or fund. The member or candidate must not allow internal or external influences to affect their independence and objectivity as they faithfully complete their performance calculation and analysis-related responsibilities.

Public Companies

Analysts may be pressured to issue favorable reports and recommendations by the companies they follow. Not every stock is a "buy," and not every research report is favorable—for many reasons, including the cyclical nature of many business activities and market fluctuations. For instance, a "good company" does not always translate into a "good stock" rating if the current stock price is fully valued. In making an investment recommendation, the analyst is responsible for anticipating, interpreting, and assessing a company's prospects and stock price performance in a factual manner. Many company managers, however, believe that their company's stock is undervalued, and these managers may find it difficult to accept critical research reports or ratings downgrades. Company managers' compensation may also be dependent on stock performance.

Due diligence in financial research and analysis involves gathering information from a wide variety of sources, including public disclosure documents (such as proxy statements, annual reports, and other regulatory filings) and also company management and investor-relations personnel, suppliers, customers, competitors, and other relevant sources. Research analysts may justifiably fear that companies will limit their ability to conduct thorough research by denying analysts who have "negative" views direct access to company managers and/or barring them from conference calls and other communication venues. Retaliatory practices include companies bringing legal action against analysts personally and/or their firms to seek monetary damages for the economic effects of negative reports and recommendations. Although few companies engage in such behavior, the perception that a reprisal is possible is a reasonable concern for analysts. This concern may make it difficult for them to conduct the comprehensive research needed to make objective recommendations. For further information and guidance, members and candidates should refer to the CFA Institute publication *Best Practice Guidelines Governing Analyst/Corporate Issuer Relations* (www.cfainstitute.org).

Credit Rating Agency Opinions

Credit rating agencies provide a service by grading the fixed-income products offered by companies. Analysts face challenges related to incentives and compensation schemes that may be tied to the final rating and successful placement of the product. Members and candidates employed at rating agencies should ensure that procedures and processes at the agencies prevent undue influences from a sponsoring company during the analysis. Members and candidates should abide by their agencies' and the industry's standards of conduct regarding the analytical process and the distribution of their reports.

The work of credit rating agencies also raises concerns similar to those inherent in investment banking relationships. Analysts may face pressure to issue ratings at a specific level because of other services the agency offers companies—namely, advising on the development of structured products. The rating agencies need to develop the necessary firewalls and protections to allow the independent operations of their different business lines.

When using information provided by credit rating agencies, members and candidates should be mindful of the potential conflicts of interest. And because of the potential conflicts, members and candidates may need to independently validate the rating granted.

Influence during the Manager Selection/Procurement Process

Members and candidates may find themselves on either side of the manager selection process. An individual may be on the hiring side as a representative of a pension organization or an investment committee member of an endowment or a charitable organization. Additionally, other members may be representing their organizations in attempts to earn new investment allocation mandates. The responsibility of members and candidates to maintain their independence and objectivity extends to the hiring or firing of those who provide business services beyond investment management.

When serving in a hiring capacity, members and candidates should not solicit gifts, contributions, or other compensation that may affect their independence and objectivity. Solicitations do not have to benefit members and candidates personally to conflict with Standard I(B). Requesting contributions to a favorite charity or political organization may also be perceived as an attempt to influence the decision-making process. Additionally, members and candidates serving in a hiring capacity should refuse gifts, donations, and other offered compensation that may be perceived to influence their decision-making process.

When working to earn a new investment allocation, members and candidates should not offer gifts, contributions, or other compensation to influence the decision of the hiring representative. The offering of these items with the intent to impair the independence and objectivity of another person would not comply with Standard I(B). Such prohibited actions may include offering donations to a charitable organization or political candidate referred by the hiring representative.

A clear example of improperly influencing hiring representatives was displayed in the "pay-to-play" scandal involving government-sponsored pension funds in the United States. Managers looking to gain lucrative allocations from the large funds made requested donations to the political campaigns of individuals directly responsible for the hiring decisions. This scandal and other similar events have led to new laws requiring additional reporting concerning political contributions and bans on hiring—or hiring delays for—managers that made campaign contributions to representatives associated with the decision-making process.

Issuer-Paid Research

In light of the recent reduction of sell-side research coverage, many companies, seeking to increase visibility both in the financial markets and with potential investors, have hired analysts to produce research reports analyzing their companies. These reports bridge the gap created by the lack of coverage and can be an effective method of communicating with investors.

Issuer-paid research conducted by independent analysts, however, is fraught with potential conflicts. Depending on how the research is written and distributed, investors may be misled into believing that the research is from an independent source when, in reality, it has been paid for by the subject company.

Members and candidates must adhere to strict standards of conduct that govern how the research is to be conducted and what disclosures must be made in the report. Analysts must engage in thorough, independent, and unbiased analysis and must fully disclose potential conflicts of interest, including the nature of their compensation. Otherwise, analysts risk misleading investors.

Investors need clear, credible, and thorough information about companies, and they need research based on independent thought. At a minimum, issuer-paid research should include a thorough analysis of the company's financial statements based on publicly disclosed information, benchmarking within a peer group, and industry analysis. Analysts must exercise diligence, independence, and thoroughness in conducting their research in an objective manner. Analysts must distinguish between fact and opinion in their reports. Conclusions must have a reasonable and adequate basis and must be supported by appropriate research.

Independent analysts must also strictly limit the type of compensation that they accept for conducting issuer-paid research. Otherwise, the content and conclusions of the reports could reasonably be expected to be determined or affected by compensation from the sponsoring companies. Compensation that might influence the research report could be direct, such as payment based on the conclusions of the report, or indirect, such as stock warrants or other equity instruments that could increase in value on the basis of positive coverage in the report. In such instances, the independent analyst has an incentive to avoid including negative information or making negative conclusions. Best practice is for independent analysts, prior to writing their reports, to negotiate only a flat fee for their work that is not linked to their conclusions or recommendations.

Travel Funding

The benefits related to accepting paid travel extend beyond the cost savings to the member or candidate and his firm, such as the chance to talk exclusively with the executives of a company or learning more about the investment options provided by an investment organization. Acceptance also comes with potential concerns; for example, members and candidates may be influenced by these discussions when flying on a corporate or chartered jet or attending sponsored conferences where many expenses, including airfare and lodging, are covered. To avoid the appearance of compromising their independence and objectivity, best practice dictates that members and candidates always use commercial transportation at their expense or at the expense of their firm rather than accept paid travel arrangements from an outside company. Should commercial transportation be unavailable, members and candidates may accept modestly arranged travel to participate in appropriate information-gathering events, such as a property tour.

5. STANDARD I(B): RECOMMENDED PROCEDURES

☐ recommend practices and procedures designed to prevent violations of the Code of Ethics and Standards of Professional Conduct

Members and candidates should adhere to the following practices and should encourage their firms to establish procedures to avoid violations of Standard I(B):

- *Protect the integrity of opinions*: Members, candidates, and their firms should establish policies stating that every research report concerning the securities of a corporate client should reflect the unbiased opinion of the analyst. Firms should also design compensation systems that protect the integrity of the investment decision process by maintaining the independence and objectivity of analysts.

- *Create a restricted list*: If the firm is unwilling to permit dissemination of adverse opinions about a corporate client, members and candidates should encourage the firm to remove the controversial company from the research universe and put it on a restricted list so that the firm disseminates only factual information about the company.

- *Restrict special cost arrangements*: When attending meetings at an issuer's headquarters, members and candidates should pay for commercial transportation and hotel charges. No corporate issuer should reimburse members or candidates for air transportation. Members and candidates should encourage issuers to limit the use of corporate aircraft to situations in which commercial transportation is not available or in which efficient movement could not otherwise be arranged. Members and candidates should take particular care that when frequent meetings are held between an individual issuer and an individual member or candidate, the issuer should not always host the member or candidate.

- *Limit gifts*: Members and candidates must limit the acceptance of gratuities and/or gifts to token items. Standard I(B) does not preclude customary, ordinary business-related entertainment as long as its purpose is not to influence or reward members or candidates. Firms should consider a strict value limit for acceptable gifts that is based on the local or regional customs and should address whether the limit is per gift or an aggregate annual value.

- *Restrict investments*: Members and candidates should encourage their investment firms to develop formal policies related to employee purchases of equity or equity-related IPOs. Firms should require prior approval for employee participation in IPOs, with prompt disclosure of investment actions taken following the offering. Strict limits should be imposed on investment personnel acquiring securities in private placements.
- *Review procedures*: Members and candidates should encourage their firms to implement effective supervisory and review procedures to ensure that analysts and portfolio managers comply with policies relating to their personal investment activities.
- *Independence policy*: Members, candidates, and their firms should establish a formal written policy on the independence and objectivity of research and implement reporting structures and review procedures to ensure that research analysts do not report to and are not supervised or controlled by any department of the firm that could compromise the independence of the analyst. More detailed recommendations related to a firm's policies regarding research objectivity are set forth in the CFA Institute statement *Research Objectivity Standards* (www.cfainstitute.org).
- *Appointed officer*: Firms should appoint a senior officer with oversight responsibilities for compliance with the firm's code of ethics and all regulations concerning its business. Firms should provide every employee with the procedures and policies for reporting potentially unethical behavior, violations of regulations, or other activities that may harm the firm's reputation.

STANDARD I(B): APPLICATION OF THE STANDARD 6

- ☐ demonstrate the application of the Code of Ethics and Standards of Professional Conduct to situations involving issues of professional integrity
- ☐ identify conduct that conforms to the Code and Standards and conduct that violates the Code and Standards

Example 1 (Travel Expenses):

Steven Taylor, a mining analyst with Bronson Brokers, is invited by Precision Metals to join a group of his peers in a tour of mining facilities in several western US states. The company arranges for chartered group flights from site to site and for accommodations in Spartan Motels, the only chain with accommodations near the mines, for three nights. Taylor allows Precision Metals to pick up his tab, as do the other analysts, with one exception—John Adams, an employee of a large trust company who insists on following his company's policy and paying for his hotel room himself.

Comment: The policy of the company where Adams works complies closely with Standard I(B) by avoiding even the appearance of a conflict of interest, but Taylor and the other analysts were not necessarily violating Standard

I(B). In general, when allowing companies to pay for travel and/or accommodations in these circumstances, members and candidates must use their judgment. They must be on guard that such arrangements not impinge on a member's or candidate's independence and objectivity. In this example, the trip was strictly for business and Taylor was not accepting irrelevant or lavish hospitality. The itinerary required chartered flights, for which analysts were not expected to pay. The accommodations were modest. These arrangements are not unusual and did not violate Standard I(B) as long as Taylor's independence and objectivity were not compromised. In the final analysis, members and candidates should consider both whether they can remain objective and whether their integrity might be perceived by their clients to have been compromised.

Example 2 (Research Independence):

Susan Dillon, an analyst in the corporate finance department of an investment services firm, is making a presentation to a potential new business client that includes the promise that her firm will provide full research coverage of the potential client.

> *Comment*: Dillon may agree to provide research coverage, but she must not commit her firm's research department to providing a favorable recommendation. The firm's recommendation (favorable, neutral, or unfavorable) must be based on an independent and objective investigation and analysis of the company and its securities.

Example 3 (Research Independence and Intrafirm Pressure):

Walter Fritz is an equity analyst with Hilton Brokerage who covers the mining industry. He has concluded that the stock of Metals & Mining is overpriced at its current level, but he is concerned that a negative research report will hurt the good relationship between Metals & Mining and the investment banking division of his firm. In fact, a senior manager of Hilton Brokerage has just sent him a copy of a proposal his firm has made to Metals & Mining to underwrite a debt offering. Fritz needs to produce a report right away and is concerned about issuing a less-than-favorable rating.

> *Comment*: Fritz's analysis of Metals & Mining must be objective and based solely on consideration of company fundamentals. Any pressure from other divisions of his firm is inappropriate. This conflict could have been eliminated if, in anticipation of the offering, Hilton Brokerage had placed Metals & Mining on a restricted list for its sales force.

Example 4 (Research Independence and Issuer Relationship Pressure):

As in Example 3, Walter Fritz has concluded that Metals & Mining stock is overvalued at its current level, but he is concerned that a negative research report might jeopardize a close rapport that he has nurtured over the years with Metals & Mining's CEO, chief finance officer, and investment relations officer. Fritz is concerned that a negative report might result also in management retaliation—for instance, cutting him off from participating in conference calls when a quarterly earnings release is made, denying him the ability to ask questions on such calls, and/or denying him access to top management for arranging group meetings between Hilton Brokerage clients and top Metals & Mining managers.

Comment: As in Example 3, Fritz's analysis must be objective and based solely on consideration of company fundamentals. Any pressure from Metals & Mining is inappropriate. Fritz should reinforce the integrity of his conclusions by stressing that his investment recommendation is based on relative valuation, which may include qualitative issues with respect to Metals & Mining's management.

Example 5 (Research Independence and Sales Pressure):

As support for the sales effort of her corporate bond department, Lindsey Warner offers credit guidance to purchasers of fixed-income securities. Her compensation is closely linked to the performance of the corporate bond department. Near the quarter's end, Warner's firm has a large inventory position in the bonds of Milton, Ltd., and has been unable to sell the bonds because of Milton's recent announcement of an operating problem. Salespeople have asked her to contact large clients to push the bonds.

Comment: Unethical sales practices create significant potential violations of the Code and Standards. Warner's opinion of the Milton bonds must not be affected by internal pressure or compensation. In this case, Warner must refuse to push the Milton bonds unless she is able to justify that the market price has already adjusted for the operating problem.

Example 6 (Research Independence and Prior Coverage):

Jill Jorund is a securities analyst following airline stocks and a rising star at her firm. Her boss has been carrying a "buy" recommendation on International Airlines and asks Jorund to take over coverage of that airline. He tells Jorund that under no circumstances should the prevailing buy recommendation be changed.

Comment: Jorund must be independent and objective in her analysis of International Airlines. If she believes that her boss's instructions have compromised her, she has two options: She can tell her boss that she cannot cover the company under these constraints, or she can take over coverage of the company, reach her own independent conclusions, and if they conflict with her boss's opinion, share the conclusions with her boss or other supervisors in the firm so that they can make appropriate recommendations. Jorund must issue only recommendations that reflect her independent and objective opinion.

Example 7 (Gifts and Entertainment from Related Party):

Edward Grant directs a large amount of his commission business to a New York–based brokerage house. In appreciation for all the business, the brokerage house gives Grant two tickets to the World Cup in South Africa, two nights at a nearby resort, several meals, and transportation via limousine to the game. Grant fails to disclose receiving this package to his supervisor.

Comment: Grant has violated Standard I(B) because accepting these substantial gifts may impede his independence and objectivity. Every member and candidate should endeavor to avoid situations that might cause or be perceived to cause a loss of independence or objectivity in recommending investments or taking investment action. By accepting the trip, Grant has opened himself up to the accusation that he may give the broker favored treatment in return.

Example 8 (Gifts and Entertainment from Client):

Theresa Green manages the portfolio of Ian Knowlden, a client of Tisbury Investments. Green achieves an annual return for Knowlden that is consistently better than that of the benchmark she and the client previously agreed to. As a reward, Knowlden offers Green two tickets to Wimbledon and the use of Knowlden's flat in London for a week. Green discloses this gift to her supervisor at Tisbury.

> *Comment*: Green is in compliance with Standard I(B) because she disclosed the gift from one of her clients in accordance with the firm's policies. Members and candidates may accept bonuses or gifts from clients as long as they disclose them to their employer because gifts in a client relationship are deemed less likely to affect a member's or candidate's objectivity and independence than gifts in other situations. Disclosure is required, however, so that supervisors can monitor such situations to guard against employees favoring a gift-giving client to the detriment of other fee-paying clients (such as by allocating a greater proportion of IPO stock to the gift-giving client's portfolio).
>
> Best practices for monitoring include comparing the transaction costs of the Knowlden account with the costs of other accounts managed by Green and other similar accounts within Tisbury. The supervisor could also compare the performance returns with the returns of other clients with the same mandate. This comparison will assist in determining whether a pattern of favoritism by Green is disadvantaging other Tisbury clients or the possibility that this favoritism could affect her future behavior.

Example 9 (Travel Expenses from External Manager):

Tom Wayne is the investment manager of the Franklin City Employees Pension Plan. He recently completed a successful search for a firm to manage the foreign equity allocation of the plan's diversified portfolio. He followed the plan's standard procedure of seeking presentations from a number of qualified firms and recommended that his board select Penguin Advisors because of its experience, well-defined investment strategy, and performance record. The firm claims compliance with the Global Investment Performance Standards (GIPS) and has been verified. Following the selection of Penguin, a reporter from the *Franklin City Record* calls to ask if there was any connection between this action and the fact that Penguin was one of the sponsors of an "investment fact-finding trip to Asia" that Wayne made earlier in the year. The trip was one of several conducted by the Pension Investment Academy, which had arranged the itinerary of meetings with economic, government, and corporate officials in major cities in several Asian countries. The Pension Investment Academy obtains support for the cost of these trips from a number of investment managers, including Penguin Advisors; the Academy then pays the travel expenses of the various pension plan managers on the trip and provides all meals and accommodations. The president of Penguin Advisors was also one of the travelers on the trip.

> *Comment*: Although Wayne can probably put to good use the knowledge he gained from the trip in selecting portfolio managers and in other areas of managing the pension plan, his recommendation of Penguin Advisors may be tainted by the possible conflict incurred when he participated in

a trip partly paid for by Penguin Advisors and when he was in the daily company of the president of Penguin Advisors. To avoid violating Standard I(B), Wayne's basic expenses for travel and accommodations should have been paid by his employer or the pension plan; contact with the president of Penguin Advisors should have been limited to informational or educational events only; and the trip, the organizer, and the sponsor should have been made a matter of public record. Even if his actions were not in violation of Standard I(B), Wayne should have been sensitive to the public perception of the trip when reported in the newspaper and the extent to which the subjective elements of his decision might have been affected by the familiarity that the daily contact of such a trip would encourage. This advantage would probably not be shared by firms competing with Penguin Advisors.

Example 10 (Research Independence and Compensation Arrangements):

Javier Herrero recently left his job as a research analyst for a large investment adviser. While looking for a new position, he was hired by an investor-relations firm to write a research report on one of its clients, a small educational software company. The investor-relations firm hopes to generate investor interest in the technology company. The firm will pay Herrero a flat fee plus a bonus if any new investors buy stock in the company as a result of Herrero's report.

> *Comment*: If Herrero accepts this payment arrangement, he will be in violation of Standard I(B) because the compensation arrangement can reasonably be expected to compromise his independence and objectivity. Herrero will receive a bonus for attracting investors, which provides an incentive to draft a positive report regardless of the facts and to ignore or play down any negative information about the company. Herrero should accept only a flat fee that is not tied to the conclusions or recommendations of the report. Issuer-paid research that is objective and unbiased can be done under the right circumstances as long as the analyst takes steps to maintain his or her objectivity and includes in the report proper disclosures regarding potential conflicts of interest.

Example 11 (Recommendation Objectivity and Service Fees):

Two years ago, Bob Wade, trust manager for Central Midas Bank, was approached by Western Funds about promoting its family of funds, with special interest in the service-fee class of funds. To entice Central to promote this class, Western Funds offered to pay the bank a service fee of 0.25%. Without disclosing the fee being offered to the bank, Wade asked one of the investment managers to review Western's funds to determine whether they were suitable for clients of Central Midas Bank. The manager completed the normal due diligence review and determined that the new funds were fairly valued in the market with fee structures on a par with competitors. Wade decided to accept Western's offer and instructed the team of portfolio managers to exclusively promote these funds and the service-fee class to clients seeking to invest new funds or transfer from their current investments.

Now, two years later, the funds managed by Western begin to underperform their peers. Wade is counting on the fees to reach his profitability targets and continues to push these funds as acceptable investments for Central's clients.

Comment: Wade is violating Standard I(B) because the fee arrangement has affected the objectivity of his recommendations. Wade is relying on the fee as a component of the department's profitability and is unwilling to offer other products that may affect the fees received.

See also Standard VI(A)–Disclosure of Conflicts.

Example 12 (Recommendation Objectivity):

Bob Thompson has been doing research for the portfolio manager of the fixed-income department. His assignment is to do sensitivity analysis on securitized subprime mortgages. He has discussed with the manager possible scenarios to use to calculate expected returns. A key assumption in such calculations is housing price appreciation (HPA) because it drives "prepays" (prepayments of mortgages) and losses. Thompson is concerned with the significant appreciation experienced over the previous five years as a result of the increased availability of funds from subprime mortgages. Thompson insists that the analysis should include a scenario run with –10% for Year 1, –5% for Year 2, and then (to project a worst-case scenario) 0% for Years 3 through 5. The manager replies that these assumptions are too dire because there has never been a time in their available database when HPA was negative.

Thompson conducts his research to better understand the risks inherent in these securities and evaluates these securities in the worst-case scenario, an unlikely but possible environment. Based on the results of the enhanced scenarios, Thompson does not recommend the purchase of the securitization. Against the general market trends, the manager follows Thompson's recommendation and does not invest. The following year, the housing market collapses. In avoiding the subprime investments, the manager's portfolio outperforms its peer group that year.

Comment: Thompson's actions in running the worst-case scenario against the protests of the portfolio manager are in alignment with the principles of Standard I(B). Thompson did not allow his research to be pressured by the general trends of the market or the manager's desire to limit the research to historical norms.

See also Standard V(A)–Diligence and Reasonable Basis.

Example 13 (Influencing Manager Selection Decisions):

Adrian Mandel, CFA, is a senior portfolio manager for ZZYY Capital Management who oversees a team of investment professionals who manage labor union pension funds. A few years ago, ZZYY sought to win a competitive asset manager search to manage a significant allocation of the pension fund of the United Doughnut and Pretzel Bakers Union (UDPBU). UDPBU's investment board is chaired by a recognized key decision maker and long-time leader of the union, Ernesto Gomez. To improve ZZYY's chances of winning the competition, Mandel made significant monetary contributions to Gomez's union reelection campaign fund. Even after ZZYY was hired as a primary manager of the pension, Mandel believed that his firm's position was not secure. Mandel continued to contribute to Gomez's reelection campaign chest as well as to entertain lavishly the union leader and his family at top restaurants on a regular basis. All of Mandel's outlays were routinely handled as marketing expenses reimbursed by ZZYY's expense accounts and were disclosed to his senior management as being instrumental in maintaining a strong close relationship with an important client.

Comment: Mandel not only offered but actually gave monetary gifts, benefits, and other considerations that reasonably could be expected to compromise Gomez's objectivity. Therefore, Mandel was in violation of Standard I(B).

Example 14 (Influencing Manager Selection Decisions):

Adrian Mandel, CFA, had heard about the manager search competition for the UDPBU Pension Fund through a broker/dealer contact. The contact told him that a well-known retired professional golfer, Bobby "The Bear" Finlay, who had become a licensed broker/dealer serving as a pension consultant, was orchestrating the UDPBU manager search. Finlay had gained celebrity status with several labor union pension fund boards by entertaining their respective board members and regaling them with colorful stories of fellow pro golfers' antics in clubhouses around the world. Mandel decided to improve ZZYY's chances of being invited to participate in the search competition by befriending Finlay to curry his favor. Knowing Finlay's love of entertainment, Mandel wined and dined Finlay at high-profile bistros where Finlay could glow in the fan recognition lavished on him by all the other patrons. Mandel's endeavors paid off handsomely when Finlay recommended to the UDPBU board that ZZYY be entered as one of three finalist asset management firms in its search.

> *Comment*: Similar to Example 13, Mandel lavished gifts, benefits, and other considerations in the form of expensive entertainment that could reasonably be expected to influence the consultant to recommend the hiring of his firm. Therefore, Mandel was in violation of Standard I(B).

Example 15 (Fund Manager Relationships):

Amie Scott is a performance analyst within her firm with responsibilities for analyzing the performance of external managers. While completing her quarterly analysis, Scott notices a change in one manager's reported composite construction. The change concealed the bad performance of a particularly large account by placing that account into a new residual composite. This change allowed the manager to remain at the top of the list of manager performance. Scott knows her firm has a large allocation to this manager, and the fund's manager is a close personal friend of the CEO. She needs to deliver her final report but is concerned with pointing out the composite change.

> *Comment*: Scott would be in violation of Standard I(B) if she did not disclose the change in her final report. The analysis of managers' performance should not be influenced by personal relationships or the size of the allocation to the outside managers. By not including the change, Scott would not be providing an independent analysis of the performance metrics for her firm.

Example 16 (Intrafirm Pressure):

Jill Stein is head of performance measurement for her firm. During the last quarter, many members of the organization's research department were removed because of the poor quality of their recommendations. The subpar research caused one larger account holder to experience significant underperformance, which resulted in the client withdrawing his money after the end of the quarter. The head of sales requests that Stein remove this account from the firm's performance composite because the performance decline can be attributed to the departed research team and not the client's adviser.

> *Comment*: Pressure from other internal departments can create situations that cause a member or candidate to violate the Code and Standards. Stein must maintain her independence and objectivity and refuse to exclude specific accounts from the firm's performance composites to which they

belong. As long as the client invested under a strategy similar to that of the defined composite, it cannot be excluded because of the poor stock selections that led to the underperformance and asset withdrawal.

7 STANDARD I(C): PROFESSIONALISM – MISREPRESENTATION

☐ demonstrate the application of the Code of Ethics and Standards of Professional Conduct to situations involving issues of professional integrity

> Members and Candidates must not knowingly make any misrepresentations relating to investment analysis, recommendations, actions, or other professional activities.

Guidance

Highlights:

- *Impact on Investment Practice*
- *Performance Reporting*
- *Social Media*
- *Omissions*
- *Plagiarism*
- *Work Completed for Employer*

Trust is the foundation of the investment profession. Investors must be able to rely on the statements and information provided to them by those with whom the investors have trusted their financial well-being. Investment professionals who make false or misleading statements not only harm investors but also reduce the level of investor confidence in the investment profession and threaten the integrity of capital markets as a whole.

A misrepresentation is any untrue statement or omission of a fact or any statement that is otherwise false or misleading. A member or candidate must not knowingly omit or misrepresent information or give a false impression of a firm, organization, or security in the member's or candidate's oral representations, advertising (whether in the press or through brochures), electronic communications, or written materials (whether publicly disseminated or not). In this context, "knowingly" means that the member or candidate either knows or should have known that the misrepresentation was being made or that omitted information could alter the investment decision-making process.

Written materials include, but are not limited to, research reports, underwriting documents, company financial reports, market letters, newspaper columns, and books. Electronic communications include, but are not limited to, internet communications, webpages, mobile applications, and e-mails. Members and candidates who use webpages should regularly monitor materials posted on these sites to ensure that they contain current information. Members and candidates should also ensure that all reasonable precautions have been taken to protect the site's integrity and security and that the site does not misrepresent any information and does provide full disclosure.

Standard I(C) prohibits members and candidates from guaranteeing clients any specific return on volatile investments. Most investments contain some element of risk that makes their return inherently unpredictable. For such investments, guaranteeing either a particular rate of return or a guaranteed preservation of investment capital (e.g., "I can guarantee that you will earn 8% on equities this year" or "I can guarantee that you will not lose money on this investment") is misleading to investors. Standard I(C) does not prohibit members and candidates from providing clients with information on investment products that have guarantees built into the structure of the products themselves or for which an institution has agreed to cover any losses.

Impact on Investment Practice

Members and candidates must not misrepresent any aspect of their practice, including (but not limited to) their qualifications or credentials, the qualifications or services provided by their firm, their performance record and the record of their firm, and the characteristics of an investment. Any misrepresentation made by a member or candidate relating to the member's or candidate's professional activities is a breach of this standard.

Members and candidates should exercise care and diligence when incorporating third-party information. Misrepresentations resulting from the use of the credit ratings, research, testimonials, or marketing materials of outside parties become the responsibility of the investment professional when it affects that professional's business practices.

Investing through outside managers continues to expand as an acceptable method of investing in areas outside a firm's core competencies. Members and candidates must disclose their intended use of external managers and must not represent those managers' investment practices as their own. Although the level of involvement of outside managers may change over time, appropriate disclosures by members and candidates are important in avoiding misrepresentations, especially if the primary activity is to invest directly with a single external manager. Standard V(B)–Communication with Clients and Prospective Clients discusses in further detail communicating the firm's investment practices.

Performance Reporting

The performance benchmark selection process is another area where misrepresentations may occur. Members and candidates may misrepresent the success of their performance record through presenting benchmarks that are not comparable to their strategies. Further, clients can be misled if the benchmark's results are not reported on a basis comparable to that of the fund's or client's results. Best practice is selecting the most appropriate available benchmark from a universe of available options. The transparent presentation of appropriate performance benchmarks is an important aspect in providing clients with information that is useful in making investment decisions.

However, Standard I(C) does not require that a benchmark always be provided in order to comply. Some investment strategies may not lend themselves to displaying an appropriate benchmark because of the complexity or diversity of the investments included. Furthermore, some investment strategies may use reference indexes that do not reflect the opportunity set of the invested assets—for example, a hedge fund comparing its performance with a "cash plus" basis. When such a benchmark is used, members and candidates should make reasonable efforts to ensure that they disclose the reasons behind the use of this reference index to avoid misrepresentations of their performance. Members and candidates should discuss with clients on a continuous basis the appropriate benchmark to be used for performance evaluations and related fee calculations.

Reporting misrepresentations may also occur when valuations for illiquid or non-traded securities are available from more than one source. When different options are available, members and candidates may be tempted to switch providers to obtain higher security valuations. The process of shopping for values may misrepresent a security's worth, lead to misinformed decisions to sell or hold an investment, and result in overcharging clients advisory fees.

Members and candidates should take reasonable steps to provide accurate and reliable security pricing information to clients on a consistent basis. Changing pricing providers should not be based solely on the justification that the new provider reports a higher current value of a security. Consistency in the reported information will improve the perception of the valuation process for illiquid securities. Clients will likely have additional confidence that they were able to make an informed decision about continuing to hold these securities in their portfolios.

Social Media

The advancement of online discussion forums and communication platforms, commonly referred to as "social media," is placing additional responsibilities on members and candidates. When communicating through social media channels, members and candidates should provide only the same information they are allowed to distribute to clients and potential clients through other traditional forms of communication. The online or interactive aspects of social media do not remove the need to be open and honest about the information being distributed.

Along with understanding and following existing and newly developing rules and regulations regarding the allowed use of social media, members and candidates should also ensure that all communications in this format adhere to the requirements of the Code and Standards. The perceived anonymity granted through these platforms may entice individuals to misrepresent their qualifications or abilities or those of their employer. Actions undertaken through social media that knowingly misrepresent investment recommendations or professional activities are considered a violation of Standard I(C).

Omissions

The omission of a fact or outcome can be misleading, especially given the growing use of models and technical analysis processes. Many members and candidates rely on such models and processes to scan for new investment opportunities, to develop investment vehicles, and to produce investment recommendations and ratings. When inputs are knowingly omitted, the resulting outcomes may provide misleading information to those who rely on it for making investment decisions. Additionally, the outcomes from models shall not be presented as fact because they represent the expected results based on the inputs and analysis process incorporated.

Omissions in the performance measurement and attribution process can also misrepresent a manager's performance and skill. Members and candidates should encourage their firms to develop strict policies for composite development to prevent cherry picking—situations in which selected accounts are presented as representative of the firm's abilities. The omission of any accounts appropriate for the defined composite may misrepresent to clients the success of the manager's implementation of its strategy.

Standard I(C): Professionalism – Misrepresentation

Plagiarism

Standard I(C) also prohibits plagiarism in the preparation of material for distribution to employers, associates, clients, prospects, or the general public. Plagiarism is defined as copying or using in substantially the same form materials prepared by others without acknowledging the source of the material or identifying the author and publisher of such material. Members and candidates must not copy (or represent as their own) original ideas or material without permission and must acknowledge and identify the source of ideas or material that is not their own.

The investment profession uses a myriad of financial, economic, and statistical data in the investment decision-making process. Through various publications and presentations, the investment professional is constantly exposed to the work of others and to the temptation to use that work without proper acknowledgment.

Misrepresentation through plagiarism in investment management can take various forms. The simplest and most flagrant example is to take a research report or study done by another firm or person, change the names, and release the material as one's own original analysis. This action is a clear violation of Standard I(C). Other practices include (1) using excerpts from articles or reports prepared by others either verbatim or with only slight changes in wording without acknowledgment, (2) citing specific quotations as attributable to "leading analysts" and "investment experts" without naming the specific references, (3) presenting statistical estimates of forecasts prepared by others and identifying the sources but without including the qualifying statements or caveats that may have been used, (4) using charts and graphs without stating their sources, and (5) copying proprietary computerized spreadsheets or algorithms without seeking the cooperation or authorization of their creators.

In the case of distributing third-party, outsourced research, members and candidates may use and distribute such reports as long as they do not represent themselves as the report's authors. Indeed, the member or candidate may add value for the client by sifting through research and repackaging it for clients. In such cases, clients should be fully informed that they are paying for the ability of the member or candidate to find the best research from a wide variety of sources. Members and candidates must not misrepresent their abilities, the extent of their expertise, or the extent of their work in a way that would mislead their clients or prospective clients. Members and candidates should disclose whether the research being presented to clients comes from another source—from either within or outside the member's or candidate's firm. This allows clients to understand who has the expertise behind the report or whether the work is being done by the analyst, other members of the firm, or an outside party.

Standard I(C) also applies to plagiarism in oral communications, such as through group meetings; visits with associates, clients, and customers; use of audio/video media (which is rapidly increasing); and telecommunications, including electronic data transfer and the outright copying of electronic media.

One of the most egregious practices in violation of this standard is the preparation of research reports based on multiple sources of information without acknowledging the sources. Examples of information from such sources include ideas, statistical compilations, and forecasts combined to give the appearance of original work. Although there is no monopoly on ideas, members and candidates must give credit where it is clearly due. Analysts should not use undocumented forecasts, earnings projections, asset values, and so on. Sources must be revealed to bring the responsibility directly back to the author of the report or the firm involved.

Work Completed for Employer

The preceding paragraphs address actions that would constitute a violation of Standard I(C). In some situations, however, members or candidates may use research conducted or models developed by others within the same firm without committing a violation.

The most common example relates to the situation in which one (or more) of the original analysts is no longer with the firm. Research and models developed while employed by a firm are the property of the firm. The firm retains the right to continue using the work completed after a member or candidate has left the organization. The firm may issue future reports without providing attribution to the prior analysts. A member or candidate cannot, however, reissue a previously released report solely under his or her name.

STANDARD I(C): RECOMMENDED PROCEDURES

☐ recommend practices and procedures designed to prevent violations of the Code of Ethics and Standards of Professional Conduct

Factual Presentations

Members and candidates can prevent unintentional misrepresentations of their qualifications or the services they or their firms provide if each member and candidate understands the limit of the firm's or individual's capabilities and the need to be accurate and complete in presentations. Firms can provide guidance for employees who make written or oral presentations to clients or potential clients by providing a written list of the firm's available services and a description of the firm's qualifications. This list should suggest ways of describing the firm's services, qualifications, and compensation that are both accurate and suitable for client or customer presentations. Firms can also help prevent misrepresentation by specifically designating which employees are authorized to speak on behalf of the firm. Regardless of whether the firm provides guidance, members and candidates should make certain that they understand the services the firm can perform and its qualifications.

Qualification Summary

In addition, to ensure accurate presentations to clients, each member and candidate should prepare a summary of his or her own qualifications and experience and a list of the services the member or candidate is capable of performing. Firms can assist member and candidate compliance by periodically reviewing employee correspondence and documents that contain representations of individual or firm qualifications.

Verify Outside Information

When providing information to clients from a third party, members and candidates share a responsibility for the accuracy of the marketing and distribution materials that pertain to the third party's capabilities, services, and products. Misrepresentation by third parties can damage the member's or candidate's reputation, the reputation of the firm, and the integrity of the capital markets. Members and candidates should encourage their employers to develop procedures for verifying information of third-party firms.

Maintain Webpages

Members and candidates who publish a webpage should regularly monitor materials posted on the site to ensure that the site contains current information. Members and candidates should also ensure that all reasonable precautions have been taken to protect the site's integrity, confidentiality, and security and that the site does not misrepresent any information and provides full disclosure.

Plagiarism Policy

To avoid plagiarism in preparing research reports or conclusions of analysis, members and candidates should take the following steps:

- *Maintain copies*: Keep copies of all research reports, articles containing research ideas, material with new statistical methodologies, and other materials that were relied on in preparing the research report.
- *Attribute quotations*: Attribute to their sources any direct quotations, including projections, tables, statistics, model/product ideas, and new methodologies prepared by persons other than recognized financial and statistical reporting services or similar sources.
- *Attribute summaries*: Attribute to their sources any paraphrases or summaries of material prepared by others. For example, to support his analysis of Brown Company's competitive position, the author of a research report on Brown might summarize another analyst's report on Brown's chief competitor, but the author of the Brown report must acknowledge in his own report the reliance on the other analyst's report.

STANDARD I(C): APPLICATION OF THE STANDARD

- ☐ demonstrate the application of the Code of Ethics and Standards of Professional Conduct to situations involving issues of professional integrity
- ☐ identify conduct that conforms to the Code and Standards and conduct that violates the Code and Standards

Example 1 (Disclosure of Issuer-Paid Research):

Anthony McGuire is an issuer-paid analyst hired by publicly traded companies to electronically promote their stocks. McGuire creates a website that promotes his research efforts as a seemingly independent analyst. McGuire posts a profile and a strong buy recommendation for each company on the website indicating that the stock is expected to increase in value. He does not disclose the contractual relationships with the companies he covers on his website, in the research reports he issues, or in the statements he makes about the companies in internet chat rooms.

> *Comment*: McGuire has violated Standard I(C) because the website is misleading to potential investors. Even if the recommendations are valid and supported with thorough research, his omissions regarding the true relationship between himself and the companies he covers constitute a

misrepresentation. McGuire has also violated Standard VI(A)–Disclosure of Conflicts by not disclosing the existence of an arrangement with the companies through which he receives compensation in exchange for his services.

Example 2 (Correction of Unintentional Errors):

Hijan Yao is responsible for the creation and distribution of the marketing materials for his firm, which claims compliance with the GIPS standards. Yao creates and distributes a presentation of performance by the firm's Asian equity composite that states the composite has ¥350 billion in assets. In fact, the composite has only ¥35 billion in assets, and the higher figure on the presentation is a result of a typographical error. Nevertheless, the erroneous material is distributed to a number of clients before Yao catches the mistake.

Comment: Once the error is discovered, Yao must take steps to cease distribution of the incorrect material and correct the error by informing those who have received the erroneous information. Because Yao did not knowingly make the misrepresentation, however, he did not violate Standard I(C). Because his firm claims compliance with the GIPS standards, it must also comply with the GIPS Guidance Statement on Error Correction in relation to the error.

Example 3 (Noncorrection of Known Errors):

Syed Muhammad is the president of an investment management firm. The promotional material for the firm, created by the firm's marketing department, incorrectly claims that Muhammad has an advanced degree in finance from a prestigious business school in addition to the CFA designation. Although Muhammad attended the school for a short period of time, he did not receive a degree. Over the years, Muhammad and others in the firm have distributed this material to numerous prospective clients and consultants.

Comment: Even though Muhammad may not have been directly responsible for the misrepresentation of his credentials in the firm's promotional material, he used this material numerous times over an extended period and should have known of the misrepresentation. Thus, Muhammad has violated Standard I(C).

Example 4 (Plagiarism):

Cindy Grant, a research analyst for a Canadian brokerage firm, has specialized in the Canadian mining industry for the past 10 years. She recently read an extensive research report on Jefferson Mining, Ltd., by Jeremy Barton, another analyst. Barton provided extensive statistics on the mineral reserves, production capacity, selling rates, and marketing factors affecting Jefferson's operations. He also noted that initial drilling results on a new ore body, which had not been made public, might show the existence of mineral zones that could increase the life of Jefferson's main mines, but Barton cited no specific data as to the initial drilling results. Grant called an officer of Jefferson, who gave her the initial drilling results over the telephone. The data indicated that the expected life of the main mines would be tripled. Grant added these statistics to Barton's report and circulated it within her firm as her own report.

Standard I(C): Application of the Standard

Comment: Grant plagiarized Barton's report by reproducing large parts of it in her own report without acknowledgment.

Example 5 (Misrepresentation of Information):

When Ricki Marks sells mortgage-backed derivatives called "interest-only strips" (IOs) to public pension plan clients, she describes them as "guaranteed by the US government." Purchasers of the IOs are entitled only to the interest stream generated by the mortgages, however, not the notional principal itself. One particular municipality's investment policies and local law require that securities purchased by its public pension plans be guaranteed by the US government. Although the underlying mortgages are guaranteed, neither the investor's investment nor the interest stream on the IOs is guaranteed. When interest rates decline, causing an increase in prepayment of mortgages, interest payments to the IOs' investors decline, and these investors lose a portion of their investment.

Comment: Marks violated Standard I(C) by misrepresenting the terms and character of the investment.

Example 6 (Potential Information Misrepresentation):

Khalouck Abdrabbo manages the investments of several high-net-worth individuals in the United States who are approaching retirement. Abdrabbo advises these individuals that a portion of their investments be moved from equity to bank-sponsored certificates of deposit and money market accounts so that the principal will be "guaranteed" up to a certain amount. The interest is not guaranteed.

Comment: Although there is risk that the institution offering the certificates of deposits and money market accounts could go bankrupt, in the United States, these accounts are insured by the US government through the Federal Deposit Insurance Corporation. Therefore, using the term "guaranteed" in this context is not inappropriate as long as the amount is within the government-insured limit. Abdrabbo should explain these facts to the clients.

Example 7 (Plagiarism):

Steve Swanson is a senior analyst in the investment research department of Ballard and Company. Apex Corporation has asked Ballard to assist in acquiring the majority ownership of stock in the Campbell Company, a financial consulting firm, and to prepare a report recommending that stockholders of Campbell agree to the acquisition. Another investment firm, Davis and Company, had already prepared a report for Apex analyzing both Apex and Campbell and recommending an exchange ratio. Apex has given the Davis report to Ballard officers, who have passed it on to Swanson. Swanson reviews the Davis report and other available material on Apex and Campbell. From his analysis, he concludes that the common stocks of Campbell and Apex represent good value at their current prices; he believes, however, that the Davis report does not consider all the factors a Campbell stockholder would need to know to make a decision. Swanson reports his conclusions to the partner in charge, who tells him to "use the Davis report, change a few words, sign your name, and get it out."

Comment: If Swanson does as requested, he will violate Standard I(C). He could refer to those portions of the Davis report that he agrees with if he identifies Davis as the source; he could then add his own analysis and conclusions to the report before signing and distributing it.

Example 8 (Plagiarism):

Claude Browning, a quantitative analyst for Double Alpha, Inc., returns from a seminar in great excitement. At that seminar, Jack Jorrely, a well-known quantitative analyst at a national brokerage firm, discussed one of his new models in great detail, and Browning is intrigued by the new concepts. He proceeds to test the model, making some minor mechanical changes but retaining the concepts, until he produces some very positive results. Browning quickly announces to his supervisors at Double Alpha that he has discovered a new model and that clients and prospective clients should be informed of this positive finding as ongoing proof of Double Alpha's continuing innovation and ability to add value.

Comment: Although Browning tested Jorrely's model on his own and even slightly modified it, he must still acknowledge the original source of the idea. Browning can certainly take credit for the final, practical results; he can also support his conclusions with his own test. The credit for the innovative thinking, however, must be awarded to Jorrely.

Example 9 (Plagiarism):

Fernando Zubia would like to include in his firm's marketing materials some "plain-language" descriptions of various concepts, such as the price-to-earnings (P/E) multiple and why standard deviation is used as a measure of risk. The descriptions come from other sources, but Zubia wishes to use them without reference to the original authors. Would this use of material be a violation of Standard I(C)?

Comment: Copying verbatim any material without acknowledgement, including plain-language descriptions of the P/E multiple and standard deviation, violates Standard I(C). Even though these concepts are general, best practice would be for Zubia to describe them in his own words or cite the sources from which the descriptions are quoted. Members and candidates would be violating Standard I(C) if they either were responsible for creating marketing materials without attribution or knowingly use plagiarized materials.

Example 10 (Plagiarism):

Through a mainstream media outlet, Erika Schneider learns about a study that she would like to cite in her research. Should she cite both the mainstream intermediary source as well as the author of the study itself when using that information?

Comment: In all instances, a member or candidate must cite the actual source of the information. Best practice for Schneider would be to obtain the information directly from the author and review it before citing it in a report. In that case, Schneider would not need to report how she found out about the information. For example, suppose Schneider read in the *Financial Times* about a study issued by CFA Institute; best practice for Schneider would be to obtain a copy of the study from CFA Institute, review it, and then cite it in her report. If she does not use any interpretation of the report from the *Financial Times* and the newspaper does not add value to the report itself, the newspaper is merely a conduit of the original information and does not need to be cited. If she does not obtain the report and review the information, Schneider runs the risk of relying on second-hand information that may misstate facts. If, for example, the *Financial Times* erroneously reported some information from the original CFA Institute study and Schneider copied that erroneous information without acknowledging CFA Institute, she could be the object of complaints. Best practice would be either to obtain the complete study from its original author and cite only that author or to use the information provided by the intermediary and cite both sources.

Example 11 (Misrepresentation of Information):

Paul Ostrowski runs a two-person investment management firm. Ostrowski's firm subscribes to a service from a large investment research firm that provides research reports that can be repackaged by smaller firms for those firms' clients. Ostrowski's firm distributes these reports to clients as its own work.

> *Comment*: Ostrowski can rely on third-party research that has a reasonable and adequate basis, but he cannot imply that he is the author of such research. If he does, Ostrowski is misrepresenting the extent of his work in a way that misleads the firm's clients or prospective clients.

Example 12 (Misrepresentation of Information):

Tom Stafford is part of a team within Appleton Investment Management responsible for managing a pool of assets for Open Air Bank, which distributes structured securities to offshore clients. He becomes aware that Open Air is promoting the structured securities as a much less risky investment than the investment management policy followed by him and the team to manage the original pool of assets. Also, Open Air has procured an independent rating for the pool that significantly overstates the quality of the investments. Stafford communicates his concerns to his supervisor, who responds that Open Air owns the product and is responsible for all marketing and distribution. Stafford's supervisor goes on to say that the product is outside of the US regulatory regime that Appleton follows and that all risks of the product are disclosed at the bottom of page 184 of the prospectus.

> *Comment*: As a member of the investment team, Stafford is qualified to recognize the degree of accuracy of the materials that characterize the portfolio, and he is correct to be worried about Appleton's responsibility for a misrepresentation of the risks. Thus, he should continue to pursue the issue of Open Air's inaccurate promotion of the portfolio according to the firm's policies and procedures.
>
> The Code and Standards stress protecting the reputation of the firm and the sustainability and integrity of the capital markets. Misrepresenting the quality and risks associated with the investment pool may lead to negative consequences for others well beyond the direct investors.

Example 13 (Avoiding a Misrepresentation):

Trina Smith is a fixed-income portfolio manager at a pension fund. She has observed that the market for highly structured mortgages is the focus of salespeople she meets and that these products represent a significant number of trading opportunities. In discussions about this topic with her team, Smith learns that calculating yields on changing cash flows within the deal structure requires very specialized vendor software. After more research, they find out that each deal is unique and that deals can have more than a dozen layers and changing cash flow priorities. Smith comes to the conclusion that, because of the complexity of these securities, the team cannot effectively distinguish between potentially good and bad investment options. To avoid misrepresenting their understanding, the team decides that the highly structured mortgage segment of the securitized market should not become part of the core of the fund's portfolio; they will allow some of the less complex securities to be part of the core.

> *Comment*: Smith is in compliance with Standard I(C) by not investing in securities that she and her team cannot effectively understand. Because she is not able to describe the risk and return profile of the securities to the pension fund beneficiaries and trustees, she appropriately limits the fund's exposure to this sector.

Example 14 (Misrepresenting Composite Construction):

Robert Palmer is head of performance for a fund manager. When asked to provide performance numbers to fund rating agencies, he avoids mentioning that the fund manager is quite liberal in composite construction. The reason accounts are included/excluded is not fully explained. The performance values reported to the rating agencies for the composites, although accurate for the accounts shown each period, may not present a true representation of the fund manager's ability.

> *Comment*: "Cherry picking" accounts to include in either published reports or information provided to rating agencies conflicts with Standard I(C). Moving accounts into or out of a composite to influence the overall performance results materially misrepresents the reported values over time. Palmer should work with his firm to strengthen its reporting practices concerning composite construction to avoid misrepresenting the firm's track record or the quality of the information being provided.

Example 15 (Presenting Out-of-Date Information):

David Finch is a sales director at a commercial bank, where he directs the bank's client advisers in the sale of third-party mutual funds. Each quarter, he holds a division-wide training session where he provides fact sheets on investment funds the bank is allowed to offer to clients. These fact sheets, which can be redistributed to potential clients, are created by the fund firms and contain information about the funds, including investment strategy and target distribution rates.

Finch knows that some of the fact sheets are out of date; for example, one long-only fund approved the use of significant leverage last quarter as a method to enhance returns. He continues to provide the sheets to the sales team without updates because the bank has no control over the marketing material released by the mutual fund firms.

> *Comment*: Finch is violating Standard I(C) by providing information that misrepresents aspects of the funds. By not providing the sales team and, ultimately, the clients with the updated information, he is misrepresenting

the potential risks associated with the funds with outdated fact sheets. Finch can instruct the sales team to clarify the deficiencies in the fact sheets with clients and ensure they have the most recent fund prospectus document before accepting orders for investing in any fund.

Example 16 (Overemphasis of Firm Results):

Bob Anderson is chief compliance officer for Optima Asset Management Company, a firm currently offering eight funds to clients. Seven of the eight had 10-year returns below the median for their respective sectors. Anderson approves a recent advertisement, which includes this statement: "Optima Asset Management is achieving excellent returns for its investors. The Optima Emerging Markets Equity fund, for example, has 10-year returns that exceed the sector median by more than 10%."

> *Comment*: From the information provided it is difficult to determine whether a violation has occurred as long as the sector outperformance is correct. Anderson may be attempting to mislead potential clients by citing the performance of the sole fund that achieved such results. Past performance is often used to demonstrate a firm's skill and abilities in comparison to funds in the same sectors.
>
> However, if all the funds outperformed their respective benchmarks, then Anderson's assertion that the company "is achieving excellent returns" may be factual. Funds may exhibit positive returns for investors, exceed benchmarks, and yet have returns below the median in their sectors.
>
> Members and candidates need to ensure that their marketing efforts do not include statements that misrepresent their skills and abilities to remain compliant with Standard I(C). Unless the returns of a single fund reflect the performance of a firm as a whole, the use of a singular fund for performance comparisons should be avoided.

STANDARD I(D): PROFESSIONALISM – MISCONDUCT 10

☐ demonstrate the application of the Code of Ethics and Standards of Professional Conduct to situations involving issues of professional integrity

> Members and Candidates must not engage in any professional conduct involving dishonesty, fraud, or deceit or commit any act that reflects adversely on their professional reputation, integrity, or competence.

Guidance

Whereas Standard I(A) addresses the obligation of members and candidates to comply with applicable law that governs their professional activities, Standard I(D) addresses *all* conduct that reflects poorly on the professional integrity, good reputation, or competence of members and candidates. Any act that involves lying, cheating, stealing, or other dishonest conduct is a violation of this standard if the offense reflects adversely on a member's or candidate's professional activities. Although CFA Institute discourages any sort of unethical behavior by members and candidates, the Code and Standards are primarily aimed at conduct and actions related to a member's or candidate's professional life.

Conduct that damages trustworthiness or competence may include behavior that, although not illegal, nevertheless negatively affects a member's or candidate's ability to perform his or her responsibilities. For example, abusing alcohol during business hours might constitute a violation of this standard because it could have a detrimental effect on the member's or candidate's ability to fulfill his or her professional responsibilities. Personal bankruptcy may not reflect on the integrity or trustworthiness of the person declaring bankruptcy, but if the circumstances of the bankruptcy involve fraudulent or deceitful business conduct, the bankruptcy may be a violation of this standard.

In some cases, the absence of appropriate conduct or the lack of sufficient effort may be a violation of Standard I(D). The integrity of the investment profession is built on trust. A member or candidate—whether an investment banker, rating or research analyst, or portfolio manager—is expected to conduct the necessary due diligence to properly understand the nature and risks of an investment before making an investment recommendation. By not taking these steps and, instead, relying on someone else in the process to perform them, members or candidates may violate the trust their clients have placed in them. This loss of trust may have a significant impact on the reputation of the member or candidate and the operations of the financial market as a whole.

Individuals may attempt to abuse the CFA Institute Professional Conduct Program by actively seeking CFA Institute enforcement of the Code and Standards, and Standard I(D) in particular, as a method of settling personal, political, or other disputes unrelated to professional ethics. CFA Institute is aware of this issue, and appropriate disciplinary policies, procedures, and enforcement mechanisms are in place to address misuse of the Code and Standards and the Professional Conduct Program in this way.

11 STANDARD I(D): RECOMMENDED PROCEDURES

☐ recommend practices and procedures designed to prevent violations of the Code of Ethics and Standards of Professional Conduct

In addition to ensuring that their own behavior is consistent with Standard I(D), to prevent general misconduct, members and candidates should encourage their firms to adopt the following policies and procedures to support the principles of Standard I(D):

- *Code of ethics*: Develop and/or adopt a code of ethics to which every employee must subscribe, and make clear that any personal behavior that reflects poorly on the individual involved, the institution as a whole, or the investment industry will not be tolerated.
- *List of violations*: Disseminate to all employees a list of potential violations and associated disciplinary sanctions, up to and including dismissal from the firm.
- *Employee references*: Check references of potential employees to ensure that they are of good character and not ineligible to work in the investment industry because of past infractions of the law.

STANDARD I(D): APPLICATION OF THE STANDARD

- [ ] demonstrate the application of the Code of Ethics and Standards of Professional Conduct to situations involving issues of professional integrity
- [ ] identify conduct that conforms to the Code and Standards and conduct that violates the Code and Standards

Example 1 (Professionalism and Competence):

Simon Sasserman is a trust investment officer at a bank in a small affluent town. He enjoys lunching every day with friends at the country club, where his clients have observed him having numerous drinks. Back at work after lunch, he clearly is intoxicated while making investment decisions. His colleagues make a point of handling any business with Sasserman in the morning because they distrust his judgment after lunch.

> *Comment*: Sasserman's excessive drinking at lunch and subsequent intoxication at work constitute a violation of Standard I(D) because this conduct has raised questions about his professionalism and competence. His behavior reflects poorly on him, his employer, and the investment industry.

Example 2 (Fraud and Deceit):

Howard Hoffman, a security analyst at ATZ Brothers, Inc., a large brokerage house, submits reimbursement forms over a two-year period to ATZ's self-funded health insurance program for more than two dozen bills, most of which have been altered to increase the amount due. An investigation by the firm's director of employee benefits uncovers the inappropriate conduct. ATZ subsequently terminates Hoffman's employment and notifies CFA Institute.

> *Comment*: Hoffman violated Standard I(D) because he engaged in intentional conduct involving fraud and deceit in the workplace that adversely reflected on his integrity.

Example 3 (Fraud and Deceit):

Jody Brink, an analyst covering the automotive industry, volunteers much of her spare time to local charities. The board of one of the charitable institutions decides to buy five new vans to deliver hot lunches to low-income elderly people. Brink offers to donate her time to handle purchasing agreements. To pay a long-standing debt to a friend who operates an automobile dealership—and to compensate herself for her trouble—she agrees to a price 20% higher than normal and splits the surcharge with her friend. The director of the charity ultimately discovers the scheme and tells Brink that her services, donated or otherwise, are no longer required.

> *Comment*: Brink engaged in conduct involving dishonesty, fraud, and misrepresentation and has violated Standard I(D).

Example 4 (Personal Actions and Integrity):

Carmen Garcia manages a mutual fund dedicated to socially responsible investing. She is also an environmental activist. As the result of her participation in nonviolent protests, Garcia has been arrested on numerous occasions for trespassing on the property of a large petrochemical plant that is accused of damaging the environment.

Comment: Generally, Standard I(D) is not meant to cover legal transgressions resulting from acts of civil disobedience in support of personal beliefs because such conduct does not reflect poorly on the member's or candidate's professional reputation, integrity, or competence.

Example 5 (Professional Misconduct):

Meredith Rasmussen works on a buy-side trading desk of an investment management firm and concentrates on in-house trades for a hedge fund subsidiary managed by a team at the investment management firm. The hedge fund has been very successful and is marketed globally by the firm. From her experience as the trader for much of the activity of the fund, Rasmussen has become quite knowledgeable about the hedge fund's strategy, tactics, and performance. When a distinct break in the market occurs and many of the securities involved in the hedge fund's strategy decline markedly in value, Rasmussen observes that the reported performance of the hedge fund does not reflect this decline. In her experience, the lack of effect is a very unlikely occurrence. She approaches the head of trading about her concern and is told that she should not ask any questions and that the fund is big and successful and is not her concern. She is fairly sure something is not right, so she contacts the compliance officer, who also tells her to stay away from the issue of the hedge fund's reporting.

Comment: Rasmussen has clearly come across an error in policies, procedures, and compliance practices within the firm's operations. According to the firm's procedures for reporting potentially unethical activity, she should pursue the issue by gathering some proof of her reason for doubt. Should all internal communications within the firm not satisfy her concerns, Rasmussen should consider reporting the potential unethical activity to the appropriate regulator.

See also Standard IV(A) for guidance on whistleblowing and Standard IV(C) for the duties of a supervisor.

13 STANDARD II(A): INTEGRITY OF CAPITAL MARKETS - MATERIAL NONPUBLIC INFORMATION

☐ demonstrate the application of the Code of Ethics and Standards of Professional Conduct to situations involving issues of professional integrity

Standard II(A) Material Nonpublic Information

> Members and Candidates who possess material nonpublic information that could affect the value of an investment must not act or cause others to act on the information.

Guidance

Highlights:

- *What Is "Material" Information?*
- *What Constitutes "Nonpublic" Information?*
- *Mosaic Theory*
- *Social Media*
- *Using Industry Experts*
- *Investment Research Reports*

Trading or inducing others to trade on material nonpublic information erodes confidence in capital markets, institutions, and investment professionals by supporting the idea that those with inside information and special access can take unfair advantage of the general investing public. Although trading on inside information may lead to short-term profits, in the long run, individuals and the profession as a whole suffer from such trading. These actions have caused and will continue to cause investors to avoid capital markets because the markets are perceived to be "rigged" in favor of the knowledgeable insider. When the investing public avoids capital markets, the markets and capital allocation become less efficient and less supportive of strong and vibrant economies. Standard II(A) promotes and maintains a high level of confidence in market integrity, which is one of the foundations of the investment profession.

The prohibition on using this information goes beyond the direct buying and selling of individual securities or bonds. Members and candidates must not use material nonpublic information to influence their investment actions related to derivatives (e.g., swaps or option contracts), mutual funds, or other alternative investments. *Any trading based on material nonpublic information constitutes a violation of Standard II(A).* The expansion of financial products and the increasing interconnectivity of financial markets globally have resulted in new potential opportunities for trading on material nonpublic information.

What Is "Material" Information?

Information is "material" if its disclosure would probably have an impact on the price of a security or if reasonable investors would want to know the information before making an investment decision. In other words, information is material if it would significantly alter the total mix of information currently available about a security in such a way that the price of the security would be affected.

The specificity of the information, the extent of its difference from public information, its nature, and its reliability are key factors in determining whether a particular piece of information fits the definition of material. For example, material information may include, but is not limited to, information on the following:

- earnings;
- mergers, acquisitions, tender offers, or joint ventures;
- changes in assets or asset quality;

- innovative products, processes, or discoveries (e.g., new product trials or research efforts);
- new licenses, patents, registered trademarks, or regulatory approval/rejection of a product;
- developments regarding customers or suppliers (e.g., the acquisition or loss of a contract);
- changes in management;
- change in auditor notification or the fact that the issuer may no longer rely on an auditor's report or qualified opinion;
- events regarding the issuer's securities (e.g., defaults on senior securities, calls of securities for redemption, repurchase plans, stock splits, changes in dividends, changes to the rights of security holders, and public or private sales of additional securities);
- bankruptcies;
- significant legal disputes;
- government reports of economic trends (employment, housing starts, currency information, etc.);
- orders for large trades before they are executed; and
- new or changing equity or debt ratings issued by a third party (e.g., sell-side recommendations and credit ratings).

In addition to the substance and specificity of the information, the source or relative reliability of the information also determines materiality. The less reliable a source, the less likely the information provided would be considered material. For example, factual information from a corporate insider regarding a significant new contract for a company is likely to be material, whereas an assumption based on speculation by a competitor about the same contract is likely to be less reliable and, therefore, not material. Additionally, information about trials of a new drug, product, or service under development from qualified personnel involved in the trials is likely to be material, whereas educated conjecture by subject experts not connected to the trials is unlikely to be material.

Also, the more ambiguous the effect of the information on price, the less material that information is considered. If it is unclear whether and to what extent the information will affect the price of a security, the information may not be considered material. The passage of time may also render information that was once important immaterial.

What Constitutes "Nonpublic" Information?

Information is "nonpublic" until it has been disseminated or is available to the marketplace in general (as opposed to a select group of investors). "Disseminated" can be defined as "made known." For example, a company report of profits that is posted on the internet and distributed widely through a press release or accompanied by a filing has been effectively disseminated to the marketplace. Members and candidates must have a reasonable expectation that people have received the information before it can be considered public. It is not necessary, however, to wait for the slowest method of delivery. Once the information is disseminated to the market, it is public information that is no longer covered by this standard.

Members and candidates must be particularly aware of information that is selectively disclosed by corporations to a small group of investors, analysts, or other market participants. Information that is made available to analysts remains nonpublic until it is made available to investors in general. Corporations that disclose information on a limited basis create the potential for insider-trading violations.

Standard II(A): Integrity of Capital Markets - Material Nonpublic Information

Issues of selective disclosure often arise when a corporate insider provides material information to analysts in a briefing or conference call before that information is released to the public. Analysts must be aware that a disclosure made to a room full of analysts does not necessarily make the disclosed information "public." Analysts should also be alert to the possibility that they are selectively receiving material nonpublic information when a company provides them with guidance or interpretation of such publicly available information as financial statements or regulatory filings.

A member or candidate may use insider information provided legitimately by the source company for the specific purpose of conducting due diligence according to the business agreement between the parties for such activities as mergers, loan underwriting, credit ratings, and offering engagements. In such instances, the investment professional would not be considered in violation of Standard II(A) by using the material information. However, the use of insider information provided by the source company for other purposes, especially to trade or entice others to trade the securities of the firm, conflicts with this standard.

Mosaic Theory

A financial analyst gathers and interprets large quantities of information from many sources. The analyst may use significant conclusions derived from the analysis of public and nonmaterial nonpublic information as the basis for investment recommendations and decisions even if those conclusions would have been material inside information had they been communicated directly to the analyst by a company. Under the "mosaic theory," financial analysts are free to act on this collection, or mosaic, of information without risking violation.

The practice of financial analysis depends on the free flow of information. For the fair and efficient operation of the capital markets, analysts and investors must have the greatest amount of information possible to facilitate making well-informed investment decisions about how and where to invest capital. Accurate, timely, and intelligible communication is essential if analysts and investors are to obtain the data needed to make informed decisions about how and where to invest capital. These disclosures must go beyond the information mandated by the reporting requirements of the securities laws and should include specific business information about items used to guide a company's future growth, such as new products, capital projects, and the competitive environment. Analysts seek and use such information to compare and contrast investment alternatives.

Much of the information used by analysts comes directly from companies. Analysts often receive such information through contacts with corporate insiders, especially investor-relations staff and financial officers. Information may be disseminated in the form of press releases, through oral presentations by company executives in analysts' meetings or conference calls, or during analysts' visits to company premises. In seeking to develop the most accurate and complete picture of a company, analysts should also reach beyond contacts with companies themselves and collect information from other sources, such as customers, contractors, suppliers, and the companies' competitors.

Analysts are in the business of formulating opinions and insights that are not obvious to the general investing public about the attractiveness of particular securities. In the course of their work, analysts actively seek out corporate information not generally known to the market for the express purpose of analyzing that information, forming an opinion on its significance, and informing their clients, who can be expected to trade on the basis of the recommendation. Analysts' initiatives to discover and analyze information and communicate their findings to their clients significantly enhance market efficiency, thus benefiting all investors (see *Dirks v. Securities and Exchange Commission*). Accordingly, violations of Standard II(A) will *not* result when a perceptive analyst reaches a conclusion about a corporate action or event through an analysis of public information and items of nonmaterial nonpublic information.

Investment professionals should note, however, that although analysts are free to use mosaic information in their research reports, they should save and document all their research [see Standard V(C)–Record Retention]. Evidence of the analyst's knowledge of public and nonmaterial nonpublic information about a corporation strengthens the assertion that the analyst reached his or her conclusions solely through appropriate methods rather than through the use of material nonpublic information.

Social Media

The continuing advancement in technology allows members, candidates, and the industry at large to exchange information at rates not previously available. It is important for investment professionals to understand the implications of using information from the internet and social media platforms because all such information may not actually be considered public.

Some social media platforms require membership in specific groups in order to access the published content. Members and candidates participating in groups with membership limitations should verify that material information obtained from these sources can also be accessed from a source that would be considered available to the public (e.g., company filings, webpages, and press releases).

Members and candidates may use social media platforms to communicate with clients or investors without conflicting with this standard. As long as the information reaches all clients or is open to the investing public, the use of these platforms would be comparable with other traditional forms of communications, such as e-mails and press releases. Members and candidates, as required by Standard I(A), should also complete all appropriate regulatory filings related to information distributed through social media platforms.

Using Industry Experts

The increased demand for insights for understanding the complexities of some industries has led to an expansion of engagement with outside experts. As the level of engagement increased, new businesses formed to connect analysts and investors with individuals who have specialized knowledge of their industry (e.g., technology or pharmaceuticals). These networks offer investors the opportunity to reach beyond their usual business circles to speak with experts regarding economic conditions, industry trends, and technical issues relating to specific products and services.

Members and candidates may provide compensation to individuals for their insights without violating this standard. However, members and candidates are ultimately responsible for ensuring that they are not requesting or acting on confidential information received from external experts, which is in violation of security regulations and laws or duties to others. As the recent string of insider-trading cases displayed, some experts are willing to provide confidential and protected information for the right incentive.

Firms connecting experts with members or candidates often require both parties to sign agreements concerning the disclosure of material nonpublic information. Even with the protections from such compliance practices, if an expert provides material nonpublic information, members and candidates would be prohibited from taking investment actions on the associated firm until the information became publicly known to the market.

Investment Research Reports

When a particularly well-known or respected analyst issues a report or makes changes to his or her recommendation, that information alone may have an effect on the market and thus may be considered material. Theoretically, under Standard II(A), such a report would have to be made public at the time it was distributed to clients. The analyst is not a company insider, however, and does not have access to inside information. Presumably, the analyst created the report from information available to the public (mosaic theory) and by using his or her expertise to interpret the information. The analyst's hard work, paid for by the client, generated the conclusions.

Simply because the public in general would find the conclusions material does not require that the analyst make his or her work public. Investors who are not clients of the analyst can either do the work themselves or become clients of the analyst to gain access to the analyst's expertise.

STANDARD II(A): RECOMMENDED PROCEDURES

☐ recommend practices and procedures designed to prevent violations of the Code of Ethics and Standards of Professional Conduct

Achieve Public Dissemination

If a member or candidate determines that information is material, the member or candidate should make reasonable efforts to achieve public dissemination of the information. These efforts usually entail encouraging the issuing company to make the information public. If public dissemination is not possible, the member or candidate must communicate the information only to the designated supervisory and compliance personnel within the member's or candidate's firm and must not take investment action or alter current investment recommendations on the basis of the information. Moreover, members and candidates must not knowingly engage in any conduct that may induce company insiders to privately disclose material nonpublic information.

Adopt Compliance Procedures

Members and candidates should encourage their firms to adopt compliance procedures to prevent the misuse of material nonpublic information. Particularly important is improving compliance in such areas as the review of employee and proprietary trading, the review of investment recommendations, documentation of firm procedures, and the supervision of interdepartmental communications in multiservice firms. Compliance procedures should suit the particular characteristics of a firm, including its size and the nature of its business.

Members and candidates are encouraged to inform their supervisor and compliance personnel of suspected inappropriate use of material nonpublic information as the basis for security trading activities or recommendations being made within their firm.

Adopt Disclosure Procedures

Members and candidates should encourage their firms to develop and follow disclosure policies designed to ensure that information is disseminated to the marketplace in an equitable manner. For example, analysts from small firms should receive the same information and attention from a company as analysts from large firms receive. Similarly, companies should not provide certain information to buy-side analysts but not to sell-side analysts, or vice versa. Furthermore, a company should not discriminate among analysts in the provision of information or "blackball" particular analysts who have given negative reports on the company in the past.

Within investment and research firms, members and candidates should encourage the development of and compliance with procedures for distributing new and updated investment opinions to clients. Recommendations of this nature may represent material market-moving information that needs to be communicated to all clients fairly.

Issue Press Releases

Companies should consider issuing press releases prior to analyst meetings and conference calls and scripting those meetings and calls to decrease the chance that further information will be disclosed. If material nonpublic information is disclosed for the first time in an analyst meeting or call, the company should promptly issue a press release or otherwise make the information publicly available.

Firewall Elements

An information barrier commonly referred to as a "firewall" is the most widely used approach for preventing the communication of material nonpublic information within firms. It restricts the flow of confidential information to those who need to know the information to perform their jobs effectively. The minimum elements of such a system include, but are not limited to, the following:

- substantial control of relevant interdepartmental communications, preferably through a clearance area within the firm in either the compliance or legal department;
- review of employee trading through the maintenance of "watch," "restricted," and "rumor" lists;
- documentation of the procedures designed to limit the flow of information between departments and of the actions taken to enforce those procedures; and
- heightened review or restriction of proprietary trading while a firm is in possession of material nonpublic information.

Appropriate Interdepartmental Communications

Although documentation requirements must, for practical reasons, take into account the differences between the activities of small firms and those of large, multiservice firms, firms of all sizes and types benefit by improving the documentation of their internal enforcement of firewall procedures. Therefore, even at small firms, procedures concerning interdepartmental communication, the review of trading activity, and the investigation of possible violations should be compiled and formalized.

Physical Separation of Departments

As a practical matter, to the greatest extent possible, firms should consider the physical separation of departments and files to prevent the communication of sensitive information that should not be shared. For example, the investment banking and corporate finance areas of a brokerage firm should be separated from the sales and research departments, and a bank's commercial lending department should be segregated from its trust and research departments.

Prevention of Personnel Overlap

There should be no overlap of personnel between the investment banking and corporate finance areas of a brokerage firm and the sales and research departments or between a bank's commercial lending department and its trust and research departments. For a firewall to be effective in a multiservice firm, an employee should be on only one side of the firewall at any time. Inside knowledge may not be limited to information about a specific offering or the current financial condition of a company. Analysts may be exposed to much information about the company, including new product developments or future budget projections that clearly constitute inside knowledge and thus preclude the analyst from returning to his or her research function. For example, an analyst who follows a particular company may provide limited assistance to the investment bankers under carefully controlled circumstances when the firm's investment banking department is involved in a deal with the company. That analyst must then be treated as though he or she were an investment banker; the analyst must remain on the investment banking side of the wall until any information he or she learns is publicly disclosed. In short, the analyst cannot use any information learned in the course of the project for research purposes and cannot share that information with colleagues in the research department.

A Reporting System

A primary objective of an effective firewall procedure is to establish a reporting system in which authorized people review and approve communications between departments. If an employee behind a firewall believes that he or she needs to share confidential information with someone on the other side of the wall, the employee should consult a designated compliance officer to determine whether sharing the information is necessary and how much information should be shared. If the sharing is necessary, the compliance officer should coordinate the process of "looking over the wall" so that the necessary information will be shared and the integrity of the procedure will be maintained.

A single supervisor or compliance officer should have the specific authority and responsibility of deciding whether information is material and whether it is sufficiently public to be used as the basis for investment decisions. Ideally, the supervisor or compliance officer responsible for communicating information to a firm's research or brokerage area would not be a member of that area.

Personal Trading Limitations

Firms should consider restrictions or prohibitions on personal trading by employees and should carefully monitor both proprietary trading and personal trading by employees. Firms should require employees to make periodic reports (to the extent that such reporting is not already required by securities laws) of their own transactions and transactions made for the benefit of family members. Securities should be placed on a restricted list when a firm has or may have material nonpublic information. The broad distribution of a restricted list often triggers the sort of trading the list was developed to avoid. Therefore, a watch list shown to only the few people responsible for compliance should be used to monitor transactions in specified securities. The use of a watch list in combination with a restricted list is an increasingly common means of ensuring effective control of personal trading.

Record Maintenance

Multiservice firms should maintain written records of the communications between various departments. Firms should place a high priority on training and should consider instituting comprehensive training programs, particularly for employees in sensitive areas.

Proprietary Trading Procedures

Procedures concerning the restriction or review of a firm's proprietary trading while the firm possesses material nonpublic information will necessarily depend on the types of proprietary trading in which the firm may engage. A prohibition on all types of proprietary activity when a firm comes into possession of material nonpublic information is *not* appropriate. For example, when a firm acts as a market maker, a prohibition on proprietary trading may be counterproductive to the goals of maintaining the confidentiality of information and market liquidity. This concern is particularly important in the relationships between small, regional broker/dealers and small issuers. In many situations, a firm will take a small issuer public with the understanding that the firm will continue to be a market maker in the stock. In such instances, a withdrawal by the firm from market-making activities would be a clear tip to outsiders. Firms that continue market-making activity while in the possession of material nonpublic information should, however, instruct their market makers to remain passive with respect to the market—that is, to take only the contra side of unsolicited customer trades.

In risk-arbitrage trading, the case for a trading prohibition is more compelling than it is in the case of market making. The impetus for arbitrage trading is neither passive nor reactive, and the potential for illegal profits is greater than in market making. The most prudent course for firms is to suspend arbitrage activity when a security is placed on the watch list. Those firms that continue arbitrage activity face a high hurdle in proving the adequacy of their internal procedures for preventing trading on material nonpublic information and must demonstrate a stringent review and documentation of firm trades.

Communication to All Employees

Members and candidates should encourage their employers to circulate written compliance policies and guidelines to all employees. Policies and guidelines should be used in conjunction with training programs aimed at enabling employees to recognize material nonpublic information. Such information is not always clearly identifiable.

Employees must be given sufficient training to either make an informed decision or to realize they need to consult a supervisor or compliance officer before engaging in questionable transactions. Appropriate policies reinforce that using material nonpublic information is illegal in many countries. Such trading activities based on material nonpublic information undermine the integrity of the individual, the firm, and the capital markets.

STANDARD II(A): APPLICATION OF THE STANDARD

- [ ] demonstrate the application of the Code of Ethics and Standards of Professional Conduct to situations involving issues of professional integrity
- [ ] identify conduct that conforms to the Code and Standards and conduct that violates the Code and Standards

Example 1 (Acting on Nonpublic Information):

Frank Barnes, the president and controlling shareholder of the SmartTown clothing chain, decides to accept a tender offer and sell the family business at a price almost double the market price of its shares. He describes this decision to his sister (SmartTown's treasurer), who conveys it to her daughter (who owns no stock in the family company at present), who tells her husband, Staple. Staple, however, tells his stockbroker, Alex Halsey, who immediately buys SmartTown stock for himself.

> *Comment*: The information regarding the pending sale is both material and nonpublic. Staple has violated Standard II(A) by communicating the inside information to his broker. Halsey also has violated the standard by buying the shares on the basis of material nonpublic information.

Example 2 (Controlling Nonpublic Information):

Samuel Peter, an analyst with Scotland and Pierce Incorporated, is assisting his firm with a secondary offering for Bright Ideas Lamp Company. Peter participates, via telephone conference call, in a meeting with Scotland and Pierce investment banking employees and Bright Ideas' CEO. Peter is advised that the company's earnings projections for the next year have significantly dropped. Throughout the telephone conference call, several Scotland and Pierce salespeople and portfolio managers walk in and out of Peter's office, where the telephone call is taking place. As a result, they are aware of the drop in projected earnings for Bright Ideas. Before the conference call is concluded, the salespeople trade the stock of the company on behalf of the firm's clients and other firm personnel trade the stock in a firm proprietary account and in employees' personal accounts.

> *Comment*: Peter has violated Standard II(A) because he failed to prevent the transfer and misuse of material nonpublic information to others in his firm. Peter's firm should have adopted information barriers to prevent the communication of nonpublic information between departments of the firm. The salespeople and portfolio managers who traded on the information have also violated Standard II(A) by trading on inside information.

Example 3 (Selective Disclosure of Material Information):

Elizabeth Levenson is based in Hanoi and covers the Vietnamese market for her firm, which is based in Singapore. She is invited, together with the other 10 largest shareholders of a manufacturing company, to meet the finance director of that company.

During the meeting, the finance director states that the company expects its workforce to strike next Friday, which will cripple productivity and distribution. Can Levenson use this information as a basis to change her rating on the company from "buy" to "sell"?

Comment: Levenson must first determine whether the material information is public. According to Standard II(A), if the company has not made this information public (a small group forum does not qualify as a method of public dissemination), she cannot use the information.

Example 4 (Determining Materiality):

Leah Fechtman is trying to decide whether to hold or sell shares of an oil-and-gas exploration company that she owns in several of the funds she manages. Although the company has underperformed the index for some time already, the trends in the industry sector signal that companies of this type might become takeover targets. While she is considering her decision, her doctor, who casually follows the markets, mentions that she thinks that the company in question will soon be bought out by a large multinational conglomerate and that it would be a good idea to buy the stock right now. After talking to various investment professionals and checking their opinions on the company as well as checking industry trends, Fechtman decides the next day to accumulate more stock in the oil-and-gas exploration company.

Comment: Although information on an expected takeover bid may be of the type that is generally material and nonpublic, in this case, the source of information is unreliable, so the information cannot be considered material. Therefore, Fechtman is not prohibited from trading the stock on the basis of this information.

Example 5 (Applying the Mosaic Theory):

Jagdish Teja is a buy-side analyst covering the furniture industry. Looking for an attractive company to recommend as a buy, he analyzes several furniture makers by studying their financial reports and visiting their operations. He also talks to some designers and retailers to find out which furniture styles are trendy and popular. Although none of the companies that he analyzes are a clear buy, he discovers that one of them, Swan Furniture Company (SFC), may be in financial trouble. SFC's extravagant new designs have been introduced at substantial cost. Even though these designs initially attracted attention, the public is now buying more conservative furniture from other makers. Based on this information and on a profit-and-loss analysis, Teja believes that SFC's next quarter earnings will drop substantially. He issues a sell recommendation for SFC. Immediately after receiving that recommendation, investment managers start reducing the SFC stock in their portfolios.

Comment: Information on quarterly earnings data is material and nonpublic. Teja arrived at his conclusion about the earnings drop on the basis of public information and on pieces of nonmaterial nonpublic information (such as opinions of designers and retailers). Therefore, trading based on Teja's correct conclusion is not prohibited by Standard II(A).

Example 6 (Applying the Mosaic Theory):

Roger Clement is a senior financial analyst who specializes in the European automobile sector at Rivoli Capital. Because he has been repeatedly nominated by many leading industry magazines and newsletters as a "best analyst" for the automobile industry, he is widely regarded as an authority on the sector. After speaking with representatives of Turgot Chariots—a European auto manufacturer with sales primarily in South Korea—and after conducting interviews with salespeople, labor leaders, his firm's Korean currency analysts, and banking officials, Clement analyzed Turgot Chariots and concluded that (1) its newly introduced model will probably not meet sales expectations, (2) its corporate restructuring strategy may well face serious opposition from unions, (3) the depreciation of the Korean won should lead to pressure on margins for the industry in general and Turgot's market segment in particular, and (4) banks could take a tougher-than-expected stance in the upcoming round of credit renegotiations with the company. For these reasons, he changes his conclusion about the company from "market outperform" to "market underperform." Clement retains the support material used to reach his conclusion in case questions later arise.

> *Comment*: To reach a conclusion about the value of the company, Clement has pieced together a number of nonmaterial or public bits of information that affect Turgot Chariots. Therefore, under the mosaic theory, Clement has not violated Standard II(A) in drafting the report.

Example 7 (Analyst Recommendations as Material Nonpublic Information):

The next day, Clement is preparing to be interviewed on a global financial news television program where he will discuss his changed recommendation on Turgot Chariots for the first time in public. While preparing for the program, he mentions to the show's producers and Mary Zito, the journalist who will be interviewing him, the information he will be discussing. Just prior to going on the air, Zito sells her holdings in Turgot Chariots. She also phones her father with the information because she knows that he and other family members have investments in Turgot Chariots.

> *Comment*: When Zito receives advance notice of Clement's change of opinion, she knows it will have a material impact on the stock price, even if she is not totally aware of Clement's underlying reasoning. She is not a client of Clement but obtains early access to the material nonpublic information prior to publication. Her trades are thus based on material nonpublic information and violate Standard II(A).
>
> Zito further violates the Standard by relaying the information to her father. It would not matter if he or any other family member traded; the act of providing the information violates Standard II(A). The fact that the information is provided to a family member does not absolve someone of the prohibition of using or communicating material nonpublic information.

Example 8 (Acting on Nonpublic Information):

Ashton Kellogg is a retired investment professional who manages his own portfolio. He owns shares in National Savings, a large local bank. A close friend and golfing buddy, John Mayfield, is a senior executive at National. National has seen its stock price drop considerably, and the news and outlook are not good. In a conversation about the economy and the banking industry on the golf course, Mayfield relays the information that National will surprise the investment community in a few days when it announces excellent earnings for the quarter. Kellogg is pleasantly surprised by this information, and thinking that Mayfield, as a senior executive, knows the law and would not disclose inside information, he doubles his position in the bank. Subsequently, National announces that it had good operating earnings but had to set aside reserves for anticipated significant losses on its loan portfolio. The combined news causes the stock to go down 60%.

> *Comment*: Even though Kellogg believes that Mayfield would not break the law by disclosing inside information and money was lost on the purchase, Kellogg should not have purchased additional shares of National. It is the member's or candidate's responsibility to make sure, before executing investment actions, that comments about earnings are not material non-public information. Kellogg has violated Standard II(A).

Example 9 (Mosaic Theory):

John Doll is a research analyst for a hedge fund that also sells its research to a select group of paying client investment firms. Doll's focus is medical technology companies and products, and he has been in the business long enough and has been successful enough to build up a very credible network of friends and experts in the business. Doll has been working on a major research report recommending Boyce Health, a medical device manufacturer. He recently ran into an old acquaintance at a wedding who is a senior executive at Boyce, and Doll asked about the business. Doll was drawn to a statement that the executive, who has responsibilities in the new products area, made about a product: "I would not get too excited about the medium-term prospects; we have a lot of work to do first." Doll incorporated this and other information about the new Boyce product in his long-term recommendation of Boyce.

> *Comment*: Doll's conversation with the senior executive is part of the mosaic of information used in recommending Boyce. When holding discussions with a firm executive, Doll would need to guard against soliciting or obtaining material nonpublic information. Before issuing the report, the executive's statement about the continuing development of the product would need to be weighed against the other known public facts to determine whether it would be considered material.

Example 10 (Materiality Determination):

Larry Nadler, a trader for a mutual fund, gets a text message from another firm's trader, whom he has known for years. The message indicates a software company is going to report strong earnings when the firm publicly announces in two days. Nadler has a buy order from a portfolio manager within his firm to purchase several hundred thousand shares of the stock. Nadler is aggressive in placing the portfolio manager's order and completes the purchases by the following morning, a day ahead of the firm's planned earnings announcement.

> *Comment*: There are often rumors and whisper numbers before a release of any kind. The text message from the other trader would most likely be considered market noise. Unless Nadler knew that the trader had an ongoing business relationship with the public firm, he had no reason to suspect he was receiving material nonpublic information that would prevent him from completing the trading request of the portfolio manager.

Example 11 (Using an Expert Network):

Mary McCoy is the senior drug analyst at a mutual fund. Her firm hires a service that connects her to experts in the treatment of cancer. Through various phone conversations, McCoy enhances her understanding of the latest therapies for successful treatment. This information is critical to Mary making informed recommendations of the companies producing these drugs.

> *Comment*: McCoy is appropriately using the expert networks to enhance her evaluation process. She has neither asked for nor received information that may be considered material and nonpublic, such as preliminary trial results. McCoy is allowed to seek advice from professionals within the industry that she follows.

Example 12 (Using an Expert Network):

Tom Watson is a research analyst working for a hedge fund. To stay informed, Watson relies on outside experts for information on such industries as technology and pharmaceuticals, where new advancements occur frequently. The meetings with the industry experts often are arranged through networks or placement agents that have specific policies and procedures in place to deter the exchange of material nonpublic information.

Watson arranges a call to discuss future prospects for one of the fund's existing technology company holdings, a company that was testing a new semiconductor product. The scientist leading the tests indicates his disappointment with the performance of the new semiconductor. Following the call, Watson relays the insights he received to others at the fund. The fund sells its current position in the company and buys many put options because the market is anticipating the success of the new semiconductor and the share price reflects the market's optimism.

> *Comment*: Watson has violated Standard II(A) by passing along material nonpublic information concerning the ongoing product tests, which the fund used to trade in the securities and options of the related company. Watson cannot simply rely on the agreements signed by individuals who participate in expert networks that state that he has not received information that would prohibit his trading activity. He must make his own determination whether information he received through these arrangements reaches a materiality threshold that would affect his trading abilities.

STANDARD II(B): INTEGRITY OF CAPITAL MARKETS - MARKET MANIPULATION   16

☐ demonstrate the application of the Code of Ethics and Standards of Professional Conduct to situations involving issues of professional integrity

> Members and Candidates must not engage in practices that distort prices or artificially inflate trading volume with the intent to mislead market participants.

Guidance

Highlights:

- *Information-Based Manipulation*
- *Transaction-Based Manipulation*

Standard II(B) requires that members and candidates uphold market integrity by prohibiting market manipulation. Market manipulation includes practices that distort security prices or trading volume with the intent to deceive people or entities that rely on information in the market. Market manipulation damages the interests of all investors by disrupting the smooth functioning of financial markets and lowering investor confidence.

Market manipulation may lead to a lack of trust in the fairness of the capital markets, resulting in higher risk premiums and reduced investor participation. A reduction in the efficiency of a local capital market may negatively affect the growth and economic health of the country and may also influence the operations of the globally interconnected capital markets. Although market manipulation may be less likely to occur in mature financial markets than in emerging markets, cross-border investing increasingly exposes all global investors to the potential for such practices.

Market manipulation includes (1) the dissemination of false or misleading information and (2) transactions that deceive or would be likely to mislead market participants by distorting the price-setting mechanism of financial instruments. The development of new products and technologies increases the incentives, means, and opportunities for market manipulation. Additionally, the increasing complexity and sophistication of the technologies used for communicating with market participants have created new avenues for manipulation.

Information-Based Manipulation

Information-based manipulation includes, but is not limited to, spreading false rumors to induce trading by others. For example, members and candidates must refrain from "pumping up" the price of an investment by issuing misleading positive information or overly optimistic projections of a security's worth only to later "dump" the investment (i.e., sell it) once the price, fueled by the misleading information's effect on other market participants, reaches an artificially high level.

Transaction-Based Manipulation

Transaction-based manipulation involves instances where a member or candidate knew or should have known that his or her actions could affect the pricing of a security. This type of manipulation includes, but is not limited to, the following:

- transactions that artificially affect prices or volume to give the impression of activity or price movement in a financial instrument, which represent a diversion from the expectations of a fair and efficient market, and
- securing a controlling, dominant position in a financial instrument to exploit and manipulate the price of a related derivative and/or the underlying asset.

Standard II(B) is not intended to preclude transactions undertaken on legitimate trading strategies based on perceived market inefficiencies. The intent of the action is critical to determining whether it is a violation of this standard.

STANDARD II(B): APPLICATION OF THE STANDARD

- [ ] demonstrate the application of the Code of Ethics and Standards of Professional Conduct to situations involving issues of professional integrity
- [ ] identify conduct that conforms to the Code and Standards and conduct that violates the Code and Standards

Example 1 (Independent Analysis and Company Promotion):

The principal owner of Financial Information Services (FIS) entered into an agreement with two microcap companies to promote the companies' stock in exchange for stock and cash compensation. The principal owner caused FIS to disseminate e-mails, design and maintain several websites, and distribute an online investment newsletter—all of which recommended investment in the two companies. The systematic publication of purportedly independent analyses and recommendations containing inaccurate and highly promotional and speculative statements increased public investment in the companies and led to dramatically higher stock prices.

> *Comment*: The principal owner of FIS violated Standard II(B) by using inaccurate reporting and misleading information under the guise of independent analysis to artificially increase the stock price of the companies. Furthermore, the principal owner violated Standard V(A)–Diligence and Reasonable Basis by not having a reasonable and adequate basis for recommending the two companies and violated Standard VI(A)–Disclosure of Conflicts by not disclosing to investors the compensation agreements (which constituted a conflict of interest).

Example 2 (Personal Trading Practices and Price):

John Gray is a private investor in Belgium who bought a large position several years ago in Fame Pharmaceuticals, a German small-cap security with limited average trading volume. He has now decided to significantly reduce his holdings owing to the poor price performance. Gray is worried that the low trading volume for the stock may cause the price to decline further as he attempts to sell his large position.

Gray devises a plan to divide his holdings into multiple accounts in different brokerage firms and private banks in the names of family members, friends, and even a private religious institution. He then creates a rumor campaign on various blogs and social media outlets promoting the company.

Gray begins to buy and sell the stock using the accounts in hopes of raising the trading volume and the price. He conducts the trades through multiple brokers, selling slightly larger positions than he bought on a tactical schedule, and over time, he is able to reduce his holding as desired without negatively affecting the sale price.

> *Comment*: John violated Standard II(B) by fraudulently creating the appearance that there was a greater investor interest in the stock through the online rumors. Additionally, through his trading strategy, he created the appearance that there was greater liquidity in the stock than actually existed. He was able to manipulate the price through both misinformation and trading practices.

Example 3 (Creating Artificial Price Volatility):

Matthew Murphy is an analyst at Divisadero Securities & Co., which has a significant number of hedge funds among its most important brokerage clients. Some of the hedge funds hold short positions on Wirewolf Semiconductor. Two trading days before the publication of a quarter-end report, Murphy alerts his sales force that he is about to issue a research report on Wirewolf that will include the following opinions:

- quarterly revenues are likely to fall short of management's guidance,
- earnings will be as much as 5 cents per share (or more than 10%) below consensus, and
- Wirewolf's highly respected chief financial officer may be about to join another company.

Knowing that Wirewolf has already entered its declared quarter-end "quiet period" before reporting earnings (and thus would be reluctant to respond to rumors), Murphy times the release of his research report specifically to sensationalize the negative aspects of the message in order to create significant downward pressure on Wirewolf's stock—to the distinct advantage of Divisadero's hedge fund clients. The report's conclusions are based on speculation, not on fact. The next day, the research report is broadcast to all of Divisadero's clients and to the usual newswire services.

Before Wirewolf's investor-relations department can assess the damage on the final trading day of the quarter and refute Murphy's report, its stock opens trading sharply lower, allowing Divisadero's clients to cover their short positions at substantial gains.

Comment: Murphy violated Standard II(B) by aiming to create artificial price volatility designed to have a material impact on the price of an issuer's stock. Moreover, by lacking an adequate basis for the recommendation, Murphy also violated Standard V(A)–Diligence and Reasonable Basis.

Example 4 (Personal Trading and Volume):

Rajesh Sekar manages two funds—an equity fund and a balanced fund—whose equity components are supposed to be managed in accordance with the same model. According to that model, the funds' holdings in stock of Digital Design Inc. (DD) are excessive. Reduction of the DD holdings would not be easy, however, because the stock has low liquidity in the stock market. Sekar decides to start trading larger portions of DD stock back and forth between his two funds to slowly increase the price; he believes market participants will see growing volume and increasing price and become interested in the stock. If other investors are willing to buy the DD stock because of such interest, then Sekar will be able to get rid of at least some of his overweight position without inducing price decreases. In this way, the whole transaction will be for the benefit of fund participants, even if additional brokers' commissions are incurred.

Comment: Sekar's plan would be beneficial for his funds' participants but is based on artificial distortion of both trading volume and the price of the DD stock and thus constitutes a violation of Standard II(B).

Example 5 ("Pump-Priming" Strategy):

ACME Futures Exchange is launching a new bond futures contract. To convince investors, traders, arbitrageurs, hedgers, and so on, to use its contract, the exchange attempts to demonstrate that it has the best liquidity. To do so, it enters into agreements

Standard II(B): Application of the Standard

with members in which they commit to a substantial minimum trading volume on the new contract over a specific period in exchange for substantial reductions of their regular commissions.

> *Comment*: The formal liquidity of a market is determined by the obligations set on market makers, but the actual liquidity of a market is better estimated by the actual trading volume and bid–ask spreads. Attempts to mislead participants about the actual liquidity of the market constitute a violation of Standard II(B). In this example, investors have been intentionally misled to believe they chose the most liquid instrument for some specific purpose, but they could eventually see the actual liquidity of the contract significantly reduced after the term of the agreement expires. If the ACME Futures Exchange fully discloses its agreement with members to boost transactions over some initial launch period, it will not violate Standard II(B). ACME's intent is not to harm investors but, on the contrary, to give them a better service. For that purpose, it may engage in a liquidity-pumping strategy, but the strategy must be disclosed.

Example 6 (Creating Artificial Price Volatility):

Emily Gordon, an analyst of household products companies, is employed by a research boutique, Picador & Co. Based on information that she has gathered during a trip through Latin America, she believes that Hygene, Inc., a major marketer of personal care products, has generated better-than-expected sales from its new product initiatives in South America. After modestly boosting her projections for revenue and for gross profit margin in her worksheet models for Hygene, Gordon estimates that her earnings projection of US$2.00 per diluted share for the current year may be as much as 5% too low. She contacts the chief financial officer (CFO) of Hygene to try to gain confirmation of her findings from her trip and to get some feedback regarding her revised models. The CFO declines to comment and reiterates management's most recent guidance of US$1.95–US$2.05 for the year.

Gordon decides to try to force a comment from the company by telling Picador & Co. clients who follow a momentum investment style that consensus earnings projections for Hygene are much too low; she explains that she is considering raising her published estimate by an ambitious US$0.15 to US$2.15 per share. She believes that when word of an unrealistically high earnings projection filters back to Hygene's investor-relations department, the company will feel compelled to update its earnings guidance. Meanwhile, Gordon hopes that she is at least correct with respect to the earnings direction and that she will help clients who act on her insights to profit from a quick gain by trading on her advice.

> *Comment*: By exaggerating her earnings projections in order to try to fuel a quick gain in Hygene's stock price, Gordon is in violation of Standard II(B). Furthermore, by virtue of previewing her intentions of revising upward her earnings projections to only a select group of clients, she is in violation of Standard III(B)–Fair Dealing. However, it would have been acceptable for Gordon to write a report that
>
> - framed her earnings projection in a range of possible outcomes,
> - outlined clearly the assumptions used in her Hygene models that took into consideration the findings from her trip through Latin America, and
> - was distributed to all Picador & Co. clients in an equitable manner.

Example 7 (Pump and Dump Strategy):

In an effort to pump up the price of his holdings in Moosehead & Belfast Railroad Company, Steve Weinberg logs on to several investor chat rooms on the internet to start rumors that the company is about to expand its rail network in anticipation of receiving a large contract for shipping lumber.

> *Comment*: Weinberg has violated Standard II(B) by disseminating false information about Moosehead & Belfast with the intent to mislead market participants.

Example 8 (Manipulating Model Inputs):

Bill Mandeville supervises a structured financing team for Superior Investment Bank. His responsibilities include packaging new structured investment products and managing Superior's relationship with relevant rating agencies. To achieve the best rating possible, Mandeville uses mostly positive scenarios as model inputs—scenarios that reflect minimal downside risk in the assets underlying the structured products. The resulting output statistics in the rating request and underwriting prospectus support the idea that the new structured products have minimal potential downside risk. Additionally, Mandeville's compensation from Superior is partially based on both the level of the rating assigned and the successful sale of new structured investment products but does not have a link to the long-term performance of the instruments.

Mandeville is extremely successful and leads Superior as the top originator of structured investment products for the next two years. In the third year, the economy experiences difficulties and the values of the assets underlying structured products significantly decline. The subsequent defaults lead to major turmoil in the capital markets, the demise of Superior Investment Bank, and the loss of Mandeville's employment.

> *Comment*: Mandeville manipulates the inputs of a model to minimize associated risk to achieve higher ratings. His understanding of structured products allows him to skillfully decide which inputs to include in support of the desired rating and price. This information manipulation for short-term gain, which is in violation of Standard II(B), ultimately causes significant damage to many parties and the capital markets as a whole. Mandeville should have realized that promoting a rating and price with inaccurate information could cause not only a loss of price confidence in the particular structured product but also a loss of investor trust in the system. Such loss of confidence affects the ability of the capital markets to operate efficiently.

Example 9 (Information Manipulation):

Allen King is a performance analyst for Torrey Investment Funds. King believes that the portfolio manager for the firm's small- and microcap equity fund dislikes him because the manager never offers him tickets to the local baseball team's games but does offer tickets to other employees. To incite a potential regulatory review of the manager, King creates user profiles on several online forums under the portfolio manager's name and starts rumors about potential mergers for several of the smaller companies in the portfolio. As the prices of these companies' stocks increase, the portfolio manager sells the position, which leads to an investigation by the regulator as King desired.

Comment: King has violated Standard II(B) even though he did not personally profit from the market's reaction to the rumor. In posting the false information, King misleads others into believing the companies were likely to be acquired. Although his intent was to create trouble for the portfolio manager, his actions clearly manipulated the factual information that was available to the market.

STANDARD III(A): DUTIES TO CLIENTS - LOYALTY, PRUDENCE, AND CARE

☐ demonstrate the application of the Code of Ethics and Standards of Professional Conduct to situations involving issues of professional integrity

Standard III(A) Loyalty, Prudence, and Care

> Members and Candidates have a duty of loyalty to their clients and must act with reasonable care and exercise prudent judgment. Members and Candidates must act for the benefit of their clients and place their clients' interests before their employer's or their own interests.

Guidance

Highlights:

- *Understanding the Application of Loyalty, Prudence, and Care*
- *Identifying the Actual Investment Client*
- *Developing the Client's Portfolio*
- *Soft Commission Policies*
- *Proxy Voting Policies*

Standard III(A) clarifies that client interests are paramount. A member's or candidate's responsibility to a client includes a duty of loyalty and a duty to exercise reasonable care. Investment actions must be carried out for the sole benefit of the client and in a manner the member or candidate believes, given the known facts and circumstances, to be in the best interest of the client. Members and candidates must exercise the same level of prudence, judgment, and care that they would apply in the management and disposition of their own interests in similar circumstances.

Prudence requires caution and discretion. The exercise of prudence by investment professionals requires that they act with the care, skill, and diligence that a reasonable person acting in a like capacity and familiar with such matters would use. In the context of managing a client's portfolio, prudence requires following the investment parameters set forth by the client and balancing risk and return. Acting with care requires members and candidates to act in a prudent and judicious manner in avoiding harm to clients.

Standard III(A) sets minimum expectations for members and candidates when fulfilling their responsibilities to their clients. Regulatory and legal requirements for such duties can vary across the investment industry depending on a variety of factors, including job function of the investment professional, the existence of an adviser/client relationship, and the nature of the recommendations being offered. From the perspective of the end user of financial services, these different standards can be arcane and confusing, leaving investors unsure of what level of service to expect from investment professionals they employ. The single standard of conduct described in Standard III(A) benefits investors by establishing a benchmark for the duties of loyalty, prudence, and care and clarifies that all CFA Institute members and candidates, regardless of job title, local laws, or cultural differences, are required to comply with these fundamental responsibilities. Investors hiring members or candidates who must adhere to the duty of loyalty, prudence, and care set forth in this standard can be confident that these responsibilities are a requirement regardless of any legally imposed fiduciary duties.

Standard III(A), however, is not a substitute for a member's or candidate's legal or regulatory obligations. As stated in Standard I(A), members and candidates must abide by the most strict requirements imposed on them by regulators or the Code and Standards, including any legally imposed fiduciary duty. Members and candidates must also be aware of whether they have "custody" or effective control of client assets. If so, a heightened level of responsibility arises. Members and candidates are considered to have custody if they have any direct or indirect access to client funds. Members and candidates must manage any pool of assets in their control in accordance with the terms of the governing documents (such as trust documents and investment management agreements), which are the primary determinant of the manager's powers and duties. Whenever their actions are contrary to provisions of those instruments or applicable law, members and candidates are at risk of violating Standard III(A).

Understanding the Application of Loyalty, Prudence, and Care

Standard III(A) establishes a minimum benchmark for the duties of loyalty, prudence, and care that are required of all members and candidates regardless of whether a legal fiduciary duty applies. Although fiduciary duty often encompasses the principles of loyalty, prudence, and care, Standard III(A) does not render all members and candidates fiduciaries. The responsibilities of members and candidates for fulfilling their obligations under this standard depend greatly on the nature of their professional responsibilities and the relationships they have with clients. The conduct of members and candidates may or may not rise to the level of being a fiduciary, depending on the type of client, whether the member or candidate is giving investment advice, and the many facts and circumstances surrounding a particular transaction or client relationship.

Fiduciary duties are often imposed by law or regulation when an individual or institution is charged with the duty of acting for the benefit of another party, such as managing investment assets. The duty required in fiduciary relationships exceeds what is acceptable in many other business relationships because a fiduciary is in an enhanced position of trust. Although members and candidates must comply with any legally imposed fiduciary duty, the Code and Standards neither impose such a legal responsibility nor require all members or candidates to act as fiduciaries. However, Standard III(A) requires members and candidates to work in the client's best interest no matter what the job function.

A member or candidate who does not provide advisory services to a client but who acts only as a trade execution professional must prudently work in the client's interest when completing requested trades. Acting in the client's best interest requires these professionals to use their skills and diligence to execute trades in the most favorable terms that can be achieved. Members and candidates operating in such positions must use care to operate within the parameters set by the client's trading instructions.

Standard III(A): Duties to Clients - Loyalty, Prudence, and Care

Members and candidates may also operate in a blended environment where they execute client trades and offer advice on a limited set of investment options. The extent of the advisory arrangement and limitations should be outlined in the agreement with the client at the outset of the relationship. For instance, members and candidates should inform clients that the advice provided will be limited to the propriety products of the firm and not include other products available on the market. Clients who want access to a wider range of investment products would have the information necessary to decide not to engage with members or candidates working under these restrictions.

Members and candidates operating in this blended context would comply with their obligations by recommending the allowable products that are consistent with the client's objectives and risk tolerance. They would exercise care through diligently aligning the client's needs with the attributes of the products being recommended. Members and candidates should place the client's interests first by disregarding any firm or personal interest in motivating a recommended transaction.

There is a large variety of professional relationships that members and candidates have with their clients. Standard III(A) requires them to fulfill the obligations outlined explicitly or implicitly in the client agreements to the best of their abilities and with loyalty, prudence, and care. Whether a member or candidate is structuring a new securitization transaction, completing a credit rating analysis, or leading a public company, he or she must work with prudence and care in delivering the agreed-on services.

Identifying the Actual Investment Client

The first step for members and candidates in fulfilling their duty of loyalty to clients is to determine the identity of the "client" to whom the duty of loyalty is owed. In the context of an investment manager managing the personal assets of an individual, the client is easily identified. When the manager is responsible for the portfolios of pension plans or trusts, however, the client is not the person or entity who hires the manager but, rather, the beneficiaries of the plan or trust. The duty of loyalty is owed to the ultimate beneficiaries.

In some situations, an actual client or group of beneficiaries may not exist. Members and candidates managing a fund to an index or an expected mandate owe the duty of loyalty, prudence, and care to invest in a manner consistent with the stated mandate. The decisions of a fund's manager, although benefiting all fund investors, do not have to be based on an individual investor's requirements and risk profile. Client loyalty and care for those investing in the fund are the responsibility of members and candidates who have an advisory relationship with those individuals.

Situations involving potential conflicts of interest with respect to responsibilities to clients may be extremely complex because they may involve a number of competing interests. The duty of loyalty, prudence, and care applies to a large number of persons in varying capacities, but the exact duties may differ in many respects in accord with the relationship with each client or each type of account in which the assets are managed. Members and candidates must not only put their obligations to clients first in all dealings but also endeavor to avoid all real or potential conflicts of interest.

Members and candidates with positions whose responsibilities do not include direct investment management also have "clients" that must be considered. Just as there are various types of advisory relationships, members and candidates must look at their roles and responsibilities when making a determination of who their clients are. Sometimes the client is easily identifiable; such is the case in the relationship between a company executive and the firm's public shareholders. At other times, the client may be the investing public as a whole, in which case the goals of independence and objectivity of research surpass the goal of loyalty to a single organization.

Developing the Client's Portfolio

The duty of loyalty, prudence, and care owed to the individual client is especially important because the professional investment manager typically possesses greater knowledge in the investment arena than the client does. This disparity places the individual client in a vulnerable position; the client must trust the manager. The manager in these situations should ensure that the client's objectives and expectations for the performance of the account are realistic and suitable to the client's circumstances and that the risks involved are appropriate. In most circumstances, recommended investment strategies should relate to the long-term objectives and circumstances of the client.

Particular care must be taken to detect whether the goals of the investment manager or the firm in conducting business, selling products, and executing security transactions potentially conflict with the best interests and objectives of the client. When members and candidates cannot avoid potential conflicts between their firm and clients' interests, they must provide clear and factual disclosures of the circumstances to the clients.

Members and candidates must follow any guidelines set by their clients for the management of their assets. Some clients, such as charitable organizations and pension plans, have strict investment policies that limit investment options to certain types or classes of investment or prohibit investment in certain securities. Other organizations have aggressive policies that do not prohibit investments by type but, instead, set criteria on the basis of the portfolio's total risk and return.

Investment decisions must be judged in the context of the total portfolio rather than by individual investment within the portfolio. The member's or candidate's duty is satisfied with respect to a particular investment if the individual has thoroughly considered the investment's place in the overall portfolio, the risk of loss and opportunity for gains, tax implications, and the diversification, liquidity, cash flow, and overall return requirements of the assets or the portion of the assets for which the manager is responsible.

Soft Commission Policies

An investment manager often has discretion over the selection of brokers executing transactions. Conflicts may arise when an investment manager uses client brokerage to purchase research services, a practice commonly called "soft dollars" or "soft commissions." A member or candidate who pays a higher brokerage commission than he or she would normally pay to allow for the purchase of goods or services, without corresponding benefit to the client, violates the duty of loyalty to the client.

From time to time, a client will direct a manager to use the client's brokerage to purchase goods or services for the client, a practice that is commonly called "directed brokerage." Because brokerage commission is an asset of the client and is used to benefit that client, not the manager, such a practice does not violate any duty of loyalty. However, a member or candidate is obligated to seek "best price" and "best execution" and be assured by the client that the goods or services purchased from the brokerage will benefit the account beneficiaries. "Best execution" refers to a trading process that seeks to maximize the value of the client's portfolio within the client's stated investment objectives and constraints. In addition, the member or candidate should disclose to the client that the client may not be getting best execution from the directed brokerage.

Proxy Voting Policies

The duty of loyalty, prudence, and care may apply in a number of situations facing the investment professional besides those related directly to investing assets.

Standard III(A): Recommended Procedures

Part of a member's or candidate's duty of loyalty includes voting proxies in an informed and responsible manner. Proxies have economic value to a client, and members and candidates must ensure that they properly safeguard and maximize this value. An investment manager who fails to vote, casts a vote without considering the impact of the question, or votes blindly with management on nonroutine governance issues (e.g., a change in company capitalization) may violate this standard. Voting of proxies is an integral part of the management of investments.

A cost–benefit analysis may show that voting all proxies may not benefit the client, so voting proxies may not be necessary in all instances. Members and candidates should disclose to clients their proxy voting policies.

STANDARD III(A): RECOMMENDED PROCEDURES

☐ recommend practices and procedures designed to prevent violations of the Code of Ethics and Standards of Professional Conduct

Regular Account Information

Members and candidates with control of client assets (1) should submit to each client, at least quarterly, an itemized statement showing the funds and securities in the custody or possession of the member or candidate plus all debits, credits, and transactions that occurred during the period, (2) should disclose to the client where the assets are to be maintained, as well as where or when they are moved, and (3) should separate the client's assets from any other party's assets, including the member's or candidate's own assets.

Client Approval

If a member or candidate is uncertain about the appropriate course of action with respect to a client, the member or candidate should consider what he or she would expect or demand if the member or candidate were the client. If in doubt, a member or candidate should disclose the questionable matter in writing to the client and obtain client approval.

Firm Policies

Members and candidates should address and encourage their firms to address the following topics when drafting the statements or manuals containing their policies and procedures regarding responsibilities to clients:

- *Follow all applicable rules and laws*: Members and candidates must follow all legal requirements and applicable provisions of the Code and Standards.
- *Establish the investment objectives of the client*: Make a reasonable inquiry into a client's investment experience, risk and return objectives, and financial constraints prior to making investment recommendations or taking investment actions.

- *Consider all the information when taking actions*: When taking investment actions, members and candidates must consider the appropriateness and suitability of the investment relative to (1) the client's needs and circumstances, (2) the investment's basic characteristics, and (3) the basic characteristics of the total portfolio.
- *Diversify*: Members and candidates should diversify investments to reduce the risk of loss, unless diversification is not consistent with plan guidelines or is contrary to the account objectives.
- *Carry out regular reviews*: Members and candidates should establish regular review schedules to ensure that the investments held in the account adhere to the terms of the governing documents.
- *Deal fairly with all clients with respect to investment actions*: Members and candidates must not favor some clients over others and should establish policies for allocating trades and disseminating investment recommendations.
- *Disclose conflicts of interest*: Members and candidates must disclose all actual and potential conflicts of interest so that clients can evaluate those conflicts.
- *Disclose compensation arrangements*: Members and candidates should make their clients aware of all forms of manager compensation.
- *Vote proxies*: In most cases, members and candidates should determine who is authorized to vote shares and vote proxies in the best interests of the clients and ultimate beneficiaries.
- *Maintain confidentiality*: Members and candidates must preserve the confidentiality of client information.
- *Seek best execution*: Unless directed by the client as ultimate beneficiary, members and candidates must seek best execution for their clients. (Best execution is defined in the preceding text.)
- *Place client interests first*: Members and candidates must serve the best interests of clients.

20 STANDARD III(A): APPLICATION OF THE STANDARD

☐ demonstrate the application of the Code of Ethics and Standards of Professional Conduct to situations involving issues of professional integrity

☐ identify conduct that conforms to the Code and Standards and conduct that violates the Code and Standards

Example 1 (Identifying the Client—Plan Participants):

First Country Bank serves as trustee for the Miller Company's pension plan. Miller is the target of a hostile takeover attempt by Newton, Inc. In attempting to ward off Newton, Miller's managers persuade Julian Wiley, an investment manager at First Country Bank, to purchase Miller common stock in the open market for the employee pension plan. Miller's officials indicate that such action would be favorably received and would probably result in other accounts being placed with the bank. Although

Wiley believes the stock is overvalued and would not ordinarily buy it, he purchases the stock to support Miller's managers, to maintain Miller's good favor toward the bank, and to realize additional new business. The heavy stock purchases cause Miller's market price to rise to such a level that Newton retracts its takeover bid.

> *Comment*: Standard III(A) requires that a member or candidate, in evaluating a takeover bid, act prudently and solely in the interests of plan participants and beneficiaries. To meet this requirement, a member or candidate must carefully evaluate the long-term prospects of the company against the short-term prospects presented by the takeover offer and by the ability to invest elsewhere. In this instance, Wiley, acting on behalf of his employer, which was the trustee for a pension plan, clearly violated Standard III(A). He used the pension plan to perpetuate existing management, perhaps to the detriment of plan participants and the company's shareholders, and to benefit himself. Wiley's responsibilities to the plan participants and beneficiaries should have taken precedence over any ties of his bank to corporate managers and over his self-interest. Wiley had a duty to examine the takeover offer on its own merits and to make an independent decision. The guiding principle is the appropriateness of the investment decision to the pension plan, not whether the decision benefited Wiley or the company that hired him.

Example 2 (Client Commission Practices):

JNI, a successful investment counseling firm, serves as investment manager for the pension plans of several large regionally based companies. Its trading activities generate a significant amount of commission-related business. JNI uses the brokerage and research services of many firms, but most of its trading activity is handled through a large brokerage company, Thompson, Inc., because the executives of the two firms have a close friendship. Thompson's commission structure is high in comparison with charges for similar brokerage services from other firms. JNI considers Thompson's research services and execution capabilities average. In exchange for JNI directing its brokerage to Thompson, Thompson absorbs a number of JNI overhead expenses, including those for rent.

> *Comment*: JNI executives are breaching their responsibilities by using client brokerage for services that do not benefit JNI clients and by not obtaining best price and best execution for their clients. Because JNI executives are not upholding their duty of loyalty, they are violating Standard III(A).

Example 3 (Brokerage Arrangements):

Charlotte Everett, a struggling independent investment adviser, serves as investment manager for the pension plans of several companies. One of her brokers, Scott Company, is close to consummating management agreements with prospective new clients whereby Everett would manage the new client accounts and trade the accounts exclusively through Scott. One of Everett's existing clients, Crayton Corporation, has directed Everett to place securities transactions for Crayton's account exclusively through Scott. But to induce Scott to exert efforts to send more new accounts to her, Everett also directs transactions to Scott from other clients without their knowledge.

> *Comment*: Everett has an obligation at all times to seek best price and best execution on all trades. Everett may direct new client trades exclusively through Scott Company as long as Everett receives best price and execution

on the trades or receives a written statement from new clients that she is *not* to seek best price and execution and that they are aware of the consequence for their accounts. Everett may trade other accounts through Scott as a reward for directing clients to Everett only if the accounts receive best price and execution and the practice is disclosed to the accounts. Because Everett does not disclose the directed trading, Everett has violated Standard III(A).

Example 4 (Brokerage Arrangements):

Emilie Rome is a trust officer for Paget Trust Company. Rome's supervisor is responsible for reviewing Rome's trust account transactions and her monthly reports of personal stock transactions. Rome has been using Nathan Gray, a broker, almost exclusively for trust account brokerage transactions. When Gray makes a market in stocks, he has been giving Rome a lower price for personal purchases and a higher price for sales than he gives to Rome's trust accounts and other investors.

Comment: Rome is violating her duty of loyalty to the bank's trust accounts by using Gray for brokerage transactions simply because Gray trades Rome's personal account on favorable terms. Rome is placing her own interests before those of her clients.

Example 5 (Client Commission Practices):

Lauren Parker, an analyst with Provo Advisors, covers South American equities for her firm. She likes to travel to the markets for which she is responsible and decides to go on a trip to Chile, Argentina, and Brazil. The trip is sponsored by SouthAM, Inc., a research firm with a small broker/dealer affiliate that uses the clearing facilities of a larger New York brokerage house. SouthAM specializes in arranging South American trips for analysts during which they can meet with central bank officials, government ministers, local economists, and senior executives of corporations. SouthAM accepts commission dollars at a ratio of 2 to 1 against the hard-dollar costs of the research fee for the trip. Parker is not sure that SouthAM's execution is competitive, but without informing her supervisor, she directs the trading desk at Provo to start giving commission business to SouthAM so she can take the trip. SouthAM has conveniently timed the briefing trip to coincide with the beginning of Carnival season, so Parker also decides to spend five days of vacation in Rio de Janeiro at the end of the trip. Parker uses commission dollars to pay for the five days of hotel expenses.

Comment: Parker is violating Standard III(A) by not exercising her duty of loyalty to her clients. She should have determined whether the commissions charged by SouthAM are reasonable in relation to the benefit of the research provided by the trip. She also should have determined whether best execution and prices could be received from SouthAM. In addition, the five extra days are not part of the research effort because they do not assist in the investment decision making. Thus, the hotel expenses for the five days should not be paid for with client assets.

Example 6 (Excessive Trading):

Vida Knauss manages the portfolios of a number of high-net-worth individuals. A major part of her investment management fee is based on trading commissions. Knauss engages in extensive trading for each of her clients to ensure that she attains the minimum commission level set by her firm. Although the securities purchased

Standard III(A): Application of the Standard

and sold for the clients are appropriate and fall within the acceptable asset classes for the clients, the amount of trading for each account exceeds what is necessary to accomplish the client's investment objectives.

> *Comment*: Knauss has violated Standard III(A) because she is using the assets of her clients to benefit her firm and herself.

Example 7 (Managing Family Accounts):

Adam Dill recently joined New Investments Asset Managers. To assist Dill in building a book of clients, both his father and brother opened new fee-paying accounts. Dill followed all the firm's procedures in noting his relationships with these clients and in developing their investment policy statements.

After several years, the number of Dill's clients has grown, but he still manages the original accounts of his family members. An IPO is coming to market that is a suitable investment for many of his clients, including his brother. Dill does not receive the amount of stock he requested, so to avoid any appearance of a conflict of interest, he does not allocate any shares to his brother's account.

> *Comment*: Dill has violated Standard III(A) because he is not acting for the benefit of his brother's account as well as his other accounts. The brother's account is a regular fee-paying account comparable to the accounts of his other clients. By not allocating the shares proportionately across *all* accounts for which he thought the IPO was suitable, Dill is disadvantaging specific clients.
>
> Dill would have been correct in not allocating shares to his brother's account if that account was being managed outside the normal fee structure of the firm.

Example 8 (Identifying the Client):

Donna Hensley has been hired by a law firm to testify as an expert witness. Although the testimony is intended to represent impartial advice, she is concerned that her work may have negative consequences for the law firm. If the law firm is Hensley's client, how does she ensure that her testimony will not violate the required duty of loyalty, prudence, and care to one's client?

> *Comment*: In this situation, the law firm represents Hensley's employer and the aspect of "who is the client" is not well defined. When acting as an expert witness, Hensley is bound by the standard of independence and objectivity in the same manner as an independent research analyst would be bound. Hensley must not let the law firm influence the testimony she provides in the legal proceedings.

Example 9 (Identifying the Client):

Jon Miller is a mutual fund portfolio manager. The fund is focused on the global financial services sector. Wanda Spears is a private wealth manager in the same city as Miller and is a friend of Miller. At a local CFA Institute society meeting, Spears mentions to Miller that her new client is an investor in Miller's fund. She states that the two of them now share a responsibility to this client.

Comment: Spears' statement is not totally correct. Because she provides the advisory services to her new client, she alone is bound by the duty of loyalty to this client. Miller's responsibility is to manage the fund according to the investment policy statement of the fund. His actions should not be influenced by the needs of any particular fund investor.

Example 10 (Client Loyalty):

After providing client account investment performance to the external-facing departments but prior to it being finalized for release to clients, Teresa Nguyen, an investment performance analyst, notices the reporting system missed a trade. Correcting the omission resulted in a large loss for a client that had previously placed the firm on "watch" for potential termination owing to underperformance in prior periods. Nguyen knows this news is unpleasant but informs the appropriate individuals that the report needs to be updated before releasing it to the client.

Comment: Nguyen's actions align with the requirements of Standard III(A). Even though the correction may lead to the firm's termination by the client, withholding information on errors would not be in the best interest of the client.

Example 11 (Execution-Only Responsibilities):

Baftija Sulejman recently became a candidate in the CFA Program. He is a broker who executes client-directed trades for several high-net-worth individuals. Sulejman does not provide any investment advice and only executes the trading decisions made by clients. He is concerned that the Code and Standards impose a fiduciary duty on him in his dealing with clients and sends an e-mail to the CFA Ethics Helpdesk (ethics@cfainstitute.org) to seek guidance on this issue.

Comment: In this instance, Sulejman serves in an execution-only capacity and his duty of loyalty, prudence, and care is centered on the skill and diligence used when executing trades—namely, by seeking best execution and making trades within the parameters set by the clients (instructions on quantity, price, timing, etc.). Acting in the best interests of the client dictates that trades are executed on the most favorable terms that can be achieved for the client. Given this job function, the requirements of the Code and Standards for loyalty, prudence, and care clearly do not impose a fiduciary duty.

21 STANDARD III(B): DUTIES TO CLIENTS - FAIR DEALING

☐ demonstrate the application of the Code of Ethics and Standards of Professional Conduct to situations involving issues of professional integrity

> Members and Candidates must deal fairly and objectively with all clients when providing investment analysis, making investment recommendations, taking investment action, or engaging in other professional activities.

Standard III(B): Duties to Clients - Fair Dealing

Guidance

Highlights:

- *Investment Recommendations*
- *Investment Action*

Standard III(B) requires members and candidates to treat all clients fairly when disseminating investment recommendations or making material changes to prior investment recommendations or when taking investment action with regard to general purchases, new issues, or secondary offerings. Only through the fair treatment of all parties can the investment management profession maintain the confidence of the investing public.

When an investment adviser has multiple clients, the potential exists for the adviser to favor one client over another. This favoritism may take various forms—from the quality and timing of services provided to the allocation of investment opportunities.

The term "fairly" implies that the member or candidate must take care not to discriminate against any clients when disseminating investment recommendations or taking investment action. Standard III(B) does not state "equally" because members and candidates could not possibly reach all clients at exactly the same time—whether by printed mail, telephone (including text messaging), computer (including internet updates and e-mail distribution), facsimile (fax), or wire. Each client has unique needs, investment criteria, and investment objectives, so not all investment opportunities are suitable for all clients. In addition, members and candidates may provide more personal, specialized, or in-depth service to clients who are willing to pay for premium services through higher management fees or higher levels of brokerage. Members and candidates may differentiate their services to clients, but different levels of service must not disadvantage or negatively affect clients. In addition, the different service levels should be disclosed to clients and prospective clients and should be available to everyone (i.e., different service levels should not be offered selectively).

Standard III(B) covers conduct in two broadly defined categories—investment recommendations and investment action.

Investment Recommendations

The first category of conduct involves members and candidates whose primary function is the preparation of investment recommendations to be disseminated either to the public or within a firm for the use of others in making investment decisions. This group includes members and candidates employed by investment counseling, advisory, or consulting firms as well as banks, brokerage firms, and insurance companies. The criterion is that the member's or candidate's primary responsibility is the preparation of recommendations to be acted on by others, including those in the member's or candidate's organization.

An investment recommendation is any opinion expressed by a member or candidate in regard to purchasing, selling, or holding a given security or other investment. The opinion may be disseminated to customers or clients through an initial detailed research report, through a brief update report, by addition to or deletion from a list of recommended securities, or simply by oral communication. A recommendation that is distributed to anyone outside the organization is considered a communication for general distribution under Standard III(B).

Standard III(B) addresses the manner in which investment recommendations or changes in prior recommendations are disseminated to clients. Each member or candidate is obligated to ensure that information is disseminated in such a manner that all clients have a fair opportunity to act on every recommendation. Communicating with all clients on a uniform basis presents practical problems for members and candidates because of differences in timing and methods of communication with various types of customers and clients. Members and candidates should encourage their firms to design an equitable system to prevent selective or discriminatory disclosure and should inform clients about what kind of communications they will receive.

The duty to clients imposed by Standard III(B) may be more critical when members or candidates change their recommendations than when they make initial recommendations. Material changes in a member's or candidate's prior investment recommendations because of subsequent research should be communicated to all current clients; particular care should be taken that the information reaches those clients who the member or candidate knows have acted on or been affected by the earlier advice. Clients who do not know that the member or candidate has changed a recommendation and who, therefore, place orders contrary to a current recommendation should be advised of the changed recommendation before the order is accepted.

Investment Action

The second category of conduct includes those members and candidates whose primary function is taking investment action (portfolio management) on the basis of recommendations prepared internally or received from external sources. Investment action, like investment recommendations, can affect market value. Consequently, Standard III(B) requires that members or candidates treat all clients fairly in light of their investment objectives and circumstances. For example, when making investments in new offerings or in secondary financings, members and candidates should distribute the issues to all customers for whom the investments are appropriate in a manner consistent with the policies of the firm for allocating blocks of stock. If the issue is oversubscribed, then the issue should be prorated to all subscribers. This action should be taken on a round-lot basis to avoid odd-lot distributions. In addition, if the issue is oversubscribed, members and candidates should forgo any sales to themselves or their immediate families in order to free up additional shares for clients. If the investment professional's family-member accounts are managed similarly to the accounts of other clients of the firm, however, the family-member accounts should not be excluded from buying such shares.

Members and candidates must make every effort to treat all individual and institutional clients in a fair and impartial manner. A member or candidate may have multiple relationships with an institution; for example, the member or candidate may be a corporate trustee, pension fund manager, manager of funds for individuals employed by the customer, loan originator, or creditor. A member or candidate must exercise care to treat all clients fairly.

Members and candidates should disclose to clients and prospective clients the documented allocation procedures they or their firms have in place and how the procedures would affect the client or prospect. The disclosure should be clear and complete so that the client can make an informed investment decision. Even when complete disclosure is made, however, members and candidates must put client interests ahead of their own. A member's or candidate's duty of fairness and loyalty to clients can never be overridden by client consent to patently unfair allocation procedures.

Treating clients fairly also means that members and candidates should not take advantage of their position in the industry to the detriment of clients. For instance, in the context of IPOs, members and candidates must make bona fide public distributions of "hot issue" securities (defined as securities of a public offering that are trading at a premium in the secondary market whenever such trading commences because of the great demand for the securities). Members and candidates are prohibited from withholding such securities for their own benefit and must not use such securities as a reward or incentive to gain benefit.

STANDARD III(B): RECOMMENDED PROCEDURES

☐ recommend practices and procedures designed to prevent violations of the Code of Ethics and Standards of Professional Conduct

Develop Firm Policies

Although Standard III(B) refers to a member's or candidate's responsibility to deal fairly and objectively with clients, members and candidates should also encourage their firms to establish compliance procedures requiring all employees who disseminate investment recommendations or take investment actions to treat customers and clients fairly. At the very least, a member or candidate should recommend appropriate procedures to management if none are in place. And the member or candidate should make management aware of possible violations of fair-dealing practices within the firm when they come to the attention of the member or candidate.

The extent of the formality and complexity of such compliance procedures depends on the nature and size of the organization and the type of securities involved. An investment adviser who is a sole proprietor and handles only discretionary accounts might not disseminate recommendations to the public, but that adviser should have formal written procedures to ensure that all clients receive fair investment action.

Good business practice dictates that initial recommendations be made available to all customers who indicate an interest. Although a member or candidate need not communicate a recommendation to all customers, the selection process by which customers receive information should be based on suitability and known interest, not on any preferred or favored status. A common practice to assure fair dealing is to communicate recommendations simultaneously within the firm and to customers.

Members and candidates should consider the following points when establishing fair-dealing compliance procedures:

- *Limit the number of people involved*: Members and candidates should make reasonable efforts to limit the number of people who are privy to the fact that a recommendation is going to be disseminated.

- *Shorten the time frame between decision and dissemination*: Members and candidates should make reasonable efforts to limit the amount of time that elapses between the decision to make an investment recommendation and the time the actual recommendation is disseminated. If a detailed institutional recommendation that might take two or three weeks to publish is in preparation, a short summary report including the conclusion might be published in advance. In an organization where both a research committee and an investment policy committee must approve a recommendation, the meetings should be held on the same day if possible. The process of reviewing reports and printing and mailing them, faxing them, or distributing them by e-mail necessarily involves the passage of time, sometimes long periods of time. In large firms with extensive review processes, the time factor is usually not within the control of the analyst who prepares the report. Thus, many firms and their analysts communicate to customers and firm personnel the new or changed recommendations by an update or "flash" report. The communication technique might be fax, e-mail, wire, or short written report.

- *Publish guidelines for pre-dissemination behavior*: Members and candidates should encourage firms to develop guidelines that prohibit personnel who have prior knowledge of an investment recommendation from discussing or taking any action on the pending recommendation.
- *Simultaneous dissemination*: Members and candidates should establish procedures for the timing of dissemination of investment recommendations so that all clients are treated fairly—that is, are informed at approximately the same time. For example, if a firm is going to announce a new recommendation, supervisory personnel should time the announcement to avoid placing any client or group of clients at an unfair advantage relative to other clients. A communication to all branch offices should be sent at the time of the general announcement. (When appropriate, the firm should accompany the announcement of a new recommendation with a statement that trading restrictions for the firm's employees are now in effect. The trading restrictions should stay in effect until the recommendation is widely distributed to all relevant clients.) Once this distribution has occurred, the member or candidate may follow up separately with individual clients, but members and candidates should not give favored clients advance information when such advance notification may disadvantage other clients.
- *Maintain a list of clients and their holdings*: Members and candidates should maintain a list of all clients and the securities or other investments each client holds in order to facilitate notification of customers or clients of a change in an investment recommendation. If a particular security or other investment is to be sold, such a list can be used to ensure that all holders are treated fairly in the liquidation of that particular investment.
- *Develop and document trade allocation procedures*: When formulating procedures for allocating trades, members and candidates should develop a set of guiding principles that ensure

    - fairness to advisory clients, both in priority of execution of orders and in the allocation of the price obtained in execution of block orders or trades,
    - timeliness and efficiency in the execution of orders, and
    - accuracy of the member's or candidate's records as to trade orders and client account positions.

With these principles in mind, members and candidates should develop or encourage their firm to develop written allocation procedures, with particular attention to procedures for block trades and new issues. Procedures to consider are as follows:

- requiring orders and modifications or cancellations of orders to be documented and time stamped;
- processing and executing orders on a first-in, first-out basis with consideration of bundling orders for efficiency as appropriate for the asset class or the security;
- developing a policy to address such issues as calculating execution prices and "partial fills" when trades are grouped, or in a block, for efficiency;
- giving all client accounts participating in a block trade the same execution price and charging the same commission;
- when the full amount of the block order is not executed, allocating partially executed orders among the participating client accounts pro rata on the basis of order size while not going below an established minimum lot size for some securities (e.g., bonds); and

Standard III(B): Application of the Standard

- when allocating trades for new issues, obtaining advance indications of interest, allocating securities by client (rather than portfolio manager), and providing a method for calculating allocations.

Disclose Trade Allocation Procedures

Members and candidates should disclose to clients and prospective clients how they select accounts to participate in an order and how they determine the amount of securities each account will buy or sell. Trade allocation procedures must be fair and equitable, and disclosure of inequitable allocation methods does not relieve the member or candidate of this obligation.

Establish Systematic Account Review

Member and candidate supervisors should review each account on a regular basis to ensure that no client or customer is being given preferential treatment and that the investment actions taken for each account are suitable for each account's objectives. Because investments should be based on individual needs and circumstances, an investment manager may have good reasons for placing a given security or other investment in one account while selling it from another account and should fully document the reasons behind both sides of the transaction. Members and candidates should encourage firms to establish review procedures, however, to detect whether trading in one account is being used to benefit a favored client.

Disclose Levels of Service

Members and candidates should disclose to all clients whether the organization offers different levels of service to clients for the same fee or different fees. Different levels of service should not be offered to clients selectively.

STANDARD III(B): APPLICATION OF THE STANDARD | 23

- ☐ demonstrate the application of the Code of Ethics and Standards of Professional Conduct to situations involving issues of professional integrity
- ☐ identify conduct that conforms to the Code and Standards and conduct that violates the Code and Standards

Example 1 (Selective Disclosure):

Bradley Ames, a well-known and respected analyst, follows the computer industry. In the course of his research, he finds that a small, relatively unknown company whose shares are traded over the counter has just signed significant contracts with some of the companies he follows. After a considerable amount of investigation, Ames decides to write a research report on the small company and recommend purchase of its shares. While the report is being reviewed by the company for factual accuracy,

Ames schedules a luncheon with several of his best clients to discuss the company. At the luncheon, he mentions the purchase recommendation scheduled to be sent early the following week to all the firm's clients.

> *Comment*: Ames has violated Standard III(B) by disseminating the purchase recommendation to the clients with whom he has lunch a week before the recommendation is sent to all clients.

Example 2 (Fair Dealing between Funds):

Spencer Rivers, president of XYZ Corporation, moves his company's growth-oriented pension fund to a particular bank primarily because of the excellent investment performance achieved by the bank's commingled fund for the prior five-year period. Later, Rivers compares the results of his pension fund with those of the bank's commingled fund. He is startled to learn that, even though the two accounts have the same investment objectives and similar portfolios, his company's pension fund has significantly underperformed the bank's commingled fund. Questioning this result at his next meeting with the pension fund's manager, Rivers is told that, as a matter of policy, when a new security is placed on the recommended list, Morgan Jackson, the pension fund manager, first purchases the security for the commingled account and then purchases it on a pro rata basis for all other pension fund accounts. Similarly, when a sale is recommended, the security is sold first from the commingled account and then sold on a pro rata basis from all other accounts. Rivers also learns that if the bank cannot get enough shares (especially of hot issues) to be meaningful to all the accounts, its policy is to place the new issues only in the commingled account.

Seeing that Rivers is neither satisfied nor pleased by the explanation, Jackson quickly adds that nondiscretionary pension accounts and personal trust accounts have a lower priority on purchase and sale recommendations than discretionary pension fund accounts. Furthermore, Jackson states, the company's pension fund had the opportunity to invest up to 5% in the commingled fund.

> *Comment*: The bank's policy does not treat all customers fairly, and Jackson has violated her duty to her clients by giving priority to the growth-oriented commingled fund over all other funds and to discretionary accounts over nondiscretionary accounts. Jackson must execute orders on a systematic basis that is fair to all clients. In addition, trade allocation procedures should be disclosed to all clients when they become clients. Of course, in this case, disclosure of the bank's policy would not change the fact that the policy is unfair.

Example 3 (Fair Dealing and IPO Distribution):

Dominic Morris works for a small regional securities firm. His work consists of corporate finance activities and investing for institutional clients. Arena, Ltd., is planning to go public. The partners have secured rights to buy an arena football league franchise and are planning to use the funds from the issue to complete the purchase. Because arena football is the current rage, Morris believes he has a hot issue on his hands. He has quietly negotiated some options for himself for helping convince Arena to do the financing through his securities firm. When he seeks expressions of interest, the institutional buyers oversubscribe the issue. Morris, assuming that the institutions have the financial clout to drive the stock up, then fills all orders (including his own) and decreases the institutional blocks.

Comment: Morris has violated Standard III(B) by not treating all customers fairly. He should not have taken any shares himself and should have prorated the shares offered among all clients. In addition, he should have disclosed to his firm and to his clients that he received options as part of the deal [see Standard VI(A)–Disclosure of Conflicts].

Example 4 (Fair Dealing and Transaction Allocation):

Eleanor Preston, the chief investment officer of Porter Williams Investments (PWI), a medium-size money management firm, has been trying to retain a client, Colby Company. Management at Colby, which accounts for almost half of PWI's revenues, recently told Preston that if the performance of its account did not improve, it would find a new money manager. Shortly after this threat, Preston purchases mortgage-backed securities (MBSs) for several accounts, including Colby's. Preston is busy with a number of transactions that day, so she fails to allocate the trades immediately or write up the trade tickets. A few days later, when Preston is allocating trades, she notes that some of the MBSs have significantly increased in price and some have dropped. Preston decides to allocate the profitable trades to Colby and spread the losing trades among several other PWI accounts.

Comment: Preston has violated Standard III(B) by failing to deal fairly with her clients in taking these investment actions. Preston should have allocated the trades prior to executing the orders, or she should have had a systematic approach to allocating the trades, such as pro rata, as soon as practical after they were executed. Among other things, Preston must disclose to the client that the adviser may act as broker for, receive commissions from, and have a potential conflict of interest regarding both parties in agency cross-transactions. After the disclosure, she should obtain from the client consent authorizing such transactions in advance.

Example 5 (Selective Disclosure):

Saunders Industrial Waste Management (SIWM) publicly indicates to analysts that it is comfortable with the somewhat disappointing earnings-per-share projection of US$1.16 for the quarter. Bernard Roberts, an analyst at Coffey Investments, is confident that SIWM management has understated the forecasted earnings so that the real announcement will cause an "upside surprise" and boost the price of SIWM stock. The "whisper number" (rumored) estimate based on extensive research and discussed among knowledgeable analysts is higher than US$1.16. Roberts repeats the US$1.16 figure in his research report to all Coffey clients but informally tells his large clients that he expects the earnings per share to be higher, making SIWM a good buy.

Comment: By not sharing his opinion regarding the potential for a significant upside earnings surprise with all clients, Roberts is not treating all clients fairly and has violated Standard III(B).

Example 6 (Additional Services for Select Clients):

Jenpin Weng uses e-mail to issue a new recommendation to all his clients. He then calls his three largest institutional clients to discuss the recommendation in detail.

Comment: Weng has not violated Standard III(B) because he widely disseminated the recommendation and provided the information to all his clients prior to discussing it with a select few. Weng's largest clients received additional personal service because they presumably pay higher fees or because they have a large amount of assets under Weng's management. If Weng had discussed the report with a select group of clients prior to distributing it to all his clients, he would have violated Standard III(B).

Example 7 (Minimum Lot Allocations):

Lynn Hampton is a well-respected private wealth manager in her community with a diversified client base. She determines that a new 10-year bond being offered by Healthy Pharmaceuticals is appropriate for five of her clients. Three clients request to purchase US$10,000 each, and the other two request US$50,000 each. The minimum lot size is established at US$5,000, and the issue is oversubscribed at the time of placement. Her firm's policy is that odd-lot allocations, especially those below the minimum, should be avoided because they may affect the liquidity of the security at the time of sale.

Hampton is informed she will receive only US$55,000 of the offering for all accounts. Hampton distributes the bond investments as follows: The three accounts that requested US$10,000 are allocated US$5,000 each, and the two accounts that requested US$50,000 are allocated US$20,000 each.

Comment: Hampton has not violated Standard III(B), even though the distribution is not on a completely pro rata basis because of the required minimum lot size. With the total allocation being significantly below the amount requested, Hampton ensured that each client received at least the minimum lot size of the issue. This approach allowed the clients to efficiently sell the bond later if necessary.

Example 8 (Excessive Trading):

Ling Chan manages the accounts for many pension plans, including the plan of his father's employer. Chan developed similar but not identical investment policies for each client, so the investment portfolios are rarely the same. To minimize the cost to his father's pension plan, he intentionally trades more frequently in the accounts of other clients to ensure the required brokerage is incurred to continue receiving free research for use by all the pensions.

Comment: Chan is violating Standard III(B) because his trading actions are disadvantaging his clients to enhance a relationship with a preferred client. All clients are benefiting from the research being provided and should incur their fair portion of the costs. This does not mean that additional trading should occur if a client has not paid an equal portion of the commission; trading should occur only as required by the strategy.

Example 9 (Limited Social Media Disclosures):

Mary Burdette was recently hired by Fundamental Investment Management (FIM) as a junior auto industry analyst. Burdette is expected to expand the social media presence of the firm because she is active with various networks, including Facebook, LinkedIn, and Twitter. Although Burdette's supervisor, Joe Graf, has never used social media, he encourages Burdette to explore opportunities to increase FIM's online presence and ability to share content, communicate, and broadcast information to clients. In response to Graf's encouragement, Burdette is working on a proposal detailing the advantages of getting FIM onto Twitter in addition to launching a company Facebook page.

As part of her auto industry research for FIM, Burdette is completing a report on the financial impact of Sun Drive Auto Ltd.'s new solar technology for compact automobiles. This research report will be her first for FIM, and she believes Sun Drive's technology could revolutionize the auto industry. In her excitement, Burdette sends a quick tweet to FIM Twitter followers summarizing her "buy" recommendation for Sun Drive Auto stock.

> *Comment*: Burdette has violated Standard III(B) by sending an investment recommendation to a select group of contacts prior to distributing it to all clients. Burdette must make sure she has received the appropriate training about FIM's policies and procedures, including the appropriate business use of personal social media networks before engaging in such activities.
>
> See Standard IV(C) for guidance related to the duties of the supervisor.

Example 10 (Fair Dealing between Clients):

Paul Rove, performance analyst for Alpha-Beta Investment Management, is describing to the firm's chief investment officer (CIO) two new reports he would like to develop to assist the firm in meeting its obligations to treat clients fairly. Because many of the firm's clients have similar investment objectives and portfolios, Rove suggests a report detailing securities owned across several clients and the percentage of the portfolio the security represents. The second report would compare the monthly performance of portfolios with similar strategies. The outliers within each report would be submitted to the CIO for review.

> *Comment*: As a performance analyst, Rove likely has little direct contact with clients and thus has limited opportunity to treat clients differently. The recommended reports comply with Standard III(B) while helping the firm conduct after-the-fact reviews of how effectively the firm's advisers are dealing with their clients' portfolios. Reports that monitor the fair treatment of clients are an important oversight tool to ensure that clients are treated fairly.

STANDARD III(C): DUTIES TO CLIENTS – SUITABILITY

24

☐ demonstrate the application of the Code of Ethics and Standards of Professional Conduct to situations involving issues of professional integrity

1. When Members and Candidates are in an advisory relationship with a client, they must:
   a. Make a reasonable inquiry into a client's or prospective client's investment experience, risk and return objectives, and financial constraints prior to making any investment recommendation or taking investment action and must reassess and update this information regularly.

> **b.** Determine that an investment is suitable to the client's financial situation and consistent with the client's written objectives, mandates, and constraints before making an investment recommendation or taking investment action.
> **c.** Judge the suitability of investments in the context of the client's total portfolio.
>
> **2.** When Members and Candidates are responsible for managing a portfolio to a specific mandate, strategy, or style, they must make only investment recommendations or take only investment actions that are consistent with the stated objectives and constraints of the portfolio.

Guidance

Highlights:

- *Developing an Investment Policy*
- *Understanding the Client's Risk Profile*
- *Updating an Investment Policy*
- *The Need for Diversification*
- *Addressing Unsolicited Trading Requests*
- *Managing to an Index or Mandate*

Standard III(C) requires that members and candidates who are in an investment advisory relationship with clients consider carefully the needs, circumstances, and objectives of the clients when determining the appropriateness and suitability of a given investment or course of investment action. An appropriate suitability determination will not, however, prevent some investments or investment actions from losing value.

In judging the suitability of a potential investment, the member or candidate should review many aspects of the client's knowledge, experience related to investing, and financial situation. These aspects include, but are not limited to, the risk profile of the investment as compared with the constraints of the client, the impact of the investment on the diversity of the portfolio, and whether the client has the means or net worth to assume the associated risk. The investment professional's determination of suitability should reflect only the investment recommendations or actions that a prudent person would be willing to undertake. Not every investment opportunity will be suitable for every portfolio, regardless of the potential return being offered.

The responsibilities of members and candidates to gather information and make a suitability analysis prior to making a recommendation or taking investment action fall on those members and candidates who provide investment advice in the course of an advisory relationship with a client. Other members and candidates may be simply executing specific instructions for retail clients when buying or selling securities, such as shares in mutual funds. These members and candidates and some others, such as sell-side analysts, may not have the opportunity to judge the suitability of a particular investment for the ultimate client.

Developing an Investment Policy

When an advisory relationship exists, members and candidates must gather client information at the inception of the relationship. Such information includes the client's financial circumstances, personal data (such as age and occupation) that are relevant to investment decisions, attitudes toward risk, and objectives in investing. This information should be incorporated into a written investment policy statement

(IPS) that addresses the client's risk tolerance, return requirements, and all investment constraints (including time horizon, liquidity needs, tax concerns, legal and regulatory factors, and unique circumstances). Without identifying such client factors, members and candidates cannot judge whether a particular investment or strategy is suitable for a particular client. The IPS also should identify and describe the roles and responsibilities of the parties to the advisory relationship and investment process, as well as schedules for review and evaluation of the IPS. After formulating long-term capital market expectations, members and candidates can assist in developing an appropriate strategic asset allocation and investment program for the client, whether these are presented in separate documents or incorporated in the IPS or in appendices to the IPS.

Understanding the Client's Risk Profile

One of the most important factors to be considered in matching appropriateness and suitability of an investment with a client's needs and circumstances is measuring that client's tolerance for risk. The investment professional must consider the possibilities of rapidly changing investment environments and their likely impact on a client's holdings, both individual securities and the collective portfolio. The risk of many investment strategies can and should be analyzed and quantified in advance.

The use of synthetic investment vehicles and derivative investment products has introduced particular issues of risk. Members and candidates should pay careful attention to the leverage inherent in many of these vehicles or products when considering them for use in a client's investment program. Such leverage and limited liquidity, depending on the degree to which they are hedged, bear directly on the issue of suitability for the client.

Updating an Investment Policy

Updating the IPS should be repeated at least annually and also prior to material changes to any specific investment recommendations or decisions on behalf of the client. The effort to determine the needs and circumstances of each client is not a one-time occurrence. Investment recommendations or decisions are usually part of an ongoing process that takes into account the diversity and changing nature of portfolio and client characteristics. The passage of time is bound to produce changes that are important with respect to investment objectives.

For an individual client, important changes might include the number of dependents, personal tax status, health, liquidity needs, risk tolerance, amount of wealth beyond that represented in the portfolio, and extent to which compensation and other income provide for current income needs. With respect to an institutional client, such changes might relate to the magnitude of unfunded liabilities in a pension fund, the withdrawal privileges in an employee savings plan, or the distribution requirements of a charitable foundation. Without efforts to update information concerning client factors, one or more factors could change without the investment manager's knowledge.

Suitability review can be done most effectively when the client fully discloses his or her complete financial portfolio, including those portions not managed by the member or candidate. If clients withhold information about their financial portfolios, the suitability analysis conducted by members and candidates cannot be expected to be complete; it must be based on the information provided.

The Need for Diversification

The investment profession has long recognized that combining several different investments is likely to provide a more acceptable level of risk exposure than having all assets in a single investment. The unique characteristics (or risks) of an individual investment may become partially or entirely neutralized when it is combined with other individual investments within a portfolio. Some reasonable amount of diversification is thus the norm for many portfolios, especially those managed by individuals or institutions that have some degree of legal fiduciary responsibility.

An investment with high relative risk on its own may be a suitable investment in the context of the entire portfolio or when the client's stated objectives contemplate speculative or risky investments. The manager may be responsible for only a portion of the client's total portfolio, or the client may not have provided a full financial picture. Members and candidates can be responsible for assessing the suitability of an investment only on the basis of the information and criteria actually provided by the client.

Addressing Unsolicited Trading Requests

Members and candidates may receive requests from a client for trades that do not properly align with the risk and return objectives outlined in the client's investment policy statement. These transaction requests may be based on the client's individual biases or professional experience. Members and candidates will need to make reasonable efforts to balance their clients' trading requests with their responsibilities to follow the agreed-on investment policy statement.

In cases of unsolicited trade requests that a member or candidate knows are unsuitable for a client, the member or candidate should refrain from making the trade until he or she discusses the concerns with the client. The discussions and resulting actions may encompass a variety of scenarios depending on how the requested unsuitable investment relates to the client's full portfolio.

Many times, an unsolicited request may be expected to have only a minimum impact on the entire portfolio because the size of the requested trade is small or the trade would result in a limited change to the portfolio's risk profile. In discussing the trade, the member or candidate should focus on educating the investor on how the request deviates from the current policy statement. Following the discussion, the member or candidate may follow his or her firm's policies regarding the necessary client approval for executing unsuitable trades. At a minimum, the client should acknowledge the discussion and accept the conditions that make the recommendation unsuitable.

Should the unsolicited request be expected to have a material impact on the portfolio, the member or candidate should use this opportunity to update the investment policy statement. Doing so would allow the client to fully understand the potential effect of the requested trade on his or her current goals or risk levels.

Members and candidates may have some clients who decline to modify their policy statements while insisting an unsolicited trade be made. In such instances, members or candidates will need to evaluate the effectiveness of their services to the client. The options available to the members or candidates will depend on the services provided by their employer. Some firms may allow for the trade to be executed in a new unmanaged account. If alternative options are not available, members and candidates ultimately will need to determine whether they should continue the advisory arrangement with the client.

Managing to an Index or Mandate

Some members and candidates do not manage money for individuals but are responsible for managing a fund to an index or an expected mandate. The responsibility of these members and candidates is to invest in a manner consistent with the stated mandate. For example, a member or candidate who serves as the fund manager for a large-cap income fund would not be following the fund mandate by investing heavily in small-cap or start-up companies whose stock is speculative in nature. Members and candidates who manage pooled assets to a specific mandate are not responsible for determining the suitability of the *fund* as an investment for investors who may be purchasing shares in the fund. The responsibility for determining the suitability of an investment for clients can be conferred only on members and candidates who have an advisory relationship with clients.

STANDARD III(C): RECOMMENDED PROCEDURES

☐ recommend practices and procedures designed to prevent violations of the Code of Ethics and Standards of Professional Conduct

Investment Policy Statement

To fulfill the basic provisions of Standard III(C), a member or candidate should put the needs and circumstances of each client and the client's investment objectives into a written investment policy statement. In formulating an investment policy for the client, the member or candidate should take the following into consideration:

- client identification—(1) type and nature of client, (2) the existence of separate beneficiaries, and (3) approximate portion of total client assets that the member or candidate is managing;
- investor objectives—(1) return objectives (income, growth in principal, maintenance of purchasing power) and (2) risk tolerance (suitability, stability of values);
- investor constraints—(1) liquidity needs, (2) expected cash flows (patterns of additions and/or withdrawals), (3) investable funds (assets and liabilities or other commitments), (4) time horizon, (5) tax considerations, (6) regulatory and legal circumstances, (7) investor preferences, prohibitions, circumstances, and unique needs, and (8) proxy voting responsibilities and guidance; and
- performance measurement benchmarks.

Regular Updates

The investor's objectives and constraints should be maintained and reviewed periodically to reflect any changes in the client's circumstances. Members and candidates should regularly compare client constraints with capital market expectations to arrive at an appropriate asset allocation. Changes in either factor may result in a fundamental change in asset allocation. Annual review is reasonable unless business or other reasons, such as a major change in market conditions, dictate more frequent review. Members and candidates should document attempts to carry out such a review if circumstances prevent it.

Suitability Test Policies

With the increase in regulatory required suitability tests, members and candidates should encourage their firms to develop related policies and procedures. The procedures will differ according to the size of the firm and the scope of the services offered to its clients.

The test procedures should require the investment professional to look beyond the potential return of the investment and include the following:

- an analysis of the impact on the portfolio's diversification,
- a comparison of the investment risks with the client's assessed risk tolerance, and
- the fit of the investment with the required investment strategy.

26 STANDARD III(C): APPLICATION OF THE STANDARD

☐ demonstrate the application of the Code of Ethics and Standards of Professional Conduct to situations involving issues of professional integrity

☐ identify conduct that conforms to the Code and Standards and conduct that violates the Code and Standards

Example 1 (Investment Suitability—Risk Profile):

Caleb Smith, an investment adviser, has two clients: Larry Robertson, 60 years old, and Gabriel Lanai, 40 years old. Both clients earn roughly the same salary, but Robertson has a much higher risk tolerance because he has a large asset base. Robertson is willing to invest part of his assets very aggressively; Lanai wants only to achieve a steady rate of return with low volatility to pay for his children's education. Smith recommends investing 20% of both portfolios in zero-yield, small-cap, high-technology equity issues.

Comment: In Robertson's case, the investment may be appropriate because of his financial circumstances and aggressive investment position, but this investment is not suitable for Lanai. Smith is violating Standard III(C) by applying Robertson's investment strategy to Lanai because the two clients' financial circumstances and objectives differ.

Example 2 (Investment Suitability—Entire Portfolio):

Jessica McDowell, an investment adviser, suggests to Brian Crosby, a risk-averse client, that covered call options be used in his equity portfolio. The purpose would be to enhance Crosby's income and partially offset any untimely depreciation in the portfolio's value should the stock market or other circumstances affect his holdings unfavorably. McDowell educates Crosby about all possible outcomes, including the risk of incurring an added tax liability if a stock rises in price and is called away and, conversely, the risk of his holdings losing protection on the downside if prices drop sharply.

Comment: When determining suitability of an investment, the primary focus should be the characteristics of the client's entire portfolio, not the characteristics of single securities on an issue-by-issue basis. The basic characteristics of the entire portfolio will largely determine whether investment recommendations are taking client factors into account. Therefore, the most important aspects of a particular investment are those that will affect the characteristics of the total portfolio. In this case, McDowell properly considers the investment in the context of the entire portfolio and thoroughly explains the investment to the client.

Example 3 (IPS Updating):

In a regular meeting with client Seth Jones, the portfolio managers at Blue Chip Investment Advisors are careful to allow some time to review his current needs and circumstances. In doing so, they learn that some significant changes have recently taken place in his life. A wealthy uncle left Jones an inheritance that increased his net worth fourfold, to US$1 million.

> *Comment*: The inheritance has significantly increased Jones's ability (and possibly his willingness) to assume risk and has diminished the average yield required to meet his current income needs. Jones's financial circumstances have definitely changed, so Blue Chip managers must update Jones's investment policy statement to reflect how his investment objectives have changed. Accordingly, the Blue Chip portfolio managers should consider a somewhat higher equity ratio for his portfolio than was called for by the previous circumstances, and the managers' specific common stock recommendations might be heavily tilted toward low-yield, growth-oriented issues.

Example 4 (Following an Investment Mandate):

Louis Perkowski manages a high-income mutual fund. He purchases zero-dividend stock in a financial services company because he believes the stock is undervalued and is in a potential growth industry, which makes it an attractive investment.

> *Comment*: A zero-dividend stock does not seem to fit the mandate of the fund that Perkowski is managing. Unless Perkowski's investment fits within the mandate or is within the realm of allowable investments the fund has made clear in its disclosures, Perkowski has violated Standard III(C).

Example 5 (IPS Requirements and Limitations):

Max Gubler, chief investment officer of a property/casualty insurance subsidiary of a large financial conglomerate, wants to improve the diversification of the subsidiary's investment portfolio and increase its returns. The subsidiary's investment policy statement provides for highly liquid investments, such as large-cap equities and government, supranational, and corporate bonds with a minimum credit rating of AA and maturity of no more than five years. In a recent presentation, a venture capital group offered very attractive prospective returns on some of its private equity funds that provide seed capital to ventures. An exit strategy was already contemplated, but investors would have to observe a minimum three-year lockup period and a subsequent laddered exit option for a maximum of one-third of their shares per year. Gubler does not want to miss this opportunity. After extensive analysis, with the intent to optimize the return on the equity assets within the subsidiary's current portfolio, he invests 4% in this seed fund, leaving the portfolio's total equity exposure still well below its upper limit.

> *Comment*: Gubler is violating Standard III(A)–Loyalty, Prudence, and Care as well as Standard III(C). His new investment locks up part of the subsidiary's assets for at least three years and up to as many as five years and possibly beyond. The IPS requires investments in highly liquid investments

and describes accepted asset classes; private equity investments with a lockup period certainly do not qualify. Even without a lockup period, an asset class with only an occasional, and thus implicitly illiquid, market may not be suitable for the portfolio. Although an IPS typically describes objectives and constraints in great detail, the manager must also make every effort to understand the client's business and circumstances. Doing so should enable the manager to recognize, understand, and discuss with the client other factors that may be or may become material in the investment management process.

Example 6 (Submanager and IPS Reviews):

Paul Ostrowski's investment management business has grown significantly over the past couple of years, and some clients want to diversify internationally. Ostrowski decides to find a submanager to handle the expected international investments. Because this will be his first subadviser, Ostrowski uses the CFA Institute model "request for proposal" to design a questionnaire for his search. By his deadline, he receives seven completed questionnaires from a variety of domestic and international firms trying to gain his business. Ostrowski reviews all the applications in detail and decides to select the firm that charges the lowest fees because doing so will have the least impact on his firm's bottom line.

> *Comment*: When selecting an external manager or subadviser, Ostrowski needs to ensure that the new manager's services are appropriate for his clients. This due diligence includes comparing the risk profile of the clients with the investment strategy of the manager. In basing the decision on the fee structure alone, Ostrowski may be violating Standard III(C).
> When clients ask to diversify into international products, it is an appropriate time to review and update the clients' IPSs. Ostrowski's review may determine that the risk of international investments modifies the risk profiles of the clients or does not represent an appropriate investment.
> See also Standard V(A)–Diligence and Reasonable Basis for further discussion of the review process needed in selecting appropriate submanagers.

Example 7 (Investment Suitability—Risk Profile):

Samantha Snead, a portfolio manager for Thomas Investment Counsel, Inc., specializes in managing public retirement funds and defined benefit pension plan accounts, all of which have long-term investment objectives. A year ago, Snead's employer, in an attempt to motivate and retain key investment professionals, introduced a bonus compensation system that rewards portfolio managers on the basis of quarterly performance relative to their peers and to certain benchmark indexes. In an attempt to improve the short-term performance of her accounts, Snead changes her investment strategy and purchases several high-beta stocks for client portfolios. These purchases are seemingly contrary to the clients' investment policy statements. Following their purchase, an officer of Griffin Corporation, one of Snead's pension fund clients, asks why Griffin Corporation's portfolio seems to be dominated by high-beta stocks of companies that often appear among the most actively traded issues. No change in objective or strategy has been recommended by Snead during the year.

> *Comment*: Snead violated Standard III(C) by investing the clients' assets in high-beta stocks. These high-risk investments are contrary to the long-term risk profile established in the clients' IPSs. Snead has changed the investment

strategy of the clients in an attempt to reap short-term rewards offered by her firm's new compensation arrangement, not in response to changes in clients' investment policy statements.

See also Standard VI(A)–Disclosure of Conflicts.

Example 8 (Investment Suitability):

Andre Shrub owns and operates Conduit, an investment advisory firm. Prior to opening Conduit, Shrub was an account manager with Elite Investment, a hedge fund managed by his good friend Adam Reed. To attract clients to a new Conduit fund, Shrub offers lower-than-normal management fees. He can do so because the fund consists of two top-performing funds managed by Reed. Given his personal friendship with Reed and the prior performance record of these two funds, Shrub believes this new fund is a winning combination for all parties. Clients quickly invest with Conduit to gain access to the Elite funds. No one is turned away because Conduit is seeking to expand its assets under management.

> *Comment*: Shrub has violated Standard III(C) because the risk profile of the new fund may not be suitable for every client. As an investment adviser, Shrub needs to establish an investment policy statement for each client and recommend only investments that match each client's risk and return profile in the IPS. Shrub is required to act as more than a simple sales agent for Elite.
>
> Although Shrub cannot disobey the direct request of a client to purchase a specific security, he should fully discuss the risks of a planned purchase and provide reasons why it might not be suitable for a client. This requirement may lead members and candidates to decline new customers if those customers' requested investment decisions are significantly out of line with their stated requirements.
>
> See also Standard V(A)–Diligence and Reasonable Basis.

STANDARD III(D): DUTIES TO CLIENTS - PERFORMANCE PRESENTATION

☐ demonstrate the application of the Code of Ethics and Standards of Professional Conduct to situations involving issues of professional integrity

> When communicating investment performance information, Members and Candidates must make reasonable efforts to ensure that it is fair, accurate, and complete.

Guidance

Standard III(D) requires members and candidates to provide credible performance information to clients and prospective clients and to avoid misstating performance or misleading clients and prospective clients about the investment performance of members or candidates or their firms. This standard encourages full disclosure of investment performance data to clients and prospective clients.

Standard III(D) covers any practice that would lead to misrepresentation of a member's or candidate's performance record, whether the practice involves performance presentation or performance measurement. This standard prohibits misrepresentations of past performance or reasonably expected performance. A member or candidate must give a fair and complete presentation of performance information whenever communicating data with respect to the performance history of individual accounts, composites or groups of accounts, or composites of an analyst's or firm's performance results. Furthermore, members and candidates should not state or imply that clients will obtain or benefit from a rate of return that was generated in the past.

The requirements of this standard are not limited to members and candidates managing separate accounts. Whenever a member or candidate provides performance information for which the manager is claiming responsibility, such as for pooled funds, the history must be accurate. Research analysts promoting the success or accuracy of their recommendations must ensure that their claims are fair, accurate, and complete.

If the presentation is brief, the member or candidate must make available to clients and prospects, on request, the detailed information supporting that communication. Best practice dictates that brief presentations include a reference to the limited nature of the information provided.

28. STANDARD III(D): RECOMMENDED PROCEDURES

- [ ] demonstrate the application of the Code of Ethics and Standards of Professional Conduct to situations involving issues of professional integrity
- [ ] identify conduct that conforms to the Code and Standards and conduct that violates the Code and Standards

Apply the GIPS Standards

For members and candidates who are showing the performance history of the assets they manage, compliance with the GIPS standards is the best method to meet their obligations under Standard III(D). Members and candidates should encourage their firms to comply with the GIPS standards.

Compliance without Applying GIPS Standards

Members and candidates can also meet their obligations under Standard III(D) by

- considering the knowledge and sophistication of the audience to whom a performance presentation is addressed,
- presenting the performance of the weighted composite of similar portfolios rather than using a single representative account,
- including terminated accounts as part of performance history with a clear indication of when the accounts were terminated,

- including disclosures that fully explain the performance results being reported (for example, stating, when appropriate, that results are simulated when model results are used, clearly indicating when the performance record is that of a prior entity, or disclosing whether the performance is gross of fees, net of fees, or after tax), and
- maintaining the data and records used to calculate the performance being presented.

STANDARD III(D): APPLICATION OF THE STANDARD

☐ recommend practices and procedures designed to prevent violations of the Code of Ethics and Standards of Professional Conduct

Example 1 (Performance Calculation and Length of Time):

Kyle Taylor of Taylor Trust Company, noting the performance of Taylor's common trust fund for the past two years, states in a brochure sent to his potential clients, "You can expect steady 25% annual compound growth of the value of your investments over the year." Taylor Trust's common trust fund did increase at the rate of 25% per year for the past year, which mirrored the increase of the entire market. The fund has never averaged that growth for more than one year, however, and the average rate of growth of all of its trust accounts for five years is 5% per year.

> *Comment*: Taylor's brochure is in violation of Standard III(D). Taylor should have disclosed that the 25% growth occurred only in one year. Additionally, Taylor did not include client accounts other than those in the firm's common trust fund. A general claim of firm performance should take into account the performance of all categories of accounts. Finally, by stating that clients can expect a steady 25% annual compound growth rate, Taylor is also violating Standard I(C)–Misrepresentation, which prohibits assurances or guarantees regarding an investment.

Example 2 (Performance Calculation and Asset Weighting):

Anna Judd, a senior partner of Alexander Capital Management, circulates a performance report for the capital appreciation accounts for the years 1988 through 2004. The firm claims compliance with the GIPS standards. Returns are not calculated in accordance with the requirements of the GIPS standards, however, because the composites are not asset weighted.

> *Comment*: Judd is in violation of Standard III(D). When claiming compliance with the GIPS standards, firms must meet *all* of the requirements, make mandatory disclosures, and meet any other requirements that apply to that firm's specific situation. Judd's violation is not from any misuse of the data but from a false claim of GIPS compliance.

Example 3 (Performance Presentation and Prior Fund/Employer):

Aaron McCoy is vice president and managing partner of the equity investment group of Mastermind Financial Advisors, a new business. Mastermind recruited McCoy because he had a proven six-year track record with G&P Financial. In developing Mastermind's advertising and marketing campaign, McCoy prepares an advertisement that includes the equity investment performance he achieved at G&P Financial. The advertisement for Mastermind does not identify the equity performance as being earned while at G&P. The advertisement is distributed to existing clients and prospective clients of Mastermind.

Comment: McCoy has violated Standard III(D) by distributing an advertisement that contains material misrepresentations about the historical performance of Mastermind. Standard III(D) requires that members and candidates make every reasonable effort to ensure that performance information is a fair, accurate, and complete representation of an individual's or firm's performance. As a general matter, this standard does not prohibit showing past performance of funds managed at a prior firm as part of a performance track record as long as showing that record is accompanied by appropriate disclosures about where the performance took place and the person's specific role in achieving that performance. If McCoy chooses to use his past performance from G&P in Mastermind's advertising, he should make full disclosure of the source of the historical performance.

Example 4 (Performance Presentation and Simulated Results):

Jed Davis has developed a mutual fund selection product based on historical information from the 1990–95 period. Davis tested his methodology by applying it retroactively to data from the 1996–2003 period, thus producing simulated performance results for those years. In January 2004, Davis's employer decided to offer the product and Davis began promoting it through trade journal advertisements and direct dissemination to clients. The advertisements included the performance results for the 1996–2003 period but did not indicate that the results were simulated.

Comment: Davis violated Standard III(D) by failing to clearly identify simulated performance results. Standard III(D) prohibits members and candidates from making any statements that misrepresent the performance achieved by them or their firms and requires members and candidates to make every reasonable effort to ensure that performance information presented to clients is fair, accurate, and complete. Use of simulated results should be accompanied by full disclosure as to the source of the performance data, including the fact that the results from 1995 through 2003 were the result of applying the model retroactively to that time period.

Example 5 (Performance Calculation and Selected Accounts Only):

In a presentation prepared for prospective clients, William Kilmer shows the rates of return realized over a five-year period by a "composite" of his firm's discretionary accounts that have a "balanced" objective. This composite, however, consisted of only a few of the accounts that met the balanced criterion set by the firm, excluded accounts under a certain asset level without disclosing the fact of their exclusion, and included accounts that did not have the balanced mandate because those accounts would boost the investment results. In addition, to achieve better results, Kilmer manipulated the narrow range of accounts included in the composite by changing the accounts that made up the composite over time.

> *Comment*: Kilmer violated Standard III(D) by misrepresenting the facts in the promotional material sent to prospective clients, distorting his firm's performance record, and failing to include disclosures that would have clarified the presentation.

Example 6 (Performance Attribution Changes):

Art Purell is reviewing the quarterly performance attribution reports for distribution to clients. Purell works for an investment management firm with a bottom-up, fundamentals-driven investment process that seeks to add value through stock selection. The attribution methodology currently compares each stock with its sector. The attribution report indicates that the value added this quarter came from asset allocation and that stock selection contributed negatively to the calculated return.

Through running several different scenarios, Purell discovers that calculating attribution by comparing each stock with its industry and then rolling the effect to the sector level improves the appearance of the manager's stock selection activities. Because the firm defines the attribution terms and the results better reflect the stated strategy, Purell recommends that the client reports should use the revised methodology.

> *Comment*: Modifying the attribution methodology without proper notifications to clients would fail to meet the requirements of Standard III(D). Purrell's recommendation is being done solely for the interest of the firm to improve its perceived ability to meet the stated investment strategy. Such changes are unfair to clients and obscure the facts regarding the firm's abilities.
>
> Had Purell believed the new methodology offered improvements to the original model, then he would have needed to report the results of both calculations to the client. The report should also include the reasons why the new methodology is preferred, which would allow the client to make a meaningful comparison to prior results and provide a basis for comparing future attributions.

Example 7 (Performance Calculation Methodology Disclosure):

While developing a new reporting package for existing clients, Alisha Singh, a performance analyst, discovers that her company's new system automatically calculates both time-weighted and money-weighted returns. She asks the head of client services and retention which value would be preferred given that the firm has various investment strategies that include bonds, equities, securities without leverage, and alternatives. Singh is told not to label the return value so that the firm may show whichever value is greatest for the period.

> *Comment*: Following these instructions would lead to Singh violating Standard III(D). In reporting inconsistent return values, Singh would not be providing complete information to the firm's clients. Full information is provided when clients have sufficient information to judge the performance generated by the firm.

Example 8 (Performance Calculation Methodology Disclosure):

Richmond Equity Investors manages a long–short equity fund in which clients can trade once a week (on Fridays). For transparency reasons, a daily net asset value of the fund is calculated by Richmond. The monthly fact sheets of the fund report month-to-date and year-to-date performance. Richmond publishes the performance based on the higher of the last trading day of the month (typically, not the last business day) or the last business day of the month as determined by Richmond. The fact sheet mentions only that the data are as of the end of the month, without giving the exact date. Maggie Clark, the investment performance analyst in charge of the calculations, is concerned about the frequent changes and asks her supervisor whether they are appropriate.

Comment: Clark's actions in questioning the changing performance metric comply with Standard III(D). She has shown concern that these changes are not presenting an accurate and complete picture of the performance generated.

30. STANDARD III(E): DUTIES TO CLIENTS - PRESERVATION OF CONFIDENTIALITY

> Members and Candidates must keep information about current, former, and prospective clients confidential unless:
>
> 1. The information concerns illegal activities on the part of the client;
> 2. Disclosure is required by law; or
> 3. The client or prospective client permits disclosure of the information.

Guidance

Highlights:

- *Status of Client*
- *Compliance with Laws*
- *Electronic Information and Security*
- *Professional Conduct Investigations by CFA Institute*

Standard III(E) requires that members and candidates preserve the confidentiality of information communicated to them by their clients, prospective clients, and former clients. This standard is applicable when (1) the member or candidate receives information because of his or her special ability to conduct a portion of the client's business or personal affairs and (2) the member or candidate receives information that arises from or is relevant to that portion of the client's business that is the subject of the special or confidential relationship. If disclosure of the information is required by law or the information concerns illegal activities by the client, however, the member or candidate may have an obligation to report the activities to the appropriate authorities.

Standard III(E): Duties to Clients - Preservation of Confidentiality

Status of Client

This standard protects the confidentiality of client information even if the person or entity is no longer a client of the member or candidate. Therefore, members and candidates must continue to maintain the confidentiality of client records even after the client relationship has ended. If a client or former client expressly authorizes the member or candidate to disclose information, however, the member or candidate may follow the terms of the authorization and provide the information.

Compliance with Laws

As a general matter, members and candidates must comply with applicable law. If applicable law requires disclosure of client information in certain circumstances, members and candidates must comply with the law. Similarly, if applicable law requires members and candidates to maintain confidentiality, even if the information concerns illegal activities on the part of the client, members and candidates should not disclose such information. Additionally, applicable laws, such as inter-departmental communication restrictions within financial institutions, can impose limitations on information flow about a client within an entity that may lead to a violation of confidentiality. When in doubt, members and candidates should consult with their employer's compliance personnel or legal counsel before disclosing confidential information about clients.

Electronic Information and Security

Because of the ever-increasing volume of electronically stored information, members and candidates need to be particularly aware of possible accidental disclosures. Many employers have strict policies about how to electronically communicate sensitive client information and store client information on personal laptops, mobile devices, or portable disk/flash drives. In recent years, regulatory authorities have imposed stricter data security laws applying to the use of mobile remote digital communication, including the use of social media, that must be considered. Standard III(E) does not require members or candidates to become experts in information security technology, but they should have a thorough understanding of the policies of their employer. The size and operations of the firm will lead to differing policies for ensuring the security of confidential information maintained within the firm. Members and candidates should encourage their firm to conduct regular periodic training on confidentiality procedures for all firm personnel, including portfolio associates, receptionists, and other non-investment staff who have routine direct contact with clients and their records.

Professional Conduct Investigations by CFA Institute

The requirements of Standard III(E) are not intended to prevent members and candidates from cooperating with an investigation by the CFA Institute Professional Conduct Program (PCP). When permissible under applicable law, members and candidates shall consider the PCP an extension of themselves when requested to provide information about a client in support of a PCP investigation into their own conduct. Members and candidates are encouraged to cooperate with investigations into the conduct of others. Any information turned over to the PCP is kept in the strictest confidence. Members and candidates will not be considered in violation of this standard by forwarding confidential information to the PCP.

31 STANDARD III(E): RECOMMENDED PROCEDURES

☐ recommend practices and procedures designed to prevent violations of the Code of Ethics and Standards of Professional Conduct

The simplest, most conservative, and most effective way to comply with Standard III(E) is to avoid disclosing any information received from a client except to authorized fellow employees who are also working for the client. In some instances, however, a member or candidate may want to disclose information received from clients that is outside the scope of the confidential relationship and does not involve illegal activities. Before making such a disclosure, a member or candidate should ask the following:

- In what context was the information disclosed? If disclosed in a discussion of work being performed for the client, is the information relevant to the work?
- Is the information background material that, if disclosed, will enable the member or candidate to improve service to the client?

Members and candidates need to understand and follow their firm's electronic information communication and storage procedures. If the firm does not have procedures in place, members and candidates should encourage the development of procedures that appropriately reflect the firm's size and business operations.

Communicating with Clients

Technological changes are constantly enhancing the methods that are used to communicate with clients and prospective clients. Members and candidates should make reasonable efforts to ensure that firm-supported communication methods and compliance procedures follow practices designed for preventing accidental distribution of confidential information. Given the rate at which technology changes, a regular review of privacy protection measures is encouraged.

Members and candidates should be diligent in discussing with clients the appropriate methods for providing confidential information. It is important to convey to clients that not all firm-sponsored resources may be appropriate for such communications.

32 STANDARD III(E): APPLICATION OF THE STANDARD

☐ demonstrate the application of the Code of Ethics and Standards of Professional Conduct to situations involving issues of professional integrity

☐ identify conduct that conforms to the Code and Standards and conduct that violates the Code and Standards

Standard III(E): Application of the Standard

Example 1 (Possessing Confidential Information):

Sarah Connor, a financial analyst employed by Johnson Investment Counselors, Inc., provides investment advice to the trustees of City Medical Center. The trustees have given her a number of internal reports concerning City Medical's needs for physical plant renovation and expansion. They have asked Connor to recommend investments that would generate capital appreciation in endowment funds to meet projected capital expenditures. Connor is approached by a local businessman, Thomas Kasey, who is considering a substantial contribution either to City Medical Center or to another local hospital. Kasey wants to find out the building plans of both institutions before making a decision, but he does not want to speak to the trustees.

> *Comment*: The trustees gave Connor the internal reports so she could advise them on how to manage their endowment funds. Because the information in the reports is clearly both confidential and within the scope of the confidential relationship, Standard III(E) requires that Connor refuse to divulge information to Kasey.

Example 2 (Disclosing Confidential Information):

Lynn Moody is an investment officer at the Lester Trust Company. She has an advisory customer who has talked to her about giving approximately US$50,000 to charity to reduce her income taxes. Moody is also treasurer of the Home for Indigent Widows (HIW), which is planning its annual giving campaign. HIW hopes to expand its list of prospects, particularly those capable of substantial gifts. Moody recommends that HIW's vice president for corporate gifts call on her customer and ask for a donation in the US$50,000 range.

> *Comment*: Even though the attempt to help the Home for Indigent Widows was well intended, Moody violated Standard III(E) by revealing confidential information about her client.

Example 3 (Disclosing Possible Illegal Activity):

Government officials approach Casey Samuel, the portfolio manager for Garcia Company's pension plan, to examine pension fund records. They tell her that Garcia's corporate tax returns are being audited and the pension fund is being reviewed. Two days earlier, Samuel had learned in a regular investment review with Garcia officers that potentially excessive and improper charges were being made to the pension plan by Garcia. Samuel consults her employer's general counsel and is advised that Garcia has probably violated tax and fiduciary regulations and laws.

> *Comment*: Samuel should inform her supervisor of these activities, and her employer should take steps, with Garcia, to remedy the violations. If that approach is not successful, Samuel and her employer should seek advice of legal counsel to determine the appropriate steps to be taken. Samuel may well have a duty to disclose the evidence she has of the continuing legal violations and to resign as asset manager for Garcia.

Example 4 (Disclosing Possible Illegal Activity):

David Bradford manages money for a family-owned real estate development corporation. He also manages the individual portfolios of several of the family members and officers of the corporation, including the chief financial officer (CFO). Based on the financial records of the corporation and some questionable practices of the CFO that Bradford has observed, Bradford believes that the CFO is embezzling money from the corporation and putting it into his personal investment account.

> *Comment*: Bradford should check with his firm's compliance department or appropriate legal counsel to determine whether applicable securities regulations require reporting the CFO's financial records.

Example 5 (Accidental Disclosure of Confidential Information):

Lynn Moody is an investment officer at the Lester Trust Company (LTC). She has stewardship of a significant number of individually managed taxable accounts. In addition to receiving quarterly written reports, about a dozen high-net-worth individuals have indicated to Moody a willingness to receive communications about overall economic and financial market outlooks directly from her by way of a social media platform. Under the direction of her firm's technology and compliance departments, she established a new group page on an existing social media platform specifically for her clients. In the instructions provided to clients, Moody asked them to "join" the group so they may be granted access to the posted content. The instructions also advised clients that all comments posted would be available to the public and thus the platform was not an appropriate method for communicating personal or confidential information.

Six months later, in early January, Moody posted LTC's year-end "Market Outlook." The report outlined a new asset allocation strategy that the firm is adding to its recommendations in the new year. Moody introduced the publication with a note informing her clients that she would be discussing the changes with them individually in their upcoming meetings.

One of Moody's clients responded directly on the group page that his family recently experienced a major change in their financial profile. The client described highly personal and confidential details of the event. Unfortunately, all clients that were part of the group were also able to read the detailed posting until Moody was able to have the comment removed.

> *Comment*: Moody has taken reasonable steps for protecting the confidentiality of client information while using the social media platform. She provided instructions clarifying that all information posted to the site would be publically viewable to all group members and warned against using this method for communicating confidential information. The accidental disclosure of confidential information by a client is not under Moody's control. Her actions to remove the information promptly once she became aware further align with Standard III(E).
>
> In understanding the potential sensitivity clients express surrounding the confidentiality of personal information, this event highlights a need for further training. Moody might advocate for additional warnings or controls for clients when they consider using social media platforms for two-way communications.

STANDARD IV(A): DUTIES TO EMPLOYERS – LOYALTY

☐ demonstrate the application of the Code of Ethics and Standards of Professional Conduct to situations involving issues of professional integrity

Standard IV(A) Loyalty

> In matters related to their employment, Members and Candidates must act for the benefit of their employer and not deprive their employer of the advantage of their skills and abilities, divulge confidential information, or otherwise cause harm to their employer.

Guidance

Highlights:

- *Employer Responsibilities*
- *Independent Practice*
- *Leaving an Employer*
- *Use of Social Media*
- *Whistleblowing*
- *Nature of Employment*

Standard IV(A) requires members and candidates to protect the interests of their firm by refraining from any conduct that would injure the firm, deprive it of profit, or deprive it of the member's or candidate's skills and ability. Members and candidates must always place the interests of clients above the interests of their employer but should also consider the effects of their conduct on the sustainability and integrity of the employer firm. In matters related to their employment, members and candidates must not engage in conduct that harms the interests of their employer. Implicit in this standard is the obligation of members and candidates to comply with the policies and procedures established by their employers that govern the employer–employee relationship—to the extent that such policies and procedures do not conflict with applicable laws, rules, or regulations or the Code and Standards.

This standard is not meant to be a blanket requirement to place employer interests ahead of personal interests in all matters. The standard does not require members and candidates to subordinate important personal and family obligations to their work. Members and candidates should enter into a dialogue with their employer about balancing personal and employment obligations when personal matters may interfere with their work on a regular or significant basis.

Employer Responsibilities

The employer–employee relationship imposes duties and responsibilities on both parties. Employers must recognize the duties and responsibilities that they owe to their employees if they expect to have content and productive employees.

Members and candidates are encouraged to provide their employer with a copy of the Code and Standards. These materials will inform the employer of the responsibilities of a CFA Institute member or a candidate in the CFA Program. The Code and Standards also serve as a basis for questioning employer policies and practices that conflict with these responsibilities.

Employers are not obligated to adhere to the Code and Standards. In expecting to retain competent employees who are members and candidates, however, they should not develop conflicting policies and procedures. The employer is responsible for a positive working environment, which includes an ethical workplace. Senior management has the additional responsibility to devise compensation structures and incentive arrangements that do not encourage unethical behavior.

Independent Practice

Included in Standard IV(A) is the requirement that members and candidates abstain from independent competitive activity that could conflict with the interests of their employer. Although Standard IV(A) does not preclude members or candidates from entering into an independent business while still employed, members and candidates who plan to engage in independent practice for compensation must notify their employer and describe the types of services they will render to prospective independent clients, the expected duration of the services, and the compensation for the services. Members and candidates should not render services until they receive consent from their employer to all of the terms of the arrangement. "Practice" means any service that the employer currently makes available for remuneration. "Undertaking independent practice" means engaging in competitive business, as opposed to making preparations to begin such practice.

Leaving an Employer

When members and candidates are planning to leave their current employer, they must continue to act in the employer's best interest. They must not engage in any activities that would conflict with this duty until their resignation becomes effective. It is difficult to define specific guidelines for those members and candidates who are planning to compete with their employer as part of a new venture. The circumstances of each situation must be reviewed to distinguish permissible preparations from violations of duty. Activities that might constitute a violation, especially in combination, include the following:

- misappropriation of trade secrets,
- misuse of confidential information,
- solicitation of the employer's clients prior to cessation of employment,
- self-dealing (appropriating for one's own property a business opportunity or information belonging to one's employer), and
- misappropriation of clients or client lists.

A departing employee is generally free to make arrangements or preparations to go into a competitive business before terminating the relationship with his or her employer as long as such preparations do not breach the employee's duty of loyalty. A member or candidate who is contemplating seeking other employment must not contact existing clients or potential clients prior to leaving his or her employer for purposes of soliciting their business for the new employer. Once notice is provided to the employer of the intent to resign, the member or candidate must follow the employer's policies and procedures related to notifying clients of his or her planned departure. In addition, the member or candidate must not take records or files to a new employer without the written permission of the previous employer.

Once an employee has left the firm, the skills and experience that an employee obtained while employed are not "confidential" or "privileged" information. Similarly, simple knowledge of the names and existence of former clients is generally not confidential information unless deemed such by an agreement or by law. Standard IV(A) does not prohibit experience or knowledge gained at one employer from being used at another employer. Firm records or work performed on behalf of the firm that is stored in paper copy or electronically for the member's or candidate's convenience while employed, however, should be erased or returned to the employer unless the firm gives permission to keep those records after employment ends.

The standard does not prohibit former employees from contacting clients of their previous firm as long as the contact information does not come from the records of the former employer or violate an applicable "noncompete agreement." Members and candidates are free to use public information after departing to contact former clients without violating Standard IV(A) as long as there is no specific agreement not to do so.

Employers often require employees to sign noncompete agreements that preclude a departing employee from engaging in certain conduct. Members and candidates should take care to review the terms of any such agreement when leaving their employer to determine what, if any, conduct those agreements may prohibit.

In some markets, there are agreements between employers within an industry that outline information that departing employees are permitted to take upon resignation, such as the "Protocol for Broker Recruiting" in the United States. These agreements ease individuals' transition between firms that have agreed to follow the outlined procedures. Members and candidates who move between firms that sign such agreements may rely on the protections provided as long as they faithfully adhere to all the procedures outlined.

For example, under the agreement between many US brokers, individuals are allowed to take some general client contact information when departing. To be protected, a copy of the information the individual is taking must be provided to the local management team for review. Additionally, the specific client information may only be used by the departing employee and not others employed by the new firm.

Use of Social Media

The growth in various online networking platforms, such as LinkedIn, Twitter, and Facebook (commonly referred to as social media platforms), is providing new opportunities and challenges for businesses. Members and candidates should understand and abide by all applicable firm policies and regulations as to the acceptable use of social media platforms to interact with clients and prospective clients. This is especially important when a member or candidate is planning to leave an employer.

Social media use makes determining how and when departure notification is delivered to clients more complex. Members and candidates may have developed profiles on these platforms that include connections with individuals who are clients of the firm, as well as individuals unrelated to their employer. Communications through social media platforms that potentially reach current clients should adhere to the employer's policies and procedures regarding notification of departing employees.

Social media connections with clients are also raising questions concerning the differences between public information and firm property. Specific accounts and user profiles of members and candidates may be created for solely professional reasons, including firm-approved accounts for client engagements. Such firm-approved business-related accounts would be considered part of the firm's assets, thus requiring members and candidates to transfer or delete the accounts as directed by their firm's policies and procedures. Best practice for members and candidates is to maintain separate accounts for their personal and professional social media activities. Members and candidates should discuss with their employers how profiles should be treated when a single account includes personal connections and also is used to conduct aspects of their professional activities.

Whistleblowing

A member's or candidate's personal interests, as well as the interests of his or her employer, are secondary to protecting the integrity of capital markets and the interests of clients. Therefore, circumstances may arise (e.g., when an employer is engaged in illegal or unethical activity) in which members and candidates must act contrary to their employer's interests in order to comply with their duties to the market and clients. In such instances, activities that would normally violate a member's or candidate's duty to his or her employer (such as contradicting employer instructions, violating certain policies and procedures, or preserving a record by copying employer records) may be justified. Such action would be permitted only if the intent is clearly aimed at protecting clients or the integrity of the market, not for personal gain.

Nature of Employment

A wide variety of business relationships exists within the investment industry. For instance, a member or candidate may be an employee or an independent contractor. Members and candidates must determine whether they are employees or independent contractors in order to determine the applicability of Standard IV(A). This issue will be decided largely by the degree of control exercised by the employing entity over the member or candidate. Factors determining control include whether the member's or candidate's hours, work location, and other parameters of the job are set; whether facilities are provided to the member or candidate; whether the member's or candidate's expenses are reimbursed; whether the member or candidate seeks work from other employers; and the number of clients or employers the member or candidate works for.

A member's or candidate's duties within an independent contractor relationship are governed by the oral or written agreement between the member and the client. Members and candidates should take care to define clearly the scope of their responsibilities and the expectations of each client within the context of each relationship. Once a member or candidate establishes a relationship with a client, the member or candidate has a duty to abide by the terms of the agreement.

34. STANDARD IV(A): RECOMMENDED PROCEDURES

☐ recommend practices and procedures designed to prevent violations of the Code of Ethics and Standards of Professional Conduct

Employers may establish codes of conduct and operating procedures for their employees to follow. Members and candidates should fully understand the policies to ensure that they are not in conflict with the Code and Standards. The following topics identify policies that members and candidates should encourage their firms to adopt if the policies are not currently in place.

Competition Policy

A member or candidate must understand any restrictions placed by the employer on offering similar services outside the firm while employed by the firm. The policy may outline the procedures for requesting approval to undertake the outside service

Termination Policy

Members and candidates should clearly understand the termination policies of their employer. Termination policies should establish clear procedures regarding the resignation process, including addressing how the termination will be disclosed to clients and staff and whether updates posted through social media platforms will be allowed. The firm's policy may also outline the procedures for transferring ongoing research and account management responsibilities. Finally, the procedures should address agreements that allow departing employees to remove specific client-related information upon resignation.

Incident-Reporting Procedures

report potentially unethical and illegal activities in the firm.

Employee Classification

Members and candidates should understand their status within their employer firm. Firms are encouraged to adopt a standardized classification structure (e.g., part time, full time, outside contractor) for their employees and indicate how each of the firm's policies applies to each employee class.

STANDARD IV(A): APPLICATION OF THE STANDARD — 35

- ☐ demonstrate the application of the Code of Ethics and Standards of Professional Conduct to situations involving issues of professional integrity
- ☐ identify conduct that conforms to the Code and Standards and conduct that violates the Code and Standards

Example 1 (Soliciting Former Clients):

Samuel Magee manages pension accounts for Trust Assets, Inc., but has become frustrated with the working environment and has been offered a position with Fiduciary Management. Before resigning from Trust Assets, Magee asks four big accounts to leave that firm and open accounts with Fiduciary. Magee also persuades several prospective clients to sign agreements with Fiduciary Management. Magee had previously made presentations to these prospects on behalf of Trust Assets.

> *Comment*: Magee violated the employee–employer principle requiring him to act solely for his employer's benefit. Magee's duty is to Trust Assets as long as he is employed there. The solicitation of Trust Assets' current clients and prospective clients is unethical and violates Standard IV(A).

Example 2 (Former Employer's Documents and Files):

James Hightower has been employed by Jason Investment Management Corporation for 15 years. He began as an analyst but assumed increasing responsibilities and is now a senior portfolio manager and a member of the firm's investment policy committee. Hightower has decided to leave Jason Investment and start his own investment management business. He has been careful not to tell any of Jason's clients that he is leaving; he does not want to be accused of breaching his duty to Jason by soliciting Jason's clients before his departure. Hightower is planning to copy and take with him the following documents and information he developed or worked on while at Jason: (1) the client list, with addresses, telephone numbers, and other pertinent client information; (2) client account statements; (3) sample marketing presentations to prospective clients containing Jason's performance record; (4) Jason's recommended list of securities; (5) computer models to determine asset allocations for accounts with various objectives; (6) computer models for stock selection; and (7) personal computer spreadsheets for Hightower's major corporate recommendations, which he developed when he was an analyst.

> *Comment*: Except with the consent of their employer, departing members and candidates may not take employer property, which includes books, records, reports, and other materials, because taking such materials may interfere with their employer's business opportunities. Taking any employer records, even those the member or candidate prepared, violates Standard IV(A). Employer records include items stored in hard copy or any other medium (e.g., home computers, portable storage devices, cell phones).

Example 3 (Addressing Rumors):

Reuben Winston manages all-equity portfolios at Target Asset Management (TAM), a large, established investment counselor. Ten years previously, Philpott & Company, which manages a family of global bond mutual funds, acquired TAM in a diversification move. After the merger, the combined operations prospered in the fixed-income business but the equity management business at TAM languished. Lately, a few of the equity pension accounts that had been with TAM before the merger have terminated their relationships with TAM. One day, Winston finds on his voice mail the following message from a concerned client: "Hey! I just heard that Philpott is close to announcing the sale of your firm's equity management business to Rugged Life. What is going on?" Not being aware of any such deal, Winston and his associates are stunned. Their internal inquiries are met with denials from Philpott management, but the rumors persist. Feeling left in the dark, Winston contemplates leading an employee buyout of TAM's equity management business.

> *Comment*: An employee-led buyout of TAM's equity asset management business would be consistent with Standard IV(A) because it would rest on the permission of the employer and, ultimately, the clients. In this case, however, in which employees suspect the senior managers or principals are not truthful or forthcoming, Winston should consult legal counsel to determine appropriate action.

Example 4 (Ownership of Completed Prior Work):

Laura Clay, who is unemployed, wants part-time consulting work while seeking a full-time analyst position. During an interview at Bradley Associates, a large institutional asset manager, Clay is told that the firm has no immediate research openings

Standard IV(A): Application of the Standard

but would be willing to pay her a flat fee to complete a study of the wireless communications industry within a given period of time. Clay would be allowed unlimited access to Bradley's research files and would be welcome to come to the offices and use whatever support facilities are available during normal working hours. Bradley's research director does not seek any exclusivity for Clay's output, and the two agree to the arrangement on a handshake. As Clay nears completion of the study, she is offered an analyst job in the research department of Winston & Company, a brokerage firm, and she is pondering submitting the draft of her wireless study for publication by Winston.

> *Comment*: Although she is under no written contractual obligation to Bradley, Clay has an obligation to let Bradley act on the output of her study before Winston & Company or Clay uses the information to their advantage. That is, unless Bradley gives permission to Clay and waives its rights to her wireless report, Clay would be in violation of Standard IV(A) if she were to immediately recommend to Winston the same transactions recommended in the report to Bradley. Furthermore, Clay must not take from Bradley any research file material or other property that she may have used.

Example 5 (Ownership of Completed Prior Work):

Emma Madeline, a recent college graduate and a candidate in the CFA Program, spends her summer as an unpaid intern at Murdoch and Lowell. The senior managers at Murdoch are attempting to bring the firm into compliance with the GIPS standards, and Madeline is assigned to assist in its efforts. Two months into her internship, Madeline applies for a job at McMillan & Company, which has plans to become GIPS compliant. Madeline accepts the job with McMillan. Before leaving Murdoch, she copies the firm's software that she helped develop because she believes this software will assist her in her new position.

> *Comment*: Even though Madeline does not receive monetary compensation for her services at Murdoch, she has used firm resources in creating the software and is considered an employee because she receives compensation and benefits in the form of work experience and knowledge. By copying the software, Madeline violated Standard IV(A) because she misappropriated Murdoch's property without permission.

Example 6 (Soliciting Former Clients):

Dennis Elliot has hired Sam Chisolm, who previously worked for a competing firm. Chisolm left his former firm after 18 years of employment. When Chisolm begins working for Elliot, he wants to contact his former clients because he knows them well and is certain that many will follow him to his new employer. Is Chisolm in violation of Standard IV(A) if he contacts his former clients?

> *Comment*: Because client records are the property of the firm, contacting former clients for any reason through the use of client lists or other information taken from a former employer without permission would be a violation of Standard IV(A). In addition, the nature and extent of the contact with former clients may be governed by the terms of any noncompete agreement signed by the employee and the former employer that covers contact with former clients after employment.

Simple knowledge of the names and existence of former clients is not confidential information, just as skills or experience that an employee obtains while employed are not "confidential" or "privileged" information. The Code and Standards do not impose a prohibition on the use of experience or knowledge gained at one employer from being used at another employer. The Code and Standards also do not prohibit former employees from contacting clients of their previous firm, in the absence of a noncompete agreement. Members and candidates are free to use public information about their former firm after departing to contact former clients without violating Standard IV(A).

In the absence of a noncompete agreement, as long as Chisolm maintains his duty of loyalty to his employer before joining Elliot's firm, does not take steps to solicit clients until he has left his former firm, and does not use material from his former employer without its permission after he has left, he is not in violation of the Code and Standards.

Example 7 (Starting a New Firm):

Geraldine Allen currently works at a registered investment company as an equity analyst. Without notice to her employer, she registers with government authorities to start an investment company that will compete with her employer, but she does not actively seek clients. Does registration of this competing company with the appropriate regulatory authorities constitute a violation of Standard IV(A)?

Comment: Allen's preparation for the new business by registering with the regulatory authorities does not conflict with the work for her employer if the preparations have been done on Allen's own time outside the office and if Allen will not be soliciting clients for the business or otherwise operating the new company until she has left her current employer.

Example 8 (Competing with Current Employer):

Several employees are planning to depart their current employer within a few weeks and have been careful to not engage in any activities that would conflict with their duty to their current employer. They have just learned that one of their employer's clients has undertaken a request for proposal (RFP) to review and possibly hire a new investment consultant. The RFP has been sent to the employer and all of its competitors. The group believes that the new entity to be formed would be qualified to respond to the RFP and be eligible for the business. The RFP submission period is likely to conclude before the employees' resignations are effective. Is it permissible for the group of departing employees to respond to the RFP for their anticipated new firm?

Comment: A group of employees responding to an RFP that their employer is also responding to would lead to direct competition between the employees and the employer. Such conduct violates Standard IV(A) unless the group of employees receives permission from their employer as well as the entity sending out the RFP.

Example 9 (Externally Compensated Assignments):

Alfonso Mota is a research analyst with Tyson Investments. He works part time as a mayor for his hometown, a position for which he receives compensation. Must Mota seek permission from Tyson to serve as mayor?

Standard IV(A): Application of the Standard

Comment: If Mota's mayoral duties are so extensive and time-consuming that they might detract from his ability to fulfill his responsibilities at Tyson, he should discuss his outside activities with his employer and come to a mutual agreement regarding how to manage his personal commitments with his responsibilities to his employer.

Example 10 (Soliciting Former Clients):

After leaving her employer, Shawna McQuillen establishes her own money management business. While with her former employer, she did not sign a noncompete agreement that would have prevented her from soliciting former clients. Upon her departure, she does not take any of her client lists or contact information and she clears her personal computer of any employer records, including client contact information. She obtains the phone numbers of her former clients through public records and contacts them to solicit their business.

Comment: McQuillen is not in violation of Standard IV(A) because she has not used information or records from her former employer and is not prevented by an agreement with her former employer from soliciting her former clients.

Example 11 (Whistleblowing Actions):

Meredith Rasmussen works on a buy-side trading desk and concentrates on in-house trades for a hedge fund subsidiary managed by a team at the investment management firm. The hedge fund has been very successful and is marketed globally by the firm. From her experience as the trader for much of the activity of the fund, Rasmussen has become quite knowledgeable about the hedge fund's strategy, tactics, and performance. When a distinct break in the market occurs, however, and many of the securities involved in the hedge fund's strategy decline markedly in value, Rasmussen observes that the reported performance of the hedge fund does not reflect this decline. In her experience, the lack of any effect is a very unlikely occurrence. She approaches the head of trading about her concern and is told that she should not ask any questions and that the fund is big and successful and is not her concern. She is fairly sure something is not right, so she contacts the compliance officer, who also tells her to stay away from the issue of this hedge fund's reporting.

Comment: Rasmussen has clearly come upon an error in policies, procedures, and compliance practices in the firm's operations. Having been unsuccessful in finding a resolution with her supervisor and the compliance officer, Rasmussen should consult the firm's whistleblowing policy to determine the appropriate next step toward informing management of her concerns. The potentially unethical actions of the investment management division are appropriate grounds for further disclosure, so Rasmussen's whistleblowing would not represent a violation of Standard IV(A).

See also Standard I(D)–Misconduct and Standard IV(C)–Responsibilities of Supervisors.

Example 12 (Soliciting Former Clients):

Angel Crome has been a private banker for YBSafe Bank for the past eight years. She has been very successful and built a considerable client portfolio during that time but is extremely frustrated by the recent loss of reputation by her current employer and subsequent client insecurity. A locally renowned headhunter contacted Crome a few days ago and offered her an interesting job with a competing private bank. This bank offers a substantial signing bonus for advisers with their own client portfolios. Crome figures that she can solicit at least 70% of her clients to follow her and gladly enters into the new employment contract.

> *Comment*: Crome may contact former clients upon termination of her employment with YBSafe Bank, but she is prohibited from using client records built by and kept with her in her capacity as an employee of YBSafe Bank. Client lists are proprietary information of her former employer and must not be used for her or her new employer's benefit. The use of written, electronic, or any other form of records other than publicly available information to contact her former clients at YBSafe Bank will be a violation of Standard IV(A).

Example 13 (Notification of Code and Standards):

Krista Smith is a relatively new assistant trader for the fixed-income desk of a major investment bank. She is on a team responsible for structuring collateralized debt obligations (CDOs) made up of securities in the inventory of the trading desk. At a meeting of the team, senior executives explain the opportunity to eventually separate the CDO into various risk-rated tranches to be sold to the clients of the firm. After the senior executives leave the meeting, the head trader announces various responsibilities of each member of the team and then says, "This is a good time to unload some of the junk we have been stuck with for a while and disguise it with ratings and a thick, unreadable prospectus, so don't be shy in putting this CDO together. Just kidding." Smith is worried by this remark and asks some of her colleagues what the head trader meant. They all respond that he was just kidding but that there is some truth in the remark because the CDO is seen by management as an opportunity to improve the quality of the securities in the firm's inventory.

Concerned about the ethical environment of the workplace, Smith decides to talk to her supervisor about her concerns and provides the head trader with a copy of the Code and Standards. Smith discusses the principle of placing the client above the interest of the firm and the possibility that the development of the new CDO will not adhere to this responsibility. The head trader assures Smith that the appropriate analysis will be conducted when determining the appropriate securities for collateral. Furthermore, the ratings are assigned by an independent firm and the prospectus will include full and factual disclosures. Smith is reassured by the meeting, but she also reviews the company's procedures and requirements for reporting potential violations of company policy and securities laws.

> *Comment*: Smith's review of the company policies and procedures for reporting violations allows her to be prepared to report through the appropriate whistleblower process if she decides that the CDO development process involves unethical actions by others. Smith's actions comply with the Code and Standards principles of placing the client's interests first and being loyal to her employer. In providing her supervisor with a copy of the Code and Standards, Smith is highlighting the high level of ethical conduct she is required to adhere to in her professional activities.

Standard IV(A): Application of the Standard

Example 14 (Leaving an Employer):

Laura Webb just left her position as portfolio analyst at Research Systems, Inc. (RSI). Her employment contract included a non-solicitation agreement that requires her to wait two years before soliciting RSI clients for any investment-related services. Upon leaving, Webb was informed that RSI would contact clients immediately about her departure and introduce her replacement.

While working at RSI, Webb connected with clients, other industry associates, and friends through her LinkedIn network. Her business and personal relationships were intermingled because she considered many of her clients to be personal friends. Realizing that her LinkedIn network would be a valuable resource for new employment opportunities, she updated her profile several days following her departure from RSI. LinkedIn automatically sent a notification to Webb's entire network that her employment status had been changed in her profile.

> *Comment*: Prior to her departure, Webb should have discussed any client information contained in her social media networks. By updating her LinkedIn profile after RSI notified clients and after her employment ended, she has appropriately placed her employer's interests ahead of her own personal interests. In addition, she has not violated the non-solicitation agreement with RSI, unless it prohibited any contact with clients during the two-year period.

Example 15 (Confidential Firm Information):

Sanjay Gupta is a research analyst at Naram Investment Management (NIM). NIM uses a team-based research process to develop recommendations on investment opportunities covered by the team members. Gupta, like others, provides commentary for NIM's clients through the company blog, which is posted weekly on the NIM password-protected website. According to NIM's policy, every contribution to the website must be approved by the company's compliance department before posting. Any opinions expressed on the website are disclosed as representing the perspective of NIM.

Gupta also writes a personal blog to share his experiences with friends and family. As with most blogs, Gupta's personal blog is widely available to interested readers through various internet search engines. Occasionally, when he disagrees with the team-based research opinions of NIM, Gupta uses his personal blog to express his own opinions as a counterpoint to the commentary posted on the NIM website. Gupta believes this provides his readers with a more complete perspective on these investment opportunities.

> *Comment*: Gupta is in violation of Standard IV(A) for disclosing confidential firm information through his personal blog. The recommendations on the firm's blog to clients are not freely available across the internet, but his personal blog post indirectly provides the firm's recommendations.
>
> Additionally, by posting research commentary on his personal blog, Gupta is using firm resources for his personal advantage. To comply with Standard IV(A), members and candidates must receive consent from their employer prior to using company resources.

36 STANDARD IV(B): DUTIES TO EMPLOYERS - ADDITIONAL COMPENSATION ARRANGEMENTS

☐ demonstrate the application of the Code of Ethics and Standards of Professional Conduct to situations involving issues of professional integrity

> Members and Candidates must not accept gifts, benefits, compensation, or consideration that competes with or might reasonably be expected to create a conflict of interest with their employer's interest unless they obtain written consent from all parties involved.

Guidance

Standard IV(B) requires members and candidates to obtain permission from their employer before accepting compensation or other benefits from third parties for the services rendered to the employer or for any services that might create a conflict with their employer's interest. Compensation and benefits include direct compensation by the client and any indirect compensation or other benefits received from third parties. "Written consent" includes any form of communication that can be documented (for example, communication via e-mail that can be retrieved and documented).

Members and candidates must obtain permission for additional compensation/benefits because such arrangements may affect loyalties and objectivity and create potential conflicts of interest. Disclosure allows an employer to consider the outside arrangements when evaluating the actions and motivations of members and candidates. Moreover, the employer is entitled to have full knowledge of all compensation/benefit arrangements so as to be able to assess the true cost of the services members or candidates are providing.

There may be instances in which a member or candidate is hired by an employer on a "part-time" basis. "Part-time" status applies to employees who do not commit the full number of hours required for a normal work week. Members and candidates should discuss possible limitations to their abilities to provide services that may be competitive with their employer during the negotiation and hiring process. The requirements of Standard IV(B) would be applicable to limitations identified at that time.

37 STANDARD IV(B): RECOMMENDED PROCEDURES

☐ recommend practices and procedures designed to prevent violations of the Code of Ethics and Standards of Professional Conduct

Members and candidates should make an immediate written report to their supervisor and compliance officer specifying any compensation they propose to receive for services in addition to the compensation or benefits received from their employer. The details of the report should be confirmed by the party offering the additional compensation, including performance incentives offered by clients. This written report should state the terms of any agreement under which a member or candidate will receive additional compensation; "terms" include the nature of the compensation, the approximate amount of compensation, and the duration of the agreement.

STANDARD IV(B): APPLICATION OF THE STANDARD

- [ ] demonstrate the application of the Code of Ethics and Standards of Professional Conduct to situations involving issues of professional integrity
- [ ] identify conduct that conforms to the Code and Standards and conduct that violates the Code and Standards

Example 1 (Notification of Client Bonus Compensation):

Geoff Whitman, a portfolio analyst for Adams Trust Company, manages the account of Carol Cochran, a client. Whitman is paid a salary by his employer, and Cochran pays the trust company a standard fee based on the market value of assets in her portfolio. Cochran proposes to Whitman that "any year that my portfolio achieves at least a 15% return before taxes, you and your wife can fly to Monaco at my expense and use my condominium during the third week of January." Whitman does not inform his employer of the arrangement and vacations in Monaco the following January as Cochran's guest.

> *Comment*: Whitman violated Standard IV(B) by failing to inform his employer in writing of this supplemental, contingent compensation arrangement. The nature of the arrangement could have resulted in partiality to Cochran's account, which could have detracted from Whitman's performance with respect to other accounts he handles for Adams Trust. Whitman must obtain the consent of his employer to accept such a supplemental benefit.

Example 2 (Notification of Outside Compensation):

Terry Jones sits on the board of directors of Exercise Unlimited, Inc. In return for his services on the board, Jones receives unlimited membership privileges for his family at all Exercise Unlimited facilities. Jones purchases Exercise Unlimited stock for the client accounts for which it is appropriate. Jones does not disclose this arrangement to his employer because he does not receive monetary compensation for his services to the board.

> *Comment*: Jones has violated Standard IV(B) by failing to disclose to his employer benefits received in exchange for his services on the board of directors. The nonmonetary compensation may create a conflict of interest in the same manner as being paid to serve as a director.

Example 3 (Prior Approval for Outside Compensation):

Jonathan Hollis is an analyst of oil-and-gas companies for Specialty Investment Management. He is currently recommending the purchase of ABC Oil Company shares and has published a long, well-thought-out research report to substantiate his recommendation. Several weeks after publishing the report, Hollis receives a call from the investor-relations office of ABC Oil saying that Thomas Andrews, CEO of the company, saw the report and really liked the analyst's grasp of the business and his company. The investor-relations officer invites Hollis to visit ABC Oil to discuss the industry further. ABC Oil offers to send a company plane to pick Hollis up and arrange for his accommodations while visiting. Hollis, after gaining the appropriate approvals, accepts the meeting with the CEO but declines the offered travel arrangements.

Several weeks later, Andrews and Hollis meet to discuss the oil business and Hollis's report. Following the meeting, Hollis joins Andrews and the investment relations officer for dinner at an upscale restaurant near ABC Oil's headquarters.

Upon returning to Specialty Investment Management, Hollis provides a full review of the meeting to the director of research, including a disclosure of the dinner attended.

> *Comment*: Hollis's actions did not violate Standard IV(B). Through gaining approval before accepting the meeting and declining the offered travel arrangements, Hollis sought to avoid any potential conflicts of interest between his company and ABC Oil. Because the location of the dinner was not available prior to arrival and Hollis notified his company of the dinner upon his return, accepting the dinner should not impair his objectivity. By disclosing the dinner, Hollis has enabled Specialty Investment Management to assess whether it has any impact on future reports and recommendations by Hollis related to ABC Oil.

39 STANDARD IV(C): DUTIES TO EMPLOYERS - RESPONSIBILITIES OF SUPERVISORS

☐ demonstrate the application of the Code of Ethics and Standards of Professional Conduct to situations involving issues of professional integrity

> Members and Candidates must make reasonable efforts to ensure that anyone subject to their supervision or authority complies with applicable laws, rules, regulations, and the Code and Standards.

Guidance

Highlights:

- *System for Supervision*
- *Supervision Includes Detection*

Standard IV(C): Duties to Employers - Responsibilities of Supervisors

Standard IV(C) states that members and candidates must promote actions by all employees under their supervision and authority to comply with applicable laws, rules, regulations, and firm policies and the Code and Standards.

Any investment professional who has employees subject to her or his control or influence—whether or not the employees are CFA Institute members, CFA charterholders, or candidates in the CFA Program—exercises supervisory responsibility. Members and candidates acting as supervisors must also have in-depth knowledge of the Code and Standards so that they can apply this knowledge in discharging their supervisory responsibilities.

The conduct that constitutes reasonable supervision in a particular case depends on the number of employees supervised and the work performed by those employees. Members and candidates with oversight responsibilities for large numbers of employees may not be able to personally evaluate the conduct of these employees on a continuing basis. These members and candidates may delegate supervisory duties to subordinates who directly oversee the other employees. A member's or candidate's responsibilities under Standard IV(C) include instructing those subordinates to whom supervision is delegated about methods to promote compliance, including preventing and detecting violations of laws, rules, regulations, firm policies, and the Code and Standards.

At a minimum, Standard IV(C) requires that members and candidates with supervisory responsibility make reasonable efforts to prevent and detect violations by ensuring the establishment of effective compliance systems. However, an effective compliance system goes beyond enacting a code of ethics, establishing policies and procedures to achieve compliance with the code and applicable law, and reviewing employee actions to determine whether they are following the rules.

To be effective supervisors, members and candidates should implement education and training programs on a recurring or regular basis for employees under their supervision. Such programs will assist the employees with meeting their professional obligations to practice in an ethical manner within the applicable legal system. Further, establishing incentives—monetary or otherwise—for employees not only to meet business goals but also to reward ethical behavior offers supervisors another way to assist employees in complying with their legal and ethical obligations.

Often, especially in large organizations, members and candidates may have supervisory responsibility but not the authority to establish or modify firm-wide compliance policies and procedures or incentive structures. Such limitations should not prevent a member or candidate from working with his or her own superiors and within the firm structure to develop and implement effective compliance tools, including but not limited to:

- a code of ethics,
- compliance policies and procedures,
- education and training programs,
- an incentive structure that rewards ethical conduct, and
- adoption of firm-wide best practice standards (e.g., the GIPS standards, the CFA Institute Asset Manager Code of Professional Conduct).

A member or candidate with supervisory responsibility should bring an inadequate compliance system to the attention of the firm's senior managers and recommend corrective action. If the member or candidate clearly cannot discharge supervisory responsibilities because of the absence of a compliance system or because of an inadequate compliance system, the member or candidate should decline in writing to accept supervisory responsibility until the firm adopts reasonable procedures to allow adequate exercise of supervisory responsibility.

System for Supervision

Members and candidates with supervisory responsibility must understand what constitutes an adequate compliance system for their firms and make reasonable efforts to see that appropriate compliance procedures are established, documented, communicated to covered personnel, and followed. "Adequate" procedures are those designed to meet industry standards, regulatory requirements, the requirements of the Code and Standards, and the circumstances of the firm. Once compliance procedures are established, the supervisor must also make reasonable efforts to ensure that the procedures are monitored and enforced.

To be effective, compliance procedures must be in place prior to the occurrence of a violation of the law or the Code and Standards. Although compliance procedures cannot be designed to anticipate every potential violation, they should be designed to anticipate the activities most likely to result in misconduct. Compliance programs must be appropriate for the size and nature of the organization. The member or candidate should review model compliance procedures or other industry programs to ensure that the firm's procedures meet the minimum industry standards.

Once a supervisor learns that an employee has violated or may have violated the law or the Code and Standards, the supervisor must promptly initiate an assessment to determine the extent of the wrongdoing. Relying on an employee's statements about the extent of the violation or assurances that the wrongdoing will not reoccur is not enough. Reporting the misconduct up the chain of command and warning the employee to cease the activity are also not enough. Pending the outcome of the investigation, a supervisor should take steps to ensure that the violation will not be repeated, such as placing limits on the employee's activities or increasing the monitoring of the employee's activities.

Supervision Includes Detection

Members and candidates with supervisory responsibility must also make reasonable efforts to detect violations of laws, rules, regulations, firm policies, and the Code and Standards. The supervisors exercise reasonable supervision by establishing and implementing written compliance procedures and ensuring that those procedures are followed through periodic review. If a member or candidate has adopted reasonable procedures and taken steps to institute an effective compliance program, then the member or candidate may not be in violation of Standard IV(C) if he or she does not detect violations that occur despite these efforts. The fact that violations do occur may indicate, however, that the compliance procedures are inadequate. In addition, in some cases, merely enacting such procedures may not be sufficient to fulfill the duty required by Standard IV(C). A member or candidate may be in violation of Standard IV(C) if he or she knows or should know that the procedures designed to promote compliance, including detecting and preventing violations, are not being followed.

40   STANDARD IV(C): RECOMMENDED PROCEDURES

☐ recommend practices and procedures designed to prevent violations of the Code of Ethics and Standards of Professional Conduct

Codes of Ethics or Compliance Procedures

Members and candidates are encouraged to recommend that their employers adopt a code of ethics. Adoption of a code of ethics is critical to establishing a strong ethical foundation for investment advisory firms and their employees. Codes of ethics formally emphasize and reinforce the client loyalty responsibilities of investment firm personnel, protect investing clients by deterring misconduct, and protect the firm's reputation for integrity.

There is a distinction, however, between codes of ethics and the specific policies and procedures needed to ensure compliance with the codes and with securities laws and regulations. Although both are important, codes of ethics should consist of fundamental, principle-based ethical and fiduciary concepts that are applicable to all of the firm's employees. In this way, firms can best convey to employees and clients the ethical ideals that investment advisers strive to achieve. These concepts need to be implemented, however, by detailed, firm-wide compliance policies and procedures. Compliance procedures assist the firm's personnel in fulfilling the responsibilities enumerated in the code of ethics and make probable that the ideals expressed in the code of ethics will be adhered to in the day-to-day operation of the firm.

Stand-alone codes of ethics should be written in plain language and should address general fiduciary concepts. They should be unencumbered by numerous detailed procedures. Codes presented in this way are the most effective in stressing to employees that they are in positions of trust and must act with integrity at all times. Mingling compliance procedures in the firm's code of ethics goes against the goal of reinforcing the ethical obligations of employees.

Separating the code of ethics from compliance procedures will also reduce, if not eliminate, the legal terminology and "boilerplate" language that can make the underlying ethical principles incomprehensible to the average person. Above all, to ensure the creation of a culture of ethics and integrity rather than one that merely focuses on following the rules, the principles in the code of ethics must be stated in a way that is accessible and understandable to everyone in the firm.

Members and candidates should encourage their employers to provide their codes of ethics to clients. In this case also, a simple, straightforward code of ethics will be best understood by clients. Unencumbered by the compliance procedures, the code of ethics will be effective in conveying that the firm is committed to conducting business in an ethical manner and in the best interests of the clients.

Adequate Compliance Procedures

A supervisor complies with Standard IV(C) by identifying situations in which legal violations or violations of the Code and Standards are likely to occur and by establishing and enforcing compliance procedures to prevent such violations. Adequate compliance procedures should

- be contained in a clearly written and accessible manual that is tailored to the firm's operations,
- be drafted so that the procedures are easy to understand,
- designate a compliance officer whose authority and responsibility are clearly defined and who has the necessary resources and authority to implement the firm's compliance procedures,
- describe the hierarchy of supervision and assign duties among supervisors,
- implement a system of checks and balances,
- outline the scope of the procedures,

- outline procedures to document the monitoring and testing of compliance procedures,
- outline permissible conduct, and
- delineate procedures for reporting violations and sanctions.

Once a compliance program is in place, a supervisor should

- disseminate the contents of the program to appropriate personnel,
- periodically update procedures to ensure that the measures are adequate under the law,
- continually educate personnel regarding the compliance procedures,
- issue periodic reminders of the procedures to appropriate personnel,
- incorporate a professional conduct evaluation as part of an employee's performance review,
- review the actions of employees to ensure compliance and identify violators, and
- take the necessary steps to enforce the procedures once a violation has occurred.

Once a violation is discovered, a supervisor should

- respond promptly,
- conduct a thorough investigation of the activities to determine the scope of the wrongdoing,
- increase supervision or place appropriate limitations on the wrongdoer pending the outcome of the investigation, and
- review procedures for potential changes necessary to prevent future violations from occurring.

Implementation of Compliance Education and Training

No amount of ethics education and awareness will deter someone determined to commit fraud for personal enrichment. But the vast majority of investment professionals strive to achieve personal success with dedicated service to their clients and employers.

Regular ethics and compliance training, in conjunction with adoption of a code of ethics, is critical to investment firms seeking to establish a strong culture of integrity and to provide an environment in which employees routinely engage in ethical conduct in compliance with the law. Training and education assist individuals in both recognizing areas that are prone to ethical and legal pitfalls and identifying those circumstances and influences that can impair ethical judgment.

By implementing educational programs, supervisors can train their subordinates to put into practice what the firm's code of ethics requires. Education helps employees make the link between legal and ethical conduct and the long-term success of the business; a strong culture of compliance signals to clients and potential clients that the firm has truly embraced ethical conduct as fundamental to the firm's mission to serve its clients.

Establish an Appropriate Incentive Structure

Even if individuals want to make the right choices and follow an ethical course of conduct and are aware of the obstacles that may trip them up, they can still be influenced to act improperly by a corporate culture that embraces a "succeed at all costs" mentality, stresses results regardless of the methods used to achieve those results, and does not reward ethical behavior. Supervisors can reinforce an individual's natural desire to "do the right thing" by building a culture of integrity in the workplace.

Supervisors and firms must look closely at their incentive structure to determine whether the structure encourages profits and returns at the expense of ethically appropriate conduct. Reward structures may turn a blind eye to how desired outcomes are achieved and encourage dysfunctional or counterproductive behavior. Only when compensation and incentives are firmly tied to client interests and *how* outcomes are achieved, rather than *how much* is generated for the firm, will employees work to achieve a culture of integrity.

STANDARD IV(C): APPLICATION OF THE STANDARD — 41

☐ demonstrate the application of the Code of Ethics and Standards of Professional Conduct to situations involving issues of professional integrity

☐ identify conduct that conforms to the Code and Standards and conduct that violates the Code and Standards

Example 1 (Supervising Research Activities):

Jane Mattock, senior vice president and head of the research department of H&V, Inc., a regional brokerage firm, has decided to change her recommendation for Timber Products from buy to sell. In line with H&V's procedures, she orally advises certain other H&V executives of her proposed actions before the report is prepared for publication. As a result of Mattock's conversation with Dieter Frampton, one of the H&V executives accountable to Mattock, Frampton immediately sells Timber's stock from his own account and from certain discretionary client accounts. In addition, other personnel inform certain institutional customers of the changed recommendation before it is printed and disseminated to all H&V customers who have received previous Timber reports.

> *Comment*: Mattock has violated Standard IV(C) by failing to reasonably and adequately supervise the actions of those accountable to her. She did not prevent or establish reasonable procedures designed to prevent dissemination of or trading on the information by those who knew of her changed recommendation. She must ensure that her firm has procedures for reviewing or recording any trading in the stock of a corporation that has been the subject of an unpublished change in recommendation. Adequate procedures would have informed the subordinates of their duties and detected sales by Frampton and selected customers.

Example 2 (Supervising Research Activities):

Deion Miller is the research director for Jamestown Investment Programs. The portfolio managers have become critical of Miller and his staff because the Jamestown portfolios do not include any stock that has been the subject of a merger or tender offer. Georgia Ginn, a member of Miller's staff, tells Miller that she has been studying a local company,

Excelsior, Inc., and recommends its purchase. Ginn adds that the company has been widely rumored to be the subject of a merger study by a well-known conglomerate and discussions between them are under way. At Miller's request, Ginn prepares a memo recommending the stock. Miller passes along Ginn's memo to the portfolio managers prior to leaving for vacation, and he notes that he has not reviewed the memo. As a result of the memo, the portfolio managers buy Excelsior stock immediately. The day Miller returns to the office, he learns that Ginn's only sources for the report were her brother, who is an acquisitions analyst with Acme Industries, the "well-known conglomerate," and that the merger discussions were planned but not held.

Comment: Miller violated Standard IV(C) by not exercising reasonable supervision when he disseminated the memo without checking to ensure that Ginn had a reasonable and adequate basis for her recommendations and that Ginn was not relying on material nonpublic information.

Example 3 (Supervising Trading Activities):

David Edwards, a trainee trader at Wheeler & Company, a major national brokerage firm, assists a customer in paying for the securities of Highland, Inc., by using anticipated profits from the immediate sale of the same securities. Despite the fact that Highland is not on Wheeler's recommended list, a large volume of its stock is traded through Wheeler in this manner. Roberta Ann Mason is a Wheeler vice president responsible for supervising compliance with the securities laws in the trading department. Part of her compensation from Wheeler is based on commission revenues from the trading department. Although she notices the increased trading activity, she does nothing to investigate or halt it.

Comment: Mason's failure to adequately review and investigate purchase orders in Highland stock executed by Edwards and her failure to supervise the trainee's activities violate Standard IV(C). Supervisors should be especially sensitive to actual or potential conflicts between their own self-interests and their supervisory responsibilities.

Example 4 (Supervising Trading Activities and Record Keeping):

Samantha Tabbing is senior vice president and portfolio manager for Crozet, Inc., a registered investment advisory and registered broker/dealer firm. She reports to Charles Henry, the president of Crozet. Crozet serves as the investment adviser and principal underwriter for ABC and XYZ public mutual funds. The two funds' prospectuses allow Crozet to trade financial futures for the funds for the limited purpose of hedging against market risks. Henry, extremely impressed by Tabbing's performance in the past two years, directs Tabbing to act as portfolio manager for the funds. For the benefit of its employees, Crozet has also organized the Crozet Employee Profit-Sharing Plan (CEPSP), a defined contribution retirement plan. Henry assigns Tabbing to manage 20% of the assets of CEPSP. Tabbing's investment objective for her portion of CEPSP's assets is aggressive growth. Unbeknownst to Henry, Tabbing frequently places S&P 500 Index purchase and sale orders for the funds and the CEPSP without providing the futures commission merchants (FCMs) who take the orders with any prior or simultaneous designation of the account for which the trade has been placed. Frequently, neither Tabbing nor anyone else at Crozet completes an internal trade ticket to record the time an order was placed or the specific account for which the order was intended. FCMs often designate a specific account only after the trade, when Tabbing provides such designation. Crozet has no written operating procedures or compliance manual concerning its futures trading, and its compliance department does not review such trading. After observing the market's movement, Tabbing assigns to CEPSP the S&P 500 positions with more favorable execution prices and assigns positions with less favorable execution prices to the funds.

> *Comment*: Henry violated Standard IV(C) by failing to adequately supervise Tabbing with respect to her S&P 500 trading. Henry further violated Standard IV(C) by failing to establish record-keeping and reporting procedures to prevent or detect Tabbing's violations. Henry must make a reasonable effort to determine that adequate compliance procedures covering all employee trading activity are established, documented, communicated, and followed.

Example 5 (Accepting Responsibility):

Meredith Rasmussen works on a buy-side trading desk and concentrates on in-house trades for a hedge fund subsidiary managed by a team at the investment management firm. The hedge fund has been very successful and is marketed globally by the firm. From her experience as the trader for much of the activity of the fund, Rasmussen has become quite knowledgeable about the hedge fund's strategy, tactics, and performance. When a distinct break in the market occurs and many of the securities involved in the hedge fund's strategy decline markedly in value, however, Rasmussen observes that the reported performance of the hedge fund does not at all reflect this decline. From her experience, this lack of an effect is a very unlikely occurrence. She approaches the head of trading about her concern and is told that she should not ask any questions and that the fund is too big and successful and is not her concern. She is fairly sure something is not right, so she contacts the compliance officer and is again told to stay away from the hedge fund reporting issue.

> *Comment*: Rasmussen has clearly come upon an error in policies, procedures, and compliance practices within the firm's operations. According to Standard IV(C), the supervisor and the compliance officer have the responsibility to review the concerns brought forth by Rasmussen. Supervisors have the responsibility of establishing and encouraging an ethical culture in the firm. The dismissal of Rasmussen's question violates Standard IV(C) and undermines the firm's ethical operations.
> See also Standard I(D)–Misconduct and, for guidance on whistleblowing, Standard IV(A)–Loyalty.

Example 6 (Inadequate Procedures):

Brendan Witt, a former junior sell-side technology analyst, decided to return to school to earn an MBA. To keep his research skills and industry knowledge sharp, Witt accepted a position with On-line and Informed, an independent internet-based research company. The position requires the publication of a recommendation and report on a different company every month. Initially, Witt is a regular contributor of new research and a participant in the associated discussion boards that generally have positive comments on the technology sector. Over time, his ability to manage his educational requirements and his work requirements begin to conflict with one another. Knowing a recommendation is due the next day for On-line, Witt creates a report based on a few news articles and what the conventional wisdom of the markets has deemed the "hot" security of the day.

Comment: Allowing the report submitted by Witt to be posted highlights a lack of compliance procedures by the research firm. Witt's supervisor needs to work with the management of On-line to develop an appropriate review process to ensure that all contracted analysts comply with the requirements.

See also Standard V(A)–Diligence and Reasonable Basis because it relates to Witt's responsibility for substantiating a recommendation.

Example 7 (Inadequate Supervision):

Michael Papis is the chief investment officer of his state's retirement fund. The fund has always used outside advisers for the real estate allocation, and this information is clearly presented in all fund communications. Thomas Nagle, a recognized sell-side research analyst and Papis's business school classmate, recently left the investment bank he worked for to start his own asset management firm, Accessible Real Estate. Nagle is trying to build his assets under management and contacts Papis about gaining some of the retirement fund's allocation. In the previous few years, the performance of the retirement fund's real estate investments was in line with the fund's benchmark but was not extraordinary. Papis decides to help out his old friend and also to seek better returns by moving the real estate allocation to Accessible. The only notice of the change in adviser appears in the next annual report in the listing of associated advisers.

Comment: Papis's actions highlight the need for supervision and review at all levels in an organization. His responsibilities may include the selection of external advisers, but the decision to change advisers appears arbitrary. Members and candidates should ensure that their firm has appropriate policies and procedures in place to detect inappropriate actions, such as the action taken by Papis.

See also Standard V(A)–Diligence and Reasonable Basis, Standard V(B)–Communication with Clients and Prospective Clients, and Standard VI(A)–Disclosure of Conflicts.

Example 8 (Supervising Research Activities):

Mary Burdette was recently hired by Fundamental Investment Management (FIM) as a junior auto industry analyst. Burdette is expected to expand the social media presence of the firm because she is active with various networks, including Facebook, LinkedIn, and Twitter. Although Burdette's supervisor, Joe Graf, has never used social media, he encourages Burdette to explore opportunities to increase FIM's online presence and ability to share content, communicate, and broadcast information to clients. In response to Graf's encouragement, Burdette is working on a proposal detailing the advantages of getting FIM onto Twitter in addition to launching a company Facebook page.

As part of her auto industry research for FIM, Burdette is completing a report on the financial impact of Sun Drive Auto Ltd.'s new solar technology for compact automobiles. This research report will be her first for FIM, and she believes Sun Drive's technology could revolutionize the auto industry. In her excitement, Burdette sends a quick tweet to FIM Twitter followers summarizing her "buy" recommendation for Sun Drive Auto stock.

Comment: Graf has violated Standard IV(C) by failing to reasonably supervise Burdette with respect to the contents of her tweet. He did not establish reasonable procedures to prevent the unauthorized dissemination of company research through social media networks. Graf must make sure all employees receive regular training about FIM's policies and procedures, including the appropriate business use of personal social media networks.

See Standard III(B) for additional guidance.

Example 9 (Supervising Research Activities):

Chen Wang leads the research department at YYRA Retirement Planning Specialists. Chen supervises a team of 10 analysts in a fast-paced and understaffed organization. He is responsible for coordinating the firm's approved process to review all reports before they are provided to the portfolio management team for use in rebalancing client portfolios.

One of Chen's direct reports, Huang Mei, covers the banking industry. Chen must submit the latest updates to the portfolio management team tomorrow morning. Huang has yet to submit her research report on ZYX Bank because she is uncomfortable providing a "buy" or "sell" opinion of ZYX on the basis of the completed analysis. Pressed for time and concerned that Chen will reject a "hold" recommendation, she researches various websites and blogs on the banking sector for whatever she can find on ZYX. One independent blogger provides a new interpretation of the recently reported data Huang has analyzed and concludes with a strong "sell" recommendation for ZYX. She is impressed by the originality and resourcefulness of this blogger's report.

Very late in the evening, Huang submits her report and "sell" recommendation to Chen without any reference to the independent blogger's report. Given the late time of the submission and the competence of Huang's prior work, Chen compiles this report with the recommendations from each of the other analysts and meets with the portfolio managers to discuss implementation.

> *Comment*: Chen has violated Standard IV(C) by neglecting to reasonably and adequately follow the firm's approved review process for Huang's research report. The delayed submission and the quality of prior work do not remove Chen's requirement to uphold the designated review process. A member or candidate with supervisory responsibility must make reasonable efforts to see that appropriate procedures are established, documented, communicated to covered personnel, and followed.

STANDARD V(A): INVESTMENT ANALYSIS, RECOMMENDATIONS, AND ACTIONS - DILIGENCE AND REASONABLE BASIS

☐ demonstrate the application of the Code of Ethics and Standards of Professional Conduct to situations involving issues of professional integrity

Standard V(A) Diligence and Reasonable Basis

Members and Candidates must:

1. Exercise diligence, independence, and thoroughness in analyzing investments, making investment recommendations, and taking investment actions.

> 2. Have a reasonable and adequate basis, supported by appropriate research and investigation, for any investment analysis, recommendation, or action.

Guidance

Highlights:

- *Defining Diligence and Reasonable Basis*
- *Using Secondary or Third-Party Research*
- *Using Quantitatively Oriented Research*
- *Developing Quantitatively Oriented Techniques*
- *Selecting External Advisers and Subadvisers*
- *Group Research and Decision Making*

The application of Standard V(A) depends on the investment philosophy the member, candidate, or firm is following, the role of the member or candidate in the investment decision-making process, and the support and resources provided by the member's or candidate's employer. These factors will dictate the nature of the diligence and thoroughness of the research and the level of investigation required by Standard V(A).

The requirements for issuing conclusions based on research will vary in relation to the member's or candidate's role in the investment decision-making process, but the member or candidate must make reasonable efforts to cover all pertinent issues when arriving at a recommendation. Members and candidates enhance transparency by providing or offering to provide supporting information to clients when recommending a purchase or sale or when changing a recommendation.

Defining Diligence and Reasonable Basis

Every investment decision is based on a set of facts known and understood at the time. Clients turn to members and candidates for advice and expect these advisers to have more information and knowledge than they do. This information and knowledge is the basis from which members and candidates apply their professional judgment in taking investment actions and making recommendations.

At a basic level, clients want assurance that members and candidates are putting forth the necessary effort to support the recommendations they are making. Communicating the level and thoroughness of the information reviewed before the member or candidate makes a judgment allows clients to understand the reasonableness of the recommended investment actions.

As with determining the suitability of an investment for the client, the necessary level of research and analysis will differ with the product, security, or service being offered. In providing an investment service, members and candidates typically use a variety of resources, including company reports, third-party research, and results from quantitative models. A reasonable basis is formed through a balance of these resources appropriate for the security or decision being analyzed.

The following list provides some, but definitely not all, examples of attributes to consider while forming the basis for a recommendation:

- global, regional, and country macroeconomic conditions,
- a company's operating and financial history,
- the industry's and sector's current conditions and the stage of the business cycle,

- a mutual fund's fee structure and management history,
- the output and potential limitations of quantitative models,
- the quality of the assets included in a securitization, and
- the appropriateness of selected peer-group comparisons.

Even though an investment recommendation may be well informed, downside risk remains for any investment. Members and candidates can base their decisions only on the information available at the time decisions are made. The steps taken in developing a diligent and reasonable recommendation should minimize unexpected downside events.

Using Secondary or Third-Party Research

If members and candidates rely on secondary or third-party research, they must make reasonable and diligent efforts to determine whether such research is sound. Secondary research is defined as research conducted by someone else in the member's or candidate's firm. Third-party research is research conducted by entities outside the member's or candidate's firm, such as a brokerage firm, bank, or research firm. If a member or candidate has reason to suspect that either secondary or third-party research or information comes from a source that lacks a sound basis, the member or candidate must not rely on that information.

Members and candidates should make reasonable enquiries into the source and accuracy of all data used in completing their investment analysis and recommendations. The sources of the information and data will influence the level of the review a member or candidate must undertake. Information and data taken from internet sources, such as personal blogs, independent research aggregation websites, or social media websites, likely require a greater level of review than information from more established research organizations.

Criteria that a member or candidate can use in forming an opinion on whether research is sound include the following:

- assumptions used,
- rigor of the analysis performed,
- date/timeliness of the research, and
- evaluation of the objectivity and independence of the recommendations.

A member or candidate may rely on others in his or her firm to determine whether secondary or third-party research is sound and use the information in good faith unless the member or candidate has reason to question its validity or the processes and procedures used by those responsible for the research. For example, a portfolio manager may not have a choice of a data source because the firm's senior managers conducted due diligence to determine which vendor would provide services; the member or candidate can use the information in good faith assuming the due diligence process was deemed adequate.

A member or candidate should verify that the firm has a policy about the timely and consistent review of approved research providers to ensure that the quality of the research continues to meet the necessary standards. If such a policy is not in place at the firm, the member or candidate should encourage the development and adoption of a formal review practice.

Using Quantitatively Oriented Research

Standard V(A) applies to the rapidly expanding use of quantitatively oriented research models and processes, such as computer-generated modeling, screening, and ranking of investment securities; the creation or valuation of derivative instruments; and quantitative portfolio construction techniques. These models and processes are being used for much more than the back testing of investment strategies, especially with continually advancing technology and techniques. The continued broad development of quantitative methods and models is an important part of capital market developments.

Members and candidates need to have an understanding of the parameters used in models and quantitative research that are incorporated into their investment recommendations. Although they are not required to become experts in every technical aspect of the models, they must understand the assumptions and limitations inherent in any model and how the results were used in the decision-making process.

The reliance on and potential limitations of financial models became clear through the investment crisis that unfolded in 2007 and 2008. In some cases, the financial models used to value specific securities and related derivative products did not adequately demonstrate the level of associated risks. Members and candidates should make reasonable efforts to test the output of investment models and other pre-programmed analytical tools they use. Such validation should occur before incorporating the process into their methods, models, or analyses.

Although not every model can test for every factor or outcome, members and candidates should ensure that their analyses incorporate a broad range of assumptions sufficient to capture the underlying characteristics of investments. The omission from the analysis of potentially negative outcomes or of levels of risk outside the norm may misrepresent the true economic value of an investment. The possible scenarios for analysis should include factors that are likely to have a substantial influence on the investment value and may include extremely positive and negative scenarios.

Developing Quantitatively Oriented Techniques

Individuals who create new quantitative models and services must exhibit a higher level of diligence in reviewing new products than the individuals who ultimately use the analytical output. Members and candidates involved in the development and oversight of quantitatively oriented models, methods, and algorithms must understand the technical aspects of the products they provide to clients. A thorough testing of the model and resulting analysis should be completed prior to product distribution.

Members and candidates need to consider the source and time horizon of the data used as inputs in financial models. The information from many commercially available databases may not effectively incorporate both positive and negative market cycles. In the development of a recommendation, the member or candidate may need to test the models by using volatility and performance expectations that represent scenarios outside the observable databases. In reviewing the computer models or the resulting output, members and candidates need to pay particular attention to the assumptions used in the analysis and the rigor of the analysis to ensure that the model incorporates a wide range of possible input expectations, including negative market events.

Selecting External Advisers and Subadvisers

Financial instruments and asset allocation techniques continue to develop and evolve. This progression has led to the use of specialized managers to invest in specific asset classes or diversification strategies that complement a firm's in-house expertise. Standard V(A) applies to the level of review necessary in selecting an external adviser or subadviser to manage a specifically mandated allocation. Members and candidates must review managers as diligently as they review individual funds and securities.

Members and candidates who are directly involved with the use of external advisers need to ensure that their firms have standardized criteria for reviewing these selected external advisers and managers. Such criteria would include, but would not be limited to, the following:

- reviewing the adviser's established code of ethics,
- understanding the adviser's compliance and internal control procedures,

- assessing the quality of the published return information, and
- reviewing the adviser's investment process and adherence to its stated strategy.

Codes, standards, and guides to best practice published by CFA Institute provide members and candidates with examples of acceptable practices for external advisers and advice in selecting a new adviser. The following guides are available at the CFA Institute website (www.cfainstitute.org): Asset Manager Code of Professional Conduct, Global Investment Performance Standards, and Model Request for Proposal (for equity, credit, or real estate managers).

Group Research and Decision Making

Commonly, members and candidates are part of a group or team that is collectively responsible for producing investment analysis or research. The conclusions or recommendations of the group report represent the consensus of the group and are not necessarily the views of the member or candidate, even though the name of the member or candidate is included on the report. In some instances, a member or candidate will not agree with the view of the group. If, however, the member or candidate believes that the consensus opinion has a reasonable and adequate basis and is independent and objective, the member or candidate need not decline to be identified with the report. If the member or candidate is confident in the process, the member or candidate does not need to dissociate from the report even if it does not reflect his or her opinion.

STANDARD V(A): RECOMMENDED PROCEDURES

☐ recommend practices and procedures designed to prevent violations of the Code of Ethics and Standards of Professional Conduct

Members and candidates should encourage their firms to consider the following policies and procedures to support the principles of Standard V(A):

- Establish a policy requiring that research reports, credit ratings, and investment recommendations have a basis that can be substantiated as reasonable and adequate. An individual employee (a supervisory analyst) or a group of employees (a review committee) should be appointed to review and approve such items prior to external circulation to determine whether the criteria established in the policy have been met.
- Develop detailed, written guidance for analysts (research, investment, or credit), supervisory analysts, and review committees that establishes the due diligence procedures for judging whether a particular recommendation has a reasonable and adequate basis.
- Develop measurable criteria for assessing the quality of research, the reasonableness and adequacy of the basis for any recommendation or rating, and the accuracy of recommendations over time. In some cases, firms may consider implementing compensation arrangements that depend on these measurable criteria and that are applied consistently to all related analysts.

- Develop detailed, written guidance that establishes minimum levels of scenario testing of all computer-based models used in developing, rating, and evaluating financial instruments. The policy should contain criteria related to the breadth of the scenarios tested, the accuracy of the output over time, and the analysis of cash flow sensitivity to inputs.
- Develop measurable criteria for assessing outside providers, including the quality of information being provided, the reasonableness and adequacy of the provider's collection practices, and the accuracy of the information over time. The established policy should outline how often the provider's products are reviewed.
- Adopt a standardized set of criteria for evaluating the adequacy of external advisers. The policy should include how often and on what basis the allocation of funds to the adviser will be reviewed.

44 STANDARD V(A): APPLICATION OF THE STANDARD

- [ ] demonstrate the application of the Code of Ethics and Standards of Professional Conduct to situations involving issues of professional integrity
- [ ] identify conduct that conforms to the Code and Standards and conduct that violates the Code and Standards

Example 1 (Sufficient Due Diligence):

Helen Hawke manages the corporate finance department of Sarkozi Securities, Ltd. The firm is anticipating that the government will soon close a tax loophole that currently allows oil-and-gas exploration companies to pass on drilling expenses to holders of a certain class of shares. Because market demand for this tax-advantaged class of stock is currently high, Sarkozi convinces several companies to undertake new equity financings at once, before the loophole closes. Time is of the essence, but Sarkozi lacks sufficient resources to conduct adequate research on all the prospective issuing companies. Hawke decides to estimate the IPO prices on the basis of the relative size of each company and to justify the pricing later when her staff has time.

> *Comment*: Sarkozi should have taken on only the work that it could adequately handle. By categorizing the issuers by general size, Hawke has bypassed researching all the other relevant aspects that should be considered when pricing new issues and thus has not performed sufficient due diligence. Such an omission can result in investors purchasing shares at prices that have no actual basis. Hawke has violated Standard V(A).

Example 2 (Sufficient Scenario Testing):

Babu Dhaliwal works for Heinrich Brokerage in the corporate finance group. He has just persuaded Feggans Resources, Ltd., to allow his firm to do a secondary equity financing at Feggans Resources' current stock price. Because the stock has been trading at higher multiples than similar companies with equivalent production, Dhaliwal presses the Feggans Resources managers to project what would be the maximum production they could achieve in an optimal scenario. Based on these numbers, he is able to justify the price his firm will be asking for the secondary issue. During a sales pitch to the brokers, Dhaliwal then uses these numbers as the base-case production levels that Feggans Resources will achieve.

> *Comment*: When presenting information to the brokers, Dhaliwal should have given a range of production scenarios and the probability of Feggans Resources achieving each level. By giving the maximum production level as the likely level of production, he has misrepresented the chances of achieving that production level and seriously misled the brokers. Dhaliwal has violated Standard V(A).

Example 3 (Developing a Reasonable Basis):

Brendan Witt, a former junior sell-side technology analyst, decided to return to school to earn an MBA. To keep his research skills and industry knowledge sharp, Witt accepted a position with On-line and Informed, an independent internet-based research company. The position requires the publication of a recommendation and report on a different company every month. Initially, Witt is a regular contributor of new research and a participant in the associated discussion boards that generally have positive comments on the technology sector. Over time, his ability to manage his educational requirements and his work requirements begin to conflict with one another. Knowing a recommendation is due the next day for On-line, Witt creates a report based on a few news articles and what the conventional wisdom of the markets has deemed the "hot" security of the day.

> *Comment*: Witt's knowledge of and exuberance for technology stocks, a few news articles, and the conventional wisdom of the markets do not constitute, without more information, a reasonable and adequate basis for a stock recommendation that is supported by appropriate research and investigation. Therefore, Witt has violated Standard V(A).
>
> See also Standard IV(C)–Responsibilities of Supervisors because it relates to the firm's inadequate procedures.

Example 4 (Timely Client Updates):

Kristen Chandler is an investment consultant in the London office of Dalton Securities, a major global investment consultant firm. One of her UK pension funds has decided to appoint a specialist US equity manager. Dalton's global manager of research relies on local consultants to cover managers within their regions and, after conducting thorough due diligence, puts their views and ratings in Dalton's manager database. Chandler accesses Dalton's global manager research database and conducts a screen of all US equity managers on the basis of a match with the client's desired philosophy/style, performance, and tracking-error targets. She selects the five managers that meet these criteria and puts them in a briefing report that is delivered to the client 10 days later. Between the time of Chandler's database search and the delivery of the report to the client, Chandler is told that Dalton has updated the database with the information that one of the firms that Chandler has recommended for consideration lost its chief investment officer, the head of its US equity research, and the majority of its portfolio managers on the US equity product—all of whom have left to establish their own firm. Chandler does not revise her report with this updated information.

Comment: Chandler has failed to satisfy the requirement of Standard V(A). Although Dalton updated the manager ratings to reflect the personnel turnover at one of the firms, Chandler did not update her report to reflect the new information.

Example 5 (Group Research Opinions):

Evelyn Mastakis is a junior analyst who has been asked by her firm to write a research report predicting the expected interest rate for residential mortgages over the next six months. Mastakis submits her report to the fixed-income investment committee of her firm for review, as required by firm procedures. Although some committee members support Mastakis's conclusion, the majority of the committee disagrees with her conclusion, and the report is significantly changed to indicate that interest rates are likely to increase more than originally predicted by Mastakis. Should Mastakis ask that her name be taken off the report when it is disseminated?

Comment: The results of research are not always clear, and different people may have different opinions based on the same factual evidence. In this case, the committee may have valid reasons for issuing a report that differs from the analyst's original research. The firm can issue a report that is different from the original report of an analyst as long as there is a reasonable and adequate basis for its conclusions.

Generally, analysts must write research reports that reflect their own opinion and can ask the firm not to put their name on reports that ultimately differ from that opinion. When the work is a group effort, however, not all members of the team may agree with all aspects of the report. Ultimately, members and candidates can ask to have their names removed from the report, but if they are satisfied that the process has produced results or conclusions that have a reasonable and adequate basis, members and candidates do not have to dissociate from the report even when they do not agree with its contents. If Mastakis is confident in the process, she does not need to dissociate from the report even if it does not reflect her opinion.

Example 6 (Reliance on Third-Party Research):

Gary McDermott runs a two-person investment management firm. McDermott's firm subscribes to a service from a large investment research firm that provides research reports. McDermott's firm makes investment recommendations on the basis of these reports.

Comment: Members and candidates can rely on third-party research but must make reasonable and diligent efforts to determine that such research is sound. If McDermott undertakes due diligence efforts on a regular basis to ensure that the research produced by the large firm is objective and reasonably based, McDermott can rely on that research when making investment recommendations to clients.

Example 7 (Due Diligence in Submanager Selection):

Paul Ostrowski's business has grown significantly over the past couple of years, and some clients want to diversify internationally. Ostrowski decides to find a submanager to handle the expected international investments. Because this will be his first subadviser, Ostrowski uses the CFA Institute model "request for proposal" to design a questionnaire for his search. By his deadline, he receives seven completed questionnaires from a variety of domestic and international firms trying to gain his business. Ostrowski reviews all the applications in detail and decides to select the firm that charges the lowest fees because doing so will have the least impact on his firm's bottom line.

> *Comment*: The selection of an external adviser or subadviser should be based on a full and complete review of the adviser's services, performance history, and cost structure. In basing the decision on the fee structure alone, Ostrowski may be violating Standard V(A).
>
> See also Standard III(C)–Suitability because it relates to the ability of the selected adviser to meet the needs of the clients.

Example 8 (Sufficient Due Diligence):

Michael Papis is the chief investment officer of his state's retirement fund. The fund has always used outside advisers for the real estate allocation, and this information is clearly presented in all fund communications. Thomas Nagle, a recognized sell-side research analyst and Papis's business school classmate, recently left the investment bank he worked for to start his own asset management firm, Accessible Real Estate. Nagle is trying to build his assets under management and contacts Papis about gaining some of the retirement fund's allocation. In the previous few years, the performance of the retirement fund's real estate investments was in line with the fund's benchmark but was not extraordinary. Papis decides to help out his old friend and also to seek better returns by moving the real estate allocation to Accessible. The only notice of the change in adviser appears in the next annual report in the listing of associated advisers.

> *Comment*: Papis violated Standard V(A). His responsibilities may include the selection of the external advisers, but the decision to change advisers appears to have been arbitrary. If Papis was dissatisfied with the current real estate adviser, he should have conducted a proper solicitation to select the most appropriate adviser.
>
> See also Standard IV(C)–Responsibilities of Supervisors, Standard V(B)–Communication with Clients and Prospective Clients, and Standard VI(A)–Disclosure of Conflicts.

Example 9 (Sufficient Due Diligence):

Andre Shrub owns and operates Conduit, an investment advisory firm. Prior to opening Conduit, Shrub was an account manager with Elite Investment, a hedge fund managed by his good friend Adam Reed. To attract clients to a new Conduit fund, Shrub offers lower-than-normal management fees. He can do so because the fund consists of two top-performing funds managed by Reed. Given his personal friendship with Reed and the prior performance record of these two funds, Shrub believes this new fund is a winning combination for all parties. Clients quickly invest with Conduit to gain access to the Elite funds. No one is turned away because Conduit is seeking to expand its assets under management.

> *Comment*: Shrub violated Standard V(A) by not conducting a thorough analysis of the funds managed by Reed before developing the new Conduit fund. Shrub's reliance on his personal relationship with Reed and his prior knowledge of Elite are insufficient justification for the investments. The

funds may be appropriately considered, but a full review of their operating procedures, reporting practices, and transparency are some elements of the necessary due diligence.

See also Standard III(C)–Suitability.

Example 10 (Sufficient Due Diligence):

Bob Thompson has been doing research for the portfolio manager of the fixed-income department. His assignment is to do sensitivity analysis on securitized subprime mortgages. He has discussed with the manager possible scenarios to use to calculate expected returns. A key assumption in such calculations is housing price appreciation (HPA) because it drives "prepays" (prepayments of mortgages) and losses. Thompson is concerned with the significant appreciation experienced over the previous five years as a result of the increased availability of funds from subprime mortgages. Thompson insists that the analysis should include a scenario run with −10% for Year 1, −5% for Year 2, and then (to project a worst-case scenario) 0% for Years 3 through 5. The manager replies that these assumptions are too dire because there has never been a time in their available database when HPA was negative.

Thompson conducts his research to better understand the risks inherent in these securities and evaluates these securities in the worst-case scenario, a less likely but possible environment. Based on the results of the enhanced scenarios, Thompson does not recommend the purchase of the securitization. Against the general market trends, the manager follows Thompson's recommendation and does not invest. The following year, the housing market collapses. In avoiding the subprime investments, the manager's portfolio outperforms its peer group that year.

> *Comment*: Thompson's actions in running the scenario test with inputs beyond the historical trends available in the firm's databases adhere to the principles of Standard V(A). His concerns over recent trends provide a sound basis for further analysis. Thompson understands the limitations of his model, when combined with the limited available historical information, to accurately predict the performance of the funds if market conditions change negatively.
>
> See also Standard I(B)–Independence and Objectivity.

Example 11 (Use of Quantitatively Oriented Models):

Espacia Liakos works in sales for Hellenica Securities, a firm specializing in developing intricate derivative strategies to profit from particular views on market expectations. One of her clients is Eugenie Carapalis, who has become convinced that commodity prices will become more volatile over the coming months. Carapalis asks Liakos to quickly engineer a strategy that will benefit from this expectation. Liakos turns to Hellenica's modeling group to fulfill this request. Because of the tight deadline, the modeling group outsources parts of the work to several trusted third parties. Liakos implements the disparate components of the strategy as the firms complete them.

Within a month, Carapalis is proven correct: Volatility across a range of commodities increases sharply. But her derivatives position with Hellenica returns huge losses, and the losses increase daily. Liakos investigates and realizes that although each of the various components of the strategy had been validated, they had never been evaluated as an integrated whole. In extreme conditions, portions of the model worked at cross-purposes with other portions, causing the overall strategy to fail dramatically.

Comment: Liakos violated Standard V(A). Members and candidates must understand the statistical significance of the results of the models they recommend and must be able to explain them to clients. Liakos did not take adequate care to ensure a thorough review of the whole model; its components were evaluated only individually. Because Carapalis clearly intended to implement the strategy as a whole rather than as separate parts, Liakos should have tested how the components of the strategy interacted as well as how they performed individually.

Example 12 (Successful Due Diligence/Failed Investment):

Alton Newbury is an investment adviser to high-net-worth clients. A client with an aggressive risk profile in his investment policy statement asks about investing in the Top Shelf hedge fund. This fund, based in Calgary, Alberta, Canada, has reported 20% returns for the first three years. The fund prospectus states that its strategy involves long and short positions in the energy sector and extensive leverage. Based on his analysis of the fund's track record, the principals involved in managing the fund, the fees charged, and the fund's risk profile, Newbury recommends the fund to the client and secures a position in it. The next week, the fund announces that it has suffered a loss of 60% of its value and is suspending operations and redemptions until after a regulatory review. Newbury's client calls him in a panic and asks for an explanation.

Comment: Newbury's actions were consistent with Standard V(A). Analysis of an investment that results in a reasonable basis for recommendation does not guarantee that the investment has no downside risk. Newbury should discuss the analysis process with the client while reminding him or her that past performance does not lead to guaranteed future gains and that losses in an aggressive investment portfolio should be expected.

Example 13 (Quantitative Model Diligence):

Barry Cannon is the lead quantitative analyst at CityCenter Hedge Fund. He is responsible for the development, maintenance, and enhancement of the proprietary models the fund uses to manage its investors' assets. Cannon reads several high-level mathematical publications and blogs to stay informed of current developments. One blog, run by Expert CFA, presents some intriguing research that may benefit one of CityCenter's current models. Cannon is under pressure from firm executives to improve the model's predictive abilities, and he incorporates the factors discussed in the online research. The updated output recommends several new investments to the fund's portfolio managers.

Comment: Cannon has violated Standard V(A) by failing to have a reasonable basis for the new recommendations made to the portfolio managers. He needed to diligently research the effect of incorporating the new factors before offering the output recommendations. Cannon may use the blog for ideas, but it is his responsibility to determine the effect on the firm's proprietary models.

See Standard VII(B) regarding the violation by "Expert CFA" in the use of the CFA designation.

Example 14 (Selecting a Service Provider):

Ellen Smith is a performance analyst at Artic Global Advisors, a firm that manages global equity mandates for institutional clients. She was asked by her supervisor to review five new performance attribution systems and recommend one that would more appropriately explain the firm's investment strategy to clients. On the list was a system she recalled learning about when visiting an exhibitor booth at a recent conference. The system is highly quantitative and something of a "black box" in how it calculates the attribution values. Smith recommended this option without researching the others because the sheer complexity of the process was sure to impress the clients.

> *Comment*: Smith's actions do not demonstrate a sufficient level of diligence in reviewing this product to make a recommendation for selecting the service. Besides not reviewing or considering the other four potential systems, she did not determine whether the "black box" attribution process aligns with the investment practices of the firm, including its investments in different countries and currencies. Smith must review and understand the process of any software or system before recommending its use as the firm's attribution system.

Example 15 (Subadviser Selection):

Craig Jackson is working for Adams Partners, Inc., and has been assigned to select a hedge fund subadviser to improve the diversification of the firm's large fund-of-funds product. The allocation must be in place before the start of the next quarter. Jackson uses a consultant database to find a list of suitable firms that claim compliance with the GIPS standards. He calls more than 20 firms on the list to confirm their potential interest and to determine their most recent quarterly and annual total return values. Because of the short turnaround, Jackson recommends the firm with the greatest total return values for selection.

> *Comment*: By considering only performance and GIPS compliance, Jackson has not conducted sufficient review of potential firms to satisfy the requirements of Standard V(A). A thorough investigation of the firms and their operations should be conducted to ensure that their addition would increase the diversity of clients' portfolios and that they are suitable for the fund-of-funds product.

Example 16 (Manager Selection):

Timothy Green works for Peach Asset Management, where he creates proprietary models that analyze data from the firm request for proposal questionnaires to identify managers for possible inclusion in the firm's fund-of-funds investment platform. Various criteria must be met to be accepted to the platform. Because of the number of respondents to the questionnaires, Green uses only the data submitted to make a recommendation for adding a new manager.

> *Comment*: By failing to conduct any additional outside review of the information to verify what was submitted through the request for proposal, Green has likely not satisfied the requirements of Standard V(A). The amount of information requested from outside managers varies among firms. Although the requested information may be comprehensive, Green should ensure sufficient effort is undertaken to verify the submitted information before recommending a firm for inclusion. This requires that he goes beyond the

Standard V(A): Application of the Standard

information provided by the manager on the request for proposal questionnaire and may include interviews with interested managers, reviews of regulatory filings, and discussions with the managers' custodian or auditor.

Example 17 (Technical Model Requirements):

Jérôme Dupont works for the credit research group of XYZ Asset Management, where he is in charge of developing and updating credit risk models. In order to perform accurately, his models need to be regularly updated with the latest market data.

Dupont does not interact with or manage money for any of the firm's clients. He is in contact with the firm's US corporate bond fund manager, John Smith, who has only very superficial knowledge of the model and who from time to time asks very basic questions regarding the output recommendations. Smith does not consult Dupont with respect to finalizing his clients' investment strategies.

Dupont's recently assigned objective is to develop a new emerging market corporate credit risk model. The firm is planning to expand into emerging credit, and the development of such a model is a critical step in this process. Because Smith seems to follow the model's recommendations without much concern for its quality as he develops his clients' investment strategies, Dupont decides to focus his time on the development of the new emerging market model and neglects to update the US model.

After several months without regular updates, Dupont's diagnostic statistics start to show alarming signs with respect to the quality of the US credit model. Instead of conducting the long and complicated data update, Dupont introduces new codes into his model with some limited new data as a quick "fix." He thinks this change will address the issue without needing to complete the full data update, so he continues working on the new emerging market model.

Several months following the quick "fix," another set of diagnostic statistics reveals nonsensical results and Dupont realizes that his earlier change contained an error. He quickly corrects the error and alerts Smith. Smith realizes that some of the prior trades he performed were due to erroneous model results. Smith rebalances the portfolio to remove the securities purchased on the basis of the questionable results without reporting the issue to anyone else.

> *Comment*: Smith violated standard V(A) because exercising "diligence, independence, and thoroughness in analyzing investments, making investment recommendations, and taking investment actions" means that members and candidates must understand the technical aspects of the products they provide to clients. Smith does not understand the model he is relying on to manage money. Members and candidates should also make reasonable enquiries into the source and accuracy of all data used in completing their investment analysis and recommendations.
>
> Dupont violated V(A) even if he does not trade securities or make investment decisions. Dupont's models give investment recommendations, and Dupont is accountable for the quality of those recommendations. Members and candidates should make reasonable efforts to test the output of pre-programed analytical tools they use. Such validation should occur before incorporating the tools into their decision-making process.
>
> See also Standard V(B)–Communication with Clients and Prospective Clients.

45. STANDARD V(B): INVESTMENT ANALYSIS, RECOMMENDATIONS, AND ACTIONS - COMMUNICATION WITH CLIENTS AND PROSPECTIVE CLIENTS

☐ demonstrate the application of the Code of Ethics and Standards of Professional Conduct to situations involving issues of professional integrity

> Members and Candidates must:
> 1. Disclose to clients and prospective clients the basic format and general principles of the investment processes they use to analyze investments, select securities, and construct portfolios and must promptly disclose any changes that might materially affect those processes.
> 2. Disclose to clients and prospective clients significant limitations and risks associated with the investment process.
> 3. Use reasonable judgment in identifying which factors are important to their investment analyses, recommendations, or actions and include those factors in communications with clients and prospective clients.
> 4. Distinguish between fact and opinion in the presentation of investment analyses and recommendations.

Guidance

Highlights:

- *Informing Clients of the Investment Process*
- *Different Forms of Communication*
- *Identifying Risk and Limitations*
- *Report Presentation*
- *Distinction between Facts and Opinions in Reports*

Standard V(B) addresses member and candidate conduct with respect to communicating with clients. Developing and maintaining clear, frequent, and thorough communication practices is critical to providing high-quality financial services to clients. When clients understand the information communicated to them, they also can understand exactly how members and candidates are acting on their behalf, which gives clients the opportunity to make well-informed decisions about their investments. Such understanding can be accomplished only through clear communication.

Standard V(B) states that members and candidates should communicate in a recommendation the factors that were instrumental in making the investment recommendation. A critical part of this requirement is to distinguish clearly between opinions and facts. In preparing a research report, the member or candidate must present the basic characteristics of the security(ies) being analyzed, which will allow the reader to evaluate the report and incorporate information the reader deems relevant to his or her investment decision-making process.

Similarly, in preparing a recommendation about, for example, an asset allocation strategy, alternative investment vehicle, or structured investment product, the member or candidate should include factors that are relevant to the asset classes that are being discussed. Follow-up communication of significant changes in the risk characteristics of a security or asset strategy is required. Providing regular updates to any changes in the risk characteristics is recommended.

Informing Clients of the Investment Process

Members and candidates must adequately describe to clients and prospective clients the manner in which they conduct the investment decision-making process. Such disclosure should address factors that have positive and negative influences on the recommendations, including significant risks and limitations of the investment process used. The member or candidate must keep clients and other interested parties informed on an ongoing basis about changes to the investment process, especially newly identified significant risks and limitations. Only by thoroughly understanding the nature of the investment product or service can a client determine whether changes to that product or service could materially affect his or her investment objectives.

Understanding the basic characteristics of an investment is of great importance in judging the suitability of that investment on a standalone basis, but it is especially important in determining the impact each investment will have on the characteristics of a portfolio. Although the risk and return characteristics of a common stock might seem to be essentially the same for any investor when the stock is viewed in isolation, the effects of those characteristics greatly depend on the other investments held. For instance, if the particular stock will represent 90% of an individual's investments, the stock's importance in the portfolio is vastly different from what it would be to an investor with a highly diversified portfolio for whom the stock will represent only 2% of the holdings.

A firm's investment policy may include the use of outside advisers to manage various portions of clients' assets under management. Members and candidates should inform the clients about the specialization or diversification expertise provided by the external adviser(s). This information allows clients to understand the full mix of products and strategies being applied that may affect their investment objectives.

Different Forms of Communication

For purposes of Standard V(B), communication is not confined to a written report of the type traditionally generated by an analyst researching a security, company, or industry. A presentation of information can be made via any means of communication, including in-person recommendation or description, telephone conversation, media broadcast, or transmission by computer (e.g., on the internet).

Computer and mobile device communications have rapidly evolved over the past few years. Members and candidates using any social media service to communicate business information must be diligent in their efforts to avoid unintended problems because these services may not be available to all clients. When providing information to clients through new technologies, members and candidates should take reasonable steps to ensure that such delivery would treat all clients fairly and, if necessary, be considered publicly disseminated.

The nature of client communications is highly diverse—from one word ("buy" or "sell") to in-depth reports of more than 100 pages. A communication may contain a general recommendation about the market, asset allocations, or classes of investments (e.g., stocks, bonds, real estate) or may relate to a specific security. If recommendations are contained in capsule form (such as a recommended stock list), members and candidates should notify clients that additional information and analyses are available from the producer of the report.

Identifying Risks and Limitations

Members and candidates must outline to clients and prospective clients significant risks and limitations of the analysis contained in their investment products or recommendations. The type and nature of significant risks will depend on the investment process that members and candidates are following and on the personal circumstances of the client. In general, the use of leverage constitutes a significant risk and should be disclosed.

Members and candidates must adequately disclose the general market-related risks and the risks associated with the use of complex financial instruments that are deemed significant. Other types of risks that members and candidates may consider disclosing include, but are not limited to, counterparty risk, country risk, sector or industry risk, security-specific risk, and credit risk.

Investment securities and vehicles may have limiting factors that influence a client's or potential client's investment decision. Members and candidates must report to clients and prospective clients the existence of limitations significant to the decision-making process. Examples of such factors and attributes include, but are not limited to, investment liquidity and capacity. Liquidity is the ability to liquidate an investment on a timely basis at a reasonable cost. Capacity is the investment amount beyond which returns will be negatively affected by new investments.

The appropriateness of risk disclosure should be assessed on the basis of what was known at the time the investment action was taken (often called an *ex ante* basis). Members and candidates must disclose significant risks known to them at the time of the disclosure. Members and candidates cannot be expected to disclose risks they are unaware of at the time recommendations or investment actions are made. In assessing compliance with Standard V(B), it is important to establish knowledge of a purported significant risk or limitation. A one-time investment loss that occurs after the disclosure does not constitute a pertinent factor in assessing whether significant risks and limitations were properly disclosed. Having no knowledge of a risk or limitation that subsequently triggers a loss may reveal a deficiency in the diligence and reasonable basis of the research of the member or candidate but may not reveal a breach of Standard V(B).

Report Presentation

Once the analytical process has been completed, the member or candidate who prepares the report must include those elements that are important to the analysis and conclusions of the report so that the reader can follow and challenge the report's reasoning. A report writer who has done adequate investigation may emphasize certain areas, touch briefly on others, and omit certain aspects deemed unimportant. For instance, a report may dwell on a quarterly earnings release or new-product introduction and omit other matters as long as the analyst clearly stipulates the limits to the scope of the report.

Investment advice based on quantitative research and analysis must be supported by readily available reference material and should be applied in a manner consistent with previously applied methodology. If changes in methodology are made, they should be highlighted.

Distinction between Facts and Opinions in Reports

Standard V(B) requires that opinion be separated from fact. Violations often occur when reports fail to separate the past from the future by not indicating that earnings estimates, changes in the outlook for dividends, or future market price information are *opinions* subject to future circumstances.

In the case of complex quantitative analyses, members and candidates must clearly separate fact from statistical conjecture and should identify the known limitations of an analysis. Members and candidates may violate Standard V(B) by failing to identify the limits of statistically developed projections because such omission leaves readers unaware of the limits of the published projections.

Members and candidates should explicitly discuss with clients and prospective clients the assumptions used in the investment models and processes to generate the analysis. Caution should be used in promoting the perceived accuracy of any model or process to clients because the ultimate output is merely an estimate of future results and not a certainty.

STANDARD V(B): RECOMMENDED PROCEDURES

- recommend practices and procedures designed to prevent violations of the Code of Ethics and Standards of Professional Conduct

Because the selection of relevant factors is an analytical skill, determination of whether a member or candidate has used reasonable judgment in excluding and including information in research reports depends heavily on case-by-case review rather than a specific checklist.

Members and candidates should encourage their firms to have a rigorous methodology for reviewing research that is created for publication and dissemination to clients.

To assist in the after-the-fact review of a report, the member or candidate must maintain records indicating the nature of the research and should, if asked, be able to supply additional information to the client (or any user of the report) covering factors not included in the report.

STANDARD V(B): APPLICATION OF THE STANDARD

- demonstrate the application of the Code of Ethics and Standards of Professional Conduct to situations involving issues of professional integrity
- identify conduct that conforms to the Code and Standards and conduct that violates the Code and Standards

Example 1 (Sufficient Disclosure of Investment System):

Sarah Williamson, director of marketing for Country Technicians, Inc., is convinced that she has found the perfect formula for increasing Country Technicians' income and diversifying its product base. Williamson plans to build on Country Technicians' reputation as a leading money manager by marketing an exclusive and expensive investment advice letter to high-net-worth individuals. One hitch in the plan is the complexity of Country Technicians' investment system—a combination of technical trading rules (based on historical price and volume fluctuations) and portfolio construction rules designed to minimize risk. To simplify the newsletter, she decides to include only each week's top five "buy" and "sell" recommendations and to leave out details of the valuation models and the portfolio structuring scheme.

> *Comment*: Williamson's plans for the newsletter violate Standard V(B). Williamson need not describe the investment system in detail in order to implement the advice effectively, but she must inform clients of Country Technicians' basic process and logic. Without understanding the basis for a recommendation, clients cannot possibly understand its limitations or its inherent risks.

Example 2 (Providing Opinions as Facts):

Richard Dox is a mining analyst for East Bank Securities. He has just finished his report on Boisy Bay Minerals. Included in his report is his own assessment of the geological extent of mineral reserves likely to be found on the company's land. Dox completed this calculation on the basis of the core samples from the company's latest drilling. According to Dox's calculations, the company has more than 500,000 ounces of gold on the property. Dox concludes his research report as follows: "Based on the fact that the company has 500,000 ounces of gold to be mined, I recommend a strong BUY."

> *Comment*: If Dox issues the report as written, he will violate Standard V(B). His calculation of the total gold reserves for the property based on the company's recent sample drilling is a quantitative opinion, not a fact. Opinion must be distinguished from fact in research reports.

Example 3 (Proper Description of a Security):

Olivia Thomas, an analyst at Government Brokers, Inc., which is a brokerage firm specializing in government bond trading, has produced a report that describes an investment strategy designed to benefit from an expected decline in US interest rates. The firm's derivative products group has designed a structured product that will allow the firm's clients to benefit from this strategy. Thomas's report describing the strategy indicates that high returns are possible if various scenarios for declining interest rates are assumed. Citing the proprietary nature of the structured product underlying the strategy, the report does not describe in detail how the firm is able to offer such returns or the related risks in the scenarios, nor does the report address the likely returns of the strategy if, contrary to expectations, interest rates rise.

> *Comment*: Thomas has violated Standard V(B) because her report fails to describe properly the basic characteristics of the actual and implied risks of the investment strategy, including how the structure was created and the degree to which leverage was embedded in the structure. The report should include a balanced discussion of how the strategy would perform in the case of rising as well as falling interest rates, preferably illustrating how the strategies might be expected to perform in the event of a reasonable variety of interest rate and credit risk–spread scenarios. If liquidity issues are relevant with regard to the valuation of either the derivatives or the underlying securities, provisions the firm has made to address those risks should also be disclosed.

Example 4 (Notification of Fund Mandate Change):

May & Associates is an aggressive growth manager that has represented itself since its inception as a specialist at investing in small-cap US stocks. One of May's selection criteria is a maximum capitalization of US$250 million for any given company. After a string of successful years of superior performance relative to its peers, May has expanded its client base significantly, to the point at which assets under management now exceed US$3 billion. For liquidity purposes, May's chief investment officer (CIO) decides to lift the maximum permissible market-cap ceiling to US$500 million and change the firm's sales and marketing literature accordingly to inform prospective clients and third-party consultants.

> *Comment*: Although May's CIO is correct about informing potentially interested parties as to the change in investment process, he must also notify May's existing clients. Among the latter group might be a number of clients who not only retained May as a small-cap manager but also retained mid-cap and large-cap specialists in a multiple-manager approach. Such clients could regard May's change of criteria as a style change that distorts their overall asset allocations.

Example 5 (Notification of Fund Mandate Change):

Rather than lifting the ceiling for its universe from US$250 million to US$500 million, May & Associates extends its small-cap universe to include a number of non-US companies.

> *Comment*: Standard V(B) requires that May's CIO advise May's clients of this change because the firm may have been retained by some clients specifically for its prowess at investing in US small-cap stocks. Other changes that require client notification are introducing derivatives to emulate a certain market sector or relaxing various other constraints, such as portfolio beta. In all such cases, members and candidates must disclose changes to all interested parties.

Example 6 (Notification of Changes to the Investment Process):

RJZ Capital Management is an active value-style equity manager that selects stocks by using a combination of four multifactor models. The firm has found favorable results when back testing the most recent 10 years of available market data in a new dividend discount model (DDM) designed by the firm. This model is based on projected inflation rates, earnings growth rates, and interest rates. The president of RJZ decides to replace its simple model that uses price to trailing 12-month earnings with the new DDM.

> *Comment*: Because the introduction of a new and different valuation model represents a material change in the investment process, RJZ's president must communicate the change to the firm's clients. RJZ is moving away from a model based on hard data toward a new model that is at least partly dependent on the firm's forecasting skills. Clients would likely view such a model as a significant change rather than a mere refinement of RJZ's process.

Example 7 (Notification of Changes to the Investment Process):

RJZ Capital Management loses the chief architect of its multifactor valuation system. Without informing its clients, the president of RJZ decides to redirect the firm's talents and resources toward developing a product for passive equity management—a product that will emulate the performance of a major market index.

> *Comment*: By failing to disclose to clients a substantial change to its investment process, the president of RJZ has violated Standard V(B).

Example 8 (Notification of Changes to the Investment Process):

At Fundamental Asset Management, Inc., the responsibility for selecting stocks for addition to the firm's "approved" list has just shifted from individual security analysts to a committee consisting of the research director and three senior portfolio managers. Eleanor Morales, a portfolio manager with Fundamental Asset Management, thinks this change is not important enough to communicate to her clients.

> *Comment*: Morales must disclose the process change to all her clients. Some of Fundamental's clients might be concerned about the morale and motivation among the firm's best research analysts after such a change. Moreover, clients might challenge the stock-picking track record of the portfolio managers and might even want to monitor the situation closely.

Example 9 (Sufficient Disclosure of Investment System):

Amanda Chinn is the investment director for Diversified Asset Management, which manages the endowment of a charitable organization. Because of recent staff departures, Diversified has decided to limit its direct investment focus to large-cap securities and supplement the needs for small-cap and mid-cap management by hiring outside fund managers. In describing the planned strategy change to the charity, Chinn's update letter states, "As investment director, I will directly oversee the investment team managing the endowment's large-capitalization allocation. I will coordinate the selection and ongoing review of external managers responsible for allocations to other classes." The letter also describes the reasons for the change and the characteristics external managers must have to be considered.

> *Comment*: Standard V(B) requires the disclosure of the investment process used to construct the portfolio of the fund. Changing the investment process from managing all classes of investments within the firm to the use of external managers is one example of information that needs to be communicated to clients. Chinn and her firm have embraced the principles of Standard V(B) by providing their client with relevant information. The charity can now make a reasonable decision about whether Diversified Asset Management remains the appropriate manager for its fund.

Example 10 (Notification of Changes to the Investment Process):

Michael Papis is the chief investment officer of his state's retirement fund. The fund has always used outside advisers for the real estate allocation, and this information is clearly presented in all fund communications. Thomas Nagle, a recognized sell-side research analyst and Papis's business school classmate, recently left the investment bank he worked for to start his own asset management firm, Accessible Real Estate. Nagle is trying to build his assets under management and contacts Papis about gaining some of the retirement fund's allocation. In the previous few years, the performance of the retirement fund's real estate investments was in line with the fund's benchmark but was not extraordinary. Papis decides to help out his old friend and also to seek better returns by moving the real estate allocation to Accessible. The only notice of the change in adviser appears in the next annual report in the listing of associated advisers.

> *Comment*: Papis has violated Standard V(B). He attempted to hide the nature of his decision to change external managers by making only a limited disclosure. The plan recipients and the fund's trustees need to be aware when changes are made to ensure that operational procedures are being followed.
>
> See also Standard IV(C)–Responsibilities of Supervisors, Standard V(A)–Diligence and Reasonable Basis, and Standard VI(A)–Disclosure of Conflicts.

Example 11 (Notification of Errors):

Jérôme Dupont works for the credit research group of XYZ Asset Management, where he is in charge of developing and updating credit risk models. In order to perform accurately, his models need to be regularly updated with the latest market data.

Dupont does not interact with or manage money for any of the firm's clients. He is in contact with the firm's US corporate bond fund manager, John Smith, who has only very superficial knowledge of the model and who from time to time asks very basic questions regarding the output recommendations. Smith does not consult Dupont with respect to finalizing his clients' investment strategies.

Dupont's recently assigned objective is to develop a new emerging market corporate credit risk model. The firm is planning to expand into emerging credit, and the development of such a model is a critical step in this process. Because Smith seems to follow the model's recommendations without much concern for its quality as he develops his clients' investment strategies, Dupont decides to focus his time on the development of the new emerging market model and neglects to update the US model.

After several months without regular updates, Dupont's diagnostic statistics start to show alarming signs with respect to the quality of the US credit model. Instead of conducting the long and complicated data update, Dupont introduces new codes into his model with some limited new data as a quick "fix." He thinks this change will address the issue without needing to complete the full data update, so he continues working on the new emerging market model.

Several months following the quick "fix," another set of diagnostic statistics reveals nonsensical results and Dupont realizes that his earlier change contained an error. He quickly corrects the error and alerts Smith. Smith realizes that some of the prior trades he performed were due to erroneous model results. Smith rebalances the portfolio to remove the securities purchased on the basis of the questionable results without reporting the issue to anyone else.

> *Comment*: Smith violated V(B) by not disclosing a material error in the investment process. Clients should have been informed about the error and the corrective actions the firm was undertaking on their behalf.
>
> See also Standard V(A)–Diligence and Reasonable Basis.

Example 12 (Notification of Risks and Limitations):

Quantitative analyst Yuri Yakovlev has developed an investment strategy that selects small-cap stocks on the basis of quantitative signals. Yakovlev's strategy typically identifies only a small number of stocks (10–20) that tend to be illiquid, but according to his backtests, the strategy generates significant risk-adjusted returns. The partners at Yakovlev's firm, QSC Capital, are impressed by these results. After a thorough examination of the strategy's risks, stress testing, historical back testing, and scenario analysis, QSC decides to seed the strategy with US$10 million of internal capital in order for Yakovlev to create a track record for the strategy.

After two years, the strategy has generated performance returns greater than the appropriate benchmark and the Sharpe ratio of the fund is close to 1.0. On the basis of these results, QSC decides to actively market the fund to large institutional investors. While creating the offering materials, Yakovlev informs the marketing team that the capacity of the strategy is limited. The extent of the limitation is difficult to ascertain with precision; it depends on market liquidity and other factors in his model that can evolve over time. Yakovlev indicates that given the current market conditions, investments in the fund beyond US$100 million of capital could become more difficult and negatively affect expected fund returns.

Alan Wellard, the manager of the marketing team, is a partner with 30 years of marketing experience and explains to Yakovlev that these are complex technical issues that will muddy the marketing message. According to Wellard, the offering material should focus solely on the great track record of the fund. Yakovlev does not object because the fund has only US$12 million of capital, very far from the US$100 million threshold.

> *Comment*: Yakovlev and Wellard have not appropriately disclosed a significant limitation associated with the investment product. Yakovlev believes this limitation, once reached, will materially affect the returns of the fund. Although the fund is currently far from the US$100 million mark, current and prospective investors must be made aware of this capacity issue. If significant limitations are complicated to grasp and clients do not have the technical background required to understand them, Yakovlev and Wellard should either educate the clients or ascertain whether the fund is suitable for each client.

Example 13 (Notification of Risks and Limitations):

Brickell Advisers offers investment advisory services mainly to South American clients. Julietta Ramon, a risk analyst at Brickell, describes to clients how the firm uses value at risk (VaR) analysis to track the risk of its strategies. Ramon assures clients that calculating a VaR at a 99% confidence level, using a 20-day holding period, and applying a methodology based on an *ex ante* Monte Carlo simulation is extremely effective. The firm has never had losses greater than those predicted by this VaR analysis.

> *Comment*: Ramon has not sufficiently communicated the risks associated with the investment process to satisfy the requirements of Standard V(B). The losses predicted by a VaR analysis depend greatly on the inputs used in the model. The size and probability of losses can differ significantly from what an individual model predicts. Ramon must disclose how the inputs were selected and the potential limitations and risks associated with the investment strategy.

Example 14 (Notification of Risks and Limitations):

Lily Smith attended an industry conference and noticed that John Baker, an investment manager with Baker Associates, attracted a great deal of attention from the conference participants. On the basis of her knowledge of Baker's reputation and the interest he received at the conference, Smith recommends adding Baker Associates to the approved manager platform. Her recommendation to the approval committee included the statement "John Baker is well respected in the industry, and his insights are consistently sought after by investors. Our clients are sure to benefit from investing with Baker Associates."

> *Comment*: Smith is not appropriately separating facts from opinions in her recommendation to include the manager within the platform. Her actions conflict with the requirements of Standard V(B). Smith is relying on her opinions about Baker's reputation and the fact that many attendees were talking with him at the conference. Smith should also review the requirements of Standard V(A) regarding reasonable basis to determine the level of review necessary to recommend Baker Associates.

STANDARD V(C): INVESTMENT ANALYSIS, RECOMMENDATIONS, AND ACTIONS - RECORD RETENTION

48

☐ demonstrate the application of the Code of Ethics and Standards of Professional Conduct to situations involving issues of professional integrity

> Members and Candidates must develop and maintain appropriate records to support their investment analyses, recommendations, actions, and other investment-related communications with clients and prospective clients.

Guidance

Highlights:

- *New Media Records*
- *Records Are Property of the Firm*
- *Local Requirements*

Members and candidates must retain records that substantiate the scope of their research and reasons for their actions or conclusions. The retention requirement applies to decisions to buy or sell a security as well as reviews undertaken that do not lead to a change in position. Which records are required to support recommendations or investment actions depends on the role of the member or candidate in the investment decision-making process. Records may be maintained either in hard copy or electronic form.

Some examples of supporting documentation that assists the member or candidate in meeting the requirements for retention are as follows:

- personal notes from meetings with the covered company,
- press releases or presentations issued by the covered company,
- computer-based model outputs and analyses,
- computer-based model input parameters,
- risk analyses of securities' impacts on a portfolio,
- selection criteria for external advisers,
- notes from clients from meetings to review investment policy statements, and
- outside research reports.

New Media Records

The increased use of new and evolving technological formats (e.g., social media) for gathering and sharing information creates new challenges in maintaining the appropriate records and files. The nature or format of the information does not remove a member's or candidate's responsibility to maintain a record of information used in his or her analysis or communicated to clients.

Members and candidates should understand that although employers and local regulators are developing digital media retention policies, these policies may lag behind the advent of new communication channels. Such lag places greater responsibility on the individual for ensuring that all relevant information is retained. Examples of non-print media formats that should be retained include, but are not limited to,

- e-mails,
- text messages,
- blog posts, and
- Twitter posts.

Records Are Property of the Firm

As a general matter, records created as part of a member's or candidate's professional activity on behalf of his or her employer are the property of the firm. When a member or candidate leaves a firm to seek other employment, the member or candidate cannot take the property of the firm, including original forms or copies of supporting records of the member's or candidate's work, to the new employer without the express consent of the previous employer. The member or candidate cannot use historical recommendations or research reports created at the previous firm because the supporting documentation is unavailable. For future use, the member or candidate must re-create the supporting records at the new firm with information gathered through public sources or directly from the covered company and not from memory or sources obtained at the previous employer.

Local Requirements

Local regulators often impose requirements on members, candidates, and their firms related to record retention that must be followed. Firms may also implement policies detailing the applicable time frame for retaining research and client communication records. Fulfilling such regulatory and firm requirements satisfies the requirements of Standard V(C). In the absence of regulatory guidance or firm policies, CFA Institute recommends maintaining records for at least seven years.

STANDARD V(C): RECOMMENDED PROCEDURES

☐ recommend practices and procedures designed to prevent violations of the Code of Ethics and Standards of Professional Conduct

The responsibility to maintain records that support investment action generally falls with the firm rather than individuals. Members and candidates must, however, archive research notes and other documents, either electronically or in hard copy, that support their current investment-related communications. Doing so will assist their firms in complying with requirements for preservation of internal or external records.

STANDARD V(C): APPLICATION OF THE STANDARD

☐ demonstrate the application of the Code of Ethics and Standards of Professional Conduct to situations involving issues of professional integrity

☐ identify conduct that conforms to the Code and Standards and conduct that violates the Code and Standards

Example 1 (Record Retention and IPS Objectives and Recommendations):

One of Nikolas Lindstrom's clients is upset by the negative investment returns of his equity portfolio. The investment policy statement for the client requires that the portfolio manager follow a benchmark-oriented approach. The benchmark for the client includes a 35% investment allocation in the technology sector. The client acknowledges that this allocation was appropriate, but over the past three years, technology stocks have suffered severe losses. The client complains to the investment manager for allocating so much money to this sector.

> *Comment*: For Lindstrom, having appropriate records is important to show that over the past three years, the portion of technology stocks in the benchmark index was 35%, as called for in the IPS. Lindstrom should also have the client's IPS stating that the benchmark was appropriate for the client's investment objectives. He should also have records indicating that the investment has been explained appropriately to the client and that the IPS was updated on a regular basis. Taking these actions, Lindstrom would be in compliance with Standard V(C).

Example 2 (Record Retention and Research Process):

Malcolm Young is a research analyst who writes numerous reports rating companies in the luxury retail industry. His reports are based on a variety of sources, including interviews with company managers, manufacturers, and economists; on-site company visits; customer surveys; and secondary research from analysts covering related industries.

Comment: Young must carefully document and keep copies of all the information that goes into his reports, including the secondary or third-party research of other analysts. Failure to maintain such files would violate Standard V(C).

Example 3 (Records as Firm, Not Employee, Property):

Martin Blank develops an analytical model while he is employed by Green Partners Investment Management, LLP (GPIM). While at the firm, he systematically documents the assumptions that make up the model as well as his reasoning behind the assumptions. As a result of the success of his model, Blank is hired to be the head of the research department of one of GPIM's competitors. Blank takes copies of the records supporting his model to his new firm.

Comment: The records created by Blank supporting the research model he developed at GPIM are the records of GPIM. Taking the documents with him to his new employer without GPIM's permission violates Standard V(C). To use the model in the future, Blank must re-create the records supporting his model at the new firm.

51 STANDARD VI(A): CONFLICTS OF INTEREST - DISCLOSURE OF CONFLICTS

☐ demonstrate the application of the Code of Ethics and Standards of Professional Conduct to situations involving issues of professional integrity

Standard VI(A) Disclosure of Conflicts

> Members and Candidates must make full and fair disclosure of all matters that could reasonably be expected to impair their independence and objectivity or interfere with respective duties to their clients, prospective clients, and employer. Members and Candidates must ensure that such disclosures are prominent, are delivered in plain language, and communicate the relevant information effectively.

Guidance

Highlights:

- *Disclosure of Conflicts to Employers*
- *Disclosure to Clients*
- *Cross-Departmental Conflicts*
- *Conflicts with Stock Ownership*
- *Conflicts as a Director*

Standard VI(A): Conflicts of Interest - Disclosure of Conflicts

Best practice is to avoid actual conflicts or the appearance of conflicts of interest when possible. Conflicts of interest often arise in the investment profession. Conflicts can occur between the interests of clients, the interests of employers, and the member's or candidate's own personal interests. Common sources for conflict are compensation structures, especially incentive and bonus structures that provide immediate returns for members and candidates with little or no consideration of long-term value creation.

Identifying and managing these conflicts is a critical part of working in the investment industry and can take many forms. When conflicts cannot be reasonably avoided, clear and complete disclosure of their existence is necessary.

Standard VI(A) protects investors and employers by requiring members and candidates to fully disclose to clients, potential clients, and employers all actual and potential conflicts of interest. Once a member or candidate has made full disclosure, the member's or candidate's employer, clients, and prospective clients will have the information needed to evaluate the objectivity of the investment advice or action taken on their behalf.

To be effective, disclosures must be prominent and must be made in plain language and in a manner designed to effectively communicate the information. Members and candidates have the responsibility of determining how often, in what manner, and in what particular circumstances the disclosure of conflicts must be made. Best practices dictate updating disclosures when the nature of a conflict of interest changes materially—for example, if the nature of a conflict of interest worsens through the introduction of bonuses based on each quarter's profits as to opposed annual profits. In making and updating disclosures of conflicts of interest, members and candidates should err on the side of caution to ensure that conflicts are effectively communicated.

Disclosure of Conflicts to Employers

Disclosure of conflicts to employers may be appropriate in many instances. When reporting conflicts of interest to employers, members and candidates must give their employers enough information to assess the impact of the conflict. By complying with employer guidelines, members and candidates allow their employers to avoid potentially embarrassing and costly ethical or regulatory violations.

Reportable situations include conflicts that would interfere with rendering unbiased investment advice and conflicts that would cause a member or candidate to act not in the employer's best interest. The same circumstances that generate conflicts to be reported to clients and prospective clients also would dictate reporting to employers. Ownership of stocks analyzed or recommended, participation on outside boards, and financial or other pressures that could influence a decision are to be promptly reported to the employer so that their impact can be assessed and a decision on how to resolve the conflict can be made.

The mere appearance of a conflict of interest may create problems for members, candidates, and their employers. Therefore, many of the conflicts previously mentioned could be explicitly prohibited by an employer. For example, many employers restrict personal trading, outside board membership, and related activities to prevent situations that might not normally be considered problematic from a conflict-of-interest point of view but that could give the appearance of a conflict of interest. Members and candidates must comply with these restrictions. Members and candidates must take reasonable steps to avoid conflicts and, if they occur inadvertently, must report them promptly so that the employer and the member or candidate can resolve them as quickly and effectively as possible.

Standard VI(A) also deals with a member's or candidate's conflicts of interest that might be detrimental to the employer's business. Any potential conflict situation that could prevent clear judgment about or full commitment to the execution of a member's or candidate's duties to the employer should be reported to the member's or candidate's employer and promptly resolved.

Disclosure to Clients

Members and candidates must maintain their objectivity when rendering investment advice or taking investment action. Investment advice or actions may be perceived to be tainted in numerous situations. Can a member or candidate remain objective if, on behalf of the firm, the member or candidate obtains or assists in obtaining fees for services? Can a member or candidate give objective advice if he or she owns stock in the company that is the subject of an investment recommendation or if the member or candidate has a close personal relationship with the company managers? Requiring members and candidates to disclose all matters that reasonably could be expected to impair the member's or candidate's objectivity allows clients and prospective clients to judge motives and possible biases for themselves.

Often in the investment industry, a conflict, or the perception of a conflict, cannot be avoided. The most obvious conflicts of interest, which should always be disclosed, are relationships between an issuer and the member, the candidate, or his or her firm (such as a directorship or consultancy by a member; investment banking, underwriting, and financial relationships; broker/dealer market-making activities; and material beneficial ownership of stock). For the purposes of Standard VI(A), members and candidates beneficially own securities or other investments if they have a direct or indirect pecuniary interest in the securities, have the power to vote or direct the voting of the shares of the securities or investments, or have the power to dispose or direct the disposition of the security or investment.

A member or candidate must take reasonable steps to determine whether a conflict of interest exists and disclose to clients any known conflicts of the member's or candidate's firm. Disclosure of broker/dealer market-making activities alerts clients that a purchase or sale might be made from or to the firm's principal account and that the firm has a special interest in the price of the stock.

Additionally, disclosures should be made to clients regarding fee arrangements, subadvisory agreements, or other situations involving nonstandard fee structures. Equally important is the disclosure of arrangements in which the firm benefits directly from investment recommendations. An obvious conflict of interest is the rebate of a portion of the service fee some classes of mutual funds charge to investors. Members and candidates should ensure that their firms disclose such relationships so clients can fully understand the costs of their investments and the benefits received by their investment manager's employer.

Cross-Departmental Conflicts

Other circumstances can give rise to actual or potential conflicts of interest. For instance, a sell-side analyst working for a broker/dealer may be encouraged, not only by members of her or his own firm but by corporate issuers themselves, to write research reports about particular companies. The buy-side analyst is likely to be faced with similar conflicts as banks exercise their underwriting and security-dealing powers. The marketing division may ask an analyst to recommend the stock of a certain company in order to obtain business from that company.

The potential for conflicts of interest also exists with broker-sponsored limited partnerships formed to invest venture capital. Increasingly, members and candidates are expected not only to follow issues from these partnerships once they are offered to the public but also to promote the issues in the secondary market after public offerings. Members, candidates, and their firms should attempt to resolve situations presenting potential conflicts of interest or disclose them in accordance with the principles set forth in Standard VI(A).

Conflicts with Stock Ownership

The most prevalent conflict requiring disclosure under Standard VI(A) is a member's or candidate's ownership of stock in companies that he or she recommends to clients or that clients hold. Clearly, the easiest method for preventing a conflict is to prohibit members and candidates from owning any such securities, but this approach is overly burdensome and discriminates against members and candidates.

Therefore, sell-side members and candidates should disclose any materially beneficial ownership interest in a security or other investment that the member or candidate is recommending. Buy-side members and candidates should disclose their procedures for reporting requirements for personal transactions. Conflicts arising from personal investing are discussed more fully in the guidance for Standard VI(B).

Conflicts as a Director

Service as a director poses three basic conflicts of interest. First, a conflict may exist between the duties owed to clients and the duties owed to shareholders of the company. Second, investment personnel who serve as directors may receive the securities or options to purchase securities of the company as compensation for serving on the board, which could raise questions about trading actions that might increase the value of those securities. Third, board service creates the opportunity to receive material nonpublic information involving the company. Even though the information is confidential, the perception could be that information not available to the public is being communicated to a director's firm—whether a broker, investment adviser, or other type of organization. When members or candidates providing investment services also serve as directors, they should be isolated from those making investment decisions by the use of firewalls or similar restrictions.

STANDARD VI(A): RECOMMENDED PROCEDURES

☐ recommend practices and procedures designed to prevent violations of the Code of Ethics and Standards of Professional Conduct

Members or candidates should disclose special compensation arrangements with the employer that might conflict with client interests, such as bonuses based on short-term performance criteria, commissions, incentive fees, performance fees, and referral fees. If the member's or candidate's firm does not permit such disclosure, the member or candidate should document the request and may consider dissociating from the activity.

Members' and candidates' firms are encouraged to include information on compensation packages in firms' promotional literature. If a member or candidate manages a portfolio for which the fee is based on capital gains or capital appreciation (a performance fee), this information should be disclosed to clients. If a member, a candidate, or a member's or candidate's firm has outstanding agent options to buy stock as part of the compensation package for corporate financing activities, the amount and expiration date of these options should be disclosed as a footnote to any research report published by the member's or candidate's firm.

STANDARD VI(A): APPLICATION OF THE STANDARD

☐ demonstrate the application of the Code of Ethics and Standards of Professional Conduct to situations involving issues of professional integrity

☐ identify conduct that conforms to the Code and Standards and conduct that violates the Code and Standards

Example 1 (Conflict of Interest and Business Relationships):

Hunter Weiss is a research analyst with Farmington Company, a broker and investment banking firm. Farmington's merger and acquisition department has represented Vimco, a conglomerate, in all of Vimco's acquisitions for 20 years. From time to time, Farmington officers sit on the boards of directors of various Vimco subsidiaries. Weiss is writing a research report on Vimco.

Comment: Weiss must disclose in his research report Farmington's special relationship with Vimco. Broker/dealer management of and participation in public offerings must be disclosed in research reports. Because the position of underwriter to a company entails a special past and potential future relationship with a company that is the subject of investment advice, it threatens the independence and objectivity of the report writer and must be disclosed.

Example 2 (Conflict of Interest and Business Stock Ownership):

The investment management firm of Dover & Roe sells a 25% interest in its partnership to a multinational bank holding company, First of New York. Immediately after the sale, Margaret Hobbs, president of Dover & Roe, changes her recommendation for First of New York's common stock from "sell" to "buy" and adds First of New York's commercial paper to Dover & Roe's approved list for purchase.

Comment: Hobbs must disclose the new relationship with First of New York to all Dover & Roe clients. This relationship must also be disclosed to clients by the firm's portfolio managers when they make specific investment recommendations or take investment actions with respect to First of New York's securities.

Example 3 (Conflict of Interest and Personal Stock Ownership):

Carl Fargmon, a research analyst who follows firms producing office equipment, has been recommending purchase of Kincaid Printing because of its innovative new line of copiers. After his initial report on the company, Fargmon's wife inherits from a distant relative US$3 million of Kincaid stock. He has been asked to write a follow-up report on Kincaid.

Comment: Fargmon must disclose his wife's ownership of the Kincaid stock to his employer and in his follow-up report. Best practice would be to avoid the conflict by asking his employer to assign another analyst to draft the follow-up report.

Example 4 (Conflict of Interest and Personal Stock Ownership):

Betty Roberts is speculating in penny stocks for her own account and purchases 100,000 shares of Drew Mining, Inc., for US$0.30 a share. She intends to sell these shares at the sign of any substantial upward price movement of the stock. A week later, her employer asks her to write a report on penny stocks in the mining industry to be published in two weeks. Even without owning the Drew stock, Roberts would recommend it in her report as a "buy." A surge in the price of the stock to the US$2 range is likely to result once the report is issued.

> *Comment*: Although this holding may not be material, Roberts must disclose it in the report and to her employer before writing the report because the gain for her will be substantial if the market responds strongly to her recommendation. The fact that she has only recently purchased the stock adds to the appearance that she is not entirely objective.

Example 5 (Conflict of Interest and Compensation Arrangements):

Samantha Snead, a portfolio manager for Thomas Investment Counsel, Inc., specializes in managing public retirement funds and defined benefit pension plan accounts, all of which have long-term investment objectives. A year ago, Snead's employer, in an attempt to motivate and retain key investment professionals, introduced a bonus compensation system that rewards portfolio managers on the basis of quarterly performance relative to their peers and to certain benchmark indexes. In an attempt to improve the short-term performance of her accounts, Snead changes her investment strategy and purchases several high-beta stocks for client portfolios. These purchases are seemingly contrary to the clients' investment policy statements. Following their purchase, an officer of Griffin Corporation, one of Snead's pension fund clients, asks why Griffin Corporation's portfolio seems to be dominated by high-beta stocks of companies that often appear among the most actively traded issues. No change in objective or strategy has been recommended by Snead during the year.

> *Comment*: Snead has violated Standard VI(A) by failing to inform her clients of the changes in her compensation arrangement with her employer, which created a conflict of interest between her compensation and her clients' IPSs. Firms may pay employees on the basis of performance, but pressure by Thomas Investment Counsel to achieve short-term performance goals is in basic conflict with the objectives of Snead's accounts.
> See also Standard III(C)–Suitability.

Example 6 (Conflict of Interest, Options, and Compensation Arrangements):

Wayland Securities works with small companies doing IPOs or secondary offerings. Typically, these deals are in the US$10 million to US$50 million range, and as a result, the corporate finance fees are quite small. To compensate for the small fees, Wayland Securities usually takes "agent options"—that is, rights (exercisable within a two-year time frame) to acquire up to an additional 10% of the current offering. Following an IPO performed by Wayland for Falk Resources, Ltd., Darcy Hunter, the head of corporate finance at Wayland, is concerned about receiving value for her Falk Resources options. The options are due to expire in one month, and the stock is not doing well. She contacts John Fitzpatrick in the research department of Wayland Securities, reminds him that he is eligible for 30% of these options, and indicates that now would be a good time to give some additional coverage to Falk Resources. Fitzpatrick agrees and immediately issues a favorable report.

> *Comment*: For Fitzpatrick to avoid being in violation of Standard VI(A), he must indicate in the report the volume and expiration date of agent options outstanding. Furthermore, because he is personally eligible for some of the options, Fitzpatrick must disclose the extent of this compensation. He also must be careful to not violate his duty of independence and objectivity under Standard I(B).

Example 7 (Conflict of Interest and Compensation Arrangements):

Gary Carter is a representative with Bengal International, a registered broker/dealer. Carter is approached by a stock promoter for Badger Company, who offers to pay Carter additional compensation for sales of Badger Company's stock to Carter's clients. Carter accepts the stock promoter's offer but does not disclose the arrangements to his clients or to his employer. Carter sells shares of the stock to his clients.

> *Comment*: Carter has violated Standard VI(A) by failing to disclose to clients that he is receiving additional compensation for recommending and selling Badger stock. Because he did not disclose the arrangement with Badger to his clients, the clients were unable to evaluate whether Carter's recommendations to buy Badger were affected by this arrangement. Carter's conduct also violated Standard VI(A) by failing to disclose to his employer monetary compensation received in addition to the compensation and benefits conferred by his employer. Carter was required by Standard VI(A) to disclose the arrangement with Badger to his employer so that his employer could evaluate whether the arrangement affected Carter's objectivity and loyalty.

Example 8 (Conflict of Interest and Directorship):

Carol Corky, a senior portfolio manager for Universal Management, recently became involved as a trustee with the Chelsea Foundation, a large not-for-profit foundation in her hometown. Universal is a small money manager (with assets under management of approximately US$100 million) that caters to individual investors. Chelsea has assets in excess of US$2 billion. Corky does not believe informing Universal of her involvement with Chelsea is necessary.

> *Comment*: By failing to inform Universal of her involvement with Chelsea, Corky violated Standard VI(A). Given the large size of the endowment at Chelsea, Corky's new role as a trustee can reasonably be expected to be time consuming, to the possible detriment of Corky's portfolio responsibilities with Universal. Also, as a trustee, Corky may become involved in the investment decisions at Chelsea. Therefore, Standard VI(A) obligates Corky to discuss becoming a trustee at Chelsea with her compliance officer or supervisor at Universal before accepting the position, and she should have disclosed the degree to which she would be involved in investment decisions at Chelsea.

Standard VI(A): Application of the Standard

Example 9 (Conflict of Interest and Personal Trading):

Bruce Smith covers eastern European equities for Marlborough Investments, an investment management firm with a strong presence in emerging markets. While on a business trip to Russia, Smith learns that investing in Russian equities directly is difficult but that equity-linked notes that replicate the performance of underlying Russian equities can be purchased from a New York–based investment bank. Believing that his firm would not be interested in such a security, Smith purchases a note linked to a Russian telecommunications company for his own account without informing Marlborough. A month later, Smith decides that the firm should consider investing in Russian equities by way of the equity-linked notes. He prepares a write-up on the market that concludes with a recommendation to purchase several of the notes. One note he recommends is linked to the same Russian telecom company that Smith holds in his personal account.

> *Comment*: Smith has violated Standard VI(A) by failing to disclose his purchase and ownership of the note linked to the Russian telecom company. Smith is required by the standard to disclose the investment opportunity to his employer and look to his company's policies on personal trading to determine whether it was proper for him to purchase the note for his own account. By purchasing the note, Smith may or may not have impaired his ability to make an unbiased and objective assessment of the appropriateness of the derivative instrument for his firm, but Smith's failure to disclose the purchase to his employer impaired his employer's ability to decide whether his ownership of the security is a conflict of interest that might affect Smith's future recommendations. Then, when he recommended the particular telecom notes to his firm, Smith compounded his problems by not disclosing that he owned the notes in his personal account—a clear conflict of interest.

Example 10 (Conflict of Interest and Requested Favors):

Michael Papis is the chief investment officer of his state's retirement fund. The fund has always used outside advisers for the real estate allocation, and this information is clearly presented in all fund communications. Thomas Nagle, a recognized sell-side research analyst and Papis's business school classmate, recently left the investment bank he worked for to start his own asset management firm, Accessible Real Estate. Nagle is trying to build his assets under management and contacts Papis about gaining some of the retirement fund's allocation. In the previous few years, the performance of the retirement fund's real estate investments was in line with the fund's benchmark but was not extraordinary. Papis decides to help out his old friend and also to seek better returns by moving the real estate allocation to Accessible. The only notice of the change in adviser appears in the next annual report in the listing of associated advisers.

> *Comment*: Papis has violated Standard VI(A) by not disclosing to his employer his personal relationship with Nagle. Disclosure of his past history with Nagle would allow his firm to determine whether the conflict may have impaired Papis's independence in deciding to change managers.
>
> See also Standard IV(C)–Responsibilities of Supervisors, Standard V(A)–Diligence and Reasonable Basis, and Standard V(B)–Communication with Clients and Prospective Clients.

Example 11 (Conflict of Interest and Business Relationships):

Bob Wade, trust manager for Central Midas Bank, was approached by Western Funds about promoting its family of funds, with special interest in the service-fee class. To entice Central to promote this class, Western Funds offered to pay the bank a service fee of 0.25%. Without disclosing the fee being offered to the bank, Wade asked one of the investment managers to review the Western Funds family of funds to determine whether they were suitable for clients of Central. The manager completed the normal due diligence review and determined that the funds were fairly valued in the market with fee structures on a par with their competitors. Wade decided to accept Western's offer and instructed the team of portfolio managers to exclusively promote these funds and the service-fee class to clients seeking to invest new funds or transfer from their current investments. So as to not influence the investment managers, Wade did not disclose the fee offer and allowed that income to flow directly to the bank.

> *Comment*: Wade is violating Standard VI(A) by not disclosing the portion of the service fee being paid to Central. Although the investment managers may not be influenced by the fee, neither they nor the client have the proper information about Wade's decision to exclusively market this fund family and class of investments. Central may come to rely on the new fee as a component of the firm's profitability and may be unwilling to offer other products in the future that could affect the fees received.
>
> See also Standard I(B)–Independence and Objectivity.

Example 12 (Disclosure of Conflicts to Employers):

Yehudit Dagan is a portfolio manager for Risk Management Bank (RMB), whose clients include retirement plans and corporations. RMB provides a defined contribution retirement plan for its employees that offers 20 large diversified mutual fund investment options, including a mutual fund managed by Dagan's RMB colleagues. After being employed for six months, Dagan became eligible to participate in the retirement plan, and she intends to allocate her retirement plan assets in six of the investment options, including the fund managed by her RMB colleagues. Dagan is concerned that joining the plan will lead to a potentially significant amount of paperwork for her (e.g., disclosure of her retirement account holdings and needing preclearance for her transactions), especially with her investing in the in-house fund.

> *Comment*: Standard VI(A) would not require Dagan to disclose her personal or retirement investments in large diversified mutual funds, unless specifically required by her employer. For practical reasons, the standard does not require Dagan to gain preclearance for ongoing payroll deduction contributions to retirement plan account investment options.
>
> Dagan should ensure that her firm does not have a specific policy regarding investment—whether personal or in the retirement account—for funds managed by the company's employees. These mutual funds may be subject to the company's disclosure, preclearance, and trading restriction procedures to identify possible conflicts prior to the execution of trades.

STANDARD VI(B): CONFLICTS OF INTEREST - PRIORITY OF TRANSACTIONS

☐ demonstrate the application of the Code of Ethics and Standards of Professional Conduct to situations involving issues of professional integrity

> Investment transactions for clients and employers must have priority over investment transactions in which a Member or Candidate is the beneficial owner.

Guidance

Highlights:

- *Avoiding Potential Conflicts*
- *Personal Trading Secondary to Trading for Clients*
- *Standards for Nonpublic Information*
- *Impact on All Accounts with Beneficial Ownership*

Standard VI(B) reinforces the responsibility of members and candidates to give the interests of their clients and employers priority over their personal financial interests. This standard is designed to prevent any potential conflict of interest or the appearance of a conflict of interest with respect to personal transactions. Client interests have priority. Client transactions must take precedence over transactions made on behalf of the member's or candidate's firm or personal transactions.

Avoiding Potential Conflicts

Conflicts between the client's interest and an investment professional's personal interest may occur. Although conflicts of interest exist, nothing is inherently unethical about individual managers, advisers, or mutual fund employees making money from personal investments as long as (1) the client is not disadvantaged by the trade, (2) the investment professional does not benefit personally from trades undertaken for clients, and (3) the investment professional complies with applicable regulatory requirements.

Some situations occur where a member or candidate may need to enter a personal transaction that runs counter to current recommendations or what the portfolio manager is doing for client portfolios. For example, a member or candidate may be required at some point to sell an asset to make a college tuition payment or a down payment on a home, to meet a margin call, or so on. The sale may be contrary to the long-term advice the member or candidate is currently providing to clients. In these situations, the same three criteria given in the preceding paragraph should be applied in the transaction so as to not violate Standard VI(B).

Personal Trading Secondary to Trading for Clients

Standard VI(B) states that transactions for clients and employers must have priority over transactions in securities or other investments for which a member or candidate is the beneficial owner. The objective of the standard is to prevent personal transactions from adversely affecting the interests of clients or employers. A member or candidate having the same investment positions or being co-invested with clients does not always create a conflict. Some clients in certain investment situations require members or candidates to have aligned interests. Personal investment positions or transactions of members or candidates or their firm should never, however, adversely affect client investments.

Standards for Nonpublic Information

Standard VI(B) covers the activities of members and candidates who have knowledge of pending transactions that may be made on behalf of their clients or employers, who have access to nonpublic information during the normal preparation of research recommendations, or who take investment actions. Members and candidates are prohibited from conveying nonpublic information to any person whose relationship to the member or candidate makes the member or candidate a beneficial owner of the person's securities. Members and candidates must not convey this information to any other person if the nonpublic information can be deemed material.

Impact on All Accounts with Beneficial Ownership

Members or candidates may undertake transactions in accounts for which they are a beneficial owner only after their clients and employers have had adequate opportunity to act on a recommendation. Personal transactions include those made for the member's or candidate's own account, for family (including spouse, children, and other immediate family members) accounts, and for accounts in which the member or candidate has a direct or indirect pecuniary interest, such as a trust or retirement account. Family accounts that are client accounts should be treated like any other firm account and should neither be given special treatment nor be disadvantaged because of the family relationship. If a member or candidate has a beneficial ownership in the account, however, the member or candidate may be subject to preclearance or reporting requirements of the employer or applicable law.

55 STANDARD VI(B): RECOMMENDED PROCEDURES

☐ recommend practices and procedures designed to prevent violations of the Code of Ethics and Standards of Professional Conduct

Policies and procedures designed to prevent potential conflicts of interest, and even the appearance of a conflict of interest, with respect to personal transactions are critical to establishing investor confidence in the securities industry. Therefore, members and candidates should urge their firms to establish such policies and procedures. Because investment firms vary greatly in assets under management, types of clients, number of employees, and so on, each firm should have policies regarding personal investing that are best suited to the firm. Members and candidates should then prominently disclose these policies to clients and prospective clients.

The specific provisions of each firm's standards will vary, but all firms should adopt certain basic procedures to address the conflict areas created by personal investing. These procedures include the following:

- *Limited participation in equity IPOs*: Some eagerly awaited IPOs rise significantly in value shortly after the issue is brought to market. Because the new issue may be highly attractive and sought after, the opportunity to participate in the IPO may be limited. Therefore, purchases of IPOs by investment personnel create conflicts of interest in two principal ways. First,

Standard VI(B): Recommended Procedures

participation in an IPO may have the appearance of taking away an attractive investment opportunity from clients for personal gain—a clear breach of the duty of loyalty to clients. Second, personal purchases in IPOs may have the appearance that the investment opportunity is being bestowed as an incentive to make future investment decisions for the benefit of the party providing the opportunity. Members and candidates can avoid these conflicts or appearances of conflicts of interest by not participating in IPOs.

Reliable and systematic review procedures should be established to ensure that conflicts relating to IPOs are identified and appropriately dealt with by supervisors. Members and candidates should preclear their participation in IPOs, even in situations without any conflict of interest between a member's or candidate's participation in an IPO and the client's interests. Members and candidates should not benefit from the position that their clients occupy in the marketplace—through preferred trading, the allocation of limited offerings, or oversubscription.

- *Restrictions on private placements*: Strict limits should be placed on investment personnel acquiring securities in private placements, and appropriate supervisory and review procedures should be established to prevent noncompliance.

  Firms do not routinely use private placements for clients (e.g., venture capital deals) because of the high risk associated with them. Conflicts related to private placements are more significant to members and candidates who manage large pools of assets or act as plan sponsors because these managers may be offered special opportunities, such as private placements, as a reward or an enticement for continuing to do business with a particular broker.

  Participation in private placements raises conflict-of-interest issues that are similar to issues surrounding IPOs. Investment personnel should not be involved in transactions, including (but not limited to) private placements, that could be perceived as favors or gifts that seem designed to influence future judgment or to reward past business deals.

  Whether the venture eventually proves to be good or bad, managers have an immediate conflict concerning private placement opportunities. If and when the investments go public, participants in private placements have an incentive to recommend the investments to clients regardless of the suitability of the investments for their clients. Doing so increases the value of the participants' personal portfolios.

- *Establish blackout/restricted periods*: Investment personnel involved in the investment decision-making process should establish blackout periods prior to trades for clients so that managers cannot take advantage of their knowledge of client activity by "front-running" client trades (trading for one's personal account before trading for client accounts).

  Individual firms must decide who within the firm should be required to comply with the trading restrictions. At a minimum, all individuals who are involved in the investment decision-making process should be subject to the same restricted period. Each firm must determine specific requirements related to blackout and restricted periods that are most relevant to the firm while ensuring that the procedures are governed by the guiding principles set forth in the Code and Standards. Size of firm and type of securities purchased are relevant factors. For example, in a large firm, a blackout requirement is, in effect, a total trading ban because the firm is continually trading in most securities. In a small firm, the blackout period is more likely to prevent the investment manager from front-running.

- *Reporting requirements*: Supervisors should establish reporting procedures for investment personnel, including disclosure of personal holdings/beneficial ownerships, confirmations of trades to the firm and the employee, and preclearance procedures. Once trading restrictions are in place, they must be enforced. The best method for monitoring and enforcing procedures to eliminate conflicts of interest in personal trading is through reporting requirements, including the following:

  - **Disclosure of holdings in which the employee has a beneficial interest**. Disclosure by investment personnel to the firm should be made upon commencement of the employment relationship and at least annually thereafter. To address privacy considerations, disclosure of personal holdings should be handled in a confidential manner by the firm.
  - **Providing duplicate confirmations of transactions**. Investment personnel should be required to direct their brokers to supply to firms duplicate copies or confirmations of all their personal securities transactions and copies of periodic statements for all securities accounts. The duplicate confirmation requirement has two purposes: (1) The requirement sends a message that there is independent verification, which reduces the likelihood of unethical behavior, and (2) it enables verification of the accounting of the flow of personal investments that cannot be determined from merely looking at holdings.
  - **Preclearance procedures**. Investment personnel should examine all planned personal trades to identify possible conflicts prior to the execution of the trades. Preclearance procedures are designed to identify possible conflicts before a problem arises.

- *Disclosure of policies*: Members and candidates should fully disclose to investors their firm's policies regarding personal investing. The information about employees' personal investment activities and policies will foster an atmosphere of full and complete disclosure and calm the public's legitimate concerns about the conflicts of interest posed by investment personnel's personal trading. The disclosure must provide helpful information to investors; it should not be simply boilerplate language, such as "investment personnel are subject to policies and procedures regarding their personal trading."

56 STANDARD VI(B): APPLICATION OF THE STANDARD

☐ demonstrate the application of the Code of Ethics and Standards of Professional Conduct to situations involving issues of professional integrity

☐ identify conduct that conforms to the Code and Standards and conduct that violates the Code and Standards

Example 1 (Personal Trading):

Research analyst Marlon Long does not recommend purchase of a common stock for his employer's account because he wants to purchase the stock personally and does not want to wait until the recommendation is approved and the stock is purchased by his employer.

> *Comment*: Long has violated Standard VI(B) by taking advantage of his knowledge of the stock's value before allowing his employer to benefit from that information.

Example 2 (Trading for Family Member Account):

Carol Baker, the portfolio manager of an aggressive growth mutual fund, maintains an account in her husband's name at several brokerage firms with which the fund and a number of Baker's other individual clients do a substantial amount of business. Whenever a hot issue becomes available, she instructs the brokers to buy it for her husband's account. Because such issues normally are scarce, Baker often acquires shares in hot issues but her clients are not able to participate in them.

> *Comment*: To avoid violating Standard VI(B), Baker must acquire shares for her mutual fund first and acquire them for her husband's account only after doing so, even though she might miss out on participating in new issues via her husband's account. She also must disclose the trading for her husband's account to her employer because this activity creates a conflict between her personal interests and her employer's interests.

Example 3 (Family Accounts as Equals):

Erin Toffler, a portfolio manager at Esposito Investments, manages the retirement account established with the firm by her parents. Whenever IPOs become available, she first allocates shares to all her other clients for whom the investment is appropriate; only then does she place any remaining portion in her parents' account, if the issue is appropriate for them. She has adopted this procedure so that no one can accuse her of favoring her parents.

> *Comment*: Toffler has violated Standard VI(B) by breaching her duty to her parents by treating them differently from her other accounts simply because of the family relationship. As fee-paying clients of Esposito Investments, Toffler's parents are entitled to the same treatment as any other client of the firm. If Toffler has beneficial ownership in the account, however, and Esposito Investments has preclearance and reporting requirements for personal transactions, she may have to preclear the trades and report the transactions to Esposito.

Example 4 (Personal Trading and Disclosure):

Gary Michaels is an entry-level employee who holds a low-paying job serving both the research department and the investment management department of an active investment management firm. He purchases a sports car and begins to wear expensive clothes after only a year of employment with the firm. The director of the investment management department, who has responsibility for monitoring the personal stock transactions of all employees, investigates and discovers that Michaels has made substantial investment gains by purchasing stocks just before they were put on the firm's recommended "buy" list. Michaels was regularly given the firm's quarterly personal transaction form but declined to complete it.

> *Comment*: Michaels violated Standard VI(B) by placing personal transactions ahead of client transactions. In addition, his supervisor violated Standard IV(C)–Responsibilities of Supervisors by permitting Michaels to continue to perform his assigned tasks without having signed the quarterly personal transaction form. Note also that if Michaels had communicated information about the firm's recommendations to a person who traded the security, that action would be a misappropriation of the information and a violation of Standard II(A)–Material Nonpublic Information.

Example 5 (Trading Prior to Report Dissemination):

A brokerage's insurance analyst, Denise Wilson, makes a closed-circuit TV report to her firm's branches around the country. During the broadcast, she includes negative comments about a major company in the insurance industry. The following day, Wilson's report is printed and distributed to the sales force and public customers. The report recommends that both short-term traders and intermediate investors take profits by selling that insurance company's stock. Seven minutes after the broadcast, however, Ellen Riley, head of the firm's trading department, had closed out a long "call" position in the stock. Shortly thereafter, Riley established a sizable "put" position in the stock. When asked about her activities, Riley claimed she took the actions to facilitate anticipated sales by institutional clients.

> *Comment*: Riley did not give customers an opportunity to buy or sell in the options market before the firm itself did. By taking action before the report was disseminated, Riley's firm may have depressed the price of the calls and increased the price of the puts. The firm could have avoided a conflict of interest if it had waited to trade for its own account until its clients had an opportunity to receive and assimilate Wilson's recommendations. As it is, Riley's actions violated Standard VI(B).

STANDARD VI(C): CONFLICTS OF INTEREST - REFERRAL FEES

☐ demonstrate the application of the Code of Ethics and Standards of Professional Conduct to situations involving issues of professional integrity

> Members and Candidates must disclose to their employer, clients, and prospective clients, as appropriate, any compensation, consideration, or benefit received from or paid to others for the recommendation of products or services.

Standard VI(C): Application of the Standard

Guidance

Standard VI(C) states the responsibility of members and candidates to inform their employer, clients, and prospective clients of any benefit received for referrals of customers and clients. Such disclosures allow clients or employers to evaluate (1) any partiality shown in any recommendation of services and (2) the full cost of the services. Members and candidates must disclose when they pay a fee or provide compensation to others who have referred prospective clients to the member or candidate.

Appropriate disclosure means that members and candidates must advise the client or prospective client, before entry into any formal agreement for services, of any benefit given or received for the recommendation of any services provided by the member or candidate. In addition, the member or candidate must disclose the nature of the consideration or benefit—for example, flat fee or percentage basis, one-time or continuing benefit, based on performance, benefit in the form of provision of research or other noncash benefit—together with the estimated dollar value. Consideration includes all fees, whether paid in cash, in soft dollars, or in kind.

STANDARD VI(C): RECOMMENDED PROCEDURES — 58

- [ ] recommend practices and procedures designed to prevent violations of the Code of Ethics and Standards of Professional Conduct

Members and candidates should encourage their employers to develop procedures related to referral fees. The firm may completely restrict such fees. If the firm does not adopt a strict prohibition of such fees, the procedures should indicate the appropriate steps for requesting approval.

Employers should have investment professionals provide to the clients notification of approved referral fee programs and provide the employer regular (at least quarterly) updates on the amount and nature of compensation received.

STANDARD VI(C): APPLICATION OF THE STANDARD — 59

- [ ] demonstrate the application of the Code of Ethics and Standards of Professional Conduct to situations involving issues of professional integrity
- [ ] identify conduct that conforms to the Code and Standards and conduct that violates the Code and Standards

Example 1 (Disclosure of Referral Arrangements and Outside Parties):

Brady Securities, Inc., a broker/dealer, has established a referral arrangement with Lewis Brothers, Ltd., an investment counseling firm. In this arrangement, Brady Securities refers all prospective tax-exempt accounts, including pension, profit-sharing, and endowment accounts, to Lewis Brothers. In return, Lewis Brothers makes available to Brady Securities on a regular basis the security recommendations and reports of its research staff, which registered representatives of Brady Securities use in serving customers. In addition, Lewis Brothers conducts monthly economic and market reviews for Brady Securities personnel and directs all stock commission business generated by referral accounts to Brady Securities.

Willard White, a partner in Lewis Brothers, calculates that the incremental costs involved in functioning as the research department of Brady Securities are US$20,000 annually.

Referrals from Brady Securities last year resulted in fee income of US$200,000 for Lewis Brothers, and directing all stock trades through Brady Securities resulted in additional costs to Lewis Brothers' clients of US$10,000.

Diane Branch, the chief financial officer of Maxwell Inc., contacts White and says that she is seeking an investment manager for Maxwell's profit-sharing plan. She adds, "My friend Harold Hill at Brady Securities recommended your firm without qualification, and that's good enough for me. Do we have a deal?" White accepts the new account but does not disclose his firm's referral arrangement with Brady Securities.

> *Comment*: White has violated Standard VI(C) by failing to inform the prospective customer of the referral fee payable in services and commissions for an indefinite period to Brady Securities. Such disclosure could have caused Branch to reassess Hill's recommendation and make a more critical evaluation of Lewis Brothers' services.

Example 2 (Disclosure of Interdepartmental Referral Arrangements):

James Handley works for the trust department of Central Trust Bank. He receives compensation for each referral he makes to Central Trust's brokerage department and personal financial management department that results in a sale. He refers several of his clients to the personal financial management department but does not disclose the arrangement within Central Trust to his clients.

> *Comment*: Handley has violated Standard VI(C) by not disclosing the referral arrangement at Central Trust Bank to his clients. Standard VI(C) does not distinguish between referral payments paid by a third party for referring clients to the third party and internal payments paid within the firm to attract new business to a subsidiary. Members and candidates must disclose all such referral fees. Therefore, Handley is required to disclose, at the time of referral, any referral fee agreement in place among Central Trust Bank's departments. The disclosure should include the nature and the value of the benefit and should be made in writing.

Example 3 (Disclosure of Referral Arrangements and Informing Firm):

Katherine Roberts is a portfolio manager at Katama Investments, an advisory firm specializing in managing assets for high-net-worth individuals. Katama's trading desk uses a variety of brokerage houses to execute trades on behalf of its clients. Roberts asks the trading desk to direct a large portion of its commissions to Naushon, Inc., a small broker/dealer run by one of Roberts' business school classmates. Katama's traders have found that Naushon is not very competitive on pricing, and although Naushon generates some research for its trading clients, Katama's other analysts have found most of Naushon's research to be not especially useful. Nevertheless, the traders do as

Roberts asks, and in return for receiving a large portion of Katama's business, Naushon recommends the investment services of Roberts and Katama to its wealthiest clients. This arrangement is not disclosed to either Katama or the clients referred by Naushon.

> *Comment*: Roberts is violating Standard VI(C) by failing to inform her employer of the referral arrangement.

Example 4 (Disclosure of Referral Arrangements and Outside Organizations):

Alex Burl is a portfolio manager at Helpful Investments, a local investment advisory firm. Burl is on the advisory board of his child's school, which is looking for ways to raise money to purchase new playground equipment for the school. Burl discusses a plan with his supervisor in which he will donate to the school a portion of his service fee from new clients referred by the parents of students at the school. Upon getting the approval from Helpful, Burl presents the idea to the school's advisory board and directors. The school agrees to announce the program at the next parent event and asks Burl to provide the appropriate written materials to be distributed. A week following the distribution of the flyers, Burl receives the first school-related referral. In establishing the client's investment policy statement, Burl clearly discusses the school's referral and outlines the plans for distributing the donation back to the school.

> *Comment*: Burl has not violated Standard VI(C) because he secured the permission of his employer, Helpful Investments, and the school prior to beginning the program and because he discussed the arrangement with the client at the time the investment policy statement was designed.

Example 5 (Disclosure of Referral Arrangements and Outside Parties):

The sponsor of a state employee pension is seeking to hire a firm to manage the pension plan's emerging market allocation. To assist in the review process, the sponsor has hired Thomas Arrow as a consultant to solicit proposals from various advisers. Arrow is contracted by the sponsor to represent its best interest in selecting the most appropriate new manager. The process runs smoothly, and Overseas Investments is selected as the new manager.

The following year, news breaks that Arrow is under investigation by the local regulator for accepting kickbacks from investment managers after they are awarded new pension allocations. Overseas Investments is included in the list of firms allegedly making these payments. Although the sponsor is happy with the performance of Overseas since it has been managing the pension plan's emerging market funds, the sponsor still decides to have an independent review of the proposals and the selection process to ensure that Overseas was the appropriate firm for its needs. This review confirms that, even though Arrow was being paid by both parties, the recommendation of Overseas appeared to be objective and appropriate.

> *Comment*: Arrow has violated Standard VI(C) because he did not disclose the fee being paid by Overseas. Withholding this information raises the question of a potential lack of objectivity in the recommendation of Overseas by Arrow; this aspect is in addition to questions about the legality of having firms pay to be considered for an allocation.
>
> Regulators and governmental agencies may adopt requirements concerning allowable consultant activities. Local regulations sometimes include having a consultant register with the regulatory agency's ethics board.

Regulator policies may include a prohibition on acceptance of payments from investment managers receiving allocations and require regular reporting of contributions made to political organizations and candidates. Arrow would have to adhere to these requirements as well as the Code and Standards.

60 STANDARD VII(A): RESPONSIBILITIES AS A CFA INSTITUTE MEMBER OR CFA CANDIDATE - CONDUCT AS PARTICIPANTS IN CFA INSTITUTE PROGRAMS

☐ demonstrate the application of the Code of Ethics and Standards of Professional Conduct to situations involving issues of professional integrity

Standard VII(A) Conduct as Participants in CFA Institute Programs

Members and Candidates must not engage in any conduct that compromises the reputation or integrity of CFA Institute or the CFA designation or the integrity, validity, or security of CFA Institute programs.

Guidance

Highlights:

- *Confidential Program Information*
- *Additional CFA Program Restrictions*
- *Expressing an Opinion*

Standard VII(A) covers the conduct of CFA Institute members and candidates involved with the CFA Program and prohibits any conduct that undermines the public's confidence that the CFA charter represents a level of achievement based on merit and ethical conduct. There is an array of CFA Institute programs beyond the CFA Program that provide additional educational and credentialing opportunities, including the Certificate in Investment Performance Measurement (CIPM) Program and the CFA Institute Investment Foundations™ Program. The standard's function is to hold members and candidates to a high ethical criterion while they are participating in or involved with any CFA Institute program. Conduct covered includes but is not limited to

- giving or receiving assistance (cheating) on any CFA Institute examinations;
- violating the rules, regulations, and testing policies of CFA Institute programs;
- providing confidential program or exam information to candidates or the public;

- disregarding or attempting to circumvent security measures established for any CFA Institute examinations;
- improperly using an association with CFA Institute to further personal or professional goals; and
- misrepresenting information on the Professional Conduct Statement or in the CFA Institute Continuing Education Program.

Confidential Program Information

CFA Institute is vigilant about protecting the integrity of CFA Institute programs' content and examination processes. CFA Institute program rules, regulations, and policies prohibit candidates from disclosing confidential material gained during the exam process.

Examples of information that cannot be disclosed by candidates sitting for an exam include but are not limited to

- specific details of questions appearing on the exam and
- broad topical areas and formulas tested or not tested on the exam.

All aspects of the exam, including questions, broad topical areas, and formulas, tested or not tested, are considered confidential until such time as CFA Institute elects to release them publicly. This confidentiality requirement allows CFA Institute to maintain the integrity and rigor of exams for future candidates. Standard VII(A) does not prohibit candidates from discussing nonconfidential information or curriculum material with others or in study groups in preparation for the exam.

Candidates increasingly use online forums and new technology as part of their exam preparations. CFA Institute actively polices blogs, forums, and related social networking groups for information considered confidential. The organization works with both individual candidates and the sponsors of online or offline services to promptly remove any and all violations. As noted in the discussion of Standard I(A)–Knowledge of the Law, candidates, members, and the public are encouraged to report suspected violations to CFA Institute.

Additional CFA Program Restrictions

The CFA Program rules, regulations, and policies define additional allowed and disallowed actions concerning the exams. Violating any of the testing policies, such as the calculator policy, personal belongings policy, or the Candidate Pledge, constitutes a violation of Standard VII(A). Candidates will find all of these policies on the CFA Program portion of the CFA Institute website (www.cfainstitute.org). Exhibit 2 provides the Candidate Pledge, which highlights the respect candidates must have for the integrity, validity, and security of the CFA exam.

Members may participate as volunteers in various aspects of the CFA Program. Standard VII(A) prohibits members from disclosing and/or soliciting confidential material gained prior to or during the exam and grading processes with those outside the CFA exam development process.

Examples of information that cannot be shared by members involved in developing, administering, or grading the exams include but are not limited to

- questions appearing on the exam or under consideration,
- deliberation related to the exam process, and
- information related to the scoring of questions.

Members may also be asked to offer assistance with other CFA Institute programs, including but not limited to the CIPM and Investment Foundations programs. Members participating in any CFA Institute program should do so with the same level of integrity and confidentiality as is required of participation in the CFA Program.

Expressing an Opinion

Standard VII(A) does *not* cover expressing opinions regarding CFA Institute, the CFA Program, or other CFA Institute programs. Members and candidates are free to disagree and express their disagreement with CFA Institute on its policies, its procedures, or any advocacy positions taken by the organization. When expressing a personal opinion, a candidate is prohibited from disclosing content-specific information, including any actual exam question and the information as to subject matter covered or not covered in the exam.

Exhibit 2: Sample of CFA Program Testing Policies

Candidate Pledge	As a candidate in the CFA Program, I am obligated to follow Standard VII(A) of the CFA Institute Standards of Professional Conduct, which states that members and candidates must not engage in any conduct that compromises the reputation or integrity of CFA Institute or the CFA designation or the integrity, validity, or security of the CFA exam.

- Prior to this exam, I have not given or received information regarding the content of this exam. During this exam, I will not give or receive any information regarding the content of this exam.
- After this exam, I will not disclose **ANY** portion of this exam and I will not remove **ANY** exam materials from the testing room in original or copied form. I understand that all exam materials, including my answers, are the property of CFA Institute and will not be returned to me in any form.
- I will follow **ALL** rules of the CFA Program as stated on the CFA Institute website and the back cover of the exam book. My violation of any rules of the CFA Program will result in CFA Institute voiding my exam results and may lead to suspension or termination of my candidacy in the CFA Program.

61 STANDARD VII(A): APPLICATION OF THE STANDARD

☐ demonstrate the application of the Code of Ethics and Standards of Professional Conduct to situations involving issues of professional integrity

☐ identify conduct that conforms to the Code and Standards and conduct that violates the Code and Standards

Standard VII(A): Application of the Standard

Example 1 (Sharing Exam Questions):

Travis Nero serves as a proctor for the administration of the CFA examination in his city. In the course of his service, he reviews a copy of the Level II exam on the evening prior to the exam's administration and provides information concerning the exam questions to two candidates who use it to prepare for the exam.

Comment: Nero and the two candidates have violated Standard VII(A). By giving information about the exam questions to two candidates, Nero provided an unfair advantage to the two candidates and undermined the integrity and validity of the Level II exam as an accurate measure of the knowledge, skills, and abilities necessary to earn the right to use the CFA designation. By accepting the information, the candidates also compromised the integrity and validity of the Level II exam and undermined the ethical framework that is a key part of the designation.

Example 2 (Bringing Written Material into Exam Room):

Loren Sullivan is enrolled to take the Level II CFA examination. He has been having difficulty remembering a particular formula, so prior to entering the exam room, he writes the formula on the palm of his hand. During the afternoon section of the exam, a proctor notices Sullivan looking at the palm of his hand. She asks to see his hand and finds the formula.

Comment: Because Sullivan wrote down information from the Candidate Body of Knowledge (CBOK) and took that written information into the exam room, his conduct compromised the validity of his exam performance and violated Standard VII(A). Sullivan's conduct was also in direct contradiction with the rules and regulations of the CFA Program, the Candidate Pledge, and the CFA Institute Code and Standards.

Example 3 (Writing after Exam Period End):

At the conclusion of the morning section of the Level I CFA examination, the proctors announce, "Stop writing now." John Davis has not completed the exam, so he continues to randomly fill in ovals on his answer sheet. A proctor approaches Davis's desk and reminds him that he should stop writing immediately. Davis, however, continues to complete the answer sheet. After the proctor asks him to stop writing two additional times, Davis finally puts down his pencil.

Comment: By continuing to complete his exam after time was called, Davis has violated Standard VII(A). By continuing to write, Davis took an unfair advantage over other candidates, and his conduct compromised the validity of his exam performance. Additionally, by not heeding the proctor's repeated instructions, Davis violated the rules and regulations of the CFA Program.

Example 4 (Sharing Exam Content):

After completing Level II of the CFA exam, Annabelle Rossi posts on her blog about her experience. She posts the following: "Level II is complete! I think I did fairly well on the exam. It was really difficult, but fair. I think I did especially well on the derivatives questions. And there were tons of them! I think I counted 18! The ethics questions were really hard. I'm glad I spent so much time on the Code and Standards. I was surprised to see there were no questions at all about IPO allocations. I expected there to be a couple. Well, off to celebrate getting through it. See you tonight?"

> *Comment*: Rossi did not violate Standard VII(A) when she wrote about how difficult she found the exam or how well she thinks she may have done. By revealing portions of the CBOK covered on the exam and areas not covered, however, she did violate Standard VII(A) and the Candidate Pledge. Depending on the time frame in which the comments were posted, Rossi not only may have assisted future candidates but also may have provided an unfair advantage to candidates yet to sit for the same exam, thereby undermining the integrity and validity of the Level II exam.

Example 5 (Sharing Exam Content):

Level I candidate Etienne Gagne has been a frequent visitor to an internet forum designed specifically for CFA Program candidates. The week after completing the Level I examination, Gagne and several others begin a discussion thread on the forum about the most challenging questions and attempt to determine the correct answers.

> *Comment*: Gagne has violated Standard VII(A) by providing and soliciting confidential exam information, which compromises the integrity of the exam process and violates the Candidate Pledge. In trying to determine correct answers to specific questions, the group's discussion included question-specific details considered to be confidential to the CFA Program.

Example 6 (Sharing Exam Content):

CFA4Sure is a company that produces test-preparation materials for CFA Program candidates. Many candidates register for and use the company's products. The day after the CFA examination, CFA4Sure sends an e-mail to all its customers asking them to share with the company the hardest questions from the exam so that CFA4Sure can better prepare its customers for the next exam administration. Marisol Pena e-mails a summary of the questions she found most difficult on the exam.

> *Comment*: Pena has violated Standard VII(A) by disclosing a portion of the exam questions. The information provided is considered confidential until publicly released by CFA Institute. CFA4Sure is likely to use such feedback to refine its review materials for future candidates. Pena's sharing of the specific questions undermines the integrity of the exam while potentially making the exam easier for future candidates.
>
> If the CFA4Sure employees who participated in the solicitation of confidential CFA Program information are CFA Institute members or candidates, they also have violated Standard VII(A).

Example 7 (Discussion of Exam Grading Guidelines and Results):

Prior to participating in grading CFA examinations, Wesley Whitcomb is required to sign a CFA Institute Grader Agreement. As part of the Grader Agreement, Whitcomb agrees not to reveal or discuss the exam materials with anyone except CFA Institute staff or other graders. Several weeks after the conclusion of the CFA exam grading,

Standard VII(A): Application of the Standard

Whitcomb tells several colleagues who are candidates in the CFA Program which question he graded. He also discusses the guideline answer and adds that few candidates scored well on the question.

> *Comment*: Whitcomb violated Standard VII(A) by breaking the Grader Agreement and disclosing information related to a specific question on the exam, which compromised the integrity of the exam process.

Example 8 (Compromising CFA Institute Integrity as a Volunteer):

Jose Ramirez is an investor-relations consultant for several small companies that are seeking greater exposure to investors. He is also the program chair for the CFA Institute society in the city where he works. Ramirez schedules only companies that are his clients to make presentations to the society and excludes other companies.

> *Comment*: Ramirez, by using his volunteer position at CFA Institute to benefit himself and his clients, compromises the reputation and integrity of CFA Institute and thus violates Standard VII(A).

Example 9 (Compromising CFA Institute Integrity as a Volunteer):

Marguerite Warrenski is a member of the CFA Institute GIPS Executive Committee, which oversees the creation, implementation, and revision of the GIPS standards. As a member of the Executive Committee, she has advance knowledge of confidential information regarding the GIPS standards, including any new or revised standards the committee is considering. She tells her clients that her Executive Committee membership will allow her to better assist her clients in keeping up with changes to the Standards and facilitating their compliance with the changes.

> *Comment*: Warrenski is using her association with the GIPS Executive Committee to promote her firm's services to clients and potential clients. In defining her volunteer position at CFA Institute as a strategic business advantage over competing firms and implying to clients that she would use confidential information to further their interests, Warrenski is compromising the reputation and integrity of CFA Institute and thus violating Standard VII(A). She may factually state her involvement with the Executive Committee but cannot infer any special advantage to her clients from such participation.

62 STANDARD VII(B): RESPONSIBILITIES AS A CFA INSTITUTE MEMBER OR CFA CANDIDATE - REFERENCE TO CFA INSTITUTE, THE CFA DESIGNATION, AND THE CFA PROGRAM

☐ demonstrate the application of the Code of Ethics and Standards of Professional Conduct to situations involving issues of professional integrity

> When referring to CFA Institute, CFA Institute membership, the CFA designation, or candidacy in the CFA Program, Members and Candidates must not misrepresent or exaggerate the meaning or implications of membership in CFA Institute, holding the CFA designation, or candidacy in the CFA Program.

Guidance

Highlights:

- *CFA Institute Membership*
- *Using the CFA Designation*
- *Referring to Candidacy in the CFA Program*

Standard VII(B) is intended to prevent promotional efforts that make promises or guarantees that are tied to the CFA designation. Individuals must not exaggerate the meaning or implications of membership in CFA Institute, holding the CFA designation, or candidacy in the CFA Program.

Standard VII(B) is not intended to prohibit factual statements related to the positive benefit of earning the CFA designation. However, statements referring to CFA Institute, the CFA designation, or the CFA Program that overstate the competency of an individual or imply, either directly or indirectly, that superior performance can be expected from someone with the CFA designation are not allowed under the standard.

Statements that highlight or emphasize the commitment of CFA Institute members, CFA charterholders, and CFA candidates to ethical and professional conduct or mention the thoroughness and rigor of the CFA Program are appropriate. Members and candidates may make claims about the relative merits of CFA Institute, the CFA Program, or the Code and Standards as long as those statements are implicitly or explicitly stated as the opinion of the speaker. Statements that do not express opinions have to be supported by facts.

Standard VII(B) applies to any form of communication, including but not limited to communications made in electronic or written form (such as on firm letterhead, business cards, professional biographies, directory listings, printed advertising, firm brochures, or personal resumes) and oral statements made to the public, clients, or prospects.

CFA Institute Membership

The term "CFA Institute member" refers to "regular" and "affiliate" members of CFA Institute who have met the membership requirements as defined in the CFA Institute Bylaws. Once accepted as a CFA Institute member, the member must satisfy the following requirements to maintain his or her status:

- remit annually to CFA Institute a completed Professional Conduct Statement, which renews the commitment to abide by the requirements of the Code and Standards and the CFA Institute Professional Conduct Program, and
- pay applicable CFA Institute membership dues on an annual basis.

If a CFA Institute member fails to meet any of these requirements, the individual is no longer considered an active member. Until membership is reactivated, individuals must not present themselves to others as active members. They may state, however, that they were CFA Institute members in the past or refer to the years when their membership was active.

Using the CFA Designation

Those who have earned the right to use the Chartered Financial Analyst designation are encouraged to do so but only in a manner that does not misrepresent or exaggerate the meaning or implications of the designation. The use of the designation may be accompanied by an accurate explanation of the requirements that have been met to earn the right to use the designation.

"CFA charterholders" are those individuals who have earned the right to use the CFA designation granted by CFA Institute. These people have satisfied certain requirements, including completion of the CFA Program and required years of acceptable work experience. Once granted the right to use the designation, individuals must also satisfy the CFA Institute membership requirements (see above) to maintain their right to use the designation.

If a CFA charterholder fails to meet any of the membership requirements, he or she forfeits the right to use the CFA designation. Until membership is reactivated, individuals must not present themselves to others as CFA charterholders. They may state, however, that they were charterholders in the past.

Given the growing popularity of social media, where individuals may anonymously express their opinions, pseudonyms or online profile names created to hide a member's identity should not be tagged with the CFA designation.

Use of the CFA designation by a CFA charterholder is governed by the terms and conditions of the annual Professional Conduct Statement Agreement, entered into between CFA Institute and its membership prior to commencement of use of the CFA designation and reaffirmed annually.

Referring to Candidacy in the CFA Program

Candidates in the CFA Program may refer to their participation in the CFA Program, but such references must clearly state that an individual is a *candidate* in the CFA Program and must not imply that the candidate has achieved any type of partial designation. A person is a candidate in the CFA Program if

- the person's application for registration in the CFA Program has been accepted by CFA Institute, as evidenced by issuance of a notice of acceptance, and the person is enrolled to sit for a specified examination or
- the registered person has sat for a specified examination but exam results have not yet been received.

If an individual is registered for the CFA Program but declines to sit for an exam or otherwise does not meet the definition of a candidate as described in the CFA Institute Bylaws, then that individual is no longer considered an active candidate. Once the person is enrolled to sit for a future examination, his or her CFA Program candidacy resumes.

CFA Program candidates must never state or imply that they have a partial designation as a result of passing one or more levels or cite an expected completion date of any level of the CFA Program. Final award of the charter is subject to meeting the CFA Program requirements and approval by the CFA Institute Board of Governors.

If a candidate passes each level of the exam in consecutive years and wants to state that he or she did so, that is not a violation of Standard VII(B) because it is a statement of fact. If the candidate then goes on to claim or imply superior ability by obtaining the designation in only three years, however, he or she is in violation of Standard VII(B).

Exhibit 3 provides examples of proper and improper references to the CFA designation.

Exhibit 3: Proper and Improper References to the CFA Designation

Proper References	Improper References
"Completion of the CFA Program has enhanced my portfolio management skills."	"CFA charterholders achieve better performance results."
"John Smith passed all three CFA Program examinations in three consecutive years."	"John Smith is among the elite, having passed all three CFA examinations in three consecutive attempts."
"The CFA designation is globally recognized and attests to a charterholder's success in a rigorous and comprehensive study program in the field of investment management and research analysis."	"As a CFA charterholder, I am the most qualified to manage client investments."
"The credibility that the CFA designation affords and the skills the CFA Program cultivates are key assets for my future career development."	"As a CFA charterholder, Jane White provides the best value in trade execution."
"I enrolled in the CFA Program to obtain the highest set of credentials in the global investment management industry."	"Enrolling as a candidate in the CFA Program ensures one of becoming better at valuing debt securities."
"I passed Level I of the CFA Program."	"CFA, Level II"
"I am a 2010 Level III candidate in the CFA Program."	"CFA, Expected 2011"
"I passed all three levels of the CFA Program and may be eligible for the CFA charter upon completion of the required work experience."	"CFA, Expected 2011" "John Smith, Charter Pending"

STANDARD VII(B): RECOMMENDED PROCEDURES

☐ recommend practices and procedures designed to prevent violations of the Code of Ethics and Standards of Professional Conduct

Misuse of a member's CFA designation or CFA candidacy or improper reference to it is common by those in a member's or candidate's firm who do not possess knowledge of the requirements of Standard VII(B). As an appropriate step to reduce this risk, members and candidates should disseminate written information about Standard VII(B) and the accompanying guidance to their firm's legal, compliance, public relations, and marketing departments (see www.cfainstitute.org).

For materials that refer to employees' affiliation with CFA Institute, members and candidates should encourage their firms to create templates that are approved by a central authority (such as the compliance department) as being consistent with Standard VII(B). This practice promotes consistency and accuracy in the firm of references to CFA Institute membership, the CFA designation, and CFA candidacy.

STANDARD VII(B): APPLICATION OF THE STANDARD — 64

- ☐ demonstrate the application of the Code of Ethics and Standards of Professional Conduct to situations involving issues of professional integrity
- ☐ identify conduct that conforms to the Code and Standards and conduct that violates the Code and Standards

Example 1 (Passing Exams in Consecutive Years):

An advertisement for AZ Investment Advisors states that all the firm's principals are CFA charterholders and all passed the three examinations on their first attempt. The advertisement prominently links this fact to the notion that AZ's mutual funds have achieved superior performance.

> *Comment*: AZ may state that all principals passed the three examinations on the first try as long as this statement is true, but it must not be linked to performance or imply superior ability. Implying that (1) CFA charterholders achieve better investment results and (2) those who pass the exams on the first try may be more successful than those who do not violates Standard VII(B).

Example 2 (Right to Use CFA Designation):

Five years after receiving his CFA charter, Louis Vasseur resigns his position as an investment analyst and spends the next two years traveling abroad. Because he is not actively engaged in the investment profession, he does not file a completed Professional Conduct Statement with CFA Institute and does not pay his CFA Institute membership dues. At the conclusion of his travels, Vasseur becomes a self-employed analyst accepting assignments as an independent contractor. Without reinstating his CFA Institute membership by filing his Professional Conduct Statement and paying his dues, he prints business cards that display "CFA" after his name.

> *Comment*: Vasseur has violated Standard VII(B) because his right to use the CFA designation was suspended when he failed to file his Professional Conduct Statement and stopped paying dues. Therefore, he no longer is able to state or imply that he is an active CFA charterholder. When Vasseur files

his Professional Conduct Statement, resumes paying CFA Institute dues to activate his membership, and completes the CFA Institute reinstatement procedures, he will be eligible to use the CFA designation.

Example 3 ("Retired" CFA Institute Membership Status):

After a 25-year career, James Simpson retires from his firm. Because he is not actively engaged in the investment profession, he does not file a completed Professional Conduct Statement with CFA Institute and does not pay his CFA Institute membership dues. Simpson designs a plain business card (without a corporate logo) to hand out to friends with his new contact details, and he continues to put "CFA" after his name.

Comment: Simpson has violated Standard VII(B). Because he failed to file his Professional Conduct Statement and ceased paying dues, his membership has been suspended and he has given up the right to use the CFA designation. CFA Institute has procedures, however, for reclassifying a member and charterholder as "retired" and reducing the annual dues. If he wants to obtain retired status, he needs to file the appropriate paperwork with CFA Institute. When Simpson receives his notification from CFA Institute that his membership has been reclassified as retired and he resumes paying reduced dues, his membership will be reactivated and his right to use the CFA designation will be reinstated.

Example 4 (Stating Facts about CFA Designation and Program):

Rhonda Reese has been a CFA charterholder since 2000. In a conversation with a friend who is considering enrolling in the CFA Program, she states that she has learned a great deal from the CFA Program and that many firms require their employees to be CFA charterholders. She would recommend the CFA Program to anyone pursuing a career in investment management.

Comment: Reese's comments comply with Standard VII(B). Her statements refer to facts: The CFA Program enhanced her knowledge, and many firms require the CFA designation for their investment professionals.

Example 5 (Order of Professional and Academic Designations):

Tatiana Prittima has earned both her CFA designation and a PhD in finance. She would like to cite both her accomplishments on her business card but is unsure of the proper method for doing so.

Comment: The order of designations cited on such items as resumes and business cards is a matter of personal preference. Prittima is free to cite the CFA designation either before or after citing her PhD. Multiple designations must be separated by a comma.

Example 6 (Use of Fictitious Name):

Barry Glass is the lead quantitative analyst at CityCenter Hedge Fund. Glass is responsible for the development, maintenance, and enhancement of the proprietary models the fund uses to manage its investors' assets. Glass reads several high-level mathematical publications and blogs to stay informed on current developments. One blog, run by Expert CFA, presents some intriguing research that may benefit

Standard VII(B): Application of the Standard

one of CityCenter's current models. Glass is under pressure from firm executives to improve the model's predictive abilities, and he incorporates the factors discussed in the online research. The updated output recommends several new investments to the fund's portfolio managers.

Comment: "Expert CFA" has violated Standard VII(B) by using the CFA designation inappropriately. As with any research report, authorship of online comments must include the charterholder's full name along with any reference to the CFA designation.

See also Standard V(A), which Glass has violated for guidance on diligence and reasonable basis.

PRACTICE PROBLEMS

Unless otherwise stated in the question, all individuals in the following questions are CFA Institute members or candidates in the CFA Program and, therefore, are subject to the CFA Institute Code of Ethics and Standards of Professional Conduct.

1. Smith, a research analyst with a brokerage firm, decides to change his recommendation for the common stock of Green Company, Inc., from a "buy" to a "sell." He mails this change in investment advice to all the firm's clients on Wednesday. The day after the mailing, a client calls with a buy order for 500 shares of Green Company. In this circumstance, Smith should:

   A. Accept the order.

   B. Advise the customer of the change in recommendation before accepting the order.

   C. Not accept the order because it is contrary to the firm's recommendation.

2. Which statement about a manager's use of client brokerage commissions violates the Code and Standards?

   A. A client may direct a manager to use that client's brokerage commissions to purchase goods and services for that client.

   B. Client brokerage commissions should be used to benefit the client and should be commensurate with the value of the brokerage and research services received.

   C. Client brokerage commissions may be directed to pay for the investment manager's operating expenses.

3. Jamison is a junior research analyst with Howard & Howard, a brokerage and investment banking firm. Howard & Howard's mergers and acquisitions department has represented the Britland Company in all of its acquisitions for the past 20 years. Two of Howard & Howard's senior officers are directors of various Britland subsidiaries. Jamison has been asked to write a research report on Britland. What is the best course of action for her to follow?

   A. Jamison may write the report but must refrain from expressing any opinions because of the special relationships between the two companies.

   B. Jamison should not write the report because the two Howard & Howard officers serve as directors for subsidiaries of Britland.

   C. Jamison may write the report if she discloses the special relationships with the company in the report.

4. Which of the following statements clearly *conflicts* with the recommended procedures for compliance presented in the CFA Institute *Standards of Practice Handbook*?

   A. Firms should disclose to clients the personal investing policies and procedures established for their employees.

Practice Problems

    B. Prior approval must be obtained for the personal investment transactions of all employees.

    C. For confidentiality reasons, personal transactions and holdings should not be reported to employers unless mandated by regulatory organizations.

5. Bronson provides investment advice to the board of trustees of a private university endowment fund. The trustees have provided Bronson with the fund's financial information, including planned expenditures. Bronson receives a phone call on Friday afternoon from Murdock, a prominent alumnus, requesting that Bronson fax him comprehensive financial information about the fund. According to Murdock, he has a potential contributor but needs the information that day to close the deal and cannot contact any of the trustees. Based on the CFA Institute Standards, Bronson should:

    A. Send Murdock the information because disclosure would benefit the client.

    B. Not send Murdock the information to preserve confidentiality.

    C. Send Murdock the information, provided Bronson promptly notifies the trustees.

6. Willier is the research analyst responsible for following Company X. All the information he has accumulated and documented suggests that the outlook for the company's new products is poor, so the stock should be rated a weak "hold." During lunch, however, Willier overhears a financial analyst from another firm whom he respects offer opinions that conflict with Willier's forecasts and expectations. Upon returning to his office, Willier releases a strong "buy" recommendation to the public. Willier:

    A. Violated the Standards by failing to distinguish between facts and opinions in his recommendation.

    B. Violated the Standards because he did not have a reasonable and adequate basis for his recommendation.

    C. Was in full compliance with the Standards.

7. An investment management firm has been hired by ETV Corporation to work on an additional public offering for the company. The firm's brokerage unit now has a "sell" recommendation on ETV, but the head of the investment banking department has asked the head of the brokerage unit to change the recommendation from "sell" to "buy." According to the Standards, the head of the brokerage unit would be permitted to:

    A. Increase the recommendation by no more than one increment (in this case, to a "hold" recommendation).

    B. Place the company on a restricted list and give only factual information about the company.

    C. Assign a new analyst to decide if the stock deserves a higher rating.

8. Albert and Tye, who recently started their own investment advisory business, have registered to take the Level III CFA examination. Albert's business card reads, "Judy Albert, CFA Level II." Tye has not put anything about the CFA designation on his business card, but promotional material that he designed for the business describes the CFA requirements and indicates that Tye participates in

the CFA Program and has completed Levels I and II. According to the Standards:

- **A.** Albert has violated the Standards, but Tye has not.
- **B.** Tye has violated the Standards, but Albert has not.
- **C.** Both Albert and Tye have violated the Standards.

9. Scott works for a regional brokerage firm. He estimates that Walkton Industries will increase its dividend by US$1.50 a share during the next year. He realizes that this increase is contingent on pending legislation that would, if enacted, give Walkton a substantial tax break. The US representative for Walkton's home district has told Scott that, although she is lobbying hard for the bill and prospects for its passage are favorable, concern of the US Congress over the federal deficit could cause the tax bill to be voted down. Walkton Industries has not made any statements about a change in dividend policy. Scott writes in his research report, "We expect Walkton's stock price to rise by at least US$8.00 a share by the end of the year because the dividend will increase by US$1.50 a share. Investors buying the stock at the current time should expect to realize a total return of at least 15% on the stock." According to the Standards:

- **A.** Scott violated the Standards because he used material inside information.
- **B.** Scott violated the Standards because he failed to separate opinion from fact.
- **C.** Scott violated the Standards by basing his research on uncertain predictions of future government action.

10. Which one of the following actions will help to ensure the fair treatment of brokerage firm clients when a new investment recommendation is made?

- **A.** Informing all people in the firm in advance that a recommendation is to be disseminated.
- **B.** Distributing recommendations to institutional clients prior to individual accounts.
- **C.** Minimizing the time between the decision and the dissemination of a recommendation.

11. The mosaic theory holds that an analyst:

- **A.** Violates the Code and Standards if the analyst fails to have knowledge of and comply with applicable laws.
- **B.** Can use material public information and nonmaterial nonpublic information in the analyst's analysis.
- **C.** Should use all available and relevant information in support of an investment recommendation.

12. Jurgen is a portfolio manager. One of her firm's clients has told Jurgen that he will compensate her beyond the compensation provided by her firm on the basis of the capital appreciation of his portfolio each year. Jurgen should:

- **A.** Turn down the additional compensation because it will result in conflicts with the interests of other clients' accounts.
- **B.** Turn down the additional compensation because it will create undue pressure on her to achieve strong short-term performance.

C. Obtain permission from her employer prior to accepting the compensation arrangement.

13. One of the discretionary accounts managed by Farnsworth is the Jones Corporation employee profit-sharing plan. Jones, the company president, recently asked Farnsworth to vote the shares in the profit-sharing plan in favor of the slate of directors nominated by Jones Corporation and against the directors sponsored by a dissident stockholder group. Farnsworth does not want to lose this account because he directs all the account's trades to a brokerage firm that provides Farnsworth with useful information about tax-free investments. Although this information is not of value in managing the Jones Corporation account, it does help in managing several other accounts. The brokerage firm providing this information also offers the lowest commissions for trades and provides best execution. Farnsworth investigates the director issue, concludes that the management-nominated slate is better for the long-run performance of the company than the dissident group's slate, and votes accordingly. Farnsworth:

    A. Violated the Standards in voting the shares in the manner requested by Jones but not in directing trades to the brokerage firm.

    B. Did not violate the Standards in voting the shares in the manner requested by Jones or in directing trades to the brokerage firm.

    C. Violated the Standards in directing trades to the brokerage firm but not in voting the shares as requested by Jones.

14. Brown works for an investment counseling firm. Green, a new client of the firm, is meeting with Brown for the first time. Green used another counseling firm for financial advice for years, but she has switched her account to Brown's firm. After spending a few minutes getting acquainted, Brown explains to Green that she has discovered a highly undervalued stock that offers large potential gains. She recommends that Green purchase the stock. Brown has committed a violation of the Standards. What should she have done differently?

    A. Brown should have determined Green's needs, objectives, and tolerance for risk before making a recommendation of any type of security.

    B. Brown should have thoroughly explained the characteristics of the company to Green, including the characteristics of the industry in which the company operates.

    C. Brown should have explained her qualifications, including her education, training, and experience and the meaning of the CFA designation.

15. Grey recommends the purchase of a mutual fund that invests solely in long-term US Treasury bonds. He makes the following statements to his clients:

    i. "The payment of the bonds is guaranteed by the US government; therefore, the default risk of the bonds is virtually zero."

    ii. "If you invest in the mutual fund, you will earn a 10% rate of return each year for the next several years based on historical performance of the market."

    Did Grey's statements violate the CFA Institute Code and Standards?

    A. Neither statement violated the Code and Standards.

    B. Only statement I violated the Code and Standards.

C. Only statement II violated the Code and Standards.

16. Anderb, a portfolio manager for XYZ Investment Management Company—a registered investment organization that advises investment firms and private accounts—was promoted to that position three years ago. Bates, her supervisor, is responsible for reviewing Anderb's portfolio account transactions and her required monthly reports of personal stock transactions. Anderb has been using Jonelli, a broker, almost exclusively for brokerage transactions for the portfolio account. For securities in which Jonelli's firm makes a market, Jonelli has been giving Anderb lower prices for personal purchases and higher prices for personal sales than Jonelli gives to Anderb's portfolio accounts and other investors. Anderb has been filing monthly reports with Bates only for those months in which she has no personal transactions, which is about every fourth month. Which of the following is *most likely* to be a violation of the Code and Standards?

    A. Anderb failed to disclose to her employer her personal transactions.

    B. Anderb owned the same securities as those of her clients.

    C. Bates allowed Anderb to use Jonelli as her broker for personal trades.

17. Which of the following is a correct statement of a member's or candidate's duty under the Code and Standards?

    A. In the absence of specific applicable law or other regulatory requirements, the Code and Standards govern the member's or candidate's actions.

    B. A member or candidate is required to comply only with applicable local laws, rules, regulations, or customs, even though the Code and Standards may impose a higher degree of responsibility or a higher duty on the member or candidate.

    C. A member or candidate who trades securities in a securities market where no applicable local laws or stock exchange rules regulate the use of material nonpublic information may take investment action based on material nonpublic information.

18. Ward is scheduled to visit the corporate headquarters of Evans Industries. Ward expects to use the information he obtains there to complete his research report on Evans stock. Ward learns that Evans plans to pay all of Ward's expenses for the trip, including costs of meals, hotel room, and air transportation. Which of the following actions would be the *best* course for Ward to take under the Code and Standards?

    A. Accept the expense-paid trip and write an objective report.

    B. Pay for all travel expenses, including costs of meals and incidental items.

    C. Accept the expense-paid trip but disclose the value of the services accepted in the report.

19. Which of the following statements is *correct* under the Code and Standards?

    A. CFA Institute members and candidates are prohibited from undertaking independent practice in competition with their employer.

    B. Written consent from the employer is necessary to permit independent practice that could result in compensation or other benefits in competition with a member's or candidate's employer.

C. Members and candidates are prohibited from making arrangements or preparations to go into a competitive business before terminating their relationship with their employer.

20. Smith is a financial analyst with XYZ Brokerage Firm. She is preparing a purchase recommendation on JNI Corporation. Which of the following situations is *most likely* to represent a conflict of interest for Smith that would have to be disclosed?

    A. Smith frequently purchases items produced by JNI.

    B. XYZ holds for its own account a substantial common stock position in JNI.

    C. Smith's brother-in-law is a supplier to JNI.

21. Michelieu tells a prospective client, "I may not have a long-term track record yet, but I'm sure that you'll be very pleased with my recommendations and service. In the three years that I've been in the business, my equity-oriented clients have averaged a total return of more than 26% a year." The statement is true, but Michelieu only has a few clients, and one of his clients took a large position in a penny stock (against Michelieu's advice) and realized a huge gain. This large return caused the average of all of Michelieu's clients to exceed 26% a year. Without this one investment, the average gain would have been 8% a year. Has Michelieu violated the Standards?

    A. No, because Michelieu is not promising that he can earn a 26% return in the future.

    B. No, because the statement is a true and accurate description of Michelieu's track record.

    C. Yes, because the statement misrepresents Michelieu's track record.

22. An investment banking department of a brokerage firm often receives material nonpublic information that could have considerable value if used in advising the firm's brokerage clients. In order to conform to the Code and Standards, which one of the following is the best policy for the brokerage firm?

    A. Permanently prohibit both "buy" and "sell" recommendations of the stocks of clients of the investment banking department.

    B. Establish physical and informational barriers within the firm to prevent the exchange of information between the investment banking and brokerage operations.

    C. Monitor the exchange of information between the investment banking department and the brokerage operation.

23. Stewart has been hired by Goodner Industries, Inc., to manage its pension fund. Stewart's duty of loyalty, prudence, and care is owed to:

    A. The management of Goodner.

    B. The participants and beneficiaries of Goodner's pension plan.

    C. The shareholders of Goodner.

24. Which of the following statements is a stated purpose of disclosure in Standard

VI(C)–Referral Fees?

- **A.** Disclosure will allow the client to request discounted service fees.
- **B.** Disclosure will help the client evaluate any possible partiality shown in the recommendation of services.
- **C.** Disclosure means advising a prospective client about the referral arrangement once a formal client relationship has been established.

25. Rose, a portfolio manager for a local investment advisory firm, is planning to sell a portion of his personal investment portfolio to cover the costs of his child's academic tuition. Rose wants to sell a portion of his holdings in Household Products, but his firm recently upgraded the stock to "strong buy." Which of the following describes Rose's options under the Code and Standards?

- **A.** Based on his firm's "buy" recommendation, Rose cannot sell the shares because he would be improperly prospering from the inflated recommendation.
- **B.** Rose is free to sell his personal holdings once his firm is properly informed of his intentions.
- **C.** Rose can sell his personal holdings but only when a client of the firm places an order to buy shares of Household.

26. A former hedge fund manager, Jackman, has decided to launch a new private wealth management firm. From his prior experiences, he believes the new firm needs to achieve US$1 million in assets under management in the first year. Jackman offers a $10,000 incentive to any adviser who joins his firm with the minimum of $200,000 in committed investments. Jackman places notice of the opening on several industry web portals and career search sites. Which of the following is *correct* according to the Code and Standards?

- **A.** A member or candidate is eligible for the new position and incentive if he or she can arrange for enough current clients to switch to the new firm and if the member or candidate discloses the incentive fee.
- **B.** A member or candidate may not accept employment with the new firm because Jackman's incentive offer violates the Code and Standards.
- **C.** A member or candidate is not eligible for the new position unless he or she is currently unemployed because soliciting the clients of the member's or candidate's current employer is prohibited.

27. Carter works for Invest Today, a local asset management firm. A broker that provides Carter with proprietary research through client brokerage arrangements is offering a new trading service. The broker is offering low-fee, execution-only trades to complement its traditional full-service, execution-and-research trades. To entice Carter and other asset managers to send additional business its way, the broker will apply the commissions paid on the new service toward satisfying the brokerage commitment of the prior full-service arrangements. Carter has always been satisfied with the execution provided on the full-service trades, and the new low-fee trades are comparable to the fees of other brokers currently used for the accounts that prohibit soft dollar arrangements.

- **A.** Carter can trade for his accounts that prohibit soft dollar arrangements under the new low-fee trading scheme.

Practice Problems

    B. Carter cannot use the new trading scheme because the commissions are prohibited by the soft dollar restrictions of the accounts.

    C. Carter should trade only through the new low-fee scheme and should increase his trading volume to meet his required commission commitment.

28. Rule has worked as a portfolio manager for a large investment management firm for the past 10 years. Rule earned his CFA charter last year and has decided to open his own investment management firm. After leaving his current employer, Rule creates some marketing material for his new firm. He states in the material, "In earning the CFA charter, a highly regarded credential in the investment management industry, I further enhanced the portfolio management skills learned during my professional career. While completing the examination process in three consecutive years, I consistently received the highest possible scores on the topics of Ethics, Alternative Investments, and Portfolio Management." Has Rule violated Standard VII(B)–Reference to CFA Institute, the CFA Designation, and the CFA Program in his marketing material?

    A. Rule violated Standard VII(B) in stating that he completed the exams in three consecutive years.

    B. Rule violated Standard VII(B) in stating that he received the highest scores in the topics of Ethics, Alternative Investments, and Portfolio Management.

    C. Rule did not violate Standard VII(B).

29. Stafford is a portfolio manager for a specialized real estate mutual fund. Her firm clearly describes in the fund's prospectus its soft dollar policies. Stafford decides that entering the CFA Program will enhance her investment decision-making skill and decides to use the fund's soft dollar account to pay the registration and exam fees for the CFA Program. Which of the following statements is *most likely* correct?

    A. Stafford did not violate the Code and Standards because the prospectus informed investors of the fund's soft dollar policies.

    B. Stafford violated the Code and Standards because improving her investment skills is not a reasonable use of the soft dollar account.

    C. Stafford violated the Code and Standards because the CFA Program does not meet the definition of research allowed to be purchased with brokerage commissions.

30. Long has been asked to be the keynote speaker at an upcoming investment conference. The event is being hosted by one of the third-party investment managers currently used by his pension fund. The manager offers to cover all conference and travel costs for Long and make the conference registrations free for three additional members of his investment management team. To ensure that the conference obtains the best speakers, the host firm has arranged for an exclusive golf outing for the day following the conference on a local championship-caliber course. Which of the following is *least likely* to violate Standard I(B)?

    A. Long may accept only the offer to have his conference-related expenses paid by the host firm.

    B. Long may accept the offer to have his conference-related expenses paid and may attend the exclusive golf outing at the expense of the hosting firm.

C. Long may accept the entire package of incentives offered to speak at this conference.

31. Andrews, a private wealth manager, is conducting interviews for a new research analyst for his firm. One of the candidates is Wright, an analyst with a local investment bank. During the interview, while Wright is describing his analytical skills, he mentions a current merger in which his firm is acting as the adviser. Andrews has heard rumors of a possible merger between the two companies, but no releases have been made by the companies concerned. Which of the following actions by Andrews is *least likely* a violation of the Code and Standards?

    A. Waiting until the next day before trading on the information to allow time for it to become public.

    B. Notifying all investment managers in his firm of the new information so none of their clients are disadvantaged.

    C. Placing the securities mentioned as part of the merger on the firm's restricted trading list.

32. Pietro, president of Local Bank, has hired the bank's market maker, Vogt, to seek a merger partner. Local is currently listed on a stock exchange and has not reported that it is seeking strategic alternatives. Vogt has discussed the possibility of a merger with several firms, but they have all decided to wait until after the next period's financial data are available. The potential buyers believe the results will be worse than the results of prior periods and will allow them to pay less for Local Bank.

    Pietro wants to increase the likelihood of structuring a merger deal quickly. Which of the following actions would *most likely* be a violation of the Code and Standards?

    A. Pietro could instruct Local Bank to issue a press release announcing that it has retained Vogt to find a merger partner.

    B. Pietro could place a buy order for 2,000 shares (or four times the average weekly volume) through Vogt for his personal account.

    C. After confirming with Local's chief financial officer, Pietro could instruct Local to issue a press release reaffirming the firm's prior announced earnings guidance for the full fiscal year.

33. ABC Investment Management acquires a new, very large account with two concentrated positions. The firm's current policy is to add new accounts for the purpose of performance calculation after the first full month of management. Cupp is responsible for calculating the firm's performance returns. Before the end of the initial month, Cupp notices that one of the significant holdings of the new accounts is acquired by another company, causing the value of the investment to double. Because of this holding, Cupp decides to account for the new portfolio as of the date of transfer, thereby allowing ABC Investment to reap the positive impact of that month's portfolio return.

    A. Cupp did not violate the Code and Standards because the GIPS standards allow composites to be updated on the date of large external cash flows.

    B. Cupp did not violate the Code and Standards because companies are allowed to determine when to incorporate new accounts into their composite calculation.

Practice Problems

C. Cupp violated the Code and Standards because the inclusion of the new account produces an inaccurate calculation of the monthly results according to the firm's stated policies.

34. Cannan has been working from home on weekends and occasionally saves correspondence with clients and completed work on her home computer. Because of worsening market conditions, Cannan is one of several employees released by her firm. While Cannan is looking for a new job, she uses the files she saved at home to request letters of recommendation from former clients. She also provides to prospective clients some of the reports as examples of her abilities.

   A. Cannan violated the Code and Standards because she did not receive permission from her former employer to keep or use the files after her employment ended.

   B. Cannan did not violate the Code and Standards because the files were created and saved on her own time and computer.

   C. Cannan violated the Code and Standards because she is prohibited from saving files on her home computer.

35. Quinn sat for the Level III CFA exam this past weekend. He updates his resume with the following statement: "In finishing the CFA Program, I improved my skills related to researching investments and managing portfolios. I will be eligible for the CFA charter upon completion of the required work experience."

   A. Quinn violated the Code and Standards by claiming he improved his skills through the CFA Program.

   B. Quinn violated the Code and Standards by incorrectly stating that he is eligible for the CFA charter.

   C. Quinn did not violate the Code and Standards with his resume update.

36. During a round of golf, Rodriguez, chief financial officer of Mega Retail, mentions to Hart, a local investment adviser and long-time personal friend, that Mega is having an exceptional sales quarter. Rodriguez expects the results to be almost 10% above the current estimates. The next day, Hart initiates the purchase of a large stake in the local exchange-traded retail fund for her personal account.

   A. Hart violated the Code and Standards by investing in the exchange-traded fund that included Mega Retail.

   B. Hart did not violate the Code and Standards because she did not invest directly in securities of Mega Retail.

   C. Rodriguez did not violate the Code and Standards because the comments made to Hart were not intended to solicit an investment in Mega Retail.

37. Park is very frustrated after taking her Level II exam. While she was studying for the exam, to supplement the curriculum provided, she ordered and used study material from a third-party provider. Park believes the additional material focused her attention on specific topic areas that were not tested while ignoring other areas. She posts the following statement on the provider's discussion board: "I am very dissatisfied with your firm's CFA Program Level II material. I found the exam extremely difficult and myself unprepared for specific questions after using your product. How could your service provide such limited instructional resources on the analysis of inventories and taxes when the exam had multiple

questions about them? I will not recommend your products to other candidates."

- **A.** Park violated the Code and Standards by purchasing third-party review material.
- **B.** Park violated the Code and Standards by providing her opinion on the difficulty of the exam.
- **C.** Park violated the Code and Standards by providing specific information on topics tested on the exam.

38. Paper was recently terminated as one of a team of five managers of an equity fund. The fund had two value-focused managers and terminated one of them to reduce costs. In a letter sent to prospective employers, Paper presents, with written permission of the firm, the performance history of the fund to demonstrate his past success.

- **A.** Paper did not violate the Code and Standards.
- **B.** Paper violated the Code and Standards by claiming the performance of the entire fund as his own.
- **C.** Paper violated the Code and Standards by including the historical results of his prior employer.

39. Townsend was recently appointed to the board of directors of a youth golf program that is the local chapter of a national not-for-profit organization. The program is beginning a new fund-raising campaign to expand the number of annual scholarships it provides. Townsend believes many of her clients make annual donations to charity. The next week in her regular newsletter to all clients, she includes a small section discussing the fund-raising campaign and her position on the organization's board.

- **A.** Townsend did not violate the Code and Standards.
- **B.** Townsend violated the Code and Standards by soliciting donations from her clients through the newsletter.
- **C.** Townsend violated the Code and Standards by not getting approval of the organization before soliciting her clients.

SOLUTIONS

1. The correct answer is B. This question involves Standard III(B)–Fair Dealing. Smith disseminated a change in the stock recommendation to his clients but then received a request contrary to that recommendation from a client who probably had not yet received the recommendation. Prior to executing the order, Smith should take additional steps to ensure that the customer has received the change of recommendation. Answer A is incorrect because the client placed the order prior to receiving the recommendation and, therefore, does not have the benefit of Smith's most recent recommendation. Answer C is also incorrect; simply because the client request is contrary to the firm's recommendation does not mean a member can override a direct request by a client. After Smith contacts the client to ensure that the client has received the changed recommendation, if the client still wants to place a buy order for the shares, Smith is obligated to comply with the client's directive.

2. The correct answer is C. This question involves Standard III(A)–Loyalty, Prudence, and Care and the specific topic of soft dollars or soft commissions. Answer C is the correct choice because client brokerage commissions may not be directed to pay for the investment manager's operating expenses. Answer B describes how members and candidates should determine how to use brokerage commissions—that is, if the use is in the best interests of clients and is commensurate with the value of the services provided. Answer A describes a practice that is commonly referred to as "directed brokerage." Because brokerage is an asset of the client and is used to benefit the client, not the manager, such practice does not violate a duty of loyalty to the client. Members and candidates are obligated in all situations to disclose to clients their practices in the use of client brokerage commissions.

3. The correct answer is C. This question involves Standard VI(A)–Disclosure of Conflicts. The question establishes a conflict of interest in which an analyst, Jamison, is asked to write a research report on a company that is a client of the analyst's employer. In addition, two directors of the company are senior officers of Jamison's employer. Both facts establish that there are conflicts of interest that must be disclosed by Jamison in her research report. Answer B is incorrect because an analyst is not prevented from writing a report simply because of the special relationship the analyst's employer has with the company as long as that relationship is disclosed. Answer A is incorrect because whether or not Jamison expresses any opinions in the report is irrelevant to her duty to disclose a conflict of interest. Not expressing opinions does not relieve the analyst of the responsibility to disclose the special relationships between the two companies.

4. The correct answer is C. This question asks about compliance procedures relating to personal investments of members and candidates. The statement in answer C clearly conflicts with the recommended procedures in the *Standards of Practice Handbook*. Employers should compare personal transactions of employees with those of clients on a regular basis regardless of the existence of a requirement by any regulatory organization. Such comparisons ensure that employees' personal trades do not conflict with their duty to their clients, and the comparisons can be conducted in a confidential manner. The statement in answer A does not conflict with the procedures in the *Handbook*. Disclosure of such policies will give full information to clients regarding potential conflicts of interest on the part of those entrusted to manage their money. Answer B is incorrect because firms are encouraged to establish policies whereby employees clear their personal holdings

and transactions with their employers.

5. The correct answer is B. This question relates to Standard III(A)–Loyalty, Prudence, and Care and Standard III(E)–Preservation of Confidentiality. In this case, the member manages funds of a private endowment. Clients, who are, in this case, the trustees of the fund, must place some trust in members and candidates. Bronson cannot disclose confidential financial information to anyone without the permission of the fund, regardless of whether the disclosure may benefit the fund. Therefore, answer A is incorrect. Answer C is incorrect because Bronson must notify the fund and obtain the fund's permission before publicizing the information.

6. The correct answer is B. This question relates to Standard V(A)–Diligence and Reasonable Basis. The opinion of another financial analyst is not an adequate basis for Willier's action in changing the recommendation. Answer C is thus incorrect. So is answer A because, although it is true that members and candidates must distinguish between facts and opinions in recommendations, the question does not illustrate a violation of that nature. If the opinion overheard by Willier had sparked him to conduct additional research and investigation that justified a change of opinion, then a changed recommendation would be appropriate.

7. The correct answer is B. This question relates to Standard I(B)–Independence and Objectivity. When asked to change a recommendation on a company stock to gain business for the firm, the head of the brokerage unit must refuse in order to maintain his independence and objectivity in making recommendations. He must not yield to pressure by the firm's investment banking department. To avoid the appearance of a conflict of interest, the firm should discontinue issuing recommendations about the company. Answer A is incorrect; changing the recommendation in any manner that is contrary to the analyst's opinion violates the duty to maintain independence and objectivity. Answer C is incorrect because merely assigning a new analyst to decide whether the stock deserves a higher rating will not address the conflict of interest.

8. The correct answer is A. Standard VII(B)–Reference to CFA Institute, the CFA Designation, and the CFA Program is the subject of this question. The reference on Albert's business card implies that there is a "CFA Level II" designation; Tye merely indicates in promotional material that he is participating in the CFA Program and has completed Levels I and II. Candidates may not imply that there is some sort of partial designation earned after passing a level of the CFA exam. Therefore, Albert has violated Standard VII(B). Candidates may communicate that they are participating in the CFA Program, however, and may state the levels that they have completed. Therefore, Tye has not violated Standard VII(B).

9. The correct answer is B. This question relates to Standard V(B)–Communication with Clients and Prospective Clients. Scott has issued a research report stating that he expects the price of Walkton Industries stock to rise by US$8 a share "because the dividend will increase" by US$1.50 per share. He has made this statement knowing that the dividend will increase only if Congress enacts certain legislation, an uncertain prospect. By stating that the dividend will increase, Scott failed to separate fact from opinion.

The information regarding passage of legislation is not material nonpublic information because it is conjecture, and the question does not state whether the US representative gave Scott her opinion on the passage of the legislation in confidence. She could have been offering this opinion to anyone who asked. Therefore, statement A is incorrect. It may be acceptable to base a recommendation, in part, on an expectation of future events, even though they may be uncertain. Therefore, answer C is incorrect.

10. The correct answer is C. This question, which relates to Standard III(B)–Fair Dealing, tests the knowledge of the procedures that will assist members and candidates in treating clients fairly when making investment recommendations. The step listed in C will help ensure the fair treatment of clients. Answer A may have negative effects on the fair treatment of clients. The more people who know about a pending change, the greater the chance that someone will inform some clients before the information's release. The firm should establish policies that limit the number of people who are aware in advance that a recommendation is to be disseminated. Answer B, distributing recommendations to institutional clients before distributing them to individual accounts, discriminates among clients on the basis of size and class of assets and is a violation of Standard III(B).

11. The correct answer is B. This question deals with Standard II(A)–Material Nonpublic Information. The mosaic theory states that an analyst may use material public information and nonmaterial nonpublic information in creating a larger picture than shown by any individual piece of information and the conclusions the analyst reaches become material only after the pieces are assembled. Answers A and C are accurate statements relating to the Code and Standards but do not describe the mosaic theory.

12. The correct answer is C. This question involves Standard IV(B)–Additional Compensation Arrangements. The arrangement described in the question—whereby Jurgen would be compensated beyond the compensation provided by her firm, on the basis of an account's performance—is not a violation of the Standards as long as Jurgen discloses the arrangement in writing to her employer and obtains permission from her employer prior to entering into the arrangement. Answers A and B are incorrect; although the private compensation arrangement could conflict with the interests of other clients and lead to short-term performance pressures, members and candidates may enter into such agreements as long as they have disclosed the arrangements to their employer and obtained permission for the arrangement from their employer.

13. The correct answer is B. This question relates to Standard III(A)–Loyalty, Prudence, and Care—specifically, a member's or candidate's responsibility for voting proxies and the use of client brokerage. According to the facts stated in the question, Farnsworth did not violate Standard III(A). Although the company president asked Farnsworth to vote the shares of the Jones Corporation profit-sharing plan a certain way, Farnsworth investigated the issue and concluded, independently, the best way to vote. Therefore, even though his decision coincided with the wishes of the company president, Farnsworth is not in violation of his responsibility to be loyal and to provide care to his clients. In this case, the participants and the beneficiaries of the profit-sharing plan are the clients, not the company's management. Had Farnsworth not investigated the issue or had he yielded to the president's wishes and voted for a slate of directors that he had determined was not in the best interest of the company, Farnsworth would have violated his responsibilities to the beneficiaries of the plan. In addition, because the brokerage firm provides the lowest commissions and best execution for securities transactions, Farnsworth has met his obligations to the client in using this brokerage firm. It does not matter that the brokerage firm also provides research information that is not useful for the account generating the commission because Farnsworth is not paying extra money of the client's for that information.

14. The correct answer is A. In this question, Brown is providing investment recommendations before making inquiries about the client's financial situation, investment experience, or investment objectives. Brown is thus violating Standard

III(C)–Suitability. Answers B and C provide examples of information members and candidates should discuss with their clients at the outset of the relationship, but these answers do not constitute a complete list of those factors. Answer A is the best answer.

15. The correct answer is C. This question involves Standard I(C)–Misrepresentation. Statement I is a factual statement that discloses to clients and prospects accurate information about the terms of the investment instrument. Statement II, which guarantees a specific rate of return for a mutual fund, is an opinion stated as a fact and, therefore, violates Standard I(C). If statement II were rephrased to include a qualifying statement, such as "in my opinion, investors may earn . . . ," it would not be in violation of the Standards.

16. The correct answer is A. This question involves three of the Standards. Anderb, the portfolio manager, has been obtaining more favorable prices for her personal securities transactions than she gets for her clients, which is a breach of Standard III(A)–Loyalty, Prudence, and Care. In addition, she violated Standard I(D)–Misconduct by failing to adhere to company policy and by hiding her personal transactions from her firm. Anderb's supervisor, Bates, violated Standard IV(C)–Responsibilities of Supervisors; although the company had requirements for reporting personal trading, Bates failed to adequately enforce those requirements. Answer B does not represent a violation because Standard VI(B)–Priority of Transactions requires that personal trading in a security be conducted after the trading in that security of clients and the employer. The Code and Standards do not prohibit owning such investments, although firms may establish policies that limit the investment opportunities of members and candidates. Answer C does not represent a violation because the Code and Standards do not contain a prohibition against employees using the same broker for their personal accounts that they use for their client accounts. This arrangement should be disclosed to the employer so that the employer may determine whether a conflict of interest exists.

17. The correct answer is A because this question relates to Standard I(A)–Knowledge of the Law—specifically, global application of the Code and Standards. Members and candidates who practice in multiple jurisdictions may be subject to various securities laws and regulations. If applicable law is more strict than the requirements of the Code and Standards, members and candidates must adhere to applicable law; otherwise, members and candidates must adhere to the Code and Standards. Therefore, answer A is correct. Answer B is incorrect because members and candidates must adhere to the higher standard set by the Code and Standards if local applicable law is less strict. Answer C is incorrect because when no applicable law exists, members and candidates are required to adhere to the Code and Standards, and the Code and Standards prohibit the use of material nonpublic information.

18. The correct answer is B. The best course of action under Standard I(B)–Independence and Objectivity is to avoid a conflict of interest whenever possible. Therefore, for Ward to pay for all his expenses is the correct answer. Answer C details a course of action in which the conflict would be disclosed, but the solution is not as appropriate as avoiding the conflict of interest. Answer A would not be the best course because it would not remove the appearance of a conflict of interest; even though the report would not be affected by the reimbursement of expenses, it could appear to be.

19. The correct answer is B. Under Standard IV(A)–Loyalty, members and candidates may undertake independent practice that may result in compensation or other benefit in competition with their employer as long as they obtain consent

from their employer. Answer C is not consistent with the Standards because the Standards allow members and candidates to make arrangements or preparations to go into competitive business as long as those arrangements do not interfere with their duty to their current employer. Answer A is not consistent with the Standards because the Standards do not include a complete prohibition against undertaking independent practice.

20. The correct answer is B. This question involves Standard VI(A)–Disclosure of Conflicts—specifically, the holdings of an analyst's employer in company stock. Answers A and C do not describe conflicts of interest that Smith would have to disclose. Answer A describes the use of a firm's products, which would not be a required disclosure. In answer C, the relationship between the analyst and the company through a relative is so tangential that it does not create a conflict of interest necessitating disclosure.

21. The correct answer is C. This question relates to Standard I(C)–Misrepresentation. Although Michelieu's statement about the total return of his clients' accounts on average may be technically true, it is misleading because the majority of the gain resulted from one client's large position taken against Michelieu's advice. Therefore, this statement misrepresents the investment performance the member is responsible for. He has not taken steps to present a fair, accurate, and complete presentation of performance. Answer B is thus incorrect. Answer A is incorrect because although Michelieu is not guaranteeing future results, his words are still a misrepresentation of his performance history.

22. The correct answer is B. The best policy to prevent violation of Standard II(A)–Material Nonpublic Information is the establishment of firewalls in a firm to prevent exchange of insider information. The physical and informational barrier of a firewall between the investment banking department and the brokerage operation prevents the investment banking department from providing information to analysts on the brokerage side who may be writing recommendations on a company stock. Prohibiting recommendations of the stock of companies that are clients of the investment banking department is an alternative, but answer A states that this prohibition would be permanent, which is not the best answer. Once an offering is complete and the material nonpublic information obtained by the investment banking department becomes public, resuming publishing recommendations on the stock is not a violation of the Code and Standards because the information of the investment banking department no longer gives the brokerage operation an advantage in writing the report. Answer C is incorrect because no exchange of information should be occurring between the investment banking department and the brokerage operation, so monitoring of such exchanges is not an effective compliance procedure for preventing the use of material nonpublic information.

23. The correct answer is B. Under Standard III(A)–Loyalty, Prudence, and Care, members and candidates who manage a company's pension fund owe these duties to the participants and beneficiaries of the pension plan, not the management of the company or the company's shareholders.

24. The correct answer is B. Answer B gives one of the two primary reasons listed in the *Handbook* for disclosing referral fees to clients under Standard VI(C)–Referral Fees. (The other is to allow clients and employers to evaluate the full cost of the services.) Answer A is incorrect because Standard VI(C) does not require members or candidates to discount their fees when they receive referral fees. Answer C is inconsistent with Standard VI(C) because disclosure of referral fees, to be effective, should be made to prospective clients before entering into a formal

client relationship with them.

25. The correct answer is B. Standard VI(B)–Priority of Transactions does not limit transactions of company employees that differ from current recommendations as long as the sale does not disadvantage current clients. Thus, answer A is incorrect. Answer C is incorrect because the Standard does not require the matching of personal and client trades.

26. Answer C is correct. Standard IV(A)–Loyalty discusses activities permissible to members and candidates when they are leaving their current employer; soliciting clients is strictly prohibited. Thus, answer A is inconsistent with the Code and Standards even with the required disclosure. Answer B is incorrect because the offer does not directly violate the Code and Standards. There may be out-of-work members and candidates who can arrange the necessary commitments without violating the Code and Standards.

27. Answer A is correct. The question relates to Standard III(A)–Loyalty, Prudence, and Care. Carter believes the broker offers effective execution at a fee that is comparable with those of other brokers, so he is free to use the broker for all accounts. Answer B is incorrect because the accounts that prohibit soft dollar arrangements do not want to fund the purchase of research by Carter. The new trading scheme does not incur additional commissions from clients, so it would not go against the prohibitions. Answer C is incorrect because Carter should not incur unnecessary or excessive "churning" of the portfolios (excessive trading) for the purpose of meeting the brokerage commitments of soft dollar arrangements.

28. Answer B is correct according to Standard VII(B)–Reference to CFA Institute, the CFA Designation, and the CFA Program. CFA Program candidates do not receive their actual scores on the exam. Topic and subtopic results are grouped into three broad categories, and the exam is graded only as "pass" or "fail." Although a candidate may have achieved a topical score of "above 70%," she or he cannot factually state that she or he received the highest possible score because that information is not reported. Thus, answer C is incorrect. Answer A is incorrect as long as the member or candidate actually completed the exams consecutively. Standard VII(B) does not prohibit the communication of factual information about completing the CFA Program in three consecutive years.

29. Answer C is correct. According to Standard III(A)–Loyalty, Prudence, and Care, the CFA Program would be considered a personal or firm expense and should not be paid for with the fund's brokerage commissions. Soft dollar accounts should be used only to purchase research services that directly assist the investment manager in the investment decision-making process, not to assist the management of the firm or to further education. Thus, answer A is incorrect. Answer B is incorrect because the reasonableness of how the money is used is not an issue; the issue is that educational expense is not research.

30. Answer A is correct. Standard I(B)–Independence and Objectivity emphasizes the need for members and candidates to maintain their independence and objectivity. Best practices dictate that firms adopt a strict policy not to accept compensation for travel arrangements. At times, however, accepting paid travel would not compromise one's independence and objectivity. Answers B and C are incorrect because the added benefits—free conference admission for additional staff members and an exclusive golf retreat for the speaker—could be viewed as inducements related to the firm's working arrangements and not solely related to the speaking engagement. Should Long wish to bring other team members or participate in the golf outing, he or his firm should be responsible for the associ-

ated fees.

31. Answer C is correct. The guidance to Standard II(A)–Material Nonpublic Information recommends adding securities to the firm's restricted list when the firm has or may have material nonpublic information. By adding these securities to this list, Andrews would uphold this standard. Because waiting until the next day will not ensure that news of the merger is made public, answer A is incorrect. Negotiations may take much longer between the two companies, and the merger may never happen. Andrews must wait until the information is disseminated to the market before he trades on that information. Answer B is incorrect because Andrews should not disclose the information to other managers; no trading is allowed on material nonpublic information.

32. Answer B is correct. Through placing a personal purchase order that is significantly greater than the average volume, Pietro is violating Standard IIB–Market Manipulation. He is attempting to manipulate an increase in the share price and thus bring a buyer to the negotiating table. The news of a possible merger and confirmation of the firm's earnings guidance may also have positive effects on the price of Local Bank, but Pietro's actions in instructing the release of the information does not represent a violation through market manipulation. Announcements of this nature are common and practical to keep investors informed. Thus, answers A and C are incorrect.

33. Answer C is correct. Cupp violated Standard III(D)–Performance Presentations when he deviated from the firm's stated policies solely to capture the gain from the holding being acquired. Answer A is incorrect because the firm does not claim GIPS compliance and the GIPS standards require external cash flows to be treated in a consistent manner with the firm's documented policies. Answer B is incorrect because the firm does not state that it is updating its composite policies. If such a change were to occur, all cash flows for the month would have to be reviewed to ensure their consistent treatment under the new policy.

34. Answer A is correct. According to Standard V(C)–Record Retention, Cannan needed the permission of her employer to maintain the files at home after her employment ended. Without that permission, she should have deleted the files. All files created as part of a member's or candidate's professional activity are the property of the firm, even those created outside normal work hours. Thus, answer B is incorrect. Answer C is incorrect because the Code and Standards do not prohibit using one's personal computer to complete work for one's employer.

35. Answer B is correct. According to Standard VII(B)–Reference to CFA Institute, the CFA Designation, and the CFA Program, Quinn cannot claim to have finished the CFA Program or be eligible for the CFA charter until he officially learns that he has passed the Level III exam. Until the results for the most recent exam are released, those who sat for the exam should continue to refer to themselves as "candidates." Thus, answer C is incorrect. Answer A is incorrect because members and candidates may discuss areas of practice in which they believe the CFA Program improved their personal skills.

36. Answer A is correct. Hart's decision to invest in the retail fund appears directly correlated with Rodriguez's statement about the successful quarter of Mega Retail and thus violates Standard II(A)–Material Nonpublic Information. Rodriguez's information would be considered material because it would influence the share price of Mega Retail and probably influence the price of the entire exchange-traded retail fund. Thus, answer B is incorrect. Answer C is also incorrect because Rodriguez shared information that was both material and nonpublic. Company officers regularly have such knowledge about their firms, which is

not a violation. The sharing of such information, however, even in a conversation between friends, does violate Standard II(A).

37. Answer C is correct. Standard VII(A)–Conduct as Members and Candidates in the CFA Program prohibits providing information to candidates or the public that is considered confidential to the CFA Program. In revealing that questions related to the analysis of inventories and analysis of taxes were on the exam, Park has violated this standard. Answer B is incorrect because the guidance for the standard explicitly acknowledges that members and candidates are allowed to offer their opinions about the CFA Program. Answer A is incorrect because candidates are not prohibited from using outside resources.

38. Answer B is correct. Paper has violated Standard III(D)–Performance Presentation by not disclosing that he was part of a team of managers that achieved the results shown. If he had also included the return of the portion he directly managed, he would not have violated the standard. Thus, answer A is incorrect. Answer C is incorrect because Paper received written permission from his prior employer to include the results.

39. Answer A is correct. Townsend has not provided any information about her clients to the leaders or managers of the golf program; thus, she has not violated Standard III(E)–Preservation of Confidentiality. Providing contact information about her clients for a direct-mail solicitation would have been a violation. Answer B is incorrect because the notice in the newsletter does not violate Standard III(E). Answer C is incorrect because the golf program's fund-raising campaign had already begun, so discussing the opportunity to donate was appropriate.

LEARNING MODULE 4

Introduction to the Global Investment Performance Standards (GIPS)

LEARNING OUTCOME

Mastery	The candidate should be able to:
☐	explain why the GIPS standards were created, who can claim compliance, and who benefits from compliance
☐	describe the key concepts of the GIPS Standards for Firms
☐	explain the purpose of composites in performance reporting
☐	describe the fundamentals of compliance, including the recommendations of the GIPS standards with respect to the definition of the firm and the firm's definition of discretion
☐	describe the concept of independent verification

INTRODUCTION

The objective of this reading is to provide candidates with an orientation to the GIPS standards. It explains why the GIPS standards were created, who can claim compliance, and who benefits from compliance. It also covers key concepts of the GIPS standards—composites, the definition of the firm, and the definition of investment discretion. Finally, the reading briefly discusses the purpose and benefits of verification. Upon completion of this reading, candidates should appreciate the benefits of an industry-wide set of standards for calculating and presenting investment performance based on the principles of fair representation and full disclosure.

The 2020 edition of the GIPS standards has three chapters:

1. GIPS Standards for Firms
2. GIPS Standards for Asset Owners
3. GIPS Standards for Verifiers

Organizations that compete for business must comply with the GIPS Standards for Firms.

Candidates are also responsible for reading the sections of the GIPS Standards for Firms specifically referenced in this reading. A complete copy of the 2020 GIPS Standards for Firms can be found here: https://www.cfainstitute.org/en/ethics/codes/gips-standards/firms.

2. WHY WERE THE GIPS STANDARDS CREATED, WHO CAN CLAIM COMPLIANCE, & WHO BENEFITS FROM COMPLIANCE?

☐ explain why the GIPS standards were created, who can claim compliance, and who benefits from compliance

☐ describe the key concepts of the GIPS Standards for Firms

The mission of the GIPS standards is to promote ethics and integrity and instill trust through the use of the GIPS standards by achieving universal demand for compliance by asset owners, adoption by asset managers, and support from regulators for the ultimate benefit of the global investment community.

Institutions and individuals are constantly scrutinizing past investment performance returns in search of the best manager to achieve their investment objectives.

In the past, the investment community had great difficulty making meaningful comparisons on the basis of accurate investment performance data. Several performance measurement practices hindered the comparability of performance returns from one firm to another, while others called into question the accuracy and credibility of performance reporting overall. Misleading practices included:

- *Representative Accounts*: Selecting a top-performing portfolio to represent the firm's overall investment results for a specific mandate.
- *Survivorship Bias*: Presenting an "average" performance history that *excludes* portfolios whose poor performance was weak enough to result in termination of the firm.
- *Varying Time Periods*: Presenting performance for a selected time period during which the mandate produced excellent returns or out-performed its benchmark—making comparison with other firms' results difficult or impossible.

Making a valid comparison of investment performance among even the most ethical investment management firms was problematic. For example, a pension fund seeking to hire an investment management firm might receive proposals from several firms, possibly from different countries, all using different methodologies for calculating their results.

The GIPS standards are a practitioner-driven set of ethical principles that establish a standardized, industry-wide approach for investment firms to follow in calculating and presenting their historical investment results to prospective clients. The GIPS standards ensure fair representation and full disclosure of investment performance. In other words, the GIPS standards lead investment management firms to avoid misrepresentations of performance and to communicate all relevant information that prospective clients and investors should know in order to evaluate past results.

The objectives of the GIPS standards are as follows:

- Promote investor interests and instill investor confidence.
- Ensure accurate and consistent data.
- Obtain worldwide acceptance of a single standard for calculating and presenting performance.
- Promote fair, global competition among investment firms.
- Promote industry self-regulation on a global basis.

Who Can Claim Compliance?

Any firm that *manages actual assets* may choose to comply with the GIPS standards. Consultants cannot make a claim of compliance unless they actually manage the assets for which they are making a claim of compliance. They can claim to endorse the GIPS standards and/or require that their investment managers comply with the GIPS standards. Similarly, software (and the vendors who supply software) cannot be "compliant." Software can assist firms in achieving compliance with the GIPS standards (e.g., by calculating performance in a manner consistent with the calculation requirements of the GIPS standards), but only a firm managing assets can claim compliance once the firm has satisfied all applicable requirements of the GIPS standards.

Asset owners may comply with the GIPS standards in the same way as firms if they compete for business. If they don't compete for business but report their performance to an oversight body, asset owners may choose to comply with the GIPS Standards for Asset Owners.

Compliance is a firm-wide process that cannot be achieved on a single product or composite. A firm has only two options with regard to compliance with the GIPS standards:

1. fully comply with *all* requirements of the GIPS standards and claim compliance through the use of the GIPS Compliance Statement; or
2. not comply with all requirements of the GIPS standards and not claim compliance with, or make any reference to, the GIPS standards.

Complying with the GIPS standards is voluntary. Compliance with the GIPS standards is not typically required by legal or regulatory authorities.

Who Benefits from Compliance?

The GIPS standards benefit firms and their prospective clients and investors, as well as asset owners and their oversight bodies.

- By choosing to comply with the GIPS standards, firms assure prospective clients and investors that the historical track record they report is both complete and fairly presented. Compliance enables the GIPS-compliant firm to participate in competitive bids against other compliant firms throughout the world. Achieving and maintaining compliance may also strengthen the firm's internal controls over performance-related policies and procedures.

- Prospective clients and investors have a greater level of confidence in the integrity of performance presentations of a GIPS-compliant firm and can more easily compare performance presentations from different investment management firms. The GIPS standards certainly do not eliminate the need for in-depth due diligence on the part of the client or investor, but compliance with the Standards enhances the credibility of investment management firms that have chosen to undertake this responsibility.

- Asset owners provide performance information to their oversight bodies that allows them to make investment decisions and evaluate the performance of the funds under their supervision. Particularly where asset owners require their external managers to comply with the GIPS standards, reporting to the oversight body using the same principles facilitates the understanding of the sources of risk and excess return in the funds under supervision.

- **Key Concepts**
- Key concepts of the GIPS standards that apply to firms include the following:

- The GIPS standards are ethical standards for investment performance presentation to ensure fair representation and full disclosure of investment performance.
- Meeting the objectives of fair representation and full disclosure is likely to require more than simply adhering to the minimum requirements of the GIPS standards. Firms should also adhere to the recommendations to achieve best practice in the calculation and presentation of performance.
- Firms must comply with all applicable requirements of the GIPS standards, including any Guidance Statements, interpretations, and Questions & Answers (Q&As) published by CFA Institute and the GIPS standards governing bodies.
- The GIPS standards do not address every aspect of performance measurement and will continue to evolve over time to address additional areas of investment performance.
- The GIPS standards require firms to create and maintain composites for all strategies for which the firm manages segregated accounts or markets to segregated accounts. Firms must include all actual, fee-paying, discretionary segregated accounts in at least one composite defined by investment mandate, objective, or strategy. Pooled funds must also be included in any composite for which the pooled fund meets the composite definition. Firms must maintain and make available information about all of the strategies they manage using composites or pooled funds. These requirements prevent firms from cherry-picking their best performance.
- The GIPS standards rely on the integrity of input data, the quality of which is critical to creating accurate performance presentations. The underlying valuations of portfolio holdings drive performance. It is essential for these and other inputs to be accurate. The GIPS standards require firms to adhere to certain calculation methodologies to allow for comparability across firms.

Please read the Preface and the Introduction to the Global Investment Performance Standards for Firms for additional insight into the history and purpose of the GIPS standards.

3. COMPOSITES

explain the purpose of composites in performance reporting

One of the key concepts of the GIPS standards is the required use of composites. A composite is an aggregation of one or more portfolios managed according to a similar investment mandate, objective, or strategy. The requirement to create, use, and maintain composites is designed to prevent firms from cherry-picking—using the best-performing accounts to represent the performance of an investment strategy. A composite must include all actual, fee-paying, discretionary portfolios managed in accordance with the same investment mandate, objective, or strategy. For example, if a GIPS-compliant firm presents its track record for a Global Equity Composite (the Composite), the Composite must include all fee-paying portfolios that are managed, or have historically been managed, in the firm's Global Equity strategy. The firm may not subjectively select which Global Equity portfolios will be included in or excluded from the calculation and presentation of the Global Equity Composite.

The determination of which portfolios to include in the Composite should be done according to pre-established criteria (i.e., on an *ex ante* basis), not after the fact. This prevents a firm from including only their best-performing portfolios in the Composite.

A firm that claims compliance must include all fee-paying, discretionary segregated accounts in at least one composite. A firm must also include all fee-paying discretionary pooled funds in any composite for which the pooled funds meet the composite definition.

Please read Section 3.A. of the GIPS Standards for Firms on composites.

FUNDAMENTALS OF COMPLIANCE

☐ describe the fundamentals of compliance, including the recommendations of the GIPS standards with respect to the definition of the firm and the firm's definition of discretion

Several core principles create the foundation for the GIPS standards, including properly defining the firm, providing GIPS Reports to all prospective clients and certain pooled fund prospective investors, adhering to applicable laws and regulations, and ensuring that information presented is not false or misleading. Two important issues that a firm must consider when becoming compliant with the GIPS standards are the definition of the firm and the firm's definition of discretion. The definition of the firm is the foundation for firm-wide compliance and creates defined boundaries whereby total firm assets can be determined.

The GIPS standards state "The firm should adopt the broadest, most meaningful definition of the firm. The scope of this definition should include all geographical (country, regional, etc.) offices operating under the same brand name, regardless of the actual name of the individual investment management company."

The firm's definition of discretion establishes criteria to judge which portfolios must be included in a composite and is based on the firm's ability to implement its investment strategies. If documented client-imposed restrictions interfere with the implementation of the intended strategy to the extent that the portfolio is no longer representative of the strategy, the firm may determine that the portfolio is non-discretionary. Non-discretionary portfolios must not be included in a firm's composites.

Section 1 of the 2020 GIPS Standards for Firms addresses the fundamentals of compliance in more detail.

VERIFICATION

☐ describe the concept of independent verification

Firms that claim compliance with the GIPS standards are responsible for their claim of compliance and for maintaining that compliance. That is, firms self-regulate their claim of compliance. Once a firm claims compliance with the GIPS standards, it may voluntarily hire an independent third party to perform a verification in order to increase confidence in the firm's claim of compliance. Verification may also increase the knowledge of the firm's performance measurement team and improve the consistency and quality of the firm's GIPS standards-related performance information.

Verification is a process by which an independent verification firm (verifier) conducts testing of a firm on a firm-wide basis in accordance with the required verification procedures of the GIPS standards. Verification provides assurance on whether the firm's policies and procedures related to composite and pooled fund maintenance, as well as the calculation, presentation, and distribution of performance, have been designed in compliance with the GIPS standards and have been implemented on a firm-wide basis.

Verification is performed with respect to an entire firm, not on specific composites or pooled funds. Verification does not ensure the accuracy of any specific performance report.

Verification must be performed by an independent third party. A firm cannot perform its own verification.

Third-party verification brings additional credibility to a firm's claim of compliance. A verified firm may provide existing and prospective clients and investors with greater assurance about its claim of compliance with the GIPS standards. Verification may also provide improved internal processes and procedures as well as marketing advantages to the firm.

PRACTICE PROBLEMS

1. A firm that does not adopt the GIPS standards could mischaracterize its overall performance by presenting a performance history:
   A. that includes terminated portfolios.
   B. composed of a single top-performing portfolio.
   C. for an investment mandate over all periods since the firm's inception.

2. Which of the following statements regarding GIPS compliance is correct?
   A. Asset owners that manage assets can claim compliance with the GIPS standards.
   B. Software that calculates performance in a manner consistent with the GIPS standards can claim compliance with the GIPS standards.
   C. Firms can comply with the GIPS standards by limiting their compliance claims to the provisions they have chosen to follow.

3. Each composite of a GIPS-compliant firm must consist of:
   A. multiple portfolios.
   B. portfolios selected on an *ex post* basis.
   C. portfolios managed according to a similar investment mandate, objective, or strategy.

4. Verification:
   A. must be performed on a firm-wide basis.
   B. may be provided by the firm's compliance department.
   C. ensures the accuracy of a specific composite presentation.

5. Which of the following *cannot* claim compliance with the GIPS standards?
   A. Investment management firms
   B. Software vendors
   C. Private pension funds

6. Which of the following is an abusive practice that the GIPS standards were designed to avoid?
   A. Presenting performance results that include terminated portfolios
   B. Comparing performance results with an appropriate benchmark
   C. Presenting performance results for select time periods

7. The process of testing a firm or asset owner that claims compliance with the

GIPS standards is referred to as a:

    A. verification.

    B. validation.

    C. certification.

8. Firms that claim compliance with the GIPS standards are required to receive a verification:

    A. before the firm can initially claim compliance.

    B. after the firm has claimed compliance for 12 months.

    C. never; verification is not required.

9. Which of the following is not a commonly perceived benefit of the GIPS standards?

    A. Comparability of results across managers that claim compliance

    B. Adherence to regulatory requirements

    C. Increased confidence by investors and beneficiaries

10. When defining the firm, the GIPS standards recommend that firms should:

    A. adopt the narrowest, most relevant definition of the firm.

    B. adopt the broadest, most meaningful definition of the firm.

    C. exclude offices operating under different brand names.

11. A composite return reflects the performance of:

    A. all portfolios managed by the firm, regardless of investment strategy.

    B. all discretionary portfolios that meet the composite definition.

    C. all discretionary and non-discretionary portfolios that meet the composite definition.

SOLUTIONS

1. B is correct. Selecting a top-performing portfolio to represent a firm's overall investment results for a specific mandate, also known as using representative accounts, is a misleading practice that is not allowed under the GIPS standards. A is incorrect because including terminated portfolios is consistent with the GIPS standards. If the firm instead presented a performance history that excludes terminated portfolios, however, such a practice would be misleading and not allowed under the GIPS standards. C is incorrect because presenting performance for its mandate covering all periods since the firm's inception is consistent with the GIPS standards. If the firm instead presented performance for a selected period during which it produced excellent returns or outperformed its benchmark, however, such a practice would be misleading and not allowed under the GIPS standards.

2. A is correct. Asset owners can claim compliance if they manage actual assets for which they are making a claim of compliance. B is incorrect because software (and the vendors that supply software) cannot be GIPS compliant. Software can assist firms in achieving compliance with the GIPS standards, but only a firm that manages actual assets can claim compliance. C is incorrect because a firm has only two options regarding compliance with the GIPS standards: fully comply with all applicable requirements of the GIPS standards and claim compliance through the use of the GIPS Compliance Statement; or not comply with all requirements of the GIPS standards and not claim compliance with, or make any reference to, the GIPS standards.

3. C is correct. A composite is an aggregation of one or more portfolios managed according to a similar investment mandate, objective, or strategy. For example, if a GIPS-compliant firm presents performance for a global equity composite (the composite), the composite must include portfolios that are managed, or have historically been managed, according to the firm's global equity strategy. A is incorrect because a composite is an aggregation of one or more portfolios managed according to a similar investment mandate, objective, or strategy. A composite may consist of a single portfolio when it is the only portfolio managed according to a particular investment mandate. B is incorrect because the determination of which portfolio(s) to include in a composite should be done according to pre-established criteria (*ex ante* basis), not after the fact (*ex post* basis).

4. A is correct. Verification is performed with respect to an entire firm, not on specific composites. B is incorrect because verification must be performed by an independent third party. C is incorrect because verification provides assurance on whether the firm's policies and procedures related to composite and pooled fund maintenance, as well as the calculation, presentation, and distribution of performance, have been designed in compliance with the GIPS standards and have been implemented on a firm-wide basis; it does not ensure the accuracy of a specific composite presentation.

5. B is correct. Only investment management firms and asset owners (including pension funds, whether public or private) that manage actual assets may claim compliance with the GIPS standards. Software vendors and other intermediaries cannot claim compliance.

6. C is correct. The GIPS standards require performance to be presented for consis-

tent, standardized time periods.

7. A is correct. Verification is the process of testing a firm or asset owner that claims compliance with the GIPS standards, in accordance with the required verification procedures of the GIPS standards.

8. C is correct. Firms are not required to be verified in order to claim compliance with the GIPS standards, although verification is recommended and viewed as best practice.

9. B is correct. Compliance with the GIPS standards is not typically required by regulators, nor are the GIPS standards intended to cover all regulatory requirements.

10. B is correct. Firms are encouraged to adopt the broadest, most meaningful definition possible of the firm.

11. B is correct. Composites must be defined based on investment mandate, objective, or strategy. Composites can include only discretionary portfolios.

LEARNING MODULE 5

Ethics Application

LEARNING OUTCOME

Mastery	The candidate should be able to:
☐	evaluate practices, policies, and conduct relative to the CFA Institute Code of Ethics and Standards of Professional Conduct
☐	explain how the practices, policies, and conduct do or do not violate the CFA Institute Code of Ethics and Standards of Professional Conduct

INTRODUCTION

This reading presents a number of short vignettes, or scenarios, inspired by real-world situations and events.[1] After reading the facts of each scenario, use your knowledge of the CFA Institute Code of Ethics and Standards of Professional Conduct to choose the best response to the multiple-choice question. After making your choice, be sure to review the correct response and case analysis, which discusses the rationale for why or why not a violation of the Code and Standards might have taken place and conduct that would comply with the Code and Standards.

PROFESSIONALISM

☐	evaluate practices, policies, and conduct relative to the CFA Institute Code of Ethics and Standards of Professional Conduct
☐	explain how the practices, policies, and conduct do or do not violate the CFA Institute Code of Ethics and Standards of Professional Conduct

---

1 Based on cases from the *Ethics in Investment Management Casebook* (CFA Institute 2019).

Knowledge of the Law

Members and Candidates must understand and comply with all applicable laws, rules, and regulations (including the CFA Institute Code of Ethics and Standards of Professional Conduct) of any government, regulatory organization, licensing agency, or professional association governing their professional activities. In the event of conflict, Members and Candidates must comply with the more strict law, rule, or regulation. Members and Candidates must not knowingly participate or assist in and must dissociate from any violation of such laws, rules, or regulations.

Mandracken

SBS Bank (SBS) serves as a custody bank for a wide range of clients. SBS offers a variety of services to its clients, including custody, clearing, payment, settlement, and record keeping. SBS charges its clients an asset-based fee for these services. Pursuant to the bank's client agreement, custody clients agree to reimburse the bank for out-of-pocket expenses for items paid by the custodian on their behalf. The majority of these expenses are for messages sent via the Society for Worldwide Interbank Financial Telecommunication (SWIFT), a secure messaging network used by banks and other financial institutions. Although SBS charges custody clients an established rate for SWIFT messages, the rate is greater than the actual cost of providing this service.

Mandracken, CFA, a vice president at SBS who oversees client service responsibilities, recognizes this discrepancy and brings it to the attention of his supervisor. In an email, Mandracken states that "although disclosure of charging for SWIFT fees is noted in the clients' fee schedules, the fees have always included an increase over actual cost, so the charge to clients is not a true pass-through because we add a margin." Mandracken's supervisor instructs him to reduce the SWIFT fee rate for new clients and to revisit the rate for existing clients when their contracts are renewed.

To meet his obligations under the CFA Institute Code and Standards, Mandracken should

A. implement the corrective procedures as directed by his supervisor.

B. implement the corrective procedures as directed by his supervisor but report his objections to the bank's board of directors.

C. refuse to participate in any client interactions using the fee schedule until the bank revises the SWIFT rate to reflect the actual cost of the service.

Analysis

C is correct. This case involves how to appropriately address the misconduct of others in carrying out your professional responsibilities. Standard I(A): Professionalism, Knowledge of the Law prohibits CFA Institute members and candidates from knowingly participating or assisting in legal or ethical violations and requires them to dissociate from any such activity. SBS is misrepresenting its reimbursable expenses to its custody clients and overcharging them. Although Mandracken brings the issue to the attention of his supervisor, his supervisor's corrective measures are inadequate because they (1) address the issue only for new clients, (2) do not immediately address the issue for existing clients, and (3) do not address the misrepresentation and overcharges to past clients. Mandracken must thus refuse to participate in any client interactions that use the fee schedule until the bank revises the SWIFT fees charged to custody clients to reflect actual out-of-pocket costs.

A is incorrect. Under the Code and Standards, Mandracken cannot continue to participate in or be associated with this misconduct. Inaction by a member and continuing association with those involved in illegal or unethical conduct might be viewed as participation or assistance in the illegal or unethical conduct.

B is incorrect. Mandracken might need to take drastic measures to dissociate from the activity and to protect client interests, such as leaving the bank or reporting the misconduct to the bank's board of directors or regulators. Several interim steps should be considered before this action, such as talking to his supervisor or the bank's compliance department about the inadequacy of the proposed corrective measures, but Mandracken cannot continue to interact with clients using a fraudulent fee schedule.

Pellie

Pellie, CFA, is CEO of Kwaume Investment Group (KIG), an investment adviser that is a wholly owned subsidiary of Kwaume Bank. A longtime bank customer that Pellie and some of the bank's board members know personally recently opened an investment account at KIG with a stated investment objective of earning income. The client made a few investments over the course of the next year, but most of the activity in the account involved several hundred bank transactions that totaled $90 million in deposits and $84 million in withdrawals.

The transactions included electronic transfers to and from individuals and entities located in bank secrecy havens and countries identified by the government as at risk for money-laundering activity. Pellie knew that the client was engaged in international business pursuits involving transactions with a higher risk potential for corruption and bribery. Given the client's longstanding relationship with the bank, Pellie assumes the transactions have a legitimate business purpose and accepts vague descriptions, such as "for services provided," "consulting fees," and "commissions." When he receives the daily anti-money-laundering (AML) reports, which are required by law when transactions trigger red flags of potentially suspicious activity, he approves them without further inquiry.

Pellie's actions are

A. a violation of the CFA Institute Code and Standards.

B. appropriate because Pellie is protecting the confidentiality of client information.

C. appropriate because Pellie can rely on the account's clearing firm to report suspicious activity for the account.

Analysis

A is correct. Pellie's actions violate Standard I(A): Professionalism, Knowledge of the Law, which states that CFA Institute members and candidates "must understand and comply with all applicable laws, rules, and regulations . . . governing their professional activities." The facts presented should have raised questions regarding the legitimacy of the client's account. The high volume of deposits and withdrawals combined with the low number of investment transactions is inconsistent with an investment account having a stated objective of earning income. The transactions in the account appeared to be high-risk transactions for money-laundering activity and should have received a greater level of scrutiny by Pellie. But rather than investigate as required by law, Pellie did not inquire further because of the client's longstanding relationship with the bank and its board members. Pellie's failure to comply with AML requirements imposed by law violates Standard I(A).

B is incorrect. The duty of loyalty to clients and the preservation of confidentiality of client information cannot be used as justification to allow clients to violate the law or otherwise damage the integrity or viability of global capital markets.

C is incorrect. Pellie cannot rely on the clearing firm to meet KIG's obligation to review the transactions for suspicious activity because that is his responsibility.

Mwangi

Mwangi, CFA, works for a firm that sells insurance products. Three of Mwangi's clients purchase one type of product (Class A) but later change their minds and ask to switch to another, lower priced product (Class B). For Mwangi to complete the transaction, the law requires that she have her clients sign new sale and purchase documents for the Class B product. Given that not all the documents are ready for signing at the time of the clients' request, Mwangi advises her clients to wait to sign until the complete set of documents has been prepared. When the full set of documents is ready, Mwangi tries unsuccessfully to reach her clients for their signatures. Because of the missing signatures, Mwangi's manager threatens to cancel the exchange, which, because of other investment purchases, would place the clients' accounts into an overdraft position. Under the firm's policies, account shortfalls are covered by selling account assets once the shortfall has been outstanding for two weeks. To prevent this from happening, Mwangi signs the necessary documents on behalf of her clients.

Mwangi's actions are

A. a violation of the CFA Institute Code and Standards.

B. acceptable because her clients had already given their permission for the exchange to be made.

C. acceptable if the clients gave Mwangi explicit permission to sign the documents on their behalf.

Analysis

A is correct. This case involves Standard I(A): Professionalism, Knowledge of the Law, which requires CFA Institute members and candidates to "comply with all applicable laws, rules, and regulations . . . governing their professional activities." To complete the exchange from the Class A to the Class B product, Mwangi's clients were legally required to sign the new sale and purchase documents, which did not happen. By signing the documents on behalf of the clients, Mwangi forged their signatures. This violation of the law constitutes a violation of Standard I(A).

B is incorrect. General approval, written or verbal, of the transaction by the clients is insufficient to meet the legal requirement for client signatures.

C is incorrect. Even if the clients fully understand what is required to make the switch and explicitly give Mwangi permission to sign the forms on their behalf, the law requires that the genuine signatures of the clients be on the documents. Although the intent of the law is to protect the clients, and the clients would be waiving their rights, Mwangi is still not permitted to circumvent the legal requirements.

Independence and Objectivity

> Members and Candidates must use reasonable care and judgment to achieve and maintain independence and objectivity in their professional activities. Members and Candidates must not offer, solicit, or accept any gift, benefit, compensation, or consideration that reasonably could be expected to compromise their own or another's independence and objectivity.

Professionalism

Myers

Myers, CFA, is a partner at Corboba, a $3 billion hedge fund that focuses on environmental, social, and governance investments. To support upcoming public office elections, Myers wants to personally donate $10,000 to one of the candidates, DeFrietas. As a passionate climate advocate and an avid proponent of responsible investment, Myers supports DeFrietas's backing of environmental policies to reduce air pollution and mitigate the effects of climate change. Myers believes his political contribution might also be beneficial for Corboba because DeFrietas is running for a position that can influence which hedge funds receive investments from the state's pension plans.

Myers's best course of action is to

A. refrain from donating to DeFrietas.

B. donate to DeFrietas because he is using personal funds in an amount that is insignificant relative to the size of the hedge fund.

C. donate to DeFrietas because he will be supporting a candidate whose environmental policies align with his beliefs.

Analysis

A is correct. If Myers makes the donation to DeFrietas's campaign, his actions would potentially violate Standard I(B): Professionalism, Independence and Objectivity, which states that CFA Institute members and candidates "must not offer . . . any gift, benefit, compensation, or consideration that reasonably could be expected to compromise . . . another's independence and objectivity." Although Myers has a legitimate reason for donating to DeFrietas, the facts clearly indicate that he believes the donation might also influence DeFrietas to choose Corboba to manage money for the state's pension plans. Standard I(B) prohibits CFA Institute members and candidates from attempting to gain lucrative allocations from government-sponsored pension funds by making donations to the political campaigns of individuals directly responsible for the manager hiring decisions.

B is incorrect. The source and the amount of the funds are irrelevant if the donation is meant to influence DeFrietas. In addition, the sum of $10,000 might be significant in the context of the campaign and thus important to DeFrietas. The critical issue is whether the donation is reasonably designed to improperly affect DeFrietas's independence and objectivity and benefit Myers or Corboba directly. Many factors would go into this determination, including the size of the donation, Myers's intent in making the donation, and how influential DeFrietas's position would be in making the hiring decision. The facts state that one of the reasons for Myers's donation is to have influence over receiving investment management business from the state.

C is incorrect. Myers seems to have both proper and improper motivations for making a political contribution to DeFrietas. Myers supports DeFrietas's positions on protecting the environment and wants to further those goals. Standard I(B) is not meant to prevent investment professionals from participating in the political process through financial or other support for candidates. But Myers recognizes that financial support of DeFrietas could benefit Corboba by gaining favor with someone who might be in a position to determine whether to invest in Corboba's fund. Therefore, Myers' actions could be perceived as inappropriate, so the best course of action would be to avoid any potential conflict by not donating to DeFrietas's campaign and finding other ways to support environmental protection policies.

Misrepresentation

> Members and Candidates must not knowingly make any misrepresentations relating to investment analysis, recommendations, actions, or other professional activities.

Lee

Lee, CFA, is a financial planner for AKC. AKC compensates its planners based on the number of AKC products they sell. Lee advises a married couple to transfer their retirement funds totaling $125,000 into a single AKC investment fund that follows a large-cap equity strategy. Lee discloses to the couple that they will have to pay a penalty totaling $30,000 for closing their retirement accounts but claims they will make up the loss with better investment returns from the AKC product.

Lee's actions are

- **A.** acceptable if the AKC product is suitable for the couple.
- **B.** a violation of the CFA Institute Code and Standards because she is promising a specific rate of return.
- **C.** acceptable because she fully discloses the negative consequences of closing their retirement accounts.

Analysis

B is correct. This case involves Standard I(C): Professionalism, Misrepresentation, which states that CFA Institute members and candidates must not knowingly make any misrepresentation related to investment analysis, recommendations, or actions. This standard prohibits members and candidates from making any statements that promise or guarantee a specific rate of return on volatile investments. Because the equity-based investment is inherently volatile, and the future return is unpredictable, Lee's promises about future returns making up for the penalty of withdrawing the funds violates Standard I(C). Trust is the foundation of the investment profession. Investment professionals who make false or misleading statements not only harm investors but also reduce the level of investor confidence in the investment profession and threaten the integrity of the capital markets.

A is incorrect. Even if the AKC product is suitable for the couple, it is an equity-based investment that is inherently volatile. Any statements that the investment will provide a certain rate of return or be worth a certain amount in the future is a misrepresentation. This case also raises questions about whether advising the couple to take such a significant loss in their retirement savings would be in their best interest and whether Lee's independence and objectivity are compromised because her recommendation is influenced by the compensation scheme of her employer.

C is incorrect. Although Lee fully discloses the negative consequences of transferring the couple's assets to the AKC product, that disclosure does not mitigate her inappropriate and misleading statement about future expected returns.

Andersen

Andersen, CFA, is the CEO of an asset management firm. Andersen and other senior investment managers at his firm make an in-person proposal to manage the investments of a large pension plan. In response to a request from the pension plan, Andersen provides a list of the key personnel who would manage the account. While waiting for the outcome of the evaluation, one of the key personnel that Andersen identified and who was part of the team that made the in-person presentation leaves the firm.

Professionalism

Andersen should

A. do nothing because the pension plan is hiring the firm, not an individual.

B. immediately inform the pension plan that one of the key personnel has left the firm.

C. hire a competent replacement for the person who left and then inform the pension plan of the change.

Analysis

B is correct. This case relates to Standard I(C): Professionalism, Misrepresentation, which prohibits members and candidates from knowingly misrepresenting anything relating to their professional activities. After the proposal is submitted to the pension plan for its investment management business, a staff member leaves Andersen's team. Andersen has identified the person leaving as a key member of the team that made the initial presentation. Given the pension plan asked for a list of individuals who would be handling the account, this information is clearly important in their decision to hire Andersen's firm. Withholding the information about the person leaving would be a misrepresentation by omission.

A is incorrect. Andersen obviously has confidence in the firm as a whole and will likely replace the person leaving with a competent professional with similar experience and talent so that the transition in service is seamless for clients. The pension plan is clearly concerned about the specific personnel involved in managing its assets because it asked for that information. If this were a junior employee, a staff member who had limited effect on the investment decision-making process, or someone who was not listed as a key employee or who had not been part of the team making the presentation, then Andersen might not need to provide an update to the pension plan. However, given the information in the case, to avoid a misrepresentation Andersen must tell the pension plan about the departure of the key staff member.

C is incorrect. Waiting until a replacement is found is too late because knowing who the managers are on the team is clearly important to the pension plan's hiring decision.

Brodeur

Brodeur, CFA, is CEO of LeTour, a global company that makes electric cars. Brodeur and LeTour disclose to the public and regulators that the company will use Brodeur's personal social media account to disseminate information to LeTour investors and the investing public. After the media reports that the company is having difficulty producing and delivering its cars to buyers, Brodeur posts on his social media that the company is "considering taking LeTour private at $420 a share. Funding is secure."

Previously, Brodeur had met with a large sovereign wealth fund (SWF) that expressed general interest in investing in the company and taking the company private. But Brodeur and the SWF had not reached any agreement or determined a share purchase price. Brodeur was also in discussions with investment banks but had not yet retained any advisers to assist with taking the company private. After the post, LeTour's stock price increased more than 6% on significantly increased volume and closed at $380 per share, 10% higher than on the previous day. When asked about the specific stock price in the post, Brodeur admitted that he had not discussed pricing with any potential investor but chose the price as a joke. Brodeur's actions are

A. inappropriate because the post was a misrepresentation of the facts.

B. inappropriate because not all investors use social media, so Brodeur is selectively disclosing information and putting some investors at a disadvantage.

C. appropriate because his post said only that he was "considering" taking the company private and thus contained only speculative, nonmaterial information.

Analysis

A is correct. This case relates to Standard I(C): Professionalism, Misrepresentation, which states that CFA Institute members and candidates must not knowingly make any misrepresentation relating to professional or investment activities. Brodeur's post was based on assumptions and contrary to the facts. Among other things, he (1) had not reached any agreement with the SWF, (2) had never discussed a share price of $420, (3) had set the price as a joke, and (4) had not formally retained any legal or financial advisers to assist with taking the company private. Unlike market participants reading his post, Brodeur knew that his supposed "secure" funding was based on a general conversation regarding a potential investment of an unspecified amount in the context of an undefined transaction structure. Because of the uncertainties that would need to be resolved before going private could be possible, Brodeur knew or should have known that his statements were false and misleading. The online or interactive aspects of social media do not remove the need to be open and honest about the information being distributed.

B is incorrect. Disseminating information to investors using social media might be appropriate and ethical under certain conditions. Distribution channels to make information public do not need to be guaranteed to reach all investors, but they must be designed to effectively make the information public. As long as the information shared reaches all clients or is available to the investing public, social media platforms would be comparable with other traditional forms of communication, such as press releases or email communication. But because the information was misleading, Brodeur's use of social media was not appropriate.

C is incorrect. The post can be considered "material" information and not speculative because (1) the source of the post was the company's CEO, (2) the subject matter was dramatic and elemental, and (3) investors would want to know the information before making an investment decision.

Misconduct

> Members and Candidates must not engage in any professional conduct involving dishonesty, fraud, or deceit or commit any act that reflects adversely on their professional reputation, integrity, or competence.

Hanse

Hanse, CFA, is a portfolio manager employed by a global investment bank. She manages an environmental, social, and governance (ESG) investment fund. In her free time, Hanse participates in civil disobedience demonstrations organized by the Extinction Rebellion, a sociopolitical movement that uses nonviolent resistance to protest climate breakdown, biodiversity loss, and ecological collapse. At several demonstrations held in the financial district, Hanse is arrested on charges of unlawful assembly, obstructing public transit, and disorderly conduct. She is ultimately convicted of several minor criminal offenses. Hanse has signed a standard employment contract with the bank that allows it to terminate any employee who is convicted of a criminal offense.

Under the CFA Institute Code and Standards, Hanse's actions

A. do not violate the Code and Standards.

B. violate the Code and Standards because she has violated her employment contract with the bank.

C. violate the Code and Standards because she is arrested for misconduct in the financial district.

Analysis

A is correct. This case relates to what constitutes professional misconduct. Standard I(D): Professionalism, Misconduct prohibits CFA Institute members and candidates from engaging "in any professional conduct involving dishonesty, fraud, or deceit" or from committing "any act that reflects adversely on their professional reputation, integrity, or competence." Generally, Standard I(D) is not meant to cover legal transgressions resulting from acts of civil disobedience in support of personal beliefs because such conduct does not reflect adversely on the member's professional reputation, integrity, or competence.

B is incorrect. Hanse's arrest is not likely an automatic violation of bank policies. Although Hanse's employment contract gives the bank the option to fire her for criminal activity, the bank can apparently use discretion in retaining employees depending on the nature and circumstances of the conviction. Further, the Code and Standards are not automatically violated with every violation of an employer's employment contract unless the violations relate to conduct addressed in the Code and Standards.

C is incorrect. The fact that Hanse is arrested in the financial district is not a sufficient link to her professional activities to make her actions a violation of the Code and Standards. The acts of civil disobedience by Hanse reflect her personal beliefs, which would generally not be considered an act involving fraud, dishonesty, or deceit or an act that reflects poorly on her professional reputation, integrity, or competence.

Mang

Mang, CFA, is an investment adviser for a regional bank that has a number of discretionary, fee-based accounts for high-net-worth individuals. The bank's policies permit trade error corrections up to 30 days following a failure to place a trade when an adviser forgets to send an order to the trading desk. To rectify the error, the adviser is permitted to buy or sell a security at the current market price, with the price differential charged to the adviser personally through an internal error account.

On many occasions, Mang uses the trade error correction policy to benefit clients who are unhappy with their account's performance. Mang identifies a security whose price has increased in the past 30 days. He then tells the trade desk he mistakenly failed to buy that particular security some days before, when the price was substantially lower than the current market price. Once the request is approved, the trade desk purchases the security and charges the price differential to Mang personally through the error account. Shortly after that trade, Mang sends an order to sell the security and net a profit for the client. Mang then tells the client that he has given them a "gift" or "no-risk" trade.

Mang's actions

A. violate the CFA Institute Code and Standards.

B. are appropriate because Mang is acting for the benefit of the client.

C. are appropriate because the bank is not harmed by Mang's actions.

Analysis

A is correct. Mang is violating Standard I(D): Professionalism, Misconduct, which prohibits CFA Institute members and candidates from engaging in professional conduct involving dishonesty, fraud, or deceit. He is engaging in a misleading, fraudulent, and deceptive practice and misusing the bank's policies to enhance the performance of his clients' accounts when no legitimate error was made. He personally compensates clients as a means to mislead them about his ability as an investment adviser as well as the actual performance of their accounts.

B is incorrect. Although the trades benefit his clients, Mang is engaging in professional misconduct by misleading his clients with fraudulent and deceptive conduct.

C is incorrect. The fact that these practices did not cause financial losses for the bank does not make Mang's conduct any less deceptive, fraudulent, or misleading.

3. INTEGRITY OF CAPITAL MARKETS

Material Nonpublic Information

Members and Candidates who possess material nonpublic information that could affect the value of an investment must not act or cause others to act on the information.

Khatri

Khatri, a candidate in the CFA Program, plays on a local cricket team with his friends, including Patel, his brother-in-law and an attorney, and Ahuja, owner of a software development company called ZeroPower (ZP). Patel handles the legal work for ZP. Khatri, Patel, and many other friends in their circle have invested in ZP. Recently, a large global information technology company (GIT) made an offer to buy ZP at a substantial premium over the company's current share price. Patel is working with lawyers from GIT to assist in their due diligence.

One weekend, during a particularly intense period of negotiations, Khatri, Patel, and Ahuja are playing in a cricket tournament. Between matches, Khatri overhears Patel speaking with representatives of GIT on his cell phone. Although mention of a ZP acquisition is not made, Khatri hears Patel repeatedly reference the name "GIT". Khatri guesses that the acquisition of ZP is happening soon after seeing Patel and Ahuja huddled in private conversation several times over the course of the weekend. On Monday, Khatri calls his broker and increases his investment in ZP by 5,000 shares. One week later, ZP announces its acquisition by GIT and its share price increases 30%.

Khatri's actions are

A. a violation of the CFA Institute Code and Standards.

B. acceptable because Khatri's investment was based on his own speculation.

C. acceptable because Khatri received the information in a public environment.

Analysis

A is correct. Khatri comes into possession of material nonpublic information by overhearing confidential information from Patel's phone calls and witnessing Patel's interactions with Ahuja that were prompted by those calls. Standard II(A): Integrity of Capital Markets, Material Nonpublic Information prohibits CFA Institute members and candidates from taking investment action based on material nonpublic information in their possession. Patel should have been more careful to keep his phone conversations private, but his failure to do so does not allow Khatri to use material nonpublic information received from overhearing those conversations.

Integrity of Capital Markets

B is incorrect. Although information about the acquisition of ZP was not explicitly stated, and Khatri was required to make some degree of deduction, he knew or should have known that this information was confidential, nonpublic, and material. His actions are different from mosaic theory, in which investment analysts combine nonmaterial and nonpublic information with public information in their analysis to derive insights.

C is incorrect. Although Patel's phone calls and interactions with Ahuja take place in a public environment, that does not mean the information is public.

Kwame

Kwame, CFA, is the chief financial officer of PH3D, a biotech firm that researches, develops, and commercializes pharmaceutical drugs for women's health. PH3D submits a drug application to the government regulator for a promising new drug. The regulator postpones two scheduled meetings with PH3D when unspecified deficiencies with the drug arise. The public announcement of the postponements results in a 10% drop in the company's stock price.

When the meeting between the regulator and PH3D finally takes place, PH3D presents unpublished preliminary test data with favorable indicators for the drug. The regulator reacts positively and gives PH3D provisional regulatory approval, contingent on further studies. Afterward, some of the sell-side research analysts covering PH3D ask Kwame about the meeting. Kwame responds by email, indicating that he believes the meeting with the regulator was "very positive and productive" and that the company was "pleasantly surprised" by the regulator's reaction. Kwame does not share the favorable preliminary test data. After Kwame's emails to the analysts, the company's stock price increases 19%.

Kwame's actions

A. violate the CFA Institute Code and Standards.

B. are appropriate because he does not share the unpublished preliminary test data with the analysts and restricts his comments to the general tenor of the meeting.

C. are appropriate because he responds to questions from research analysts covering the company.

Analysis

A is correct. This case relates to selective disclosure of material nonpublic information. Standard II(A): Integrity of Capital Markets, Material Nonpublic Information prohibits CFA Institute members and candidates from causing others to act on material nonpublic information. Information is material if its disclosure would affect the price of a security or if reasonable investors would want to know the information before making an investment decision. Information is "nonpublic" until it has been disseminated or made available to the marketplace in general, and Kwame's response to select sell-side analysts inquiring about PH3D's meeting with the regulator would not be considered public dissemination of the information. In this case, both the drug's positive preliminary test results and the regulator's positive reaction to the new drug is information that would have an impact on the price of the security in addition to information that reasonable investors would want to know.

B is incorrect. Although Kwame does not share the test results with the analysts, he shares that the meeting with the regulator was "very positive and productive". This is information that reasonable investors would want to know.

C is incorrect. Kwame shares this information with a select group of analysts who regularly cover PH3D and not the general investing public. The fact that Kwame is only responding to questions is irrelevant. Kwame and PH3D should have issued a public announcement about the meeting with the regulator before, or at the same time, information was disclosed to analysts.

Market Manipulation

Members and Candidates must not engage in practices that distort prices or artificially inflate trading volume with the intent to mislead market participants.

Abbha

Abbha, CFA, is a securities contractor working to assist Superior Energy (SE) with listing its shares on the Regional Security Exchange (RSX). SE files a prospectus for an offer of up to five million shares at $2 each to raise $10 million. The RSX current applicable listing rule requires that entities seeking admission to the RSX must meet a "minimum spread requirement" of at least 300 shareholders with a minimum value holding to qualify for listing. In their listing application, representatives of SE inform RSX that the minimum spread requirement of 300 shareholders has been met. These disclosures include as shareholders 31 people or companies arranged by Abbha, though none are actual buyers of SE securities. Abbha provides false names and addresses for the 31 shareholders. The SE share offer raises more than $3.5 million, with more than 1.75 million shares issued. SE is admitted to the official list of the RSX, with its shares quoted on the exchange. Over time, the price of SE shares steadily increases, the company attracts hundreds of investors and shareholders, and early investors achieve an excellent investment return.

Abbha's actions

A. violate the CFA Institute Code and Standards.

B. are acceptable because SE proved to be a strong company with excellent performance.

C. are acceptable because no investors were harmed by the technical violation of RSX rules.

Analysis

A is correct. Abbha engaged in information-based manipulation by inflating the number of initial shareholders in SE securities to create the impression that its shares would have sufficient liquidity, and giving new investors comfort in buying them. Standard II(B): Integrity of Capital Markets, Market Manipulation prohibits CFA Institute members and candidates from engaging in practices that artificially inflate trading volume to mislead market participants. To circumvent regulatory requirements and drive investor interest, Abbha's misrepresentations overstated initial interest in SE securities, thereby creating false pretenses under which the company was listed.

B is incorrect. The fact that SE ultimately proved to be a bona fide and well performing investment does not mitigate Abbha's unethical, misleading, and deceitful conduct.

C is incorrect. The purpose of the minimum spread requirement for RSX security listings is to demonstrate that investor interest in a company is sufficient to justify the company's listing. Th minimum spread requirement ensures some level of liquidity at the time a company is listed and prevents lower quality applicants, that are unable

Duties to Clients

to attract sufficient investor interest, from being listed. Falsifying the number of initial investors goes beyond a technical violation of RSX rules and has substantial consequences.

DUTIES TO CLIENTS

Loyalty, Prudence, and Care

Members and Candidates have a duty of loyalty to their clients and must act with reasonable care and exercise prudent judgment. Members and Candidates must act for the benefit of their clients and place their clients' interests before their employer's or their own interests.

Maste

Maste, CFA, is the sole director of Dov Services (Dov), a firm that sells financial products and advice. Maste directs Dov's authorized representatives to incorporate the Dov Client Protection Policy into their contracts with clients. The protection policy, which sets forth the terms for providing financial advice, states that it "contains a number of client protections designed to ensure that you (the client) receive the best possible advice and the maximum protection available under the law." The protection policy's terms (1) excuse Dov and its authorized representatives from various liabilities arising from their failure to act in a client's best interest, (2) relieve Dov and its authorized representatives of their duty to conduct suitability analyses of clients and investments, and (3) lead clients to believe that they cannot make claims against Dov or its representatives for violating securities law.

Maste's actions

A. violate the CFA Institute Code and Standards.

B. are appropriate because Dov and Maste fully disclose the terms of the Dov Client Protection Policy to clients.

C. are appropriate because Dov and Maste are free to negotiate the terms of advisory agreements with clients.

Analysis

A is correct. The terms of the Dov Client Protection Policy improperly attempt to use disclosure to relieve Dov and Maste of their fundamental ethical (and very likely legal) obligations to clients by limiting liability for failures to act in the client's best interests or to provide appropriate advice. Standard III(A): Duties to Clients, Loyalty, Prudence, and Care sets forth a duty of loyalty on the part of CFA Institute members and candidates to their clients and requires them to act for the benefit of their clients and to place their clients' interests before their own. In addition, Standard V(A): Investment Analysis, Recommendations, and Actions, Diligence and Reasonable Basis requires members and candidates to provide diligent, independent, and thorough advice and to have a reasonable and adequate basis for investment action; Standard III(B): Duties to Clients, Fair Dealing requires members and candidates to conduct a suitability analysis for any investment recommendation to their clients; and Standard I(C): Professionalism, Misrepresentation says that members and candidates cannot make any misrepresentations relating to investment services. These components of the CFA Institute Code and Standards define the fundamental principles applicable to investment professionals and detail the conduct investors should expect from their financial advisers.

B is incorrect. Disclosure cannot be used to relieve advisers of their fundamental ethical obligations to clients. The Dov Client Protection Policy is also deceptive because it misrepresents the client's right to bring legal action for ethical and regulatory violations and appears to give the false impression that a client would benefit from its terms.

C is incorrect. Although in general, clients and advisers are free to negotiate the terms of advisory agreements, for advisers to use the client agreement to create a significant imbalance between the rights and obligations of the adviser and their client or to limit the fundamental ethical obligations of loyalty, prudence, and care to their client is improper.

Gaini

Gaini, CFA, is a commodities trader with a number of retail clients, including Laube, who opens a self-directed foreign exchange retail account for which Gaini does not advise on any trades. Laube signs Gaini's standard customer agreement, which contains provisions relating to margin requirements and liquidation in the event of margin deficits. The agreement authorizes Gaini, at his discretion, "to liquidate, without notice, any or all open positions in an account with insufficient margin."

Laube initially purchases two 100,000 US dollar/Swiss franc (USD/CHF) contracts and sets her margin requirement to $4,000. Laube then places two additional 100,000 USD/CHF "pending limit" orders that will execute if the contract trading prices reach a specified level. Each order has a different limit price, so one will execute before the other. Shortly after placing the orders, Laube goes on an extended vacation. While she is away, execution on the first limit order occurs, and the margin requirement increases to $6,000. Then, the next limit price is reached, and the second order executes, increasing the margin requirement to $8,000. Post trades, while Laube is still on vacation, her account balance drops to $6,900. Without notice, Gaini liquidates all positions in Laube's account, realizing a loss of $37,000 from the liquidation.

Gaini's actions

A. are appropriate because Gaini followed the policy and procedures set forth in Laube's client agreement.

B. violate the CFA Institute Code and Standards because Gaini has a duty to act in the best interest of Laube by protecting her financial position.

C. are inappropriate because Gaini could have met the margin requirement by liquidating only one foreign exchange contract position.

Analysis

A is correct. This case relates to Standard III(A): Duties to Clients, Loyalty, Prudence, and Care, which imposes on CFA Institute members and candidates a duty to act with loyalty, prudence, and care in their clients' best interests as well as in relation to other clients and the markets. However the conduct that fulfills this responsibility depends on the nature of the relationship with the client. Laube self-directs her trades which are executed by Gaini, who does not provide investment advice. Additionally, Laube freely contracts with Gaini regarding the consequences of insufficient margins in her account, and these policies and procedures are clearly set forth in her client agreement. Nothing indicates that Gaini misled Laube about the margin requirements or the liquidation procedures. Although the contractual provision authorizing liquidation without notice does not waive Laube's right to be dealt with in good faith, the margin and liquidation provisions are not an attempt by Gaini to waive his duty of loyalty, prudence, and care. They simply set forth the parameters of the relationship, which

Duties to Clients

Gaini and Laube are free to negotiate. Although Laube suffered significant trading losses, Gaini liquidated Laube's open positions in accordance with the terms of the customer agreement, serving to protect the integrity of the market.

B is incorrect. Given the facts of this case, Gaini's responsibility to protect his own financial position and that of his other customers supersedes any duties he owes to Laube when she defaults on the margin requirements. Because of the limited nature of the relationship between Laube and Gaini, Gaini is not obligated to actively monitor Laube's account to protect her financial interests. Doing so would require Gaini to continuously monitor a potentially deteriorating market or to take on additional risk management measures that he has not agreed to and that Laube has not contracted for.

C is incorrect. Gaini is not obligated to use a less drastic alternative by closing only one foreign exchange contract position and does not breach a duty to Laube by liquidating all open positions when the parties have contractually agreed that total liquidation to meet a margin deficit may be done at Gaini's discretion without notice.

Braung

A regional government hires Braung, CFA, and his firm to serve as its financial adviser for issuing general obligation bonds. The municipality conducts several bond offerings over the years for constructing municipal facilities, including a maximum-security detention facility and two school buildings. In connection with the bond issues, Braung makes a number of trips to New York City to meet with ratings agencies. The trips are typically planned for a Monday or Friday because the costs for weekend travel are less. Braung's wife accompanies him on the trips, and they typically spend the weekend either before or after the meetings in New York City to enjoy sporting events, theater performances, and museums. Braung often makes a number of train and hotel changes after a trip is booked to accommodate meetings with other clients. Braung submits his travel expenses to his supervisor, who deducts costs she believes are unrelated to the business purpose of the trip and submits the bills to the municipality for reimbursement.

Which of the following expenses can most likely be billed to the government entity issuing the bonds?

- **A.** Braung's accommodation and meal expenses for the weekend days because the travel rates are less expensive over a weekend
- **B.** Tickets to the sporting and theater events, as long as they do not exceed a reasonable amount for business entertainment
- **C.** Flight and hotel change fees that result from the regular course of Braung's business activities

Analysis

A is correct. This case relates to Standard III(A): Duties to Clients, Loyalty, Prudence, and Care, which states that CFA Institute members and candidates have a duty of loyalty to their clients, must act for their clients' benefit, and must place client interests before their own. Under this standard, investment professionals, including municipal security dealers, must not engage in any deceptive, dishonest, or unfair practice when handling client accounts. The savings in travel fees for booking a weekend travel schedule could be greater than the additional accommodation and meal expenses for Braung to stay in New York City the extra days, making the cost to the client lower. Under these circumstances, Braung would be meeting his duty of loyalty to the client by choosing the most inexpensive travel schedule overall, thus limiting costs to the client. Charging personal theater and sporting event tickets or travel change fees associated with seeing unrelated clients would not qualify as chargeable expenses to the client. The best scenario would be to detail in writing at the outset of the engagement which expenses would be considered reimbursable.

B is incorrect. In the context of conflicts of interest, the CFA Institute Code and Standards allow members and candidates to accept or provide modest gifts and entertainment in the ordinary course of business (a gift basket at the holidays from a vendor or to a client, for example). But that "ordinary course of business" does not allow investment professionals to charge clients for obviously extraneous entertainment expenses not connected to a business meeting. Charging excessive or lavish expenses for the personal benefit of the investment professional at the expense of the client can constitute a deceptive, dishonest, or unfair practice that violates Standard III(A).

C is incorrect. Although busy investment professionals might be forced by other priorities to change travel arrangements when a client trip has already been scheduled, additional expenses resulting from the change most likely must be borne by the investment professional (Braung) as an overhead cost, not charged to the client. (Under some limited circumstances, those expenses might be charged to the client who necessitates the travel changes.)

Fair Dealing

> Members and Candidates must deal fairly and objectively with all clients when providing investment analysis, making investment recommendations, taking investment action, or engaging in other professional activities.

Scherzer

Scherzer, CFA, is the head of research at a large investment management firm. She publishes monthly "Recommendation Update Reports" to communicate to clients any investment recommendation changes her firm has made. The reports are sent to clients via email on the first Friday of the month and posted on the firm's website the following Monday. The firm's internal policy is that a change in recommendation can only be made once a month through this report. Scherzer also publishes weekly reports with information gathered by analysts that might implicitly signal a future change in recommendation or lead a reader to infer that a recommendation will be changing. Although the monthly "Recommendation Update Reports" are sent to all clients, clients who wish to receive the weekly publication must pay an annual fee of $1,000. This option is available to any client and is fully disclosed as part of every client agreement.

To comply with the CFA Institute Code and Standards, Scherzer is required to

A. do nothing because her actions comply with the Code and Standards.

B. publish the monthly report on the firm's website at the same time it is sent to clients.

C. send the weekly reports to all clients at no additional charge.

Analysis

A is correct. Standard III(B): Duties to Clients, Fair Dealing requires CFA Institute members and candidates to deal fairly and objectively with all clients when providing investment analysis and making investment recommendations. It also requires that information about investment recommendations be disseminated in such a manner that all clients have a fair opportunity to act on the information. Scherzer distributes the recommendation update reports to all clients simultaneously via email, giving each an opportunity to act on the information. Scherzer is also not limited by the Code and Standards in communicating with clients about investments only when an investment recommendation is provided and can provide updated or clarifying information to clients as appropriate. In addition, Scherzer does not violate the Code and Standards

Duties to Clients

by providing weekly reports to clients who pay a subscription fee for the service as long as (1) all clients are eligible to purchase the service, (2) the different levels of service are disclosed to clients, and (3) no change in recommendations is made that would disadvantage existing clients who receive only the monthly report.

B is incorrect. The Code and Standards do not require Scherzer to publish the reports to the public on the firm's website.

C is incorrect. The Code and Standards allow CFA Institute members and candidates to provide more personal, specialized, or in-depth service to clients who are willing to pay for premium services through additional fees as long as (1) those services do not disadvantage other clients who do not pay additional fees, (2) the differing levels of service are disclosed to clients, and (3) the services are made available to all.

Suitability

1. When Members and Candidates are in an advisory relationship with a client, they must:

    a. Make a reasonable inquiry into a client's or prospective client's investment experience, risk and return objectives, and financial constraints prior to making any investment recommendation or taking investment action and must reassess and update this information regularly.

    b. Determine that an investment is suitable to the client's financial situation and consistent with the client's written objectives, mandates, and constraints before making an investment recommendation or taking investment action.

    c. Judge the suitability of investments in the context of the client's total portfolio.

2. When Members and Candidates are responsible for managing a portfolio to a specific mandate, strategy, or style, they must make only investment recommendations or take only investment actions that are consistent with the stated objectives and constraints of the portfolio.

Marte

Marte, CFA, is an asset manager in Puerto Rico, a US territory. Residents of Puerto Rico receive significant tax advantages when they invest in local securities. To capitalize on this advantage, Marte's firm offers its clients shares in a closed-end investment fund, organized under Puerto Rico's financial laws and regulations, that holds at least 67% local securities and is permitted to borrow against up to 50% of its assets. The fund is usually leveraged to the extent legally permitted. Many of Marte's clients have a modest net worth and conservative or moderate investment objectives. Marte convinces them to invest 85% or more of their assets in shares of the closed-end fund.

Marte's actions

   A. violate the CFA Institute Code and Standards.
   B. are appropriate because they take advantage of the fund's unique tax benefits for his clients.
   C. are appropriate as long as Marte fully discloses the risks and benefits of the fund to his clients.

Analysis

A is correct. Standard III(C): Duties to Clients, Suitability states that CFA Institute members and candidates in an advisory relationship with clients must "determine that an investment is suitable to the client's financial situation and consistent with the client's written objectives, mandates, and constraints before making an investment recommendation or taking investment action." Given the financial circumstances and conservative investment objectives of his clients, the high concentration of the fund's shares in his clients' accounts, combined with the leverage, makes the large investment in the fund unsuitable because greater portfolio diversification is needed. Despite the favorable tax advantages, highly concentrated investments carry an increased risk that a single market event affecting the value of the fund's shares would significantly decrease the total account value. This risk is exacerbated by the fact that the closed-end fund is internally leveraged, which could magnify the fund's loss during a market event that causes share values to drop steeply.

B is incorrect. Given the favorable tax advantages of the investment vehicle, investment in shares of the closed-end fund might be suitable and appropriate for his clients at some level. But given the financial circumstances and investment objectives of his clients, the high concentration, combined with the leverage, makes the large investment in the fund unsuitable.

C is incorrect. Although Marte should always fully disclose the risks and benefits of his recommendations to his clients, doing so does not take away the need for the investment to be suitable for the clients' financial circumstances, risk tolerance, and investment goals.

Duri

Duri, CFA, is a registered account representative providing financial advice to retail clients. She is also a principal partner of Tabak Accountants. Duri assists a number of advisory clients who want to move their retirement assets from existing superannuation (pension) accounts to establish self-managed superannuation funds (SMSFs) that have the goal of investing in direct residential property. When clients express interest in these types of SMSFs, Duri accepts their reasons for wanting to invest in direct property and assumes that they have the time and expertise to manage their superannuation affairs. She reclassifies their investment objectives as "growth" to match the new investment strategy. Duri charges her clients for establishing the SMSFs and recommends that her firm, Tabak Accountants, prepare the clients' annual accounts and tax returns.

Duri's actions

A. violate the CFA Institute Code and Standards.

B. are acceptable because she is following the directives of her clients.

C. are acceptable if the services provided by Tabak Accountants are reasonable and the costs of services are competitive.

Analysis

A is correct. Standard III(C): Duties to Clients, Suitability requires CFA Institute members and candidates in an advisory relationship to make a reasonable inquiry into a client's investment experience, risk and return objectives, and financial constraints to determine whether an investment is suitable for the client's financial situation and consistent with the client's objectives and mandates before taking investment action. When Duri's clients want to switch their retirement assets into an SMSF that invests in direct residential property, Duri appears to accept their reasoning without doing a suitability analysis. The case does not indicate whether Duri did any of the following:

- Assess the reasons a client wants to invest in direct property
- Consider the client's financial goals

Duties to Clients

- Compare the benefits, risks, and costs associated with establishing an SMSF or owning rental property to existing superannuation account investment alternatives
- Consider asset diversification
- Determine whether the client intends to draw a pension from the SMSF once the individual reaches retirement, or how the client will do that with an illiquid asset such as investment property
- Evaluate whether the client has the time and expertise to manage his or her superannuation affairs, including managing a rental property
- Consider whether the SMSF investment strategy will remain viable if the client's income is reduced or the property is unoccupied for a period of time

Without analyzing these and other factors, for Duri to move her clients to the SMSFs would be inappropriate.

B is incorrect. If her clients request a change in their investment strategy, Duri has a responsibility as their investment adviser to conduct an analysis to ensure that the new direction is suitable and appropriate. Duri appears to have classified all clients as growth investors to superficially justify their investment in an SMSF vehicle without doing an analysis of whether this classification was an accurate assessment.

C is incorrect. Duri appears to be recommending that her firm provide clients' accounting services for the SMSF investments to create additional income for herself. But Standard III(A): Duties to Clients, Loyalty, Prudence, and Care requires members and candidates to act for the benefit of their clients and to place their clients' interests before their own. At a minimum, Duri's relationship with Tabak must be fully disclosed to clients as a potential conflict of interest.

Performance Presentation

> When communicating investment performance information, Members and Candidates must make reasonable efforts to ensure that it is fair, accurate, and complete.

Jergenn

Jergenn, CFA, is the portfolio manager for the Volare Investment Management (VIM) fund, a registered collective investment scheme (CIS) organized under the laws of South Africa. VIM's 2022 regulatory disclosure and marketing material for the fund, produced by Jergenn, presents annual investment performance data for the 2014–2020 period that is accurate and calculated correctly. The performance history is that of a composite of separate accounts that followed the strategy used by the VIM fund before the assets were moved over to the CIS environment in 2021.

In presenting the fund's performance history, Jergenn's actions

- **A.** violate the CFA Institute Code and Standards.
- **B.** are appropriate because the investment performance is accurate.
- **C.** are appropriate as long as the performance calculations are net of fees.

Analysis

A is correct. Standard III(D): Duties to Clients, Performance Presentation states that CFA Institute members and candidates must make a reasonable effort to ensure that investment performance information is fair, accurate, and complete. Although the performance information presented by Jergenn is calculated correctly and includes technically accurate data, Jergenn's failure to indicate clearly that the performance data applied to a period before the VIM fund was registered as a CIS has the potential to mislead investors into believing that the CIS fund had a long track record. To meet the "fair, accurate, and complete" requirement of the standard, Jergenn should disclose that the 2014–2020 performance history was for a prior but similar entity with the same investment strategy and objectives and that the VIM fund, as a CIS, has been in existence since only 2021.

B is incorrect. Although the performance is accurate and correctly calculated, the lack of disclosure about the nature of the accounts makes the presentation misleading.

C is incorrect. Performance can be presented either net or gross of fees as long as investors are sufficiently informed about how the performance is calculated and what effect fees might have on the returns.

Preservation of Confidentiality

> Members and Candidates must keep information about current, former, and prospective clients confidential unless:
> 1. The information concerns illegal activities on the part of the client or prospective client,
> 2. Disclosure is required by law, or
> 3. The client or prospective client permits disclosure of the information.

Giddings and Marsh

Giddings, CFA, is responsible for compliance at GWH, a large broker/dealer and investment adviser. In connection with GWH's wealth management business, the company maintains personally identifiable information (names, addresses, phone numbers, account numbers, balances, and holdings) of its clients. Giddings adopts a number of policies and restrictions, including a Code of Conduct, that address employees' access to and handling of this confidential information. Marsh, CFA, who works for GWH as a client services associate, decides to download client data to his personal server located at his residence to facilitate his telecommuting. Marsh's server is hacked, and portions of the personal client information Marsh downloaded are posted for sale on the internet.

Did either Marsh or Giddings violate the CFA Institute Code and Standards?

A. Marsh violated the Code and Standards.

B. Giddings violated the Code and Standards.

C. Both Marsh and Giddings violated the Code and Standards.

Analysis

C is correct. Standard III(E): Duties to Clients, Preservation of Confidentiality requires that CFA Institute members and candidates keep information about current, former, and prospective clients confidential unless the information concerns illegal activities, disclosure is required by law, or the client permits disclosure. Although the standard does not require investment professionals to be information security experts, they must make reasonable efforts to prevent the accidental distribution of confidential information by following compliance procedures. Assuming Marsh did not have permission to download client data to his personal server, his misappropriation of client information for his own purposes is a violation of Standard III(E). And although he was not responsible for the distribution of the information, his misconduct facilitated the publication of the information. Marsh needed to understand and follow the firm's electronic information communication and storage procedures.

As the compliance officer, Giddings is responsible for implementing sufficient compliance policies and procedures reasonably designed to protect client information. He is responsible for ensuring the confidentiality of customer information, protecting against any potential threats to the security or integrity of the records, and preventing unauthorized access or use of client information that could harm GWH clients. Although GWH has policies restricting access to and handling of client information, the extent of those safeguards was apparently insufficient because Marsh was able to download company files to his personal computer. The fact that client information was accessed and published makes the effectiveness of Giddings's compliance efforts questionable. Even if the policies were sufficient, nothing indicates that Giddings audited and/or tested the effectiveness of the safeguards meant to keep client information confidential.

A is incorrect. Both Marsh and Giddings violated the Code and Standards.

B is incorrect. Both Marsh and Giddings violated the Code and Standards.

DUTIES TO EMPLOYERS

Loyalty

In matters related to their employment, Members and Candidates must act for the benefit of their employer and not deprive their employer of the advantage of their skills and abilities, divulge confidential information, or otherwise cause harm to their employer.

Nickoli

Nickoli, CFA, is an investment counselor with HHI Capital Management (HHI). A colleague at her local society encourages Nickoli to leave HHI and join her at Vesuvius Asset Advisers. Nickoli eventually agrees and decides to leave at the beginning of the new year. In the weeks before submitting her resignation, she tells her clients that they will likely be working with a new investment counselor because she is leaving HHI. Her clients express surprise, and when asked for details about why she is leaving, Nickoli shares that she is frustrated by the firm's structure, disagrees with the direction the firm is going, lacks confidence in the current leadership, doubts the firm will be able to attract and retain good people, and believes other HHI employees have been mistreated and will also be leaving soon. Several of Nickoli's HHI clients indicate that they would like information about Vesuvius and might be interested in switching their accounts. After submitting her resignation, Nickoli immediately shares the names of the interested clients with Vesuvius, and after the first of the year, she begins soliciting them to transfer their accounts from HHI to her new firm.

Nickoli's conduct is

A. a violation of the Code and Standards.

B. acceptable because she did not solicit clients until after she left HHI.

C. acceptable because she is looking out for her clients' best interests and believes Vesuvius provides better service.

Analysis

A is correct. Standard IV(A): Duties to Employers, Loyalty states that CFA Institute members and candidates "must act for the benefit of their employer and not . . . otherwise cause harm to their employer." Although a departing employee is generally free to make arrangements or preparations to change firms before terminating the relationship, those preparations must not conflict with the employee's continued duty to act in the best interests of the current employer and not otherwise undermine, disparage, or cause harm to that employer. In this case, Nickoli decides to leave HHI and join Vesuvius weeks before she notifies the firm and submits her resignation. During that time, Standard IV(A) obligates her to continue to act in her current employer's best interests and not engage in any activities that would conflict with this duty until her resignation becomes effective. Nickoli violates her duty of loyalty to HHI by making disparaging and harmful statements about the firm to its clients in the weeks before she submits her resignation and by promoting Vesuvius to HHI clients while she is still employed by HHI.

B is incorrect. Although she did not make actual solicitations until after she left HHI, Nickoli used the final weeks of her employment with HHI to determine which of the firm's clients might be interested in receiving information about Vesuvius and possibly transferring their accounts from HHI and then contacted them after her move to Vesuvius.

C is incorrect. Although investment professionals should protect their clients' best interests, even if Nickoli believes the clients will be better off with her at Vesuvius, the clients' relationship is with HHI. She is a representative of HHI, so she must not act in a manner harmful to the firm while still employed there.

Kuznetsov

Kuznetsov, CFA, is a portfolio manager for a medium-sized investment firm that encourages its employees to sell proprietary investment products to their clients. Kuznetsov follows the encouragement, and within a year, he becomes the firm's top seller of these investment products. He receives glowing performance reviews and a large bonus. However, Kuznetsov begins to realize that the firm's investment products are underperforming, and more expensive than other, external investment options that are suitable for his clients and present stronger growth opportunities. He stops selling the firm's investment products to his clients. Although his supervisor puts increasing pressure on him to resume selling the firm's products, Kuznetsov refuses. He complains several times to management that he is being pressured to place the firm's interests above his clients. He secretly records several conversations with his supervisor and makes copies of client records that document what he considers inappropriate conduct by his supervisor. When management ignores his complaints and Kuznetsov's supervisor begins giving him poor performance reviews, he files a complaint with the local regulator against his supervisor and his firm, providing the recordings and copies of client files as evidence. After the firm becomes aware of Kuznetsov's actions, he is let go.

Kuznetsov's actions are

A. appropriate because he is protecting his clients' interests.

B. a violation of the CFA Institute Code and Standards because he fails to keep client information confidential.

C. a violation of the CFA Institute Code and Standards because he violates his duty of loyalty to his employer by taking his dispute with his supervisor to the regulator and exposing the employer to financial and reputational harm.

Analysis

A is correct. Standard IV(A): Duties to Employers, Loyalty states that CFA Institute members and candidates "must act for the benefit of their employer and not . . . divulge confidential information, or otherwise cause harm to their employer." But occasionally, circumstances might arise in which investment professionals need to engage in conduct contrary to their employer's interests to protect clients' interests. In pressuring Kuznetsov to sell more expensive, suboptimal investment products to his clients, the employer is acting in its own interests and not in the clients' best interests. Kuznetsov is clearly acting in the best interests of the clients by notifying the regulators of his employer's unethical practices.

B is incorrect. Copying client records to give to the regulator is a justifiable step for Kuznetsov to take to protect his clients' interests.

C is incorrect. In general, Kuznetsov's decision to record conversations with his supervisor and report the employer to the regulator is justified because he is attempting to protect his clients' interests by calling out his employer's unethical (and possibly illegal) conduct. However, certain jurisdictions might have laws against recording conversations without the other party's consent. Under these circumstances, his "whistle-blowing" activity is not a violation of the Code and Standards.

Clemence

Clemence, CFA, is a wealth management adviser for DeLaurier Strategic Advisers, where she is responsible for financial planning and wealth management for more than 400 retail clients. She met many of her clients through her spouse, who is a well-known attorney, and her sister, who is a physician. Clemence decides to leave DeLaurier to take a position at another firm, where she will not be expected to generate new advisory clients but will take on more research and investment management responsibilities. She leaves DeLaurier on good terms, providing her supervisor with all the background and information to seamlessly transition her clients to a new account manager. Not all of Clemence's clients have sufficient assets under management to become clients at her new firm. On the day Clemence leaves DeLaurier, she downloads a spreadsheet of DeLaurier's clients, prospects, and former clients and sends it to her personal email. The list includes names, assets under management, addresses, and phone numbers. Clemence intends to contact her clients as a courtesy to inform them of her new position, thank them for being clients, and express her confidence that DeLaurier will continue to provide them with competent and professional service even though she has left the firm.

Clemence's actions are

- **A.** a violation of the CFA Institute Code and Standards.
- **B.** appropriate because she is protecting the interests of her clients.
- **C.** appropriate as long as she contacts only those clients who are personal friends to inform them of her new position.

Analysis

A is correct. Standard IV(A): Duties to Employers, Loyalty requires that CFA Institute members and candidates "act for the benefit of their employer and not . . . divulge confidential information, or otherwise cause harm to their employer." Clemence has violated her duty of loyalty to her employer by downloading the client list and taking it with her for use after she leaves DeLaurier. The client list is DeLaurier's property. The list also contains proprietary confidential information about DeLaurier clients that Clemence is improperly using for her own purposes, no matter how well intentioned those purposes might be. Clemence could have asked her employer's permission to send a "thank you" note to her clients immediately before leaving DeLaurier, thus eliminating the need to take client information with her.

B is incorrect. Clemence is clearly not motivated to use the client list and information to benefit her new firm but appears rather to be working for DeLaurier to protect the interests of her former clients and make them feel comfortable in continuing to use DeLaurier as their financial adviser. But in obtaining information about her clients, Clemence goes too far and also takes more information than perhaps intended. In addition to information about her clients she has also obtained information about the firm's former, current, and prospective clients.

C is incorrect. Clemence may contact her former clients who are friends through personal channels, such as social media or a personal contact, but she cannot use DeLaurier's property to facilitate this communication. As an alternative, she could ask DeLaurier's permission to take her clients' contact information so she can send them a final "thank you" correspondence.

Additional Compensation Arrangements

> Members and Candidates must not accept gifts, benefits, compensation, or consideration that competes with or might reasonably be expected to create a conflict of interest with their employer's interest unless they obtain written consent from all parties involved.

Estevez

Estevez, CFA, is a senior research analyst with BIR, a boutique investment research firm covering micro- and small-cap companies that hire BIR to provide research coverage (called issuer-paid research) to promote their stock to investors. Because of BIR's stellar reputation, its research services are in high demand among both investors and companies seeking potential investors. Estevez helps BIR select the companies it covers and oversees a team of junior research analysts. Some companies encourage Estevez to select their company for BIR research coverage by giving her a separate bonus if they are included in the BIR research universe. Estevez's actions are

A. a violation of the CFA Institute Code and Standards because her independence and objectivity in conducting the research are compromised.

B. acceptable as long as Estevez does not use material nonpublic information from the company.

C. acceptable as long as her company approves in writing the payments offered by covered companies.

Analysis

C is correct. Standard IV(B): Duties to Employers, Additional Compensation Arrangements requires members and candidates to obtain written consent from their employer before they accept any gift, benefit, or compensation that "might reasonably be expected to create a conflict of interest with their employer's interest." Estevez receives a benefit from companies that BIR selects to receive research coverage. Estevez's involvement in the process of choosing the companies that BIR agrees to research presents a conflict of interest because she might favor those companies that pay her the bonus. Estevez would have to disclose to her company that she is receiving the benefit from the selected company, and BIR would have to disclose to the users of the report that the company paid Estevez the bonus and is paying for the research coverage.

Duties to Employers

A is incorrect. Issuer-paid research itself is not automatically unethical nor does it automatically compromise an analyst's independence and objectivity. However this area is filled with potential conflicts, so important safeguards must be observed. BIR must adopt strict procedures to protect the analyst's objectivity from being influenced by the company. Such safeguards must also include full disclosure of any conflicts of interest on the part of the analyst conducting the research; full disclosure of any compensation arrangements, including the source of the payment for the research; and policies that separate the research recommendations from the level or nature of the payment.

B is incorrect. Even if she is not using material nonpublic information from the company, this does not alleviate Estevez's need for full disclosure and employer consent regarding her bonuses from companies.

Responsibilities of Supervisors

> Members and Candidates must make reasonable efforts to ensure that anyone subject to their supervision or authority complies with applicable laws, rules, regulations, and the Code and Standards.

Duhih

RC Group (RCG) is a registered futures commission merchant with several branch offices, including one in Memphis, Tennessee (USA). Duhih, CFA, is hired to be the branch manager of the Memphis office, supervising several employees, including Lewes, CFA. Duhih allows Lewes to work from home, so Lewes does not have a physical workspace in the Memphis office or even access to the building, and Duhih only occasionally checks in with Lewes regarding work. Unknown to either Duhih or RCG, Lewes also works for another futures commission merchant, called AFCM. Lewes arranges swap agreements for AFCM, including orders with several cattle feed yard clients. Working with another employee at RCG, Lewes opens new futures accounts for the feed yard clients RCG represents. Although the other RCG employee receives all the commissions for the accounts, she secretly splits them with Lewes. Duhih is unaware of Lewes' participation in this commission sharing arrangement.

Duhih's actions as a supervisor are

A. a violation of the CFA Institute Code and Standards.

B. acceptable if the RCG headquarters conducts regular audits of the Memphis branch.

C. acceptable if RCG did not develop adequate policies and procedures for the detection and deterrence of possible employee misconduct.

Analysis

A is correct. Standard IV(C): Duties to Employers, Responsibilities of Supervisors states that members and candidates "must make reasonable efforts to ensure that anyone subject to their supervision or authority complies with applicable laws, rules, regulations, and the Code and Standards." At a minimum, supervisors must make reasonable efforts to detect and prevent legal, regulatory, and policy violations by ensuring that effective compliance systems have been established. Although the case does not clearly present what steps Duhih took to diligently exercise supervisory responsibility, the fact that Lewes works from home and did not have access to the branch office suggests that Duhih's supervision is minimal at best and noticeably ineffective. In addition, Duhih should support his company by encouraging it to adopt a code of ethics, have clearly written compliance policies and procedures, and employee training on appropriate ethical behavior.

B is not correct. A regular audit of the Memphis branch by compliance personnel from RCG headquarters could be an excellent way to ensure that branch employees are complying with applicable law, regulations, and RCG policies. However, it would not be a substitute for effective and regular supervision by Duhih, the onsite branch manager.

C is incorrect. Supervisors must understand what constitutes an adequate compliance system and make reasonable efforts to ensure that appropriate compliance procedures are established, documented, communicated to covered personnel, and followed. If Duhih knew that RCG did not have adequate policies and procedures for detecting and deterring potential employee misconduct, he was obligated to tell management about the shortcoming, help develop adequate compliance policies, or decline supervisory responsibility. A lack of adequate policies is not an excuse for failing to detect potential misconduct by RCG employees, including Lewes. Duhih should not have accepted supervisory responsibility until he understood not only RCG's policies and procedures but also the company's expectations of him with regard to maintaining his subordinates' compliance with them.

Denikin & Denikin

Sasha Denikin, CFA, began his investment career as a research analyst for Galak Investment Partners, a company founded and controlled by his father, Franz Denikin, CFA. After several years, Franz transfers ownership of Galak to Sasha, who becomes a director of the company. Franz tells the firm's clients that he retains management of all client accounts. When the longtime CCO announces her retirement, Sasha is promoted to chief compliance officer (CCO). While Sasha has no previous compliance experience, the plan is for the prior CCO to retain compliance responsibilities as a consultant while mentoring and training Sasha. Despite his title, Sasha has no actual authority to supervise his father's conduct and Franz continues to exert absolute control over Galak. Sasha also does not have permission to contact clients or review Galak communications with clients because his father insists that all client contact go through him. During his tenure as CCO, Sasha raises multiple compliance issues to his father regarding his father's actions, but Sasha is powerless to enforce company policies and procedures concerning his father's conduct. After continuing to serve as Galak CCO for a time, Sasha finally resigns in frustration.

Sasha Denikin's actions are

A. a violation of the CFA Institute Code and Standards.

B. acceptable because Franz holds the actual power and client responsibilities at the firm and thus cannot be under the supervision of a subordinate.

C. acceptable because Sasha resigns as CCO when he is frustrated by his inability to exercise his compliance responsibilities.

Analysis

A is correct. Standard IV(C): Duties to Employers, Responsibilities of Supervisors requires CFA Institute members and candidates to "make reasonable efforts to ensure that anyone subject to their supervision or authority complies with applicable laws, rules, regulations, and the Code and Standards." Members and candidates with supervisory responsibility must make reasonable efforts to prevent and detect violations by ensuring that effective compliance systems are established. If they cannot carry out their supervisory responsibilities because of an inadequate compliance system, they should decline in writing to accept the supervisory responsibility until the firm adopts reasonable procedures to allow for the adequate exercise of that supervisory responsibility. Sasha knows that he is not qualified to serve as CCO of Galak, but still accepts the role. As CCO, Sasha has supervisory responsibility for all firm employees in compliance matters. However Sasha has difficulty performing his CCO duties because the firm's structure gives him no real authority over his father to ensure that his father's conduct complies with internal policies and regulatory rules. Sasha knows that his father is ignoring firm rules, but despite being CCO and a director of the company, Sasha has no real authority or ability to supervise and influence Franz's conduct.

B is incorrect. Franz's status as the founder and the one truly controlling the company does not exempt him from oversight by the CCO.

C is incorrect. If Sasha is unable to fulfill his responsibilities because of an inadequate compliance system or a lack of experience, he should refuse the CCO role until he has been fully trained and Galak adopts procedures allowing him to effectively exercise supervisory responsibility over his father. For example, Sasha could work with the outgoing CCO to establish a compliance program that includes a code of ethics, compliance policies and procedures, education and training programs, an incentive structure rewarding ethical behavior, and firmwide best practice standards to help meet his supervisory obligations. However, Sasha chooses to quit the CCO job and resign from the firm only after a significant period during which he fails to adequately meet his supervisory responsibilities, and, likely, the best interests of the firm's clients.

INVESTMENT ANALYSIS, RECOMMENDATIONS, AND ACTIONS

Diligence and Reasonable Basis

Members and Candidates must:

1. Exercise diligence, independence, and thoroughness in analyzing investments, making investment recommendations, and taking investment actions.

2. Have a reasonable and adequate basis, supported by appropriate research and investigation, for any investment analysis, recommendation, or action.

Harrel and Chong

Corix Bioscience is a startup company in the manufacturing and distribution of cannabidiol (CBD) products. To promote the company, the Corix CEO hires Harrel, an independent research analyst and CFA Program candidate, to write and distribute a research report on the company. The CEO tells Harrel the following:

- Corix has an agreement with indigenous tribes that allows it to access tribal lands for commercial hemp and cannabis farming and to sell hemp and cannabis products in retail outlets on tribal lands.
- Corix has a certificate of compliance from the national regulator that permits the company to transport, process, and export industrial hemp products.
- The prior year's harvest of hemp exceeded expectations in both quality and quantity, resulting in a substantial inventory of product.

Harrelson includes all this information in a research report and provides a positive analysis of the company. However, Corix does not have agreements with indigenous tribes; nor does it have regulatory approval, the certificate of compliance is a forgery; and Corix never cultivated, or harvested significant quantities of commercial hemp.

Chong, a CFA charterholder and research analyst at Nature's Harvest Investment Management (NHIM), incorporates the information and conclusions from Harrel's research report into his own research on Corix and includes a "buy" recommendation on the company. Chong's report is distributed to portfolio managers at NHIM. Corix is ultimately shown to be a fake operation, leading to substantial losses for NHIM's clients.

Which individual(s) most likely violated the CFA Institute Code and Standards?

A. Harrel only
B. Chong only
C. Both Harrel and Chong

Analysis
C is correct. Standard V(A): Investment Analysis, Recommendations, and Actions, Diligence and Reasonable Basis states that CFA Institute members and candidates must exercise diligence and thoroughness in analyzing investments and must have a reasonable and adequate basis that is supported by appropriate research and investigation for any investment recommendation. Harrel and Chong do not meet the requirements of this standard. By relying on the statements given by Corix and not conducting an independent investigation into the accuracy of the information, Harrel did not exercise diligence and thoroughness in analyzing the company. Chong seemingly relied on Harrel's research to formulate his "buy" recommendation without conducting his own independent research. Investment professionals who rely on third-party research must make reasonable and diligent efforts to determine whether that research is correct. The facts do not indicate that Chong independently verified the information, critically assessed Harrel's research, or had reason to rely on Harrel's report based on past experience and familiarity with the quality of Harrel's work. In addition, Harrel works as an independent researcher and thus has no management structure that could enforce due diligence standards, which should raise concerns about the quality of Harrel's due diligence. Chong also did not recognize that Harrel's work was issuer-paid research and thus subject to increased scrutiny. NHIM should have had clear due diligence policies and procedures in place that Chong would need to follow before completing and disseminating research on behalf of the firm.

A is incorrect. Both Harrel and Chong violated the Code and Standards.
B is incorrect. Both Harrel and Chong violated the Code and Standards.

Communication with Clients and Prospective Clients

Members and Candidates must:
1. Disclose to clients and prospective clients the basic format and general principles of the investment processes they use to analyze investments, select securities, and construct portfolios and must promptly disclose any changes that might materially affect those processes.
2. Disclose to clients and prospective clients significant limitations and risks associated with the investment process.
3. Use reasonable judgment in identifying which factors are important to their investment analyses, recommendations, or actions and include those factors in communications with clients and prospective clients.
4. Distinguish between fact and opinion in the presentation of investment analysis and recommendations.

Maalouf

Maalouf, CFA, works for a large wealth management firm. The firm's fees are calculated as a percentage of the asset value managed for each client account. The firm has a standard method for valuing assets and calculating fees, which is disclosed to clients when they open their account. Over time, the firm transitions to (1) using the market value of client assets at the end of the billing cycle instead of the average daily balance of the account; (2) including assets that were previously excluded, such as cash or cash equivalents, in the fee calculation; and (3) charging clients for a full billing period rather than prorating fees for clients that start or terminate accounts mid-billing period.

Under the CFA Institute Code and Standards, Maalouf

- **A.** must notify clients of the changes in the valuation and fee calculation method.
- **B.** cannot use end-of-cycle valuations, include cash equivalents, or charge fees for a full billing cycle for partial cycle accounts.
- **C.** can change the valuation and fee calculation methodology as long as actual fees charged to clients are lower.

Analysis

A is correct. Standard V(B): Investment Analysis, Recommendations, and Actions, Communication with Clients and Prospective Clients requires CFA Institute members and candidates to disclose to clients the basic format and general principles of the investment process. Advisory fees are a critical part of that process. Developing and maintaining clear, frequent, and thorough communication with clients allows those clients to make well-informed decisions about their investments, including whether to engage or retain an investment adviser. Any changes to the method for valuing assets or calculating fees that are different from the process the client originally agreed to must be disclosed. Maalouf must notify his clients ahead of the changes.

B is incorrect. Using end-of-cycle valuations, including cash equivalents, or not prorating fees for new or terminated clients are acceptable methods for calculating fees as long as those policies are disclosed and agreed to by the client.

C is incorrect. Changing valuation and fee calculation policies over time for existing accounts in a way that might result in higher fees is permissible, however Maalouf and his firm should negotiate with their clients on fees and changing the calculation methodology that were disclosed when the clients opened their accounts. Changing the methodology for the fee calculation without disclosing the change is improper, even if it results in lower fees.

Dukis

Dukis, CFA, is a managing director at a global credit ratings service. She is responsible for the group that assigns new issue and surveillance credit ratings to commercial mortgage-backed securities (CMBSs). To determine the ratings, Dukis and her group calculate the debt service coverage ratio (DSCR) of each security, a key quantitative metric used to rate CMBSs. Shortly after the global financial crisis, the ratings agency changes its methodology for calculating the DSCR for certain securities so that it more accurately reflects risk. Dukis's group publishes subsequent credit ratings without disclosing the change. When the new methodology is used, the securities receive higher credit ratings than they would have received if the original methodology had been used.

Dukis's actions are

- **A.** appropriate because the new methodology more accurately reflects risk.
- **B.** a violation of the CFA Institute Code and Standards because she did not disclose the change in methodology to the investing public.

C. appropriate because no disclosure is necessary, given that calculating DSCR is only one element in determining the overall rating of the security.

Analysis

B is correct. Standard V(B): Investment Analysis, Recommendations, and Actions, Communication with Clients and Prospective Clients requires CFA Institute members and candidates to disclose to investors the basic format and general principles of the investment process they use to analyze investments as well as any changes that might materially affect those processes. Ratings agencies' consistency and transparency are important to investors. If rating methodologies are not applied consistently, ratings might not be easily comparable. Similarly, without transparency, investors cannot assess the methodologies used by the credit ratings agency or the application of those methodologies, which means they cannot determine how much weight to give the rating. Dukis should have disclosed to investors the change in methodology for calculating the DSCR.

A is incorrect. Even if the new methodology does more accurately reflect risk, the change must still be communicated to investors.

C is incorrect. The DSCR is clearly a key quantitative metric used to rate the securities because the change in methodology materially affected the credit ratings by rating them higher than the original method. A change in such a key factor must be disclosed.

Record Retention

> Members and Candidates must develop and maintain appropriate records to support their investment analyses, recommendations, actions, and other investment-related communications with clients and prospective clients.

Duermott

Duermott, CFA, is president of Enhanced Investment Strategies (EIS), a small investment firm. Most clients of EIS are longtime associates of Duermott who have had their investment portfolios with the firm for decades. Because of his close personal relationship with his clients, Duermott is very familiar with their investment profile, income and retirement requirements, and risk tolerance. He keeps up with all his clients' life-changing events—such as health issues, real estate purchases, children's university expenses, and retirement—and adjusts the clients' portfolios accordingly. Duermott regularly meets with his clients at EIS's offices, and he also sees them on numerous occasions outside the office, which give him additional opportunities to update them on their investments. EIS clients complete a client agreement and risk profile when opening their account, and those profiles are updated whenever Duermott finds the time to do so.

Duermott's business practices are

A. a violation of the CFA Institute Code and Standards.

B. acceptable because he regularly communicates with clients about their investments.

C. acceptable because he adjusts clients' investments to ensure that they are suitable for the clients' needs given their changing income and risk profile.

Analysis

Conflicts of Interest

A is correct. Standard V(C): Investment Analysis, Recommendations, and Actions, Record Retention states that CFA Institute members and candidates must "develop and maintain appropriate records to support their investment analyses, recommendations, actions, and other investment-related communications with clients and prospective clients." In this case, Duermott is personally close to his clients, but he updates client records only when he "finds the time to do so," which does not appear to be promptly or regularly. Duermott has a responsibility as his clients' adviser and as the president of his company to maintain appropriate records when client circumstances change. Without necessary, relevant, and up-to-date know-your-client information, Duermott would have difficulty establishing and proving that EIS has identified the needs and circumstances of its clients and has taken them into account in recommending investments. When client circumstances, investment goals, risk tolerances, or income needs change, records should be promptly updated and reviewed regularly to document these changes.

B is incorrect. Although Duermott is fulfilling his ethical obligations as an investment manager by communicating regularly with his clients, he is not keeping regular, up-to-date client records.

C is incorrect. Although Duermott is reviewing and adjusting client portfolios on a timely basis to meet clients' changing financial circumstances, he is not keeping regular, up-to-date client records.

CONFLICTS OF INTEREST

Disclosure of Conflicts

> Members and Candidates must make full and fair disclosure of all matters that could reasonably be expected to impair their independence and objectivity or interfere with respective duties to their clients, prospective clients, and employer. Members and Candidates must ensure that such disclosures are prominent, are delivered in plain language, and communicate the relevant information effectively.

Reebh

Reebh, CFA, is the CEO and founding partner of Lux Asset Management (Lux). Reebh provides asset management and allocation services for high-net-worth individuals and several small institutional clients. His services include investing client funds with third-party subadvisers who have a specialty in a particular asset class. Reebh's clients are aware, and approve, of Lux's allocation of their assets to subadvisers. The third-party subadvisers make payments to Lux based on the total value of a client's assets placed or invested in the subadvisers' funds.

Reebh's actions are

A. appropriate because Reebh has disclosed the use of subadvisers.

B. inappropriate because the payments are an improper referral fee.

C. inappropriate unless Reebh discloses the financial arrangement he has with the subadvisers to his clients.

Analysis

C is correct. Standard VI(A): Conflicts of Interest, Disclosure of Conflicts requires CFA Institute members and candidates to "make full and fair disclosure of all matters that could reasonably be expected to impair their independence and objectivity or interfere with respective duties to their clients." The payments subadvisers make to Lux based on the value of the client assets Lux places with the subadvisers creates a potential conflict of interest because Reebh is thereby incentivized to hire subadvisers who pay the fee but who might not necessarily be the best subadvisers for his clients. To mitigate this conflict, Reebh must disclose the financial incentive to clients.

A is incorrect. Reebh has disclosed Lux's use of subadvisers, but he has not disclosed the financial incentive for Lux to use those subadvisers.

B is incorrect. Although referral arrangements might be acceptable with full disclosure to clients, Reebh is not referring clients to the subadvisers but hiring them directly on his clients' behalf.

Priority of Transactions

> Investment transactions for clients and employers must have priority over investment transactions in which a Member or Candidate is the beneficial owner.

Yang

Yang, CFA, is a research analyst at Dacco, a registered broker/dealer and investment adviser. While employed with Dacco, Yang establishes Prestige Trade Investments Limited (Prestige) and acts as investment adviser for the firm's clients. Yang is responsible for formulating Prestige's investment strategy and directs all trades on behalf of Prestige. Over several days, Yang purchases 50,000 shares of Zhongpin stock and 1,978 Zhongpin call options for his personal account at Dacco. Shortly after, Yang uses $29.8 million of Prestige's funds to purchase more than 3 million shares of Zhongpin stock.

Yang's actions are

- **A.** a violation of the CFA Institute Code and Standards.
- **B.** acceptable because Yang's personal investments are not in conflict with the investment advice being given to his clients at Prestige.
- **C.** acceptable as long as Prestige clients are not negatively affected by Yang's prior purchase of Zhongpin securities through his account at Dacco.

Analysis

A is correct. Standard VI(B): Conflicts of Interest, Priority of Transactions states that "investment transactions for clients . . . must have priority over investment transactions in which a [CFA Institute] Member or Candidate is the beneficial owner." Yang is "front-running" his Prestige clients' trades. Front-running involves trading for one's personal account before trading for client accounts. Yang purchases Zhongpin stock and call options in his personal account at Dacco before directing the Zhongpin trades for clients at Prestige. The $29.8 million of Prestige funds invested in Zhongpin stock could have a material upward effect on the price of the stock and options Yang holds. Even the perception that Yang could profit by using Prestige's funds will diminish investors' trust in Yang and the capital markets.

B is incorrect. Yang's personal investments are tracking with his client investments, so no conflict exists between his personal trading and the investment actions/advice for clients. However the timing of the trades is the issue in this case because Yang is "front-running" his clients' trades.

Conflicts of Interest

C is incorrect. The fact that Prestige clients are not harmed by Yang's earlier trades for his personal accounts does not make his actions acceptable.

Kapadia

Kapadia, CFA, is a trader for an asset management company that manages several large global mutual funds. Kapadia executes the equity buy-and-sell orders for the portfolio managers of one of the company's mutual funds. He has the discretion to execute the orders at any time during the day, depending on market conditions. Before executing the orders, Kapadia contacts several close friends and relatives to give them information on which securities the mutual fund will be trading. In turn, these friends and relatives make trades that mirror the imminent trades to be executed by Kapadia on behalf of the mutual fund.

Kapadia's actions are

- **A.** a violation of the CFA Institute Code and Standards.
- **B.** inappropriate only if the client is harmed financially by the conduct.
- **C.** appropriate because he does not share confidential information about individual clients.

Analysis

A is correct. Standard VI(B): Conflicts of Interest, Priority of Transactions states that "investment transactions for clients must have priority over investment transactions" for a member or candidate's personal benefit. Kapadia is facilitating front-running by his friends and relatives on the trades of his employer's mutual fund. Front-running is the unethical and often illegal practice of trading on advance information for one's personal account before trading for client accounts to gain an economic advantage. Although Kapadia might not directly benefit financially, he benefits personally by providing the information to those with whom he has close relationships.

B is incorrect. Kapadia's engagement in the practice of front-running, which involves trading in personal accounts before trading for client accounts, is unethical and inappropriate even if the trades of Kapadia's friends and relatives do not disadvantage the mutual fund by moving the price of the security or causing the fund to lose the price advantage or any profit from its own trades.

C is incorrect. Although Kapadia does not share the confidential information of individual clients or individual investors in the fund, he does share confidential information about the fund itself.

Perrkins

Perrkins, CFA, is the chief investment officer of GT Financial (GTF). Perrkins's wife is GTF's compliance officer. GTF has several dozen retail clients and total assets under management of $70 million. All client assets are managed on a discretionary basis. Perrkins frequently makes trades for his clients using an omnibus trading account through a broker/dealer, which allows Perrkins to buy and sell securities in a block trade on behalf of multiple clients simultaneously. Perrkins regularly allocates the securities purchases to individual client accounts after the market closes. Over one six-month period, Perrkins allocates 75% of the profitable trades to nine accounts that Perrkins and his wife own or control. At the same time, he allocates 82% of the unprofitable trades to the account of the three largest GTF clients.

Perrkins's actions are

- **A.** a violation of the CFA Institute Code and Standards.
- **B.** acceptable as long as he discloses the trade allocation practices to his clients.

C. acceptable as long as he reverses his trade allocation practices to favor the larger clients so that they are not harmed over the long term.

Analysis

A is correct. Standard VI(B): Conflicts of Interest, Priority of Transactions states that investment transactions for clients have priority over personal transactions. By trading in the firm's omnibus account and then delaying the allocation of trades to a specific account until he has an opportunity to observe the security's intraday performance, Perrkins can pick the winning trades for accounts in which he has a beneficial interest. This practice is a violation of Standard VI(B). He then allocates the losing trades to clients' accounts that are large enough to absorb incremental trading losses without arousing suspicion that the losses are due to fraud. Perrkins's actions are also likely a violation of Standard III(B): Duties to Clients, Fair Dealing, which states that members and candidates "must deal fairly and objectively with all clients when . . . taking investment action, or engaging in other professional activities."

B is incorrect. Disclosure to his clients as to how he is allocating the trades does not make Perrkins unethical, fraudulent behavior acceptable.

C is incorrect. Perrkins cannot temporarily favor his personal interests over his clients' interests with the intent of rectifying the situation for his clients in the future. Ethical conduct is not subject to a ledger-keeping exercise. CFA Institute members and candidates must comply with the ethical principles and requirements of the Code and Standards at all times.

Referral Fees

> Members and Candidates must disclose to their employer, clients, and prospective clients, as appropriate, any compensation, consideration, or benefit received from or paid to others for the recommendation of products or services.

Kiang

Kiang, CFA, is a successful investment adviser with several high-net-worth clients who are very happy with his services. Many of Kiang's clients recommend his advisory services to their friends and family, and Kiang encourages these recommendations to build his business. Each year, Kiang hosts an elaborate party for clients who have referred new clients to his advisory firm. At the party, Kiang distributes nominal gift cards to attendees. In some cases, Kiang offers discounts on advisory fees to clients who sent him referrals that proved particularly lucrative. Many of the clients attending these celebrations were referred to Kiang by other clients, and they, in turn, continue the cycle of recommending Kiang to a wider circle of friends and family.

Kiang's actions most likely are

A. acceptable as a reward for client loyalty.

B. acceptable because he treats all clients fairly.

C. a violation of the CFA Institute Code and Standards.

Analysis

C is correct. Standard VI(C): Conflicts of Interest, Referral Fees states that members and candidates "must disclose to their employer, clients, and prospective clients, as appropriate, any compensation, consideration, or benefit . . . paid to others for the recommendation of . . . services." In this case, Kiang hosts an elaborate party, distributes gift cards, and, in some cases, offers discounted advisory fees to clients who have referred particularly lucrative clients. Under the standard, these benefits would be considered referral fees that must be disclosed. The facts do not indicate that Kiang makes any disclosure to potential clients. The fact that some prospects, upon becoming clients, become aware that he pays for referrals when they receive discounted fees is insufficient disclosure. It would be acceptable if Kiang were to host a party or give gift cards to all his clients to reward their loyalty, regardless as to whether or not they provided referrals.

A is incorrect. The party, gift cards, and discounted advisory fees are more than a reward for client loyalty and would be considered referral fees that are provided only to existing clients for recommending Kiang's services.

B is incorrect. Arguably, Kiang treats his clients fairly because he offers all of his clients the opportunity to receive these benefits and fee discounts as long as they refer others to his business and whether the clients access these benefits by making referrals is up to them. However regardless as to whether Kiang is treating all clients fairly, he is violating Standard VI(C) by not disclosing the benefits and compensation he awards for referrals.

RESPONSIBILITIES AS A CFA INSTITUTE MEMBER OR CFA CANDIDATE   8

Conduct as Participants in CFA Institute Programs

> Members and Candidates must not engage in any conduct that compromises the reputation or integrity of CFA Institute or the CFA designation or the integrity, validity, or security of the CFA Institute programs.

Taveras

Taveras, CFA, leads an exam preparation course sponsored by his local society. The society hosts a celebration for the students after the exam is over. During the celebration, several of Taveras's students describe their experience of taking the exam. Most give their opinion on the relative difficulty of the exam compared to their expectations, and some describe their surprise about areas of the curriculum that were not tested. Taveras asks his students for their opinions on the most difficult exam questions.

Under the CFA Institute Code and Standards, Taveras is most likely

A. prohibited from discussing the exam with students after it is over.

B. free to pass along information about the exam to candidates in future prep courses to help prepare them for the exam.

C. allowed to share the opinions of his students about the difficulty of the exam with candidates in future prep courses to emphasize the need to thoroughly prepare.

Analysis

B is correct. Standard VII(A): Responsibilities as a CFA Institute Member or CFA Candidate, Conduct as Participants in CFA Institute Programs states that candidates "must not engage in any conduct that compromises... the integrity, validity, or security of CFA Institute programs. For Taveras to share with future prep course participants the opinions of his previous students who found the CFA exam more difficult than expected is acceptable as a way to encourage future students to study the curriculum thoroughly and prepare as much as possible. However, Tavares should not solicit or pass on information regarding the specifics of the exam.

A is incorrect. A group of candidates who collectively completed the rigorous process of studying for and taking the CFA exam will naturally want to celebrate the accomplishment and discuss the exam after it is over. Candidates are allowed to discuss their exam experience with Taveras in general terms, but they cannot provide specific information about the exam regarding the questions or the general areas tested.

C is incorrect. Taveras cannot pass along specific information to future candidates and should not be soliciting information about specific questions; doing so would be a violation of Standard VII(A), which is designed to protect the integrity and security of future exams.

Reference to CFA Institute, the CFA Designation, and the CFA Program

> When referring to CFA Institute, CFA Institute membership, the CFA designation, or candidacy in the CFA Program, Members and Candidates must not misrepresent or exaggerate the meaning or implications of membership in CFA Institute, holding the CFA designation, or candidacy in the CFA program.

Ahmed

Ahmed recently earned his CFA designation and joined a medium-sized hedge fund as a senior analyst. His supervisor, Bennett, the firm's founder, earned her CFA designation 10 years ago and proudly uses the CFA designation on her business card and on all marketing materials for the fund. Bennett shares with Ahmed that she has not paid her CFA Institute membership dues for the past four years and no longer participates in the organization's continuing education program. When Ahmed asks Bennett about her use of the designation, she states that by passing the CFA exam she earned the CFA charter, and that the credential is like a university degree that cannot be taken away. Later, during a marketing meeting by the two to a potential investor, the investor notes that he narrowed his manager search to only firms that employ CFA charterholders in senior positions. When he asks Bennett if everyone in the firm on the investment side is a CFA charterholder, she responds, "Yes, that is correct." Ahmed does not respond.

Did either Ahmed or Bennett violate the CFA Institute Code and Standards?

- **A.** Ahmed violated the Code and Standards, but Bennett did not.
- **B.** Bennett violated the Code and Standards, but Ahmed did not.
- **C.** Both Ahmed and Bennett violated the Code and Standards.

Analysis

C is correct. Standard VII(B): Responsibilities as a CFA Institute Member or CFA Candidate, Reference to CFA Institute, the CFA Designation, and the CFA Program states that when referring to the CFA designation, members and candidates "must not misrepresent . . . holding the CFA designation." The CFA designation is not like a degree from a university because once individuals have been granted the right to use the designation, they must also satisfy CFA Institute membership requirements, which include paying dues, to maintain the right to refer to themselves as CFA charterholders. Participation in the CFA Institute Professional Learning program is not mandatory for members to maintain their designation, but it is encouraged as a way to meet the

Responsibilities as a CFA Institute Member or CFA Candidate

CFA Institute Code of Ethics provision that members maintain and improve their professional competence. Bennett's membership is considered lapsed because she has not been paying dues to CFA Institute. Until she reactivates her membership, Bennett is violating Standard VII(B) by continuing to use the CFA designation and representing herself as a charterholder to a potential client. Ahmed knows that Bennett's CFA Institute membership has lapsed. Standard I(A): Professionalism, Knowledge of the Law prohibits members and candidates from knowingly participating or assisting in the violations of others and requires members and candidates to dissociate from any unethical or illegal conduct. By staying silent in a sales meeting in which he knows false information is being given to a potential investor that could cause harm to that investor, Ahmed would be seen as assisting Bennett in providing that false information, even though Ahmed is not actively engaging in the misconduct himself. Best practice would be for Ahmed to address Bennett directly about her conduct and ask her to reinstate her membership or correct the statement she made to the potential investor. If Bennett refuses to take corrective action, Ahmed should report her conduct to the fund's compliance department for it to address and should dissociate himself from the activity by not participating in any additional sales meetings with Bennett.

A is not correct because both Ahmed and Bennett violated the Code and Standards

B is not correct because both Ahmed and Bennett violated the Code and Standards.

Glossary

A priori probability A probability based on logical analysis rather than on observation or personal judgment.

Abandonment option The option to terminate an investment at some future time if the financial results are disappointing.

Abnormal return The amount by which a security's actual return differs from its expected return, given the security's risk and the market's return.

Absolute advantage A country's ability to produce a good or service at a lower absolute cost than its trading partner.

Absolute dispersion The amount of variability present without comparison to any reference point or benchmark.

Absolute frequency The actual number of observations counted for each unique value of the variable (also called raw frequency).

Accelerated book build An offering of securities by an investment bank acting as principal that is accomplished in only one or two days.

Accelerated methods Depreciation methods that allocate a relatively large proportion of the cost of an asset to the early years of the asset's useful life.

Accounting costs Monetary value of economic resources used in performing an activity. These can be explicit, out-of-pocket, current payments, or an allocation of historical payments (depreciation) for resources. They do not include implicit opportunity costs.

Accounting profit Income as reported on the income statement, in accordance with prevailing accounting standards, before the provisions for income tax expense. Also called *income before taxes* or *pretax income*.

Accounts payable Amounts that a business owes to its vendors for goods and services that were purchased from them but which have not yet been paid.

Accredited investors Those who are considered sophisticated enough to take greater risks and to have a reduced need for regulatory oversight and protection. In some jurisdictions, these investors are referred to as professional, eligible, or qualified investors.

Accrued expenses Liabilities related to expenses that have been incurred but not yet paid as of the end of an accounting period—an example of an accrued expense is rent that has been incurred but not yet paid, resulting in a liability "rent payable." Also called *accrued liabilities*.

Accrued interest Interest earned but not yet paid.

Acquisition method A method of accounting for a business combination where the acquirer is required to measure each identifiable asset and liability at fair value. This method was the result of a joint project of the IASB and FASB aiming at convergence in standards for the accounting of business combinations.

Action lag Delay from policy decisions to implementation.

Active investment An approach to investing in which the investor seeks to outperform a given benchmark.

Active return The return on a portfolio minus the return on the portfolio's benchmark.

Activity ratios Ratios that measure how well a company is managing key current assets and working capital over time.

Add-on rates Bank certificates of deposit, repos, and indexes such as Libor and Euribor are quoted on an add-on rate basis (bond equivalent yield basis).

Addition rule for probabilities A principle stating that the probability that A or B occurs (both occur) equals the probability that A occurs, plus the probability that B occurs, minus the probability that both A and B occur.

Affiliate marketing The generation of commission revenues for sales generated on other's websites.

Agency bond See *quasi-government bond*.

Agency costs Costs associated with conflicts of interest between principals and agents when a company is managed by non-owners. Agency costs result from the inherent conflicts of interest between managers and debtholders (referred to as agency costs of debt) and between managers and shareholders (referred to as agency costs of equity).

Agency RMBS In the United States, securities backed by residential mortgage loans and guaranteed by a federal agency or guaranteed by either of the two GSEs (Fannie Mae and Freddie Mac).

Aggregate demand The quantity of goods and services that households, businesses, government, and non-domestic customers want to buy at any given level of prices.

Aggregate demand curve Inverse relationship between the price level and real output.

Aggregate income The value of all the payments earned by the suppliers of factors used in the production of goods and services.

Aggregate output The value of all the goods and services produced during a specified period.

Aggregate supply The quantity of goods and services producers are willing to supply at any given level of price.

Aggregate supply curve The level of domestic output that companies will produce at each price level.

Aggregators Similar to marketplaces, but the aggregator re-markets products and services under its own brand.

All-or-nothing (AON) orders An order that includes the instruction to trade only if the trade fills the entire quantity (size) specified.

Allocationally efficient A characteristic of a market, a financial system, or an economy that promotes the allocation of resources to their highest value uses.

Alternative data Non-traditional data types generated by the use of electronic devices, social media, satellite and sensor networks, and company exhaust.

Alternative hypothesis The hypothesis that is accepted if the null hypothesis is rejected.

Alternative investment markets Market for investments other than traditional securities investments (i.e., traditional common and preferred shares and traditional fixed income instruments). The term usually encompasses direct and indirect investment in real estate (including timberland and farmland) and commodities (including precious metals); hedge funds, private equity, and other investments requiring specialized due diligence.

Alternative trading systems (ATS) Non-exchange trading venues that bring together buyers and sellers to find transaction counterparties. Also called *multilateral trading facilities (MTF)*.

American depository receipt A US dollar-denominated security that trades like a common share on US exchanges.

American depository share The underlying shares on which American depository receipts are based. They trade in the issuing company's domestic market.

American options Options that may be exercised at any time from contract inception until maturity.

American-style Type of option contract that can be exercised at any time up to the option's expiration date.

Amortisation The process of allocating the cost of intangible long-term assets having a finite useful life to accounting periods; the allocation of the amount of a bond premium or discount to the periods remaining until bond maturity.

Amortised cost The historical cost (initially recognised cost) of an asset, adjusted for amortisation and impairment.

Amortizing bond Bond with a payment schedule that calls for periodic payments of interest and repayments of principal.

Amortizing loans Loans with a payment schedule that calls for periodic payments of interest and repayments of principal.

Analysis of variance (ANOVA) The analysis that breaks the total variability of a dataset (such as observations on the dependent variable in a regression) into components representing different sources of variation.

Analytical duration The use of mathematical formulas to estimate the impact of benchmark yield-to-maturity changes on bond prices.

Anchoring and adjustment bias An information-processing bias in which the use of a psychological heuristic influences the way people estimate probabilities.

Annual percentage rate The cost of borrowing expressed as a yearly rate.

Annuity A finite set of level sequential cash flows.

Annuity due An annuity having a first cash flow that is paid immediately.

Anomalies Apparent deviations from market efficiency.

Antidilutive With reference to a transaction or a security, one that would increase earnings per share (EPS) or result in EPS higher than the company's basic EPS—antidilutive securities are not included in the calculation of diluted EPS.

Arbitrage 1) The simultaneous purchase of an undervalued asset or portfolio and sale of an overvalued but equivalent asset or portfolio, in order to obtain a riskless profit on the price differential. Taking advantage of a market inefficiency in a risk-free manner. 2) The condition in a financial market in which equivalent assets or combinations of assets sell for two different prices, creating an opportunity to profit at no risk with no commitment of money. In a well-functioning financial market, few arbitrage opportunities are possible. 3) A risk-free operation that earns an expected positive net profit but requires no net investment of money.

Arbitrageurs Traders who engage in arbitrage. See *arbitrage*.

Arithmetic mean The sum of the observations divided by the number of observations.

Artificial intelligence Computer systems that exhibit cognitive and decision-making ability comparable (or superior) to that of humans.

Ask The price at which a dealer or trader is willing to sell an asset, typically qualified by a maximum quantity (ask size). See *offer*.

Ask size The maximum quantity of an asset that pertains to a specific ask price from a trader. For example, if the ask for a share issue is $30 for a size of 1,000 shares, the trader is offering to sell at $30 up to 1,000 shares.

Asset allocation The process of determining how investment funds should be distributed among asset classes.

Asset-backed securities A type of bond issued by a legal entity called a *special purpose entity* (SPE) on a collection of assets that the SPE owns. Also, securities backed by receivables and loans other than mortgages.

Asset-based valuation models Valuation based on estimates of the market value of a company's assets.

Asset beta The unlevered beta, which reflects the business risk of the assets; the asset's systematic risk.

Asset class A group of assets that have similar characteristics, attributes, and risk–return relationships.

Asset-light business models Business models that minimize required capital investment by shifting the ownership of high-cost assets to other firms.

Asset swap Converts the periodic fixed coupon of a specific bond to an MRR plus or minus a spread.

Asset utilization ratios Ratios that measure how efficiently a company performs day-to-day tasks, such as the collection of receivables and management of inventory.

Assets Resources controlled by an enterprise as a result of past events and from which future economic benefits to the enterprise are expected to flow.

Assignment of accounts receivable The use of accounts receivable as collateral for a loan.

Asymmetric information Also known as information asymmetry. The differential of information between corporate insiders and outsiders regarding the company's performance and prospects. Managers typically have more information about the company's performance and prospects than owners and creditors.

At-the-money Describes a unique situation in which the price of the underlying is equal to an option's exercise price. Like an out-of-the-money option, the intrinsic value is zero.

Auction A type of bond issuing mechanism often used for sovereign bonds that involves bidding.

Auction/reverse auction models Pricing models that establish prices through bidding (by sellers in the case of reverse auctions).

Autarkic price The price of a good or service in an autarkic economy.

Autarky Countries seeking political self-sufficiency with little or no external trade or finance. State-owned enterprises control strategic domestic industries.

Automatic stabilizer A countercyclical factor that automatically comes into play as an economy slows and unemployment rises.

Availability bias An information-processing bias in which people take a heuristic approach to estimating the probability of an outcome based on how easily the outcome comes to mind.

Available-for-sale Under US GAAP, debt securities not classified as either held-to-maturity or held-for-trading securities. The investor is willing to sell but not actively planning to sell. In general, available-for-sale debt securities are reported at fair value on the balance sheet, with unrealized gains included as a component of other comprehensive income.

Average fixed cost Total fixed cost divided by quantity produced.

Average life See *weighted average life*.
Average product Measures the productivity of inputs on average and is calculated by dividing total product by the total number of units for a given input that is used to generate that output.
Average revenue Total revenue divided by quantity sold.
Average total cost Total cost divided by quantity produced.
Average variable cost Total variable cost divided by quantity produced.
Backtesting The process that approximates the real-life investment process, using historical data, to assess whether an investment strategy would have produced desirable results.
Backfill bias A problem whereby certain surviving hedge funds are added to databases and various hedge fund indexes only after they are initially successful and start to report their returns.
Backtesting The process that approximates the real-life investment process, using historical data, to assess whether an investment strategy would have produced desirable results.
Backup line of credit A type of credit enhancement provided by a bank to an issuer of commercial paper to ensure that the issuer will have access to sufficient liquidity to repay maturing commercial paper if issuing new paper is not a viable option.
Backwardation A condition in the futures markets in which the spot price exceeds the futures price, the forward curve is downward sloping, and the convenience yield is high.
Balance of payments A double-entry bookkeeping system that summarizes a country's economic transactions with the rest of the world for a particular period of time, typically a calendar quarter or year.
Balance of trade deficit When the domestic economy is spending more on non-domestic goods and services than non-domestic economies are spending on domestic goods and services.
Balance sheet The financial statement that presents an entity's current financial position by disclosing resources the entity controls (its assets) and the claims on those resources (its liabilities and equity claims), as of a particular point in time (the date of the balance sheet). Also called *statement of financial position* or *statement of financial condition*.
Balance sheet ratios Financial ratios involving balance sheet items only.
Balanced With respect to a government budget, one in which spending and revenues (taxes) are equal.
Balloon payment Large payment required at maturity to retire a bond's outstanding principal amount.
Bar chart A chart for plotting the frequency distribution of categorical data, where each bar represents a distinct category and each bar's height is proportional to the frequency of the corresponding category. In technical analysis, a bar chart that plots four bits of data for each time interval—the high, low, opening, and closing prices. A vertical line connects the high and low prices. A cross-hatch left indicates the opening price and a cross-hatch right indicates the closing price.
Barter economy An economy where economic agents as house-holds, corporations, and governments "pay" for goods and services with another good or service.
Base-rate neglect A type of representativeness bias in which the base rate or probability of the categorization is not adequately considered.
Base rates The reference rate on which a bank bases lending rates to all other customers.

Basic EPS Net earnings available to common shareholders (i.e., net income minus preferred dividends) divided by the weighted average number of common shares outstanding.
Basis point Used in stating yield spreads, one basis point equals one-hundredth of a percentage point, or 0.01%.
Basis risk The possibility that the expected value of a derivative differs unexpectedly from that of the underlying.
Basket of listed depository receipts An exchange-traded fund (ETF) that represents a portfolio of depository receipts.
Bayes' formula The rule for updating the probability of an event of interest—given a set of prior probabilities for the event, information, and information given the event—if you receive new information.
Bearer bonds Bonds for which ownership is not recorded; only the clearing system knows who the bond owner is.
Bearish crossover A technical analysis term that describes a situation where a short-term moving average crosses a longer-term moving average from above; this movement is considered bearish. A **death cross** is a bearish crossover based on 50-day and 200-day moving averages.
Behavioral finance A field of finance that examines the psychological variables that affect and often distort the investment decision making of investors, analysts, and portfolio managers.
Behind the market Said of prices specified in orders that are worse than the best current price; e.g., for a limit buy order, a limit price below the best bid.
Benchmark A comparison portfolio; a point of reference or comparison.
Benchmark issue The latest sovereign bond issue for a given maturity. It serves as a benchmark against which to compare bonds that have the same features but that are issued by another type of issuer.
Benchmark rate Typically the yield-to-maturity on a government bond having the same or close to the same time-to-maturity.
Benchmark spread The yield spread over a specific benchmark, usually measured in basis points.
Bernoulli random variable A random variable having the outcomes 0 and 1.
Bernoulli trial An experiment that can produce one of two outcomes.
Best bid The highest bid in the market.
Best effort offering An offering of a security using an investment bank in which the investment bank, as agent for the issuer, promises to use its best efforts to sell the offering but does not guarantee that a specific amount will be sold.
Best-efforts offering An offering of a security using an investment bank in which the investment bank, as agent for the issuer, promises to use its best efforts to sell the offering but does not guarantee that a specific amount will be sold.
Best-in-class An ESG implementation approach that seeks to identify the most favorable companies and sectors based on ESG considerations. Also called *positive screening*.
Best offer The lowest offer (ask price) in the market.
Beta A measure of the sensitivity of a given investment or portfolio to movements in the overall market.
Bid The price at which a dealer or trader is willing to buy an asset, typically qualified by a maximum quantity.
Bid size The maximum quantity of an asset that pertains to a specific bid price from a trader.
Bid–ask spread The ask price minus the bid price.

Bid–offer spread The difference between the prices at which dealers will buy from a customer (bid) and sell to a customer (offer or ask). It is often used as an indicator of liquidity.

Big Data The vast amount of data being generated by industry, governments, individuals, and electronic devices that arises from both traditional and non-traditional data sources.

Bilateral loan A loan from a single lender to a single borrower.

Bilateralism The conduct of political, economic, financial, or cultural cooperation between two countries. Countries engaging in bilateralism may have relations with many different countries but in one-at-a-time agreements without multiple partners. Typically, countries exist on a spectrum between bilateralism and multilateralism.

Bimodal A distribution that has two most frequently occurring values.

Binomial random variable The number of successes in n Bernoulli trials for which the probability of success is constant for all trials and the trials are independent.

Binomial tree The graphical representation of a model of asset price dynamics in which, at each period, the asset moves up with probability p or down with probability $(1 - p)$.

Bitcoin A cryptocurrency using blockchain technology that was created in 2009.

Bivariate correlation See *Pearson correlation*.

Black swan risk An event that is rare and difficult to predict but has an important impact.

Block brokers A broker (agent) that provides brokerage services for large-size trades.

Blockchain A type of digital ledger in which information is recorded sequentially and then linked together and secured using cryptographic methods.

Blue chip Widely held large market capitalization companies that are considered financially sound and are leaders in their respective industry or local stock market.

Bollinger Bands A price-based technical analysis indicator consisting of a line representing the moving average, a higher line representing the moving average plus a set number of standard deviations from the average (for the same number of periods as was used to calculate the moving average), and a lower line representing the moving average minus the same number of standard deviations.

Bond Contractual agreement between the issuer and the bondholders.

Bond equivalent yield A calculation of yield that is annualized using the ratio of 365 to the number of days to maturity. Bond equivalent yield allows for the restatement and comparison of securities with different compounding periods.

Bond indenture A legal contract specifying the terms of a bond issue.

Bond market vigilantes Bond market participants who might reduce their demand for long-term bonds, thus pushing up their yields.

Bond yield plus risk premium approach An estimate of the cost of common equity that is produced by summing the before-tax cost of debt and a risk premium that captures the additional yield on a company's stock relative to its bonds. The additional yield is often estimated using historical spreads between bond yields and stock yields.

Bonus issue of shares A type of dividend in which a company distributes additional shares of its common stock to shareholders instead of cash.

Book building Investment bankers' process of compiling a "book" or list of indications of interest to buy part of an offering.

Book value The net amount shown for an asset or liability on the balance sheet; book value may also refer to the company's excess of total assets over total liabilities. Also called *carrying value*.

Boom An expansionary phase characterized by economic growth "testing the limits" of the economy.

Bootstrap A resampling method that repeatedly draws samples with replacement of the selected elements from the original observed sample. Bootstrap is usually conducted by using computer simulation and is often used to find standard error or construct confidence intervals of population parameters.

Borrowed capital (debt) Money that is lent by debtholders to a company.

Bottom-up analysis An investment selection approach that focuses on company-specific circumstances rather than emphasizing economic cycles or industry analysis.

Box and whisker plot A graphic for visualizing the dispersion of data across quartiles. It consists of a "box" with "whiskers" connected to the box.

Breakdown A breakdown occurs when the price of an asset moves below a support level.

Breakeven point Represents the price of the underlying in a derivative contract in which the profit to both counterparties would be zero.

Breakout A breakout occurs when the price of an asset moves above a resistance level.

Bridge financing Interim financing that provides funds until permanent financing can be arranged.

Broad money Encompasses narrow money plus the entire range of liquid assets that can be used to make purchases.

Broker 1) An agent who executes orders to buy or sell securities on behalf of a client in exchange for a commission. 2) See *futures commission merchants*.

Broker–dealer A financial intermediary (often a company) that may function as a principal (dealer) or as an agent (broker) depending on the type of trade.

Brokered market A market in which brokers arrange trades among their clients.

Brownfield investment Investing in existing infrastructure assets.

Bubble line chart A line chart that uses varying-sized bubbles to represent a third dimension of the data. The bubbles are sometimes color-coded to present additional information.

Budget surplus/deficit The difference between government revenue and expenditure for a stated fixed period of time.

Bullet bond Bond in which the principal repayment is made entirely at maturity.

Bullish crossover A technical analysis term that describes a situation where a short-term moving average crosses a longer-term moving average from below; this movement is considered bullish. A **golden cross** is a bullish crossover based on 50-day and 200-day moving averages.

Bundling A pricing approach that refers to combining multiple products or services so that customers are incentivized or required to buy them together.

Business cycles are recurrent expansions and contractions in economic activity affecting broad segments of the economy.

Business risk The risk that the firm's operating results will fall short of expectations, independently of how the business is financed.

Buy-side firm An investment management company or other investor that uses the services of brokers or dealers (i.e., the client of the sell side firms).

Buyback A transaction in which a company buys back its own shares. Unlike stock dividends and stock splits, share repurchases use corporate cash.

CBOE Volatility Index (VIX) A measure of near-term market volatility as conveyed by S&P 500 stock index option prices.

CDS credit spread Reflects the credit spread of a credit default swap (CDS) derivative contract. As with cash bonds, CDS credit spreads depend on the probability of default (POD) and the loss given default (LGD).

CVaR Conditional VaR, a tail loss measure. The weighted average of all loss outcomes in the statistical distribution that exceed the VaR loss.

Cabotage The right to transport passengers or goods within a country by a foreign firm. Many countries—including those with multilateral trade agreements—impose restrictions on cabotage across transportation subsectors, meaning that shippers, airlines, and truck drivers are not allowed to transport goods and services within another country's borders.

Call market A market in which trades occur only at a particular time and place (i.e., when the market is called).

Call money rate The interest rate that buyers pay for their margin loan.

Call option The right to buy an underlying.

Call protection The time during which the issuer of the bond is not allowed to exercise the call option.

Callable bond A bond containing an embedded call option that gives the issuer the right to buy the bond back from the investor at specified prices on pre-determined dates.

Calmar ratio A ratio of the average annual compounded return to the maximum drawdown risk over a limited time period, typically three years.

Candlestick chart A price chart with four bits of data for each time interval. A candle indicates the opening and closing price for the interval. The body of the candle is shaded if the opening price was higher than the closing price, and the body is white (or clear) if the opening price was lower than the closing price. Vertical lines known as wicks or shadows extend from the top and bottom of the candle to indicate, respectively, the high and low prices for the interval.

Cannibalization Cannibalization occurs when an investment takes customers and sales away from another part of the company.

Cap rate A metric by which real estate managers are often judged; the annual rent actually earned (net of any vacancies) divided by the price originally paid for the property.

Capacity The ability of the borrower to make its debt payments on time.

Capital account A component of the balance of payments account that measures transfers of capital.

Capital allocation The process that companies use for decision making on capital investments—those projects with a life of one year or longer.

Capital allocation line (CAL) A graph line that describes the combinations of expected return and standard deviation of return available to an investor from combining the optimal portfolio of risky assets with the risk-free asset.

Capital asset pricing model (CAPM) An equation describing the expected return on any asset (or portfolio) as a linear function of its beta relative to the market portfolio.

Capital consumption allowance A measure of the wear and tear (depreciation) of the capital stock that occurs in the production of goods and services.

Capital deepening investment Increases the stock of capital relative to labor.

Capital expenditure Expenditure on physical capital (fixed assets).

Capital investment risk The risk of sub-optimal investment by a firm.

Capital light Also known as asset light. Capital-light businesses require little incremental investment in fixed assets or working capital to enable revenue growth.

Capital market expectations An investor's expectations concerning the risk and return prospects of asset classes.

Capital market line (CML) The line with an intercept point equal to the risk-free rate that is tangent to the efficient frontier of risky assets; represents the efficient frontier when a risk-free asset is available for investment.

Capital market securities Securities with maturities at issuance longer than one year.

Capital markets Financial markets that trade securities of longer duration, such as bonds and equities.

Capital providers Investors who provide capital proceeds to a company in return for holding the corporation's debt or equity securities. Equity investors are referred to as shareholders or owners, while debt investors are referred to as bondholders or debtholders.

Capital restrictions Controls placed on foreigners' ability to own domestic assets and/or domestic residents' ability to own foreign assets.

Capital stock The accumulated amount of buildings, machinery, and equipment used to produce goods and services.

Capital structure The mix of debt and equity that a company uses to finance its business; a company's specific mix of long-term financing.

Carrying Investing and holding an asset for a period of time.

Carrying amount The amount at which an asset or liability is valued according to accounting principles.

Carrying value The net amount shown for an asset or liability on the balance sheet; book value may also refer to the company's excess of total assets over total liabilities. For a bond, the purchase price plus (or minus) the amortized amount of the discount (or premium).

Cartel Participants in collusive agreements that are made openly and formally.

Cash collateral account Form of external credit enhancement whereby the issuer immediately borrows the credit-enhancement amount and then invests that amount, usually in highly rated short-term commercial paper.

Cash conversion cycle A financial metric that measures the length of time required for a company to convert cash invested in its operations to cash received as a result of its operations; equal to days of inventory on hand + days of sales outstanding − number of days of payables. Also called *net operating cycle*.

Cash flow additivity principle The principle that dollar amounts indexed at the same point in time are additive.

Cash flow from operating activities The net amount of cash provided from operating activities.

Cash flow from operations The net amount of cash provided from operating activities.

Cash flow hedge Refers to a specific **hedge accounting** classification in which a derivative is designated as absorbing the variable cash flow of a floating-rate asset or liability, such as foreign exchange, interest rates, or commodities.

Cash flow yield The internal rate of return on a series of cash flows.

Cash market securities Money market securities settled on a "same day" or "cash settlement" basis.

Cash markets Markets in which specific assets are exchanged at current prices. Cash markets are often referred to as **spot markets**.

Cash prices The current prices prevailing in **cash markets**.

Catch-up clause A clause in an agreement that favors the GP. For a GP who earns a 20% performance fee, a catch-up clause allows the GP to receive 100% of the distributions above the hurdle rate *until* she receives 20% of the profits generated, and then every excess dollar is split 80/20 between the LPs and GP.

Categorical data Values that describe a quality or characteristic of a group of observations and therefore can be used as labels to divide a dataset into groups to summarize and visualize (also called qualitative data).

Central bank funds market The market in which deposit-taking banks that have an excess reserve with their national central bank can lend money to banks that need funds for maturities ranging from overnight to one year. Called the Federal or Fed funds market in the United States.

Central bank funds rate Interest rate at which central bank funds are bought (borrowed) and sold (lent) for maturities ranging from overnight to one year. Called Federal or Fed funds rate in the United States.

Central banks The dominant bank in a country, usually with official or semi-official governmental status.

Central clearing mandate A requirement instituted by global regulatory authorities following the 2008 global financial crisis that most **over-the-counter** (OTC) derivatives be **cleared** by a **central counterparty** (CCP).

Central counterparty (CCP) An economic entity that assumes the **counterparty credit risk** between derivative **counterparties**, one of which is typically a financial intermediary. CCPs provide **clearing** and **settlement** for most **derivative contracts**.

Central limit theorem The theorem that states the sum (and the mean) of a set of independent, identically distributed random variables with finite variances is normally distributed, whatever distribution the random variables follow.

Certificate of deposit An instrument that represents a specified amount of funds on deposit with a bank for a specified maturity and interest rate. CDs are issued in various denominations and can be negotiable or non-negotiable.

Change in polarity principle A tenet of technical analysis that states that once a support level is breached, it becomes a resistance level. The same holds true for resistance levels: Once breached, they become support levels.

Change of control put A covenant giving bondholders the right to require the issuer to buy back their debt, often at par or at some small premium to par value, in the event that the borrower is acquired.

Character The quality of a debt issuer's management.

Chartist An individual who uses charts or graphs of a security's historical prices or levels to forecast its future trends.

Chi-square test of independence A statistical test for detecting a potential association between categorical variables.

Circuit breaker A pause in intraday trading for a brief period if a price limit is reached.

Classical cycle refers to fluctuations in the level of economic activity when measured by GDP in volume terms.

Classified balance sheet A balance sheet organized so as to group together the various assets and liabilities into subcategories (e.g., current and noncurrent).

Clawback A requirement that the general partner return any funds distributed as incentive fees until the limited partners have received back their initial investment and a percentage of the total profit.

Clearing An exchange's process of verifying the execution of a transaction, exchange of payments, and recording of participants.

Clearing instructions Instructions that indicate how to arrange the final settlement ("clearing") of a trade.

Clearinghouse An entity associated with a futures market that acts as middleman between the contracting parties and guarantees to each party the performance of the other.

Closed economy An economy that does not trade with other countries; an *autarkic economy*.

Closed-end fund A mutual fund in which no new investment money is accepted. New investors invest by buying existing shares, and investors in the fund liquidate by selling their shares to other investors.

Cluster sampling A procedure that divides a population into subpopulation groups (clusters) representative of the population and then randomly draws certain clusters to form a sample.

Clustered bar chart See *grouped bar chart*.

Co-investing In co-investing, the investor invests in assets *indirectly* through the fund but also possesses rights (known as co-investment rights) to invest *directly* in the same assets. Through co-investing, an investor is able to make an investment *alongside* a fund when the fund identifies deals.

Code of ethics An established guide that communicates an organization's values and overall expectations regarding member behavior. A code of ethics serves as a general guide for how community members should act.

Coefficient of determination The percentage of the variation of the dependent variable that is explained by the independent variables. Also referred to as the R-squared or R^2.

Coefficient of variation The ratio of a set of observations' standard deviation to the observations' mean value.

Cognitive cost The effort involved in processing new information and updating beliefs.

Cognitive dissonance The mental discomfort that occurs when new information conflicts with previously held beliefs or cognitions.

Cognitive errors Behavioral biases resulting from faulty reasoning; cognitive errors stem from basic statistical, information-processing, or memory errors.

Coincident economic indicators Turning points that are usually close to those of the overall economy; they are believed to have value for identifying the economy's present state.

Collateral Assets or financial guarantees underlying a debt obligation that are above and beyond the issuer's promise to pay.

Collateral manager Buys and sells debt obligations for and from the CDO's portfolio of assets (i.e., the collateral) to generate sufficient cash flows to meet the obligations to the CDO bondholders.

Collateral trust bonds Bonds secured by securities, such as common shares, other bonds, or other financial assets.

Glossary

Collateralized debt obligation Generic term used to describe a security backed by a diversified pool of one or more debt obligations.

Collateralized mortgage obligations Securities created through the securitization of a pool of mortgage-related products (mortgage pass-through securities or pools of loans).

Collaterals Assets or financial guarantees underlying a debt obligation that are above and beyond the issuer's promise to pay.

Combination A listing in which the order of the listed items does not matter.

Combination formula (binomial formula) The number of ways that we can choose r objects from a total of n objects, when the order in which the r objects are listed does not matter, is $_nC_r = \binom{n}{r} = \frac{n!}{(n-r)!r!}$.

Commercial paper A short-term, negotiable, unsecured promissory note that represents a debt obligation of the issuer.

Committed capital The amount that the limited partners have agreed to provide to the private equity fund.

Committed (regular) lines of credit A bank commitment to extend credit; the commitment is considered a short-term liability and is usually in effect for 364 days (one day short of a full year).

Commodity swap A type of swap involving the exchange of payments over multiple dates as determined by specified reference prices or indexes relating to commodities.

Common market Level of economic integration that incorporates all aspects of the customs union and extends it by allowing free movement of factors of production among members.

Common shares A type of security that represent an ownership interest in a company.

Common-size analysis The restatement of financial statement items using a common denominator or reference item that allows one to identify trends and major differences; an example is an income statement in which all items are expressed as a percent of revenue.

Common stock See *common shares*.

Company analysis Analysis of an individual company.

Comparable company A company that has similar business risk, usually in the same industry and preferably with a single line of business.

Comparative advantage A country's ability to produce a good or service at a lower relative cost, or opportunity cost, than its trading partner.

Competitive risk The risk of a loss of market share or pricing power to competitors.

Competitive strategy A company's plans for responding to the threats and opportunities presented by the external environment.

Complement The event not-S, written S^C, given the event S. Note that $P(S) + P(S^C) = 1$.

Complements Goods that tend to be used together; technically, two goods whose cross-price elasticity of demand is negative.

Complete markets Informally, markets in which the variety of distinct securities traded is so broad that any desired payoff in a future state-of-the-world is achievable.

Component cost of capital The rate of return required by suppliers of capital for an individual source of a company's funding, such as debt or equity.

Compounding The process of accumulating interest on interest.

Comprehensive income All changes in equity other than contributions by, and distributions to, owners; income under clean surplus accounting; includes all changes in equity during a period except those resulting from investments by owners and distributions to owners. Comprehensive income equals net income plus other comprehensive income.

Conditional expected value The expected value of a stated event given that another event has occurred.

Conditional pass-through covered bonds Covered bonds that convert to pass-through securities after the original maturity date if all bond payments have not yet been made and the sponsor is in default.

Conditional probability The probability of an event given (conditioned on) another event.

Conditional variances The variance of one variable, given the outcome of another.

Confidence level The complement of the level of significance.

Confirmation bias A belief perseverance bias in which people tend to look for and notice what confirms their beliefs, to ignore or undervalue what contradicts their beliefs, and to misinterpret information as support for their beliefs.

Confusion matrix A grid used for error analysis in classification problems, it presents values for four evaluation metrics including true positive (TP), false positive (FP), true negative (TN), and false negative (FN).

Conservatism bias A belief perseverance bias in which people maintain their prior views or forecasts by inadequately incorporating new information.

Consolidation The movement of a stock's price within a well-defined range of trading levels for a period of time. The price consolidates between a support level and a resistance level.

Constant-yield price trajectory A graph that illustrates the change in the price of a fixed-income bond over time assuming no change in yield-to-maturity. The trajectory shows the "pull to par" effect on the price of a bond trading at a premium or a discount to par value.

Constituent securities With respect to an index, the individual securities within an index.

Consumer surplus The difference between the value that a consumer places on units purchased and the amount of money that was required to pay for them.

Contango A condition in the futures markets in which the spot price is lower than the futures price, the forward curve is upward sloping, and there is little or no convenience yield.

Contingency provision Clause in a legal document that allows for some action if a specific event or circumstance occurs.

Contingency table A table of the frequency distribution of observations classified on the basis of two discrete variables.

Contingent claim A type of derivative in which one of the **counterparties** determines whether and when the trade will settle. An **option** is a common type of contingent claim.

Contingent convertible bonds Bonds that automatically convert into equity if a specific event or circumstance occurs, such as the issuer's equity capital falling below the minimum requirement set by the regulators. Also called *CoCos*.

Continuation pattern A type of pattern used in technical analysis to predict the resumption of a market trend that was in place prior to the formation of a pattern.

Continuous data Data that can be measured and can take on any numerical value in a specified range of values.

Continuous random variable A random variable for which the range of possible outcomes is the real line (all real numbers between $-\infty$ and $+\infty$) or some subset of the real line.

Continuous trading market A market in which trades can be arranged and executed any time the market is open.

Continuously compounded return The natural logarithm of 1 plus the holding period return, or equivalently, the natural logarithm of the ending price over the beginning price.

Contra account An account that offsets another account.

Contract rate See *mortgage rate*.

Contract size Amount(s) used for calculation to price and value the derivative. The contract size is often referred to as "notional amount or notional principal."

Contraction The period of a business cycle after the peak and before the trough; often called a *recession* or, if exceptionally severe, called a *depression*.

Contraction risk The risk that when interest rates decline, the security will have a shorter maturity than was anticipated at the time of purchase because borrowers refinance at the new, lower interest rates.

Contractionary Tending to cause the real economy to contract.

Contractionary fiscal policy A fiscal policy that has the objective to make the real economy contract.

Contribution margin The amount available for fixed costs and profit after paying variable costs; revenue minus variable costs.

Controlling shareholders A particular shareholder or group of shareholders holding a percentage of shares that gives them significant voting power.

Convenience sampling A procedure of selecting an element from a population on the basis of whether or not it is accessible to a researcher or how easy it is for a researcher to access the element.

Convenience yield A non-cash benefit of holding a physical commodity versus a derivative.

Conventional bond See *plain vanilla bond*.

Conventional cash flow pattern A conventional cash flow pattern is one with an initial outflow followed by a series of inflows.

Convergence The tendency for differences in output per capita across countries to diminish over time. In technical analysis, the term describes the case when an indicator moves in the same manner as the security being analyzed.

Conversion premium The difference between the convertible bond's price and its conversion value.

Conversion price For a convertible bond, the price per share at which the bond can be converted into shares.

Conversion ratio For a convertible bond, the number of common shares that each bond can be converted into.

Conversion value For a convertible bond, the value of the bond if it is converted at the market price of the shares. Also called *parity value*.

Convertible bond Bond that gives the bondholder the right to exchange the bond for a specified number of common shares in the issuing company.

Convertible preference shares A type of equity security that entitles shareholders to convert their shares into a specified number of common shares.

Convexity adjustment For a bond, one half of the annual or approximate convexity statistic multiplied by the change in the yield-to-maturity squared.

Convexity bias Refers to the difference in price changes for a given change in yield between interest rate futures and interest rate forward contracts. That is, interest rate forwards exhibit a non-linear or convex relationship between price and yield, while the price–yield relationship is linear for interest rate futures.

Cooperation The process by which countries work together toward some shared goal or purpose. These goals may, and often do, vary widely—from strategic or military concerns, to economic influence, to cultural preferences.

Cooperative country A country that engages and reciprocates in rules standardization; harmonization of tariffs; international agreements on trade, immigration, or regulation; and allowing the free flow of information, including technology transfer.

Core inflation Refers to the inflation rate calculated based on a price index of goods and services except food and energy.

Corporate governance The system of internal checks, balances, and incentives that exists to manage conflicting interests among a company's stakeholders.

Correlation A measure of the linear relationship between two random variables.

Correlation coefficient A number between –1 and +1 that measures the consistency or tendency for two investments to act in a similar way. It is used to determine the effect on portfolio risk when two assets are combined.

Cost averaging The periodic investment of a fixed amount of money.

Cost-based pricing Pricing set primarily by reference to the firm's costs.

Cost of capital (opportunity cost of funds) The cost of financing to a company; the rate of return that suppliers of capital require as compensation for their contribution of capital.

Cost of carry The net of the costs and benefits related to owning an underlying asset for a specific period.

Cost of debt The required return on debt financing to a company, such as when it issues a bond, takes out a bank loan, or leases an asset through a finance lease.

Cost of equity The return required by equity investors to compensate for both the time value of money and the risk. Also referred to as the required rate of return on common stock or the required return on equity.

Cost of preferred stock The cost to a company of issuing preferred stock; the dividend yield that a company must commit to pay preferred stockholders.

Cost structure The mix of a company's variable costs and fixed costs.

Counterparty Legal entities entering a **derivative contract**.

Counterparty credit risk The likelihood that a **counterparty** is unable to meet its financial obligations under the contract.

Counterparty risk The risk that the other party to a contract will fail to honor the terms of the contract.

Coupon rate The interest rate promised in a contract; this is the rate used to calculate the periodic interest payments.

Cournot assumption Assumption in which each firm determines its profit-maximizing production level assuming that the other firms' output will not change.

Covariance A measure of the co-movement (linear association) between two random variables.

Covariance matrix A matrix or square array whose entries are covariances; also known as a variance–covariance matrix.

Covenants The terms and conditions of lending agreements that the issuer must comply with; they specify the actions that an issuer is obligated to perform (affirmative covenant) or prohibited from performing (negative covenant).

Covered bond Debt obligation secured by a segregated pool of assets called the cover pool. The issuer must maintain the value of the cover pool. In the event of default, bondholders have recourse against both the issuer and the cover pool.

Covered bonds A senior debt obligation of a financial institution that gives recourse to the originator/issuer and a predetermined underlying collateral pool.

Credit analysis The evaluation of credit risk; the evaluation of the creditworthiness of a borrower or counterparty.

Credit default swap (CDS) A type of credit derivative in which one party, the credit protection buyer who is seeking credit protection against a third party, makes a series of regularly scheduled payments to the other party, the credit protection seller. The seller makes no payments until a credit event occurs.

Credit default swaps (CDS) Derivative contracts that allow an investor to manage the risk of loss from borrower default separately from the bond market.

Credit enhancements Provisions that may be used to reduce the credit risk of a bond issue.

Credit event An event that defines a payout in a credit derivative. Events are usually defined as bankruptcy, failure to pay an obligation, or an involuntary debt restructuring.

Credit-linked coupon bond Bond for which the coupon changes when the bond's credit rating changes.

Credit-linked note (CLN) Fixed-income security in which the holder of the security has the right to withhold payment of the full amount due at maturity if a credit event occurs.

Credit migration risk The risk that a bond issuer's creditworthiness deteriorates, or migrates lower, leading investors to believe the risk of default is higher. Also called *downgrade risk*.

Credit risk The risk of loss caused by a counterparty's or debtor's failure to make a promised payment. Also called *default risk*.

Credit tranching A structure used to redistribute the credit risk associated with the collateral; a set of bond classes created to allow investors a choice in the amount of credit risk that they prefer to bear.

Creditworthiness The perceived willingness and ability of the borrower to pay its debt obligations in a timely manner; it represents the ability of a company to withstand adverse impacts on its cash flows.

Critical values Values of the test statistic at which the decision changes from fail to reject the null hypothesis to reject the null hypothesis.

Cross-default Covenant or contract clause that specifies a borrower is considered in default if they default on another debt obligation.

Cross-default provisions Provisions whereby events of default, such as non-payment of interest on one bond, trigger default on all outstanding debt; implies the same default probability for all issues.

Cross-price elasticity of demand The percentage change in quantity demanded for a given percentage change in the price of another good; the responsiveness of the demand for Product A that is associated with the change in price of Product B.

Cross-sectional analysis Analysis that involves comparisons across individuals in a group over a given time period or at a given point in time.

Cross-sectional data A list of the observations of a specific variable from multiple observational units at a given point in time. The observational units can be individuals, groups, companies, trading markets, regions, etc.

Crossing networks Trading systems that match buyers and sellers who are willing to trade at prices obtained from other markets.

Crowding out The thesis that government borrowing may divert private sector investment from taking place.

Crowdsourcing A business model that enables users to contribute directly to a product, service, or online content.

Cryptocurrency An electronic medium of exchange that lacks physical form.

Cryptography An algorithmic process to encrypt data, making the data unusable if received by unauthorized parties.

Cumulative absolute frequency Cumulates (i.e., adds up) in a frequency distribution the absolute frequencies as one moves from the first bin to the last bin.

Cumulative distribution function A function giving the probability that a random variable is less than or equal to a specified value.

Cumulative frequency distribution chart A chart that plots either the cumulative absolute frequency or the cumulative relative frequency on the y-axis against the upper limit of the interval and allows one to see the number or the percentage of the observations that lie below a certain value.

Cumulative preference shares Preference shares for which any dividends that are not paid accrue and must be paid in full before dividends on common shares can be paid.

Cumulative relative frequency A sequence of partial sums of the relative frequencies in a frequency distribution.

Cumulative voting A voting process whereby shareholders can accumulate and vote all their shares for a single candidate in an election, as opposed to having to allocate their voting rights evenly among all candidates.

Currencies Monies issued by national monetary authorities.

Currency option bonds Bonds that give bondholders the right to choose the currency in which they want to receive interest payments and principal repayments.

Currency swap A swap in which each party makes interest payments to the other in different currencies.

Current account A component of the balance of payments account that measures the flow of goods and services.

Current assets Assets that are expected to be consumed or converted into cash in the near future, typically one year or less. *Also called liquid assets*.

Current cost With reference to assets, the amount of cash or cash equivalents that would have to be paid to buy the same or an equivalent asset today; with reference to liabilities, the undiscounted amount of cash or cash equivalents that would be required to settle the obligation today.

Current government spending With respect to government expenditures, spending on goods and services that are provided on a regular, recurring basis including health, education, and defense.

Current liabilities Short-term obligations, such as accounts payable, wages payable, or accrued liabilities, that are expected to be settled in the near future, typically one year or less.

Current yield The sum of the coupon payments received over the year divided by the flat price; also called the *income* or *interest yield* or *running yield*.

Curve duration The sensitivity of the bond price (or the market value of a financial asset or liability) with respect to a benchmark yield curve.

Customs union Extends the free trade area (FTA) by not only allowing free movement of goods and services among members, but also creating a common trade policy against nonmembers.

Cyclical A cyclical company is one whose profits are strongly correlated with the strength of the overall economy.

Cyclical companies Companies with sales and profits that regularly expand and contract with the business cycle or state of economy.

Daily settlement A specific process of mark-to-market by a central clearing party in which the profits and losses of all counterparties to derivatives contracts are determined using settlement prices for each contract.

Dark pools Alternative trading systems that do not display the orders that their clients send to them.

Data A collection of numbers, characters, words, and text—as well as images, audio, and video—in a raw or organized format to represent facts or information.

Data mining The practice of determining a model by extensive searching through a dataset for statistically significant patterns.

Data science An interdisciplinary field that brings computer science, statistics, and other disciplines together to analyze and produce insights from Big Data.

Data snooping The practice of determining a model by extensive searching through a dataset for statistically significant patterns.

Data table see two-dimensional rectangular array.

Day order An order that is good for the day on which it is submitted. If it has not been filled by the close of business, the order expires unfilled.

Days of inventory on hand An activity ratio equal to the number of days in the period divided by inventory turnover over the period.

Dealers Financial intermediaries, such as commercial banks or investment banks, who transact as **counterparties** with derivative end users.

Dealing securities Securities held by banks or other financial intermediaries for trading purposes.

Death cross See **Bearish crossover**.

Debentures Type of bond that can be secured or unsecured.

Debt-rating approach A method for estimating a company's before-tax cost of debt based on the yield on comparably rated bonds for maturities that closely match that of the company's existing debt.

Debt tax shield The tax benefit from interest paid on debt being tax-deductible from income, equal to the marginal tax rate multiplied by the value of the debt.

Debt-to-assets ratio A solvency ratio calculated as total debt divided by total assets.

Debt-to-capital ratio A solvency ratio calculated as total debt divided by total debt plus total shareholders' equity.

Debt-to-equity ratio A solvency ratio calculated as total debt divided by total shareholders' equity.

Deciles Quantiles that divide a distribution into 10 equal parts.

Declaration date The day that the corporation issues a statement declaring a specific dividend.

Decreasing returns to scale When a production process leads to increases in output that are proportionately smaller than the increase in inputs.

Deductible temporary differences Temporary differences that result in a reduction of or deduction from taxable income in a future period when the balance sheet item is recovered or settled.

Deep-in-the-money option An option that is highly likely to be exercised.

Deep learning Machine learning using neural networks with many hidden layers.

Deep learning nets Machine learning using neural networks with many hidden layers.

Deep-out-of-the-money option An option that is highly unlikely to be exercised.

Default probability The probability that a borrower defaults or fails to meet its obligation to make full and timely payments of principal and interest, according to the terms of the debt security. Also called *default risk*.

Default risk See *credit risk*.

Default risk premium An extra return that compensates investors for the possibility that the borrower will fail to make a promised payment at the contracted time and in the contracted amount.

Defensive companies Companies with sales and profits that have little sensitivity to the business cycle or state of the economy.

Defensive interval ratio A liquidity ratio that estimates the number of days that an entity could meet cash needs from liquid assets; calculated as (cash + short-term marketable investments + receivables) divided by daily cash expenditures.

Deferred coupon bond Bond that pays no coupons for its first few years but then pays a higher coupon than it otherwise normally would for the remainder of its life. Also called *split coupon bond*.

Deferred income A liability account for money that has been collected for goods or services that have not yet been delivered; payment received in advance of providing a good or service.

Deferred revenue A liability account for money that has been collected for goods or services that have not yet been delivered; payment received in advance of providing a good or service.

Deferred tax assets A balance sheet asset that arises when an excess amount is paid for income taxes relative to accounting profit. The taxable income is higher than accounting profit and income tax payable exceeds tax expense. The company expects to recover the difference during the course of future operations when tax expense exceeds income tax payable.

Deferred tax liabilities A balance sheet liability that arises when a deficit amount is paid for income taxes relative to accounting profit. The taxable income is less than the accounting profit and income tax payable is less than tax expense. The company expects to eliminate the liability over the course of future operations when income tax payable exceeds tax expense.

Defined benefit pension plans Plans in which the company promises to pay a certain annual amount (defined benefit) to the employee after retirement. The company bears the investment risk of the plan assets.

Defined contribution pension plans Individual accounts to which an employee and typically the employer makes contributions during their working years and expect to draw on the accumulated funds at retirement. The employee bears the investment and inflation risk of the plan assets.

Deflation Negative inflation.

Degree of confidence The probability that a confidence interval includes the unknown population parameter.

Degree of financial leverage (DFL) The ratio of the percentage change in net income to the percentage change in operating income; the sensitivity of the cash flows available to owners when operating income changes.

Degree of operating leverage (DOL) The ratio of the percentage change in operating income to the percentage change in units sold; the sensitivity of operating income to changes in units sold.

Degree of total leverage The ratio of the percentage change in net income to the percentage change in units sold; the sensitivity of the cash flows to owners to changes in the number of units produced and sold.

Degrees of freedom The number of independent variables used in defining sample statistics, such as variance, and the probability distributions they measure.

Delta The relationship between the option price and the underlying price, which reflects the sensitivity of the price of the option to changes in the price of the underlying. Delta is a good approximation of how an option price will change for a small change in the stock.

Demand curve Graph of the inverse demand function. A graph showing the demand relation, either the highest quantity willingly purchased at each price or the highest price willingly paid for each quantity.

Demand function A relationship that expresses the quantity demanded of a good or service as a function of own-price and possibly other variables.

Demand shock A typically unexpected disturbance to demand, such as an unexpected interruption in trade or transportation.

Dependent With reference to events, the property that the probability of one event occurring depends on (is related to) the occurrence of another event.

Dependent variable The variable whose variation about its mean is to be explained by the regression; the left-side variable in a regression equation. Also referred to as the *explained variable*.

Depository bank A bank that raises funds from depositors and other investors and lends it to borrowers.

Depository institutions Commercial banks, savings and loan banks, credit unions, and similar institutions that raise funds from depositors and other investors and lend it to borrowers.

Depository receipt A security that trades like an ordinary share on a local exchange and represents an economic interest in a foreign company.

Depreciation The process of systematically allocating the cost of long-lived (tangible) assets to the periods during which the assets are expected to provide economic benefits.

Derivative A financial instrument that derives its value from the performance of an underlying asset.

Derivative contract A legal agreement between counterparties with a specific **maturity**, or length of time, until the closing of the transaction, or **settlement**.

Derivative pricing rule A pricing rule used by crossing networks in which a price is taken (derived) from the price that is current in the asset's primary market.

Derivatives A financial instrument whose value depends on the value of some underlying asset or factor (e.g., a stock price, an interest rate, or exchange rate).

Descriptive statistics The study of how data can be summarized effectively.

Diffuse prior The assumption of equal prior probabilities.

Diffusion index Reflects the proportion of the index's components that are moving in a pattern consistent with the overall index.

Diluted EPS The EPS that would result if all dilutive securities were converted into common shares.

Diluted shares The number of shares that would be outstanding if all potentially dilutive claims on common shares (e.g., convertible debt, convertible preferred stock, and employee stock options) were exercised.

Diminishing balance method An accelerated depreciation method, i.e., one that allocates a relatively large proportion of the cost of an asset to the early years of the asset's useful life.

Diminishing marginal productivity When each additional unit of an input, keeping the other inputs unchanged, increases output by a smaller increment.

Direct format With reference to the cash flow statement, a format for the presentation of the statement in which cash flow from operating activities is shown as operating cash receipts less operating cash disbursements. Also called *direct method*.

Direct investing Occurs when an investor makes a direct investment in an asset without the use of an intermediary.

Direct listing (DL) A process whereby a company becomes public by listing on an exchange and shares are sold by existing shareholders.

Direct method See *direct format*.

Direct sales A sales strategy used by businesses to sell directly to the end customer, which bypasses ("disintermediates") the distributor or retailer.

Direct taxes Taxes levied directly on income, wealth, and corporate profits.

Direct write-off method An approach to recognizing credit losses on customer receivables in which the company waits until such time as a customer has defaulted and only then recognizes the loss.

Discount To reduce the value of a future payment in allowance for how far away it is in time; to calculate the present value of some future amount. Also, the amount by which an instrument is priced below its face value.

Discount factor The price equivalent of a zero rate. Also may be stated as the present value of a currency unit on a future date.

Discount margin The discount (or required) margin is the yield spread versus the MRR such that the FRN is priced at par on a rate reset date.

Discount rates In general, the interest rates used to calculate present values. In the money market, however, a discount rate is a specific type of quoted rate.

Discounted cash flow models Valuation models that estimate the intrinsic value of a security as the present value of the future benefits expected to be received from the security.

Discouraged worker A person who has stopped looking for a job or has given up seeking employment.

Discrete data Numerical values that result from a counting process; therefore, practically speaking, the data are limited to a finite number of values.

Discrete random variable A random variable that can take on at most a countable number of possible values.

Discriminatory pricing rule A pricing rule used in continuous markets in which the limit price of the order or quote that first arrived determines the trade price.

Diseconomies of scale Increase in cost per unit resulting from increased production.

Dispersion The variability of a population or sample of observations around the central tendency.

Display size The size of an order displayed to public view.

Disposition effect As a result of loss aversion, an emotional bias whereby investors are reluctant to dispose of losers. This results in an inefficient and gradual adjustment to deterioration in fundamental value.

Disruption When new or potential competitors using new technology or business models take market share rather than known or established competitors using established business models.

Distributed ledger A type of database that can be shared among entities in a network.

Distributed ledger technology Technology based on a distributed ledger.

Divergence In technical analysis, a term that describes the case when an indicator moves differently from the security being analyzed.

Diversification ratio The ratio of the standard deviation of an equally weighted portfolio to the standard deviation of a randomly selected security.

Dividend A distribution paid to shareholders based on the number of shares owned.

Dividend discount model (DDM) A present value model of stock value that views the intrinsic value of a stock as present value of the stock's expected future dividends.

Dividend payout ratio The ratio of cash dividends paid to earnings for a period.

Divisor A number (denominator) used to determine the value of a price return index. It is initially chosen at the inception of an index and subsequently adjusted by the index provider, as necessary, to avoid changes in the index value that are unrelated to changes in the prices of its constituent securities.

Doji In the Japanese terminology used in candlestick charting, the doji signifies that after a full day of trading, the positive price influence of buyers and the negative price influence of sellers exactly counteracted each other—with opening and closing prices that are virtually equal—which suggests that the market under analysis is in balance.

Domestic content provisions Stipulate that some percentage of the value added or components used in production should be of domestic origin.

Double bottom In technical analysis, a reversal pattern that is formed when the price reaches a low, rebounds, and then declines back to the first low level. A double bottom is used to predict a change from a downtrend to an uptrend.

Double coincidence of wants A prerequisite to barter trades, in particular that both economic agents in the transaction want what the other is selling.

Double declining balance depreciation An accelerated depreciation method that involves depreciating the asset at double the straight-line rate. This rate is multiplied by the book value of the asset at the beginning of the period (a declining balance) to calculate depreciation expense.

Double top In technical analysis, a reversal pattern that is formed when an uptrend reverses twice at roughly the same high price level. A double top is used to predict a change from an uptrend to a downtrend.

Down transition probability The probability that an asset's value moves down in a model of asset price dynamics.

Downgrade risk The risk that a bond issuer's creditworthiness deteriorates, or migrates lower, leading investors to believe the risk of default is higher. Also called *credit migration risk*.

Downside risk Risk of incurring returns below a specified value.

Downtrend A pattern that occurs when the price of an asset moves lower over a period of time.

Drag on liquidity When receipts (inflows) lag, creating pressure from the decreased available funds.

Drawdown A percentage peak-to-trough reduction in net asset value.

Drop shipping Often used in e-commerce, when goods are delivered directly from manufacturer to end customer, enabling the marketer to avoid taking the goods into inventory.

DuPont analysis An approach to decomposing return on investment, e.g., return on equity, as the product of other financial ratios.

Dual-currency bonds Bonds that make coupon payments in one currency and pay the par value at maturity in another currency.

Duration A measure of the approximate sensitivity of a security to a change in interest rates (i.e., a measure of interest rate risk).

Duration gap A bond's Macaulay duration minus the investment horizon.

Dutch Book Theorem A result in probability theory stating that inconsistent probabilities create profit opportunities.

Dynamic pricing A pricing approach that charges different prices at different times. Specific examples include off-peak pricing, "surge" pricing, and "congestion" pricing.

ESG An acronym that encompasses environmental, social, and governance factors.

ESG integration An ESG investment approach that focuses on systematic consideration of material ESG factors in asset allocation, security selection, and portfolio construction decisions for the purpose of achieving the product's stated investment objectives. Used interchangeably with **ESG investing**.

ESG risk The risk associated with environmental, social, and governance–related factors.

Early repayment option See *prepayment option*.

Earnings per share The amount of income earned during a period per share of common stock.

Earnings surprise The portion of a company's earnings that is unanticipated by investors and, according to the efficient market hypothesis, merits a price adjustment.

Economic costs All the remuneration needed to keep a productive resource in its current employment or to acquire the resource for productive use; the sum of total accounting costs and implicit opportunity costs.

Economic indicator A variable that provides information on the state of the overall economy.

Economic loss The amount by which accounting profit is less than normal profit.

Economic profit Equal to accounting profit less the implicit opportunity costs not included in total accounting costs; the difference between total revenue (TR) and total cost (TC). Also called *abnormal profit* or *supernormal profit*.

Economic stabilization Reduction of the magnitude of economic fluctuations.

Economic union Incorporates all aspects of a common market and in addition requires common economic institutions and coordination of economic policies among members.

Economies of scale A situation in which average costs per unit of good or service produced fall as volume rises. In reference to mergers, the savings achieved through the consolidation of operations and elimination of duplicate resources.

Effective annual rate The amount by which a unit of currency will grow in a year with interest on interest included.

Effective convexity A *curve convexity* statistic that measures the secondary effect of a change in a benchmark yield curve on a bond's price.

Effective duration Sensitivity of the bond's price to a 100 bps parallel shift of the benchmark yield curve, assuming no change in the bond's credit spread.

Effective interest rate The borrowing rate or market rate that a company incurs at the time of issuance of a bond.

Efficient market A market in which asset prices reflect new information quickly and rationally.

Elastic Said of a good or service when the magnitude of elasticity is greater than one.

Elasticity The percentage change in one variable for a percentage change in another variable; a general measure of how sensitive one variable is to a change in the value of another variable.

Elasticity of demand A measure of the sensitivity of quantity demanded to a change in a product's own price: $\%\Delta Q^D/\%\Delta P$.

Elasticity of supply A measure of the sensitivity of quantity supplied to a change in price: $\%\Delta Q^S/\%\Delta P$.

Electronic communications networks See *alternative trading systems*.

Embedded derivative A derivative within an underlying, such as a callable, putable, or convertible bond.

Embedded option Contingency provisions that provide the issuer or the bondholders the right, but not the obligation, to take action. These options are part of the security and cannot be traded separately.

Embedded options Contingency provisions found in a bond's indenture or offering circular representing rights that enable their holders to take advantage of interest rate movements. They can be exercised by the issuer, by the bondholder, or automatically depending on the course of interest rates.

Emotional biases Behavioral biases resulting from reasoning influenced by feelings; emotional biases stem from impulse or intuition.

Empirical duration The use of statistical methods and historical bond prices to estimate the price–yield relationship for a specific bond or portfolio of bonds.

Empirical probability The probability of an event estimated as a relative frequency of occurrence.

Employed The number of people with a job.

Endowment bias An emotional bias in which people value an asset more when they hold rights to it than when they do not.

Engagement/active ownership An ESG investment approach that uses shareholder power to influence corporate behavior through direct corporate engagement (i.e., communicating with senior management and/or boards of companies), filing or co-filing shareholder proposals, and proxy voting directed by ESG guidelines.

Enterprise risk management An overall assessment of a company's risk position. A centralized approach to risk management sometimes called firmwide risk management.

Enterprise value Total company value (the market value of debt, common equity, and preferred equity) minus the value of cash and investments.

Equal weighting An index weighting method in which an equal weight is assigned to each constituent security at inception.

Equipment trust certificates Bonds secured by specific types of equipment or physical assets.

Equity Assets less liabilities; the residual interest in the assets after subtracting the liabilities.

Equity risk premium The expected return on equities minus the risk-free rate; the premium that investors demand for investing in equities.

Equity swap A swap transaction in which at least one cash flow is tied to the return on an equity portfolio position, often an equity index.

Error term The difference between an observation and its expected value, where the expected value is based on the true underlying population relation between the dependent and independent variables. Also known simply as the *error*.

Estimate The particular value calculated from sample observations using an estimator.

Estimated parameters With reference to a regression analysis, the estimated values of the population intercept and population slope coefficients in a regression.

Estimator An estimation formula; the formula used to compute the sample mean and other sample statistics are examples of estimators.

Ethical principles Beliefs regarding what is good, acceptable, or obligatory behavior and what is bad, unacceptable, or forbidden behavior.

Ethics The study of moral principles or of making good choices. Ethics encompasses a set of moral principles and rules of conduct that provide guidance for our behavior.

Eurobonds Type of bond issued internationally, outside the jurisdiction of the country in whose currency the bond is denominated.

European options Options that may be exercised only at contract maturity.

European-style Said of an option contract that can only be exercised on the option's expiration date.

Event Any outcome or specified set of outcomes of a random variable.

Event risk Risk that evolves around set dates, such as elections, new legislation, or other date-driven milestones, such as holidays or political anniversaries, known in advance. Example: Brexit referendum.

Ex-dividend date The first date that a share trades without (i.e., "ex") the right to receive the declared dividend for the period.

Excess kurtosis Degree of kurtosis (fatness of tails) relative to the kurtosis of the normal distribution.

Exchange-traded derivative (ETD) Futures, options, and other financial contracts available on exchanges.

Exchanges Places where traders can meet to arrange their trades.

Execution instructions Instructions that indicate how to fill an order.

Execution risk The risk that management will be unable to do what is needed to deliver the expected results.

Exercise The decision to transact the underlying by an option buyer.

Exercise price The pre-agreed execution price specified in an option contract. Sometimes, this price is referred to as the strike price.

Exhaustive An index construction strategy that selects every constituent of a universe.

Exogenous risk A sudden or unanticipated risk that impacts either a country's cooperative stance, the ability of non-state actors to globalize, or both. Examples include sudden uprisings, invasions, or the aftermath of natural disasters.

Expansion The period of a business cycle after its lowest point and before its highest point.

Expansionary Tending to cause the real economy to grow.

Expansionary fiscal policy Fiscal policy aimed at achieving real economic growth.

Expected inflation The level of inflation that economic agents expect in the future.

Expected loss Default probability times loss severity given default.

Expected return on the portfolio ($E(R_p)$) The weighted average of the expected returns (R_1 to R_n) on the component securities using their respective weights (w_1 to w_n).

Expected value The probability-weighted average of the possible outcomes of a random variable.

Expenses Outflows of economic resources or increases in liabilities that result in decreases in equity (other than decreases because of distributions to owners); reductions in net assets associated with the creation of revenues.

Export subsidy Paid by the government to the firm when it exports a unit of a good that is being subsidized.

Exports Goods and services that an economy sells to other countries.

Extension risk The risk that when interest rates rise, fewer prepayments will occur because homeowners are reluctant to give up the benefits of a contractual interest rate that now looks low. As a result, the security becomes longer in maturity than anticipated at the time of purchase.

Externalities Spillover effects of production and consumption activities onto others who are not directly involved in a particular transaction, activity, or decision.

Externality An effect of a market transaction that is borne by parties other than those who transacted.

Extra dividend A dividend paid by a company that does not pay dividends on a regular schedule, or a dividend that supplements regular cash dividends with an extra payment.

Extreme value theory A branch of statistics that focuses primarily on extreme outcomes.

FIFO method The first in, first out, method of accounting for inventory, which matches sales against the costs of items of inventory in the order in which they were placed in inventory.

FX swap The combination of a spot and a forward FX transaction.

Face value The amount of cash payable by a company to the bondholders when the bonds mature; the promised payment at maturity separate from any coupon payment.

Factoring arrangement When a company sells its accounts receivable to a lender (known as a factor) who assumes responsibility for the credit-granting and collection process.

Fair value The amount at which an asset could be exchanged, or a liability settled, between knowledgeable, willing parties in an arm's-length transaction; the price that would be received to sell an asset or paid to transfer a liability in an orderly transaction between market participants.

Fair value hedge Refers to a specific **hedge accounting** designation that applies when a derivative is deemed to offset the fluctuation in fair value of an asset or liability.

False discovery approach An adjustment in the *p*-values for tests performed multiple times.

False discovery rate The rate of Type I errors in testing a null hypothesis multiple times for a given level of significance.

Fat-Tailed Describes a distribution that has fatter tails than a normal distribution (also called leptokurtic).

Fed funds rate The US interbank lending rate on overnight borrowings of reserves.

Federal funds rate The US interbank lending rate on overnight borrowings of reserves.

Fiat money Money that is not convertible into any other commodity.

Fiduciary An entity designated to represent the rights and responsibilities of a beneficiary whose assets they are managing, such as a bond trustee acting on behalf of fixed-income investors.

Fiduciary call A combination of a purchased call option and investment in a risk-free bond with face value of the option's exercise price.

Fill or kill See *immediate or cancel order*.

Finance lease A type of lease which is more akin to the purchase or sale of the underlying asset.

Financial account A component of the balance of payments account that records investment flows.

Financial distress Heightened uncertainty regarding a company's ability to meet its various obligations because of diminished earnings power or actual current losses.

Financial flexibility The ability to react and adapt to financial adversity and opportunities.

Financial leverage The use of fixed sources of capital, such as debt, relative to sources without fixed costs, such as equity.

Financial leverage ratio A measure of financial leverage calculated as average total assets divided by average total equity.

Financial risk The risk arising from a company's capital structure and, specifically, from the level of debt and debt-like obligations.

Financing activities Activities related to obtaining or repaying capital to be used in the business (e.g., equity and long-term debt).

Fintech Technological innovation in the design and delivery of financial services and products in the financial industry.

Firm commitment A pre-determined amount (price and quantity) is agreed to be exchanged at settlement. Examples of firm commitments include forward contracts, futures contracts, and swaps.

Firm commitment offering See *underwritten offering*.

First-degree price discrimination Where a monopolist is able to charge each customer the highest price the customer is willing to pay.

First lien debt Debt secured by a pledge of certain assets that could include buildings, but it may also include property and equipment, licenses, patents, brands, etc.

First mortgage debt Debt secured by a pledge of a specific property.

Fiscal multiplier The ratio of a change in national income to a change in government spending.

Fiscal policy The use of taxes and government spending to affect the level of aggregate expenditures.

Fisher effect The thesis that the real rate of interest in an economy is stable over time so that changes in nominal interest rates are the result of changes in expected inflation.

Fixed charge coverage A solvency ratio measuring the number of times interest and lease payments are covered by operating income, calculated as (EBIT + lease payments) divided by (interest payments + lease payments).

Fixed costs Costs that remain at the same level regardless of a company's level of production and sales.

Fixed-rate payer The counterparty paying fixed cash flows in a swap contract. May also be referred to as the floating-rate receiver.

Fixed-rate perpetual preferred stock Nonconvertible, noncallable preferred stock that has a fixed dividend rate and no maturity date.

Flag A technical analysis continuation pattern formed by parallel trendlines, typically over a short period.

Flat price The full price of a bond minus the accrued interest; also called the *quoted* or *clean* price.

Float-adjusted market-capitalization weighting An index weighting method in which the weight assigned to each constituent security is determined by adjusting its market capitalization for its market float.

Floaters See *floating-rate notes*.

Floating-rate notes Notes on which interest payments are not fixed but instead vary from period to period depending on the current level of a reference interest rate.

Floating-rate payer The counterparty paying the variable cash flows in a swap contract. May also be referred to as the fixed-rate receiver.

Flotation cost Fees charged to companies by investment bankers and other costs associated with raising new capital.

Foreclosure Allows the lender to take possession of a mortgaged property if the borrower defaults and then sell it to recover funds.

Foreign currency reserves Holding by the central bank of non-domestic currency deposits and non-domestic bonds.

Foreign direct investment Direct investment by a firm in one country (the source country) in productive assets in a foreign country (the host country).

Foreign direct investments (FDI) Long-term investments in the productive capacity of a foreign country.

Foreign exchange gains (or losses) Gains (or losses) that occur when the exchange rate changes between the investor's currency and the currency that foreign securities are denominated in.

Foreign portfolio investment Shorter-term investment by individuals, firms, and institutional investors (e.g., pension funds) in foreign financial instruments such as foreign stocks and foreign government bonds.

Forward contract A **derivative contract** for the future exchange of an **underlying** at a fixed price set at contract signing.

Forward curve A series of forward rates, each having the same time frame.

Forward market For future delivery, beyond the usual settlement time period in the cash market.

Forward price Represents the price agreed upon in a forward contract to be exchanged at the contract's maturity date, T. This price is shown in equations as $F_0(T)$.

Forward rate An interest rate determined today for a loan that will be initiated in a future period.

Forward rate agreement (FRA) An OTC derivatives contract in which counterparties agree to apply a specific interest rate to a future time period.

Fractile A value at or below which a stated fraction of the data lies. Also called quantile.

Fractional reserve banking Banking in which reserves constitute a fraction of deposits.

Fractionalization The creation of value by selling something in parts.

Framing bias An information-processing bias in which a person answers a question differently based on the way in which it is asked (framed).

Franchising An owner of an asset and associated intellectual property divests the asset and licenses intellectual property to a third-party operator (franchisee) in exchange for royalties. Franchisees operate under the constraints of a franchise agreement.

Free cash flow The actual cash that would be available to the company's investors after making all investments necessary to maintain the company as an ongoing enterprise (also referred to as free cash flow to the firm); the internally generated funds that can be distributed to the company's investors (e.g., shareholders and bondholders) without impairing the value of the company.

Free cash flow hypothesis The hypothesis that higher debt levels discipline managers by forcing them to make fixed debt service payments and by reducing the company's free cash flow.

Free-cash-flow-to-equity models Valuation models based on discounting expected future free cash flow to equity.

Free float The number of shares that are readily and freely tradable in the secondary market.

Free trade When there are no government restrictions on a country's ability to trade.

Free trade areas One of the most prevalent forms of regional integration, in which all barriers to the flow of goods and services among members have been eliminated.

Freemium pricing A pricing approach that allows customers a certain level of usage or functionality at no charge. Those who wish to use more must pay.

Frequency distribution A tabular display of data constructed either by counting the observations of a variable by distinct values or groups or by tallying the values of a numerical variable into a set of numerically ordered bins (also called a one-way table).

Frequency polygon A graph of a frequency distribution obtained by drawing straight lines joining successive points representing the class frequencies.

Frequency table A representation of the frequency of occurrence of two discrete variables.

Full price The price of a security with accrued interest; also called the *invoice* or *dirty* price.

Fundamental analysis The examination of publicly available information and the formulation of forecasts to estimate the intrinsic value of assets.

Fundamental value The underlying or true value of an asset based on an analysis of its qualitative and quantitative characteristics. Also called *intrinsic value*.

Fundamental weighting An index weighting method in which the weight assigned to each constituent security is based on its underlying company's size. It attempts to address the disadvantages of market-capitalization weighting by using measures that are independent of the constituent security's price.

Funds of hedge funds Funds that hold a portfolio of hedge funds, more commonly shortened to *funds of funds*.

Fungible Freely exchangeable, interchangeable, or substitutable with other things of the same type. Money and commodities are the most common examples.

Future value (FV) The amount to which a payment or series of payments will grow by a stated future date.

Futures contract A variation of a forward contract that has essentially the same basic definition but with some additional features, such as a clearinghouse guarantee against credit losses, a daily settlement of gains and losses, and an organized electronic or floor trading facility.

Futures contract basis point value (BPV) The change in price of a futures contract given a 1 basis point (0.01%) change in yield.

Futures contracts Forward contracts with standardized sizes, dates, and underlyings that trade on futures exchanges.

Futures margin account An account held by an exchange clearinghouse for each derivatives counterparty. The funds in such an account are used to ensure that counterparties do not default on their contract obligation.

Futures price The pre-agreed price at which a futures contract buyer (seller) agrees to pay (receive) for the underlying at the maturity date of the futures contract.

GDP deflator A gauge of prices and inflation that measures the aggregate changes in prices across the overall economy.

G-spread The yield spread in basis points over an actual or interpolated government bond.

Gains Asset inflows not directly related to the ordinary activities of the business.

Game theory The set of tools decision makers use to incorporate responses by rival decision makers into their strategies.

Gamma A numerical measure of how sensitive an option's delta (the sensitivity of the derivative's price) is to a change in the value of the underlying.

Gap opening A gap is an area of a chart where a security's price either rises or falls from the previous day's close with no trading occurring in between. A gap opening is the start of a new trading session with a gap.

Gate A fund provision that limits or restricts redemptions from the fund for a period of time.

General partner Individual(s) in a limited partnership responsible for managing the business with unlimited liability.

Geometric mean A measure of central tendency computed by taking the nth root of the product of n non-negative values.

Geophysical resource endowment Includes such factors as livable geography and climate as well as access to food and water, which are necessary for sustainable growth. Geophysical resource endowment is highly unequal among countries.

Geopolitical risk The risk associated with tensions or actions between actors that affect the normal and peaceful course of international relations. Geopolitical risk can have a tangible impact on investment outcomes.

Geopolitics The study of how geography affects politics and international relations. These relations matter for investments because they contribute to important drivers of investment performance, including economic growth, business performance, market volatility, and transaction costs.

Giffen goods Goods that are consumed more as the price of the good rises because it is a very inferior good whose income effect overwhelms its substitution effect when price changes.

Gilts Bonds issued by the UK government.

Global depository receipt A depository receipt that is issued outside of the company's home country and outside of the United States.

Global minimum-variance portfolio The portfolio on the minimum-variance frontier with the smallest variance of return.

Global registered share A common share that is traded on different stock exchanges around the world in different currencies.

Globalization The process of interaction and integration among people, companies, and governments worldwide. It is marked by the spread of products, information, jobs, and culture across borders.

Gold standard With respect to a currency, if a currency is on the gold standard a given amount can be converted into a prespecified amount of gold.

Golden Cross See **Bullish crossover**.

Good-on-close An execution instruction specifying that an order can only be filled at the close of trading. Also called *market on close*.

Good-on-open An execution instruction specifying that an order can only be filled at the opening of trading.

Good-till-cancelled order An order specifying that it is valid until the entity placing the order has cancelled it (or, commonly, until some specified amount of time such as 60 days has elapsed, whichever comes sooner).

Goodwill An intangible asset that represents the excess of the purchase price of an acquired company over the value of the net identifiable assets acquired.

Government equivalent yield A yield that restates a yield-to-maturity based on a 30/360 day count to one based on actual/actual.

Green bonds Bonds used in green finance whereby the proceeds are earmarked toward environmental-related products.

Green finance A type of finance that addresses environmental concerns while achieving economic growth.

Green loans Any loan instruments made available exclusively to finance or re-finance, in whole or in part, new and/or existing eligible green projects. Green loans are commonly aligned in the market with the Green Loan Principles.

Greenfield investment Investing in infrastructure assets that are to be constructed.

Grey market The forward market for bonds about to be issued. Also called "when issued" market.

Gross domestic product The market value of all final goods and services produced within the economy during a given period (output definition) or, equivalently, the aggregate income earned by all households, all companies, and the government within the economy during a given period (income definition).

Gross margin Sales minus the cost of sales (i.e., the cost of goods sold for a manufacturing company).

Gross profit Sales minus the cost of sales (i.e., the cost of goods sold for a manufacturing company).

Gross profit margin The ratio of gross profit to revenues.

Grouped bar chart A bar chart for showing joint frequencies for two categorical variables (also known as a clustered bar chart).

Grouping by function With reference to the presentation of expenses in an income statement, the grouping together of expenses serving the same function, e.g. all items that are costs of goods sold.

Grouping by nature With reference to the presentation of expenses in an income statement, the grouping together of expenses by similar nature, e.g., all depreciation expenses.

Groupthink The practice of thinking or making decisions as a group in a way that discourages creativity or individual responsibility. For scenario analysis to be useful in portfolio management, teams must work hard to build creative processes, identify scenarios, track these scenarios, and assess the need for action on a regular cadence.

Growth cycle Refers to fluctuations in economic activity around the long-term potential trend growth level, focusing on how much actual economic activity is below or above trend growth in economic activity.

Growth cyclical A term sometimes used to describe companies that are growing rapidly on a long-term basis but that still experience above-average fluctuation in their revenues and profits over the course of a business cycle.

Growth investors With reference to equity investors, investors who seek to invest in high-earnings-growth companies.

Growth option The option to make additional investments in a project at some future time if the financial results are strong. Also called an *expansion option*.

Growth rate cycle Refers to fluctuations in the growth rate of economic activity.

Guarantee certificate A type of structured financial instrument that provides investors with capital protection. It combines a zero-coupon bond and a call option on some underlying asset.

Haircut See *repo margin*.

Halo effect An emotional bias that extends a favorable evaluation of some characteristics to other characteristics.

Hard-bullet covered bonds Covered bonds for which a bond default is triggered and bond payments are accelerated in the event of sponsor default if payments do not occur according to the original maturity schedule.

Hard commodities Traded natural resources, such as crude oil and metals, with markets often involving the physical delivery of the underlying upon settlement.

Harmonic mean A type of weighted mean computed as the reciprocal of the arithmetic average of the reciprocals.

Head and shoulders pattern In technical analysis, a reversal pattern that is formed in three parts: a left shoulder, a head, and a right shoulder. A head and shoulders pattern is used to predict a change from an uptrend to a downtrend.

Headline inflation Refers to the inflation rate calculated based on the price index that includes all goods and services in an economy.

Heat map A type of graphic that organizes and summarizes data in a tabular format and represents it using a color spectrum.

Hedge The **derivative contract** used in **hedging** an exposure.

Hedge accounting Accounting standard(s) that allow an issuer to offset a hedging instrument (usually a derivative) against a hedged transaction or balance sheet item to reduce financial statement volatility.

Hedge funds Private investment vehicles that typically use leverage, derivatives, and long and short investment strategies.

Hedge ratio The proportion of an underlying that will offset the risk associated with a derivative position.

Hedging The use of a derivative contract to offset or neutralize existing or anticipated exposure to an **underlying**.

Hegemony Countries that are regional or even global leaders and use their political or economic influence of others to control resources.

Held-to-maturity Debt (fixed-income) securities that a company intends to hold to maturity; these are presented at their original cost, updated for any amortisation of discounts or premiums.

Herding Clustered trading that may or may not be based on information.

Heteroskedasticity The property of having a nonconstant variance; refers to an error term with the property that its variance differs across observations.

Hidden order An order that is exposed not to the public but only to the brokers or exchanges that receive it.

Hidden revenue business models Business models that provide services to users at no charge and generate revenues elsewhere.

High-frequency trading A form of algorithmic trading that makes use of vast quantities of data to execute trades on ultra-high-speed networks in fractions of a second.

High-water mark The highest value, net of fees, that a fund has reached in history. It reflects the highest cumulative return used to calculate an incentive fee.

Hindsight bias A bias with selective perception and retention aspects in which people may see past events as having been predictable and reasonable to expect.

Histogram A chart that presents the distribution of numerical data by using the height of a bar or column to represent the absolute frequency of each bin or interval in the distribution.

Historical cost In reference to assets, the amount paid to purchase an asset, including any costs of acquisition and/or preparation; with reference to liabilities, the amount of proceeds received in exchange in issuing the liability.

Historical equity risk premium approach An estimate of a country's equity risk premium that is based on the historical averages of the risk-free rate and the rate of return on the market portfolio.

Holder-of-record date The date that a shareholder listed on the corporation's books will be deemed to have ownership of the shares for purposes of receiving an upcoming dividend.

Holding period return The return that an investor earns during a specified holding period; a synonym for total return.

Home bias A preference for securities listed on the exchanges of one's home country.

Homogeneity of expectations The assumption that all investors have the same economic expectations and thus have the same expectations of prices, cash flows, and other investment characteristics.

Homoskedasticity The property of having a constant variance; refers to an error term that is constant across observations.

Horizon yield The internal rate of return between the total return (the sum of reinvested coupon payments and the sale price or redemption amount) and the purchase price of the bond.

Horizontal analysis Common-size analysis that involves comparing a specific financial statement with that statement in prior or future time periods; also, cross-sectional analysis of one company with another.

Horizontal demand schedule Implies that at a given price, the response in the quantity demanded is infinite.

Hostile takeover An attempt by one entity to acquire a company without the consent of the company's management.

Household A person or a group of people living in the same residence, taken as a basic unit in economic analysis.

Human capital An implied asset; the net present value of an investor's future expected labor income weighted by the probability of surviving to each future age. Also called *net employment capital*.

Hurdle rate The rate of return that a project's IRR must exceed for the project to be accepted by the company.

Hypothesis A proposed explanation or theory that can be tested.

Hypothesis testing The process of testing of hypotheses about one or more populations using statistical inference.

I-spread The yield spread of a specific bond over the standard swap rate in that currency of the same tenor.

Iceberg order An order in which the display size is less than the order's full size.

If-converted method A method for accounting for the effect of convertible securities on earnings per share (EPS) that specifies what EPS would have been if the convertible securities had been converted at the beginning of the period, taking account of the effects of conversion on net income and the weighted average number of shares outstanding.

Illusion of control bias A bias in which people tend to believe that they can control or influence outcomes when, in fact, they cannot.

Immediate or cancel order An order that is valid only upon receipt by the broker or exchange. If such an order cannot be filled in part or in whole upon receipt, it cancels immediately. Also called *fill or kill*.

Impact investing Investment approach that seeks to achieve targeted social or environmental objectives along with measurable financial returns through engagement with a company or by direct investment in projects or companies.

Impact lag The lag associated with the result of actions affecting the economy with delay.

Implicit price deflator for GDP A gauge of prices and inflation that measures the aggregate changes in prices across the overall economy.

Implicit selection bias One type of selection bias introduced through the presence of a threshold that filters out some unqualified members.

Implied forward rate (IFR) The breakeven reinvestment rate linking a short-dated and long-dated zero-coupon bond. More specifically, the interest rate for a period in the future at which an investor earns the same return from: 1) investing for a period from today until the forward start date and rolling over the proceeds at the implied forward rate, or 2) investing today through the final maturity of the forward rate.

Implied forward rates Calculated from spot rates, an implied forward rate is a breakeven reinvestment rate that links the return on an investment in a shorter-term zero-coupon bond to the return on an investment in a longer-term zero-coupon bond.

Import license Specifies the quantity of a good that can be imported into a country.

Imports Goods and services that a domestic economy (i.e., house-holds, firms, and government) purchases from other countries.

In-the-money Describes an option with a positive intrinsic value.

Income Increases in economic benefits in the form of inflows or enhancements of assets, or decreases of liabilities that result in an increase in equity (other than increases resulting from contributions by owners).

Income elasticity of demand A measure of the responsiveness of demand to changes in income, defined as the percentage change in quantity demanded divided by the percentage change in income.

Income tax paid The actual amount paid for income taxes in the period; not a provision, but the actual cash outflow.

Income tax payable The income tax owed by the company on the basis of taxable income.

Increasing marginal returns When the marginal product of a resource increases as additional units of that input are employed.

Increasing returns to scale When a production process leads to increases in output that are proportionately larger than the increase in inputs.

Incremental cash flow The net cash flow that is realized because of a decision; the changes or increments to cash flows resulting from a decision or action.

Indenture A written contract between a lender and borrower that specifies the terms of the loan, such as interest rate, interest payment schedule, or maturity.

Independent With reference to events, the property that the occurrence of one event does not affect the probability of another event occurring. With reference to two random variables X and Y, they are independent if and only if $P(X,Y) = P(X)P(Y)$.

Independent projects Independent projects are capital investments whose cash flows are independent of each other.

Independent variable A variable used to explain the dependent variable in a regression; a right-side variable in a regression equation. Also referred to as the *explanatory variable*.

Independently and identically distributed With respect to random variables, the property of random variables that are independent of each other but follow the identical probability distribution.

Index-linked bond Bond for which coupon payments and/or principal repayment are linked to a specified index.

Indexing An investment strategy in which an investor constructs a portfolio to mirror the performance of a specified index.

Indicator variable A variable that takes on only one of two values, 0 or 1, based on a condition. In simple linear regression, the slope is the difference in the dependent variable for the two conditions. Also referred to as a *dummy variable*.

Indifference curve A curve representing all the combinations of two goods or attributes such that the consumer is entirely indifferent among them.

Indirect format With reference to cash flow statements, a format for the presentation of the statement which, in the operating cash flow section, begins with net income then shows additions and subtractions to arrive at operating cash flow. Also called *indirect method*.

Indirect method See *indirect format*.

Indirect taxes Taxes such as taxes on spending, as opposed to direct taxes.

Industry A group of companies offering similar products and/or services.

Industry analysis The analysis of a specific branch of manufacturing, service, or trade.

Industry risks Risks that apply to all competitors in the same industry and include risk factors likely to affect the overall level of demand, pricing, and profitability in the industry.

Inelastic Said of a good or service when the magnitude of elasticity is less than one. Insensitive to price changes.

Inferior goods A good whose consumption decreases as income increases.

Inflation The percentage increase in the general price level from one period to the next; a sustained rise in the overall level of prices in an economy.

Inflation-linked bond Type of index-linked bond that offers investors protection against inflation by linking the bond's coupon payments and/or the principal repayment to an index of consumer prices. Also called *linkers*.

Inflation premium An extra return that compensates investors for expected inflation.

Inflation reports A type of economic publication put out by many central banks.

Inflation uncertainty The degree to which economic agents view future rates of inflation as difficult to forecast.

Information cascade The transmission of information from those participants who act first and whose decisions influence the decisions of others.

Information-motivated traders Traders that trade to profit from information that they believe allows them to predict future prices.

Informationally efficient market A market in which asset prices reflect new information quickly and rationally.

Initial coin offering An unregulated process whereby companies raise capital by selling crypto tokens to investors in exchange for fiat money or another agreed-upon cryptocurrency.

Initial margin The required sum that each counterparty must deposit upon entering into the futures contract. This amount is deposited into a futures margin account held at the exchange clearinghouse to settle the daily mark to market.

Initial margin requirement The margin requirement on the first day of a transaction as well as on any day in which additional margin funds must be deposited.

Initial public offering (IPO) The first issuance of common shares to the public by a formerly private corporation.

Initial public offering (IPO) A process used by companies to raise capital and offer shares to the public for the first time.

Input productivity The amount of output produced by workers in a given period of time—for example, output per hour worked; measures the efficiency of labor.

Insolvency Refers to the condition in which firm value is below the face value of debt used to finance the firm's assets.

Institution An established organization or practice in a society or culture. An institution can be a formal structure, such as a university, organization, or process backed by law; or it can be informal, such as a custom or behavioral pattern important to society. Institutions can, but need not be, formed by national governments. Examples of institutions include non-governmental organizations, charities, religious customs, family units, the media, political parties, and educational practice.

Intangible assets Assets without a physical form, such as patents and trademarks.

Interbank market The market of loans and deposits between banks for maturities ranging from overnight to one year.

Intercept The expected value of the dependent variable when the independent variable in a simple linear regression is equal to zero.

Interest Payment for lending funds.

Interest coverage A solvency ratio calculated as EBIT divided by interest payments.

Interest-only mortgage A loan in which no scheduled principal repayment is specified for a certain number of years.

Interest rate A rate of return that reflects the relationship between differently dated cash flows; a discount rate.

Interest rate effect The effect through which price level changes, through demand for money, impact interest rate, which in turn impacts investment and consumption.

Interest rate swap A swap in which the underlying is an interest rate. Can be viewed as a currency swap in which both currencies are the same and can be created as a combination of currency swaps.

Intermarket analysis A field within technical analysis that combines analysis of the major categories of securities—namely, equities, bonds, currencies, and commodities—to identify market trends and possible inflections in trends.

Internal rate of return The discount rate that makes net present value equal 0; the discount rate that makes the present value of an investment's costs (outflows) equal to the present value of the investment's benefits (inflows).

Internet of Things A network arrangement of structures and devices whereby the objects on the network are able to interact and share information.

Interpolated spread The yield spread of a specific bond over the standard swap rate in that currency of the same tenor.

Interquartile range The difference between the third and first quartiles of a dataset.

Interval With reference to grouped data, a set of values within which an observation falls.

Intrinsic value The amount gained (per unit) by an option buyer if an option is exercised at any given point in time. May be referred to as the exercise value of the option.

Inventory investment Net change in business inventory.

Inventory turnover An activity ratio calculated as cost of goods sold divided by average inventory.

Inverse demand function A restatement of the demand function in which price is stated as a function of quantity.

Inverse floater A type of leveraged structured financial instrument. The cash flows are adjusted periodically and move in the opposite direction of changes in the reference rate.

Inverse transformation method A method using randomly generated numbers from the continuous uniform distribution to generate random observations from any distribution.

Investing activities Activities associated with the acquisition and disposal of property, plant, and equipment; intangible assets; other long-term assets; and both long-term and short-term investments in the equity and debt (bonds and loans) issued by other companies.

Investment banks Financial intermediaries that provide advice to their mostly corporate clients and help them arrange transactions such as initial and seasoned securities offerings.

Investment policy statement A written planning document that describes a client's investment objectives and risk tolerance over a relevant time horizon, along with the constraints that apply to the client's portfolio.

Investment property Property used to earn rental income or capital appreciation (or both).

Jackknife A resampling method that repeatedly draws samples by taking the original observed data sample and leaving out one observation at a time (without replacement) from the set.

January effect Calendar anomaly that stock market returns in January are significantly higher compared to the rest of the months of the year, with most of the abnormal returns reported during the first five trading days in January. Also called *turn-of-the-year effect*.

Joint frequencies The entry in the cells of the contingency table that represent the joining of one variable from a row and the other variable from a column to count observations.

Joint probability The probability of the joint occurrence of stated events.

Joint probability function A function giving the probability of joint occurrences of values of stated random variables.

Judgmental Sampling A procedure of selectively handpicking elements from the population based on a researcher's knowledge and professional judgment.

Key rate duration A method of measuring the interest rate sensitivities of a fixed-income instrument or portfolio to shifts in key points along the yield curve.

Keynesians Economists who believe that fiscal policy can have powerful effects on aggregate demand, output, and employment when there is substantial spare capacity in an economy.

Kurtosis The statistical measure that indicates the combined weight of the tails of a distribution relative to the rest of the distribution.

LIFO layer liquidation With respect to the application of the LIFO inventory method, the liquidation of old, relatively low-priced inventory; happens when the volume of sales rises above the volume of recent purchases so that some sales are made from relatively old, low-priced inventory. Also called *LIFO liquidation*.

LIFO method The last in, first out, method of accounting for inventory, which matches sales against the costs of items of inventory in the reverse order the items were placed in inventory (i.e., inventory produced or acquired last are assumed to be sold first).

LIFO reserve The difference between the reported LIFO inventory carrying amount and the inventory amount that would have been reported if the FIFO method had been used (in other words, the FIFO inventory value less the LIFO inventory value).

Labor force Everyone of working age (ages 16 to 64) who either is employed or is available for work but not working.

Labor productivity The quantity of goods and services (real GDP) that a worker can produce in one hour of work.

Lagging economic indicators Turning points that take place later than those of the overall economy; they are believed to have value in identifying the economy's past condition.

Law of demand The principle that as the price of a good rises, buyers will choose to buy less of it, and as its price falls, they will buy more.

Law of diminishing marginal returns The observation that a variable factor's marginal product must eventually fall as more of it is added to a fixed amount of the other factors.

Law of diminishing returns The smallest output that a firm can produce such that its long run average costs are minimized.

Law of one price A principle that states that if two investments have the same or equivalent future cash flows regardless of what will happen in the future, then these two investments should have the same current price.

Lead underwriter The lead investment bank in a syndicate of investment banks and broker–dealers involved in a securities underwriting.

Leading economic indicators A set of economic variables whose values vary with the business cycle but at a fairly consistent time interval before a turn in the business cycle.

Lean startups A form of asset-light business model that attempts to outsource as many functions as possible in order to minimize both capital investment and fixed operating expenses.

Lease A contract that conveys the right to use an asset for a period of time in exchange for consideration.

Leasing The right to use an asset for a specified time, without ownership rights, for a fee.

Legal tender Something that must be accepted when offered in exchange for goods and services.

Lender of last resort An entity willing to lend money when no other entity is ready to do so.

Leptokurtic Describes a distribution that has fatter tails than a normal distribution (also called fat-tailed).

Lessee The party obtaining the use of an asset through a lease.

Lessor The owner of an asset that grants the right to use the asset to another party.

Letter of credit Form of external credit enhancement whereby a financial institution provides the issuer with a credit line to reimburse any cash flow shortfalls from the assets backing the issue.

Level of significance The probability of a Type I error in testing a hypothesis.

Leverage A measure for identifying a potentially influential high-leverage point.

Leveraged buyout A transaction whereby the target company management team converts the target to a privately held company by using heavy borrowing to finance the purchase of the target company's outstanding shares.

Leveraged buyout (LBO) An acquirer (typically an investment fund specializing in LBOs) uses a significant amount of debt to finance the acquisition of a target and then pursues restructuring actions, with the goal of exiting the target with a sale or public listing.

Leveraged buyouts Transactions whereby the target company's management team converts the target to a privately held company by using heavy borrowing to finance the purchase of the target company's outstanding shares.

Liabilities Present obligations of an enterprise arising from past events, the settlement of which is expected to result in an outflow of resources embodying economic benefits; creditors' claims on the resources of a company.

Liability-driven investment (LDI) An investment approach which takes the size, timing and/or relative certainty of future investor financial obligations into account when establishing portfolio risk and return objectives.

Licensing arrangements The right to produce a product or have access to intangible assets using someone else's brand name in return for a royalty (often a percentage of revenues).

Likelihood The probability of an observation, given a particular set of conditions.

Limit order Instructions to a broker or exchange to obtain the best price immediately available when filling an order, but in no event accept a price higher than a specified (limit) price when buying or accept a price lower than a specified (limit) price when selling.

Limit order book The book or list of limit orders to buy and sell that pertains to a security.

Limitations on liens Meant to put limits on how much secured debt an issuer can have.

Limited partners The partners in a limited partnership who cannot lose more than their investment in the partnership due to having limited liability.

Limited partnership A special form of partnership in which there is at least one general partner with unlimited liability and responsibility for management of the business. The remaining limited partners have limited liability in the business.

Limited partnership agreements (LPAs) Legal documents that outline the rules of a partnership and establish the framework that ultimately guides the fund's operations throughout its life.

Lin-log model A regression model in which the independent variable is in logarithmic form.

Line chart A type of graph used to visualize ordered observations. In technical analysis, a plot of price data, typically closing prices, with a line connecting the points.

Linear derivatives Firm commitment derivative contracts in which the contract's payoff/profit function is linear with respect to the price of the underlying.

Linear interpolation The estimation of an unknown value on the basis of two known values that bracket it, using a straight line between the two known values.

Linear regression Regression that models the straight-line relationship between the dependent and independent variables. Also known as *least squares regression* and *ordinary least squares regression*.

Linear scale A scale in which equal distances correspond to equal absolute amounts. Also called an *arithmetic scale*.

Linker See *inflation-linked bond*.

Liquid market Said of a market in which traders can buy or sell with low total transaction costs when they want to trade.

Liquidation To sell the assets of a company, division, or subsidiary piecemeal, typically because of bankruptcy; the form of bankruptcy that allows for the orderly satisfaction of creditors' claims after which the company ceases to exist.

Liquidity The extent to which a company is able to meet its short-term obligations using cash flows and those assets that can be readily transformed into cash.

Liquidity management The company's ability to generate cash when needed, at the lowest possible cost.

Liquidity premium An extra return that compensates investors for the risk of loss relative to an investment's fair value if the investment needs to be converted to cash quickly.

Liquidity ratios Financial ratios measuring the company's ability to meet its short-term obligations to creditors as they come due.

Liquidity risk A divergence in the cash flow timing of a derivative versus that of an underlying transaction.

Liquidity trap A condition in which the demand for money becomes infinitely elastic (horizontal demand curve) so that injections of money into the economy will not lower interest rates or affect real activity.

Load fund A mutual fund in which, in addition to the annual fee, a percentage fee is charged to invest in the fund and/or for redemptions from the fund.

Loan-to-value ratio The ratio of a property's purchase price to the amount of its mortgage.

Lockup periods Minimum fund holding periods before investors are allowed to make withdrawals or redeem shares.

Log-lin model A regression model in which the dependent variable is in logarithmic form.

Log-log model A regression model in which both the dependent and independent variables are in logarithmic form. Also known as the *double-log model*.

Logarithmic scale A scale in which equal distances represent equal proportional changes in the underlying quantity.

London interbank offered rate (Libor) Collective name for multiple rates at which a select set of banks believes they could borrow unsecured funds from other banks in the London interbank market for different currencies and different borrowing periods ranging from overnight to one year.

Long A trading position in a **derivative contract** that gains value as the price of the **underlying** moves higher.

Long-lived assets Assets that are expected to provide economic benefits over a future period of time, typically greater than one year. Also called *long-term assets*.

Long position A position in an asset or contract in which one owns the asset or has an exercisable right under the contract.

Long-run average total cost The curve describing average total cost when no costs are considered fixed.

Look-ahead bias A bias caused by using information that was unavailable on the test date.

Loss aversion The tendency of people to dislike losses more than they like comparable gains.

Loss-aversion bias A bias in which people tend to strongly prefer avoiding losses as opposed to achieving gains.

Loss severity Portion of a bond's value (including unpaid interest) an investor loses in the event of default.

Losses Asset outflows not directly related to the ordinary activities of the business.

Lower bound The lowest possible value of an option.

M^2 A measure of what a portfolio would have returned if it had taken on the same total risk as the market index.

M^2 alpha Difference between the risk-adjusted performance of the portfolio and the performance of the benchmark.

MAR ratio A ratio of the average annual compounded return to the maximum drawdown risk over the full history of the investment. A variation of the Calmar ratio.

Macaulay duration The approximate amount of time a bond would have to be held for the market discount rate at purchase to be realized if there is a single change in interest rate. It indicates the point in time when the coupon reinvestment and price effects of a change in yield-to-maturity offset each other.

Machine learning Computer based techniques that seek to extract knowledge from large amounts of data by "learning" from known examples and then generating structure or predictions. ML algorithms aim to "find the pattern, apply the pattern."

Macro risk The risk from political, economic, legal, and other institutional risk factors that impact all businesses in an economy, a region, or a country.

Macroeconomics The branch of economics that deals with aggregate economic quantities, such as national output and national income.

Maintenance covenants Covenants in bank loan agreements that require the borrower to satisfy certain financial ratio tests while the loan is outstanding.

Maintenance margin Minimum balance set below the initial margin that each contract buyer and seller must hold in the futures margin account from trade initiation until final settlement at maturity.

Maintenance margin requirement The margin requirement on any day other than the first day of a transaction.

Management buy-ins Leveraged buyouts in which the current management team is replaced with the acquiring team.

Management buyout A leveraged buyout event in which a group of investors consisting primarily of the company's existing management purchases at least controlling interest in its outstanding shares. At the extreme, they may purchase all shares and take the company private.

Management buyout (MBO) A process used to take a public company private, involving significant amounts of debt to finance the acquisition by members of the company's current management team.

Management buyouts Leveraged buyout events in which a group of investors consisting primarily of the company's existing management purchases at least a controlling interest in its outstanding shares. At the extreme, they may purchase all shares and take the company private.

Management fee A fee based on assets under management or committed capital, as applicable—also called a *base fee*.

Margin call Request to a derivatives contract counterparty to immediately deposit funds to return the futures margin account balance to the initial margin.

Margin loan Money borrowed from a broker to purchase securities.

Marginal cost The cost of producing an additional unit of a good.

Marginal frequencies The sums determined by adding joint frequencies across rows or across columns in a contingency table.

Marginal product Measures the productivity of each unit of input and is calculated by taking the difference in total product from adding another unit of input (assuming other resource quantities are held constant).

Marginal propensity to consume The proportion of an additional unit of disposable income that is consumed or spent; the change in consumption for a small change in income.

Marginal propensity to save The proportion of an additional unit of disposable income that is saved (not spent).

Marginal revenue The change in total revenue divided by the change in quantity sold; simply, the additional revenue from selling one more unit.

Marginal value curve A curve describing the highest price consumers are willing to pay for each additional unit of a good.

Mark-to-market Refers to the current expected fair market value for which a security would likely be available for purchase or sale if traded in current market conditions.

Mark to market (MTM) The practice in which a central clearing party assigns profits and losses to counterparties to derivative contracts. In exchange-traded markets, this practice takes place daily and is often referred to as daily settlement.

Market anomaly Change in the price or return of a security that cannot directly be linked to current relevant information known in the market or to the release of new information into the market.

Market bid–ask spread The difference between the best bid and the best offer.

Market-capitalization weighting An index weighting method in which the weight assigned to each constituent security is determined by dividing its market capitalization by the total market capitalization (sum of the market capitalization) of all securities in the index. Also called *value weighting*.

Market discount rate The rate of return required by investors given the risk of the investment in a bond; also called the *required yield* or the *required rate of return*.

Market float The number of shares that are available to the investing public.

Market liquidity risk The risk that the price at which investors can actually transact—buying or selling—may differ from the price indicated in the market.

Market makers Over-the-counter (OTC) dealers who typically enter into offsetting bilateral transactions with one another to transfer risk to other parties.

Market model A regression model with the return on a stock as the dependent variable and the returns on a market index as the independent variable.

Market multiple models Valuation models based on share price multiples or enterprise value multiples.

Market-on-close An execution instruction specifying that an order can only be filled at the close of trading.

Market order Instructions to a broker or exchange to obtain the best price immediately available when filling an order.

Market-oriented investors With reference to equity investors, investors whose investment disciplines cannot be clearly categorized as value or growth.

Market rate of interest The rate demanded by purchasers of bonds, given the risks associated with future cash payment obligations of the particular bond issue.

Market reference rate (MRR) The interest rate underlying used in interest rate swaps. These rates typically match those of loans or other short-term obligations. Survey-based Libor rates used as reference rates in the past have been replaced by rates based on a daily average of observed market transaction rates. For example, the Secured Overnight Financing Rate (SOFR) is an overnight cash borrowing rate collateralized by US Treasuries. Other MRRs include the euro short-term rate (€STR) and the Sterling Overnight Index Average (SONIA).

Market risk The risk that arises from movements in interest rates, stock prices, exchange rates, and commodity prices.

Market value The price at which an asset or security can currently be bought or sold in an open market.

Marketable limit order A buy limit order in which the limit price is placed above the best offer, or a sell limit order in which the limit price is placed below the best bid. Such orders generally will partially or completely fill right away.

Marketplace businesses Businesses that create networks of buyers and sellers without taking ownership of the goods during the process.

Markowitz efficient frontier The graph of the set of portfolios offering the maximum expected return for their level of risk (standard deviation of return).

Matching principle The accounting principle that expenses should be recognized in the same period in which the associated revenue is recognized.

Matrix pricing Process of estimating the market discount rate and price of a bond based on the quoted or flat prices of more frequently traded comparable bonds.

Maturity Length of time until the closing of a derivative contract, or **settlement**.

Maturity premium An extra return that compensates investors for the increased sensitivity of the market value of debt to a change in market interest rates as maturity is extended.

Maturity structure A factor explaining the differences in yields on similar bonds; also called *term structure*.

Mean absolute deviation With reference to a sample, the mean of the absolute values of deviations from the sample mean.

Mean square error (MSE) The sum of squares error divided by the degrees of freedom, $n - k - 1$; in a simple linear regression, $n - k - 1 = n - 2$.

Mean square regression (MSR) The sum of squares regression divided by the number of independent variables k; in a simple linear regression, $k = 1$.

Mean–variance analysis An approach to portfolio analysis using expected means, variances, and covariances of asset returns.

Measure of central tendency A quantitative measure that specifies where data are centered.

Measure of value A standard for measuring value; a function of money.

Measures of location Quantitative measures that describe the location or distribution of data. They include not only measures of central tendency but also other measures, such as percentiles.

Median The value of the middle item of a set of items that has been sorted into ascending or descending order (i.e., the 50th percentile).

Medium of exchange Any asset that can be used to purchase goods and services or to repay debts; a function of money.

Medium-term note A corporate bond offered continuously to investors by an agent of the issuer, designed to fill the funding gap between commercial paper and long-term bonds.

Mental accounting bias An information-processing bias in which people treat one sum of money differently from another equal-sized sum based on which mental account the money is assigned to.

Menu costs A cost of inflation in which businesses constantly have to incur the costs of changing the advertised prices of their goods and services.

Mesokurtic Describes a distribution with kurtosis equal to that of the normal distribution, namely, kurtosis equal to three.

Microeconomics The branch of economics that deals with markets and decision making of individual economic units, including consumers and businesses.

Minimum efficient scale The smallest output that a firm can produce such that its long-run average total cost is minimized.

Minimum-variance portfolio The portfolio with the minimum variance for each given level of expected return.

Minority shareholders Particular shareholders or a block of shareholders holding a small proportion of a company's outstanding shares, resulting in a limited ability to exercise control in voting activities.

Minsky moment Named for Hyman Minksy. A point in a business cycle when, after individuals become overextended in borrowing to finance speculative investments, people start realizing that something is likely to go wrong and a panic ensues, leading to asset sell-offs.

Modal interval With reference to grouped data, the interval containing the greatest number of observations (i.e., highest frequency).

Mode The most frequently occurring value in a distribution.

Modern portfolio theory (MPT) The analysis of rational portfolio choices based on the efficient use of risk.

Modified duration A measure of the percentage price change of a bond given a change in its yield-to-maturity.

Momentum oscillator A graphical representation of market sentiment that is constructed from price data and calculated so that it oscillates either between a low and a high or around some number.

Monetarists Economists who believe that the rate of growth of the money supply is the primary determinant of the rate of inflation.

Monetary policy Actions taken by a nation's central bank to affect aggregate output and prices through changes in bank reserves, reserve requirements, or its target interest rate.

Monetary transmission mechanism The process whereby a central bank's interest rate gets transmitted through the economy and ultimately affects the rate of increase of prices.

Monetary union An economic union in which the members adopt a common currency.

Money A generally accepted medium of exchange and unit of account.

Money convexity For a bond, the annual or approximate convexity multiplied by the full price.

Money creation The process by which changes in bank reserves translate into changes in the money supply.

Money duration A measure of the price change in units of the currency in which the bond is denominated given a change in its yield-to-maturity.

Money market The market for short-term debt instruments (one-year maturity or less).

Money market securities Fixed-income securities with maturities at issuance of one year or less.

Money multiplier Describes how a change in reserves is expected to affect the money supply; in its simplest form, 1 divided by the reserve requirement.

Money neutrality The thesis that an increase in the money supply leads in the long-run to an increase in the price level, while leaving real variables like output and employment unaffected.

Money-weighted return The internal rate of return on a portfolio, taking account of all cash flows.

Moneyness Expresses the relationship between an option's value and its exercise price across the full range of possible underlying prices.

Monopolistic competition Highly competitive form of imperfect competition; the competitive characteristic is a notably large number of firms, while the monopoly aspect is the result of product differentiation.

Monopoly In pure monopoly markets, there are no substitutes for the given product or service. There is a single seller, which exercises considerable power over pricing and output decisions.

Monte Carlo simulation A technique that uses the inverse transformation method for converting a randomly generated uniformly distributed number into a simulated value of a random variable of a desired distribution. Each key decision variable in a Monte Carlo simulation requires an assumed statistical distribution; this assumption facilitates incorporating non-normality, fat tails, and tail dependence as well as solving high-dimensionality problems.

Moral principles Beliefs regarding what is good, acceptable, or obligatory behavior and what is bad, unacceptable, or forbidden behavior.

Mortgage-backed securities Debt obligations that represent claims to the cash flows from pools of mortgage loans, most commonly on residential property.

Mortgage loan A loan secured by the collateral of some specified real estate property that obliges the borrower to make a predetermined series of payments to the lender.

Mortgage pass-through security A security created when one or more holders of mortgages form a pool of mortgages and sell shares or participation certificates in the pool.

Mortgage rate The interest rate on a mortgage loan; also called *contract rate* or *note rate*.

Moving average The average of the closing price of a security over a specified number of periods. With each new period, the average is recalculated.

Moving-average convergence/divergence oscillator A momentum oscillator that is based on the difference between short-term and long-term moving averages of a security's price.

Multi-factor model A model that explains a variable in terms of the values of a set of factors.

Multi-market indexes Comprised of indexes from different countries, designed to represent multiple security markets.

Multi-step format With respect to the format of the income statement, a format that presents a subtotal for gross profit (revenue minus cost of goods sold).

Multilateral trading facilities (MTF) See *Alternative trading systems (ATS)*.

Multilateralism The conduct of countries who participate in mutually beneficial trade relationships and extensive rules harmonization. Private firms are fully integrated into global supply chains with multiple trade partners. Examples of multilateral countries include Germany and Singapore.

Multinational corporation A company operating in more than one country or having subsidiary firms in more than one country.

Multinomial formula (general formula for labeling problems) The number of ways that n objects can be labeled with k different labels, with n_1 of the first type, n_2 of the second type, and so on, with $n_1 + n_2 + ... + n_k = n$, is given by $\frac{n!}{n_1! n_2!...n_k!}$.

Multiple of invested capital (MOIC) A simplified calculation that measures the total value of all distributions and residual asset values relative to an initial total investment—also known as a *money multiple*.

Multiple testing problem The risk of getting statistically significant test results when performing a test multiple times.

Multiplication rule for counting If one task can be done in n_1 ways, and a second task, given the first, can be done in n_2 ways, and a third task, given the first two tasks, can be done in n_3 ways, and so on for k tasks, then the number of ways the k tasks can be done is $(n_1)(n_2)(n_3) ... (n_k)$.

Multiplication rule for independent events The rule that when two events are independent, the joint probability of A and B equals the product of the individual probabilities of A and B.

Multiplication rule for probability The rule that the joint probability of events A and B equals the probability of A given B times the probability of B.

Multiplier models Valuation models based on share price multiples or enterprise value multiples.

Multivariate distribution A probability distribution that specifies the probabilities for a group of related random variables.

Multivariate normal distribution A probability distribution for a group of random variables that is completely defined by the means and variances of the variables plus all the correlations between pairs of the variables.

Muni See *municipal bond*.

Municipal bond A type of non-sovereign bond issued by a state or local government in the United States. It very often (but not always) offers income tax exemptions.

Mutual fund A comingled investment pool in which investors in the fund each have a pro-rata claim on the income and value of the fund.

Mutually exclusive Indicates that only one event can occur at a time.

Mutually exclusive projects Mutually exclusive projects compete directly with each other. For example, if Projects A and B are mutually exclusive, you can choose A or B but you cannot choose both.

n Factorial For a positive integer n, the product of the first n positive integers; 0 factorial equals 1 by definition. n factorial is written as $n!$.

Narrow money The notes and coins in circulation in an economy, plus other very highly liquid deposits.

Nash equilibrium When two or more participants in a non-coop-erative game have no incentive to deviate from their respective equilibrium strategies given their opponent's strategies.

National income The income received by all factors of production used in the generation of final output. National income equals gross domestic product (or, in some countries, gross national product) minus the capital consumption allowance and a statistical discrepancy.

Nationalism The promotion of a country's own economic interests to the exclusion or detriment of the interests of other nations. Nationalism is marked by limited economic and financial cooperation. These actors may focus on national production and sales, limited cross-border investment and capital flows, and restricted currency exchange.

Natural language processing Computer programs developed to analyze and interpret human language.

Natural rate of unemployment Effective unemployment rate, below which pressure emerges in labor markets.

Negative screening An ESG investment style that focuses on the exclusion of certain sectors, companies, or practices in a fund or portfolio on the basis of specific ESG criteria.

Net book value The remaining (undepreciated) balance of an asset's purchase cost. For liabilities, the face value of a bond minus any unamortized discount, or plus any unamortized premium.

Net exports The difference between the value of a country's exports and the value of its imports (i.e., value of exports minus imports).

Net income The difference between revenue and expenses; what remains after subtracting all expenses (including depreciation, interest, and taxes) from revenue.

Net investment hedge Refers to a specific **hedge accounting** designation that applies when either a foreign currency bond or a derivative, such as an FX swap or forward, is used to offset the exchange rate risk of the equity of a foreign operation.

Net present value The present value of an investment's cash inflows (benefits) minus the present value of its cash outflows (costs).

Net profit margin An indicator of profitability, calculated as net income divided by revenue; indicates how much of each dollar of revenues is left after all costs and expenses. Also called *profit margin* or *return on sales*.

Net realisable value Estimated selling price in the ordinary course of business less the estimated costs necessary to make the sale.

Net revenue Revenue after adjustments (e.g., for estimated returns or for amounts unlikely to be collected).

Net tax rate The tax rate net of transfer payments.

Network effects The increase in value or utility for some services and products as more users join and wider adoption occurs.

Neural networks Computer programs based on how our own brains learn and process information.

Neutral rate of interest The rate of interest that neither spurs on nor slows down the underlying economy.

No-load fund A mutual fund in which there is no fee for investing in the fund or for redeeming fund shares, although there is an annual fee based on a percentage of the fund's net asset value.

Node Each value on a binomial tree from which successive moves or outcomes branch.

Nominal data Categorical values that are not amenable to being organized in a logical order. An example of nominal data is the classification of publicly listed stocks into sectors.

Nominal GDP The value of goods and services measured at current prices.

Nominal risk-free interest rate The sum of the real risk-free interest rate and the inflation premium.

Non-accelerating inflation rate of unemployment Effective unemployment rate below which pressure emerges in labor markets.

Non-agency RMBS In the United States, securities issued by private entities that are not guaranteed by a federal agency or a GSE.

Non-bank lenders Unlike typical banks, which make loans and take deposits, these lenders only make loans and may provide specific financial services to targeted consumers and firms such as mortgage services, lease financing, and venture capital.

Non-cooperative country A country with inconsistent and even arbitrary rules; restricted movement of goods, services, people, and capital across borders; retaliation; and limited technology exchange.

Non-cumulative preference shares Preference shares for which dividends that are not paid in the current or subsequent periods are forfeited permanently (instead of being accrued and paid at a later date).

Non-current assets Assets that are expected to benefit the company over an extended period of time (usually more than one year).

Non-current liabilities Obligations that broadly represent a probable sacrifice of economic benefits in periods generally greater than one year in the future.

Non-cyclical A company whose performance is largely independent of the business cycle. Also known as defensive.

Non-financial risks Risks that arise from sources other than changes in the external financial markets, such as changes in accounting rules, legal environment, or tax rates.

Non-linear derivatives Derivatives, such as options or other contingent claims, with payoff/profit profiles that are non-linear (asymmetric) with respect to the price of the underlying.

Non-participating preference shares Preference shares that do not entitle shareholders to share in the profits of the company. Instead, shareholders are only entitled to receive a fixed dividend payment and the par value of the shares in the event of liquidation.

Non-probability sampling A sampling plan dependent on factors other than probability considerations, such as a sampler's judgment or the convenience to access data.

Non-recourse loan A loan in which the lender does not have a shortfall claim against the borrower, so the lender can look only to the property to recover the outstanding mortgage balance.

Non-renewable resources Finite resources that are depleted once they are consumed; oil and coal are examples.

Non-sovereign bond A bond issued by a government below the national level, such as a province, region, state, or city.

Non-state actors Those that participate in global political, economic, or financial affairs but do not directly control national security or country resources. Examples of non-state actors are non-governmental organizations (NGOs), multinational companies, charities, and even influential individuals, such as business leaders or cultural icons.

Nonconventional cash flow pattern In a nonconventional cash flow pattern, the initial outflow is not followed by inflows only, but the cash flows can flip from positive (inflows) to negative (outflows) again or even change signs several times.

Nonparametric test A test that is not concerned with a parameter or that makes minimal assumptions about the population from which a sample comes.

Nonprofit corporations (Nonprofits) Corporations formed with the specific purpose of promoting a public benefit, religious benefit, or charitable mission. The motive of nonprofits is not expressly profit driven.

Nonsystematic risk Unique risk that is local or limited to a particular asset or industry that need not affect assets outside of that asset class.

Normal distribution A continuous, symmetric probability distribution that is completely described by its mean and its variance.

Normal goods Goods that are consumed in greater quantities as income increases.

Normal profit The level of accounting profit needed to just cover the implicit opportunity costs ignored in accounting costs.

Notching Ratings adjustment methodology where specific issues from the same borrower may be assigned different credit ratings.

Note rate See *mortgage rate*.

Notice periods The length of time (typically 30–90 days) of prior notice that a fund receives from investors who may be required to express their intent to redeem some or all of their investment.

Novation process A process that substitutes the initial **swap execution facility(SEF)** contract with identical trades facing the **central counterparty (CCP)**. The CCP serves as **counterparty** for both financial intermediaries, eliminating bilateral **counterparty credit risk** and providing **clearing** and **settlement** services.

Null hypothesis The hypothesis that is tested.

Numerical data Values that represent measured or counted quantities as a number. Also called quantitative data.

Objective probabilities Probabilities that generally do not vary from person to person; includes a priori and empirical probabilities.

Observation The value of a specific variable collected at a point in time or over a specified period of time.

Odds against E The reciprocal of odds for E.

Odds for E The probability of E divided by 1 minus the probability of E.

Off-the-run A series of securities or indexes that were issued/created prior to the most recently issued/created series.

Offer The price at which a dealer or trader is willing to sell an asset, typically qualified by a maximum quantity (ask size).

Official interest rate An interest rate that a central bank sets and announces publicly; normally the rate at which it is willing to lend money to the commercial banks. Also called *official policy rate* or *policy rate*.

Official policy rate An interest rate that a central bank sets and announces publicly; normally the rate at which it is willing to lend money to the commercial banks.

Oligopoly Market structure with a relatively small number of firms supplying the market.

Omnichannel A distribution strategy that integrates both digital and physical sales channels, so that both can be used together to complete a sale.

On-the-run The most recently issued and most actively traded sovereign securities.

One-dimensional array The simplest format for representing a collection of data of the same data type.

One-sided hypothesis test A test in which the null hypothesis is rejected only if the evidence indicates that the population parameter is greater than or less than the hypothesized parameter; occurs when the alternative hypothesis is stated either as greater than or less than the hypothesized population parameter.

Open economy An economy that trades with other countries.

Open-end fund A mutual fund that accepts new investment money and issues additional shares at a value equal to the net asset value of the fund at the time of investment.

Open interest The number of outstanding contracts.

Open market operations The purchase or sale of bonds by the national central bank to implement monetary policy. The bonds traded are usually sovereign bonds issued by the national government.

Operating activities Activities that are part of the day-to-day business functioning of an entity, such as selling inventory and providing services.

Operating breakeven The number of units produced and sold at which the company's operating profit is zero (revenues = operating costs).

Operating cash flow The net amount of cash provided from operating activities.

Operating efficiency ratios Ratios that measure how efficiently a company performs day-to-day tasks, such as the collection of receivables and management of inventory.

Operating lease A type of lease which is more akin to the rental of the underlying asset.

Operating leverage The sensitivity of a firm's operating profit to a change in revenues.

Operating profit A company's profits on its usual business activities before deducting taxes. Also called *operating income*.

Operating profit margin A profitability ratio calculated as operating income (i.e., income before interest and taxes) divided by revenue. Also called *operating margin*.

Operating risk The risk attributed to the operating cost structure, in particular the use of fixed costs in operations; the risk arising from the mix of fixed and variable costs; the risk that a company's operations may be severely affected by environmental, social, and governance risk factors.

Operational independence A bank's ability to execute monetary policy and set interest rates in the way it thought would best meet the inflation target.

Operational risk The risk that arises from inadequate or failed people, systems, and internal policies, procedures, and processes, as well as from external events that are beyond the control of the organization but that affect its operations.

Operationally efficient Said of a market, a financial system, or an economy that has relatively low transaction costs.

Opportunity cost Reflects the foregone opportunity of investing in a different asset. It is typically denoted by the risk-free rate of interest, r.

Optimal capital structure The capital structure at which the value of the company is maximized.

Option A primary example of a **contingent claim**. A **derivative contract** that provides the buyer the right, but not the obligation, to buy or sell an **underlying**.

Option-adjusted price The value of the embedded option plus the flat price of the bond.

Option-adjusted spread (OAS) Constant spread that, when added to all the one-period forward rates on the interest rate tree, makes the arbitrage-free value of the bond equal to its market price.

Option-adjusted yield The required market discount rate whereby the price is adjusted for the value of the embedded option.

Option contract See *option*.

Option premium An amount that is paid upfront from the option buyer to the option seller. Reflects the value of the option buyer's right to exercise in the future.

Optional product pricing A pricing approach that applies when a customer buys additional services or product features, either at the time of purchase or afterward.

Order A specification of what instrument to trade, how much to trade, and whether to buy or sell.

Order-driven markets A market (generally an auction market) that uses rules to arrange trades based on the orders that traders submit; in their pure form, such markets do not make use of dealers.

Order precedence hierarchy With respect to the execution of orders to trade, a set of rules that determines which orders execute before other orders.

Ordinal data Categorical values that can be logically ordered or ranked.

Ordinary annuity An annuity with a first cash flow that is paid one period from the present.

Ordinary shares Equity shares that are subordinate to all other types of equity (e.g., preferred equity). Also called *common stock* or *common shares*.

Organized exchange A securities marketplace where buyers and seller can meet to arrange their trades.

Other comprehensive income Items of comprehensive income that are not reported on the income statement; comprehensive income minus net income.

Out-of-sample test A test of a strategy or model using a sample outside the period on which the strategy or model was developed.

Out-of-the-money Describes an option with zero intrinsic value because the option buyer would not rationally exercise the option. An example of such would be the case in which the price of the underlying is less than the option's exercise price for a call option.

Outcome A possible value of a random variable.

Over-the-counter (OTC) Refers to derivative markets in which **derivative contracts** are created and traded between derivatives end users and **dealers**, or financial intermediaries, such as commercial banks or investment banks.

Over-the-counter (OTC) market A decentralized market where buy and sell orders initiated from various locations are matched through a communications network.

Overbought When a market has trended too far in one direction and is vulnerable to a trend reversal, or correction.

Overcollateralization Form of internal credit enhancement that refers to the process of posting more collateral than needed to obtain or secure financing.

Overconfidence bias A bias in which people demonstrate unwarranted faith in their own intuitive reasoning, judgments, and/or cognitive abilities.

Overfitting Situation in which the model has too many independent variables relative to the number of observations in the sample, such that the coefficients on the independent variables represent noise rather than relationships with the dependent variable.

Oversold The opposite of overbought; see *overbought*.

Own price The price of a good or service itself (as opposed to the price of something else).

Own-price elasticity of demand The percentage change in quantity demanded for a percentage change in good's own price, holding all other things constant.

Owners' equity The excess of assets over liabilities; the residual interest of shareholders in the assets of an entity after deducting the entity's liabilities. Also called *shareholders' equity* or *shareholders' funds*.

Ownership capital (equity) Money invested by the owners of the company.

***p*-Value** The smallest level of significance at which the null is rejected.

Paired comparisons test See *test of the mean of the differences*.

Panel data A mix of time-series and cross-sectional data that contains observations through time on characteristics of across multiple observational units.

Par curve A sequence of yields-to-maturity such that each bond is priced at par value. The bonds are assumed to have the same currency, credit risk, liquidity, tax status, and annual yields stated for the same periodicity.

Par swap rate The fixed swap rate that equates the present value of all future expected floating cash flows to the present value of fixed cash flows.

Par value The amount of principal on a bond.

Parallel shift A parallel yield curve shift implies that all rates change by the same amount in the same direction.

Parameter A descriptive measure computed from or used to describe a population of data, conventionally represented by Greek letters.

Parametric test Any test (or procedure) concerned with parameters or whose validity depends on assumptions concerning the population generating the sample.

Pari passu Covenant or contract clause that ensures a debt obligation is treated the same as the borrower's other senior debt instruments and is not subordinated to similar obligations.

Partial duration See *key rate duration*.

Participating preference shares Preference shares that entitle shareholders to receive the standard preferred dividend plus the opportunity to receive an additional dividend if the company's profits exceed a pre-specified level.

Partnership agreement A legal document used in a partnership business structure that details how much of the business each partner owns, how the profits are to be shared, and what the duties are of each partner.

Pass-through rate The coupon rate of a mortgage pass-through security.

Passive investment A buy and hold approach in which an investor does not make portfolio changes based on short-term expectations of changing market or security performance.

Pay-in-advance A business model that requires payment from customers before a product or service is delivered, in order to reduce or eliminate the need for working capital.

Payable date The day that the company actually mails out (or electronically transfers) a dividend payment.

Payment date The day that the company actually mails out (or electronically transfers) a dividend payment.

Payments system The system for the transfer of money.

Pearson correlation A parametric measure of the relationship between two variables.

Pecking order theory The theory that managers consider how their actions might be interpreted by outsiders and thereby order their preferences for various forms of corporate financing. Forms of financing that are least visible to outsiders (e.g., internally generated funds) are most preferable to managers, and those that are most visible (e.g., equity) are least preferable.

Peer company See *comparable company*.

Peer group A group of companies engaged in similar business activities whose economics and valuation are influenced by closely related factors.

Penetration pricing A discount pricing approach used when a firm willingly sacrifices margins in order to build scale and market share.

Pennant A technical analysis continuation pattern formed by trendlines that converge to form a triangle, typically over a short period.

Per capita real GDP Real GDP divided by the size of the population, often used as a measure of a country's average standard of living.

Per unit contribution margin The amount that each unit sold contributes to covering fixed costs—that is, the difference between the price per unit and the variable cost per unit.

Percentiles Quantiles that divide a distribution into 100 equal parts that sum to 100.

Perfect capital markets Markets in which, by assumption, there are no taxes, transaction costs, or bankruptcy costs and in which all investors have equal ("symmetric") information.

Perfect competition A market structure in which the individual firm has virtually no impact on market price, because it is assumed to be a very small seller among a very large number of firms selling essentially identical products.

Perfectly elastic When the quantity demanded or supplied of a given good is infinitely sensitive to a change in the value of a specified variable (e.g., price).

Perfectly inelastic When the quantity demanded or supplied of a given good is completely insensitive to a change in the value of a specified variable (e.g., price).

Performance evaluation The measurement and assessment of the outcomes of investment management decisions.

Period costs Costs (e.g., executives' salaries) that cannot be directly matched with the timing of revenues and which are thus expensed immediately.

Periodicity The assumed number of periods in the year; typically matches the frequency of coupon payments.

Permanent differences Differences between tax and financial reporting of revenue (expenses) that will not be reversed at some future date. These result in a difference between the company's effective tax rate and statutory tax rate and do not result in a deferred tax item.

Permissioned networks Networks that are fully open only to select participants on a DLT network.

Permissionless networks Networks that are fully open to any user on a DLT network.

Permutation An ordered listing.

Permutation formula The number of ways that we can choose r objects from a total of n objects, when the order in which the r objects are listed does matter, is $_nP_r = \frac{n!}{(n-r)!}$.

Perpetual bonds Bonds with no stated maturity date.

Perpetuity A perpetual annuity, or a set of never-ending level sequential cash flows, with the first cash flow occurring one period from now.

Personal income A broad measure of household income that includes all income received by households, whether earned or unearned; measures the ability of consumers to make purchases.

Pet projects Investments in which influential managers want the corporation to invest. Often, unfortunately, pet projects are selected without undergoing normal capital allocation analysis.

Plain vanilla bond Bond that makes periodic, fixed coupon payments during the bond's life and a lump-sum payment of principal at maturity. Also called *conventional bond*.

Platykurtic Describes a distribution that has relatively less weight in the tails than the normal distribution (also called thin-tailed).

Point estimate A single numerical estimate of an unknown quantity, such as a population parameter.

Policy rate An interest rate that a central bank sets and announces publicly; normally the rate at which it is willing to lend money to the commercial banks.

Population All members of a specified group.

Portfolio companies In private equity, the companies in which the private equity fund is investing.

Portfolio demand for money The demand to hold speculative money balances based on the potential opportunities or risks that are inherent in other financial instruments.

Portfolio investment flows Short-term investments in foreign assets, such as stocks or bonds.

Portfolio planning The process of creating a plan for building a portfolio that is expected to satisfy a client's investment objectives.

Position The quantity of an asset that an entity owns or owes.

Positive screening An ESG implementation approach that seeks to identify the most favorable companies and sectors based on ESG considerations. Also called *best-in-class*.

Posterior probability An updated probability that reflects or comes after new information.

Potential GDP The maximum amount of output an economy can sustainably produce without inducing an increase in the inflation rate. The output level that corresponds to full employment with consistent wage and price expectations.

Power of a test The probability of correctly rejecting the null—that is, rejecting the null hypothesis when it is false.

Precautionary money balances Money held to provide a buffer against unforeseen events that might require money.

Preference shares A type of equity interest which ranks above common shares with respect to the payment of dividends and the distribution of the company's net assets upon liquidation. They have characteristics of both debt and equity securities. Also called *preferred stock*.

Preferred stock See *preference shares*.

Premium In the case of bonds, premium refers to the amount by which a bond is priced above its face (par) value. In the case of an option, the amount paid for the option contract.

Prepaid expense A normal operating expense that has been paid in advance of when it is due.

Prepayment option Contractual provision that entitles the borrower to prepay all or part of the outstanding mortgage principal prior to the scheduled due date when the principal must be repaid. Also called *early repayment option*.

Prepayment penalty mortgages Mortgages that stipulate a monetary penalty if a borrower prepays within a certain time period after the mortgage is originated.

Prepayment risk The uncertainty that the timing of the actual cash flows will be different from the scheduled cash flows as set forth in the loan agreement due to the borrowers' ability to alter payments, usually to take advantage of interest rate movements.

Present value models Valuation models that estimate the intrinsic value of a security as the present value of the future benefits expected to be received from the security. Also called *discounted cash flow models*.

Present value (PV) The present discounted value of future cash flows: For assets, the present discounted value of the future net cash inflows that the asset is expected to generate; for liabilities, the present discounted value of the future net cash outflows that are expected to be required to settle the liabilities.

Pretax margin A profitability ratio calculated as earnings before taxes divided by revenue.

Price discrimination A pricing approach that charges different prices to different customers based on their willingness to pay.

Price elasticity of demand Measures the percentage change in the quantity demanded, given a percentage change in the price of a given product.

Price index Represents the average prices of a basket of goods and services.

Price limits Establish a band relative to the previous day's settlement price within which all trades must occur.

Price multiple A ratio that compares the share price with some sort of monetary flow or value to allow evaluation of the relative worth of a company's stock.

Price priority The principle that the highest priced buy orders and the lowest priced sell orders execute first.

Price relative A ratio of an ending price over a beginning price; it is equal to 1 plus the holding period return on the asset.

Price return Measures *only* the price appreciation or percentage change in price of the securities in an index or portfolio.

Price return index An index that reflects *only* the price appreciation or percentage change in price of the constituent securities. Also called *price index*.

Price-setting option The option to adjust prices when demand varies from what is forecast.

Price stability In economics, refers to an inflation rate that is low on average and not subject to wide fluctuation.

Price takers Producers that must accept whatever price the market dictates.

Price to book value A valuation ratio calculated as price per share divided by book value per share.

Price to cash flow A valuation ratio calculated as price per share divided by cash flow per share.

Price-to-earnings ratio (P/E) The ratio of share price to earnings per share.

Price to sales A valuation ratio calculated as price per share divided by sales per share.

Price value of a basis point A version of money duration, it is an estimate of the change in the full price of a bond given a 1 basis point change in the yield-to-maturity.

Price weighting An index weighting method in which the weight assigned to each constituent security is determined by dividing its price by the sum of all the prices of the constituent securities.

Priced risk Risk for which investors demand compensation for bearing (e.g., equity risk, company-specific factors, macroeconomic factors).

Primary bond market A market in which issuers first sell bonds to investors to raise capital.

Primary capital markets (primary markets) The market where securities are first sold and the issuers receive the proceeds.

Primary dealer Financial institution that is authorized to deal in new issues of sovereign bonds and that serves primarily as a trading counterparty of the office responsible for issuing sovereign bonds.

Primary market The market where securities are first sold and the issuers receive the proceeds.

Prime brokers Brokers that provide services commonly including custody, administration, lending, short borrowing, and trading.

Principal The amount of funds originally invested in a project or instrument; the face value to be paid at maturity.

Principal amount Amount that an issuer agrees to repay the debtholders on the maturity date.

Principal business activity The business activity from which a company derives a majority of its revenues and/or earnings.

Principal value Amount that an issuer agrees to repay the debtholders on the maturity date.

Principal–agent relationship A relationship in which a principal hires an agent to perform a particular task or service; also known as an *agency relationship*.

Prior probabilities Probabilities reflecting beliefs prior to the arrival of new information.

Priority of claims Priority of payment, with the most senior or highest ranking debt having the first claim on the cash flows and assets of the issuer.

Private equity fund A hedge fund that seeks to buy, optimize, and ultimately sell portfolio companies to generate profits. See *venture capital fund*.

Private equity funds Funds that seek to invest in, optimize, and eventually exit portfolio companies to generate profits. See venture capital funds.

Private equity securities Securities that are not listed on public exchanges and have no active secondary market. They are issued primarily to institutional investors via non-public offerings, such as private placements.

Private investment in public equity (PIPE) An investment in the equity of a publicly traded firm that is made at a discount to the market value of the firm's shares.

Private label or "contract" manufacturers Manufacturers that produce goods to be marketed by others.

Private placement Typically, a non-underwritten, unregistered offering of securities that are sold only to an investor or a small group of investors. It can be accomplished directly between the issuer and the investor(s) or through an investment bank.

Private placement memorandum (PPM) A legal document used in the purchase of private company shares that describes the business, the terms of the offering, and the risks involved in making an investment in the company. Also termed an offering memorandum.

Probability A number between 0 and 1 describing the chance that a stated event will occur.

Probability density function A function with non-negative values such that probability can be described by areas under the curve graphing the function.

Probability distribution A distribution that specifies the probabilities of a random variable's possible outcomes.

Probability function A function that specifies the probability that the random variable takes on a specific value.

Probability sampling A sampling plan that allows every member of the population to have an equal chance of being selected.

Probability tree diagram A diagram with branches emanating from nodes representing either mutually exclusive chance events or mutually exclusive decisions.

Product market risk The risk that the market for a new product or service will fall short of expectations.

Production-flexibility option The option to alter production when demand varies from what is forecast.

Production function Provides the quantitative link between the levels of output that the economy can produce and the inputs used in the production process.

Productivity The amount of output produced by workers during a given period—for example, output per hour worked measures the efficiency of labor.

Profession An occupational group that has specific education, expert knowledge, and a framework of practice and behavior that underpins community trust, respect, and recognition.

Profit The return that owners of a company receive for the use of their capital and the assumption of financial risk when making their investments.

Profit and loss (P&L) statement A financial statement that provides information about a company's profitability over a stated period of time. Also called the *income statement*.

Profit margin An indicator of profitability, calculated as net income divided by revenue; indicates how much of each dollar of revenues is left after all costs and expenses.

Profitability ratios Ratios that measure a company's ability to generate profitable sales from its resources (assets).

Project sequencing To defer the decision to invest in a future project until the outcome of some or all of a current investment is known. Investments are sequenced over time, so that making an investment creates the option to invest in future projects.

Promissory note A written promise to pay a certain amount of money on demand.

Property, plant, and equipment Tangible assets that are expected to be used for more than one period in either the production or supply of goods or services, or for administrative purposes.

Prospectus The document that describes the terms of a new bond issue and helps investors perform their analysis on the issue.

Protective put A strategy of purchasing an underlying asset and purchasing a put on the same asset.

Proxy contest Corporate takeover mechanism in which shareholders are persuaded to vote for a group seeking a controlling position on a company's board of directors.

Proxy voting A process that enables shareholders who are unable to attend a meeting to authorize another individual to vote on their behalf.

Public offer See *public offering*.

Public offering An offering of securities in which any member of the public may buy the securities. Also called *public offer*.

Public–private partnership (PPP) An agreement between the public and private sector to finance, build, and operate public infrastructure, such as hospitals and toll roads.

Pull on liquidity When disbursements (outflows) are paid too quickly or trade credit availability is limited, requiring companies to expend funds before they receive funds from sales that could cover the liability.

Pure discount bonds See *zero-coupon bond*.

Put An option that gives the holder the right to sell an underlying asset to another party at a fixed price over a specific period of time.

Put option The right to sell an underlying.

Putable bonds Bonds that give the bondholder the right to sell the bond back to the issuer at a predetermined price on specified dates.

Put–call forward parity Describes the no-arbitrage condition in which at $t = 0$ the present value of the price of a long forward commitment plus the price of the long put must equal the price of the long call plus the price of the risk-free asset (with face value of the exercise price of both the call and the put).

Put–call parity Describes the no-arbitrage condition in which at $t = 0$ the price of the long underlying asset plus the price of the long put must equal the price of the long call plus the price of the risk-free asset (with face value of the exercise price of both the call and the put).

Put/call ratio A technical analysis indicator that evaluates market sentiment based on the volume of put options traded divided by the volume of call options traded for a particular financial instrument.

Qualitative data see *categorical data*.

Quantile A value at or below which a stated fraction of the data lies. Also referred to as a fractile.

Quantitative data see *numerical data*.

Quantitative easing An expansionary monetary policy based on aggressive open market purchase operations.

Quantity equation of exchange An expression that over a given period, the amount of money used to purchase all goods and services in an economy, $M \times V$, is equal to monetary value of this output, $P \times Y$.

Quantity theory of money Asserts that total spending (in money terms) is proportional to the quantity of money.

Quartiles Quantiles that divide a distribution into four equal parts.

Quasi-fixed cost A cost that stays the same over a range of production but can change to another constant level when production moves outside of that range.

Quasi-government bond A bond issued by an entity that is either owned or sponsored by a national government. Also called *agency bond*.

Quintiles Quantiles that divide a distribution into five equal parts.

Quota rents Profits that foreign producers can earn by raising the price of their goods higher than they would without a quota.

Quotas Government policies that restrict the quantity of a good that can be imported into a country, generally for a specified period of time.

Quote-driven market A market in which dealers acting as principals facilitate trading.

Quoted interest rate A quoted interest rate that does not account for compounding within the year. Also called *stated annual interest rate*.

Quoted margin The yield spread over the MRR established upon issuance of an FRN to compensate investors for assuming an issuer's credit risk.

Random number An observation drawn from a uniform distribution.

Random number generator An algorithm that produces uniformly distributed random numbers between 0 and 1.

Random variable A quantity whose future outcomes are uncertain.

Range The difference between the maximum and minimum values in a dataset.

Raw data Data available in their original form as collected.

Razors-and-blades pricing A pricing approach that combines a low price on a piece of equipment and high-margin pricing on repeat-purchase consumables.

Real estate investment trusts (REITs) Tax-advantaged entities (companies or trusts) that own, operate, and—to a limited extent—develop income-producing real estate property.

Real exchange rate effect The effect through which changing price level impacts real exchange rate which in turn impacts net exports and aggregate demand.

Real GDP The value of goods and services produced, measured at base year prices.

Real income Income adjusted for the effect of inflation on the purchasing power of money. Also known as the *purchasing power of income*. If income remains constant and a good's price falls, real income is said to rise, even though the number of monetary units (e.g., dollars) remains unchanged.

Real interest rate Nominal interest rate minus the expected rate of inflation.

Real risk-free interest rate The single-period interest rate for a completely risk-free security if no inflation were expected.

Realizable (settlement) value With reference to assets, the amount of cash or cash equivalents that could currently be obtained by selling the asset in an orderly disposal; with reference to liabilities, the undiscounted amount of cash or cash equivalents expected to be paid to satisfy the liabilities in the normal course of business.

Rebalancing In the context of asset allocation, a discipline for adjusting the portfolio to align with the strategic asset allocation.

Rebalancing policy The set of rules that guide the process of restoring a portfolio's asset class weights to those specified in the strategic asset allocation.

Recession A period during which real GDP decreases (i.e., negative growth) for at least two successive quarters, or a period of significant decline in total output, income, employment, and sales usually lasting from six months to a year.

Glossary

Recognition lag The lag in government response to an economic problem resulting from the delay in confirming a change in the state of the economy.

Recourse loan A loan in which the lender has a claim against the borrower for any shortfall between the outstanding mortgage balance and the proceeds received from the sale of the property.

Recurring revenue/subscription pricing A pricing approach that enables customers to "rent" a product or service for as long as they need it.

Redemption yield See *yield-to-maturity*.

Refinancing rate A type of central bank policy rate.

Regionalism In between the two extremes of bilateralism and multilateralism. In regionalism, a group of countries cooperate with one another. Both bilateralism and regionalism can be conducted at the exclusion of other groups. For example, regional blocs may agree to provide trade benefits to one another and increase barriers for those outside of that group.

Registered bonds Bonds for which ownership is recorded by either name or serial number.

Regression analysis A tool for examining whether a variable is useful for explaining another variable.

Regression coefficients The intercept and slope coefficient(s) of a regression.

Regret The feeling that an opportunity has been missed; typically, an expression of *hindsight bias*.

Regret-aversion bias An emotional bias in which people tend to avoid making decisions that will result in action out of fear that the decision will turn out poorly.

Relative dispersion The amount of dispersion relative to a reference value or benchmark.

Relative frequency The absolute frequency of each unique value of the variable divided by the total number of observations of the variable.

Relative price The price of a specific good or service in comparison with those of other goods and services.

Relative strength analysis A comparison of the performance of one asset with the performance of another asset or a benchmark, based on changes in the ratio of the two assets' prices over time.

Relative strength index (RSI) A technical analysis momentum oscillator that compares a security's gains with its losses over a set period.

Renewable resources Resources that can be replenished, such as a forest.

Rent Payment for the use of property.

Reorganization A court-supervised restructuring process available in some jurisdictions for companies facing insolvency from burdensome debt levels. A bankruptcy court assumes control of the company and oversees an orderly negotiation process between the company and its creditors for asset sales, conversion of debt to equity, refinancing, and so on.

Replication A strategy in which a derivative's cash flow stream may be recreated using a combination of long or short positions in an underlying asset and borrowing or lending cash.

Repo A form of collateralized loan involving the sale of a security with a simultaneous agreement by the seller to buy back the same security from the purchaser at an agreed-on price and future date. The party who sells the security at the inception of the repurchase agreement and buys it back at maturity is borrowing money from the other party, and the security sold and subsequently repurchased represents the collateral.

Repo margin The difference between the market value of the security used as collateral and the value of the loan. Also called *haircut*.

Repo rate The interest rate on a repurchase agreement.

Representativeness bias A belief perseverance bias in which people tend to classify new information based on past experiences and classifications.

Repurchase agreement See *Repo*.

Repurchase date The date when the party who sold the security at the inception of a repurchase agreement buys back the security from the cash lending counterparty.

Repurchase price The price at which the party who sold the security at the inception of the repurchase agreement buys back the security from the cash lending counterparty.

Required margin The yield spread over or under the reference rate such that an FRN is priced at par value on a rate reset date.

Required rate of return The minimum rate of return required by an investor to invest in an asset, given the asset's riskiness.

Required yield See *market discount rate*.

Required yield spread The difference between the yield-to-maturity on a new bond and the benchmark rate; additional compensation required by investors for the difference in risk and tax status of a bond relative to a government bond. Sometimes called the *spread over the benchmark*.

Resampling A statistical method that repeatedly draws samples from the original observed data sample for the statistical inference of population parameters.

Reserve accounts Form of internal credit enhancement that relies on creating accounts and depositing in these accounts cash that can be used to absorb losses. Also called *reserve funds*.

Reserve funds See *reserve accounts*.

Reserve requirement The requirement for banks to hold reserves in proportion to the size of deposits.

Residual The difference between an observation and its predicted value, where the predicted value is based on the estimated linear relation between the dependent and independent variables using sample data.

Resistance In technical analysis, a price range in which selling activity is sufficient to stop the rise in the price of a security.

Responsible investing A broad (umbrella) term to describe investing that incorporates environmental, social, and governance factors into investment decisions.

Restricted payments A bond covenant meant to protect creditors by limiting how much cash can be paid out to shareholders over time.

Retracement In technical analysis, a reversal in the movement of a security's price such that it is counter to the prevailing longer-term price trend.

Return-generating model A model that can provide an estimate of the expected return of a security given certain parameters and estimates of the values of the independent variables in the model.

Return on assets (ROA) A profitability ratio calculated as net income divided by average total assets; indicates a company's net profit generated per dollar invested in total assets.

Return on equity (ROE) A profitability ratio calculated as net income divided by average shareholders' equity.

Return on invested capital A measure of the profitability of a company relative to the amount of capital invested by the equity- and debtholders.

Return on sales An indicator of profitability, calculated as net income divided by revenue; indicates how much of each dollar of revenues is left after all costs and expenses. Also referred to as *net profit margin*.

Return on total capital A profitability ratio calculated as EBIT divided by the sum of short- and long-term debt and equity.

Revaluation model Under IFRS, the process of valuing long-lived assets at fair value, rather than at cost less accumulated depreciation. Any resulting profit or loss is either reported on the income statement and/or through equity under revaluation surplus.

Revenue The amount charged for the delivery of goods or services in the ordinary activities of a business over a stated period; the inflows of economic resources to a company over a stated period.

Reversal pattern A type of pattern used in technical analysis to predict the end of a trend and a change in the direction of a security's price.

Reverse repo A repurchase agreement viewed from the perspective of the cash lending counterparty.

Reverse repurchase agreement A repurchase agreement viewed from the perspective of the cash lending counterparty.

Reverse stock split A reduction in the number of shares outstanding with a corresponding increase in share price, but no change to the company's underlying fundamentals.

Revolving credit agreements (also known as revolvers) The most reliable form of short-term bank borrowing facilities; they are in effect for multiple years (e.g., three to five years) and can have optional medium-term loan features.

Rho The change in a given derivative instrument for a given small change in the risk-free interest rate, holding everything else constant. Rho measures the sensitivity of the option to the risk-free interest rate.

Ricardian equivalence An economic theory that implies that it makes no difference whether a government finances a deficit by increasing taxes or issuing debt.

Risk Exposure to uncertainty. The chance of a loss or adverse outcome as a result of an action, inaction, or external event.

Risk averse The assumption that an investor will choose the least risky alternative.

Risk aversion The degree of an investor's unwillingness to take risk; the inverse of risk tolerance.

Risk budgeting The establishment of objectives for individuals, groups, or divisions of an organization that takes into account the allocation of an acceptable level of risk.

Risk exposure The state of being exposed or vulnerable to a risk. The extent to which an organization is sensitive to underlying risks.

Risk governance The top-down process and guidance that directs risk management activities to align with and support the overall enterprise.

Risk management The process of identifying the level of risk an organization wants, measuring the level of risk the organization currently has, taking actions that bring the actual level of risk to the desired level of risk, and monitoring the new actual level of risk so that it continues to be aligned with the desired level of risk.

Risk management framework The infrastructure, process, and analytics needed to support effective risk management in an organization.

Risk-neutral pricing A no-arbitrage derivative value established separately from investor views on risk that uses underlying asset volatility and the risk-free rate to calculate the present value of future cash flows.

Risk-neutral probability The computed probability used in binomial option pricing by which the discounted weighted sum of expected values of the underlying equal the current option price. Specifically, this probability is computed using the risk-free rate and assumed up gross return and down gross return of the underlying.

Risk premium An extra return expected by investors for bearing some specified risk.

Risk shifting Actions to change the distribution of risk outcomes.

Risk tolerance The amount of risk an investor is willing and able to bear to achieve an investment goal.

Risk transfer Actions to pass on a risk to another party, often, but not always, in the form of an insurance policy.

Robo-adviser A machine-based analytical tool or service that provides technology-driven investment solutions through online platforms.

Rule of 72 The principle that the approximate number of years necessary for an investment to double is 72 divided by the stated interest rate.

Running yield See *current yield*.

Safety-first rules Rules for portfolio selection that focus on the risk that portfolio value or portfolio return will fall below some minimum acceptable level over some time horizon.

Sales Generally, a synonym for revenue; "sales" is generally understood to refer to the sale of goods, whereas "revenue" is understood to include the sale of goods or services.

Sales risk The uncertainty regarding the price and number of units sold of a company's products.

Sample A subset of a population.

Sample correlation coefficient A standardized measure of how two variables in a sample move together. It is the ratio of the sample covariance to the product of the two variables' standard deviations.

Sample covariance A measure of how two variables in a sample move together.

Sample excess kurtosis A sample measure of the degree of a distribution's kurtosis in excess of the normal distribution's kurtosis.

Sample mean The sum of the sample observations divided by the sample size.

Sample selection bias Bias introduced by systematically excluding some members of the population according to a particular attribute—for example, the bias introduced when data availability leads to certain observations being excluded from the analysis.

Sample-size neglect A type of representativeness bias in which financial market participants incorrectly assume that small sample sizes are representative of populations (or "real" data).

Sample skewness A sample measure of the degree of asymmetry of a distribution.

Sample standard deviation The positive square root of the sample variance.

Sample statistic A quantity computed from or used to describe a sample.

Sample variance The sum of squared deviations around the mean divided by the degrees of freedom.

Sampling The process of obtaining a sample.

Sampling distribution   The distribution of all distinct possible values that a statistic can assume when computed from samples of the same size randomly drawn from the same population.

Sampling error   The difference between the observed value of a statistic and the estimate resulting from using subsets of the population.

Sampling plan   The set of rules used to select a sample.

Say on pay   A process whereby shareholders may vote on executive remuneration (compensation) matters.

Scatter plot   A chart in which two variables are plotted along the axis and points on the chart represent pairs of the two variables. In regression, the dependent variable is plotted on the vertical axis and the independent variable is plotted along the horizontal axis. Also known as a scattergram and a *scatter diagram*.

Scatter plot matrix   A tool for organizing scatter plots between pairs of variables, making it easy to inspect all pairwise relationships in one combined visual.

Scenario analysis   A technique for exploring the performance and risk of investment strategies in different structural regimes.

Screening   The application of a set of criteria to reduce a set of potential investments to a smaller set having certain desired characteristics.

Seasoned offering   An offering in which an issuer sells additional units of a previously issued security.

Second-degree price discrimination   When the monopolist charges different per-unit prices using the quantity purchased as an indicator of how highly the customer values the product.

Second lien   A secured interest in the pledged assets that ranks below first lien debt in both collateral protection and priority of payment.

Secondary bond markets   Markets in which existing bonds are traded among investors.

Secondary market   The market where securities are traded among investors.

Secondary precedence rules   Rules that determine how to rank orders placed at the same time.

Sector   A group of related industries (GICS definition).

Sector indexes   Indexes that represent and track different economic sectors—such as consumer goods, energy, finance, health care, and technology—on either a national, regional, or global basis.

Secured bonds   Bonds secured by assets or financial guarantees pledged to ensure debt repayment in case of default.

Secured debt   Debt in which the debtholder has a direct claim—a pledge from the issuer—on certain assets and their associated cash flows.

Secured ("asset-based") loans   Loan that are backed by specific, secured company assets.

Securitization   A process that involves moving assets into a special legal entity, which then uses the assets as guarantees to secure a bond issue.

Securitized assets   Assets that are typically used to create asset-backed bonds; for example, when a bank securitizes a pool of loans, the loans are said to be securitized.

Security characteristic line   A plot of the excess return of a security on the excess return of the market.

Security market index   A portfolio of securities representing a given security market, market segment, or asset class.

Security market line   (SML) The graph of the capital asset pricing model.

Security selection   The process of selecting individual securities; typically, security selection has the objective of generating superior risk-adjusted returns relative to a portfolio's benchmark.

Self-attribution bias   A bias in which people take too much credit for successes (*self-enhancing*) and assign responsibility to others for failures (*self-protecting*).

Self-control bias   A bias in which people fail to act in pursuit of their long-term, overarching goals because of a lack of self-discipline.

Self-investment limits   With respect to investment limitations applying to pension plans, restrictions on the percentage of assets that can be invested in securities issued by the pension plan sponsor.

Sell-side firm   A broker/dealer that sells securities and provides independent investment research and recommendations to their clients (i.e., buy-side firms).

Semi-strong-form efficient market   A market in which security prices reflect all publicly known and available information.

Semiannual bond basis yield   An annual rate having a periodicity of two; also known as a *semiannual bond equivalent yield*.

Semiannual bond equivalent yield   See *semiannual bond basis yield*.

Seniority ranking   Priority of payment of various debt obligations.

Sensitivity analysis   Analysis that shows the range of possible outcomes as specific assumptions are changed.

Separately managed account   (SMA) An investment portfolio managed exclusively for the benefit of an individual or institution.

Serial maturity structure   Structure for a bond issue in which the maturity dates are spread out during the bond's life; a stated number of bonds mature and are paid off each year before final maturity.

Settlement   The closing date at which the **counterparties** of a **derivative contract** exchange payment for the **underlying** as required by the contract.

Settlement date   Date when the buyer makes cash payment and the seller delivers the security.

Settlement price   The price determined by an exchange's clearinghouse in the daily settlement of the mark-to-market process. The price reflects an average of the final futures trades of the day.

Share repurchase   A transaction in which a company buys back its own shares. Unlike stock dividends and stock splits, share repurchases use corporate cash.

Shareholder activism   Strategies used by shareholders to attempt to compel a company to act in a desired manner.

Shareholder engagement   The process whereby companies engage with their shareholders.

Shareholders' equity   Total assets minus total liabilities.

Sharpe ratio   The average return in excess of the risk-free rate divided by the standard deviation of return; a measure of the average excess return earned per unit of standard deviation of return.

Shelf registration   A type of public offering that allows the issuer to file a single, all-encompassing offering circular that covers a series of bond issues.

Short   A trading position in a **derivative contract** that gains value as the price of the **underlying** moves lower.

Short position   A position in an asset or contract in which one has sold an asset one does not own, or in which a right under a contract can be exercised against oneself.

Short-run average total cost The curve describing average total cost when some costs are considered fixed.

Short selling A transaction in which borrowed securities are sold with the intention to repurchase them at a lower price at a later date and return them to the lender.

Shortfall risk The risk that portfolio value or portfolio return will fall below some minimum acceptable level over some time horizon.

Shutdown point The point at which average revenue is equal to the firm's average variable cost.

Side letters Side agreements created between the GP and specific LPs. These agreements exist *outside* the LPA. These agreements provide additional terms and conditions related to the investment agreement.

Signpost An indicator, market level, data piece, or event that signals a risk is becoming more or less likely. An analyst can think of signposts like a traffic light.

Simple interest The interest earned each period on the original investment; interest calculated on the principal only.

Simple linear regression (SLR) A regression that summarizes the relation between the dependent variable and a single independent variable.

Simple random sample A subset of a larger population created in such a way that each element of the population has an equal probability of being selected to the subset.

Simple random sampling The procedure of drawing a sample to satisfy the definition of a simple random sample.

Simple yield The sum of the coupon payments plus the straight-line amortized share of the gain or loss, divided by the flat price.

Simulation A technique for exploring how a target variable (e.g. portfolio returns) would perform in a hypothetical environment specified by the user, rather than a historical setting.

Simulation trial A complete pass through the steps of a simulation.

Single-step format With respect to the format of the income statement, a format that does not subtotal for gross profit (revenue minus cost of goods sold).

Sinking fund arrangement Provision that reduces the credit risk of a bond issue by requiring the issuer to retire a portion of the bond's principal outstanding each year.

Situational influences External factors, such as environmental or cultural elements, that shape our behavior.

Skewed Not symmetrical.

Skewness A quantitative measure of skew (lack of symmetry); a synonym of skew. It is computed as the average cubed deviation from the mean standardized by dividing by the standard deviation cubed.

Slope coefficient The coefficient of an independent variable that represents the average change in the dependent variable for a one-unit change in the independent variable.

Small country A country that is a price taker in the world market for a product and cannot influence the world market price.

Smart beta Involves the use of simple, transparent, rules-based strategies as a basis for investment decisions.

Smart contract A computer program that is designed to self-execute on the basis of pre-specified terms and conditions agreed to by parties to a contract.

Socially responsible investing (SRI) Investing in assets and companies with favorable profiles or attributes based on the investor's social, moral, or faith-based beliefs.

Soft-bullet covered bonds Covered bonds for which bond default and payment acceleration of bond cash flows may be delayed upon sponsor default until a new final maturity date is reached.

Soft commodities Standardized agricultural products, such as cattle and corn, with markets often involving the physical delivery of the underlying upon settlement.

Soft power A means of influencing another country's decisions without force or coercion. Soft power can be built over time through actions, such as cultural programs, advertisement, travel grants, and university exchange.

Solvency Refers to the condition in which firm value exceeds the face value of debt used to finance the firm's assets.

Solvency ratios Ratios that measure a company's ability to meet its long-term obligations.

Solvency risk The risk that an organization does not survive or succeed because it runs out of cash, even though it might otherwise be solvent.

Sovereign bond A bond issued by a national government. Also called "Sovereign."

Spearman rank correlation coefficient A measure of correlation applied to ranked data.

Special dividend A dividend paid by a company that does not pay dividends on a regular schedule, or a dividend that supplements regular cash dividends with an extra payment.

Special purpose acquisition company (SPAC) A publicly listed shell company, also referred to as a "blank check" company, that exists solely for the purpose of acquiring an unspecified private company sometime in the future.

Special purpose entity A non-operating entity created to carry out a specified purpose, such as leasing assets or securitizing receivables; can be a corporation, partnership, trust, or limited liability partnership formed to facilitate a specific type of business activity. Also called *special purpose vehicle*, *special purpose company*, or *variable interest entity*.

Special purpose vehicle See *special purpose entity*.

Specific identification method An inventory accounting method that identifies which specific inventory items were sold and which remained in inventory to be carried over to later periods.

Speculative demand for money The demand to hold speculative money balances based on the potential opportunities or risks that are inherent in other financial instruments. Also called *portfolio demand for money*.

Speculative money balances Monies held in anticipation that other assets will decline in value.

Split coupon bond See *deferred coupon bond*.

Sponsored A type of depository receipt in which the foreign company whose shares are held by the depository has a direct involvement in the issuance of the receipts.

Spot curve A sequence of yields-to-maturity on zero-coupon bonds. Sometimes called *zero* or *strip curve* (because coupon payments are "stripped" off the bonds).

Spot markets Markets in which specific assets are exchanged at current prices. Spot markets are often referred to as **cash markets**.

Spot prices The current prices prevailing in **spot markets**.

Spot rates A sequence of market discount rates that correspond to the cash flow dates; yields-to-maturity on zero-coupon bonds maturing at the date of each cash flow.

Spread In general, the difference in yield between different fixed-income securities. Often used to refer to the difference between the yield-to-maturity and the benchmark.

Spread over the benchmark See *required yield spread*.

Spread risk Bond price risk arising from changes in the yield spread on credit-risky bonds; reflects changes in the market's assessment and/or pricing of credit migration (or downgrade) risk and market liquidity risk.

Spurious correlation Refers to: 1) correlation between two variables that reflects chance relationships in a particular dataset; 2) correlation induced by a calculation that mixes each of two variables with a third variable; and 3) correlation between two variables arising not from a direct relation between them but from their relation to a third variable.

Stacked bar chart An alternative form for presenting the frequency distribution of two categorical variables, where bars representing the sub-groups are placed on top of each other to form a single bar. Each sub-section is shown in a different color to represent the contribution of each sub-group, and the overall height of the stacked bar represents the marginal frequency for the category.

Stackelberg model A prominent model of strategic decision making in which firms are assumed to make their decisions sequentially.

Stagflation The combination of a high inflation rate with a high level of unemployment and a slowdown of the economy.

Staggered boards Board-related election process whereby directors are typically divided into multiple classes that are elected separately in consecutive years — that is, one class every year.

Stakeholder management The identification, prioritization, and understanding of the interests of stakeholder groups and managing the company's relationships with these groups.

Stakeholders Individuals or groups of individuals who may be affected either directly or indirectly by a decision and thus have an interest, or stake, in the decision.

Standard deviation The positive square root of the variance; a measure of dispersion in the same units as the original data.

Standard error of the estimate A measure of the fit of a regression line, calculated as the square root of the mean square error. Also known as the *standard error of the regression* and the *root mean square error*.

Standard error of the forecast A measure of the uncertainty associated with a forecasted value of the dependent variable that depends on the standard error of the estimate, the variability of the independent variable, the deviation of the forecasted independent variable from the mean in the regression, and the number of observations.

Standard error of the slope coefficient The standard error of the slope, which in a simple linear regression is the ratio of the model's standard error of the estimate (s_e) to the square root of the variation of the independent variable.

Standard normal distribution The normal density with mean (μ) equal to 0 and standard deviation (σ) equal to 1.

Standardization The process of creating protocols for the production, sale, transport, or use of a product or service. Standardization occurs when relevant parties agree to follow these protocols together. It helps support expanded economic and financial activities, such as trade and capital flows that support higher economic growth and standards of living, across borders.

Standardizing A transformation that involves subtracting the mean and dividing the result by the standard deviation.

Standards of conduct Behaviors required by a group; established benchmarks that clarify or enhance a group's code of ethics.

Standing limit orders A limit order at a price below market and which therefore is waiting to trade.

State actors Typically national governments, political organizations, or country leaders that exert authority over a country's national security and resources. The South African President, Sultan of Brunei, Malaysia's Parliament, and the British Prime Minister are all examples of state actors.

Stated annual interest rate A quoted interest rate that does not account for compounding within the year. Also called *quoted interest rate*.

Statement of changes in equity (statement of owners' equity) A financial statement that reconciles the beginning-of-period and end-of-period balance sheet values of shareholders' equity; provides information about all factors affecting shareholders' equity. Also called *statement of owners' equity*.

Statement of financial condition The financial statement that presents an entity's current financial position by disclosing resources the entity controls (its assets) and the claims on those resources (its liabilities and equity claims), as of a particular point in time (the date of the balance sheet).

Statement of financial position The financial statement that presents an entity's current financial position by disclosing resources the entity controls (its assets) and the claims on those resources (its liabilities and equity claims), as of a particular point in time (the date of the balance sheet).

Statement of operations A financial statement that provides information about a company's profitability over a stated period of time.

Static trade-off theory of capital structure A theory pertaining to a company's optimal capital structure. The optimal level of debt is found at the point where additional debt would cause the costs of financial distress to increase by a greater amount than the benefit of the additional tax shield.

Statistic A summary measure of a sample of observations.

Statistically significant A result indicating that the null hypothesis can be rejected; with reference to an estimated regression coefficient, frequently understood to mean a result indicating that the corresponding population regression coefficient is different from zero.

Status quo bias An emotional bias in which people do nothing (i.e., maintain the status quo) instead of making a change.

Statutory voting A common method of voting where each share represents one vote.

Step-up coupon bond Bond for which the coupon, fixed or floating, increases by specified margins at specified dates.

Stochastic oscillator A momentum indicator that compares a particular closing price of a security to a range of the security's prices over a certain period of time.

Stock dividend A type of dividend in which a company distributes additional shares of its common stock to shareholders instead of cash.

Stock split An increase in the number of shares outstanding with a consequent decrease in share price, but no change to the company's underlying fundamentals.

Stop-loss order See *stop order*.

Stop order An order in which a trader has specified a stop price condition. Also called *stop-loss order*.

Store of value The quality of tending to preserve value.

Store of wealth Goods that depend on the fact that they do not perish physically over time, and on the belief that others would always value the good.

Straight-line method A depreciation method that allocates evenly the cost of a long-lived asset less its estimated residual value over the estimated useful life of the asset.

Straight voting A shareholder voting process in which shareholders receive one vote for each share owned.

Strategic analysis Analysis of the competitive environment with an emphasis on the implications of the environment for corporate strategy.

Strategic asset allocation The set of exposures to IPS-permissible asset classes that is expected to achieve the client's long-term objectives given the client's investment constraints.

Stratified random sampling A procedure that first divides a population into subpopulations (strata) based on classification criteria and then randomly draws samples from each stratum in sizes proportional to that of each stratum in the population.

Street convention A yield measure that neglects weekends and holidays; the internal rate of return on cash flows assuming payments are made on the scheduled dates, even when the scheduled date falls on a weekend or holiday.

Stress testing A specific type of scenario analysis that estimates losses in rare and extremely unfavorable combinations of events or scenarios.

Strong-form efficient market A market in which security prices reflect all public and private information.

Structural subordination Arises in a holding company structure when the debt of operating subsidiaries is serviced by the cash flow and assets of the subsidiaries before funds can be passed to the holding company to service debt at the parent level.

Structural (or cyclically adjusted) budget deficit The deficit that would exist if the economy was at full employment (or full potential output).

Structured data Data that are highly organized in a pre-defined manner, usually with repeating patterns.

Structured financial instrument A financial instrument that shares the common attribute of repackaging risks. Structured financial instruments include asset-backed securities, collateralized debt obligations, and other structured financial instruments such as capital protected, yield enhancement, participation, and leveraged instruments.

Structured notes A broad category of securities that incorporate the features of debt instruments and one or more embedded derivatives designed to achieve a particular issuer or investor objective.

Subjective probability A probability drawing on personal or subjective judgment.

Subordinated debt A class of unsecured debt that ranks below a firm's senior unsecured obligations.

Subordination A form of internal credit enhancement that relies on creating more than one bond tranche and ordering the claim priorities for ownership or interest in an asset between the tranches. The ordering of the claim priorities is called a senior/subordinated structure, where the tranches of highest seniority are called senior, followed by subordinated or junior tranches. Also called *credit tranching*.

Substitutes Said of two goods or services such that if the price of one increases the demand for the other tends to increase, holding all other things equal (e.g., butter and margarine).

Sum of squares error (SSE) The sum of the squared deviations of (1) the value of the dependent variable and (2) the value of the dependent variable based on the estimated regression line. Also referred to as the *residual sum of squares*.

Sum of squares regression (SSR) The sum of the squared deviations of (1) the value of the dependent variable based on the estimated regression line and (2) the mean of the dependent variable.

Sum of squares total (SST) The sum of the squared deviations of the dependent variable from its mean; the variation of the dependent variable. Also referred to as the *total sum of squares*.

Sunk cost A cost that has already been incurred.

Supervised learning A machine learning approach that makes use of labeled training data.

Supply chain The sequence of processes involved in the creation and delivery of a physical product to the end customer, both within and external to a firm, regardless of whether those steps are performed by a single firm.

Supply shock A typically unexpected disturbance to supply.

Support In technical analysis, a price range in which buying activity is sufficient to stop the decline in the price of a security.

Support tranches Classes or tranches in CMOs that protect PAC tranches from prepayment risk.

Supranational bond A bond issued by a supranational agency such as the World Bank.

Surety bond Form of external credit enhancement whereby a rated and regulated insurance company guarantees to reimburse bondholders for any losses incurred up to a maximum amount if the issuer defaults.

Survey approach An estimate of the equity risk premium that is based on estimates provided by a panel of finance experts.

Survivorship bias The exclusion of poorly performing or defunct companies from an index or database, biasing the index or database toward financially healthy companies.

Sustainability linked loans These are any types of loan instruments and/or contingent facilities (such as bonding lines, guarantee lines, or letters of credit) that incentivize the borrower's achievement of ambitious, pre-determined sustainability performance objectives.

Sustainable growth rate The rate of dividend (and earnings) growth that can be sustained over time for a given level of return on equity, keeping the capital structure constant and without issuing additional common stock.

Sustainable investing Investing in assets and companies based on their perceived ability to deliver value by advancing economic, environmental, and social sustainability.

Sustainable rate of economic growth The rate of increase in the economy's productive capacity or potential GDP.

Swap A firm commitment involving a periodic exchange of cash flows.

Swap contract An agreement between two parties to exchange a series of future cash flows.

Swap execution facility (SEF) A swap trading platform accessed by multiple **dealers**.

Swap rate The fixed rate to be paid by the fixed-rate payer specified in a swap contract.

Switching barriers Factors that make it more difficult or more costly to switch suppliers.

Syndicated loan A loan from a group of lenders to a single borrower.

Syndicated offering A bond issue underwritten by a group of investment banks.

Synthetic protective put The combination of a synthetic long underlying position (i.e., a long forward and risk-free borrowing) and a purchased put on the underlying.

Systematic risk Risk that affects the entire market or economy; it cannot be avoided and is inherent in the overall market. Systematic risk is also known as non-diversifiable or market risk.

Systematic sampling A procedure of selecting every kth member until reaching a sample of the desired size. The sample that results from this procedure should be approximately random.

Systemic risk Refers to risks supervisory authorities believe are likely to have broad impact across the financial market infrastructure and affect a wide swath of market participants.

Tactical asset allocation Asset allocation that involves making short-term adjustments to asset class weights based on short-term predictions of relative performance among asset classes.

Tactical asset allocation (TAA) A portfolio strategy that shifts the percentages of assets held in various asset classes (or categories) to take advantage of market opportunities. Allocation shifts can occur within an asset class or across asset classes.

Tag cloud see *word cloud*.

Target capital structure A company's chosen proportions of debt and equity.

Target independent A bank's ability to determine the definition of inflation that they target, the rate of inflation that they target, and the horizon over which the target is to be achieved.

Target semideviation A measure of downside risk, calculated as the square root of the average of the squared deviations of observations below the target (also called target downside deviation).

Tariffs Taxes that a government levies on imported goods.

Tax base The amount at which an asset or liability is valued for tax purposes.

Tax expense An aggregate of an entity's income tax payable (or recoverable in the case of a tax benefit) and any changes in deferred tax assets and liabilities. It is essentially the income tax payable or recoverable if these had been determined based on accounting profit rather than taxable income.

Tax loss carry forward A taxable loss in the current period that may be used to reduce future taxable income.

Taxable income The portion of an entity's income that is subject to income taxes under the tax laws of its jurisdiction.

Taxable temporary differences Temporary differences that result in a taxable amount in a future period when determining the taxable profit as the balance sheet item is recovered or settled.

Technical analysis A form of security analysis that uses price and volume data, often displayed graphically, in decision making.

Technology The process a company uses to transform inputs into outputs.

Tender offer A public offer whereby the acquirer invites target shareholders to submit ("tender") their shares in return for the proposed payment.

Tenor The time-to-maturity for a bond or derivative contract. Also called *term to maturity*.

Term maturity structure Structure for a bond issue in which the bond's notional principal is paid off in a lump sum at maturity.

Term structure See *maturity structure*.

Term structure of credit spreads The relationship between the spreads over the "risk-free" (or benchmark) rates and times-to-maturity.

Term structure of yield volatility The relationship between the volatility of bond yields-to-maturity and times-to-maturity.

Terminal stock value The expected value of a share at the end of the investment horizon—in effect, the expected selling price. Also called *terminal value*.

Terminal value The expected value of a share at the end of the investment horizon—in effect, the expected selling price.

Terms of trade The ratio of the price of exports to the price of imports, representing those prices by export and import price indexes, respectively.

Test of the mean of the differences A statistical test for differences based on paired observations drawn from samples that are dependent on each other.

Text analytics The use of computer programs to analyze and derive meaning from typically large, unstructured text- or voice-based datasets.

Thematic investing An investment approach that focuses on companies within a specific sector or following a specific theme, such as energy efficiency or climate change.

Thematic risks Known risks that evolve and expand over a period of time. Climate change, pattern migration, the rise of populist forces, and the ongoing threat of terrorism fall into this category.

Thin-Tailed Describes a distribution that has relatively less weight in the tails than the normal distribution (also called platykurtic).

Third-degree price discrimination When the monopolist segregates customers into groups based on demographic or other characteristics and offers different pricing to each group.

Tiered pricing A pricing approach that charges different prices to different buyers, commonly based on volume purchased.

Time-period bias The possibility that when we use a time-series sample, our statistical conclusion may be sensitive to the starting and ending dates of the sample.

Time-series data A sequence of observations for a single observational unit of a specific variable collected over time and at discrete and typically equally spaced intervals of time (such as daily, weekly, monthly, annually, or quarterly).

Time tranching The creation of classes or tranches in an ABS/MBS that possess different (expected) maturities.

Time value The difference between an option's premium and its intrinsic value.

Time value decay The process by which the time value of an option declines toward zero as the option's expiration date is approached.

Time value of money The principles governing equivalence relationships between cash flows with different dates.

Time-weighted rate of return The compound rate of growth of one unit of currency invested in a portfolio during a stated measurement period; a measure of investment performance that is not sensitive to the timing and amount of withdrawals or additions to the portfolio.

Title Document representing real estate property ownership covering building and land-use rights along with air, mineral, and surface rights. Titles can be purchased, leased, sold, mortgaged, or transferred together or separately, in whole or in part.

Title search Crucial part of buyer and lender due diligence, ensuring the seller/borrower owns the property without any liens or other claims against the asset, such as from other owners, lenders, or investors or from the government for unpaid taxes.

Tokenization The process of representing ownership rights to physical assets on a blockchain or distributed ledger.

Top-down analysis An investment selection approach that begins with consideration of macroeconomic conditions and then evaluates markets and industries based upon such conditions.

Total comprehensive income The change in equity during a period resulting from transaction and other events, other than those changes resulting from transactions with owners in their capacity as owners.

Total cost The summation of all costs, for which costs are classified as fixed or variable.

Total cost of ownership The aggregate direct and indirect costs associated with owning an asset over its life span.

Total factor productivity A variable which accounts for that part of Y not directly accounted for by the levels of the production factors (K and L).

Total fixed cost The summation of all expenses that do not change as the level of production varies.

Total invested capital The sum of market value of common equity, book value of preferred equity, and face value of debt.

Total probability rule A rule explaining the unconditional probability of an event in terms of probabilities of the event conditional on mutually exclusive and exhaustive scenarios.

Total probability rule for expected value A rule explaining the expected value of a random variable in terms of expected values of the random variable conditional on mutually exclusive and exhaustive scenarios.

Total return Measures the price appreciation, or percentage change in price of the securities in an index or portfolio, plus any income received over the period.

Total return index An index that reflects the price appreciation or percentage change in price of the constituent securities plus any income received since inception.

Total variable cost The summation of all variable expenses.

Tracking error The standard deviation of the differences between a portfolio's returns and its benchmark's returns; a synonym of *active risk*. Also called *tracking risk*.

Tracking risk The standard deviation of the differences between a portfolio's returns and its benchmarks returns. Also called *tracking error*.

Trade creation When regional integration results in the replacement of higher cost domestic production by lower cost imports from other members.

Trade credit A spontaneous form of credit in which a purchaser of the goods or service is financing its purchase by delaying the date on which payment is made.

Trade diversion When regional integration results in lower-cost imports from non-member countries being replaced with higher-cost imports from members.

Trade payables Amounts that a business owes to its vendors for goods and services that were purchased from them but which have not yet been paid.

Trade protection Government policies that impose restrictions on trade, such as tariffs and quotas.

Trade surplus (deficit) When the value of exports is greater (less) than the value of imports.

Trading securities Under US GAAP, a category of debt securities held by a company with the intent to trade them. Also called *held-for-trading securities*.

Traditional investment markets Markets for traditional investments, which include all publicly traded debts and equities and shares in pooled investment vehicles that hold publicly traded debts and/or equities.

Transactions money balances Money balances that are held to finance transactions.

Transfer payments Welfare payments made through the social security system that exist to provide a basic minimum level of income for low-income households.

Treasury stock method A method for accounting for the effect of options (and warrants) on earnings per share (EPS) that specifies what EPS would have been if the options and warrants had been exercised and the company had used the proceeds to repurchase common stock.

Tree-Map Another graphical tool for displaying categorical data. It consists of a set of colored rectangles to represent distinct groups, and the area of each rectangle is proportional to the value of the corresponding group.

Trend A long-term pattern of movement in a particular direction.

Treynor ratio A measure of risk-adjusted performance that relates a portfolio's excess returns to the portfolio's beta.

Triangle pattern In technical analysis, a continuation chart pattern that forms as the range between high and low prices narrows, visually forming a triangle.

Trimmed mean A mean computed after excluding a stated small percentage of the lowest and highest observations.

Trimodal A distribution that has the three most frequently occurring values.

Triple bottom In technical analysis, a reversal pattern that results when the price forms three troughs at roughly the same price level. A triple bottom is used to predict a change from a downtrend to an uptrend.

Triple top In technical analysis, a reversal pattern that results when the price forms three peaks at roughly the same price level. A triple top is used to predict a change from an uptrend to a downtrend.

True yield The internal rate of return on cash flows using the actual calendar, including weekends and bank holidays.

Trust deed The governing legal credit agreement, typically incorporated by reference in the prospectus. Also called *bond indenture*.

Turn-of-the-year effect Calendar anomaly that stock market returns in January are significantly higher compared to the rest of the months of the year, with most of the abnormal returns reported during the first five trading days in January.

Two-dimensional rectangular array A popular form for organizing data for processing by computers or for presenting data visually. It is comprised of columns and rows to hold multiple variables and multiple observations, respectively (also called a data table).

Two-fund separation theorem The theory that all investors regardless of taste, risk preferences, and initial wealth will hold a combination of two portfolios or funds: a risk-free asset and an optimal portfolio of risky assets.

Two-sided hypothesis test A test in which the null hypothesis is rejected in favor of the alternative hypothesis if the evidence indicates that the population parameter is either

Glossary

smaller or larger than a hypothesized value; occurs when the alternative hypothesis is stated as not equal to the hypothesized population parameters.

Two-way table See *contingency table*.

Two-week repo rate The interest rate on a two-week repurchase agreement; may be used as a policy rate by a central bank.

Type I error The error of rejecting a true null hypothesis; a false positive.

Type II error The error of not rejecting a false null hypothesis; false negative.

Unanticipated (unexpected) inflation The component of inflation that is a surprise.

Uncommitted lines of credit The least reliable form of bank borrowing in which a bank offers, without formal commitment, a line of credit for an extended period of time but reserves the right to refuse any request for its use.

Unconditional probability The probability of an event *not* conditioned on another event.

Underemployed A person who has a job but has the qualifications to work a significantly higher-paying job.

Underlying The asset referred to in a **derivative contract**.

Underwriter A firm, usually an investment bank, that takes the risk of buying the newly issued securities from the issuer and then reselling them to investors or to dealers, thus guaranteeing the sale of the securities at the offering price negotiated with the issuer.

Underwritten offering A type of securities issue mechanism in which the investment bank guarantees the sale of the securities at an offering price that is negotiated with the issuer. Also known as *firm commitment offering*.

Unearned revenue A liability account for money that has been collected for goods or services that have not yet been delivered; payment received in advance of providing a good or service. Also called *deferred revenue* or *deferred income*.

Unemployed People who are actively seeking employment but are currently without a job.

Unemployment rate The ratio of unemployed to the labor force.

Unexpected inflation The component of inflation that is a surprise.

Unimodal A distribution with a single value that is most frequently occurring.

Unit economics The expression of revenues and costs on a per-unit basis.

Unit elastic An elasticity with a magnitude of negative one. Also called *unitary elastic*.

Unit labor cost The average labor cost to produce one unit of output.

Unit normal distribution The normal density with mean (μ) equal to 0 and standard deviation (σ) equal to 1.

Unitranche debt Consists of a hybrid or blended loan structure that combines different tranches of secured and unsecured debt into a single loan with a single, blended interest rate.

Units-of-production method A depreciation method that allocates the cost of a long-lived asset based on actual usage during the period.

Univariate distribution A distribution that specifies the probabilities for a single random variable.

Unsecured debt Debt that gives the debtholder only a general claim on an issuer's assets and cash flow.

Unsponsored A type of depository receipt in which the foreign company whose shares are held by the depository has no involvement in the issuance of the receipts.

Unstructured data Data that do not follow any conventionally organized forms.

Unsupervised learning A machine learning approach that does not make use of labeled training data.

Up transition probability The probability that an asset's value moves up.

Uptrend A pattern that occurs when the price of an asset moves higher over a period of time.

VaR See *value at risk*.

Validity instructions Instructions which indicate when the order may be filled.

Valuation allowance A reserve created against deferred tax assets, based on the likelihood of realizing the deferred tax assets in future accounting periods.

Valuation ratios Ratios that measure the quantity of an asset or flow (e.g., earnings) in relation to the price associated with a specified claim (e.g., a share or ownership of the enterprise).

Value added resellers Businesses that distribute a product and also handle more complex aspects of product installation, customization, service, or support.

Value at risk A money measure of the minimum value of losses expected during a specified time period at a given level of probability.

Value-based pricing Pricing set primarily by reference to the value of the product or service to customers.

Value chain The systems and processes within a firm that create value for its customers.

Value investors With reference to equity investors, investors who are focused on paying a relatively low share price in relation to earnings or assets per share.

Value proposition The product or service attributes valued by a firm's target customer that lead those customers to prefer that firm's offering.

Variable A characteristic or quantity that can be measured, counted, or categorized and that is subject to change (also called a field, an attribute, or a feature).

Variable costs Costs that fluctuate with the level of production and sales.

Variance The expected value (the probability-weighted average) of squared deviations from a random variable's expected value.

Variation margin The amount required to replenish the futures margin account back to the initial margin.

Veblen goods Goods that increase in desirability with increasing price.

Vega The change in a given derivative instrument for a given small change in volatility, holding everything else constant. A sensitivity measure for options that reflects the effect of volatility.

Velocity The pace at which geopolitical risk impacts an investor portfolio.

Venture capital Investments that provide "seed" or start-up capital, early-stage financing, or later-stage financing (including mezzanine-stage financing) to companies in early development stages and requiring more capital for expansion or preparation for an initial public offering.

Venture capital fund A hedge fund that seeks to buy, optimize, and ultimately sell portfolio companies to generate profits. See *private equity fund*.

Vertical analysis Common-size analysis using only one reporting period or one base financial statement; for example, an income statement in which all items are stated as percentages of sales.

Vertical demand schedule Implies that some fixed quantity is demanded, regardless of price.

Visual technique The most common and readily available method of initial data assessment. Experts in pattern recognition maintain that the visual (or "eyeball") technique is still the most effective way of searching for recognizable patterns.

Visualization The presentation of data in a pictorial or graphical format for the purpose of increasing understanding and for gaining insights into the data.

Volatility The standard deviation of the continuously compounded returns on the underlying asset.

Voluntarily unemployed A person voluntarily outside the labor force, such as a jobless worker refusing an available vacancy.

Voluntary export restraint A trade barrier under which the exporting country agrees to limit its exports of the good to its trading partners to a specific number of units.

Vote by proxy A mechanism that allows a designated party—such as another shareholder, a shareholder representative, or management—to vote on the shareholder's behalf.

Warrant Attached option that gives its holder the right to buy the underlying stock of the issuing company at a fixed exercise price until the expiration date.

Waterfall Represents the distribution method that defines the order in which allocations are made to LPs and GPs. There are two major types of waterfall: *deal by deal* (or *American*) and *whole of fund* (or *European*).

Weak-form efficient market hypothesis The belief that security prices fully reflect all past market data, which refers to all historical price and volume trading information.

Wealth effect An increase (decrease) in household wealth increases (decreases) consumer spending out of a given level of current income.

Web-based lenders Lenders that operate primarily on the internet, offering loans in relatively small amounts, typically to small businesses in need of cash.

Weighted average cost method An inventory accounting method that averages the total cost of available inventory items over the total units available for sale.

Weighted average cost of capital A weighted average of the after-tax required rates of return on a company's common stock, preferred stock, and long-term debt, where the weights are the fraction of each source of financing in the company's target capital structure.

Weighted average coupon rate Weighting the mortgage rate of each mortgage loan in the pool by the percentage of the mortgage outstanding relative to the outstanding amount of all the mortgages in the pool.

Weighted average life A measure that gives investors an indication of how long they can expect to hold the MBS before it is paid off; the convention-based average time to receipt of all principal repayments. Also called *average life*.

Weighted average maturity Weighting the remaining number of months to maturity for each mortgage loan in the pool by the amount of the outstanding mortgage balance.

Weighted mean An average in which each observation is weighted by an index of its relative importance.

Winsorized mean A mean computed after assigning a stated percentage of the lowest values equal to one specified low value and a stated percentage of the highest values equal to one specified high value.

Word cloud A visual device for representing textual data, which consists of words extracted from a source of textual data. The size of each distinct word is proportional to the frequency with which it appears in the given text (also known as tag cloud).

Working capital The difference between current assets and current liabilities.

Working capital management The management of a company's short-term assets (such as inventory) and short-term liabilities (such as money owed to suppliers).

World price The price prevailing in the world market.

Yield duration The sensitivity of the bond price with respect to the bond's own yield-to-maturity.

Yield-to-maturity Annual return that an investor earns on a bond if the investor purchases the bond today and holds it until maturity. It is the discount rate that equates the present value of the bond's expected cash flows until maturity with the bond's price. Also called *yield-to-redemption* or *redemption yield*.

Yield-to-redemption See *yield-to-maturity*.

Yield-to-worst The lowest of the sequence of yields-to-call and the yield-to-maturity.

Zero-coupon bond A bond that does not pay interest during its life. It is issued at a discount to par value and redeemed at par. Also called *pure discount bond*.

Zero-volatility spread (Z-spread) Calculates a constant yield spread over a government (or interest rate swap) spot curve.